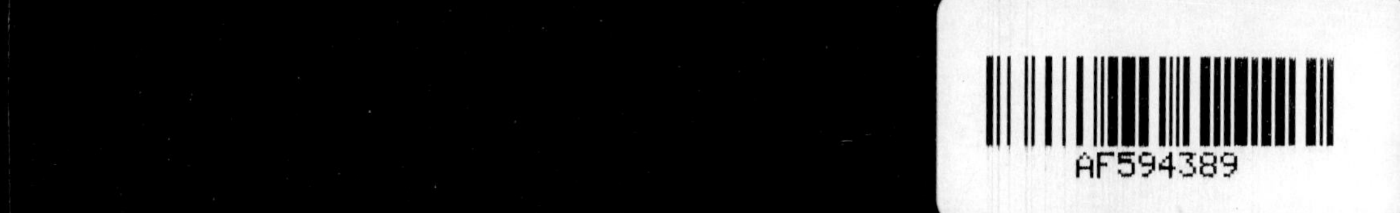
AF594389

EDITED BY
CHARLES AUBIN

PHOTOGRAPHS BY
PAULA COURT

ROSELEE
GOLDBERG

ON THE TOWN

A PERFORMA
COMPENDIUM
2016–2021

ON THE TOWN

FOREWORD
Yvonne Rainer

I am continually amazed at Performa's scope and long-standing involvement in inducing different kinds of artists to create live performances, many of which, unfortunately and over the years, I have not always been able to follow as closely as I would have liked. Several stand out in my memory, such as Jérôme Bel's pared-down *Ballet* at Marian Goodman Gallery and *Reanimation*, Joan Jonas's concert of dance and drawings with Jason Moran at Roulette in Brooklyn.

Over the past fourteen years, with the oversight of Director RoseLee Goldberg and her energetic team, I myself have been a consistent beneficiary of Performa's investment in my work, the most recent example being the reconstruction of *Parts of Some Sextets*, a 1965 epic I call my "mattress monster," a dance for ten people and twelve mattresses.

At the outset, I was initially invited to conceive a new work named *RoS Indexical* for Performa 07 (2007). This was an ambitious reimagining of Nijinsky's *Rite of Spring*, presented at a Broadway theater and inspired by the BBC's film dramatization, *Riot at the Rite*. Since then, the organization has produced and toured my work, including *Spiraling Down* (2008), *Assisted Living: Good Sports 2* (2010), and *Assisted Living: Do You Have Any Money?* (2013). In 2014, Performa and the Getty Institute co-commissioned and co-produced *The Concept of Dust: Continuous Project—Altered Annually*, and, most recently, Performa's commitment was essential to the reconstruction of the aforementioned "mattress monster."

A brief diversion regarding my repeated use of titles like *Continuous Project* and my predilection for revising and reworking older material: I should point out that the origin for variations on that particular title lies with a 1969 installation by Robert Morris called *Continuous Project Altered Daily*, which consisted of a pile of dirt in which were lodged a number of objects, the whole rearranged and augmented by the artist every day during the run of the show. My titles refer to a longer process and period of time, with the temporal adjustments of Altered *Annually, Sixty Years*, etc., which is more characteristic of a performance-based event than one usually encountered in a gallery show. My titles also attest to my reassessment of the works as I re-entered a choreographic career after almost thirty years as a filmmaker and writer (1972–2000).

Performa has organized tours of my works to Fundação de Serralves in Porto, Portugal; Dia Art Foundation in Beacon, New York, MACBA in Barcelona; the Getty Center in Los Angeles; Fondazione Antonio Ratti in Como, Italy; the Louvre in Paris, and Marseille Objectif Danse in France.

My working relationship with Performa has been instrumental in enabling me to excavate and extend my artistic practice. RoseLee's passion for both instigation and disinterment is unparalleled in the arena of so-called *avant-garde art*, so much of which disappears under the critical radar or emerges like a flash in the pan before vanishing from memory. Among innumerable others, I remain indebted to her unflagging zeal.

BEYOND THE BIENNIAL

RoseLee Goldberg

On the Town, A Performa Compendium: 2016–2021 is a book about two biennials, Performa 17 and Performa 19, and the actions of artists, curators, and producers, before, during, and after each biennial. Spanning a period of five years, it encapsulates much of the thinking, imagining, inventing, and producing that goes into the preparation of each biennial, but it also provides information about everything else that Performa does on a year-round basis. Together, these activities have established the organization as a world leader, not only in the field of live performance by visual artists but as an entirely new kind of arts institution, capable of responding to shifting political, social, and media landscapes as they occur, and devising highly visible platforms for artists in a broad range of disciplines to directly engage audiences.

Performa, from the start, has always been much more than a biennial. It is a museum without walls, a research center, a think tank, a highly specialized commissioning and production house, a training ground for emerging curators and producers, a repository of contemporary performance from around the world. Its various departments and programs—Performa Archives, Performa Institute, Pavilions Without Walls, Radical Broadcast, *Performa Magazine*, Performa Radio, Performa publications, and the Performa Telethon—have been added year by year to our organization's core mission of making the extensive history of performance by visual artists known to wide audiences and to instigating new directions for performance in the twenty-first century.

Performa's unique commissioning process—working closely with each artist to realize their vision and ideas as well as providing support at all levels, including dramaturgy, technical expertise, and context-setting educational programs—have catapulted Performa Commissions into the spotlight, changing public perception of artists' performance through riveting, unforgettable experiences created by some of the most remarkable artists of our times. Since the first Performa Biennial in 2005, our commissions opened new possibilities and transformed art institutions' approach to visual art performance, now a staple in museums, art centers, and galleries worldwide. Indeed, the centrality of performance in art today reflects Performa's instrumental role in establishing both the history of performance and its current manifestations in contemporary conversations about art and culture. International interest in our biennials and exhibitions, both touring and online, and our public programs and publications, indicates the immense significance of live interaction, sought after by humankind, now more than ever, as an antidote to living inside the overwhelming matrix of our media-saturated globe.

Focusing on the city of New York has been Performa's driving force from the very beginning. Starting with the storied streets of "Downtown"—with their cast-iron buildings emptied out except for a single artist or two on each block-long floor, the alternative spaces of SoHo, nearby Judson Memorial Church, clubs and bars on the Bowery, and empty parking lots along the Hudson River—these spaces and places of the sixties and seventies where artists gathered, performed, argued, and collaborated, and the streets and alleyways that connected them, provide a physical history, a walking tour of artists' performance and avant-garde dance, film, and music in New York. It was a remarkable era. Performa, in 2005, picked up the baton, adding with each biennial unexpected dimensions to each borough, layering new memories amongst them and inviting local communities to follow wherever our programs led them—uptown, downtown, east or west—and to use their city differently.

A night *on the town* in New York is very different from a night (or a week for that matter) in any other city. This town is so compact, its inhabitants so energized by and addicted to its constant charge, that the Performa Biennial chose, without hesitation, to harness its underlying engine to the city itself, using its rich history as fuel for its programs and research. The pages of this book celebrate the extraordinary vitality, inventiveness, and resilience of New York City as the performance capital of the world. As the song goes: "New York, New York, It's a wonderful town! The Bronx is up and the Battery's down."

THE SHAPE OF A CITY

Charles Aubin

Securing a site for a Performa Commission is often the most nerve-racking stage of the production process. Hurdles abound: scheduling conflicts, ludicrous fees, change of leadership, you name it. Yet, for Performa 17, not one but two artists decided to multiply the challenges of finding even one corner of New York to work in, and instead went big: They embraced the entire city. Barbara Kruger's provocative questions appeared on a roving school bus that crisscrossed boroughs, emerged on thousands of MetroCards sold to commuters, popped up on billboards, and overran a skateboarding park on the Lower East Side. The formidable self-portraits of Zanele Muholi stood at heroic scale on giant LED screens in Times Square and throughout information displays in the subway system. For both artists, New York became a canvas and ubiquity a modus operandi, not only across town but also online: in ricochets of stories, posts, and reposts.

The city is often an implied performer in our biennial. However, each commission originates first in an artist's idea; we look for the ideal venue to frame the piece afterward. We're fortunate to have wonderful peers in theaters and museums to whom we can return, as well as good friends in the municipal Department of Parks & Recreation, but we also consistently scout for new locations. And New York ain't easy, as the Estonian artist Anu Vahtra showed with *Open House Closing. A Walk* (2017), her tour of storefronts in SoHo: Once a bohemian enclave of artists, filmmakers, and writers, now a paragon of a pop-up economy championing temporary "experiential retail." In her precisely documented guided tour, she lucidly portrayed this new condition while sending an earnest love letter to the ghosts of Gordon Matta-Clark and his fellow SoHo-resident artists of the 1970s. In a way, Vahtra's negotiation between past and present encapsulated Performa's relationship to its hometown: As we adapt to its ever-changing parameters for presenting live art, each biennial channels New York's history while renewing it.

Vahtra's wasn't the only procession at Performa 17: With *Zion* (2017), the South African artist Mohau Modisakeng directed a dozen performers to walk south from Harlem. Members of the Harambee Dance Group intertwined histories of migration and segregation, of South Africa and the United States, as they marched through Central Park to the site of Seneca Village, a community of African American homeowners displaced in the 1850s to make way for the park's creation. With music and movement, the African dance company brought to the fore the overlooked story of the village. *Zion* came to add a new layer on the park's topography.

That same year, the American architects and scholars Bryony Roberts and Mabel O. Wilson collaborated with an after-school dance and drumline program in Harlem, whose dozens of teenage performers are known as the Marching Cobras of New York. Their performance *Marching On*, which Storefront for Art and Architecture presented during Performa 17, brought to Marcus Garvey Park a rhythmic procession whose costumes recalled another march exactly a century previously: the 1917 Silent March against racial violence. Other parts of the performance alluded to the Harlem Hellfighters Band as they paraded through Manhattan on their return from the First World War. *Marching On* was what the architects called a *counter-monument*, one that forswore the stability and monumentality of New York's memorials for a more transient, more participatory embodiment of history. It's worth recalling that in 2017, after the white supremacist "Unite the Right" rally in Charlottesville, North Carolina, New York's mayor Bill de Blasio convened a commission to inspect public monuments—of which Mabel O. Wilson was a member. She knew well that temporary assemblies can become tactical tools to engage with the meaning of a place. They offer modes to construct civic identity. If the built environment is a container of history, performance provides the means to upset, reframe, and retell it.

The widespread protests that followed the murder of George Floyd in 2020 brought to center stage the role monuments and memorials play in the politics of representation. Citizens, working together, toppled statues that promoted racial injustice for centuries. After months of lockdowns and isolation due to the COVID-19 pandemic, these gatherings also reaffirmed the centrality of the body in urban life. Black Lives Matter needed social media to galvanize and organize, certainly. Yet BLM and its fellow social justice movements across the country and abroad used those digital tools to reinscribe human interactions into the fabric of the city (in a balancing act of communal experience and the need to protect one's health).

Art today often finds itself in this state of constant arbitration between physical presence and the pervasive digitalization of our days. If live art seems to evade social media's packaging of human beings into data (which can then be aggregated and sold off), it also, through posts, likes, and shares, nevertheless participates in our image-driven epoch. Taiwanese artist Yu Cheng-Ta made the most of this with *FAMEME*, at Performa 19, using Instagram to garner attention for his faux museum and prank influencer "reveal" in Times Square. *FAMEME* lived both online and IRL, and then returned to the web through the dissemination of its documentation.

Performa has been driven by the desire to stir up our experience of the urban environment (as well as its online extensions). If architecture shapes behavior and conditions our use of a space, performance in turn might conjure new familiarities and memories. In fact, the biennial might be better thought of as an exercise in how people and their actions can infuse new qualities to a space, be it with the murmurs of Tarik Kiswanson's young actors at the Alexander Hamilton U.S. Custom House or the stomach-churning smell of Éva Mag's clay in Judson Memorial Church's gym. For the spaces of New York never stop taking on new residents, new meanings, new histories, not least after a pandemic that froze this most dynamic of cities. It is through the eyes of artists that we can see what kind of new life we want to build in this reemerging town, and how we can get there together.

CHOREOGRAPHY OF PRODUCTION

Esa Nickle

Performa was launched with the intention of commissioning new works of live performance by visual artists, providing full curatorial and production support to realize their ambitions. Borrowing some production strategies from the performing arts world, we adapted them to accommodate the immense range of material that artists envision, encouraging them to pursue their ideas, almost without limitation. Without a set venue or an existing technical team, Performa's approach is often "producing without a net," or, as RoseLee Goldberg likes to say, "100% risk. 100% trust." Our method is purposely loose and nimble, allowing artists to experiment and be ambitious, but also to be ready to change direction and take advantage of a sudden opportunity or an unexpected location about to be forever lost or transformed, such as the vacant James A. Farley Building, New York City's former general post office. We are always up for a challenge and an artist with an outlandish idea. It is all possible until it is impossible.

The process begins when one of our curators invites an artist to participate in the biennial. Soon after, a producer is assigned to work closely with the artist and curator to realize the project, with equal emphasis placed on both curatorial and production. The timeframe of six months up to two years before the debut is an ongoing discussion and a learning process for everyone involved: There must be extensive planning, research, scenario testing, and trust built into each commission, or there will be cracks in the confidence of the piece. For those who are creating in unfamiliar territory—outside of an institutional or gallery context—and for many who have never worked live before, this entirely new way of working can be a moment of transformation or one-off experimentation, often leading artists to make more live performances. For an artist with a studio practice, relinquishing control over a performance that involves, on average, about twenty performers and crew members, a hundred moving parts, and an audience of three hundred people or more, can be a stressful but ultimately exhilarating experience.

The artist Francis Alÿs describes his method as a "choreography of production," in which the work of art is the very action of making it. Similarly, as we work with an artist through the production process, we hope to encounter revelations, radical ideas, and inspiration both in its completion and after it ends, feeling the effects of every work's long tail and wide net. For those accustomed to operating alone or with a studio staff, realizing their Performa Commissions is often surprising and unpredictable—identifying possible collaborators, organizing specialized technical teams, scouting numerous potential settings and contexts, forming partnerships, and incessantly tweaking financial scenarios as funds are raised. For artists working with moving image, the multiple specialties on set are par for the course, although they often lose their ultimate oversight in the final cut of editing. For both kinds of artists, perhaps the most important consideration is the audience; how they will arrive; how they will sit, stand, or move about; how they might behave or respond; and how we can best connect them to the performance experience and to the artist's intentions.

With each Commission, there are inevitable hurdles, complications, stretched budgets, and minor disappointments that are well balanced with invigorating epiphanies, coincidences, surprise opportunities, and happy accidents. From start to finish, our small team will have joined forces with the artist to scout and consider multiple venues, put together a tight-knit team, review dozens of rental quotes, track down hard-to-find props, fabricate objects of all kinds, conduct citywide casting calls, search high and low for affordable housing for arriving performers, plan for documentation, and remember to include budget lines for drinks, snacks, and food for hardworking casts and crews. Finally, when it's time for the premiere, we are all there together with the expectation that everything that can go wrong will go wrong, but always ready and excited to see what will happen. Perhaps the two greatest pleasures of the process are the giddy exploration of all of the possibilities at the very beginning and the sense of fatigued wonderment after the final applause.

A few production highlights from the most recent biennials include installing Barbara Kruger's billboard-sized double-entendre phrases on the walls and ramps of the Coleman Skate Park on the Lower East Side; watching unexpected police helicopters circle Samson Young's outdoor opera above Castle Williams on Governors Island; having two tons of clay delivered to Éva Mag at the gym of the Judson Memorial Church, getting sixteen blue ticking mattresses fabricated by the oldest mattress factory in the Bronx for Yvonne Rainer's *Parts of Some Sextets*; transporting, housing, and feeding fifty college marching-band members from Athens, Georgia for Paul Pfeiffer's live staging of their musical accompaniment to a football game at the Apollo Theater in Harlem; filling a giant bowl suspended from the ceiling with one ton of clear gel for Kelly Nipper's performance; recruiting an army of zombies for Bunny Rogers's *Sanctuary* at a Lower East Side high school; hanging five hundred feet of canvas and ropes from scaffolding to celebrate Christo and Jeanne-Claude at a gala evening; finding banana leaves and black ink for Wangechi Mutu's performance at the Metropolitan Museum of Art; forming a quartet of retired émigré Chinese opera musicians for Lap-See Lam's live and virtual transportation of a Chinese restaurant from Stockholm to New York; sourcing an array of durian-flavored snacks for Yu Cheng-Ta's Museum of Durian on Canal Street; and seeing Estonian artist Anu Vahtra break down in tears of joy at the nineteenth-century Putnam Rolling Ladder Company on Howard Street in SoHo shortly before it closed down, now memorialized in her performance *Open House Closing. A Walk*.

PERFORMA 17

CIRCULATIONS

BALTIC CURRENTS

AROUND TOWN

BARBARA KRUGER

IN CONVERSATION WITH

ROSELEE GOLDBERG

&

JOB PISTON

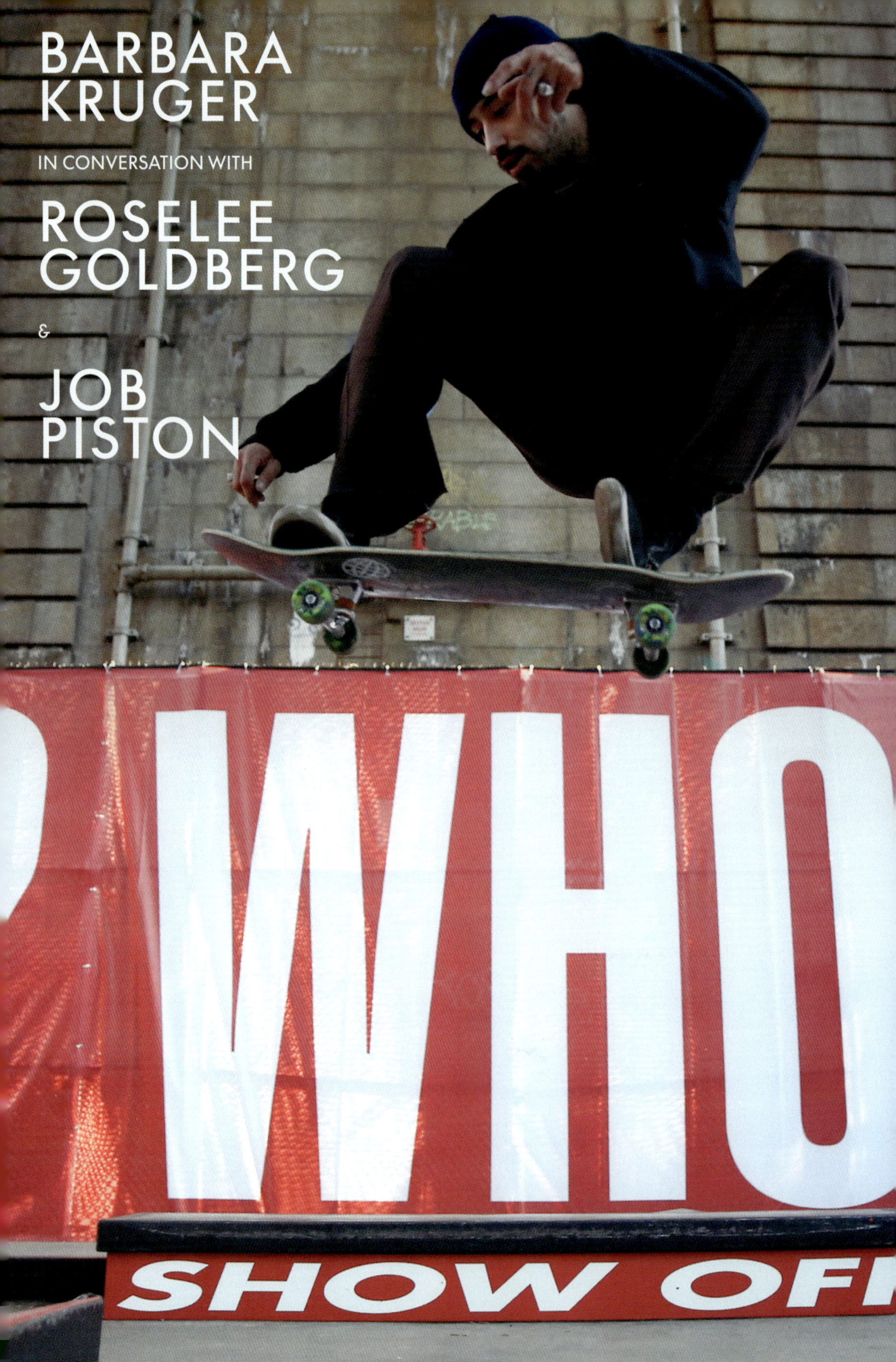

Untitled (School)
Untitled (Skate)
Untitled (Know, Believe, Forget)
Untitled (The Drop)

Curated by
RoseLee Goldberg
with Job Piston

Coleman Playground Skatepark, Performa 17 Hub, 10th Avenue Billboard, and New York City Subway

November 1–19, 2017

*Barbara Kruger's instantly recognizable—and frequently appropriated—visual style of white Futura Bold text over red blocks is as widely known to millennials as it is to museum veterans. Her terse phrases addressing consumerism, feminism, and civil rights capture the intensity of life in the city and the impact of marketing messaging on our daily lives. For Performa 17, Kruger collaborated with the design firm Project Projects to reconceive the visual identity of the whole biennial. By redesigning the organization's logo, website, social media, digital and print marketing materials, as well as merchandise, Kruger blurred the lines between branding, public art, performance, commerce, and appropriation even further. Her commission infiltrated New York City: It included 50,000 subway cards distributed across the MTA network, a roving yellow school bus [*Untitled (School)*], a full takeover of the Coleman Playground Skatepark on the Lower East Side [*Untitled (Skate)*], and a billboard in Chelsea [*Untitled (Know, Believe, Forget)*]. At the Performa 17 Hub,* Untitled (The Drop) *was a live performance riffing on the phenomenon of "drops" pioneered by streetwear brands, where boutiques expect their customers to queue on the sidewalk before entering the store one by one to peruse a limited number of exclusive products—t-shirts, beanies, skate decks—whose extremely limited quantities are only available for a limited time. The performance also hinted at the marketing strategies of these brands that have often used Kruger's slogan style in the past. For* The Drop, *the biennial partnered with the skating and clothing brand Volcom, co-opting a legitimate corporate machine to create and foster an endless cycle of appropriation and re-appropriation.*

ROSELEE GOLDBERG
Barbara, I know you'd been following Performa at a distance, but when we came to you and said, "Will you be part of it?," what did you think? "Are they crazy?"

BARBARA KRUGER

I was thrilled! I had been watching Performa grow over the years and enjoyed how it both reflected and developed the visibility of live works, which ebbed and flowed over time. I knew of your work at the Kitchen early on, when you were insistent on performance's revelatory promise, and its weight on the art world, in New York and elsewhere. There was a prevalence of them in the 1970s, and then, with the rise of the market and commodified objects, it reversed. It's here again now.

When you approached me, you came with a Dada reader, which was an incredible effort to put together. I read a lot of it and thought about what my contribution could be to the scattering of meaning, nonsense, supposition, and doubt within a dense urban area. But I knew your capabilities to make connections and make things visible in a kind of "aerosol" way. Not locked to a specific setting or a white cube.

RLG

When you read the reader, did you make notes? Were there specific texts that you were particularly drawn to? How did you physically and intellectually respond to those texts?

BK

I started taking notes. I got so into the history, much of which I'd known, but it refreshed me in a way. I'd visited some of those sites in Europe, too. I felt the incredible chaos and destruction of war there, the damage and pathology that we do to one another and the place of culture.

RLG

My mantra for the piece was "Barbara takes New York." I like what you said about aerosol, the idea that we're reaching people in every possible way, in the air around them, throughout the city. But what was your next thought regarding what you wanted to do?

BK

It was about simultaneity. I thought of all these different sites that could be engaged rather than one site, because I knew that your team could make it happen. With much effort and struggle, I do understand that. Just the ambitiousness of your schedule, having twenty things happen at once. I can't think of any other sort of structure that would have allowed for it.

The subway came to my mind very quickly and when Esa [Nickle] suggested a skate park, I just felt it was perfect! Then the bus came up, and then the pop-up store, which you guys were so plugged in about. I have to say there was a certain comfort level but also an OMG reaction because of my long history with you, Job. We would sit in your studio at UCLA talking pop subcultures, the real estate and neighborhood situation just above Canal Street, the street scene, consumerism, the *garmentos* who became sneakerheads... So, it started as a group conversation with Performa, a wacky, disjointed one.

JOB PISTON

As an artwork, *The Drop* was able to instigate a critical distance from the consumerism that drives these street-style labels, and fashion in general.

BK

In some ways, it was a return for me because as a young woman, I started out at Condé Nast. I worked at *Mademoiselle*, then I was at *Vogue* for a little bit, and later I went to *House & Garden*. The art department was a marginalized place at those magazines. But nevertheless, I understood the quick turnaround and the brutal fickleness of clothing, commodities, and fashion. And these issues are rife with questions of class, race, and gender that remain unexamined on so many levels. The street, the notion of the street—

JP

—Like a public square where passersby

of different backgrounds move by one another randomly. What I also liked about your piece was that you used social media influencers' marketing strategies to promote the project in quite a subversive way.

BK

I'm not romantic enough to say I'm subversive. I'm not contradicting you, but *subversion*, I think, means that you're doing something that you feel you're getting away with. And I never make those claims for my work.

JP

You're using fashion as a political tool, though. You turned art and design into a political tool.

BK

But fashion has long been a political tool.

JP

It's also a business, a means to make a profit.

BK

It is. Absolutely. It is the most appropriative visual practice. I remember when I used to go to the Picture Collection at the New York Public Library. We all used to go there and look at images, and it was full of young fashion designers appropriating looks from the fifteenth century.

RLG

This is such an important aspect of living here in the late seventies: We all talked about pictures or images back then. All the artists whom I knew had the walls of their lofts covered with images; the television would be on, without sound, just for the pictures. I find it interesting that you were using the Public Library as your picture source.

BK

I used to go there and go through those files. It came from my experience working at magazines, like so many of us were at the time. Richard [Prince] worked at magazines; David Salle, too.

RLG

And Nancy Dwyer.

BK

Yes!

RLG

There was a group of artists working in the design department at Barnes & Noble, designing book covers, posters, and signage.

BK

It was the way we received things. The way images fed us and then we spit them out and retooled them for our own usage.

RLG

Let's get into the various convolutions with Supreme. Can you talk about the back and forth with them about their appropriating your typeface style?

BK

With Supreme, there was no back and forth. They've been doing that for years. The brand uses Futura white on red. I was aware of it and they were aware of what I was doing, too. I had no problems with it. I would not have said anything and certainly would have never sued them. I don't do that. I don't own the typeface. I'm not a corporation. Then Foster Kamer from *Complex* magazine contacted me and explained that Supreme was suing a designer who made "Supreme Bitch" merch using the same font. There's a picture of Rihanna wearing a hat with that phrase. He asked me what my take on it was. I just wrote three sentences back and that was it.[1]

They're in some kind of corporate imbroglio now, suing each other over copyright infringement. It's just not my trip. I remember years ago, RoseLee, there were a bunch of artists marching down to D.C. to defend artists' copyrights. And I just said, "How can I join them, since people call me an appropriation artist?" (Although I don't see myself that way.) Who am I suing? That's ridiculous. I'm not against copyright

1 "What a ridiculous clusterfuck of totally uncool jokers. I make my work about this kind of sadly foolish farce. I'm waiting for all of them to sue me for copyright infringement." Email from Barbara Kruger to Foster Kamer, senior editor of *Complex*, sent on May 1, 2013.

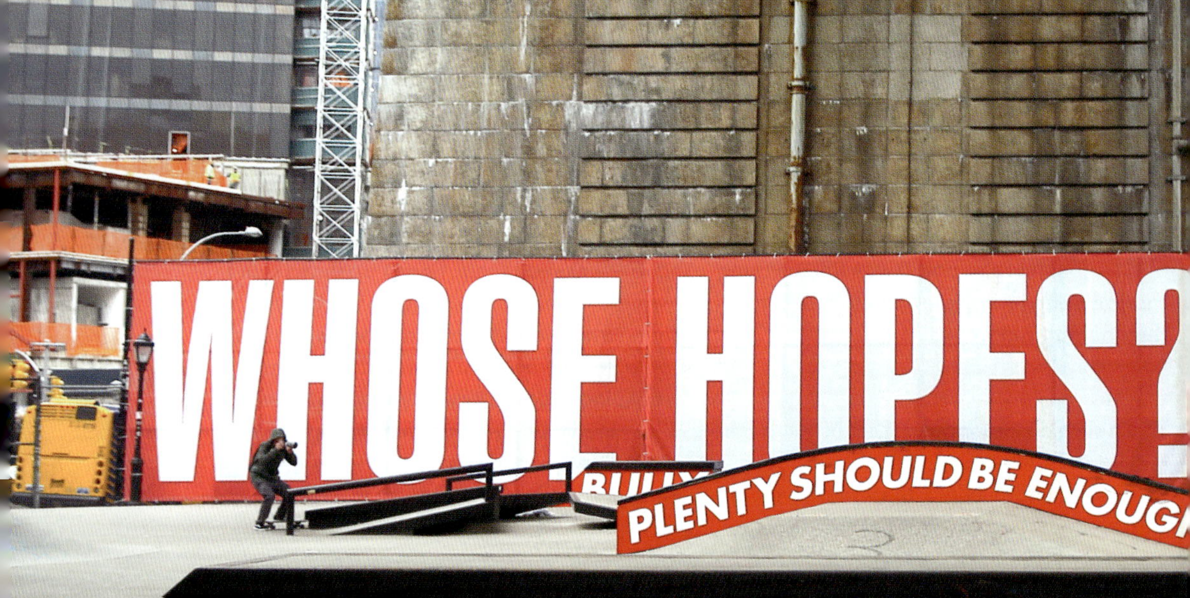
WHOSE HOPES?
PLENTY SHOULD BE
VALUES?
DOES THE CRIME?

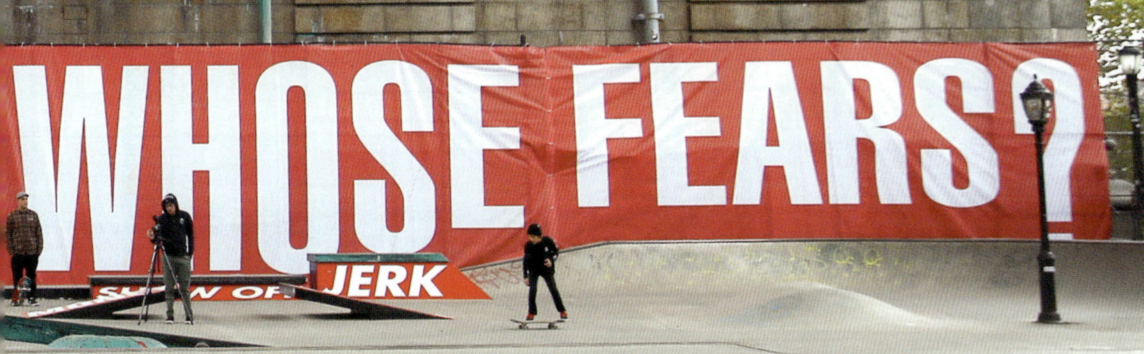
WHOSE FEARS?
JERK
SHOVE IT. PRAISE IT.
WHOSE JUSTIC
WHO DOES THE TIME?

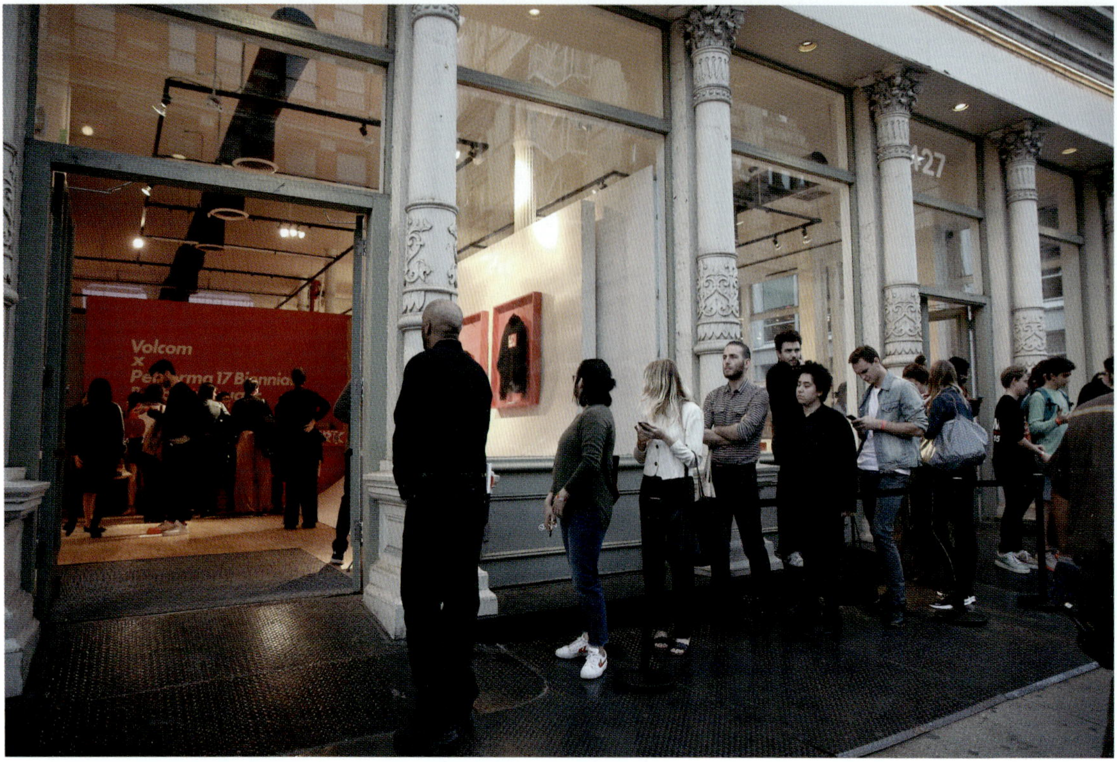

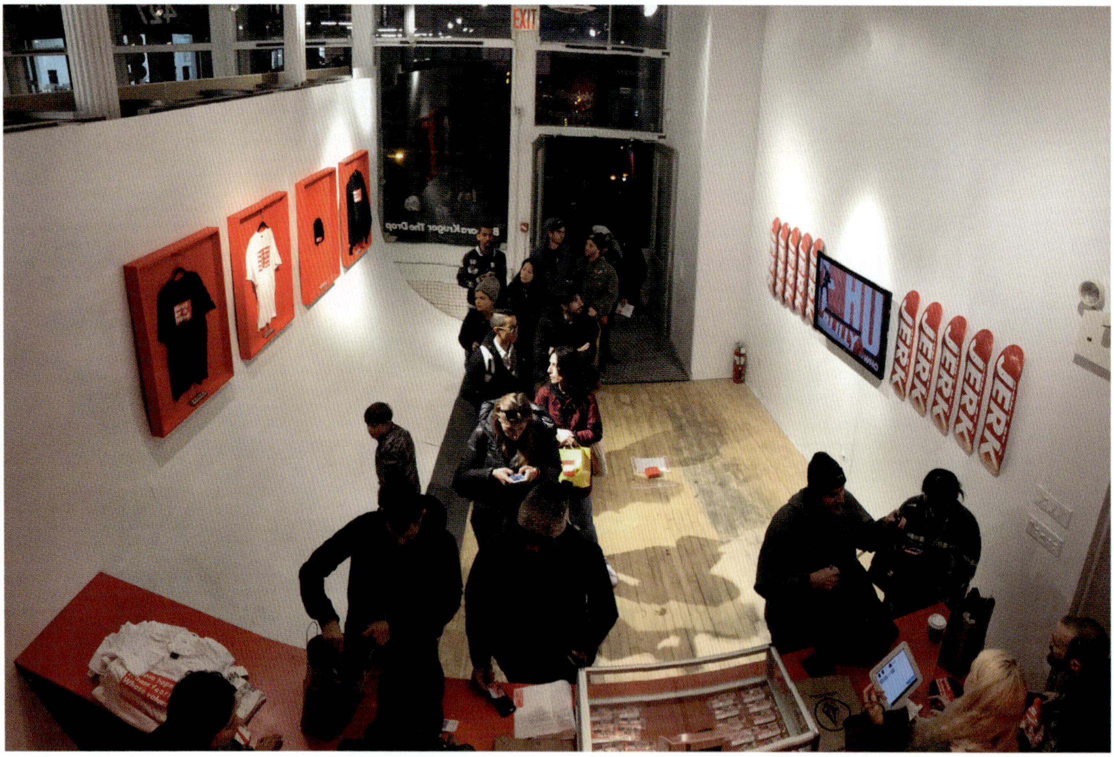

at all, but I do feel that, in many ways, it has become a euphemism for intellectual property and corporate control.

Let them sue each other into oblivion. Lucky me that my work has become part of the parlance, or cultural vocabulary.

JP

How did you react when you discovered the skate park? I remember, you were fascinated by its sound.

BK

It was just amazing! (And I hate to use the word *amazing*. Everything is *amazing* now.) I was struck by the sound reverberations from the cars and the trains overhead, on the Manhattan Bridge. It was industrial—not postindustrial—an industrial cathedral of the twentieth century. And its scale! All those noises. All the traffic. And—because it's New York and America—it has rotting infrastructure: You looked up at the bridge and parts of it looked like they were falling apart.

JP

I love this idea of a skate park that comes out of a rotting infrastructure. It's the least desirable place and yet, the skaters took it over. We should mention Steve Rodriguez, a skating legend and Volcom ambassador, who designed the park. He came by way of Sasha [Okshteyn], our producer. He's a crucial part of the story.

BK

He was amazing! We walked in there with him, and the waves parted. Everybody there knew who he was and had great respect for him. You couldn't walk through there otherwise, with everyone moving around, but everyone parted for him during our walkthrough. It wouldn't have happened without his wonderful support.

RLG

I remember going down to the skate park and watching the skaters as they whooshed across the park in one long horizontal ride, then turning around and going back again, and other skaters going by in parallel rows. I felt like I was standing on a beach watching the ocean. You know how the water just keeps coming to the shoreline and then receding, back and forth without end.

BK

And the sound!

RLG

The sound. So many sensations. I could sit and watch forever. The skaters would start out moving slowly on their boards, their bodies sometimes covering one word or another. It was poetry in motion. I loved the way they would arrive at the park and begin their ride: there seemed to be a kind of agreed upon choreography as each skater made their entrance from the wings as it were. And the sound. Each one walked casually to the edge, carrying their board, then there's a loud crash as their board hits the ground. The rider then places one foot on the board, pushes hard against the ground with the other, and they're off! Watching their movements over your language was so beautiful. Regulars were upset when we took it down at the end of the biennial, after only three weeks in place.

JP

There was disappointment at *The Drop*, too.

BK

Yes. I was getting all these emails and texts from my friends who wanted to meet me there but there was absolutely no reason for me to be present. This event was about ritual, waiting, the procession, and the commodification of ideas in objects. It wasn't an opening for me.

RLG

It's true, it was quite difficult for us to be anywhere near the storefront with *The Drop*, because people had to understand that waiting was part of the work.

JP

I felt first-hand the roller coaster of emotions that your performance produced. At one point, I was downstairs [at the Performa Hub] with Sasha. We were preparing new orders. I felt both pressure and anxiety, and I realized we were embodying the intent of this project. I was going through joy, pleasure, frustration, all at the same moment, from this frenzy to consume.

BK

And the confusion! This often has to do with performance and how cultural productions are coded within them. Some works are totally accessible, but others are deeply coded and become unreadable or questionable, which can cause chaos and a sort of wariness or even rage.

The act of waiting in line on the sidewalk for a commodity is something which has arisen so much with these pop-up drops. They usually happen on Thursdays and I'd see so many of them walking through SoHo. There was one on Greene Street, for Louis Vuitton, where they had chic black chairs one after another down the block. Everyone understood what they were doing there. These situations were already performative.

JP

"Where does *The Drop* start and end?" became the question.

RLG

Well, the other interesting thing was who knew exactly what it was and who didn't. For some, a drop was a completely unfamiliar phenomenon. They hadn't walked past the lines that you describe, Barbara, or if they had, they didn't actually see them, or notice the built-in drama. Shoppers show up at seven in the morning, come rain or shine, and stay all day to buy a pair of sneakers. At your drop, visitors were asking: "What are we supposed to do?" "We're paying to stand in line?" That was the biggest confusion. They were mystified. They just didn't get the irony.[2]

BK

Exactly.

JP

Some guests asked for a special treatment, and I'd respond: "I know you've traveled to come see this. For you to experience its intention, you should get in the line and wait. The meaning could evade you if you don't participate from beginning to end."

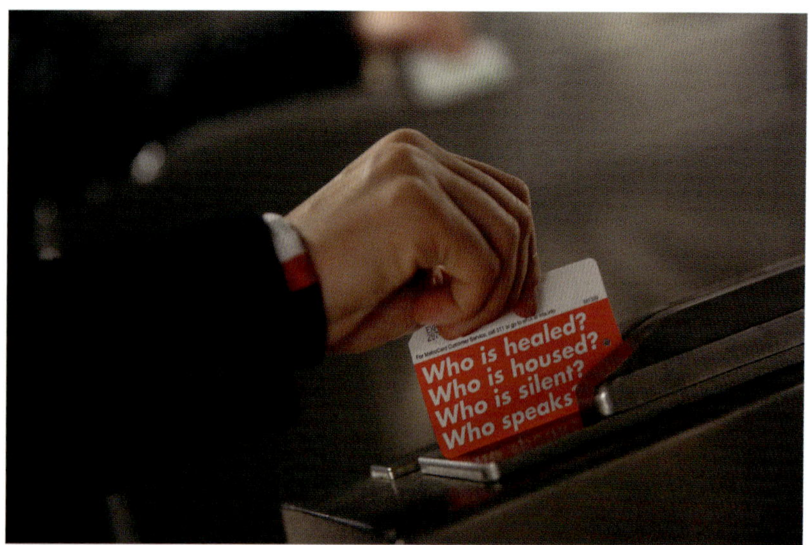

2
See Finlay Renwick, "How Waiting in Line Became the Biggest Fashion Trend of the 2010s," *Esquire*, December 20, 2019. https://www.esquire.com/uk/style/fashion/a30292432/queue-supreme-palace-louis-vuitton-2010s-fashion/

BK

I felt ambivalent about that, because I didn't want it to be a contemptuous gesture. It was problematic to me, like I was some kind of a trickster. In many ways, I saw it as a framing of something which happens quite regularly—literally every Thursday—within those few blocks. It was a commentary of sorts. That hectic moment connected to Dada for me. It was just so chaotic and kind of fabulous.

RLG

What a great way to look at Dada in the city.

JP

The formation we had to create reminded me of Roman Ondak's line for *Good Feelings in Good Times* (2003). But Ondak's queue came out of his experience of seeing them outside grocery stores while growing up in communist Slovakia; yours comes out of late capitalism. I thought a lot about the different meanings of these two different lines. With one major difference: Ondak cast performers. For yours, the audience was voluntarily lining up.

BK

Don't forget the influencers we hired.

JP

True. That was the other exciting part of *The Drop*—to see how the piece lived online. It was not just the drop on the corner of Broadway and Howard in SoHo. It had a real presence on Instagram. We were engaging within a consumerist space, one that co-exists online. To this day, *The Drop* is still expanding through eBay auctions and resale sites. The virtual queue is still growing.

BK

And the skating videos are on Instagram, Facebook, etc. And there was the bus. There was the MTA. The billboard on Tenth Avenue.

JP

And the branding of Performa 17.

BK

I remember the day that RoseLee dropped that on me.

RLG

It was like a month before the biennial and we weren't happy with the designs we'd seen so far. Suddenly there it was—the perfect solution.

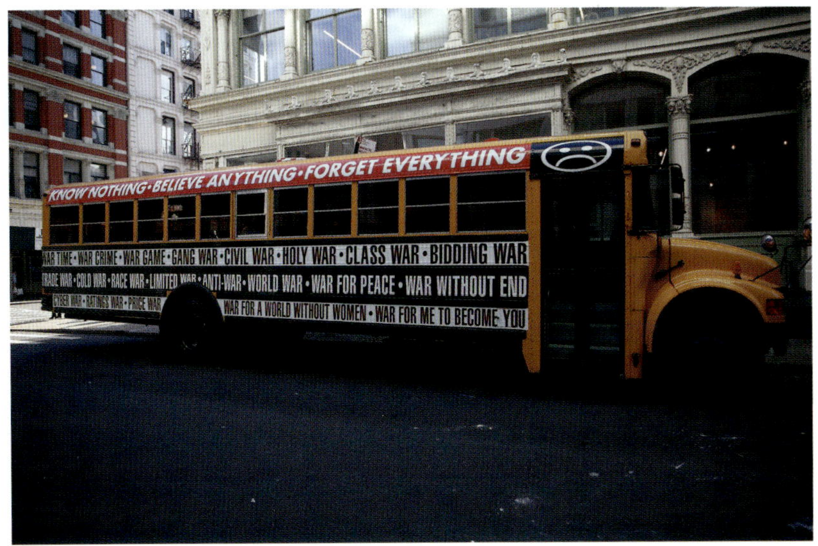

JP

Art solves problems! What did you think about branding an arts organization, especially one based in New York?

BK

I mean, it's Performa, so of course I would do it. But it was a lot. The bus itself was hugely difficult to fit into the plan. We had everything to do in the skate park and then we had the branding to do. Oh my god. The fact that I could do this with Project Projects made a huge difference. I usually don't do logos. I only did one previously, for Benjamin Millepied and the Los Angeles Dance Project.

RLG

You know Barbara, this has been a dream—Performa taking an artist's ideas to the outermost edges of engagement, with an entire city. Returning to your comment of touching so many people, of being "aerosol," it truly achieved that. I wore my "Want it / Buy it / Forget it" hat again today. It's such an instructional piece—it has meaning in an instant. I had someone stop me on the subway and go, "Uh huh. Yeah." It's certainly the hat to wear at art fairs, too!

Getting back to the question of language: The texts that you come up with quickly become central to the conversation. When do you come up with these slogans like "Whose Values?" Do you find yourself responding to the TV while you're watching Fox News?

BK

"Whose Values?" was originally done for a *Newsweek* cover in 1992. It was during the Bush era, when the right wing had appropriated the notion of values. They called me and said, "We want you to do a cover about values." I said I didn't want to be appropriated by that right-wing discourse and that's when I first did that work, asking whose values we (you) are talking about. I've since used that question repeatedly. It is unfortunately still relevant. I'm not a fortune teller. This goes back centuries.

JP

When I was your student at UCLA, I learned how you use words the same way you can use colors or paint: You can bring forth multiple new meanings from the same material simply by changing the arrangement.

BK

Yes, that is so horrifyingly true. I remember I had done a work at Mary Boone's gallery around 1994. It was the first work I made using audio, and it went like: "Think like us / Look like us / Pray like us / Hate like us." The immersive wall and floor wrap had a sonic backdrop of a mix of brutal sounds—crowds, laughter, jeering. I was asked to redo it in Lucerne, Switzerland, in 2003 ["me & more," Kunstmuseum Luzern]. The reaction was strong: The audience, as well as the press, said it was my response to 9/11. But it wasn't. It was from 1994. The same issues of subjugation, murder, power, and dominance have been going on for ages.

RLG

What has changed, though, is the scale of your work. You've done a lot of projects that are about architecture, opening up the notion of the urban environment—just breaking it apart, changing the way we see our surroundings. During the biennial, we could follow you across town and see entirely different sections outside of our routines, discovering places we'd never been. I just wondered if this led you to other ways of thinking?

BK

For the past thirty years, the big difference, the change in my practice, has been in the ability to spatialize the work. Having to do mainly with finances, I started making little prints, and then they got bigger. I wanted to engage with architecture, and then, with this Performa Commission, the built environment, rather than the singularity of working within a building. I'm not a Santa's Workshop type of artist. I don't have a studio (literally) or any assistants, or a workplace full of stuff that I turn out. That's not wrong, but it's not the way I do things. So, the opportunity to spatialize the work and engage viewers has been so appreciated.

RLG

A beautiful way to say it—the spatialization of your work.

BK

But that's the armature of what you do at Performa.

JP

Barbara, I also have to remind us that we had our initial visit to your studio in January 2017, and we were able to pull it off by November 2017 . . . You move quickly.

RLG

Like skateboarding through the city.

BK

It's the urbanization of surf culture. "Under the cobblestones, the beach."

JP

May '68! Students dug up cobblestones to throw at the police and a layer of sand appeared.

RLG

For me, it speaks to what you say about the spatialization of the work and this notion of activism at a profound level. Somebody the other day said to me, "Nowadays more artists do politics." I replied, "It's the only work I follow." I look back on all the works that have been in Performa, starting with Shirin Neshat and Isaac Julian, which have been visually stunning, but at the same time deeply political and meaningful. As the song goes, "a spoonful of sugar makes the medicine go down." These artists talk about performance as a profound way to get closer to politics and the public. They have this sense of humanism and humanity and are asking what we're doing to the world. "Whose Values?" was literally in your hand, on your subway card.

BK

The other thing that was important to me is that most of the people who had the MTA card didn't know who "Barbara Kruger" is, and that's fine by me. The visual arts do not loom large in America, except around the speculations of investments in luxury goods.

RLG

Isn't that fantastic? The anonymity of it. It's what makes someone go, "What's on your hat?" as I experienced today on the train.

JP

Or when you walked past the skate park.

BK

It was such a satisfying experience for me. Performa's support made it all possible. I couldn't see it ever happening without you.

This conversation between Barbara Kruger, RoseLee Goldberg, and Job Piston took place in New York on November 3, 2018. It has been edited for clarity.

Ever since the inaugural Performa Biennial in 2005, which featured Capetonian image maker Berni Searle, the organization and its Durban, South Africa-born Founding Director, RoseLee Goldberg, have presented the nation as a point of constant inspiration. Over the past decade, Performa has staged the work of Candice Breitz, Athi-Patra Ruga, Robin Rhode, William Kentridge, and the collective Chimurenga, who all shared their distinct visions with New York City audiences.

Performa 17's South African Pavilion Without Walls took a deeper look into post-apartheid practices: Since the 1990s, multiple generations of South African artists simultaneously shifted away from modern and contemporary Western art and expanded their modes of production, informed by a culture of ongoing resistance and global change; art and politics were not separate spheres but intricate, interlocked societal and intellectual systems in which they played important roles. Performance, in particular, emerged as a direct, accessible, and versatile vehicle to reach across a multitude of languages, tribes, identities, and landscapes. Bringing together artists who have developed deeply personal and individual vocabularies, Performa 17 sought to shed light on the complex strategies and conceptual frameworks defined by the contradictions, disparities, and skepticism generated in the midst of dramatic political shifts.

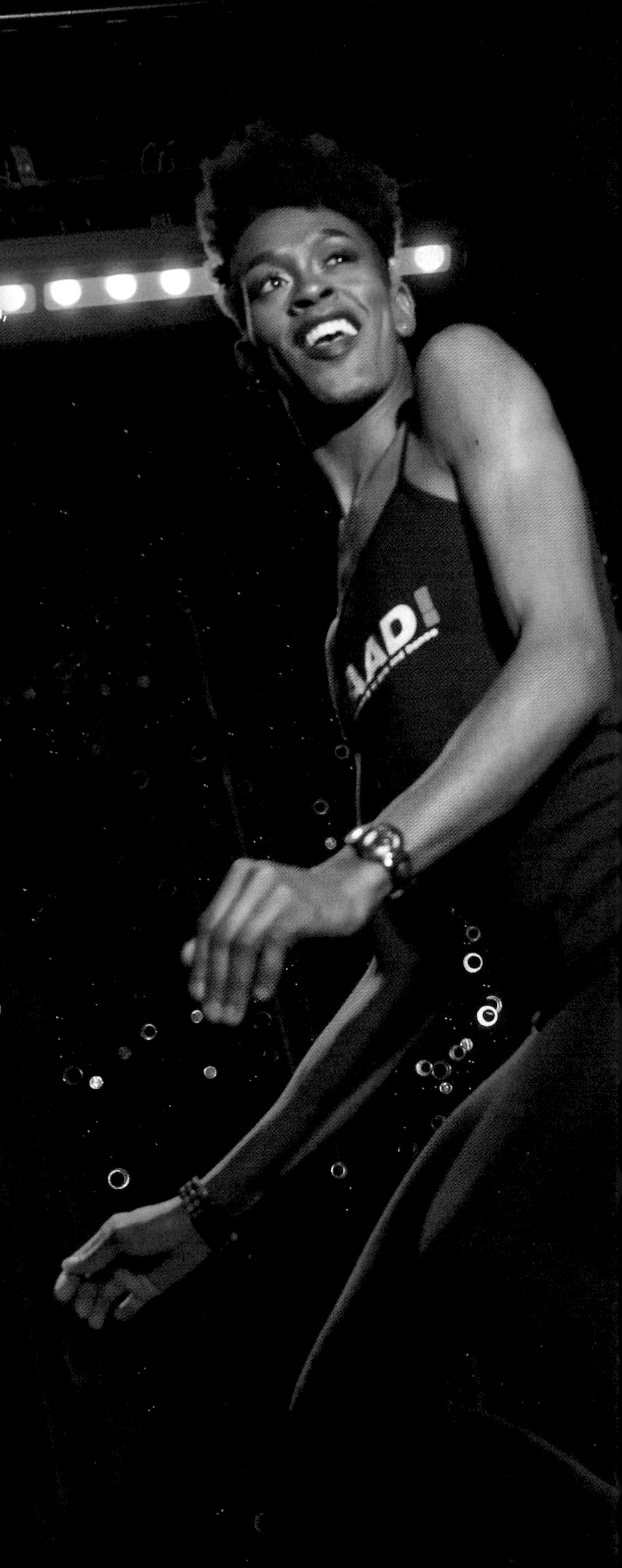

BELOVED COUNTRY

HE TAKES LIBRARIES WITH HIM: A PERSONAL REMEMBRANCE OF OKWUI ENWEZOR

Sue Williamson

Okwui Enwezor has left us. He died of cancer on the 15th of March, 2019, in Munich, where he had been, until recent months, director of the Haus der Kunst. His departure at the early age of 55 is almost unthinkable and infinitely sad to contemplate. He was a visionary curator with an unparalleled understanding of the depth and sweep of African—and global—art history and its contemporary practitioners. He had a sense of exactly how all the disparate and complex histories fitted into and influenced international art practice and discourse. His curatorial and art historical achievements have radically expanded the boundaries of artistic endeavor.

In person, Okwui was a stylish, gracious man, with an easy laugh and an insatiable curiosity. He had a way of listening which seldom failed to elicit respect and admiration. Received information would be considered, reflected upon, and given back, placed swiftly and fluidly within a new, expanded framework.

It was an honor and a privilege to have known him for more than twenty years, and our meetings have been here in Cape Town on a number of occasions, but also in Dakar, Chicago, Venice, Bern, London, and New York.

Okwui was peripatetic, and, after his early successes, in demand everywhere.

The first time we lunched together was at the Obz Cafe, Cape Town, along with Ashraf Jamal, my co-author on the then newly published *Art in South Africa: the future present*. It must have been the beginning of 1997, or perhaps even late 1996, and Okwui had recently been appointed artistic director of the 2nd Johannesburg Biennale, scheduled to open in the fall of 1997. I had heard news of the young New York-based Nigerian curator: that he was beginning to make his mark, and had curated a show for the Guggenheim Museum in New York titled "In/Sight: African Photographers, 1940 to the Present," an exhibition which moved beyond the ethnographic and exotic images taken by Westerners in favor of work by African photographers. I also knew that two years before that, together with his fellow Nigerian curator Chika Okeke-Agulu, the art historian Salah M. Hassan, and the artist Olu Oguibe, he had launched the magazine *Nka* specifically to cover contemporary African art. I was excited to meet Okwui and to hear his plans for the upcoming biennale.

The 1st Johannesburg Biennale had been held in 1995, and had followed the biennale model of national pavilions, or exhibitions, but Okwui explained over lunch that he had decided on a different approach for his edition. His theme "Trade Routes: History and Geography" explored the hybridity of the contemporary art world, and, as he wrote in his catalog essay, "owes something to the restless contingent histories of people who in the last half of the twentieth century have gathered at the edge of events, under a common heading called *globalization*." Thus, instead of national pavilions, Okwui took a global approach, and appointed a roster of like-minded curators to bring to Johannesburg—and to Cape Town—one of the most exciting series of exhibitions ever to be seen in this country. The artists he invited, if not already well-known, were to rise to the top of their fields in the next twenty years: Sophie Calle, Shirin

Neshat, Isaac Julien, Steve McQueen, Carrie Mae Weems, Cildo Meireles, Stan Douglas, Wangechi Mutu, David Hammons, Pascale Marthine Tayou, Hans Haacke, and Sam Taylor-Wood (now Sam Taylor-Johnson).

Many South African artists were also part of the Biennale: Patrick Mautloa, Penny Siopis, William Kentridge, Tracey Rose, Kendell Geers, Santu Mofokeng, Kay Hassan, Moshekwa Langa, and myself, to mention just a few. "South African art is so formidable because South Africans have this passionate deep belief that there is no separation between the imagination and the reality of every day," Okwui has said.

Writing about that Johannesburg Biennale in *Artforum* in 1997, curator Dan Cameron commented: "it's a profound relief to be able to report that this is the artistic payoff that everyone who's been traipsing the globe this year has been waiting for [...] the first global exhibition to transform the promise of postcolonial theory into a tangible reality, thereby almost completely exorcising the ghost of 1989's "Magiciens de la Terre" (Pompidou Centre) from the curatorial lexicon."

The accolades which followed the success of the Johannesburg Biennale led to Enwezor's invitation to be the artistic director of the 2002 edition of the world's most prestigious exhibition: Documenta, held in Kassel, Germany, once every five years. It was the first time the position had gone to an African curator.

Speaking at a gala dinner in New York on November 1, 2016, hosted by Performa Director RoseLee Goldberg, Okwui, the gala's honoree, reflected on the importance of his 1997 curatorial success, and that very auspicious beginning as a 32-year-old being appointed artistic director of the Johannesburg Biennale, and, three years later, as a 35-year-old, being appointed artistic director of Documenta.

"South Africa gave me the opportunity for the very first time in my career to produce something in Africa, something that was deep, important, and in many ways enabled me to travel the world. And without South Africa I would not be standing on this stage and that is why I am so indebted to South Africa."

At that dinner, Okwui, who was born Okwuchukwu Emmanuel Enwezor on October 23, 1963, in Calabar, a port city in southern Nigeria near the border with Cameroon, also spoke about his early years in New York.

"I came (to New York) simply because it was the thing to do, like many young people who came from Nigeria, or from different parts of West Africa in the 1980s. It was about being at home in the world. It was not in any sense about arriving at a place in which you transform yourself. You wanted to be a contributor to that transformation. So I fell into the art world by accident. And it was a very happy accident. I went into the art world because I wanted to construct and place myself, to create an emotional geography and an intellectual and cultural biography. But my journey is a journey that is not individual. It is a collective journey of all the people in our field. And when I step into one of my favorite museums in the world, the Metropolitan Museum, here in New York, it reaffirms the fact, of the reason why I started here in the art world.

And that is, it is not a museum of art. It is a museum of the human imagination. And I was first and foremost interested in the human imagination."

Following the success of the Johannesburg Biennale, Enwezor's next major curatorial coup was the highly lauded "The Short Century: Independence and Liberation Movements in Africa, 1945- 1994," a landmark exhibition of work and documentation by African, Asian, and Oceanic artists which challenged the appropriation of modernism by the West.

"I give you one reason why my commitment to contemporary art was really palpable. I wanted to understand why, in African art, the representations which had been realistic up until the 16th and 17th centuries suddenly shifted. I wanted to understand that. That what we call *primitive* shifted from very representational and became completely abstract. The destruction of the picture. And that for me was so incredible, giving me confidence, so that I could look at Picasso, and say, 'You're just only beginning.' It's really true."

In 2013, Enwezor became artistic director of the 56th Venice Biennale, taking as his overarching theme "All the World's Futures," selecting the work of 136 artists from 53 countries, almost two-thirds of whom had never shown in a biennale before. Criticized by some as too dense and too political, lauded by the most respected reviewers, the Biennale highlighted the precarious situation of artists and their communities across the world, and shifted the boundaries of contemporary art history.

With all that Okwui had going on at any one moment, it was hardly surprising that it was difficult to get his attention. Emails would sometimes go unanswered for some time, but one knew he had read them, and he might pick up the phone and call to announce an imminent arrival, or, just when a deadline was about to hit, send that email.

Thus, he would grant a Venice interview to *ArtThrob*, the online journal which had launched in August 1997 with a preview of the 2nd Johannesburg Biennale, or write an essay for my book, *South African Art Now* (2009), or give up time to spend two days in Switzerland with me and the young fellows of the Sommerakademie of the Zentrum Paul Klee in Bern in 2011, the year I was guest curator.

Our last meal together was a coffee shop breakfast the morning after the Performa gala dinner in November 2016. It was known that he had cancer, but he looked the same as ever, and talked with enthusiasm about the night before, and how much he had enjoyed Athi-Patra Ruga's musical procession into the dinner, and how honored he had felt by the occasion, accompanied as he was by his partner, Louise Neri. He talked about the imminent election, and how excited his daughter was about the prospect of a woman president of the United States. Little did we know.

At Okwui's suggestion, we did a final project together in the spring of 2017, an interview-style essay for the catalog of the Fondation Louis Vuitton exhibition "Being There," conducted over Skype and email. I had hoped to see Okwui at the opening of the exhibition in Paris, but apparently, he was not well enough to leave Munich. His absence cast a shadow over the proceedings.

When the sad news came last month, the tributes started to pour in. He was not only a giant in the art world but was held in deep affection by hundreds who had worked with him over the years, and there is no one who can fill his shoes. As RoseLee Goldberg texted me, "Even though we knew it was coming, the finality was heartbreaking. Such a brilliant mind and generous heart. He takes libraries with him."

This text was initially published online on artthrob.co.za on April 5, 2019. Reprinted courtesy the author and artthrob.co.za.

RoseLee Goldberg and Okwui Enwezor at the Performa 2016 Gala.

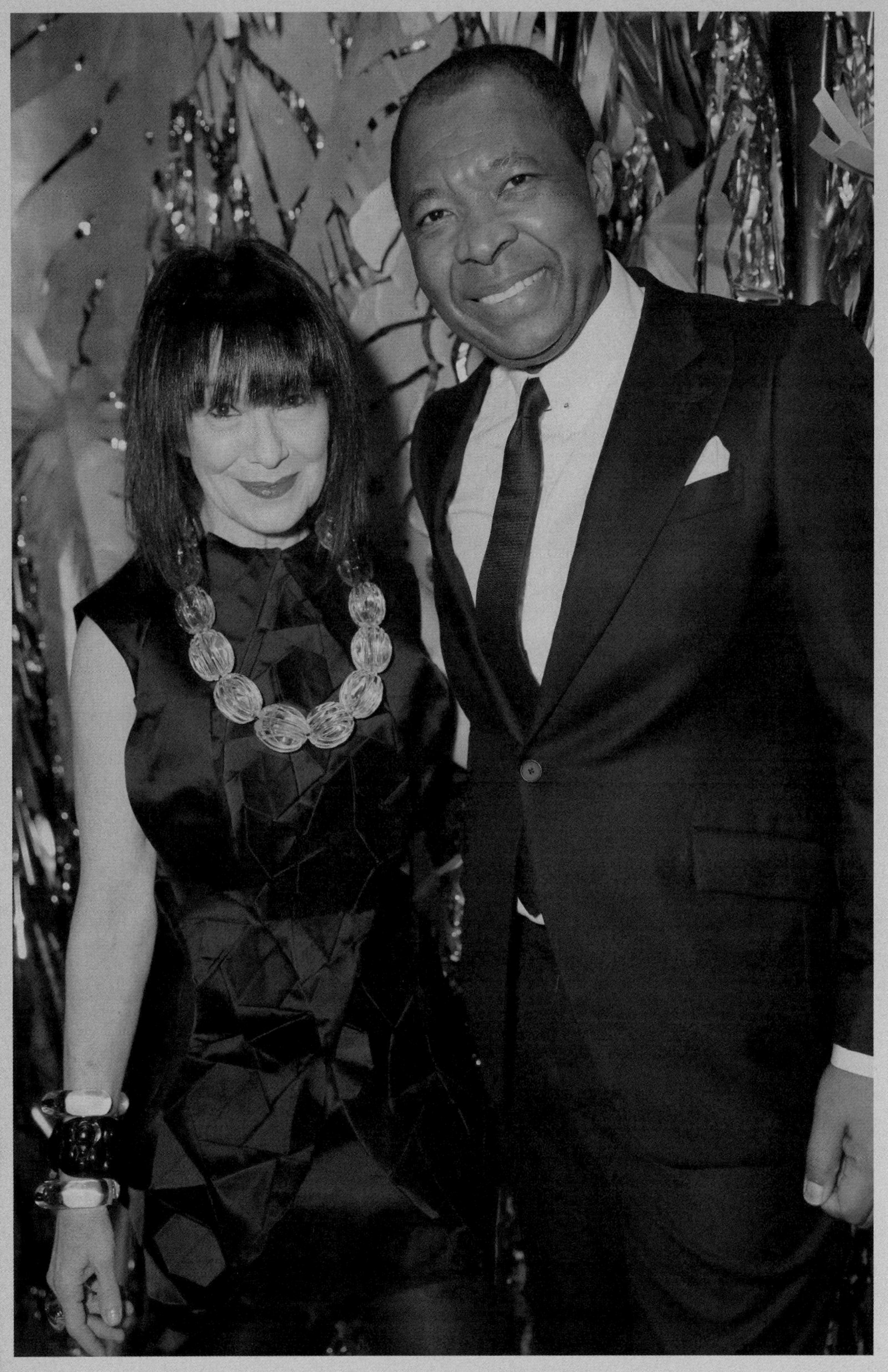

WILLIAM KENTRIDGE
Ursonate

Curated by
RoseLee Goldberg

Harlem Parish

November 5–6, 2017

At a lectern in the historic Harlem Parish, score booklet in front of him, William Kentridge stood to deliver Kurt Schwitters's iconic Dada sound poem "Ursonate." In his white dress shirt and glasses, the South African artist resembled something between a preacher and a teacher. With booming vocalizations, expansive gestures, and rapid-fire images projecting behind him, he began to speak: "Fümms bö wö tää zää Uu, / pögiff, / kwii E."

"Ursonate" starts with this line and maintains the same emphatic, thrilling gibberish over the course of its four movements, introduction, coda, and credenza. A German artist, poet, and graphic designer, Schwitters circled Dada after the first World War, embracing its intentional nonsensicality in his practice. "Ursonate" began in 1921, when he tried reading aloud "fmsbwtözäu," a poster poem by his friend Raoul Hausmann. By fragmenting language, picking and pulling and recombining letters into new combinations and exaggerating their pronunciation, the poet sought to compose a sonata in "primordial sounds." The style offered a mirror for the chaos of modern life, and breaking language provided access to communication beyond it, demonstrating that illegibility—a world-opening Dada tactic—still offers a striking critique of social hegemony and radically expands the possibilities of language.

Nearly a century after its completion, Kentridge added stop-motion projections to the score and expanded its script with live music by an ensemble comprised of a soprano, a French horn player, and a percussionist. He also thrust it into new global contexts, inserting maps, dates, and combative characters, alluding to the historical and ongoing violent residues of South African apartheid. His iteration oscillated between enlightenment and indecipherability, contouring Dadaism with the realities of racial violence entangled in the Western avant-garde's fetishization of African "primitivism."

Commanding the parish, Kentridge moved through each sound—rolling and staccato, stretched and clipped—with a bravado almost paradoxical to the text's incoherence. As a theater student in late 1970s Paris, he trained with Jacques Lecoq, the pioneering movement coach and mime. As he gained momentum through the work's progression, the artist's motions and intonation imbued a sense of urgency to each line. If the phonemes, some repeated, some new, troubled interpretation, then the artist's authorial, electric physicality suggested meaning in their combinations.

In the meticulous instructions Schwitters wrote for his poem, leaving directives on tone, tempo, and enunciation for future performers, he remarked

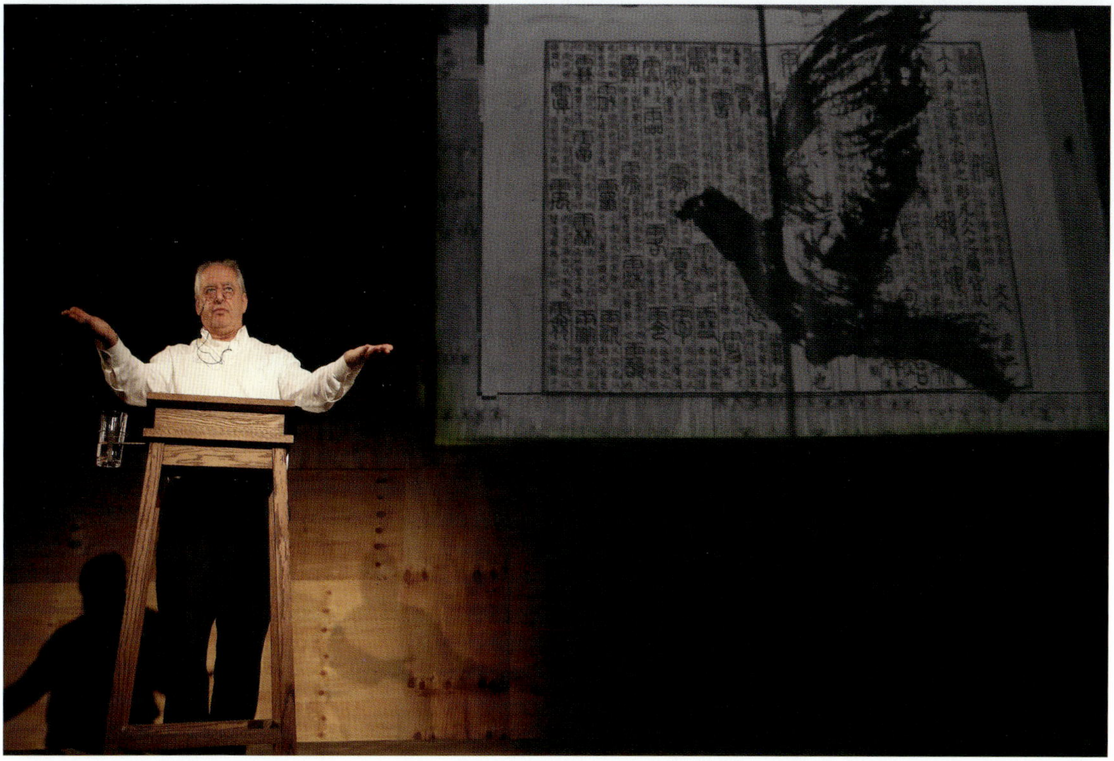

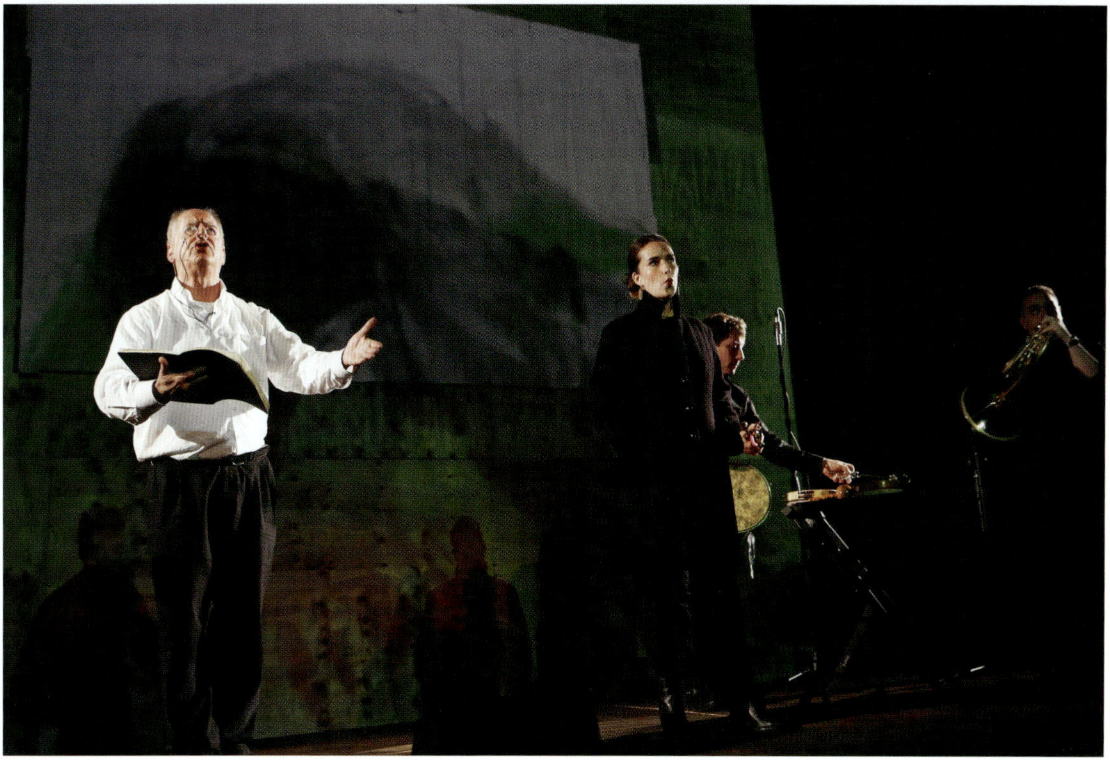

that listening to "Ursonate" is "better than reading it." Kentridge transformed the work into something not simply to hear but to see, expanding the sonata into the visual and heightening its political resonance. Overlaid on double-page book spreads, abstract shapes, text, and his signature charcoal drawings—of figures, birds, even himself—the images counterbalanced and echoed his oration. Certain projections—a map of the African continent, a young Black ballerina holding a rifle, the Soweto uprising against the forced instruction of Afrikaans in 1976—ricocheted the speech into the legacies of racial inequity, which the artist frequently addresses in his work. Fragments aligned: As the artist thundered "Bumm bimbimm bamm bimbimm," edging *bomb* and punctuating each word with force, the flower genus *brunfelsia* (the Yesterday, Today, and Tomorrow shrub) ran on the pages, followed by a "A SAFE SPACE FOR STUPIDITY," washed over by a plume of smoke. These suggestive intersections came and went without firm explanation, allowing for the explosive associative potentials of nonsensicality.

Alone, Kentridge continued through the melodious incantations, building toward its final section, when a French horn interrupted him. He looked up and hurriedly flipped through his sheets as a woman's voice rang out. Soprano Ariadne Greif stormed the stage, delivering lines to the artist as the two vocally sparred. They chanted back and forth, a two-member band assembling around them to orchestrate their delirious repartee. At moments they appeared in spirited debate; at others, in raucous play. At one point, he instructed Greif on a particularly roaring "Rrrrrrum!" As the credenza closed, he slowly and patiently recited the last section: "Gee äff Ee dee zee beeee." Amplified and shaped by his masterful performance and interjections, the evening took on a fraught transcendence, pushing against its expressive limits. QUINN SCHOEN

William Kentridge,
drawing for *Ursonate*, 2017.

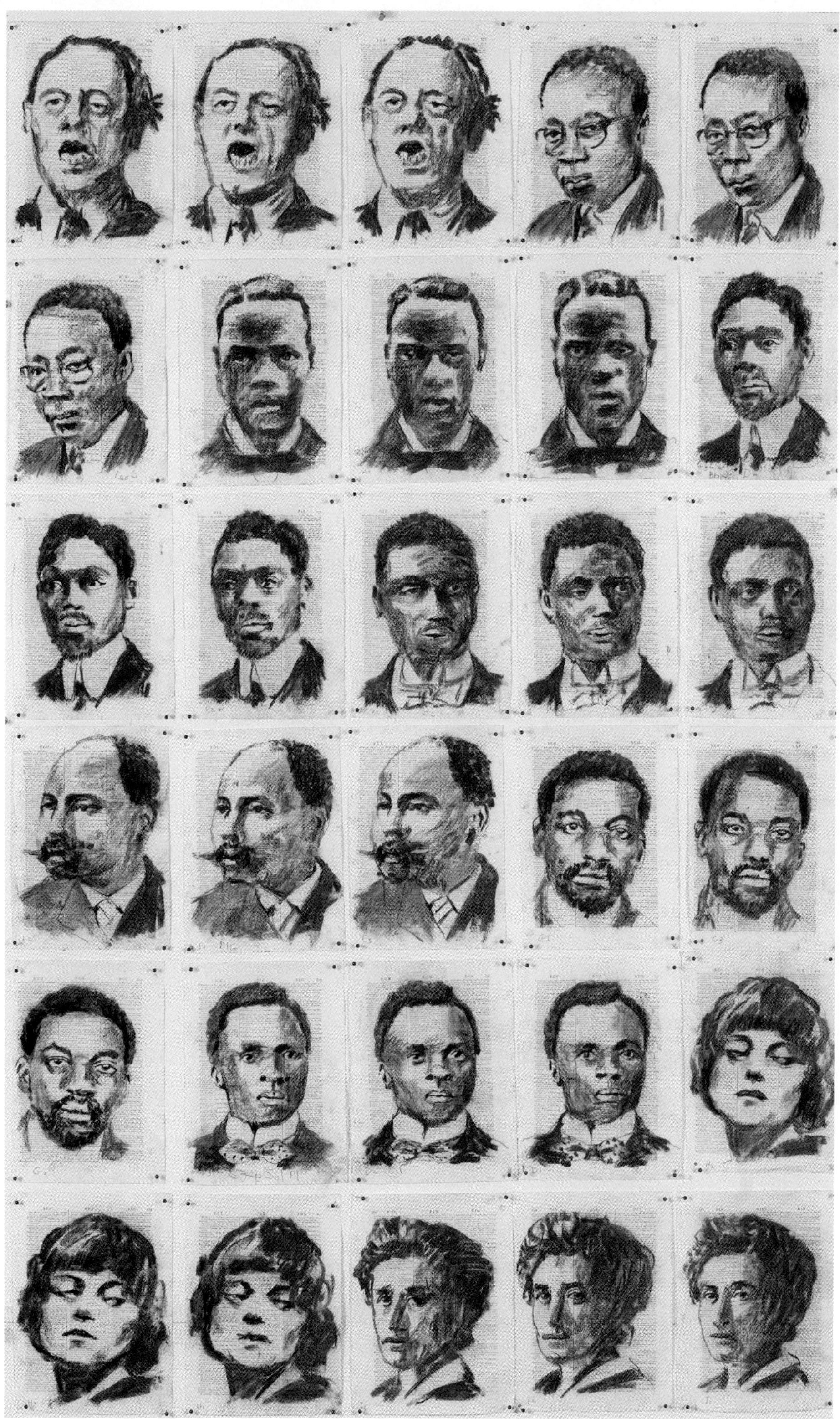

KEMANG WA LEHULERE

IN CONVERSATION WITH

EVAN MOFFITT

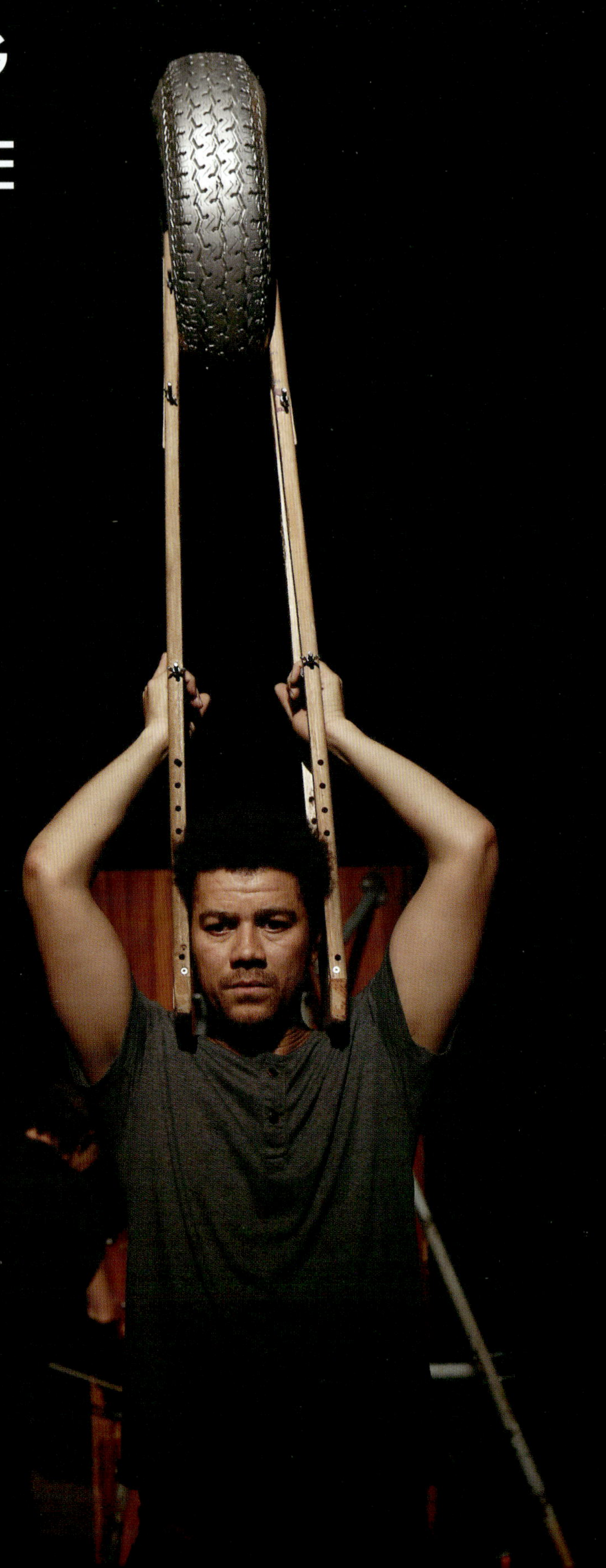

I cut my skin to liberate the splinter

Curated by RoseLee Goldberg

Connelly Theater

November 3–5, 2017

Kemang Wa Lehulere was a rebellious student. Growing up in Gugulethu, a township near Cape Town, South Africa, he refused to accept instruction in Afrikaans, and insisted that his primary school curriculum—largely a holdover from the apartheid-era education system—make room for Black African history, art, and literature. Wa Lehulere has since repurposed rough-hewn wooden desks from township schools for sculptures and installations that pick at the physical and psychic legacies of colonialism. At first glance, his chimeric oeuvre, which includes video and performance as well as drawings on a variety of surfaces, such as chalkboard, has a kind of Dadaist whimsy: mesmerizing in its cacophony, laced with non sequiturs that conceal deeper meaning. See, for instance, the plastic African gray parrots that perch on birdhouse pegs in many of his works: A species known for its ability to mimic human elocution, the bird could be an apt metaphor for Sotho children forced to parrot Afrikaans language and culture. Birdhouses, too—like slanted township homes—provide shelter even as they confine their inhabitants to the control of others. Other works by Wa Lehulere feature the cheerful ceramic German Shepherds that dot many South African lawns—domesticated animals colonized by training, valued for their obeisance to the will of their masters.

In I cut my skin to liberate the splinter, *winner of the 2017 Malcolm McLaren Prize, the artist assembles these images of submission like troops in an armed resistance. As the performance unfolds over the course of an hour, performers dance on school desks and truck tires, march in sand-filled suitcases, shuffle birdhouses, and read poetic messages written on notes curled inside glass bottles from the top of a large wooden pyramid onstage. Along with real trumpets and makeshift horns, many of the sculptures are activated as musical instruments, with a group of trained musicians playing a mournful, clattering jazz on them. Detritus can't be weaponized if it's used instead for play. The ambivalence of Wa Lehulere's work is that of post-apartheid South Africa: democratic yet dysfunctional, violent yet vibrant. In light of past national traumas, his objects give room to express anger and frustration, but also hope for the future.*

EVAN MOFFITT

Thank you Performa for the invitation; Kemang, congratulations again. I had the pleasure of seeing the piece on Friday and there were a lot of moving parts that I'd like to discuss in greater detail. But first, I wanted to talk about your diverse background in terms of media and disciplines. One of the most distinct elements of I cut my skin to liberate the splinter is the band of sculptures activated as instruments, and you are a performer along with all of the musicians involved. You have a background as an actor, correct?

KEMANG WA LEHULERE

A little bit, yeah.

EM

And you also started as a painter. I'd like to know how you came to performance and how that began to play a central role in your work. How do you see performance relating to this insistently sculptural, multimedia, physical aspect of your practice?

KWL

Okay, so, painting, acting, theater. When I was growing up, I had two cousins who were involved in theater, film, and television…The older one of the two is named Tumele Walule. I met Chuma Sopotela, who's performing with me in the piece, through him probably more than fifteen years ago. After school, I would go to the theater where Tumele would be working on productions, and I'd sit in the rehearsal room and do my homework. I'd watch him working with young actors; that's how I really got to know Chuma.

As a result, I became quite fascinated by theater. I joined a space called Cape Town Theatre Laboratory while I was still in high school. I became part of Bax Teens, a theater group for teenagers at the Baxter Theatre. Through this, I did a little bit of work in theater and had really marginal roles in television and film projects. This really excited me at the time, and initially I thought I'd become an actor; that was my dream. But this was the late 1990s; we had just transitioned to a democratic South Africa, and, with the history of apartheid, things were really fragile, as they still are. And, because—how do I say it—I'm light-skinned, but I'm Black, right? In South Africa, that's a major mind fuck for a lot of people. Elsewhere isn't a problem, but in South Africa, it's like, "Oh my God, what do we do with this guy? He's Black." I'd audition for roles and be told I wasn't credible enough to play a Black person onscreen. As a result, I shifted away from my dream of being an actor.

Throughout high school, I was doing art, which I hated, because I didn't get along with my art teacher. I only did art because I had fights with my math teacher, so, automatically, I had to take art, which I also hated. But I enjoyed painting and drawing; I painted voraciously and made drawings throughout this time. When I left high school, I was like, "Okay, fuck! What do I do now?" Then I went to a space which no longer exists called the Community Arts Projects (CAP), which was an art center built during apartheid, because Blacks weren't allowed to go to university and study art at that time.

The Community Arts Project was education and theater, visual arts and music. A lot of musicians and artists who were prominent toward the end of apartheid and immediately after had been through this institution. I went there and initially did theater, but within a space of six months, I felt really bored because I'd been doing the workshops in high school. So, I was like, "Okay, let me challenge myself and do the visual arts program." That's how I transitioned into painting. I thought I was going to be a painter, but that also fell to

1 The final year of high school in South Africa.

the side. We started an art collective called Gugulective in 2006 and were pushing experimental work together. We all came from different backgrounds: we had painters, we had people coming from theater, poets, writers, and musicians. In fact, the most important education I've ever received was working within the collective.

EM

It sounds like performance actually enabled you to get back to your original passion, theater, while still keeping an art practice.

I want to go back to the theme of academic frustration, which seems to come up in your work. You've used salvaged school desks to make your sculptures, and your recent show at Stevenson Gallery [in Johannesburg] addressed the troubling history of education in apartheid and post-apartheid South Africa. I'm wondering if you could talk a little bit about that. It's my understanding that you studied woodworking too—

KWL

In high school.

EM

—which was one of those things that they taught Black students in order to emphasize practical education. Diminishing literature and politics was used as a form of segregation.

KWL

I received quite an incredible education, actually, by all of the challenges. The challenges were designed as obstacles, but these obstacles were very important for me in terms of how I think today. As you mentioned, the experience was geared toward practicality. During apartheid, one of the presidents actually said, "Why teach someone something that they will never use?" That spoke to how education was engineered to create a working class out of the Black population.

I come from a family of very vocal people. My uncle, my mother's brother, became a student activist after my aunt, my mom's sister, was shot in the head in 1976 during the student uprising. She survived, and he became fiercely political. He went to study math during apartheid, which was an anomaly at the time. In fact, when he was doing his matric,[1] his results were so good that they thought he was cheating, so they forced him to strip naked, and then they watched him repeat his final exam this way. By the time I got to school, I was hyperaware of this political history in my own family. In high school, the history books ended as we touched the Soweto uprising of 1976. I protested: I refused to speak Afrikaans. The school had to change the Afrikaans teacher and get someone who could also speak Xhosa, and I was the only student allowed to avoid speaking Afrikaans: I made the case that I refused to do so on political grounds, which I now regret, actually, but that was me at the time. In terms of literature, we never read any Black writers. As a result, my high school English teacher developed a curriculum outside of the main one for a small group of us. We met during lunch breaks and after school; we'd sit and read African writers. And then again, by the time I got to university, it was very Western-oriented, and we were, like, "Where are the Black artists? Where is the African history?"

This is not to say that I am against European or Western knowledge, but I felt it wasn't balanced. I couldn't see myself in that history. This is really why I've chosen the school desk as a material in my work. It's because of my own experience, but in many ways it's also a critique of the education system, both historically and in the present sense. I use it as a vehicle to teach myself a lot of things that I was denied. For example, I don't play a musical instrument, but I've worked with Dan [Daniel Bruce Gray] to build these musical instruments, or these objects that become musical.

EM

Do you consider yourself a musician?

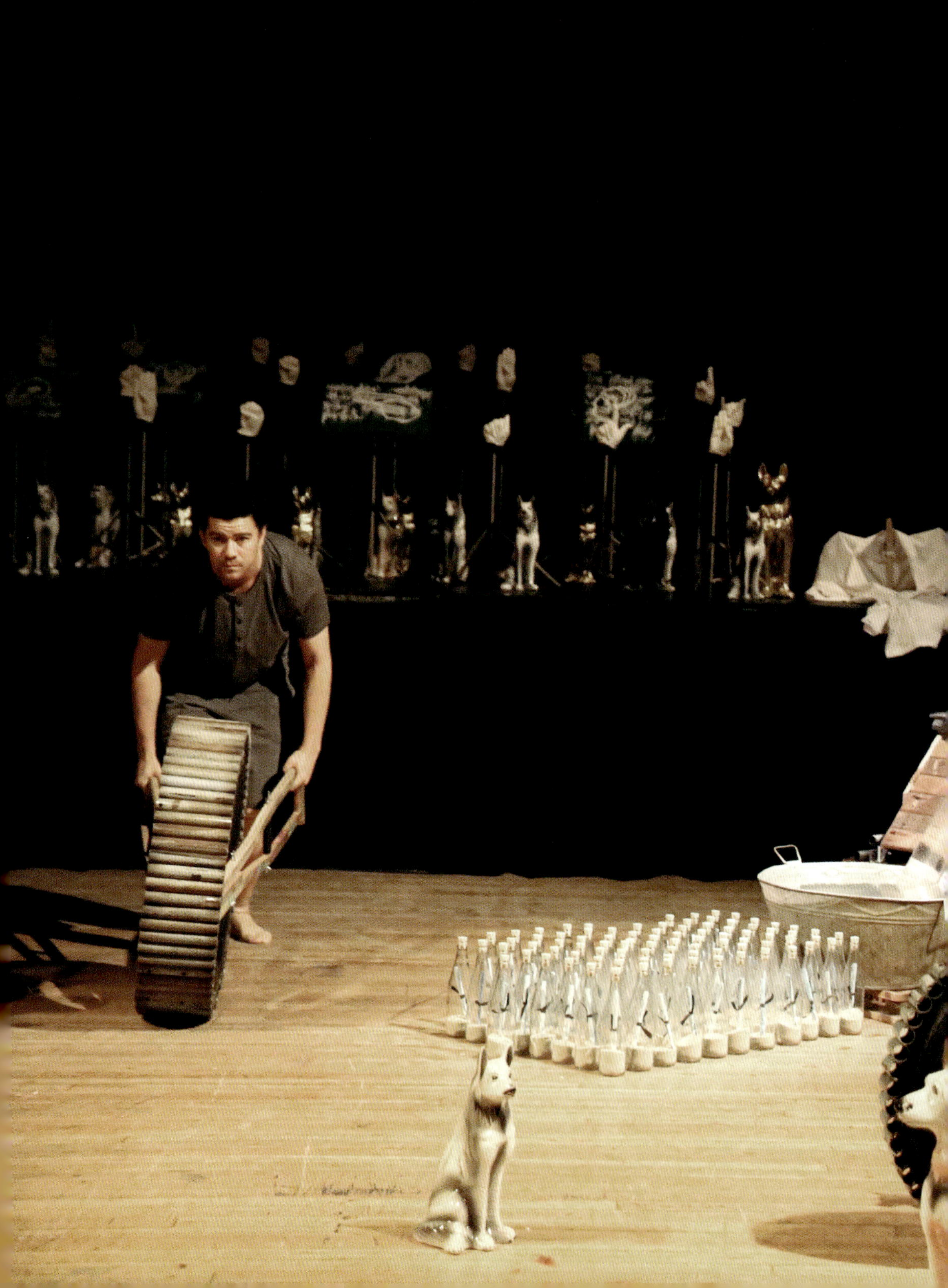

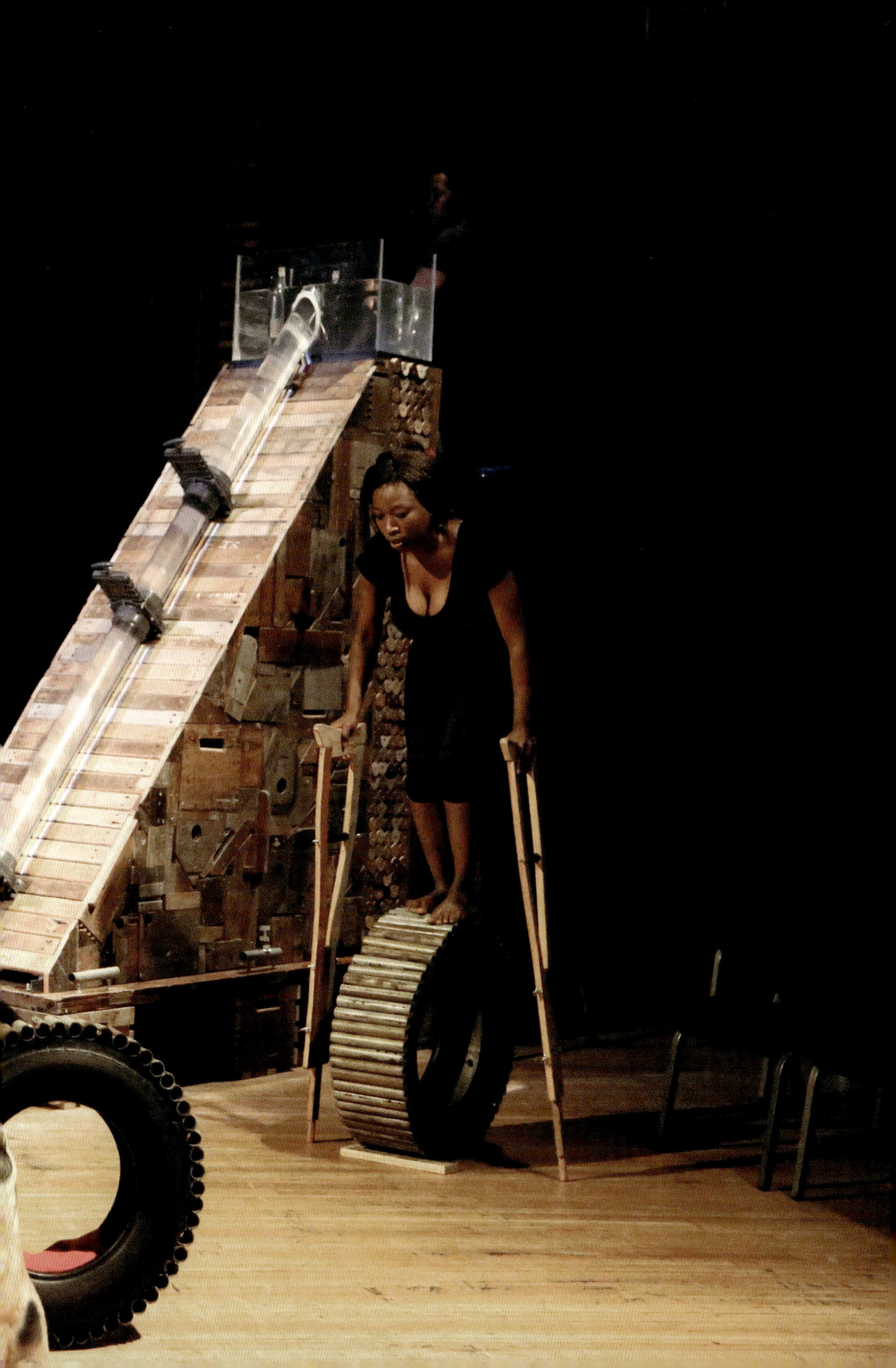

KWL

That's a tough question. I think, for a long time, I didn't consider myself an artist. Last year, when I was about to open my show at the Art Institute of Chicago, for the first time, I was like, "Fuck, I think I'm an artist, I have a solo show in a museum in the U.S." And I was like, "I'm an artist? Okay. I'm an artist." In that sense, I think it would take years for me to consider myself a musician. Someone came up to me after the show and said, "Wow, the musicians were great." I was like, "These guys aren't musicians." Dan is the only one who has a musical background. Lesedi plays the trumpet, but everyone else, myself included, had no experience. Dan was interested in making musical instruments that are designed so that anyone can come and play with them. At the same time, it makes it incredibly difficult to write music for these instruments, which for me is more exciting because it demands that you be spontaneous and free.

EM

Are you kind of a conductor in the piece? How does the musical improvisation get organized during the run of a performance?

KWL

Well, we had a lot of conversations about that. The project was conceived when I initially approached Chuma, and RoseLee [Goldberg] came with the commission. Chuma and I had worked together a decade ago. She'd been wanting to do something again, but I was like, "Yeah, let's wait until the right moment," and the right moment came when RoseLee approached me. We sat down and looked at the body of work that I had built over the last decade because I'd been interested in making sculptures that I could perform with.

We had long conversations about this, and I was also in the process of producing a jazz album ["the bird song album"], so a sense of musicality was quite strong in my mind at the time. My mother died just after she'd finished writing an album and didn't have the chance to record it, so, last year, I produced and co-composed a jazz album with a friend, because I wanted to complete something for her. Earlier this year, Dan and I staged an experiment, an intervention in the studio called Dr. Mshini's Laboratory, and used simple objects and every kind of thing we could get our hands on to make music and sounds with.

I wanted to create a performance that could encapsulate the entire body of work I've been producing over the last ten years, but not in a didactic manner. We started building objects, and Chuma was present in the studio throughout—we were working on the choreography during the actual manufacture and production of the sculptures. While the machines were going and the welding and the cutting of wood was happening, Chuma and I were there, doing workshops and thinking about movement and gestures. It was unscripted, and as a result it was a continuous response to the process. I wanted to treat the process like a painting, where you make a mark, you paint over it, you paint over it, you paint a new layer, or you take away a new layer.

EM

Was the actual construction of the instruments somewhat improvisatory? I'm sure it takes a lot of engineering to make a working electric cello that's six feet tall and made out of a salvaged swing set. Did you have any kind of acoustical advice on that, or was it just try, fail, and try again?

KWL

There are three kinds of elements to the project. There's a choreography, which I worked on with Chuma; then there's the musical element, which I worked on with Dan. We actually built more things than we brought to New York. I mean, RoseLee came to me and said, "Just dream." I was like, "Really? Let's just go wild, let's imagine something, let's try this."

2
Maya Angelou, *I Know Why the Caged Bird Sings* (New York: Random House, 1969).

EM

I'm wondering, given that the instruments in your performance are sculptures, whether you feel that they're only completed as actual works when they're played, or whether your sculptural objects take on a life of their own outside the context of the performance?

KWL

Initially, I imagined them as standalone pieces, which was challenging because, as I said, there are other pieces that didn't make it here in the end, so we had to edit. But the idea was that they could exist as things on their own, but can also be activated. That is what I was interested in, and it really came because of Chuma. When we were looking at the work I'd been making, she said there was a lot of suggestion toward mobility or something that can be activated in them.

From the swing, to tires, to paper planes made out of these school desk materials, that's really how we came into the piece—from Chuma's interest in wanting to activate this thing. With her coming from the theater, where it's very physical, it became about movement. That's how we began thinking about this project. Previously in my work, there was an evocation or suggestion toward music, but there was intentionally never any music produced.

Then, thinking about the element of performance, it was, "Okay, how do we activate these things?" The music that was always silent is enhanced, even in this piece: There is a kind of silent orchestra with sign language and the hands on the stage. The text reads, "Please remember on my behalf," and the hands I cast were my aunt's, the one who got shot in the head in '76. It was about finding a balance, and, for the first time, I've really managed to do that in a way that is quite satisfying.

EM

As I mentioned, there are a lot of moving parts in your work. There are moments of frenetic energy in the performance, but it also feels quite mediated, perhaps because of a parallel sense of precarity—like the moments when you're balancing on a pipe or standing on top of a suitcase. There's a really poignant moment where one of the performers is reordering birdhouses, faster and faster and faster, and it becomes this really exhausting, harrowing activity. I'm curious if that precarity was an intentional allusion to something individual or collective. I felt exhausted—in a productive way—watching the performance, and I wonder whether that was intended as an expression of a specific kind of frustration in response to a sociopolitical context.

KWL

With the birdhouses, one can evoke Maya Angelou when she says, "I know why the caged bird sings." For me, this kind of expression is about years of frustration about forced removals.[2] It's about migration; it's about ideas of home and exile. The thing is, while the work starts from a very personal place, I intentionally direct it toward a place to where the work can be accessible and meaningful to people anywhere in the world.

Whether one is speaking about the current political situation in the U.S. and issues around migration since Trump took office, or the refugee crisis in Europe, or South Africa, we're talking about forced removals in the colonial period to apartheid to now, with this major housing problem—Cape Town has been gentrifying over the last year; I've never seen this extent of homelessness before. It's insane, to be honest.

I like to approach my work in a way where it's open, it's metaphorical, it's poetic. I search for a slippery slope where nothing is ever really definite because I'm suspicious. I'm an incredibly suspicious person. I'm suspicious of my own belief systems, I'm suspicious of politics, I'm suspicious of politicians. So, as a result, I never want to settle for anything, I chose to be on this kind of slippery ground, almost like having a wet bar of soap in your hand: It's something that you can almost grab, but it can also always slip away.

That's how I approach the work and how I try and find balance. In fact, one of the lines in the piece came from my dad's journal. It reads, "Here I am, a concrete man throwing himself into abstraction." I think, for me, that really defines my practice in a way. It's kind of like this balance between the concrete and the abstract.

EM

I have one more question about writing, because one of the organizing structures in the performance is the system of bottles with messages inside them—I have to say, it was an amazing piece of stagecraft that I've never seen before. A bottle gets dunked into a tank of water and is released and pulled up into a chute, and then it's read by a performer at the top of a tall pyramid. Were those pre-determined messages? And is there a message in every single one of the bottles? I had no idea where you—

KWL

Wouldn't you like to know? (laughter)

EM

You don't have to answer that. But, at first, I thought it was really going to be a durational performance; I was like, "Okay, they're going to be dancing for five hours."

KWL

Okay, to answer your question honestly, there were only five messages there because we only did five, but it was an aesthetic consideration. I had considered having more, but then I considered that we were going to New York, we'd be presenting this in New York. I had to consider the New York audience, which in a way is kind of like a Johannesburg audience, because the city is so busy and people don't have time; they're always rushing. I had to be like, "Okay, to what extent can this go?"

The duration of the piece was really informed by an idea of what I thought a New York audience would be like; I don't really know what the New York audience is like, but I have an idea, right? That influenced the duration and certain choices. We cut out a lot of things. It was longer, in fact, up until Friday. Before we premiered, we were still cutting things down, but there is a kind of sense among all of us that we'd like to extend it, actually, because we performed the piece for the first time in its fullness on Friday just before the actual performance for the public.

In a way it was also a kind of delivery thing, because, coming back to the initial

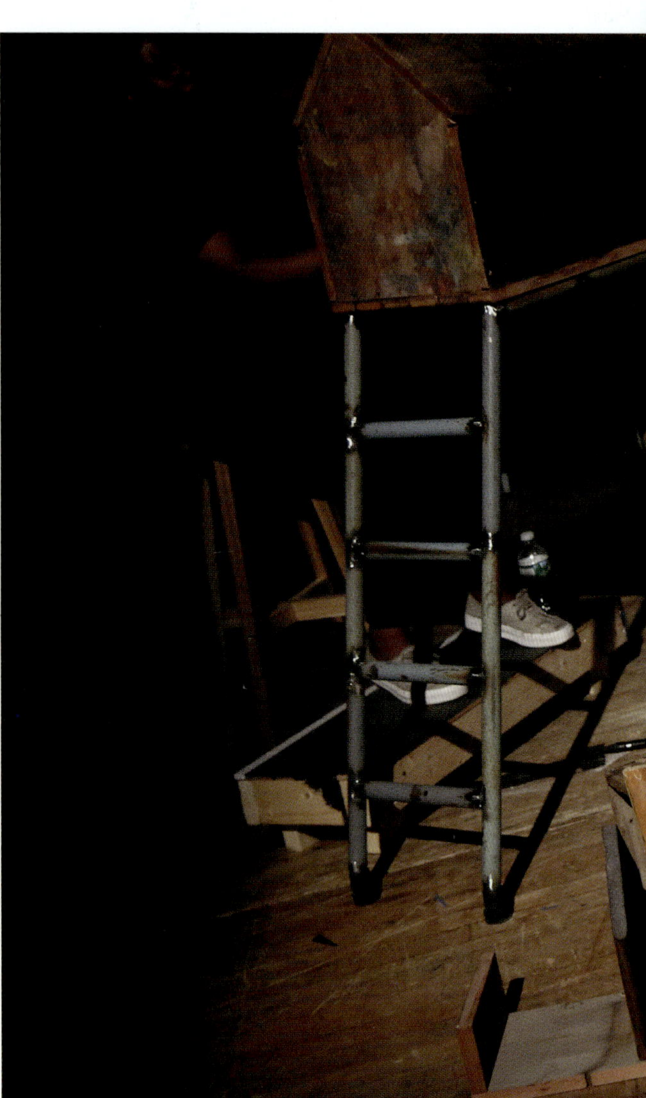

discussion about the theater and my journey, it's knowing the process of theater-making, and the amount of rehearsals that go into it. I didn't want the piece to be dead, so to speak, or stiff. I wanted to leave some room for discovery up until the last moment. When we were working on the choreography with Chuma, we'd work to a certain point, then I was like, "It feels like it's too subtle, it's too fixed, it's too finished."

So, I said, "Okay, let's stop, let's do something else." We'd leave that and then come back to it later because we had five months of intensity in the studio every day, like Monday to Friday, eight to ten hours a day, just working on this thing. I wanted to leave kind of an uncertainty for all of us. In the studio, of course, we came knowing the movements like we'd rehearsed, and we practiced certain things, but I didn't want to—I don't know how to say it. It's like uncertainty, but also knowing and unknowing, I wanted that slipperiness.

This conversation between Evan Moffitt and Kemang Wa Lehulere took place in front of an audience at the Performa 17 Hub on November 6, 2017. It has been edited for clarity.

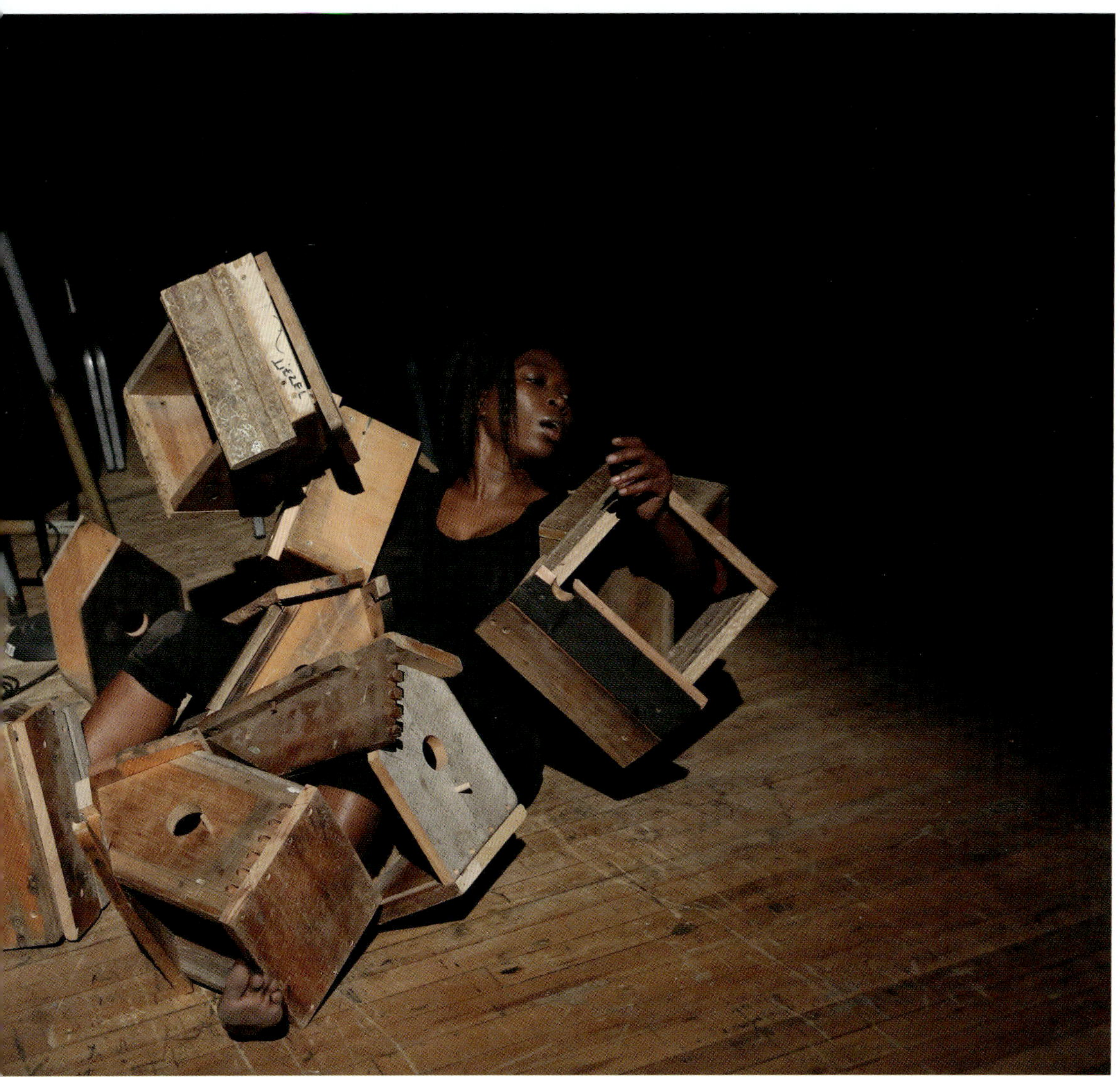

ZANELE MUHOLI

Masihambisane - On Visual Activism

"This is beyond ads," announced South African photographer and visual activist Zanele Muholi, speaking on the occasion of their interdisciplinary, city-spanning endeavor (the artist uses 'they/them' pronouns). "I want to share information and knowledge that our people possess," they stated, "especially Black LGBTI people," and, true to its title—Masihambisane means "let's go together" in Zulu—their objective brought them to New York along with the Sisonke collective and its nearly two dozen members of artists, musicians, drag performers, and poets.

A longtime advocate for queer rights in their home country, Muholi delivered an expansive, multi-iterative platform that wove together photography, digital screens, and live performance over several boroughs. The artist staged a large-scale takeover of the city's topography: Their striking self-portraits were disseminated throughout the ubiquitous screens in subway stations and platforms and appeared on the colossal video billboards of Times Square.

Stark, arresting grayscale photographs from the series *Somnyama Ngonyama* ("Hail, the Dark Lioness") show a dexterity both behind and before the camera, using what's at hand—including plastic tubes, clothespins, and inflated gloves—as makeshift garments and hair accessories. Muholi's subjects uncover some of the invention inherent in any portrait or presentation; digitally enhanced, they also challenge the pervasive exotification of the Black subject in mass media.

Masihambisane proliferated these images in public; it also took the form of public programs, performances, and nightlife festivities. The artist and their entourage were equally at home at the Bronx Museum as they were at the Stonewall Inn in the West Village. Talks at Harlem's Schomburg Center for Research in Black Culture and "Information Station," their temporary resource center on queer media from South Africa at the Leslie-Lohman Museum of Art—a SoHo institution dedicated to LGBTQI art and history—supported the project's mission of activism and outreach in New York while celebrating the resilience and vitality of South Africa's LGBTQI community.

Curated by RoseLee Goldberg with Maaike Gouwenberg, Lydia Brawner, and Job Piston

BAAD! Bronx Academy of Arts & Dance, Bronx Museum of the Arts, Leslie-Lohman Museum of Art, Schomburg Center for Research in Black Culture, Stonewall Inn, Times Square, and PUBLIC Arts.

November 2–14, 2017

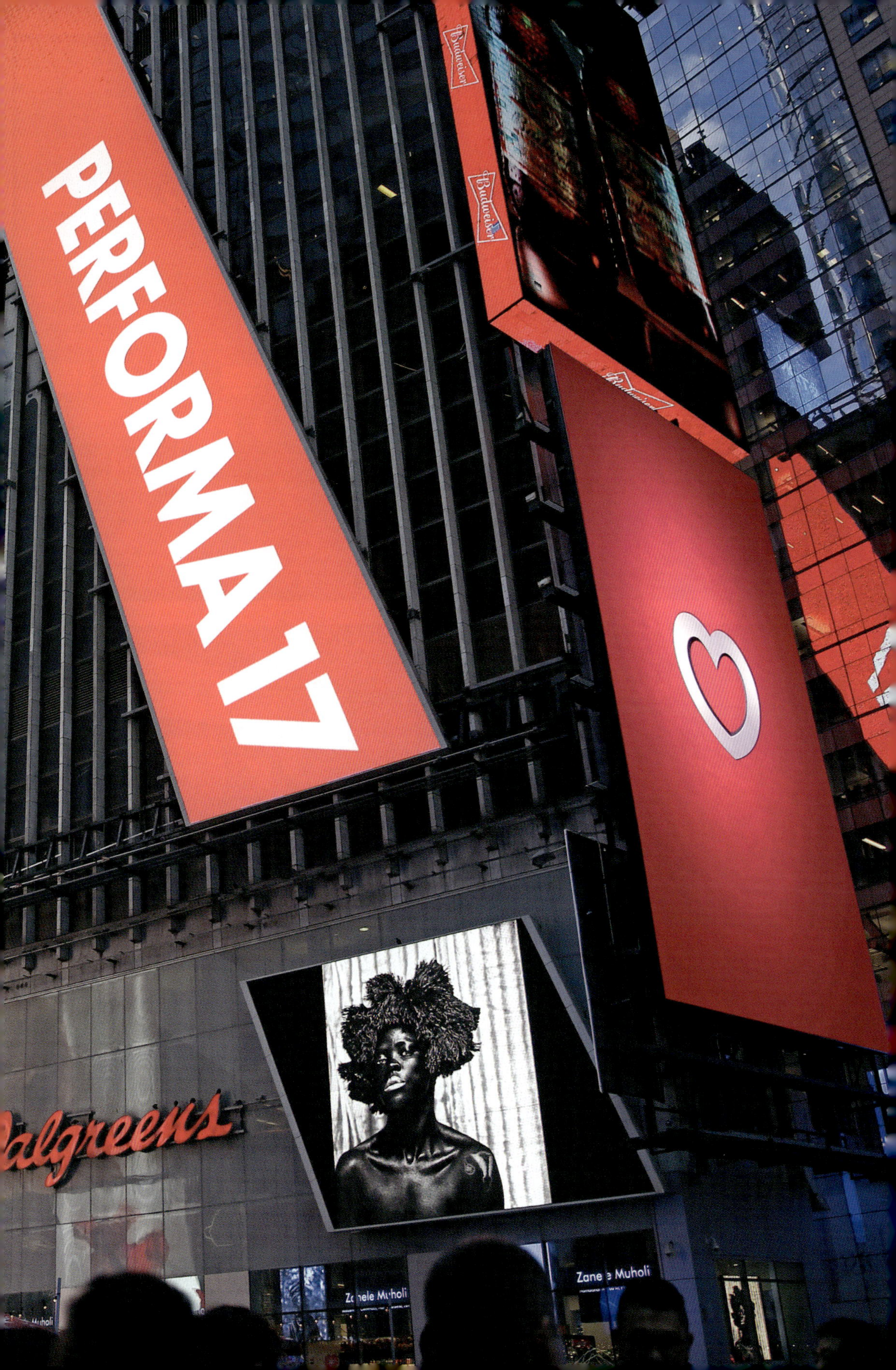
PERFORMA 17
Budweiser
algreens
Zanele Muholi
Zanele Muholi

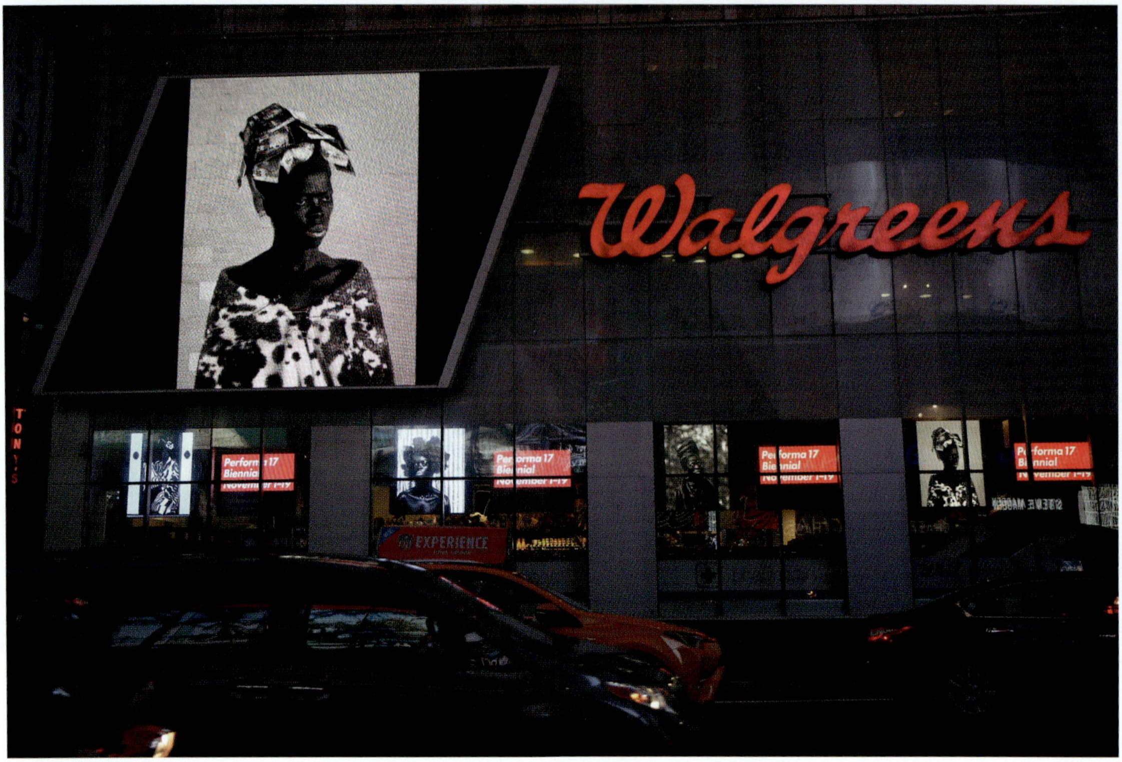

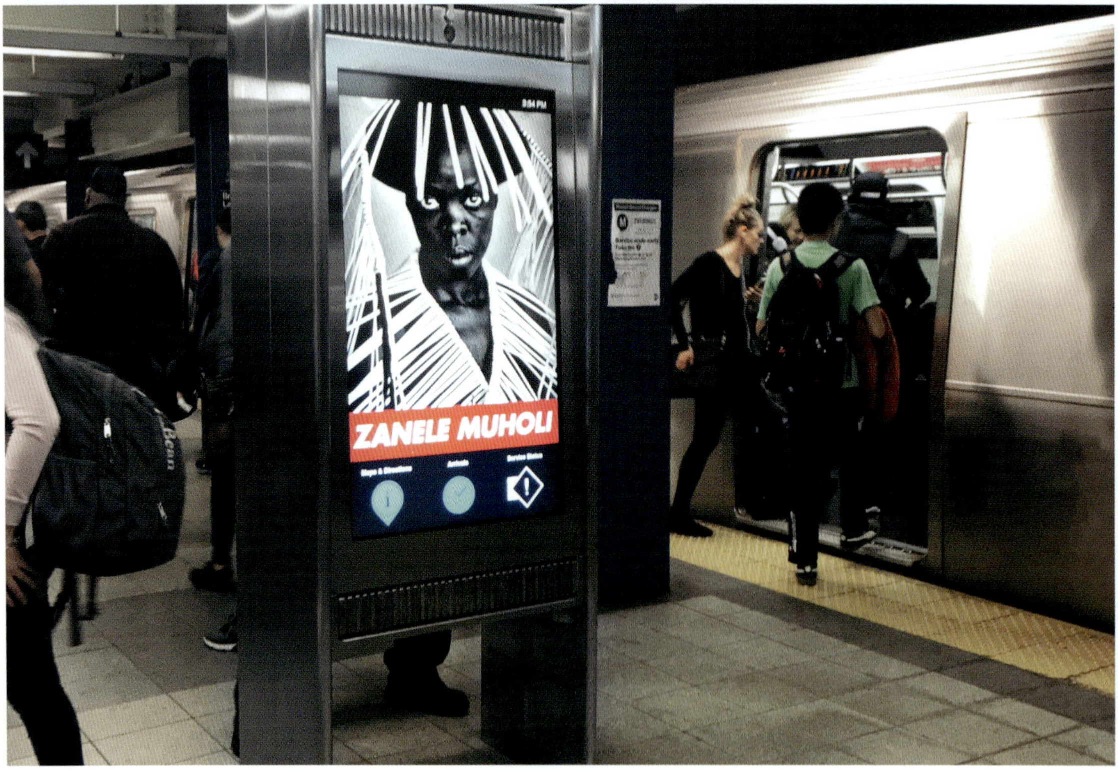

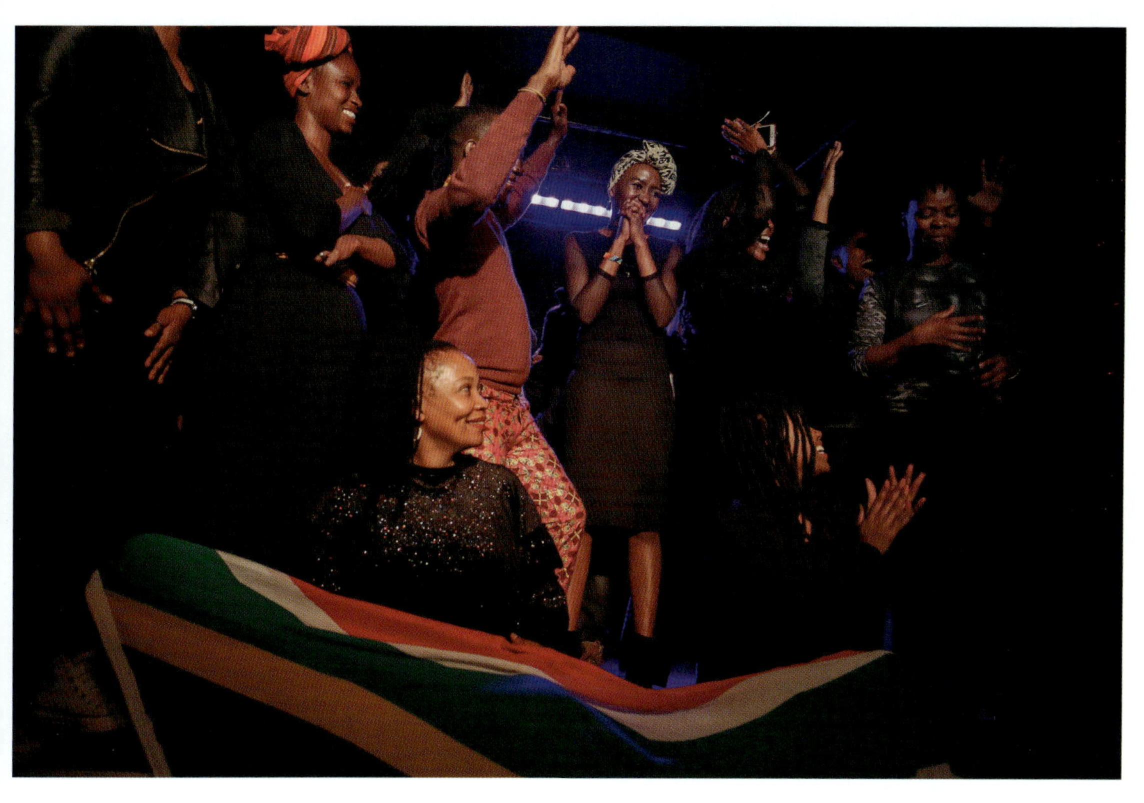

Masihambisane at the Bronx Museum of the Arts

The Bronx Museum of the Arts

November 10, 2017

Zanele Muholi's citywide #VisualActivism tour culminated with a song. At the Bronx Museum of the Arts, Muholi and their[1] traveling posse of fellow South African performers, activists, and artists filled the institution's South Wing and took to the stage with "Nkosi Sikelel' iAfrika" (God Save Africa), a rousing Xhosa hymn that is the first verse of South Africa's national anthem. The chorus was indicative of the artist's approach to the night, which was a tribute to the South African LGBTQI+ community. Muholi watched proudly from the back of the room, and when they made their way to the stage for a heartfelt speech at the end of the night, admitted that the decision to highlight this community was an intentional one that came to them the minute they were invited to make their Performa debut.

"*Home* became the first thought," said Muholi. "I said to myself, I can't do this thing in New York alone, not this time, not ever."

Describing themselves as a "visual activist," Muholi considers the visibility of South Africa's LGBTQI+ community very much part of their artistry. "It doesn't make sense to shine alone," they said. The performers included Odidi Mfenyana, also known as "Odi Diva," a drag performer, writer, and poet who also served as the night's master of ceremonies, and Eva Mofokeng, a model who appears in Muholi's "Brave Beauties" photography series. Yanela Ncetani-Mhlawuli, a singer whose blend of jazz and R&B styles, as well as lyrics in Xhosa, Zulu, and English, conveyed the horrors of corrective rape, shedding light on this troubling history that has plagued South African lesbians for several decades. The most uncommon addition to the night's lineup was a song by Dr. Mpume Simelane, an activist and gynecologist traveling with the group, who warned about the ways in which hostility toward members of the LGBTQI+ community in hospitals and mainstream medical spaces in South Africa further discriminate and isolate, leaving many of them without access to necessary healthcare and education.

Before Muholi invited all of the South Africans in the large audience to join them onstage, the crowd and performers had feasted on overflowing tables of Indian food and nonalcoholic beverages at the artist's request. As the night came to an end, Muholi urged guests to think about art and community as one. "This is not for me," they said referring to their work at Performa. "It's for us." ASHLEY OKWUOSA

1 Zanele Muholi uses they/them/their pronouns.

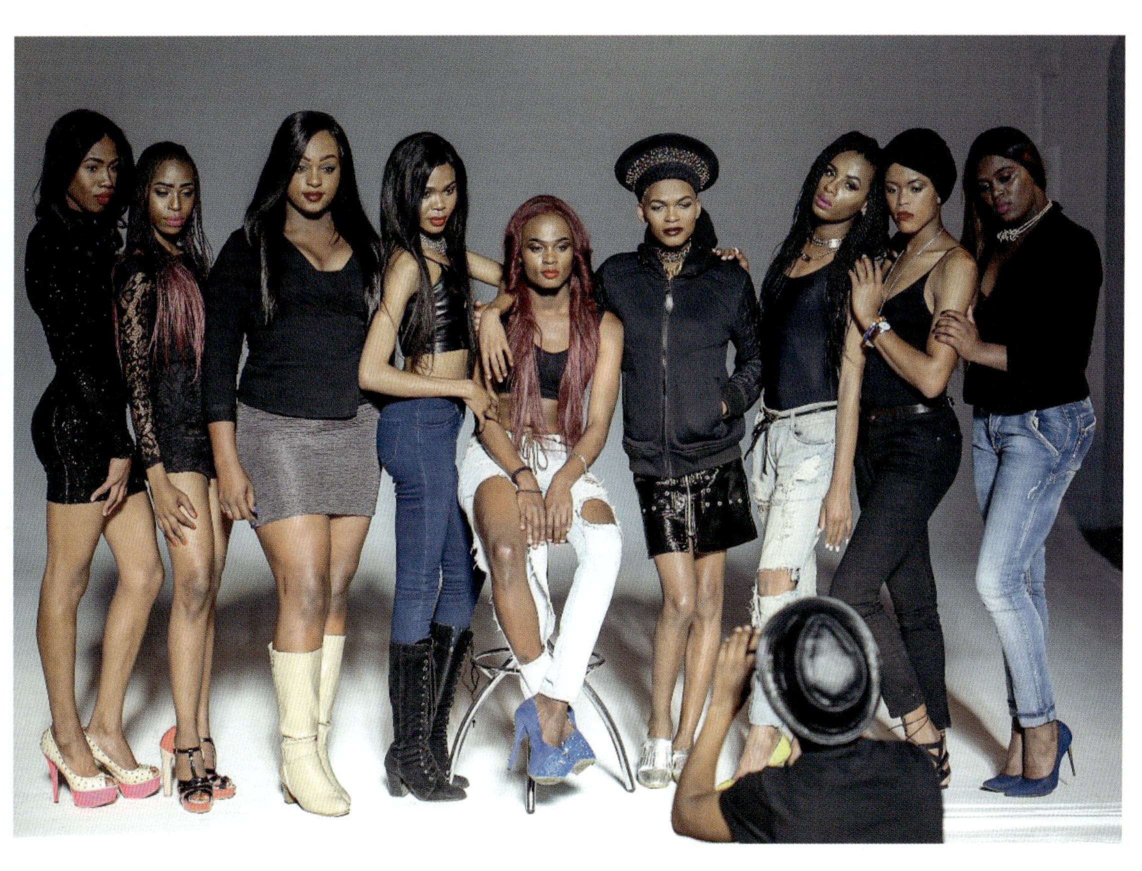

MOHAU MODISAKENG

Zion

Referencing both the forced removals of the Black population during apartheid in South Africa as well as the Great Migration of African Americans in the United States, Mohau Modisakeng's performance presented a street procession of twenty dancers, carrying luggage and furniture and clad in white costumes reminiscent of the cotton that fueled the U.S. slave trade. The procession started at the Mother African Methodist Episcopal Zion Church in Harlem, known as "Mother Zion," the oldest Black church in the state of New York, founded in 1796. It continued to various important historical sites, one being near the intersection of Eighty-Sixth Street and Central Park West, the former location of Seneca Village, an early enclave of free Black people who were forcibly removed in the mid-nineteenth century to create Central Park. The procession—its dancers in continuous movement, symbolizing the society's seemingly never-ending uprooting—created a profound experience of loss, one that eventually came to an end in Times Square, that American monument to consumption. The dancers, kicking up white dust with their movements across the plaza, channeled a powerful aesthetic force that recalled heart-wrenching memories of the inflicted migration, subjugation, and violence of apartheid, where Black communities were driven off of their ancestral lands into so-called Bantustans, as well as histories of African American slavery and segregation.[1] It also recalled modern-day South Africa, where increased post-apartheid calls for redistribution of the Bantustan lands from out of the hands of the white minority remain unanswered. VINCENT BEZUIDENHOUT

Curated by
RoseLee Goldberg

Mother AME Zion Church, Central Park, and Times Square

November 11, 2017

This text was initially published online on artthrob.co.za on November 22, 2017. Reprinted courtesy the author and artthrob.co.za.

1
In the 1960s and 1970s, the white National Party administration of South Africa established Bantustans (or Black homelands) to concentrate Black inhabitants of South Africa and South West Africa (now Namibia) in autonomous territories, depriving them of their South African national civil rights.

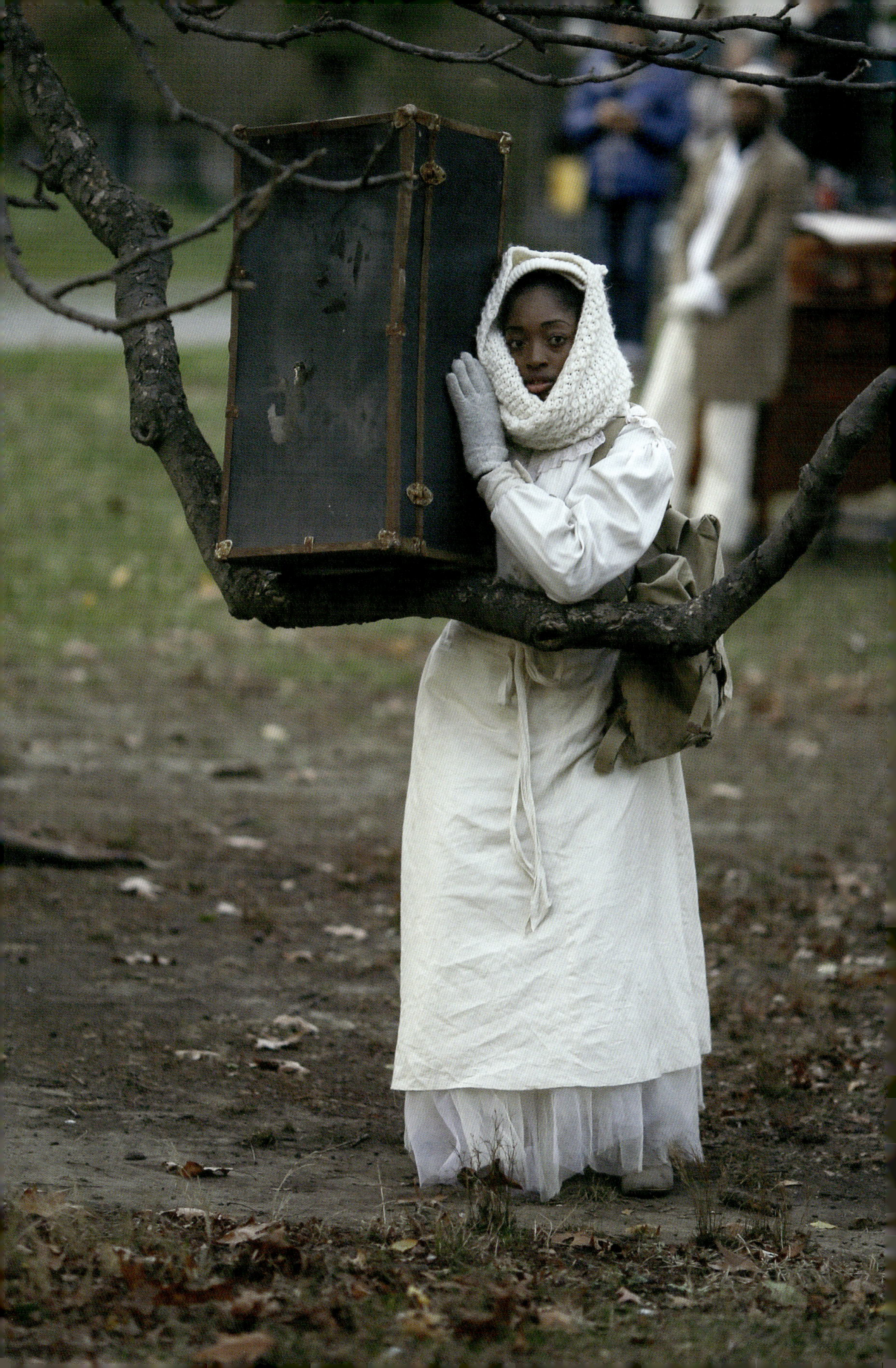

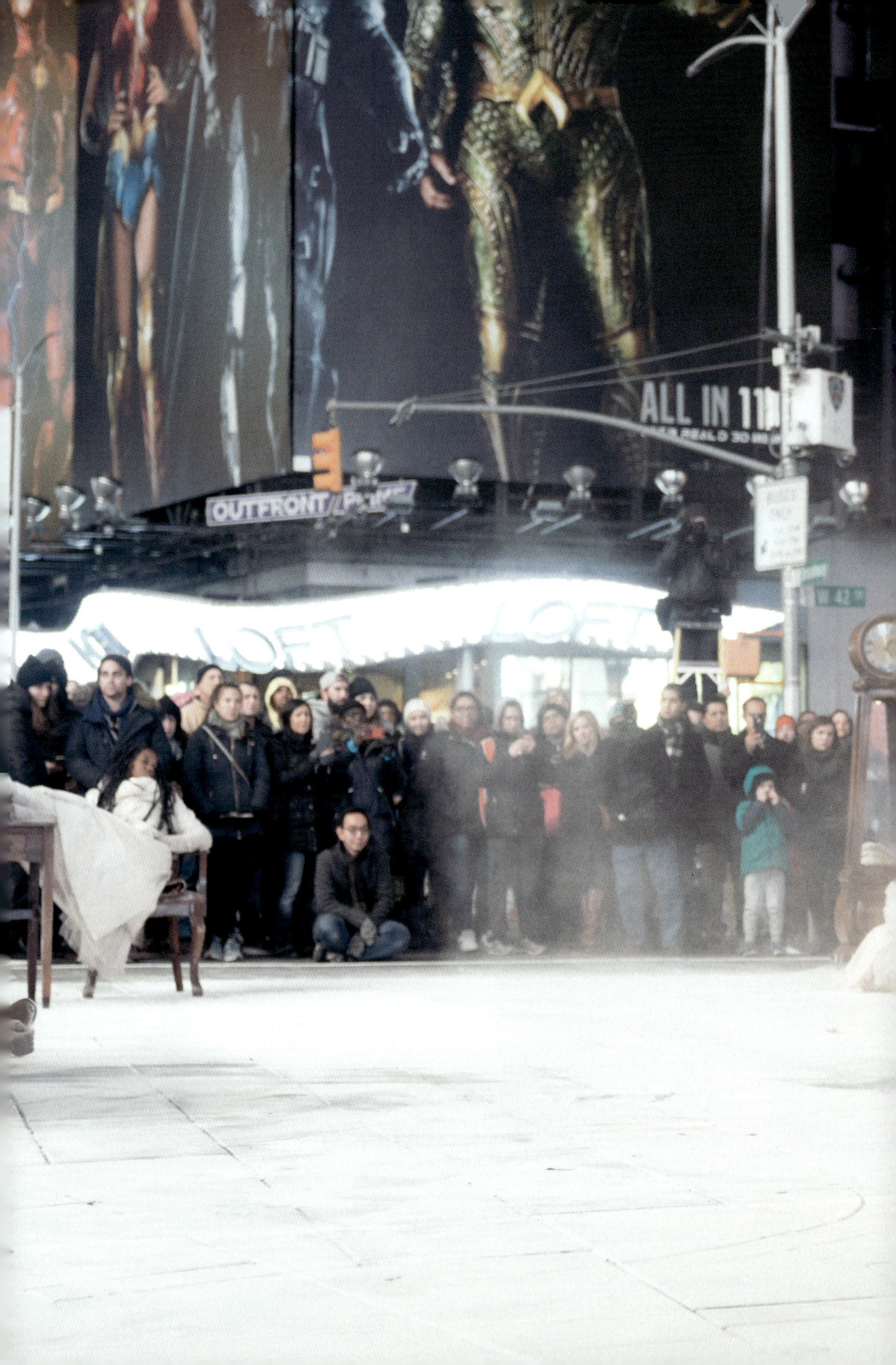
ALL IN 11
OUTFRONT

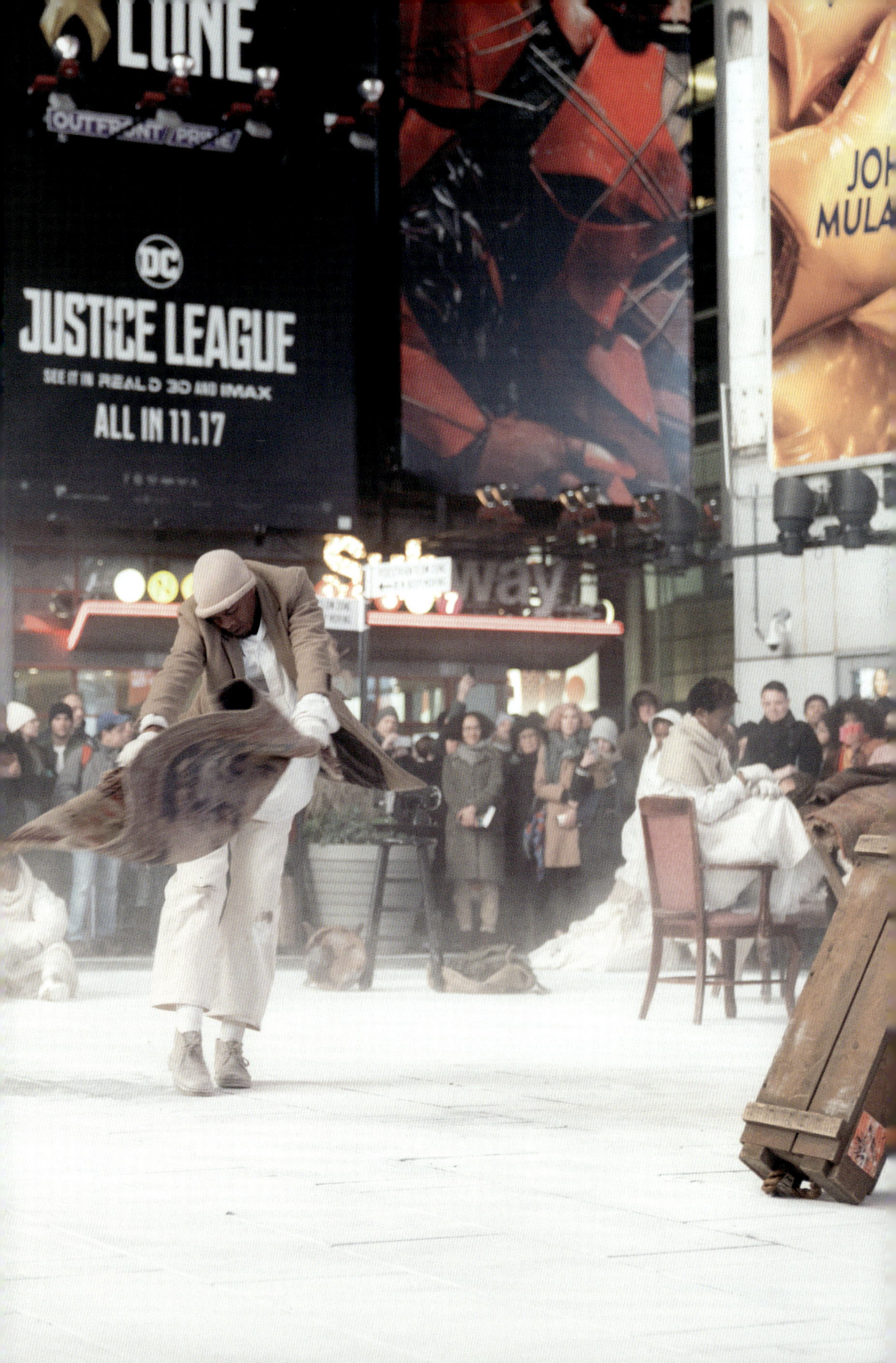

JUSTICE LEAGUE
SEE IT IN REAL D 3D AND IMAX
ALL IN 11.17

KENDELL GEERS
RitualResist

Curated by
Juan Puntes
and Amanda Ryan

WhiteBox

November 8, 2017

A man and a woman engaged in the martial art of vanity. Neither can see the other and both struggle against their own reflection in a square mirror. The square is the symbol of all things in balance: the four elements, the four directions, and four corners of the Earth, the Four Evangelists, four seasons, and Four Noble Truths. The instructions are simple: to keep the mirror afloat, suspended in time and space by pressure alone. The sides may never be grasped, the top and bottom never supported, the mirror may never be caught, held, or contained. It floats only by the force and pressure of the two blinded, visually eclipsed bodies, both in resistance but needing the other. Each person depends upon the force of the other as they slowly move, trying to maintain their individual center of gravity on the other side of the mirror, in the domain of the other. If either makes a false step or slips, if either loses their balance, then they shall both fall and the mirror will shatter.

Stasis is not an option.

The palms of their open hands, arms, shoulders, breast, back, neck, head, and every part of the upper body is used to support the mirror that should always be held in such a way that neither person ever sees the face of the other. As the hands and skin begin to sweat, so the mirror starts slipping, and ever more force is required to maintain the double mirror of the slow *RitualResist*. As more pressure is demanded, the body tires and begins to groan, and even more resistance and pressure is then needed to stop the mirror from falling and cracking.

The visitor is, in the meanwhile, transformed into voyeur, watching a naked couple sweating in a slow, combative struggle. The act of looking is interrupted, as a slight shift in the mirror suddenly reflects the image of their own gaze and they are caught in the act of looking. The exhibitionist fantasy is dissected, for the upper half of the female torso is visually joined with the sex and legs of the male beyond and vice versa. The androgynous child of the trickster Hermes and lover Aphrodite, Hermaphroditus, is borne.

The mirror stares out onto all who dare gaze upon its secret domain, a reflection of vanity and of fear as age patinates youth and the body re-members the traces of lived experience, the physical expression of an inner emotional condition. The conventional beauty of youth evolves into the sophisticated unequivocal imprints of truthful time. The looking glass transports those who do not fear into dimensions beyond the three of conventional understanding, into the spaces of spirit and the chambers of imagination. The mirror flips over into a double reflection when time and space stop at once. Alice chases the rabbit through the wormhole of shamanic perception.

The square of four balanced elements is infinitely multiplied within the implicit infinity of a double reflection, two mirrors back to back caught between the struggle of male and female forces, the duality of binary oppositional worlds caught in loopback, flesh and spirit at the precipice of the space-time continuum. Neither one, nor another, both all ways, always, the struggle continues. A luta continua.

KENDELL GEERS

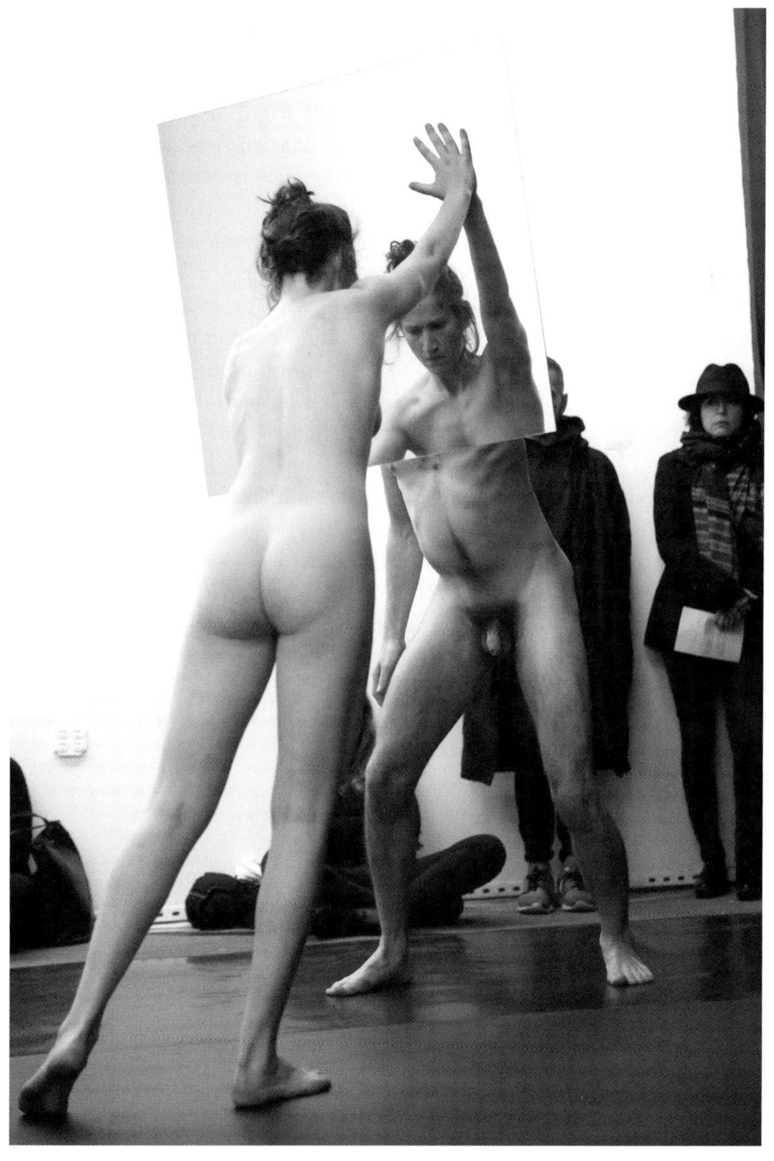

NICHOLAS HLOBO

umBhovuzo: The Parable of the Sower

Curated by RoseLee Goldberg

Harlem Parish

November 18–19, 2017

The Harlem Parish, a deconsecrated Catholic church built in 1907 to serve the neighborhood's immigrant communities, and which has featured a distinguished list of African American attendees throughout its history, aptly channeled the work of Nicholas Hlobo. With his nine-person ensemble, *umBhovuzo: The Parable of the Sower* continued the artist's exploration of Xhosa traditions and gender through emphasizing masculinity and the use of rituals. Hlobo, who grew up in the former apartheid "homeland" of rural Transkei,[1] uses the sewing of cloth, silk, rubber, and ribbon, and these materials' strong connection with femininity, to comment both on his own identity as well as on notions of patriarchy in Xhosa and the greater South African culture.

Hlobo's use of sewing in particular as a metaphor for ideas around gender was expanded upon in *umBhovuzo*, as performers patched together large pieces of fabric while seated on absurdly high tables and chairs. The noise of the sewing machines at work echoed dramatically in the sweeping arches and confessional booths of the otherwise silent church. New York performer John-Deric Mitchell, his head covered with a wooden sewing machine box, addressed both the sewers and the audience. Mitchell transformed what was originally a silent experience into one of immense power by connecting with the South African ensemble as an African American artist and reflecting on the cultures' mutual history of destruction and renewal. The simple act of sewing characterizes the act of remaking—one that all South Africans are still aware of, even more than twenty-five years after the advent of their state's democracy. But it is also about remembrance, holding on to the thread of memory as they remake their nation anew. VINCENT BEZUIDENHOUT

This text was initially published online on artthrob.co.za on November 22, 2017. Reprinted courtesy the author and artthrob.co.za.

1 Transkei, a southeastern region of South Africa, was given nominal autonomy in 1963 as a Bantustan (Bantu homeland) by the white National Party administration: an area set aside for black South Africans of Xhosa descent. It became an independent republic in 1976 and existed as an unrecognized state until 1994, when it was re-incorporated into South Africa.

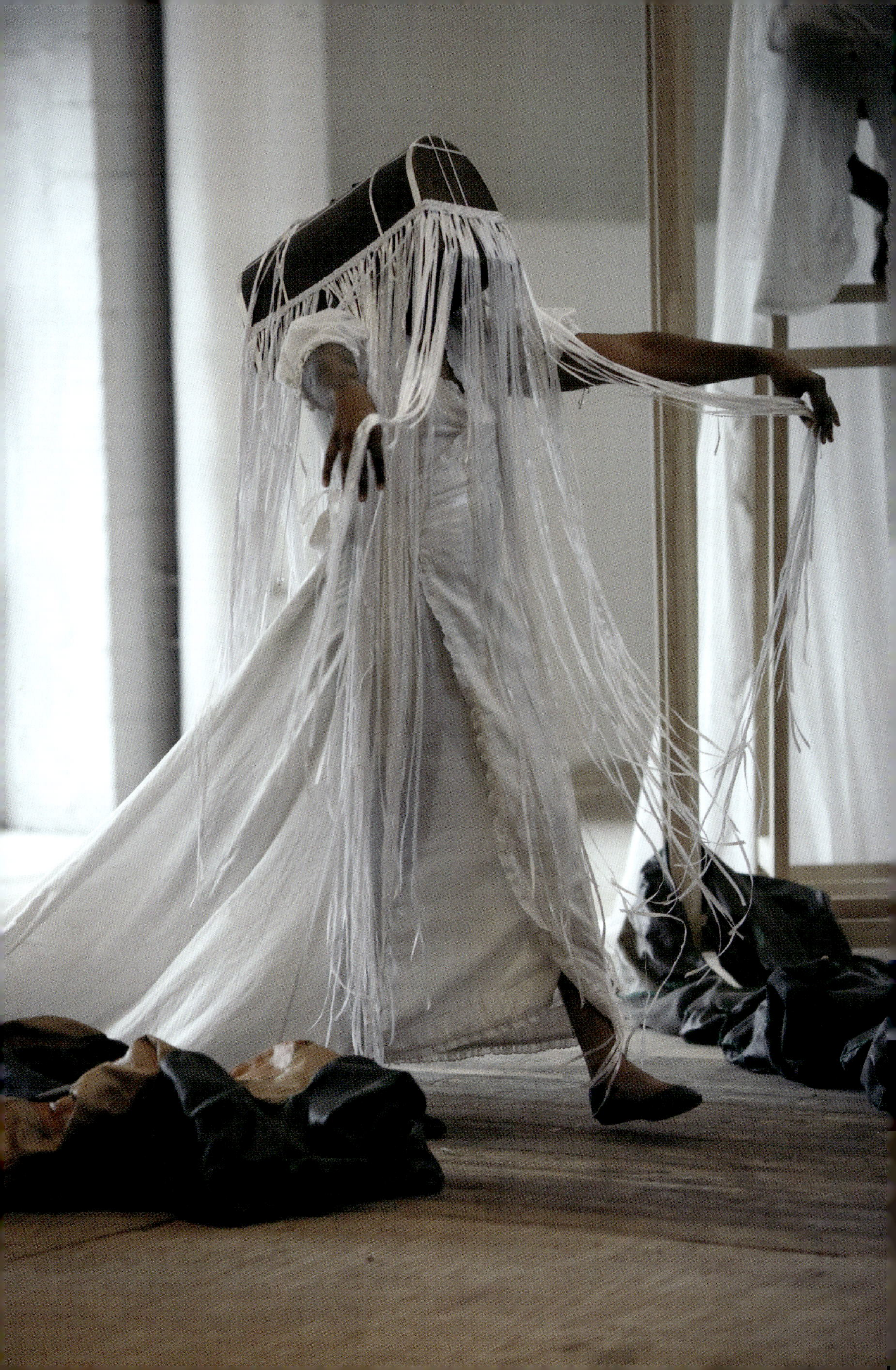

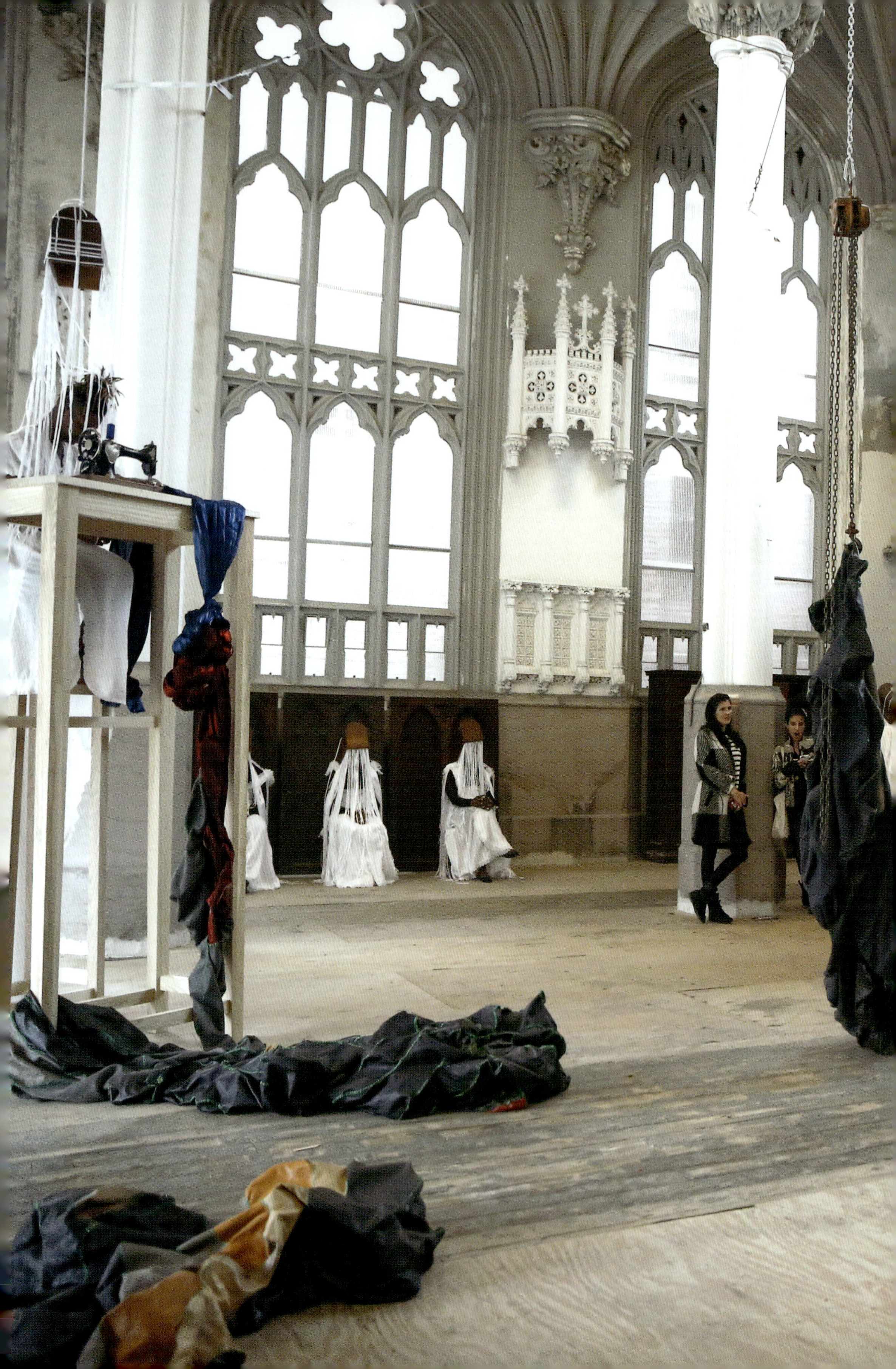

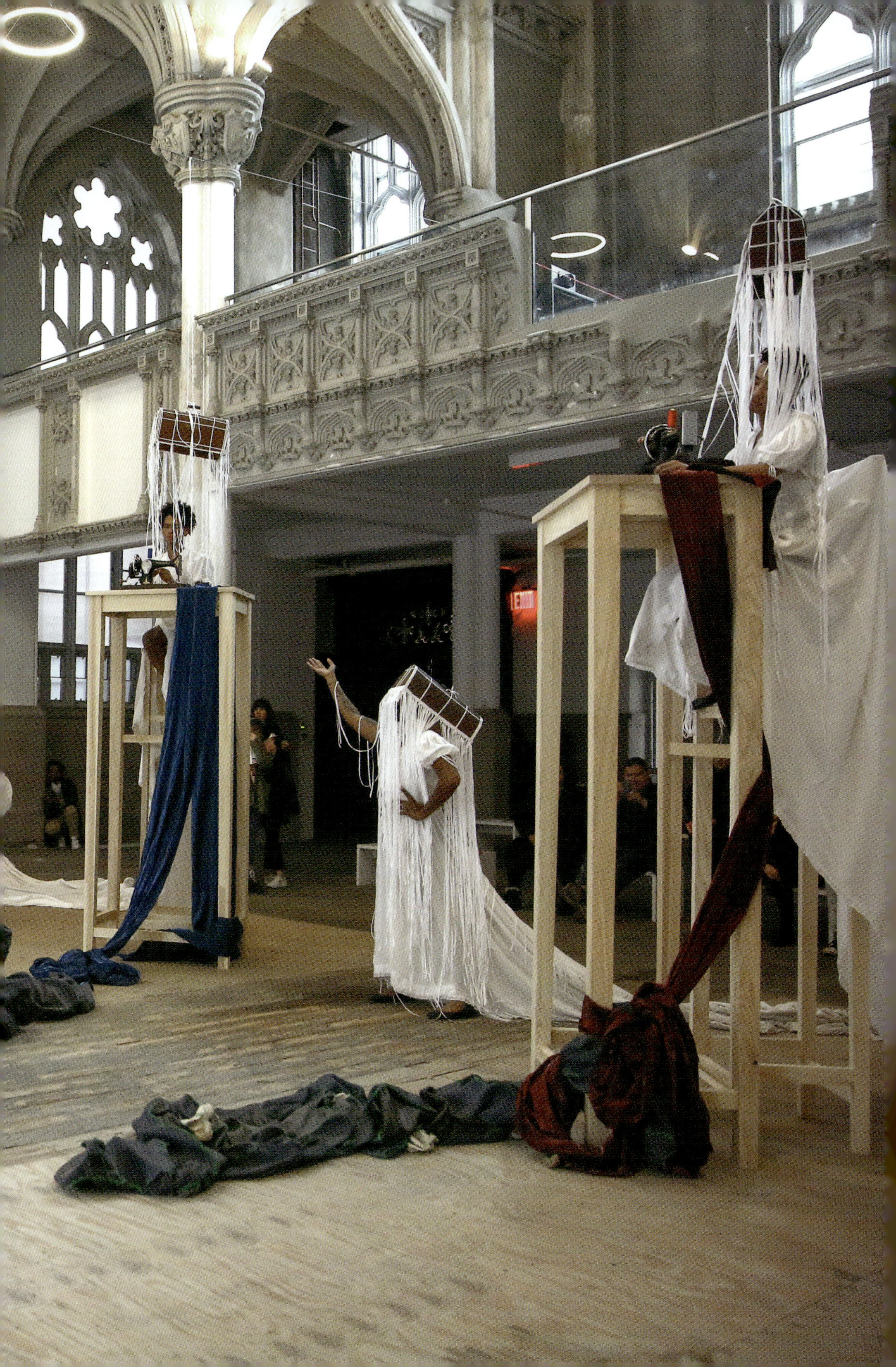

Afroglossia, a neologism coined by Performa Curator Adrienne Edwards, riffed on the term *polyglossia* (numerous languages spoken in one area) and incorporated the abbreviation *Afro* to emphasize the incredible complexity, heterogeneity, and multiplicity of the African continent. This program highlighted a range of voices and coalesced diverse perspectives from various regions into a single lineup, allowing viewers to encounter multiple approaches to interdisciplinary art and ideas by contemporary artists from Ethiopia, Kenya, Morocco, Nigeria, and South Africa, all underpinned by questions such as "What is radical?," "How do the conditions of everyday life inform aesthetic choices?," and "What constitutes experimentation in cross-boundary performance?" The presentation's commissions were points of convergence, taking up social, historical, political, and economic scenarios and experiences in their own distinctly formal ways.

Intermingling fiction, poetry, essays, films, performances, painting, music, videos, and photography, *Afroglossia* provided a means through which we could contemplate the intersection of radical art and radical politics as articulated by artists from Africa and its diaspora. Given the United States' civic climate in 2017, the power of the voice, the resonating ways that an individual can speak to the concerns and realities of the collective, became the thrust of this curatorial platform. These voices were often challenging, even opaque, obscure, and defiant, which made them an especially compelling focus, reflective of individuals' creative lives and values. For the artists who made up *Afroglossia*—the vast majority of whom were born in the 1970s and came of age in the aftermath of several of these states' independence movements—exploring and making work with a distinct ethical dimension was a natural and logical expression of rule-bending.

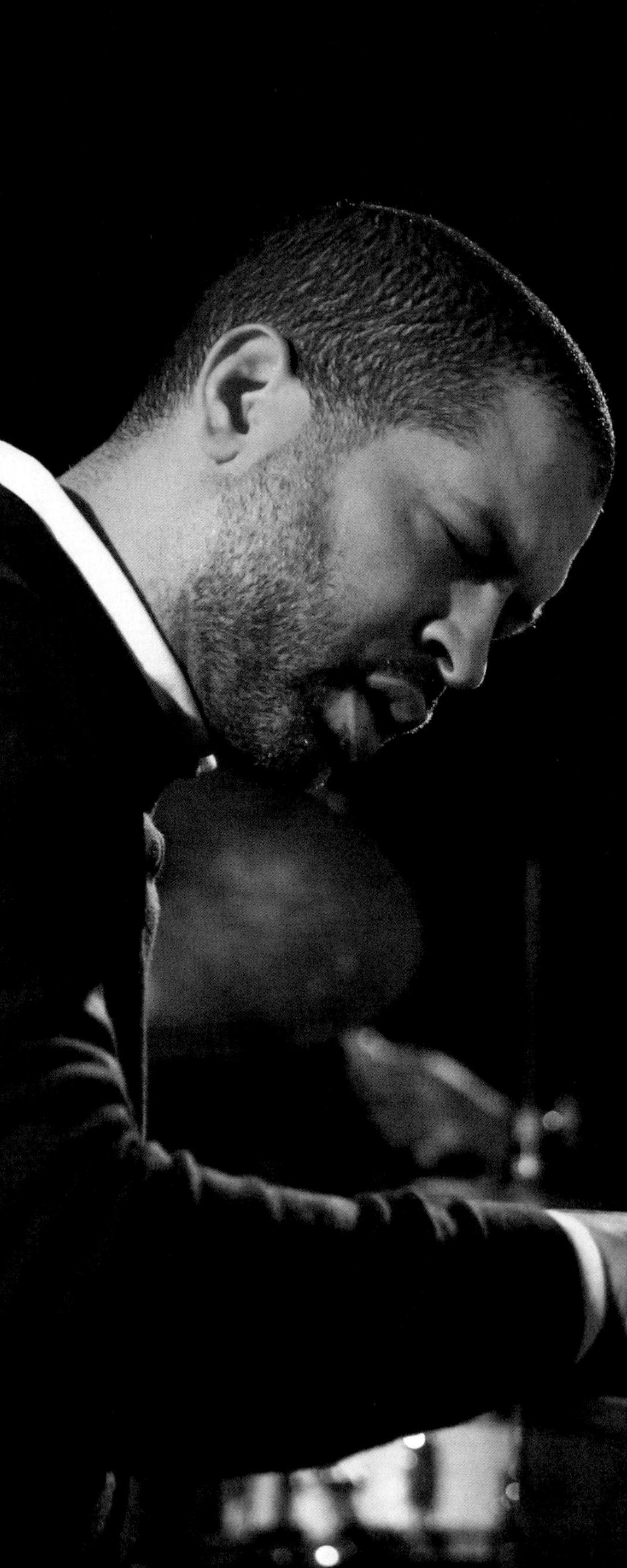

AFROGLOSSIA

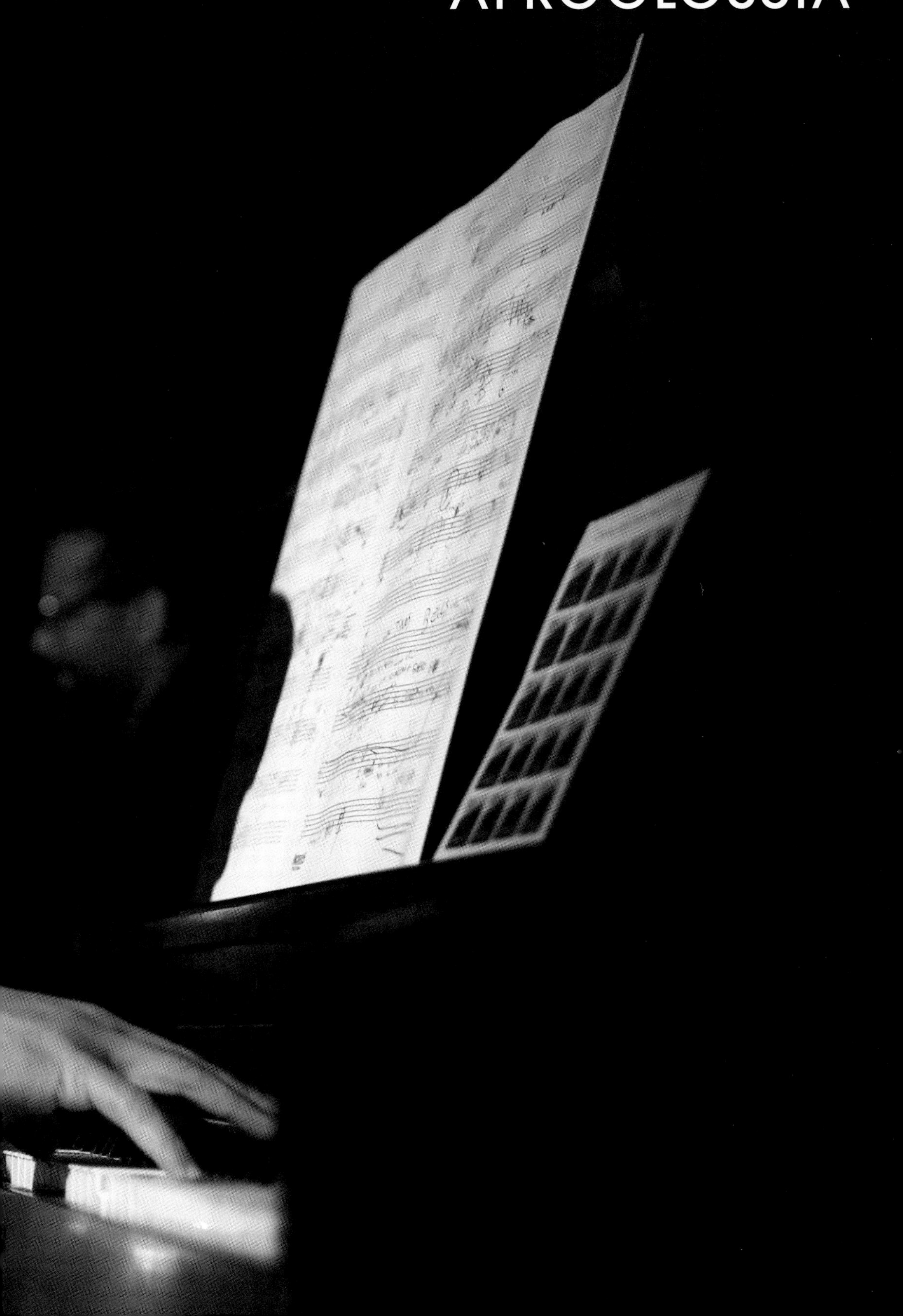

TEJU COLE

Black Paper

Curated by
Adrienne Edwards

BKLYN Studios at
City Point

November 2–4, 2017

Known for his vivid storytelling, Teju Cole, the Nigerian American writer, photographer, and photography critic for *The New York Times Magazine*, delivered a powerful, immersive experience within a continuously evolving installation. *Black Paper* featured Cole's photographs and videos accompanied by a score of field recordings and readings of incisive texts, all presented as one artwork. It was Cole's first foray into sound, the moving image, and live performance. The subtly sober mosaic presentation was an intuitive multimedia response to the 2016 presidential election by addressing deeply buried emotions, haunted spaces, dreams and premonitions, shadows and darkness.

Staged in Downtown Brooklyn, the seating was configured in an arena-style formation, with the audience facing one another in four delineated sections. Suspended overhead were six large screens, divided into two groupings of three on each side. Cole, who mingled with attendees in the lobby as they awaited entry, was the last to enter the low-lit space, walking down a central aisle, dressed in his typical clothing—white shirt, dark suit, and dress shoes, replete with porkpie hat and rectangular-shaped glasses. He changed into modest sleeping attire, a billowy shirt and drawstring pants. He settled into a simple twin-sized bed at the center of the performance space and drew a knit cap over his head and a blanket over his body as the six screens came to life with a single image, which seemed to be one of his photographs of a bucolic landscape of the Swiss Alps. The image was actually a video projection of a *trompe-l'œil* scene painted on the closet doors of a hotel in Zürich where the artist has stayed many times.

After a few minutes, the video fell back to two screens, one each on the left side of the space, shining an animation of the front page of *The New York Times* from the day after Donald Trump won the 2016 U.S. presidential election. Over the course of the performance, a collage of election-related headlines began to blur and darken, seeming to collapse and disintegrate before one's very eyes. All the while, the artist's cacophonous sound montage of crickets, car horns, muffled voices, Cole and friends singing along to a recording of Andrea Bocelli's aria "Con Te Partirò," family conversations spoken in Yoruba, a chat with a Muslim female taxi driver, and repetitions of pings, chimes, and a single piano note played from speakers placed at cardinal points throughout the installation.

The center screen showed hundreds of his photographs taken over the course of the previous year, from election day up to the day of the performance. Paced at the rate of Cole's heartbeat, the images resonated as flashes across the screen, one's eyes barely able to take in the fleeting landscapes, streetscapes, and people living their lives that Cole traversed and encountered during his international travels. The sense of bombardment and dissonance intensified as the photographs grew darker and the sound crescendoed and quickened into loud booms and throbbing pounds. Midway through the performance, Cole arose from the bed as if sleepwalking; at its conclusion, he arose from his slumber, screamed, and jumped out of bed, desperate to escape the nightmare that is our current reality. ADRIENNE EDWARDS

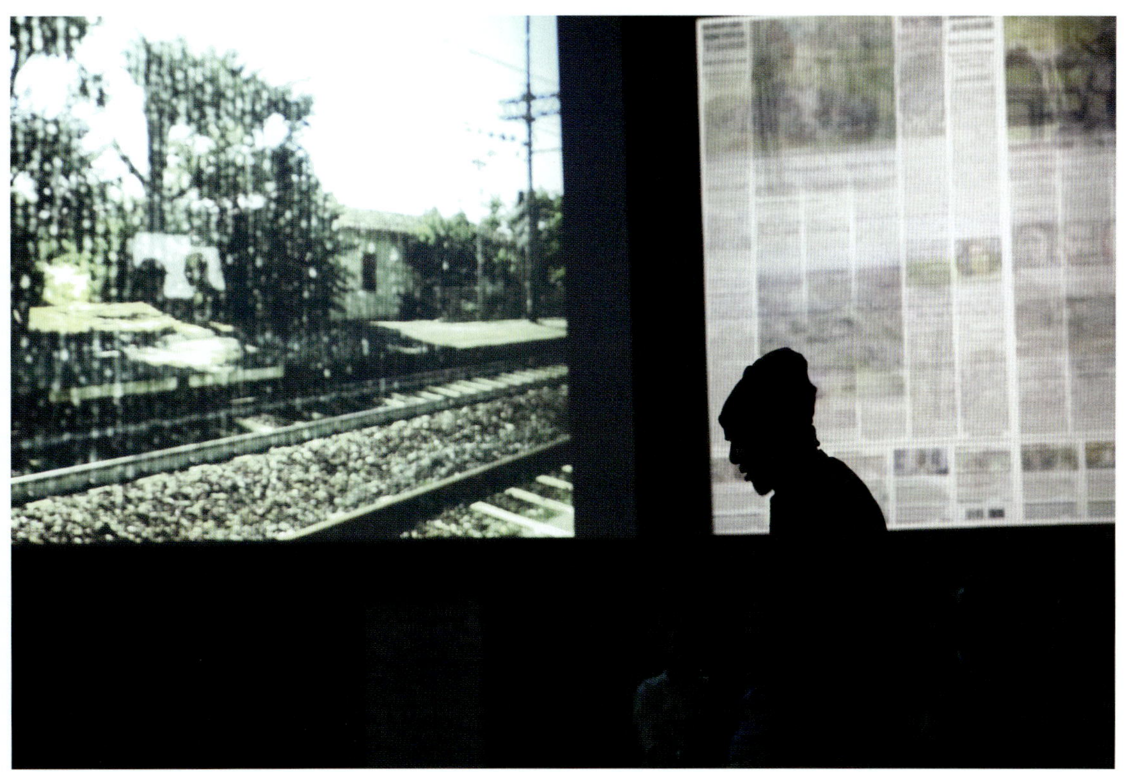

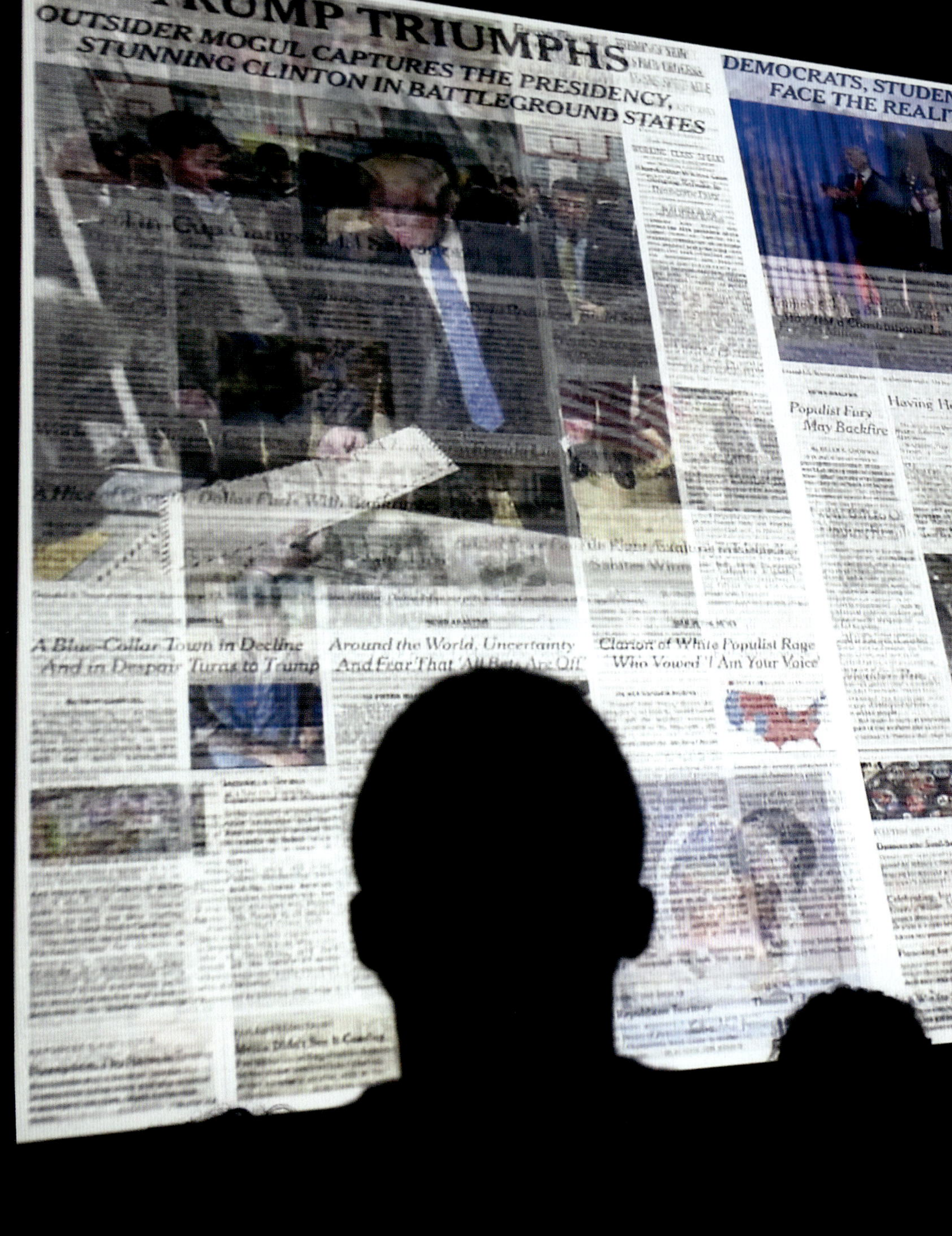
TRUMP TRIUMPHS
OUTSIDER MOGUL CAPTURES THE PRESIDENCY,
STUNNING CLINTON IN BATTLEGROUND STATES
Populist Fury
May Backfire
A Blue-Collar Town in Decline
And in Despair Turns to Trump
Around the World, Uncertainty
And Fear That 'All Bets Are Off'
Clarion of White Populist Rage
Who Vowed 'I Am Your Voice'

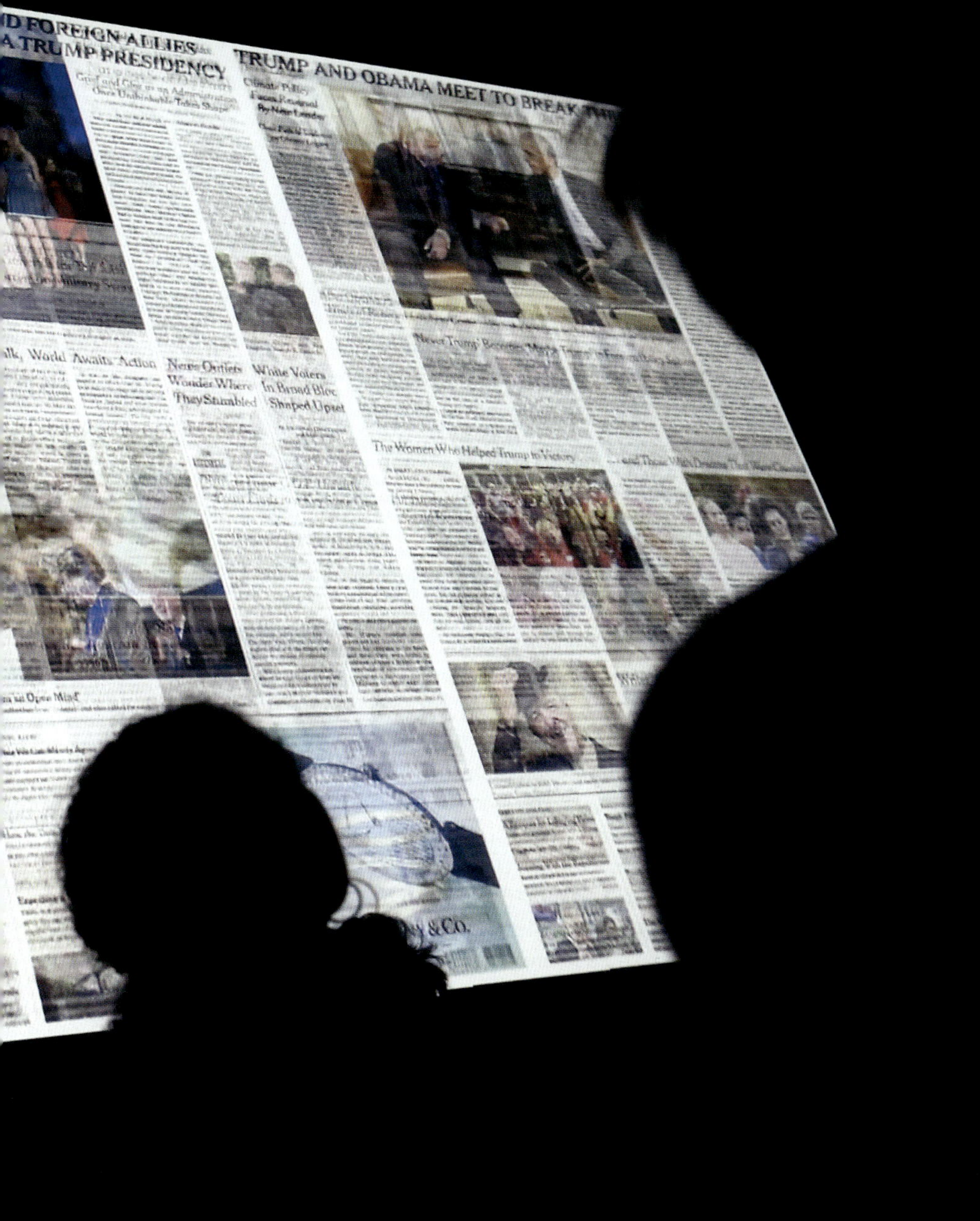
A TRUMP PRESIDENCY
TRUMP AND OBAMA MEET TO BREAK
News Outlets Wonder Where They Stumbled
White Voters In Broad Bloc Shaped Upset
The Women Who Helped Trump to Victory

TRACEY ROSE

THE TRACEY ROSE SHOW IN COLLABORATION WITH PERFORMA17 AND AFROGLOSSIA PRESENTS: THE GOOD SHIP JESUS VS THE BLACK STAR LINE HITCHING A RIDE WITH DIE ALIBAMA [WORKING TITLE]

Curated by
Adrienne Edwards

Black Lady Theatre

November 9–11, 2017

Chaos, even *anarchy*, readily describes the experience of a Tracey Rose performance. But such an impression merely reflects the veneer of her acts—they give us an immediate and profound feeling of discombobulation, a reaction to unwieldy skidding on the surface of her ephemeral assaults. These immediate feelings do not reflect the more profound formal interventions with which her works are concerned. Over a more than twenty-year career, Rose has developed her live artworks from modes of direct address about the political, social, and economic realities of her native South Africa, buttressed by considerations of race, gender, and sexuality, to oblique performances unfolding in rather ambiguous ways. Her initial representational works were primarily performed by Rose through a range of characters. Recently, she has shifted to a more subtle and obtuse sensibility (that is no less forceful), in which the complexities of such violence and its ongoing aftermath is transferred to the viewing audience. In other words, Rose no longer enacts the issues with which she is concerned. Rather, she structures experiences in which their repercussions are felt. The impossibility of representing these histories and their aftermaths leaves us gobsmacked and disoriented. In the melee, astonishment is mistaken for pandemonium.

This departure in Rose's performance style was made evident in her Performa 17 Commission *THE TRACEY ROSE SHOW IN COLLABORATION WITH PERFORMA17 AND AFROGLOSSIA PRESENTS: THE GOOD SHIP JESUS VS THE BLACK STAR LINE HITCHING A RIDE WITH DIE ALIBAMA [WORKING TITLE]*. Workshopped over three days of open rehearsals and culminating in a public show at the Black Lady Theatre in Crown Heights, Brooklyn, each night, it came at you in waves, carried along by Rose's singular verve. The battle as epic journey is indicated in the title, which references the first British slave ship to the Americas; the United Negro Improvement Association (UNIA) founder Marcus Garvey's shipping line; and the

Confederate screw sloop that visited Cape Town in 1863. These references point to the complexity of relations and the intricacies of identity between those stolen or sent away from Africa and those who remained.

Staged in the round, Rose created a dynamic theatrical installation structured by three freestanding mesh screens at its center and platforms of various shapes in red, black, and green, in reference to the Blaupunkt TV set as well as to the colors of the flags for UNIA, Pan-African, Black American nationalist, and Black Liberation movements. The television fulfilled a series of theatrical tropes, although obtusely—the frames were a visual layering of the "tell-lie-vision" and what Gil Scott-Heron referred to when he explained why the revolution would not be televised. This abstraction has its aesthetic basis in the absurdism of Dada's concern for language and language as noise—a product of the colonial encounter with Africa, which profoundly influenced Dadaist art.

The live event seemed provisional, as if the entire production was done on a whim—day to day, minute to minute, impulse to impulse, word to word. Its unpredictable quality was as much a part of the evening performances as the open rehearsals. It was only the intensity that changed, as the artist determined. Rose's DIY style cultivated a sense of fraying and unraveling, with the center, or anchor, shifting among the players: The Voice (M. Lamar), White Bitches (Jahmal B. Gordon and Lirael O'Neil), Cheetah Cape (Christopher Wessels), Elephant (Keitu Gwangwa), and Ship Builder (Tito Valery). Even one of the producers (Bob Wuss) was instrumentalized on the spot to play the Money character. There was no clear "narrative." Instead, utterances, symbols, and speech all contributed to a sensation of dissonance, culling the holes, slippages, and frays of existing myths, their heroes, and heroines.

THE TRACEY ROSE SHOW drew upon the often citational nature of her work, in which elements and concepts from one artwork are referenced in another. TV, for instance, was alluded to in both *The Cockpit* (2008), a film she made specifically for television, and the exhibition "The World Is Not Fair" (2012) at Hebbel am Ufer in Berlin, where she staged a soap opera within a reconstructed black-and-white Blaupunkt television set. Some of the props too originated in previous works. Her eccentric sculpture series *A Dream Deferred (Mandela Balls)* (2013–14), referred to the 1951 Langston Hughes book-length poem and the precarity of post-apartheid South African idealism (a legacy of its founding president). The objects have been featured in a range of Rose's presentations, most notably the 32nd Bienal de São Paulo in 2016 and Koyo Kouoh's 2015 touring exhibition "Body Talk: Feminism, Sexuality and the Body in the Work of Six African Artists." For Performa, she assembled her environment from materials at hand, such as packing tape, newspapers, and cardboard boxes. Meanwhile, the phrase "Stop the Muslim Holocaust" was painted on a bed sheet. The text first appeared in *Muster of Peacocks: THE SHOAH* (2012), a single-color video played on an iPad. The show also took the structure of a boxing match, a theme she explored in an earlier self-portrait, *TKO* (2000), a performance for the camera that had her pummeling a punching bag containing the three cameras recording the action. The obscured black-and-white images vacillate, at once corporeal apparitions and physically present, as we hear the artist panting, scuffling, and groaning. The video, like *THE TRACEY ROSE SHOW*, recalls the violence of surveillance and self-reflexivity as a means to expose and deconstruct subjectivity. Rose has employed the feint as an artistic device to drive home its deceptive intentions and results. ADRIENNE EDWARDS

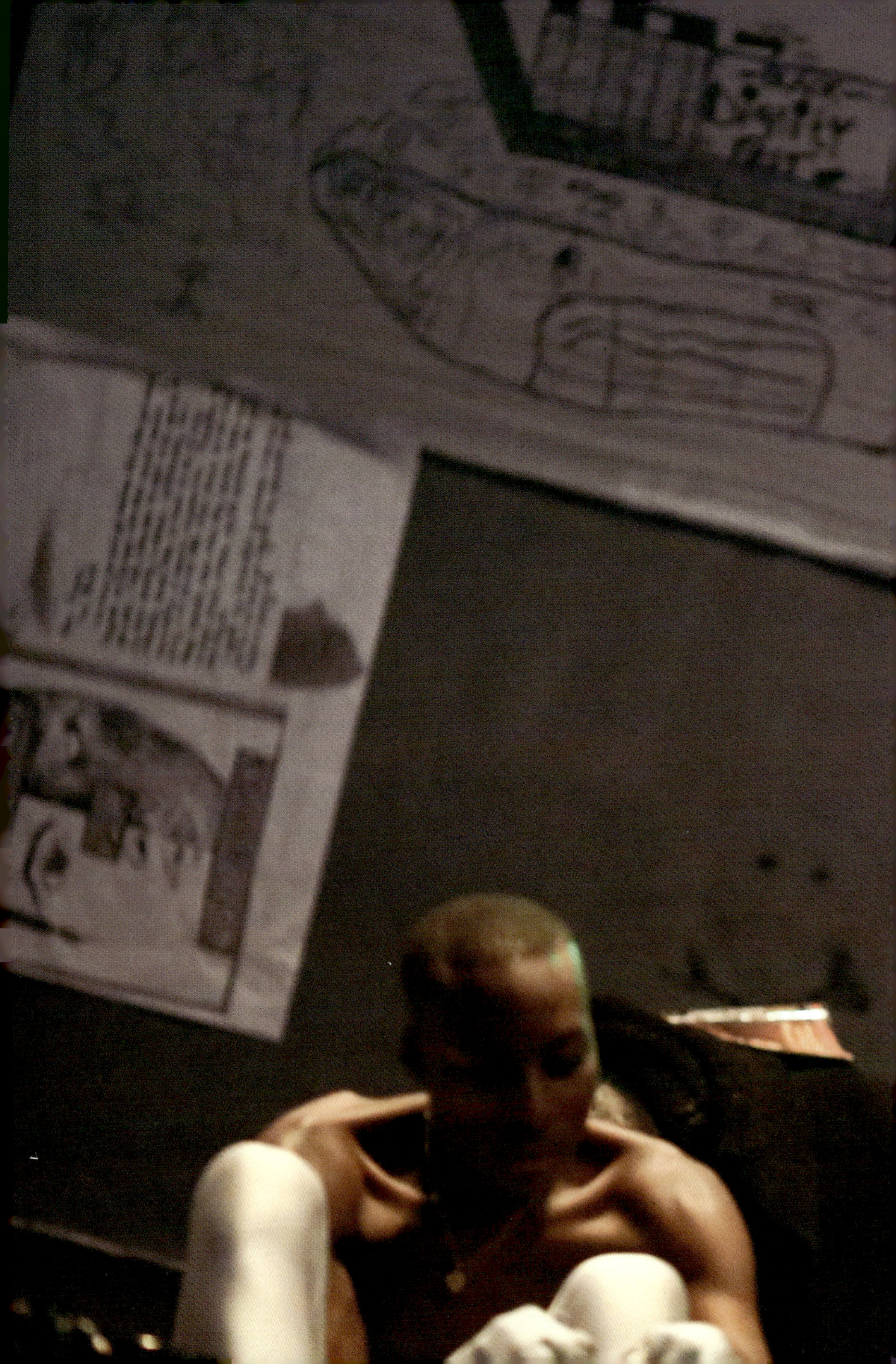

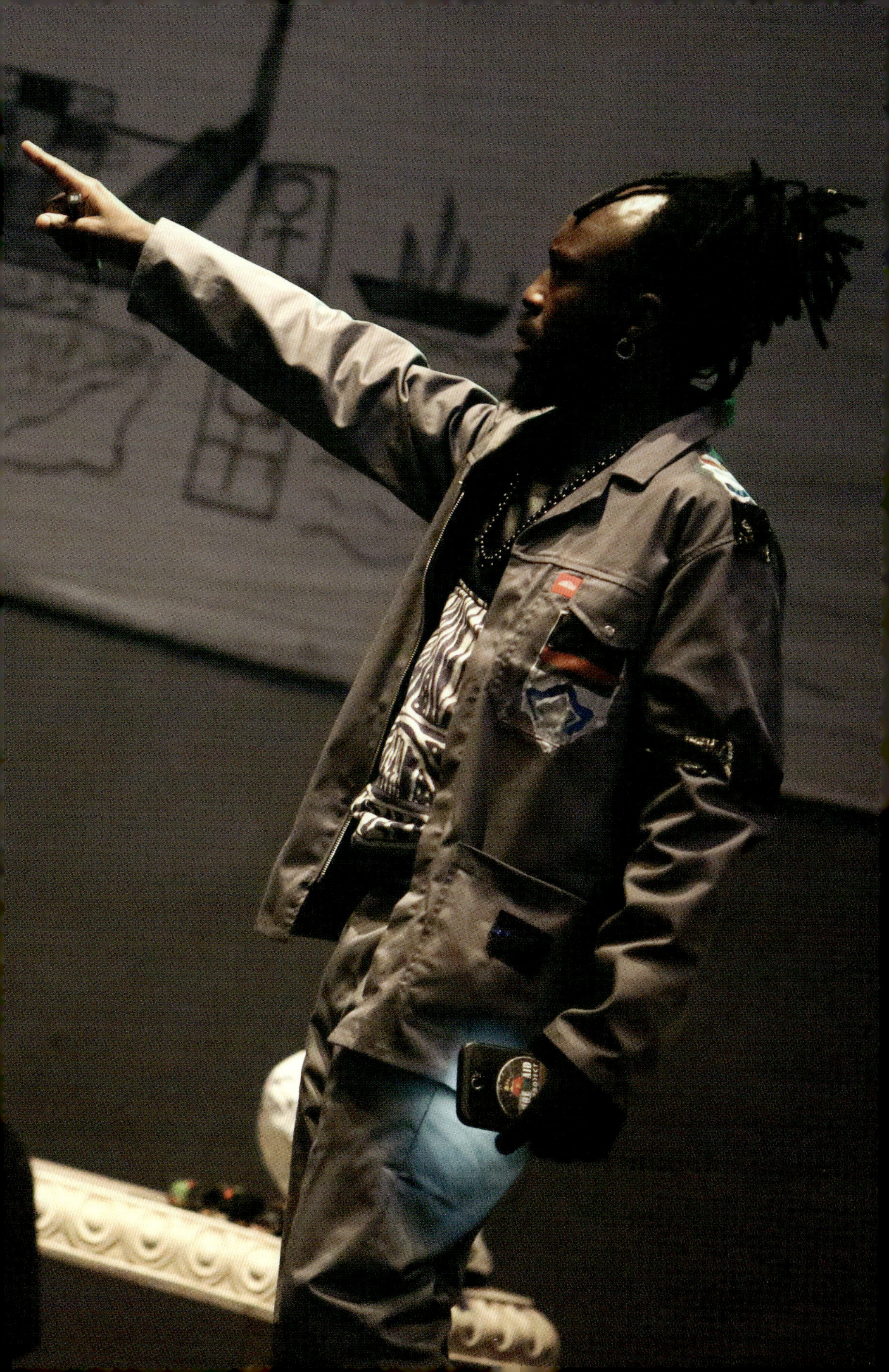

WANGECHI MUTU
Banana Stroke

Curated by
Adrienne Edwards

The Grace Rainey Rogers Auditorium at the Metropolitan Museum of Art

November 13–14, 2017

While New York- and Nairobi-based artist Wangechi Mutu is best known for her lush, surreal, otherworldly paintings and collages, she has worked in performance since her graduate studies at Yale University's School of Art. Her art traverses a range of themes such as the Black female body, popular culture, mysticism, mythology, the supernatural, ethnography, anthropology, colonialism, sexism, mass overconsumption, and the environment.

Such ideas have been brought forth in innovative and striking ways as the artist expanded her explorations in installation and performance, often realizing cross-boundary art that disregards distinctions between forms. Whether live or for the camera, Mutu's performances dynamically embody the hybrid configured personas revered in her two-dimensional works. Beginning in late 2014, Mutu began to transform paper she would typically use for her paintings and collages by shredding, dying, saturating, and fermenting it in large batches. The pulverized matter was incorporated into the sculptural installation element of her multimedia contribution to the 2015 Venice Biennale titled *The End of Carrying It All*, and again in 2016 in *Throw*, a private performance enacted over two evenings in which the artist used this dark, pulpy material to create a site-specific, monochromatic abstract painting on a floating white gallery wall. The exhibition was part of "Blackness in Abstraction" at Pace Gallery in New York.[1]

For Performa 17, I asked Mutu to create an evening-length piece, one that would expand upon her 2016 performance and be shown to a public audience. This was Mutu's second Performa Commission, following her debut in the 2007 biennial. Presented on the Metropolitan Museum of Art's Grace Rainey Rogers's Auditorium stage, Mutu designed a set that was part arena, part white cube gallery, with two floating white walls situated over a span of white marley flooring and custom white seating of varying sizes and widths; it was a theater turned into a blank canvas. Audience members entered an empty auditorium, proceeded down the aisles, and took their places on the stage. The lights dimmed, and a video of Mutu performing in tall grass and amongst ancient trees in Nairobi, wearing dark casual clothing and boots with enormous palm fronds and gigantic cow horns adorning her arms, played on the white walls. A voiceover of Mutu reading Derek Walcott's poem "A Far Cry from Africa" accompanied the film. In near-total darkness, Mutu entered, the sound of faint swooshes heard as she approached the stage; you could hear her, but not see her. As the lights came up, Mutu was there, in a black velvet jumpsuit, head turbaned. As in the video, the length of her arms was extended by four-foot-long

1
"Blackness in Abstraction" at Pace Gallery, New York, June 24–August 19, 2016. Curated by Adrienne Edwards.

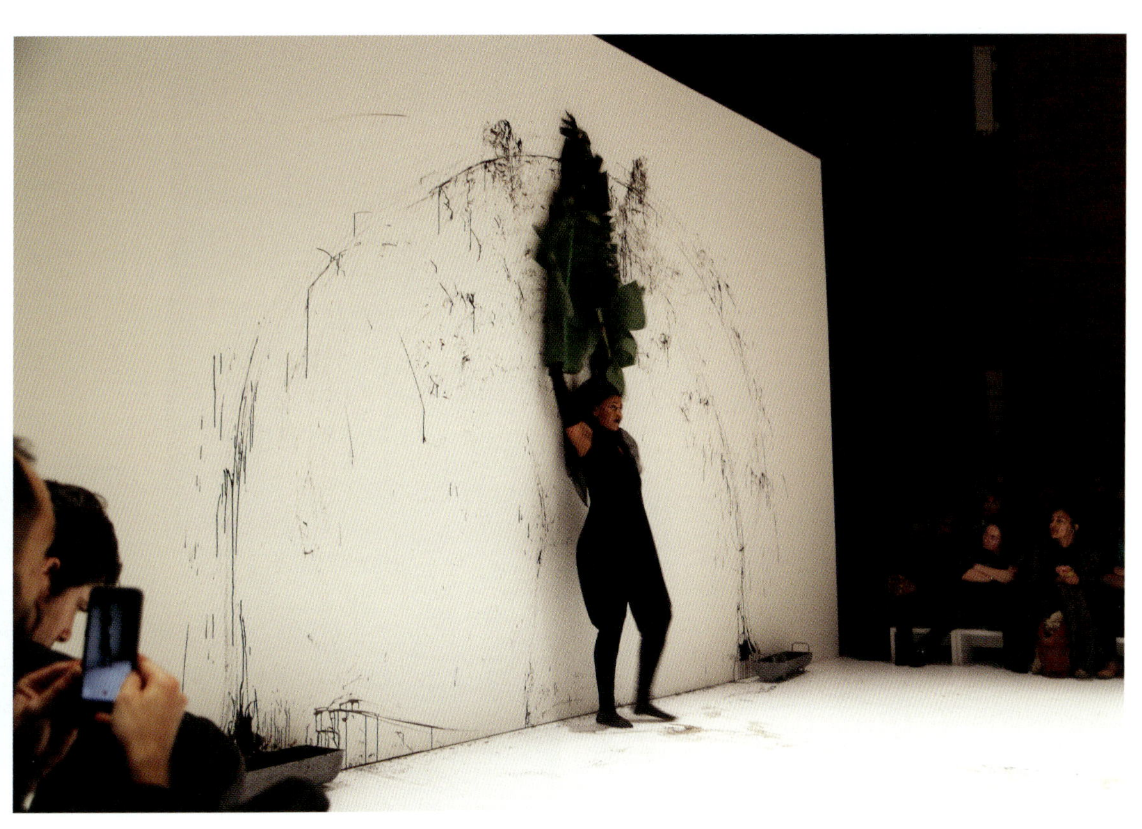

banana leaves, striking ornaments that doubled as paintbrushes. Mutu dragged the leaves through troughs filled with the same black viscous matter used in *Throw*, though less dense and more liquefied. Drawing upon movements, gestures, and choreographies employed in earlier works and harnessing the energy of improvisation and chance, Mutu made a site-specific, live-action painting over the course of thirty minutes as the accumulating aftermath of thick marks, wispy strokes, and furtive gestures clung to walls and floor, sullying their pristine veneer with the remainder of her fierce, forthright, and poignant dance. As a coda to the event, a subtly altered version of the opening videos was cast over the paintings, which eventually were destroyed after the performance. ADRIENNE EDWARDS

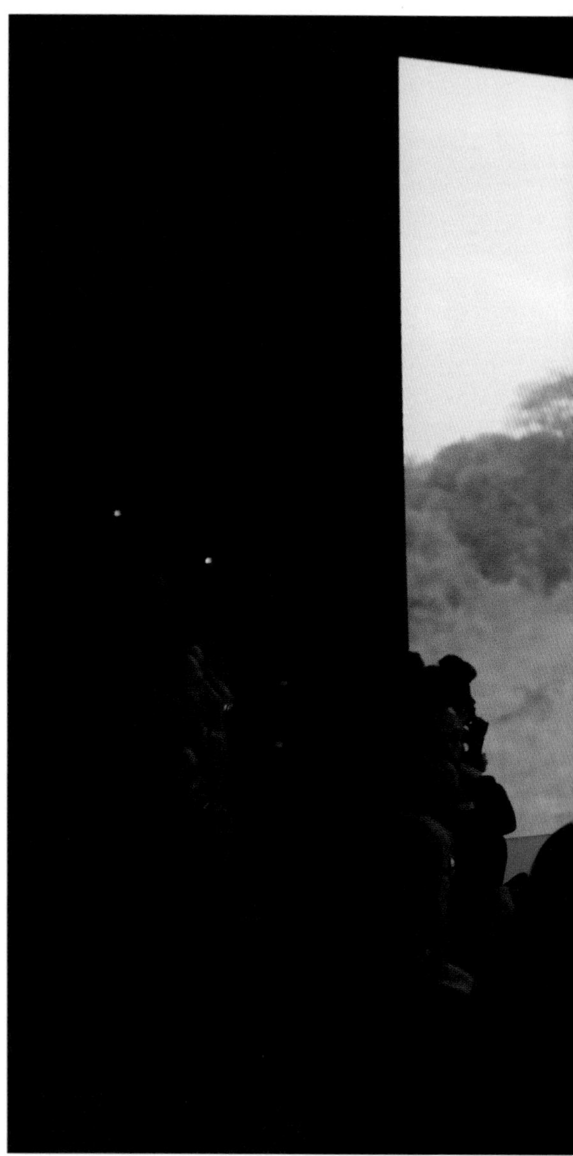

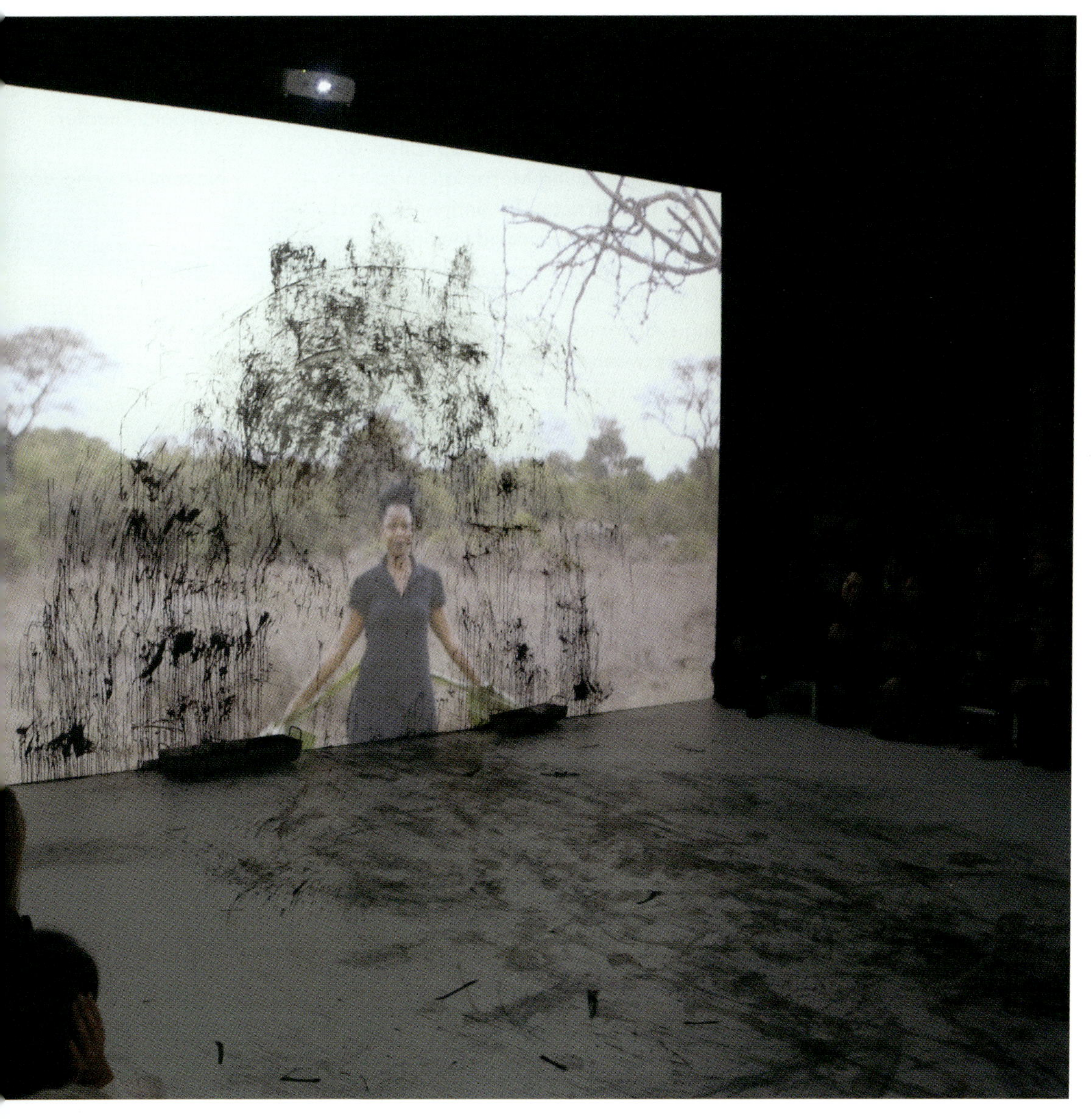

YTO BARRADA
Tree Identification for Beginners

Curated by
Adrienne Edwards

Connelly Theater

November 17–19, 2017

In *Tree Identification for Beginners,* artist Yto Barrada wove a multimedia refraction of her mother's first visit to the United States in 1966 as part of a group of African students participating in the Operation Crossroads Africa program, a precursor to the Peace Corps, founded in 1958 by Harlem-based Black American clergyman James Herman Robinson. Rather than accept the capitalism-and-democracy narrative proposed by her hosts, the young Moroccan socialist saw instead the revolutionary potential of the Pan-African, Tricontinental Black Power, and anti-Vietnam War movements. Barrada chronicled multiple layers of this history—overlapping, subjective, and unreliable—using archival materials, film, textile painting, and educational toys. *Tree Identification for Beginners* extended Barrada's practice of creating synchronously across various mediums, often centering her work in the dialogue between social, historical, and political machinations and family history. As in her earlier work, Barrada delves into ethnography, paleontology, natural history, and "abstract geology," exploring child-centered educational methods and cataloguing personal objects and ephemera.

> *My mother ended up in Hollywood with a guy who had a jaguar.*
> *And in Michigan she drowned.*
> *She walked through a crowd in a church to meet Stokely Carmichael with her green passport, saying, "I'm African." And the way she described it is like Moses opening the ocean.*
> *We're from a family of pirates.*
> *My mother is a self-invented hero.*

This is how Barrada recounted her mother's fantastical stories and her marvelous reasoning for their creation during one of our earliest conversations about her visit to the United States, a "founding journey in her character," as the artist described it. *Tree Identification for Beginners* illuminated the intersection of Cold War and postcolonial anxieties, as well as possibilities concerning leadership, radical intellectualism, and politics through the force of autobiographical mythology and the fraught utopian desire for Pan-Africanism in the mid-1960s. Barrada draws upon myth as a compelling recourse to challenge history, facts, and authenticated narratives as their suspect, unauthorized, and animated counterpoint. Told through a series of vignettes drawn from cardinal moments of Barrada's mother's visit, the work is comprised of a stop-motion animation film with recorded sound as its centerpiece, a lush hand-dyed and sewn two-sided, multi-paneled theater curtain (her largest textile work to date), and live foley sound accompaniment enacted by Barrada and a collaborator, alternating nightly between Steve Cossman (who was also director of photography and the film's animator) and Rachel Abernathy-Guma. In the approximately forty-minute-long work, Barrada entwined events as accumulations of individual and collective history assembled through archives and reports sourced from the Amistad Research Center at Tulane University. The resource material was excerpted and presented in two registers: as mundane data as well as slyly suspect, yet marvelous, even sometimes heartbreaking, personal accounts recited in the recording by Barrada and a host of participants, including Sean Gullette (also a producer of the project) and fellows at the American Academy in Rome, where the artist was in residence in 2017. An array of educational toys were the actors: These animated characters stand in as abstract proxies for people and places. The film concludes with four geometric forms—one is translucent, the others are yellow, pink, and blue—dancing to jazz pianist and composer Duke Ellington's 1962 recording of "The African Flower." ADRIENNE EDWARDS

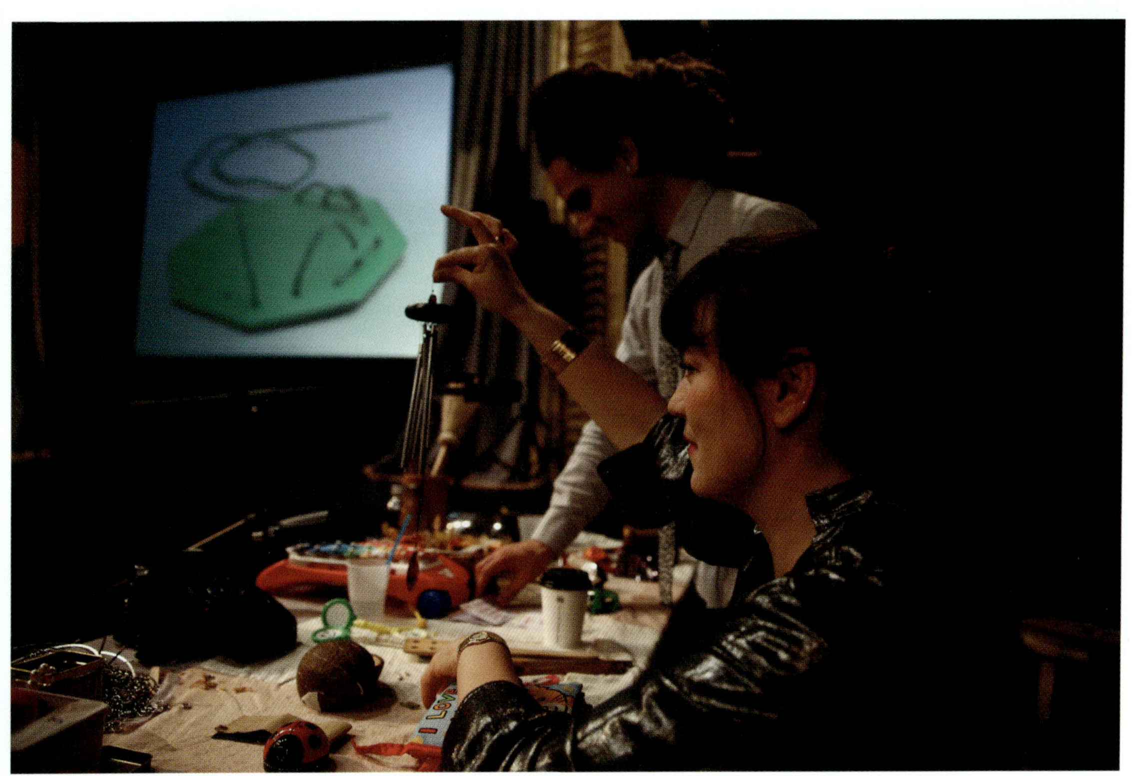

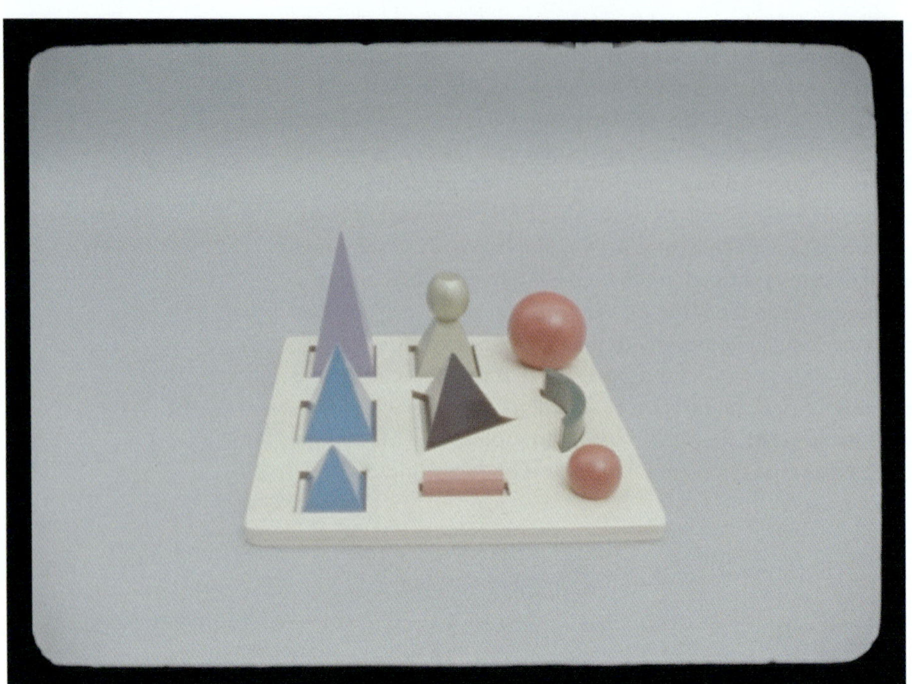

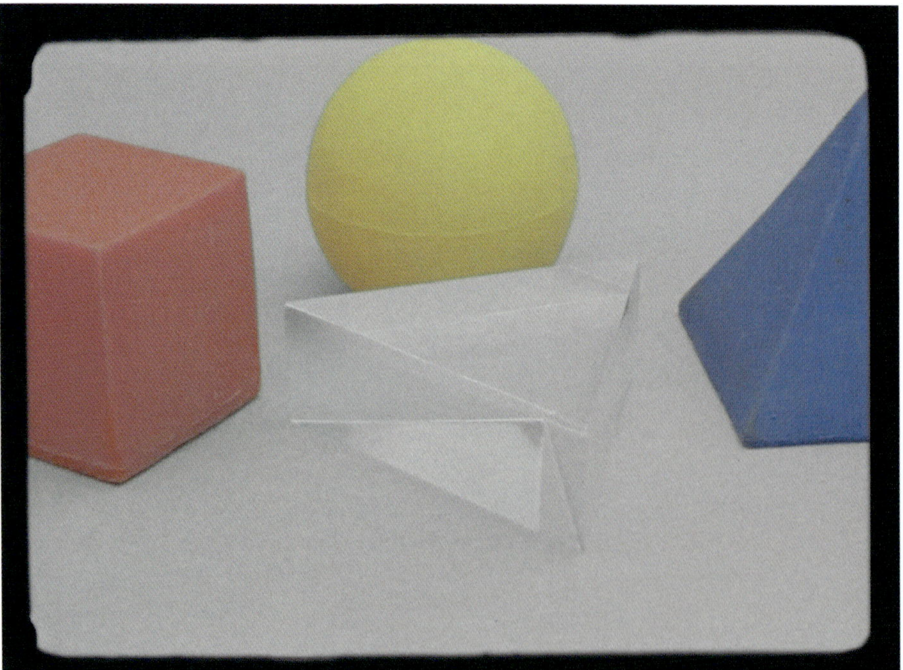

Yto Barrada, *Tree Identification for Beginners*, 2017. Film stills.

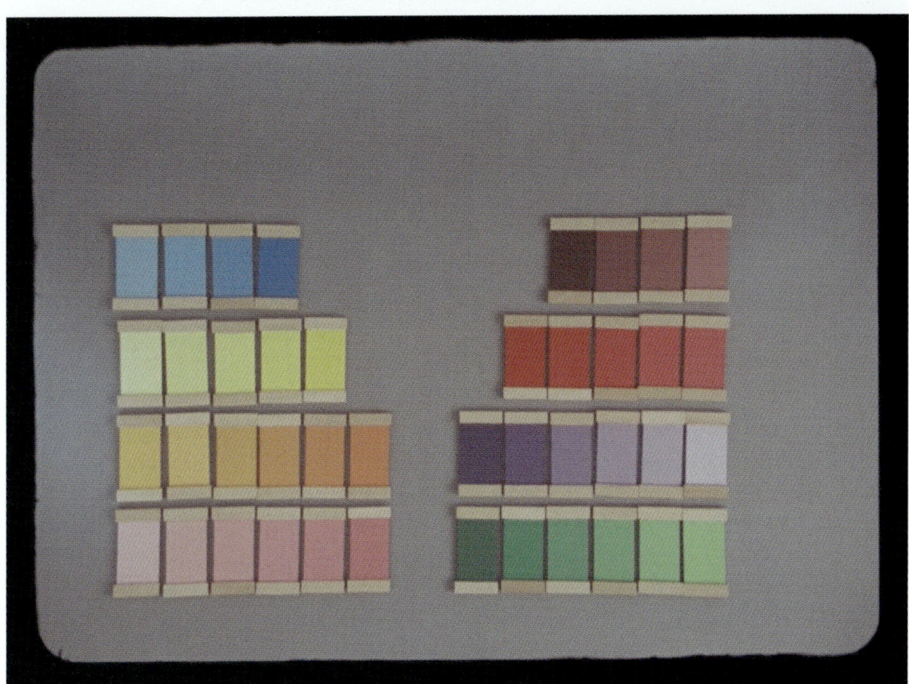

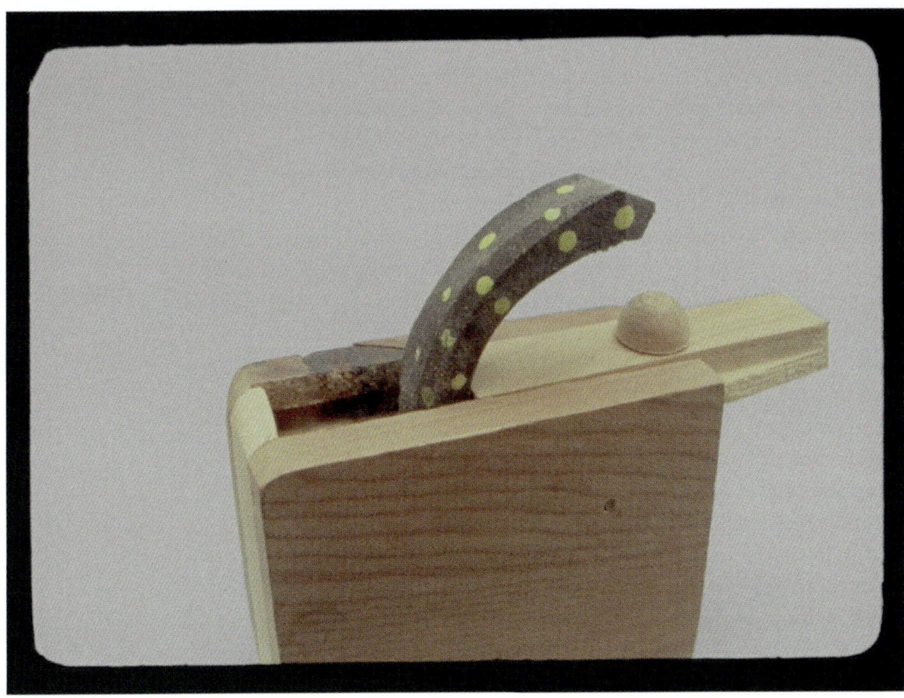

JULIE MEHRETU & JASON MORAN

MASS (HOWL, eon)

Curated by Adrienne Edwards and RoseLee Goldberg

Harlem Parish

November 16, 2017

The collaboration between painter Julie Mehretu and interdisciplinary artist Jason Moran, best known as a jazz musician, was an intimate and observational duet. In the months following the 2016 U.S. presidential election, Mehretu had temporarily moved her studio into a decommissioned neo-Gothic church in Harlem, where Moran would start visiting regularly. There, she was creating a pair of monumental paintings titled *HOWL, eon (I, II)*, commissioned by the San Francisco Museum of Modern Art for its atrium. Mehretu invited Moran to join her as she worked, often perched on a cherry picker to reach the height of her canvases. On an electric piano ensconced on the balcony, Moran composed and improvised a set of phrases and gestures into an hour-long score that responded to and was redolent of the sonic residue within the church—its bygone hymns, sacred voids, and calibrated light—as much as it was tied to the repetitions and disquieting erasures of the painter's bold mark-making.

The paintings examine the competing and contradictory narratives of slavery, emancipation, annihilation, and preservation at the heart of our nation's mid-nineteenth-century westward expansion, and explore the colonialism, capitalism, class conflicts, uprisings, and technological innovations that have transformed its social and physical landscape. The underpaintings are based on distorted digital images of contemporary race riots (following the extra-judicial killings of young Black men in London; Ferguson, Missouri; and Baltimore), recent land protests, and mid-nineteenth-century depictions of the sublime and the American West.

MASS (HOWL, eon) took place in the wake of a political reckoning anachronistic in scope and kind, and in a Harlem vastly different from the one in which the original parish was established. Because the expressionistic diptych had already been shipped to SFMOMA, Mehretu made her first video work for the occasion. The virtual semblance of these paintings was also a return to an earlier stage in their making, revisiting the digital process that she uses to create her underpaintings. The audience was taken on an intensive tour of the canvases, magnified in great detail, the focus dynamically shifting across two towering, cinematically scaled projection screens set on an angle from each other. Moran, set up in the center of the former sanctuary, offered a counterpoint to the lush visual experience by alternately playing an upright and an electric piano, accompanied by Graham Haynes on coronet and sound effects and Jamire Williams on drums. The seated audience was divided into two sections, facing each other and enveloping the screens and the band.

While the sets of the two performances were remarkably distinct, they shared a structural through-line. The music began slow and low, soft and sweeping; then haunting and surging, symphonic and staticky. At times the elements ran parallel; at others, they coalesced. Ultimately, there was an urgency to their playing, particularly in the climactic moments when they, too, seemed to face off, sonically encircling one another in moments of percolating and perplexingly seductive crescendos. Only to come down from such heights to return to the ethereal, echoing, and lulling resonance with which they began, now punctuated by silences, but different this time around, more dissonant, much like the reality of the times to which these paintings give form. ADRIENNE EDWARDS

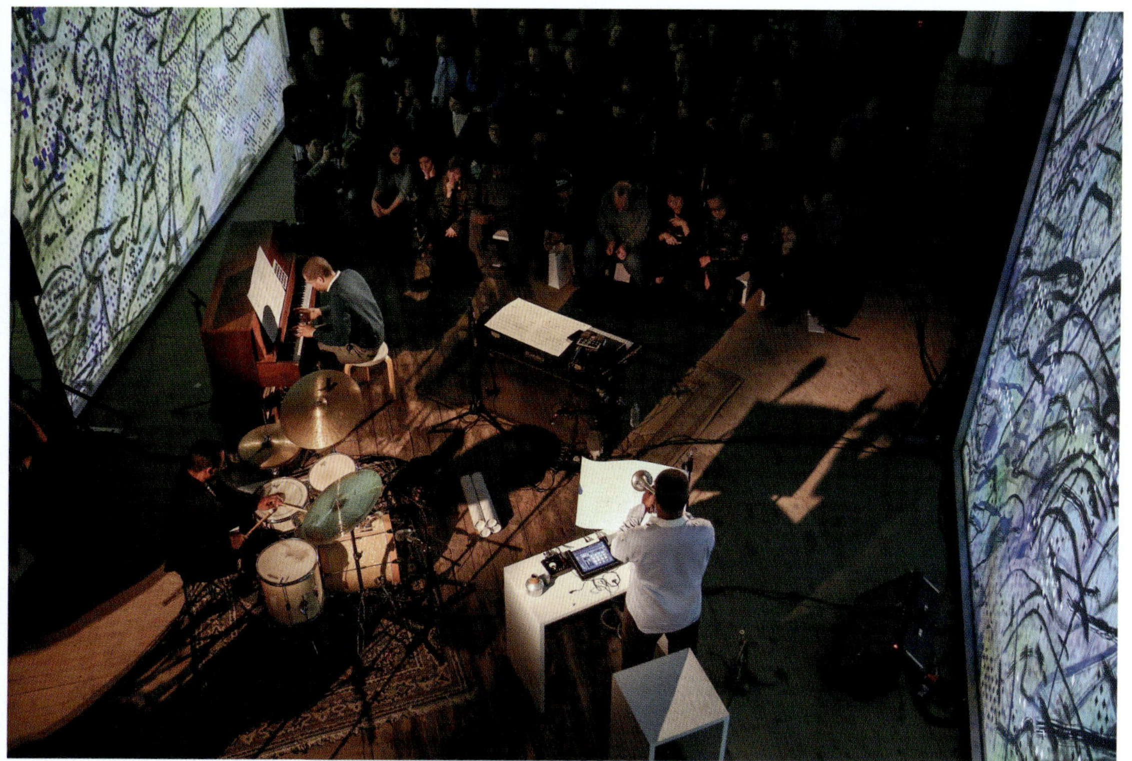

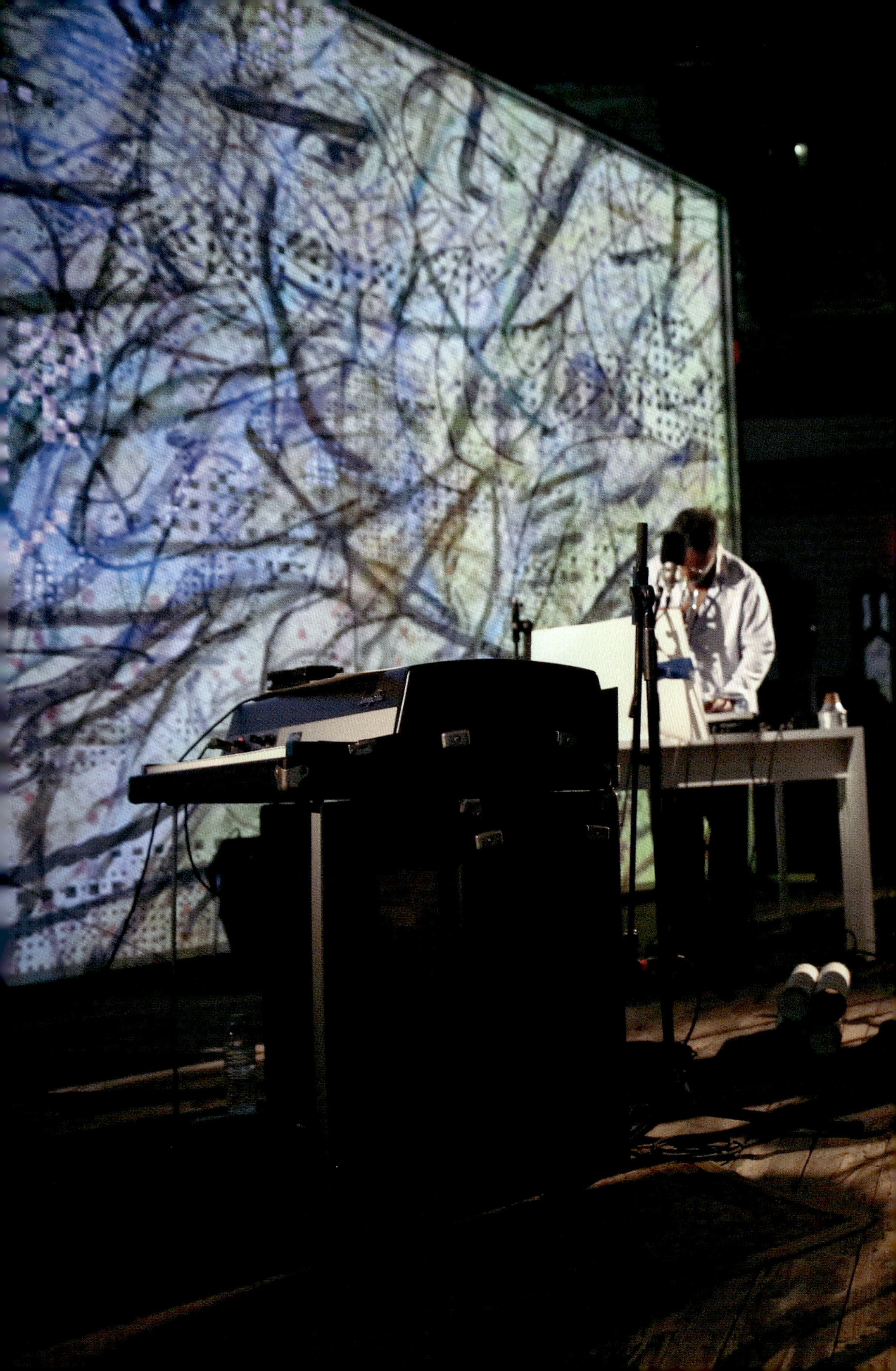

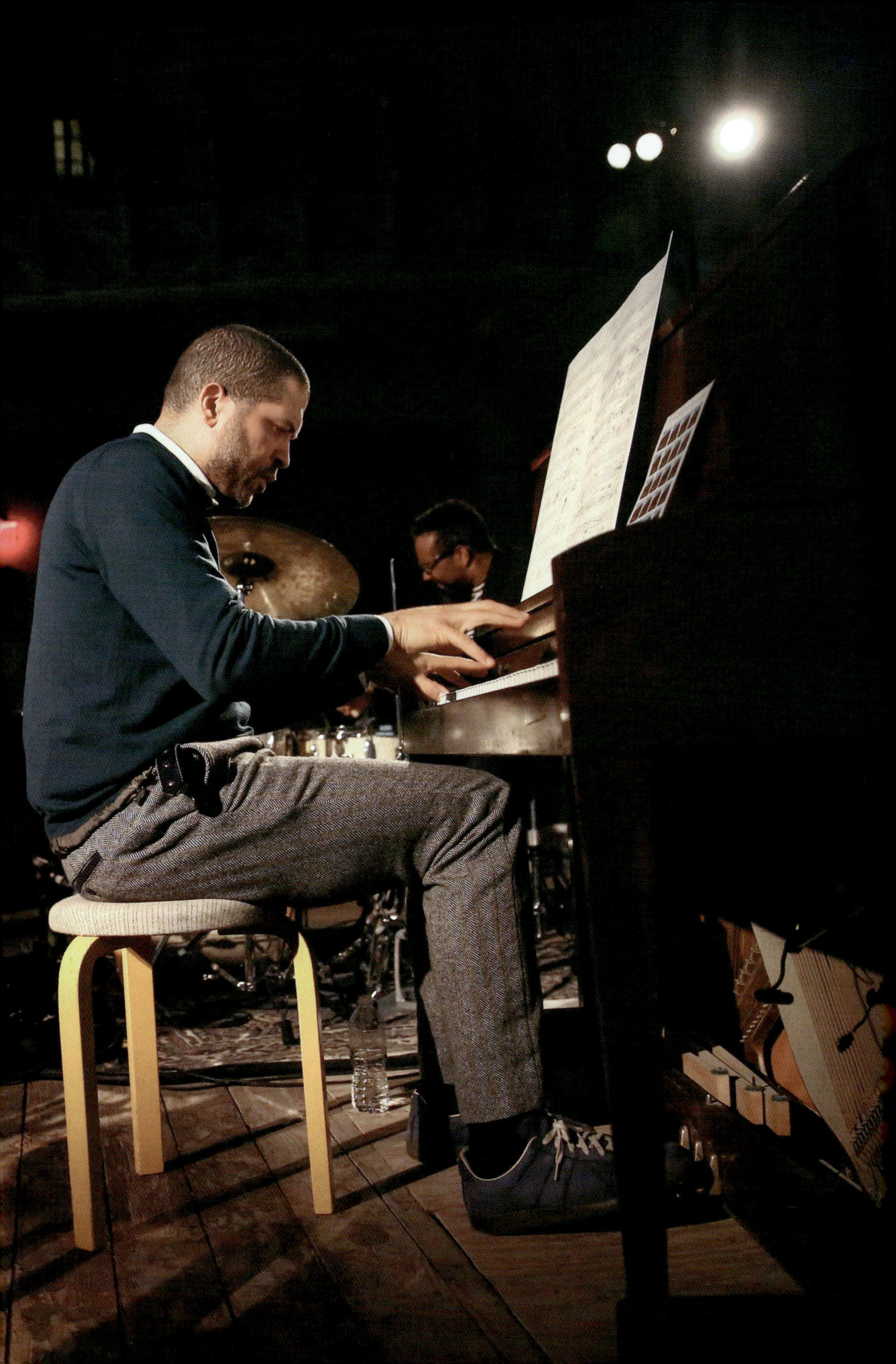

ADRIENNE EDWARDS

&

CHARLES AUBIN

IN CONVERSATION WITH

AGNIESZKA

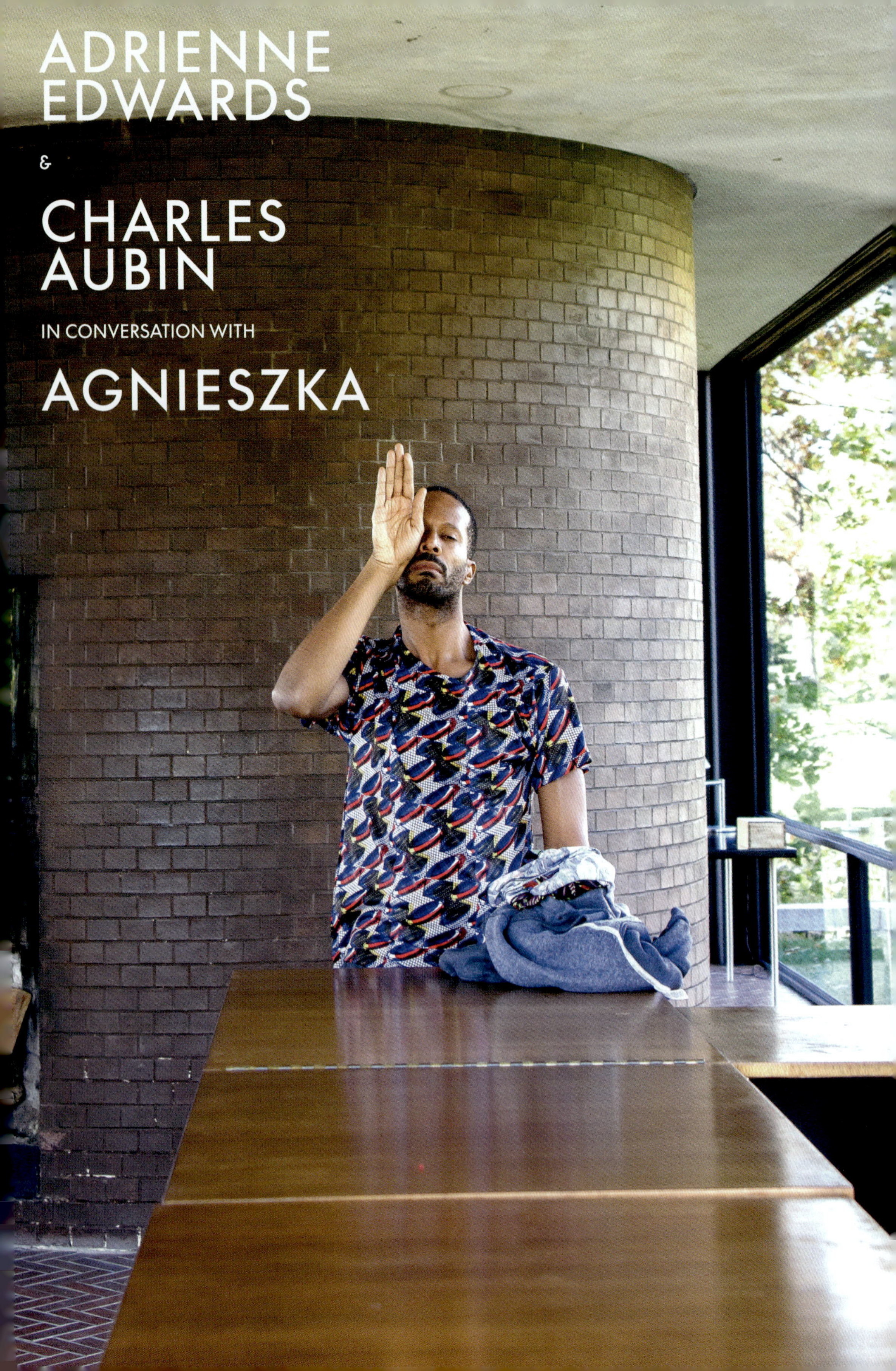

A month before the opening of Performa 17, curators Adrienne Edwards and Charles Aubin spoke to art writer Agnieszka Gratza about several curatorial investigations underpinning the Biennial's program—the South African Pavilion, Afroglossia, *and* Circulations*—and the role of Dada, the historical "anchor" for the Biennial. Edwards and Aubin explain how these areas of study became of interest as well as where they overlap. They also highlight the importance of this year's focus on artists from the African continent and its diaspora.*

AGNIESZKA GRATZA (TO ADRIENNE EDWARDS)
As well as being Performa's chief curator and director, RoseLee Goldberg is overseeing the South African pavilion this year, and you're looking after *Afroglossia* while Charles Aubin is curating *Circulations*, Performa 17's performance and architecture program. Perhaps you could start by explaining how you divide tasks.

ADRIENNE EDWARDS
Typically, what happens is that RoseLee has some instinct or inclination about what she might like to focus on in the next biennial. And so, in 2015, she said to me, "I think we should do a geographical focus on Africa," and I thought, great, since my areas of expertise have always been the African diaspora and the Global South. There's a profound openness at Performa; you might get a prompt, but the curators themselves actually develop programs. Each curator owns their platform in the context of the biennial, and then that platform gets assigned a set of producers who work closely with the curators and the artists to make whatever we've dreamed up over a two-year period happen.

AG
Besides *Afroglossia* and *Circulations*, there's a third research theme, which is Dada. Who looks after that? Or is it subsumed into the other themes?

Jimmy Robert, *Imitation of Lives*, 2017. Performance view.

AE

With each biennial, there's a historical research anchor that operates a little differently than the curatorial platforms. That historical anchor doesn't always end up as a program in the biennial. In 2009, we did Futurism, and then Russian Constructivism in 2011, and Surrealism in 2013. Dada came up early on as a result of the centenary of Dada. It is something we were thinking about over the two-year period leading up to the biennial. For example, I did a program called "100 Degrees Above Dada." I invited Yvonne Rainer and Adam Pendleton to collaborate. I saw in both Adam's "Black Dada" project and the way Yvonne works with language some Dada sensibilities. They developed a beautiful film together called *Just Back from Los Angeles*, which features the two of them.

AG

Let's focus on *Afroglossia*, which is a term you coined, I gather. Could you explain what you mean by it?

AE

"Polyglossia" is the word I'm drawing from. The *afro* is replacing the *poly*. The "many" of this term has been used to point to the multiplicity and complexity that is Africa. *Glossia* is referencing the voice, the fact that there are many voices from one geographical area. All the artists in *Afroglossia* are born in the 1970s, except the guys in the Nest Collective.
So, they came of age around independence, and there's a historical fashioning of the individual in that context and its relationship to the collective. There were some shared sensibilities, a desire to point to something opaque but working with it in a fairly abstract way, whether that be in language, the way they use imagery, or how they draw upon sound and music.

AG

Africa is vast, and yet it's often treated as if it were a country—the United States of Africa. But it isn't. Why should Morocco and South Africa have any more in common than, say, two countries at opposite ends of Europe?

AE

You're right, Africa is not a country, and I remember having extensive discussions about the fact that there's a kind of impossibility to even trying to approach Africa in such a way. And yet there's also a historical, utopian project around pan-Africanism that's even bigger than just the continent of Africa. It encompasses the entire diaspora. Even if pan-Africanism is a complicated, historically failed project, it's been useful in imagining the possibility of a kind of African commons. That said, that's not really what *Afroglossia* is about. These are different voices out of various countries, and I don't think I'm trying to connect them any more closely than that.

AG

I noticed that there's a particular focus—despite the diversity of the places where the artists come from (many of them also live in New York and other Western places)—on Nairobi and East Africa. The Kwani Trust, Wangechi Mutu, and the Nest Collective all have ties with this region.

AE

The number of things happening in Kenya is mind-boggling. It is just so rich in terms of real experimentation that is interdisciplinary. The Nest is primarily known for their video and film work, but they're also in fashion, and they make art animations and drawings. Performance itself as a notion gets stretched a bit in the context of the biennial. With Kwani, the journalists, writers, and people who collect oral histories are looking at lived experience in a way that is politically engaged and also cultural. They have poetry and music nights, all kinds of ways in which they animate the cultural scene of Nairobi.

AG

Would you say that there's an emphasis on literature and the spoken word in your program, as the *glossia* in the title suggests?

Yto Barrada, *Tree Identification for Beginners*, 2017. Performance view.

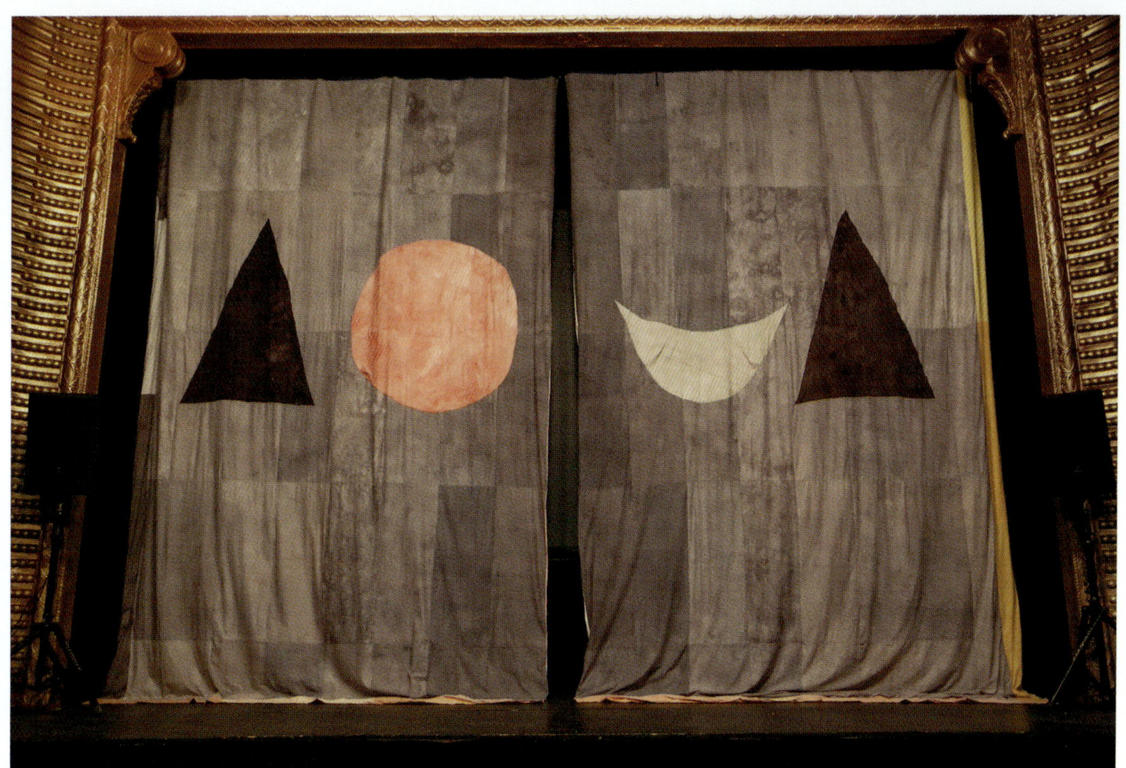

AE

It's certainly evident in the work Yto Barrada is doing, something that is all about voice: her mother's voice, correspondence, records, and interviews of figures her mother was with on a tour of the United States in 1966. Teju Cole is known not only as a critic but also as a novelist and an essayist. And Tracey Rose is working with two writers: one in the United States, one in Cameroon. They're developing a script as part of a poetic performance that, like Yto's, is about sieving archives, narratives, and oral histories.

AG

You said that the notion of performance is stretched in the Performa biennial, which seems right to me; as a result, the performative element is somewhat elusive.

AE

Each project is like a container for the various ways an artist works. So, with Yto, for example, you'll see her textile works, her photo prints, her film, you'll hear her sing; they're all these things that people could experience in one way or another in relation to Yto's work, but this time, it's all sitting in one space.

AG

But that one space doesn't appear to be very distinctly about performance.

AE

It depends on what your expectations of performance are. For me, performance is interdisciplinarity. There's a live component, but it's not the only one. These kinds of commissions have always had various visual art elements in the experience.

AG

Would you say that there are any overlaps between *Afroglossia* and the South African pavilion?

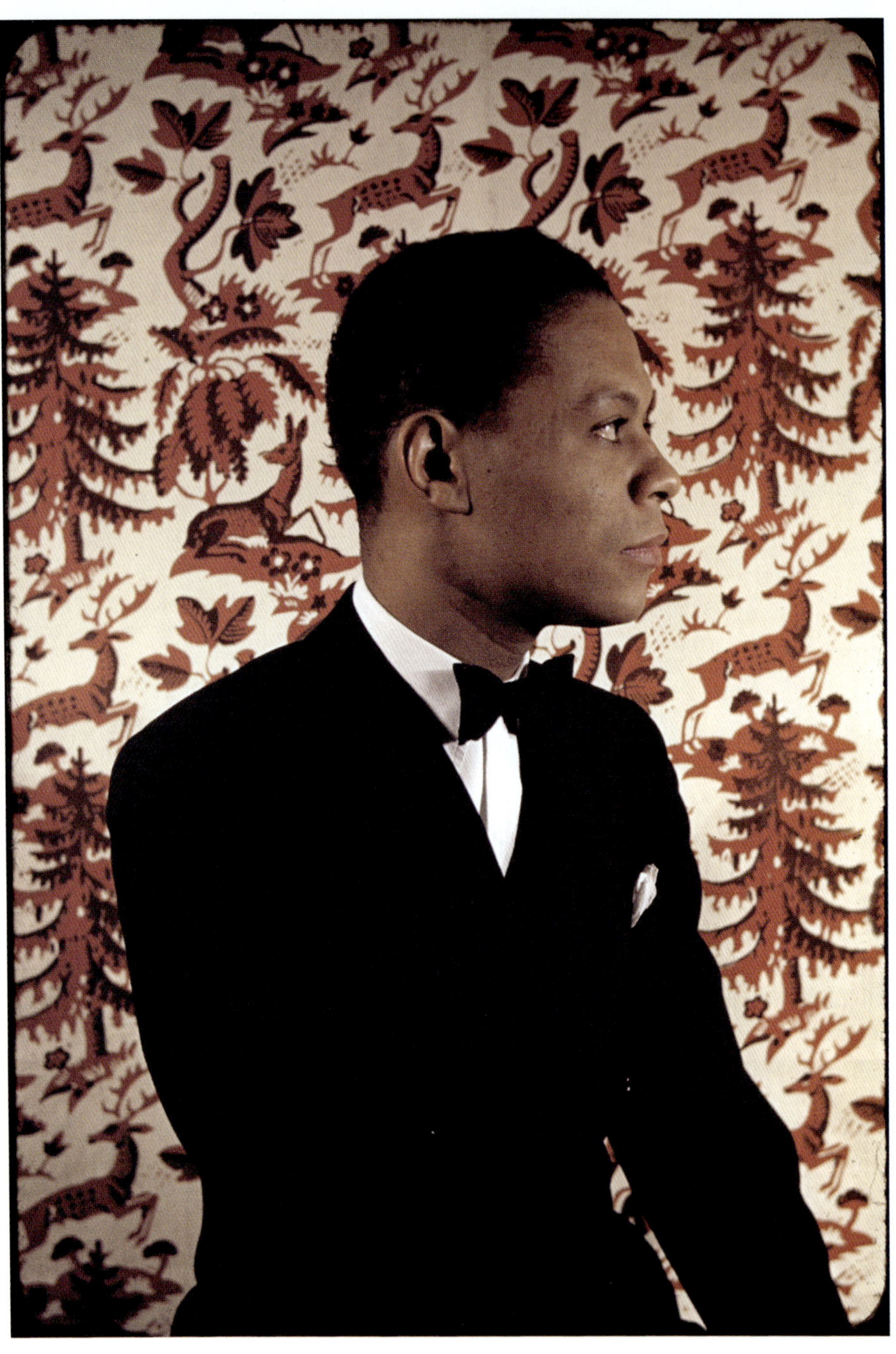

Carl Van Vechten,
Jimmie Daniels, 1940.

AE

All the other pavilions, since we started the Pavilions Without Walls in 2013, have been with European countries. There's an infrastructure and an apparatus in place to support the presentation of European artists around the world. Such a thing does not exist for a country like South Africa, so it was very important for us and RoseLee in particular, who is from South Africa, to do a deep dive into that country. There are some overlaps with *Afroglossia* and shared sensibilities, certainly an interest in the ethical, social, political dimensions of art making.

AG (TO CHARLES AUBIN)

The Glass House, where you are working today, is one of the iconic architectural venues your program will occupy. How did this particular project within your program come about?

CHARLES AUBIN

A year and a half ago, I mentioned in passing to Jimmy Robert that the Glass House is a strange extension of the New York architectural landscape, with all the different pavilions that Philip Johnson built here on the site. Jimmy told me about Dan Graham's *Kammerspiel*, a book he'd read by Jeff Wall on Graham's work. In Jeff Wall's text, there's a whole section discussing how, at dusk, the artificial light inside and the darkness outside create a choreography of reflections of the self in which the transparent walls become mirrors. And this is where Jimmy started bringing in questions of identity and representation.

AG

And in particular Black representation, I gather.

CA

Exactly. And the more research we did, the more interesting this site became because of either repressed histories or some elements of Philip Johnson's biography, in particular his romantic relationship with the Harlem Renaissance cabaret figure Jimmie Daniels.

AG

Which seems fitting given the overall emphasis on Africa and its diaspora in *Afroglossia* especially.

CA

Adrienne and I have conceived of the two programs *Afroglossia* and *Circulations* on their own, but we have sometimes posed similar questions that can be addressed through performance. With the Glass House but also *Marching On*—a project with Mabel O. Wilson and Bryony Roberts commissioned by Storefront for Art and Architecture—political questions of identity were very much our concern. Bryony and Mabel have been researching the political role of marching bands in African American communities and parades coming from U.S. military tradition at a time when African Americans had participated in world wars but were still not granted the same civil rights at home.

AG

You're also editing a publication with Carlos Mínguez Carrasco from Storefront for Art and Architecture.

CA

The way that I conceived of *Circulations* was as a curatorial platform with a discursive aspect in the shape of a symposium on November 11, 2017 and a book that Carlos and I are co-editing called *Bodybuilding*. One of the impulses for the book and the program is the renewal of interest in ephemeral, event-based actions by architects since the 2008 financial crisis. That's something you can see in "The Other Architect" exhibition that Giovanna Borasi, who spoke at the symposium, curated at the Canadian Centre for Architecture in Montreal.

AG

I was struck by the variety of "performative"

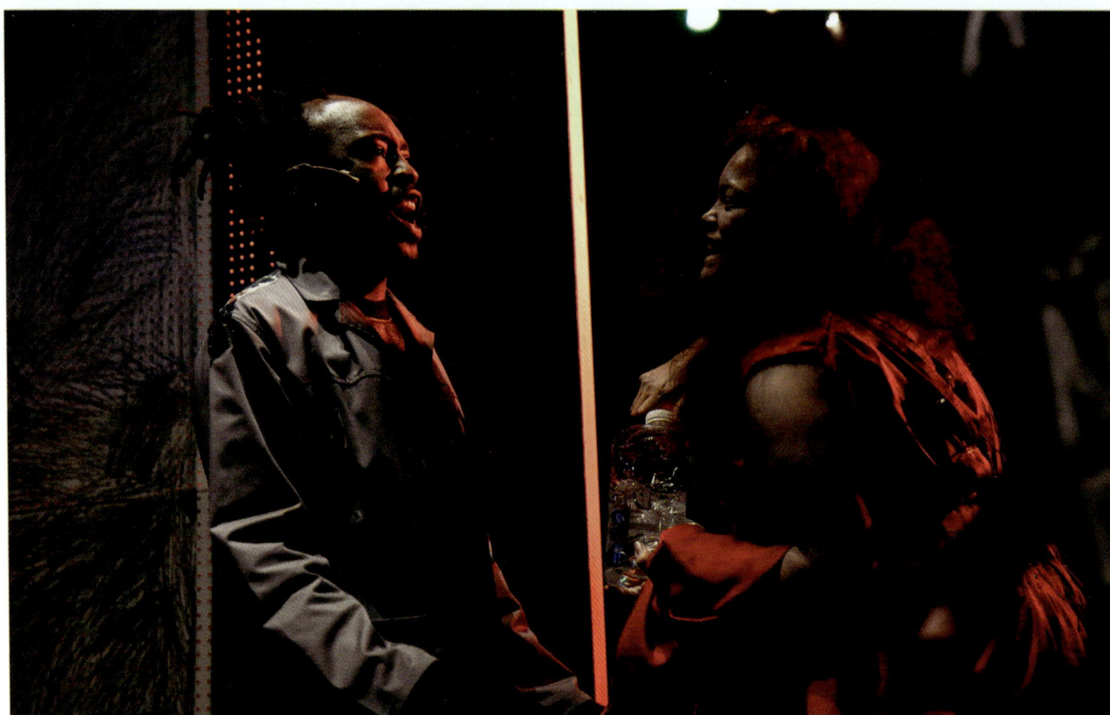

disciplines in *Circulations*, from poetry to singing to choreography and marching bands. Did you opt to give as wide a spread of possible fields that architecture can have an impact on, and vice versa?

CA

For me, performance is not so much a discipline as a tool. It allows visual artists to expand on their work in space, and it's this kind of nexus where an artist can actually borrow from different disciplines. It's more of a strategy, if that makes sense.

AG

Could you comment on the title *Circulations*?

CA

I was interested in this idea that architecture is a space where bodies are allowed or not allowed to circulate in different ways, and that there's a kind of implicit choreography that is somehow directed. Politically, it's a complicated moment, and I wanted to open up this notion of circulation toward more political concerns: Who gets to circulate, and how does that happen? This question is embedded in François Dallegret's *Environment-Bubble*, circulating in different parts of the city, trying to create this kind of movement.

AG

Dallegret's *Bubble*, which embodies the degree zero of architecture, has never been realized until now. Was it easy to construct?

CA

The Los Angeles–based architect François Perrin, who had curated a retrospective of Dallegret's work, came up with the idea that we should build *The Environment-Bubble* for the first time. To be honest, the most simple and minimal forms are somehow the most complicated ones to make. The *Bubble*, as Dallegret conceived of it, is a place for reprogramming interactions between its inhabitants. That's why the choreographer Dimitri Chamblas was brought in as a dance

Tracey Rose, *THE TRACEY ROSE SHOW*, 2017. Performance view.

François Dallegret with Dimitri Chamblas and François Perrin, *The Environment-Bubble* 2017. Performance view.

workshop leader. For us, dance was going to be a tool to activate the *Bubble*.

AG

This kind of reprogramming is also at the heart of Alex Schweder and Ward Shelley's practice. Their biennial offering, *The Newcomers*, was originally going to be a nomadic architectural installation. What came of that?

CA

The very initial idea, which proved impossible to realize for security reasons, was a suspended structure that would be assembled and disassembled and moved every day for ten days. We were looking at various sites. Among the different options we had was 28 Liberty, an iconic International-style skyscraper downtown, which contrasted with what Ward and Alex were planning in terms of a more nimble, ephemeral mode of thinking about architecture: an architecture that mutates or produces its own constant reshaping.

This text was initially published online by Mousse Magazine *on November 14, 2017. Reprinted courtesy the authors and* Mousse Magazine.

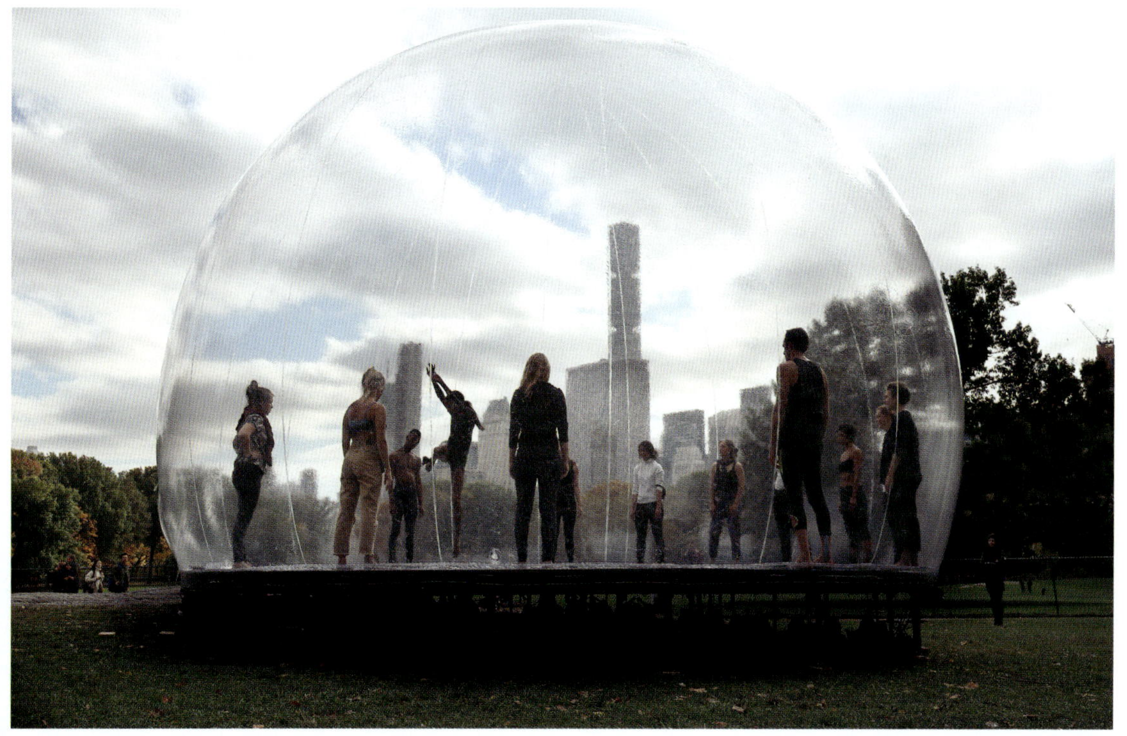

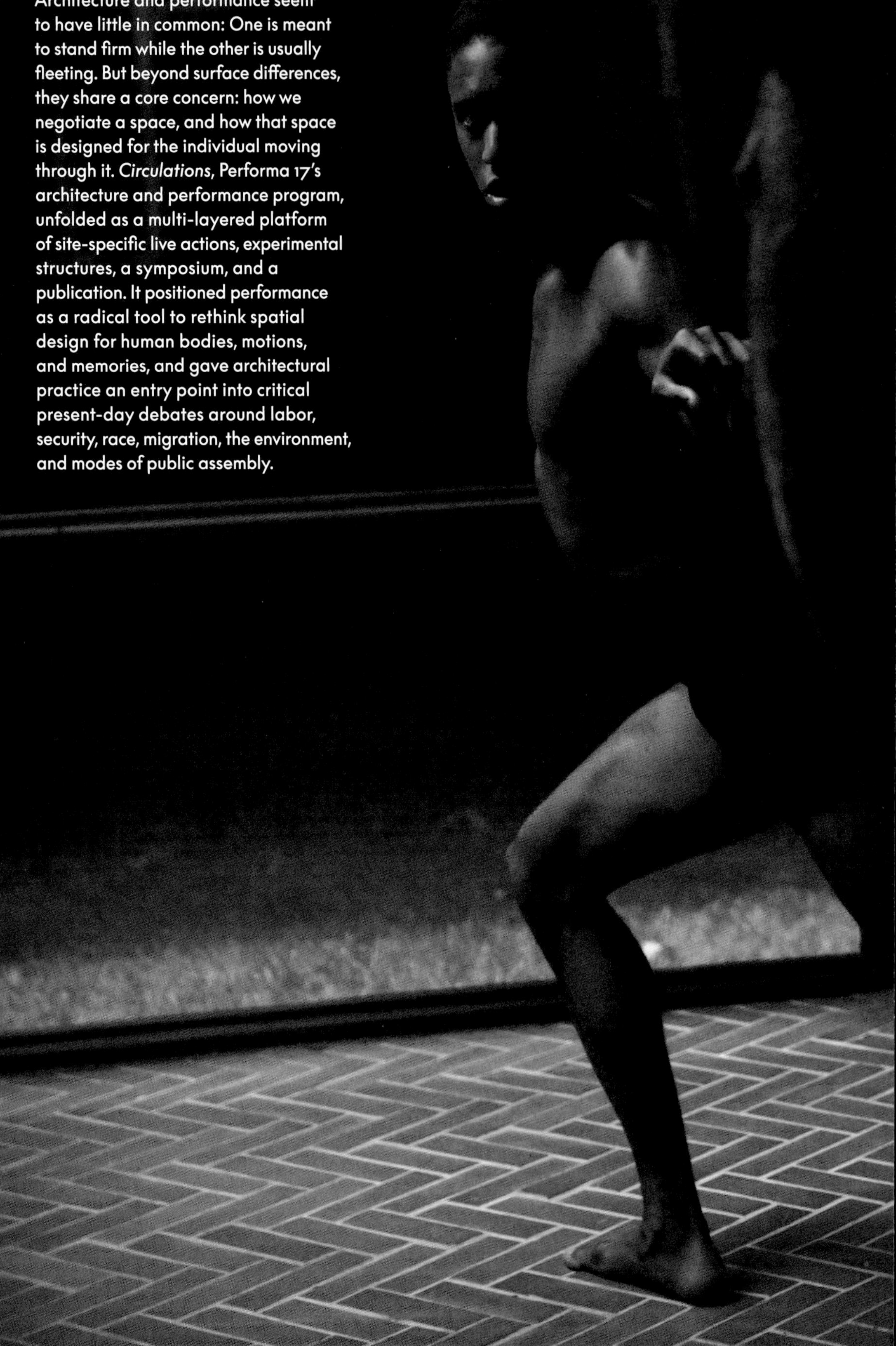

Architecture and performance seem to have little in common: One is meant to stand firm while the other is usually fleeting. But beyond surface differences, they share a core concern: how we negotiate a space, and how that space is designed for the individual moving through it. *Circulations*, Performa 17's architecture and performance program, unfolded as a multi-layered platform of site-specific live actions, experimental structures, a symposium, and a publication. It positioned performance as a radical tool to rethink spatial design for human bodies, motions, and memories, and gave architectural practice an entry point into critical present-day debates around labor, security, race, migration, the environment, and modes of public assembly.

CIRCULATIONS

JIMMY ROBERT
Imitation of Lives

Curated by
Charles Aubin
and Cole Akers

The Glass House

November 3–5, 2017

In *Orpheus*, Jean Cocteau's iconic 1950 French film-poem, a mirror offers access to the underworld. Similarly, the Glass House, Philip Johnson's residence built in 1949 in New Canaan, Connecticut, acts as a threshold to the complex and controversial past of its American architect. It's within these glass walls that French artist Jimmy Robert created *Imitation of Lives*, an intimate drama of dance and poetry that collapsed multiple identities inside the house's interplay of reflection and transparency—optics that can be both uncanny and anxiety-inducing. Throughout his hourlong performance, with performers NIC Kay and Quenton Stuckey, Robert conjured tableaux that slipped back and forth between present and past, classical and postmodern dance. The series of vignettes that emerged examined desires alongside politics of sexuality, gender, and race.

Two uniformed security personnel stood silently near the entrance of the house, which is now owned by the National Trust for Historic Preservation, as the audience entered, unaware that the performance had already begun. The visitors were free to casually inspect the room, while Robert and Stuckey acted out the stereotypical Black male bodies hired to be the silent and invisible guards in most cultural institutions. Moving amongst the assembled crowd, they reached at their waists for a red lipstick (rather than a weapon); as their dance unfolded, the duo carefully reddened their lips. Finally, this sequence of movements culminated in Stuckey lying face-down on the floor in a disturbing invocation of Black men, women, and children murdered by police violence. The audience remained eerily silent.

Then, a pair of gray-hooded, ghostlike figures mirrored each other's movements, one walking inside the perimeter of the house, the other outside. The hoodies brought to mind Trayvon Martin, the seventeen-year-old African American high school student murdered in 2012, who was wearing a similar hooded sweatshirt on the night he was gunned down, and the Black Lives Matter movement. During the evening performance, the figures were rendered anonymous by the darkness. The silence of the first two parts of the performance was followed by a transitional vignette that included texts by Josephine Baker, Marguerite Duras, Lorenzo Thomas, and Audre Lorde. Sitting on the floor, leaning over a large horizontal mirror placed on the house's daybed, NIC Kay performed a poem by Jayne Cortez. This scene recalled the cinematic moment from Cocteau's film where the poet Orpheus was lying in the sand while gazing upon his reflection in a pool of water. In their respective solos through the piece, Robert, Kay, and Stuckey filled out the desire for the dark surfaces and dark skins that serviced architectural modernism's historical white elite.

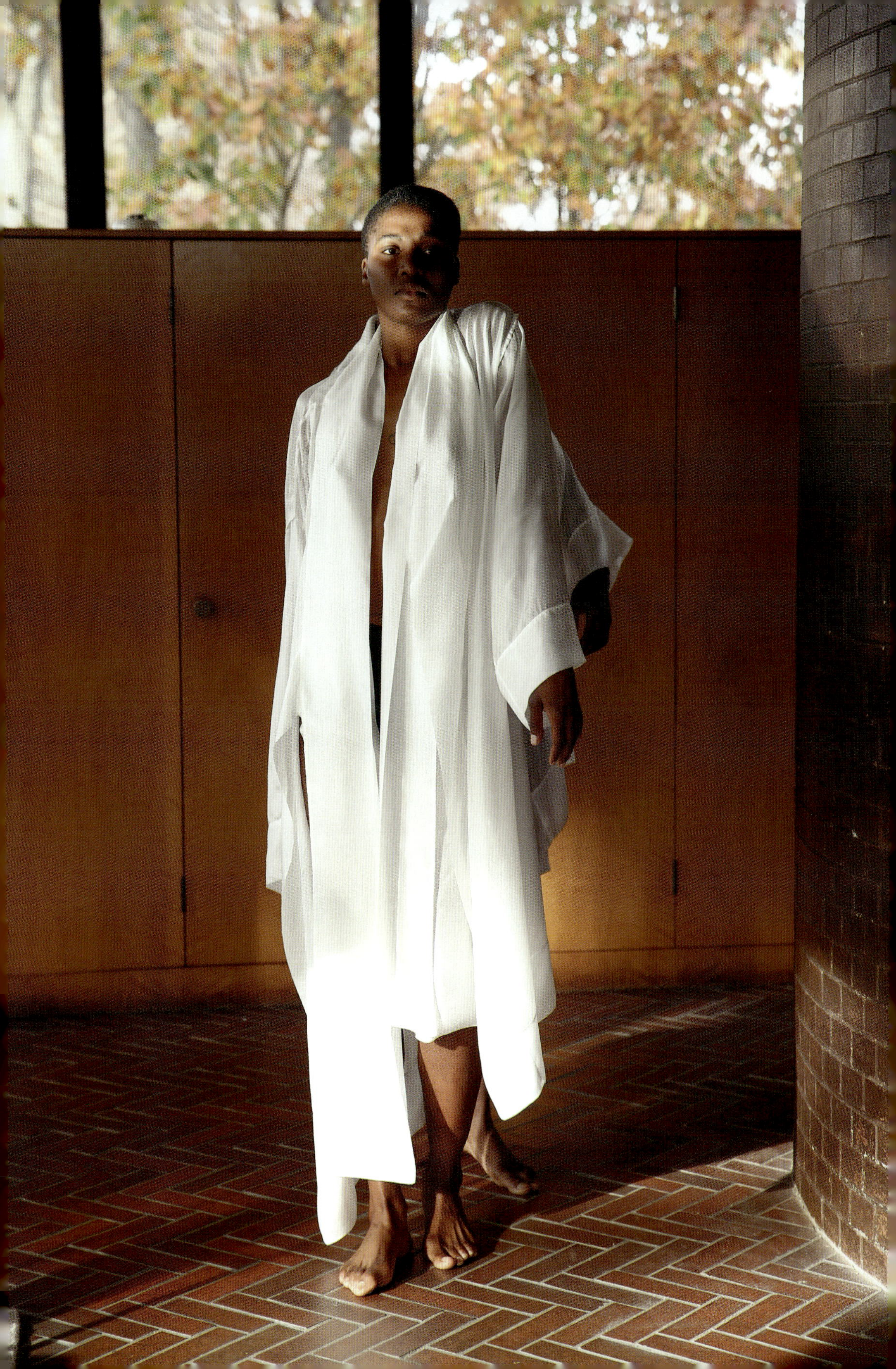

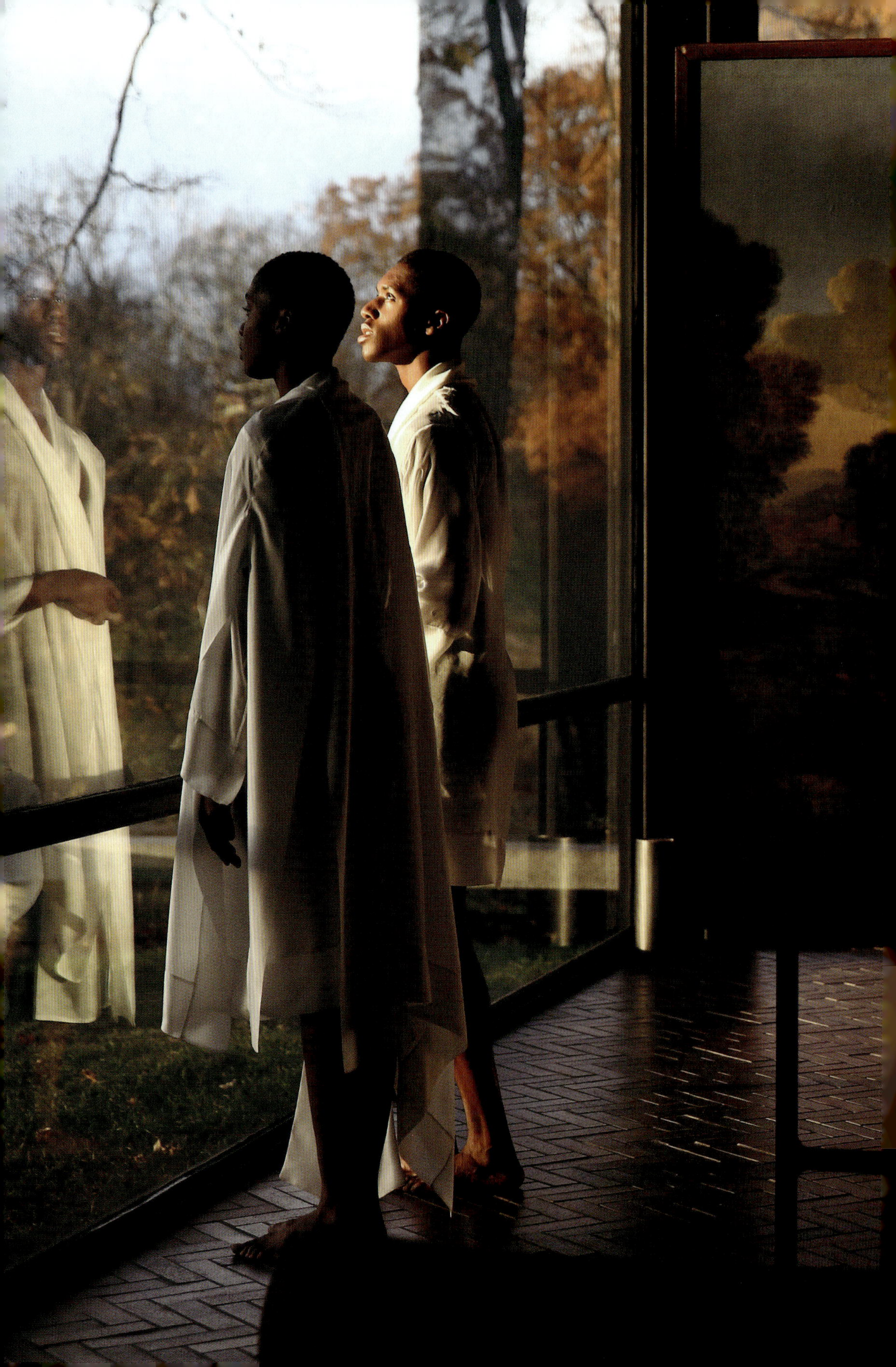

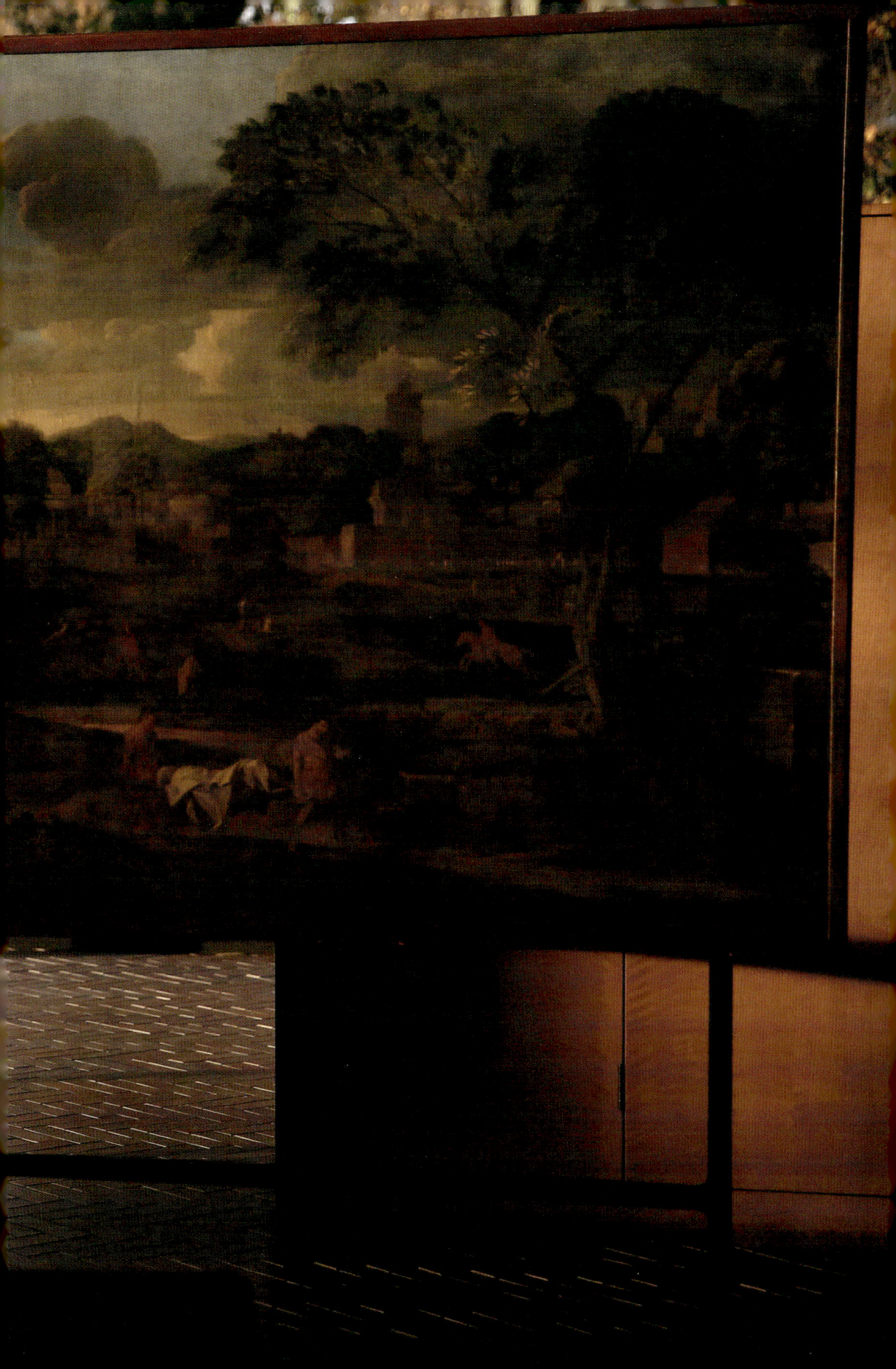

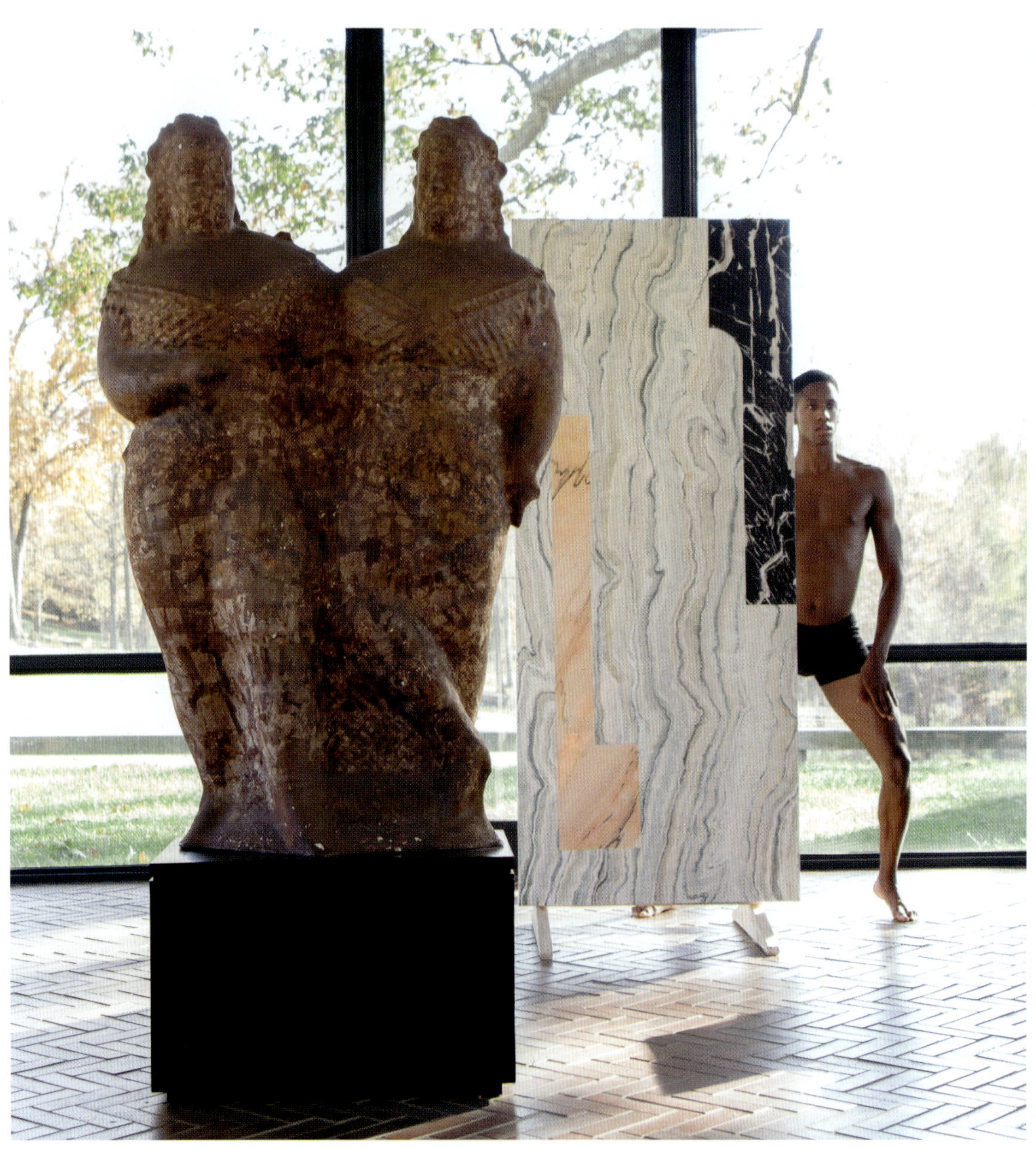

Indeed, Philip Johnson's well-documented desire for a young Black cabaret singer from Harlem named Jimmie Daniels was woven into the fabric of the performance. Described as one of Harlem's most popular café singers, Daniels met Johnson in 1934, and after a brief affair, described his lover as "the first Mrs. Johnson," bragging that he "was the envy of all Downtown." "It was so chic," Johnson added, "those were the days when you just automatically went to Harlem." Robert channeled Daniels in a soliloquy of lyrics from his song "Chez Moi," combining it with prose and slow voguing movements—hinting at Harlem's ballroom culture. First, Robert stripped away his gray hoodie to reveal a multicolored Matisse leaf-patterned T-shirt, a reference to the backgrounds of Carl Van Vechten's Harlem Renaissance portraits, then removing it to show an African wax-print shirt beneath it.

Following a brief interlude of "Naked Lunch" by jazz avant-gardist Ornette Coleman and Howard Shore, the final part of the performance challenged the marginalization of the Black body in art history. Here, Stuckey danced between Elie Nadelman's large *papier-mâché* sculpture, a pair of voluptuous female figures titled *Two Circus Women* (1930) permanently installed in the house, and a trompe l'oeil painting of a marble slab by Lucy McKenzie titled *Loos / De Bruycker marble* (2017) that was created for the performance as a reference to architect Adolf Loos's designs for Josephine Baker. Then the two dancers changed into sheer white robes behind Nicolas Poussin's painting *The Burial of Phocion* (ca.1648) on an easel, and recited Audre Lorde's poem "Touring" as they sat upon Johnson's bed. The denouement of the performance gave presence to past (and future) beings that bring forth culture and meaning. In the final moments, these are the ghosts of buried ancestors who appeared as Kay and Stuckey emerged into the living area of the house in a crescendo of explosive movements. The pair danced with angular shoulder gestures and flowing limbs of white cloth, set to Bro Safari & UFO!'s propulsive "Burn the Block," a climax that reframed the Glass House as an indefinite, elusive, and intersectional space. MARIO GOODEN

FRANÇOIS DALLEGRET WITH 'DIMITRI CHAMBLAS & FRANÇOIS PERRIN

The Environment-Bubble

Curated by Charles Aubin and François Perrin

Mineral Springs, Central Park and Brooklyn Bridge Park

November 8–9, 2017

More than fifty years after its initial conception, architect and artist François Dallegret's *The Environment-Bubble* was finally realized—twice in New York in one season. This twenty-four-foot-wide transparent plastic inflatable bubble was a contemporary rendition of Dallegret's original design—first published in *Art in America* in April 1965 as a series of illustrations for architecture historian and theorist Reyner Banham's canonical essay "A Home is Not a House."

Banham's essay identified what he called "the junk that kept the pad swinging," including the prevalence of relatively new and particularly American mechanical services—kitchen appliances, bathroom plumbing, thermostats, and even television, radio, and stereo systems—that were absent from European buildings. Banham extended this logic to the absurdly rational conclusion of an "un-house," where absolute technical functionality would be more important than any aesthetic considerations by decoupling a building's envelope from its insides. Dallegret's original sectional drawing notoriously included a collage of figures, specifically himself and Banham, alongside a totem of modern technological conveniences, for scale. The imagined "un-house" paralleled larger sixties countercultural off-the-grid trends that used design to imagine utopian, technological, and ecological futures.

Around the time Dallegret conceived of the project, there were a number of similar architectural utopian endeavors, including inflatable designs by architects and designers such as Hans Hollein's *Mobiles Büro* (1969) and Ant Farm's *Berkeley Clean Air Pod* (1970), as well as the *Cushicle* (1964) and *Suitaloon* (1967) projects by Archigram's Michael Webb. These all shared a desire to spatially disconnect from society yet remain connected through technology, embodied by Dallegret's "transportable standard-of-living package." This custom "package" was designed to include all of the creature comforts one would need in a modern dwelling, like a home entertainment system, air conditioning unit, and stovetop, all enclosed by a thin, plastic membrane dividing interior from exterior. Together, these two elements of the bubble—the package and its transparent plastic enclosure—presented a new technological form of social space, one that we might now recognize as prescient of today's contested notions of privacy.

Performa's *The Environment-Bubble,* initiated by the late French American architect François Perrin, realized Dallegret's design for the first time. Instead of Dallegret and Banham seated at the center, French choreographer Dimitri

François Dallegret, *The Environment-Bubble*, published in April 1965 in *Art in America*.

In the present state of the environmental art, no mechanical device can make the rain go back to Spain; the standard-of-living package is apt to need some sort of an umbrella for emergencies, and it could well be a plastic dome inflated by conditioned air blown out by the package itself.

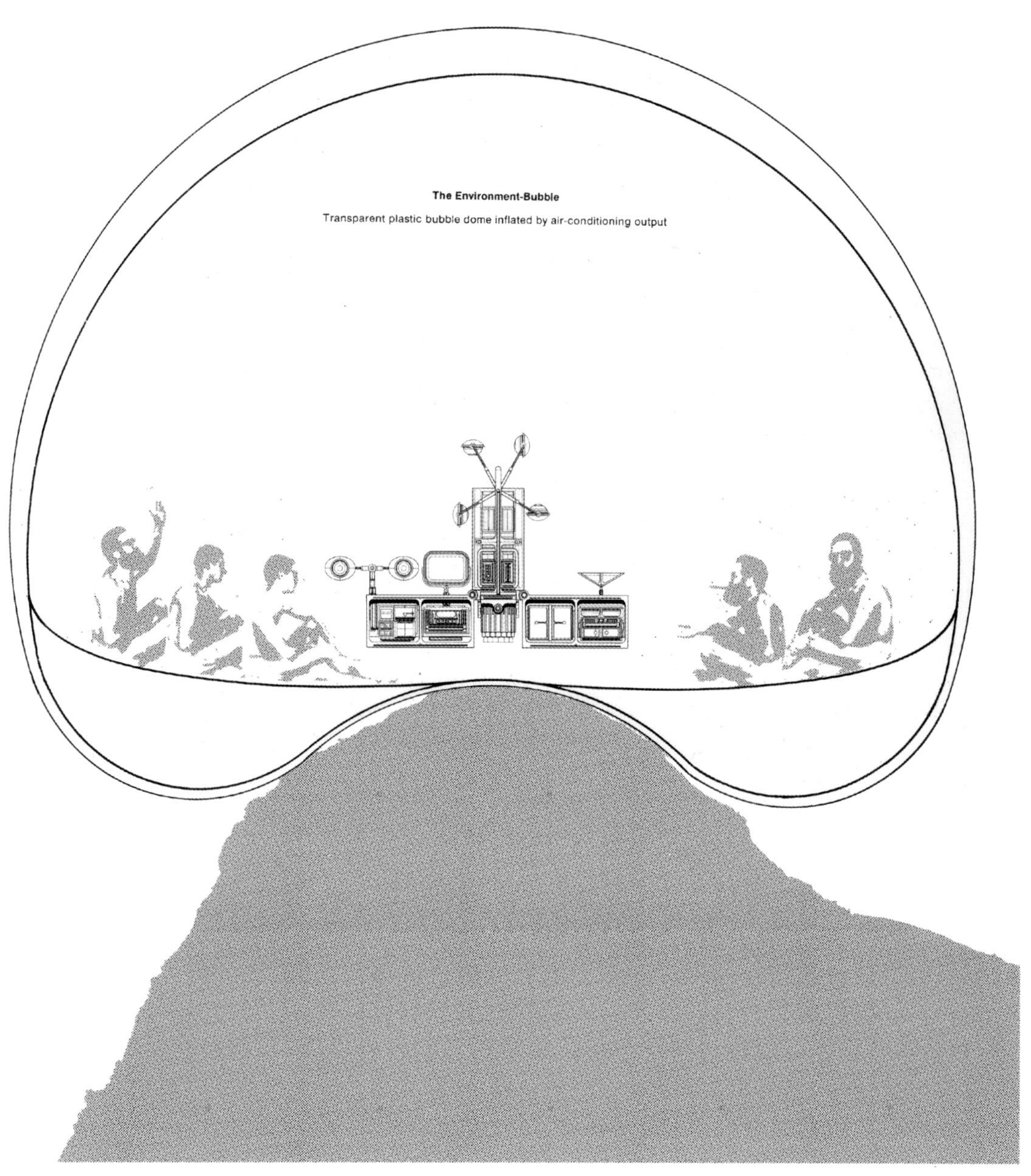

Chamblas activated the bubble with a series of dance workshops in Brooklyn Bridge Park and Mineral Springs in Central Park.

While *The Environment-Bubble* can be seen in its historical context as remarking on architecture's relationship to environmental control, as well as speculating on the potential of technological progress, in 2017, we might say that its revealing capacity lay in its potential to represent our interpersonal digital communication technologies—social media. The dance workshops inside the transparent membrane were the daily activities that participants collected and broadcast to their networks. Furthermore, the acoustics inside the bubble amplified its inhabitants' every move and noise to each other on the inside, but they did not reach outside of the inflatable. The bubble created a voyeuristic relationship between the performers and their audience. They were protected from the elements by just twenty-thousandths of an inch of crystal-clear PVC plastic. The experience was not unlike our phone's screen, which is another transparent technology that we can use to insulate ourselves from the world outside of the bubbles of our own choosing.

While *The Environment-Bubble* of 1965 brought the outdoors into the domestic space, the 2017 iteration in public parks equally focused on the passerby's gaze on the activity inside the inflatable. Dallegret's transportable standard-of-living-package has become decentralized (for better or worse), embedded within the smartphones and social media platforms which increasingly choreograph much of our cultural awareness. Our acquiescence to these surveillance capabilities oscillates between basking in the attention that these platforms promise and wrestling with their omniscience, from which we find ourselves unable to look away.

With the benefit of hindsight, the twenty-first century technology of social media—Instagram and its parent company, Facebook, in particular—may be altering humanity's coexistence on our planet just as much as Dallegret's transportable standard-of-living package would have. Whereas Dallegret's combination of energy-consuming HVAC machinery and audiovisual media equipment eventually ballooned into dual crises of climate change and the Debordian spectacle over the ensuing decades, the 2017 *Environment-Bubble* at Performa disclosed our compulsive obligation to self-brand online at every opportunity, laying bare the self-commodification of our own image-forms. Very few options are left to avert our gaze from it—being in public now means being forced to contribute, IRL and online, to this collective social experiment. Like some kind of cultural Newtonian law of physics in which every action has an equal yet opposite reaction, both the original 1965 and the 2017 *Environment-Bubbles* allow us to understand how each techno-utopian promise may contain its equal yet opposite latent techno-dystopia. JESSE SEEGERS

In memoriam François Perrin (1969–2019)

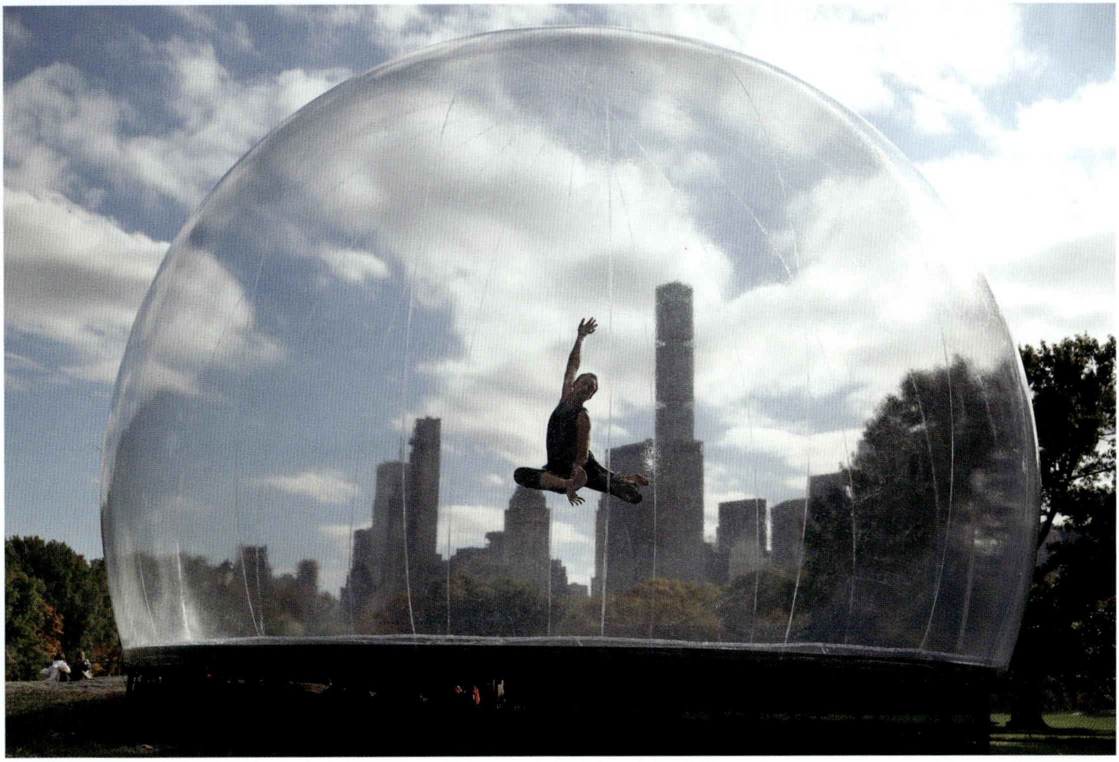

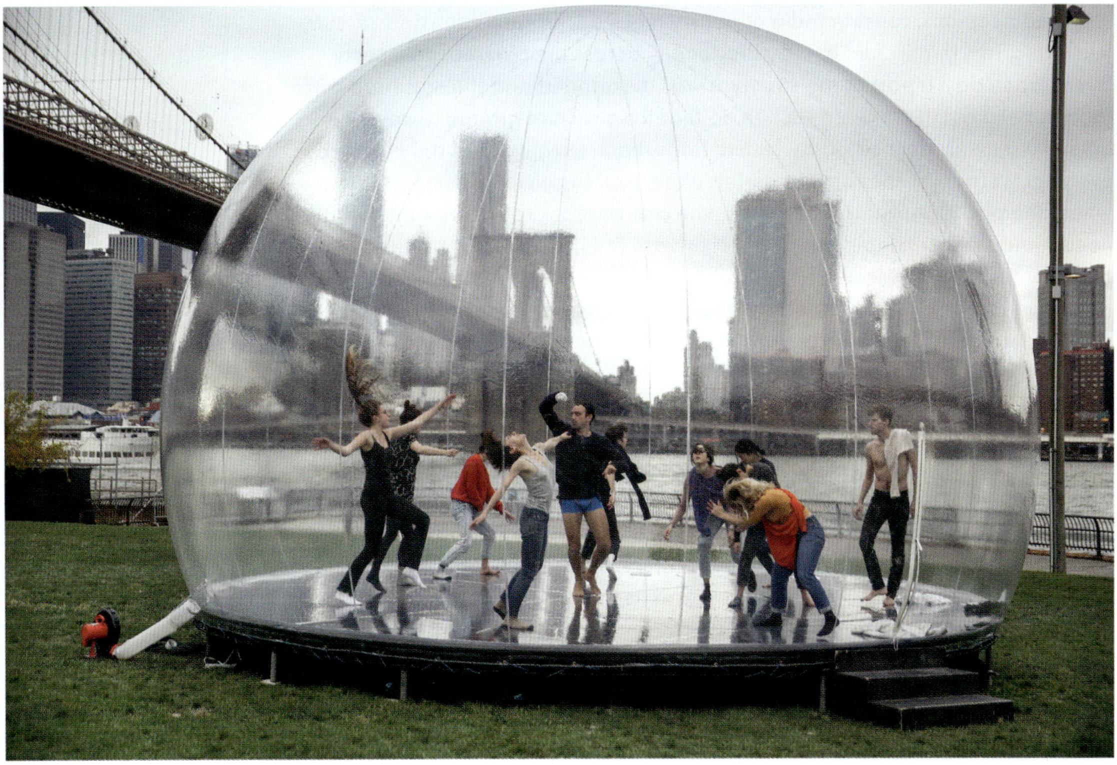

ALEX SCHWEDER & WARD SHELLEY

The Newcomers

28 Liberty Plaza

November 10–19, 2017

Since its first biennial, in 2005, Performa has pioneered an expansive understanding of performance, welcoming and commissioning innovative projects that radically extend the medium. *The Newcomers* by architects and artists Alex Schweder and Ward Shelley, in collaboration with Sarah Burns and Lena Kouvela, was an idiosyncratic, durational architectural performance, an experiment in cooperative work and living, and a celebration of shared social space, taking place outdoors in the heart of New Yorks Financial District, in public, day and night. Construction and real estate promotion are central to this dense, hyper-commercial location. *The Newcomers* diverted both for eccentric and evocative purposes, realizing a wild card structure-in-process governed by a completely alternative logic.

For ten days and nights, using bare-bones materials like plywood, extension cords, pulleys with constraints, and paint, the participants, never leaving their elevated positions, constructed a curiously mobile sculpture-cum-bridge-cum-living quarters that inched its way diagonally across the plaza of 28 Liberty Street. Each day, a part of the structure was dismantled and the materials were used to build out the forward section, so that the structure gradually advanced in ten increments delineated by festive flags. Each evening (and the November evenings were *cold*), the same materials were used to construct living quarters, where the participants ate, interacted with one another, took care of their bodily needs, and slept in sleeping bags; their private lives became part of this very public enterprise.

In one sense, *The Newcomers* was all no-nonsense practicality—the construction of a flat, raised, utilitarian structure made mostly of black boards and panels that jutted (and also moved in ultra-slow motion) across the plaza. Interspersed with vibrant colors from flags, orange and blue closets, red painted beams, the bright orange suits worn by Burns and Kouvela and magenta ones worn by Schweder and Shelley, this practical construction also had visual flair. Dwarfed by a sixty-floor-high skyscraper, this very special construction jettisoned just about every rule and assumption pertaining to buildings in the immediate area. It was inviting, not imposing; impermanent; mobile, not static. It highlighted daily street life, not business and money, and its focus was on process, not an ultimate goal.

It is no wonder that permission to build was hard to come by. In supporting *The Newcomers*, officials from the FOSUN Group, the new owners of 28 Liberty, were courageous, but this project presented unexpected problems. Securing insurance proved almost insurmountable, in part because of liability questions,

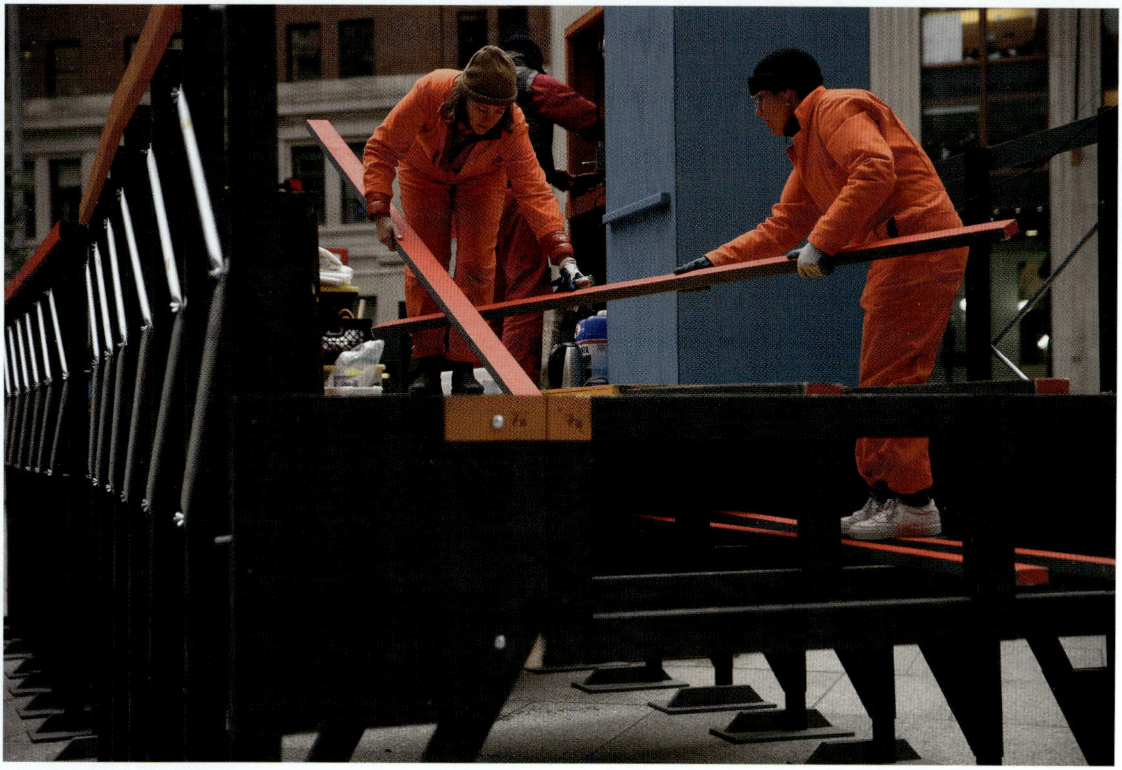

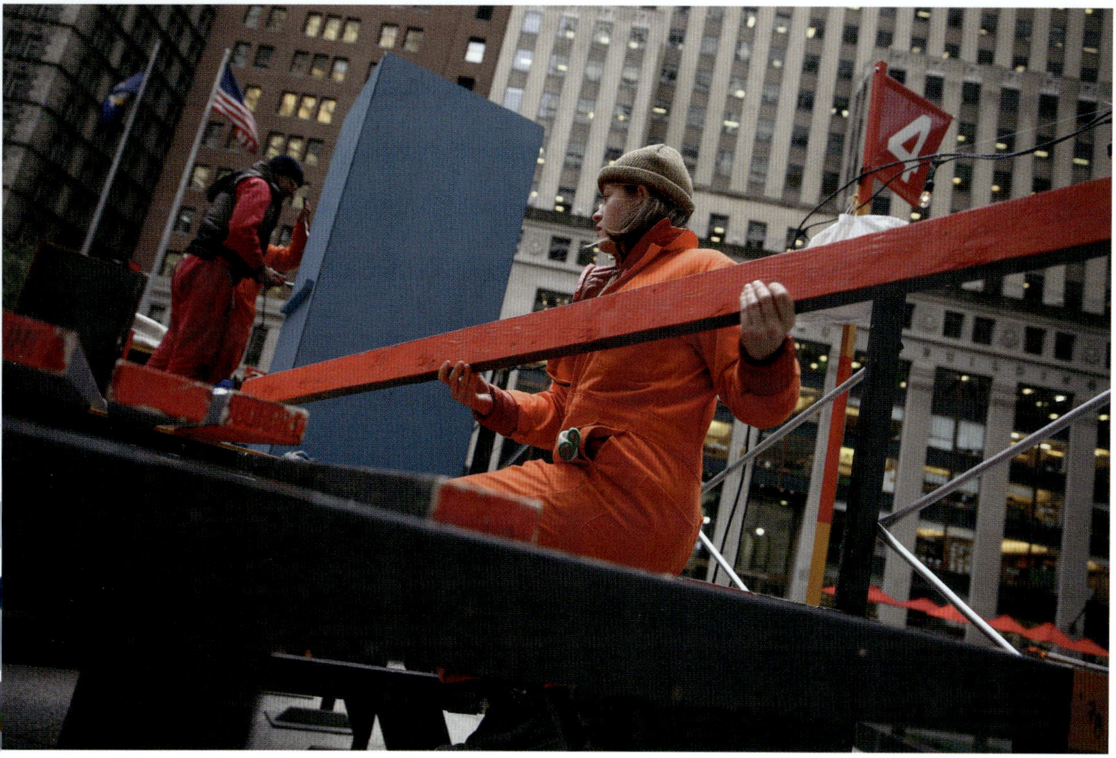

but also because this looked nothing like anything insurers had seen before in terms of risk assessment. An official New York City building permit was required (this also proved to be tricky), and, when received, was hilariously taped to one of the upright closets inside of the mobile structure. Schweder and Shelley infiltrated a complex system of rules and regulations pertaining to commercial real estate. Passersby in this commercial district might have had a tough time grasping why anyone would do something so arduous and outlandish with no financial reward in sight.

Hard, purposeful work was on display throughout the project by this quirky and convivial team on a mission, yet the participants frequently took time out from their work to talk with viewers, some of them Performa visitors versed in contemporary art and performance, but many others quizzical and at times totally baffled locals or workers. Thus, this oddball construction site doubled as a forum for impromptu interaction, both within the tightly knit community of makers and between the community and public at large. *The Newcomers* forged a building of sorts, a peculiar, horizontal, carnivalized one that moved and transformed, however slowly. This peculiar building was also a stage, a temporary home, a viewing platform, a strange spectacle, and a meeting ground.

While *The Newcomers* had a wacky and antic side, it also had potent political and social connotations. Its participants placed themselves as newcomers in an alien place—intrepid artists in a site dominated by money and corporate power—and then set about realizing a decidedly eccentric, yet marvelous and meaningful, enterprise. This project suggested that it might be a good idea to welcome, not condemn, outsiders of all stripes and to honor their contributions and achievements. GREGORY VOLK

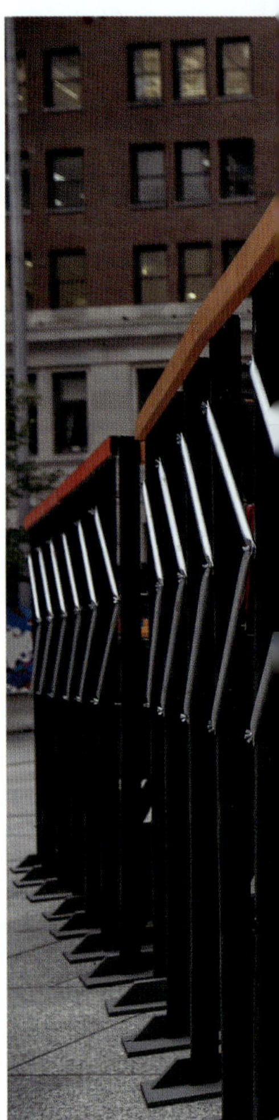

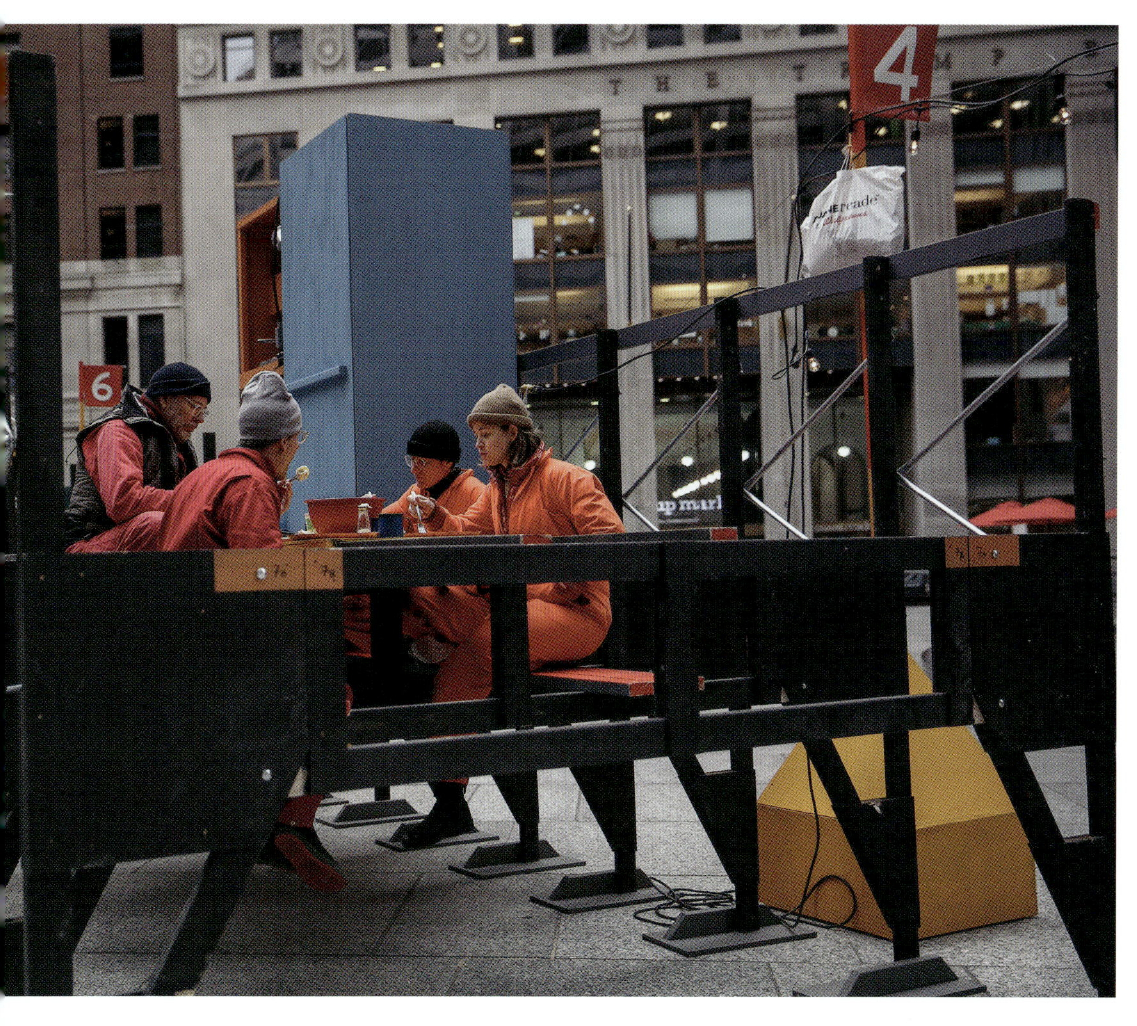

BRYONY ROBERTS & MABEL O. WILSON WITH THE MARCHING COBRAS OF NEW YORK

Marching On

Curated by
Eva Franch i Gilabert

Marcus Garvey Park

November 11–12, 2017

On February 17, 1919, the Harlem Hellfighters Band, an early jazz marching band composed of Black soldiers from the 369th Infantry Regiment, proudly walked up Fifth and Lenox Avenues in Manhattan to celebrate their own remarkable contribution to the U.S. military in the European theater of the First World War. Two years earlier, on July 28, 1917, thousands of Black New Yorkers, all dressed in white, made the same walk, silently, and in the opposite direction, moving from 57th Street to Madison Square to protest the racial violence that Jim Crow laws had brought to the South, particularly the recent gruesome lynchings in Waco, Memphis, and East St. Louis.

With *Marching On*, American architects and architecture scholars Bryony Roberts and Mabel O. Wilson explored the legacies of organized forms of marching in African American communities. From pageants and parades to demonstrations and protests, these group actions have been powerful agents of cultural and political expression to honor collective identities and assert their right to public space. Roberts and Wilson collaborated with the Marching Cobras, a Harlem-based after-school drumline and dance team, to weave together references to the silent movement a century earlier as well as the revered Hellfighters. Simply gathering people in the street was—and still is—both a form of civic engagement and an act of resistance. Presented at Marcus Garvey Park in Harlem, the performance began with two dozen members of the youth group getting into linear formations. The drummers wore olive-green shirts, pants, and capes just as the Hellfighters did; the dancers donned white garments to pay homage to the silent activists of 1917. Their choreography hybridized strains of traditional routines with contemporary drill-team formations. Halfway through, the performance exploded in free-form action that revealed the cloaks' colorful linings, all in a nod to student bands' theatrical flair at historically Black colleges and universities. *Marching On* took over the famed park and its adjacent streets for an entire weekend, creating a rhythmic, live celebration of Harlem's rich and vibrant legacy. CHARLES AUBIN

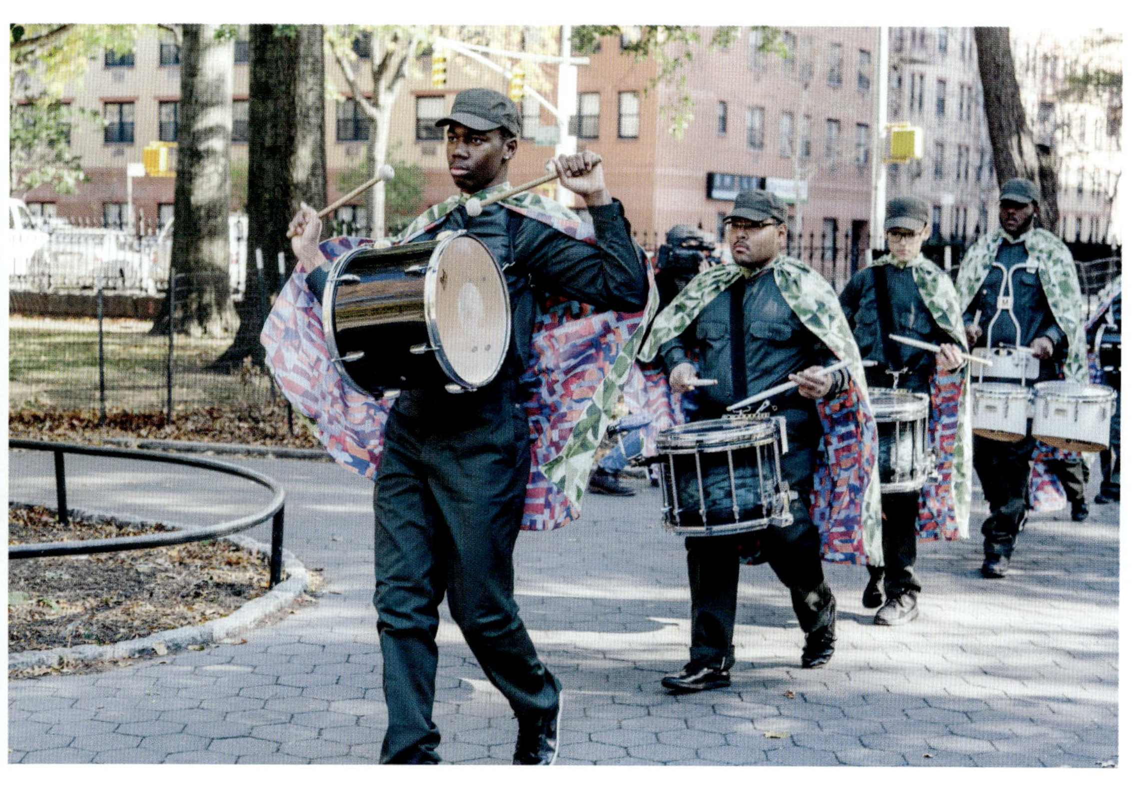

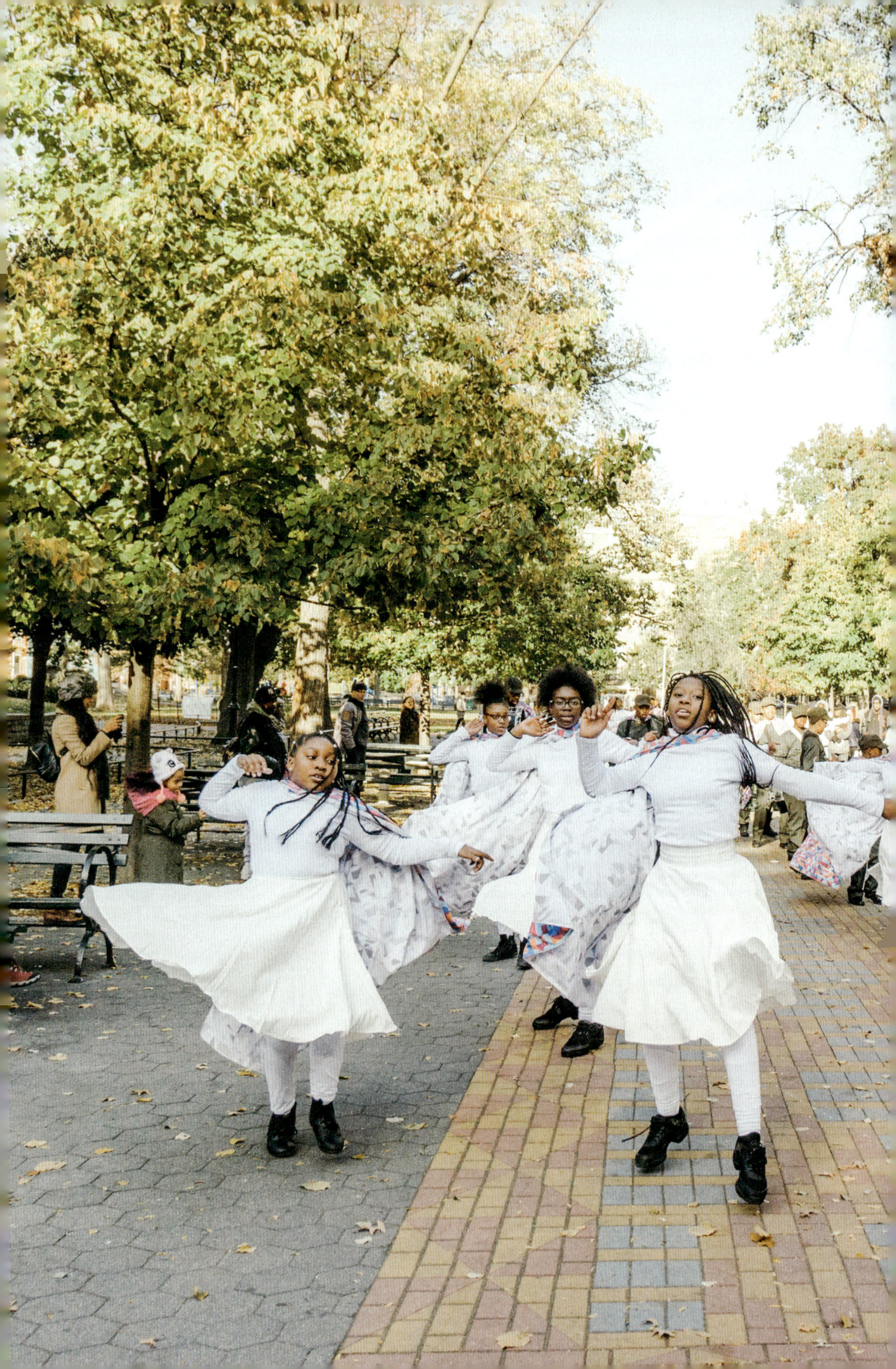

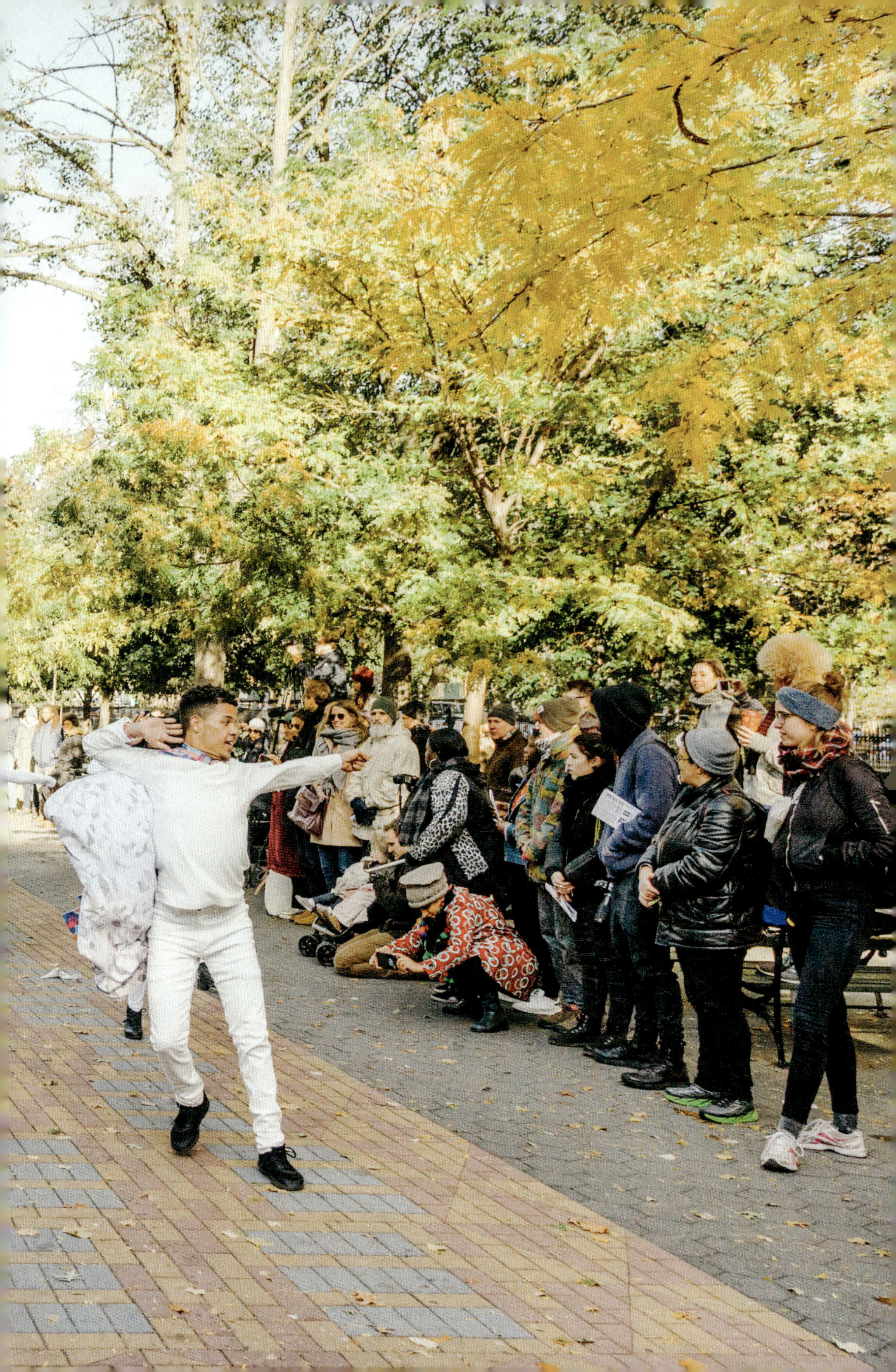

EIKO OTAKE

A Body in Places —The Met Edition

Curated by
Limor Tomer

The Met Cloisters,
the Met Breuer,
and the Metropolitan
Museum of Art

November 5, 12, and
19, 2017

November 5, 2017. The Fuentidueña Chapel of the Met Cloisters. Eiko watches herself moving. She's behind a black cart loaded with a speaker and a huge projector beaming a video she's produced from photographs of her dancing in Fukushima, Japan in the years following the earthquake, tsunami, and nuclear meltdowns of March 2011. She pushes the cart slowly, and the images animate, changing size and slipping in and out of focus. Fragments of narrative text appear and give context to the endless stream of desolate landscapes in which Eiko has placed her body. It's a gray November day, and the flat light filters through the clerestory windows high above her. This performance is the first of three daylong events that make up the 21-hour-and-45-minute work.

I've collaborated with Eiko since 2014, helping her shape her solo performances to best fit into and disrupt their site. I've seen her perform in countless spaces: a small boutique in the East Village, a cavernous cathedral uptown, in front of the New York Stock Exchange downtown. But this project feels different. It's longer, definitely, conceived as a durational work, unfolding over three consecutive Sundays. But, more important, it's explicit in a way that's even more direct than her previous work. The text in the projections, written in the first person, speaks frankly of her despair and anger over this continuing disaster.

Over their forty years together, Eiko & Koma's work was rooted in an austere and insular aesthetic. Theirs was a choreography of relation, each piece built around two bodies locked in a hermetic, deeply private exchange. In contrast, Eiko's solo work is rooted in porousness and collaboration. William Johnston photographed Eiko in Fukushima and then allowed her to shape those images into a time-based object. During *A Body in Places: The Met Edition*, I sometimes stepped in and moved the projector, giving Eiko the chance to dance more actively with her own image, making a brief trio out of a duet. With this project, Eiko has opened her work by engaging with collaborators, historical events, and the site of the museum.

As the day at the Cloisters wore on, Eiko moved through many different levels of time and space. She'd been working for months to make this video, choreographing the way her photographic image would move within the frame of the projection. She foreshadowed and echoed the poses and movements of her projected self, sometimes mirroring, sometimes aligning her body with her body's projection, sometimes just watching, and sometimes turning away. The chapel's stone walls gave the photographs a new texture, blurring them slightly.

As the photos were projected to become Eiko's duet partner, they felt charged, urgent, and new.

November 12, 2017. The fifth-floor galleries of the Met Breuer. The rooms are smooth, empty, anodyne. Here, in the contemporary art building of the Metropolitan Museum of Art, Eiko moves her body and the projection more aggressively, sometimes projecting her video straight onto the audience. Surprisingly, when this happens, most people didn't move. They sat still. They breathed. Some closed their eyes. I imagined them as plants, absorbing the light of the video. Eiko sat next to a woman and leaned into her as a way of underscoring the reality of Fukushima with the weight of her body, its warmth, its movement. I was there, her body said. The distance between New York City and ruined Fukushima collapsed.

Eiko has referred to *A Body in Places* as her "late work." Pressed on what she meant by this, she said she is learning to be less precious about what she makes and that she is no longer afraid to fail by being explicit. For example, she initially worried that performing while wearing the same costume she wore in the video might be too obvious. But this visual doubling made it clear to anyone watching that the body in the room was an extension of the body in Fukushima.

Eiko is often a paradox: an artist of singular vision who nevertheless remains open to working with whatever she has at hand. For this project, she's choreographed herself meticulously, taking into account the image of the projection, its size and placement, the text threaded between the photos, where

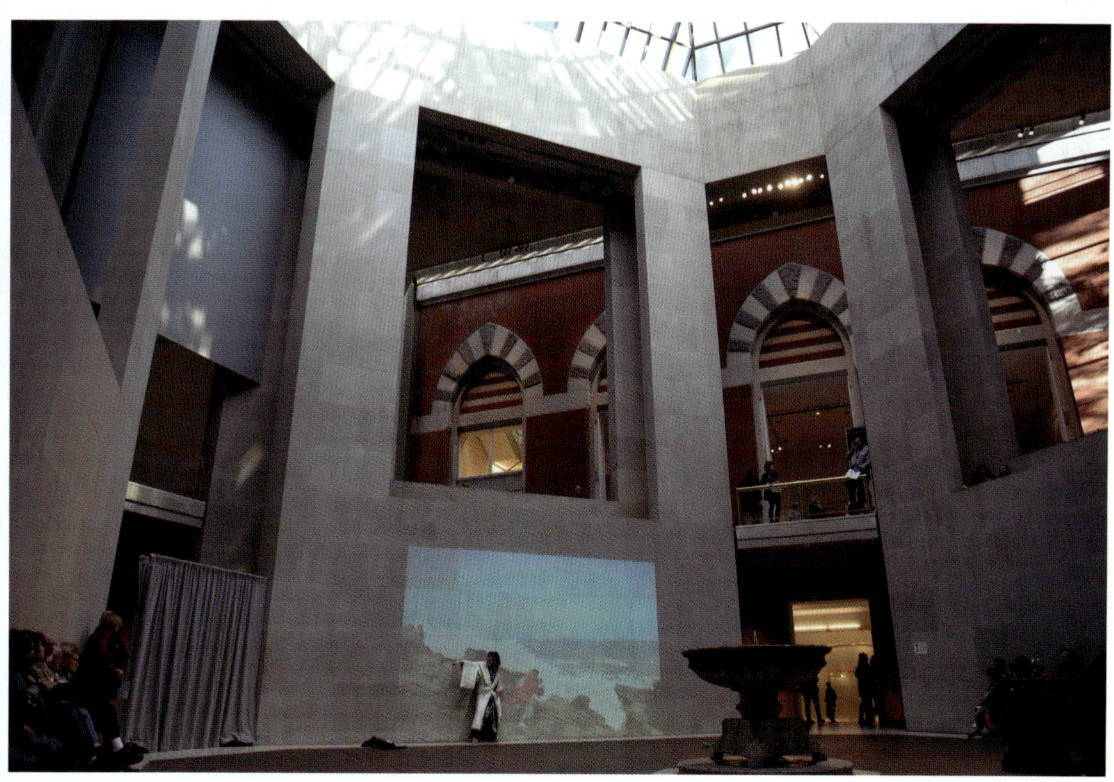

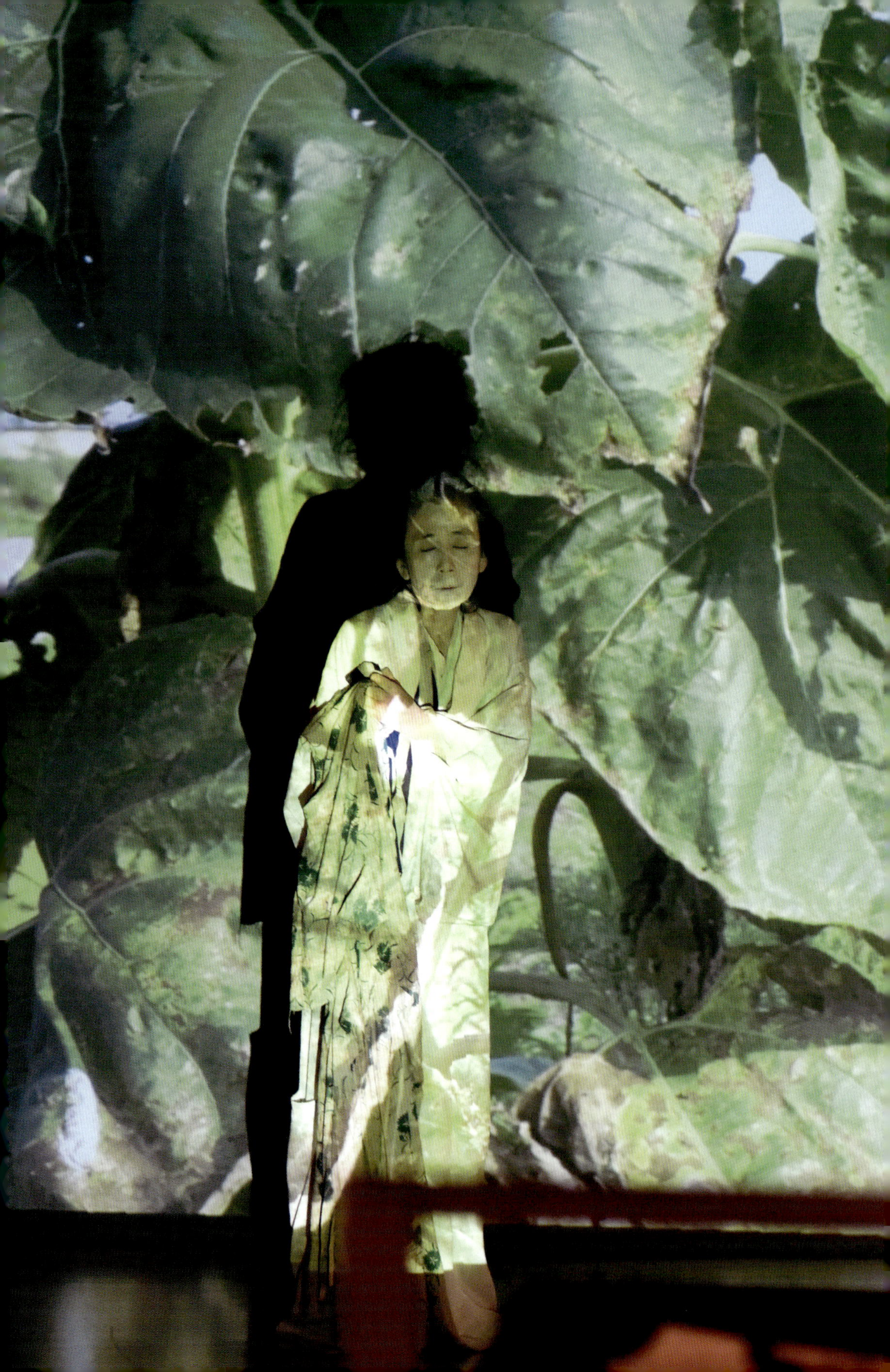

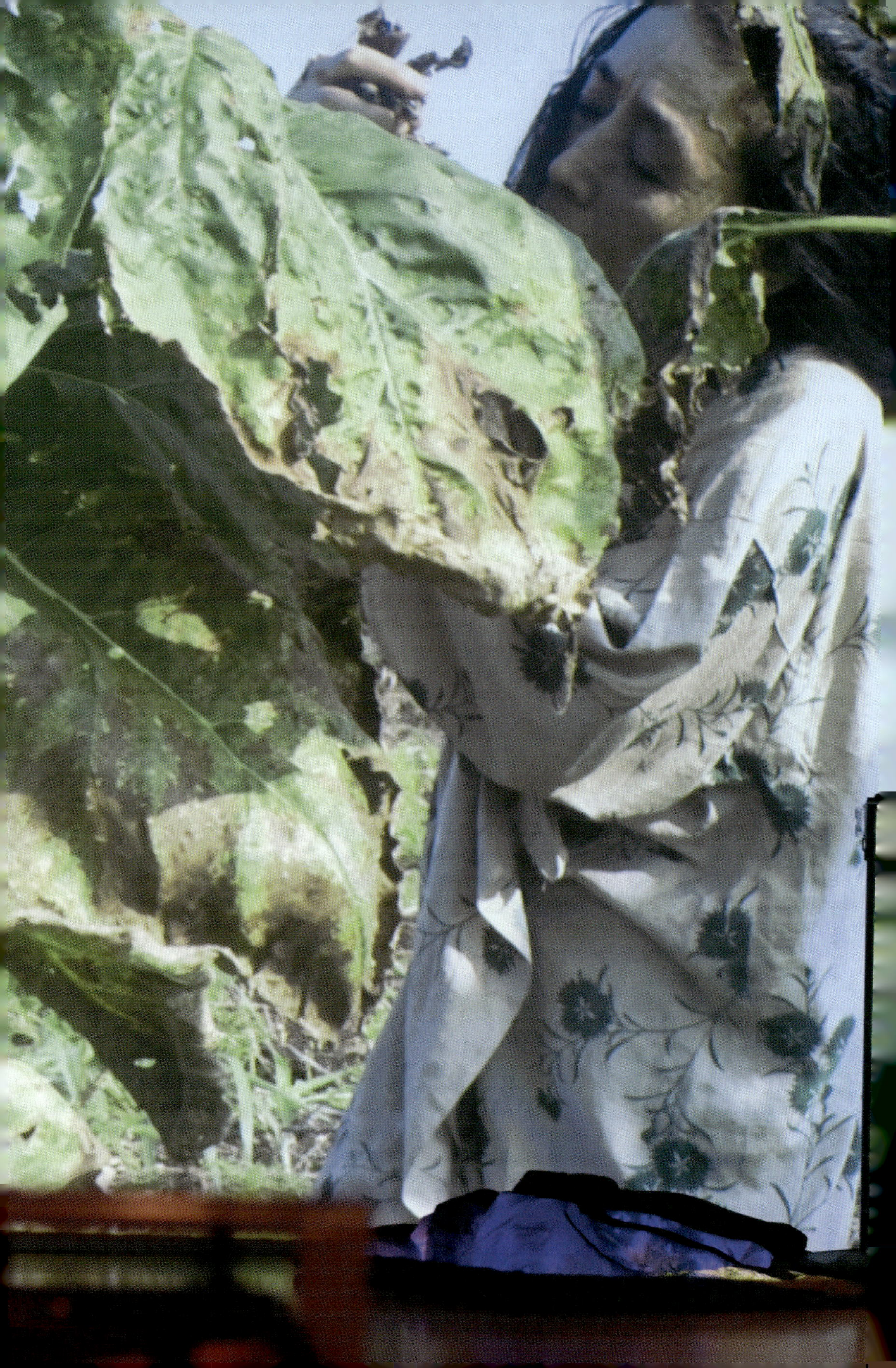

to place her body and the projector within the galleries, and how and when to use objects. Yet, as the work unfolded, she often betrayed this preparation, making different decisions in the moment of performance, responding to the site and the audience watching her.

November 19, 2017. The Robert Lehman Collection, Metropolitan Museum of Art. The final week. A newly installed exhibition of delicate drawings in the surrounding galleries has resulted in the Met's sudden decision to prohibit Eiko from moving the projector during the performance as planned. Even after agreeing to adjust the work, she kept looking for ways to inhabit the space more fully, probing the site to see what she might be able to get away with. She can be a bit of a nuisance (a word she loves, one she repeats over and over), always on the lookout for new ways to disrupt the place into which she's putting her body.

During a last-minute work session in the space, Eiko saw members of the custodial staff washing the walls with wet cloths, leaving a temporary stain. Quickly and insistently, she asked for permission to do the same. The museum granted it, and at several points during this third and final part of the project, she mournfully washed the projected images, trying and failing to cleanse them of all the radiation they carried. This literal staining, the water temporarily darkening the walls of the museum, inspired other decisions that allowed Eiko to fill the space without moving the projector. She audibly drank a bowl of water, the sound of her sipping drawing the audience's attention. She danced with a long, dirty garden hose she brought into the space, threatening even more water, a flood that might overwhelm the museum. Eiko's responsiveness allowed the parameters of the project to expand.

At the beginning of the performance, Eiko wore several kimonos, shedding them one by one over the course of the day. Now, as the end of the work approached, Eiko danced, wildly; she wanted to stain the walls of the Met with Fukushima. I saw how her body, both in projection and in the flesh, was the staining agent, carrying radioactivity and a potent grief back from the exclusion zone. She gathered the kimonos in a bundle and slowly left the gallery, disappearing into the vast vascular system of hallways that are off-limits to the public. Though security funneled the audience toward the exit, the video projection continued to play. In the now-empty gallery, I watched a short coda: a series of blurred shots of Eiko dancing in overgrown grass, evening glories blooming all around her. Eiko brought Fukushima into the Met and let it live there, however briefly, the reality of it blooming like the flowers in these final photos: temporary, and somehow all the more powerful because of it. IRIS MCCLOUGHAN

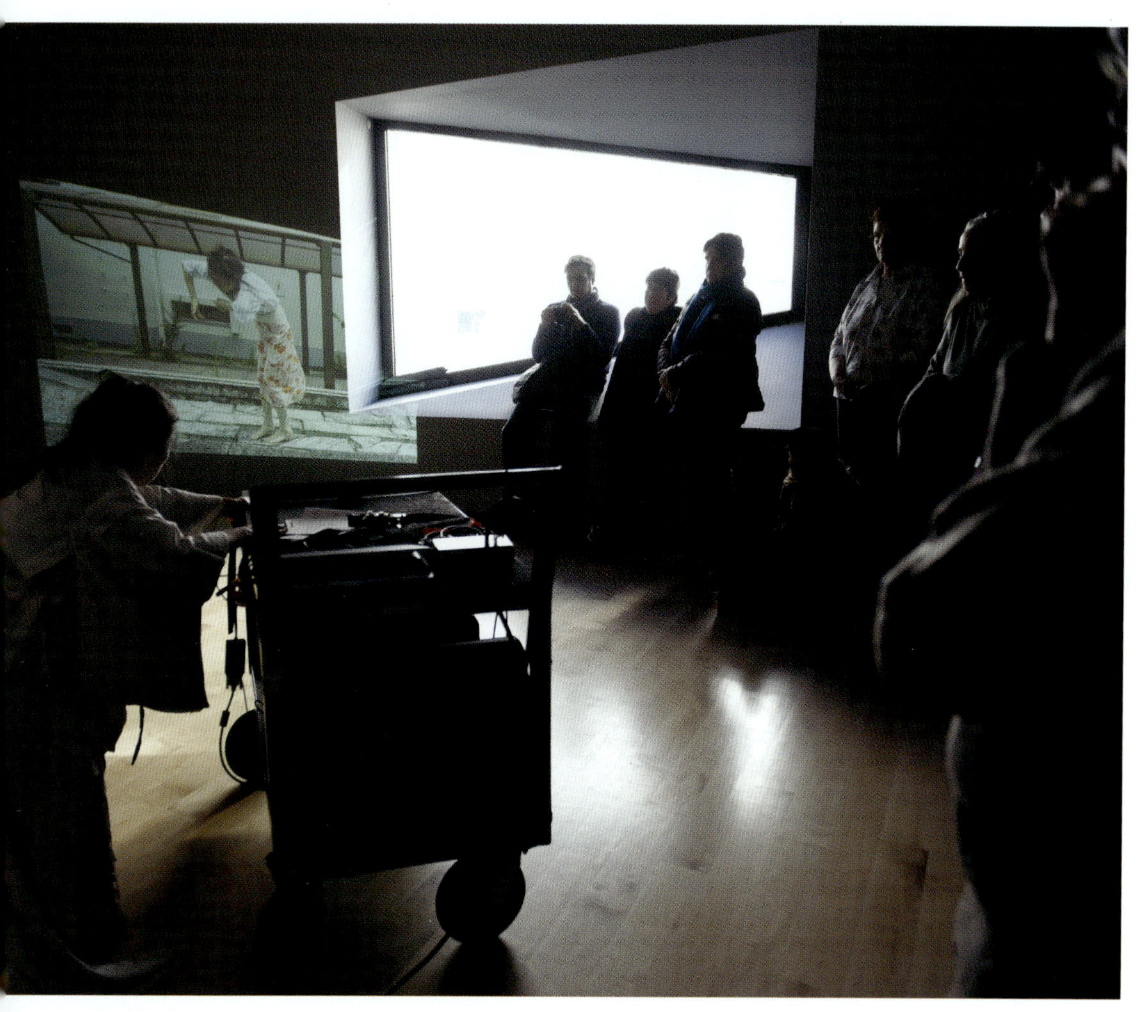

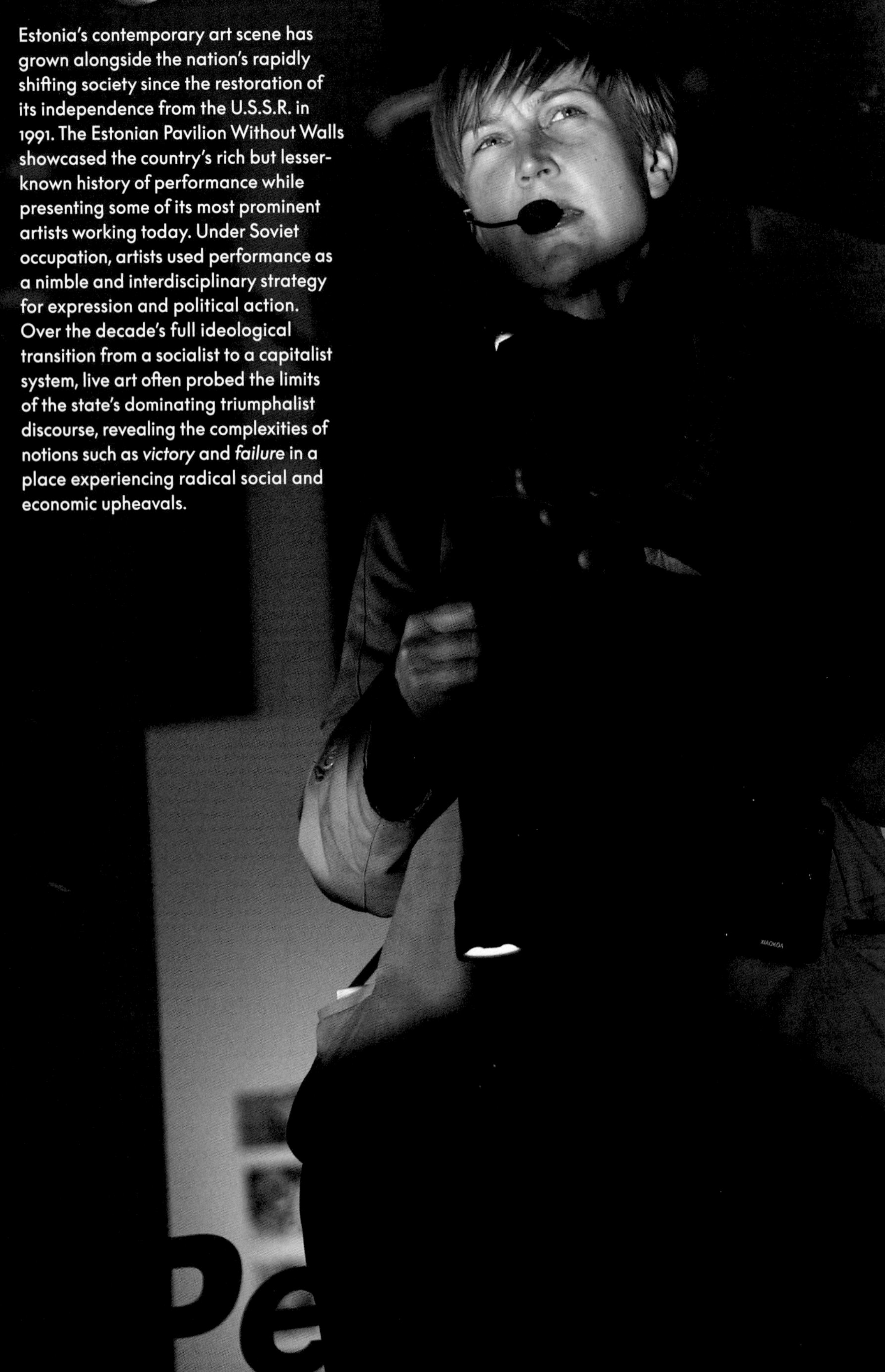

Estonia's contemporary art scene has grown alongside the nation's rapidly shifting society since the restoration of its independence from the U.S.S.R. in 1991. The Estonian Pavilion Without Walls showcased the country's rich but lesser-known history of performance while presenting some of its most prominent artists working today. Under Soviet occupation, artists used performance as a nimble and interdisciplinary strategy for expression and political action. Over the decade's full ideological transition from a socialist to a capitalist system, live art often probed the limits of the state's dominating triumphalist discourse, revealing the complexities of notions such as *victory* and *failure* in a place experiencing radical social and economic upheavals.

Pe

BALTIC CURRENTS

FLO KASEARU

Ainult liikmetele (Members Only)

With an unrelenting penchant for absurdist humor, Estonian artist Flo Kasearu grapples with systems of classification—social, geopolitical, or otherwise. Since 2013, the artist has served as director of the *Flo Kasearu House Museum*, in which she transformed her living space in Tallinn into an institution, bypassing the local gallery system and admitting the visiting public to view her work by appointment. During *Ainult liikmetele (Members Only)* Kasearu likewise converted the New York Estonian House, a cultural club for the local Estonian American community, into a "museum" where irony and uncertainty obscure the distinction between who is a "member" and who is not.

Organized by
Esa Nickle and
Maaike Gouwenberg

Estonian House

November 3 and 10, 2017

Over two evenings, the Beaux-Arts building's doors opened to non-members as Kasearu guided small groups of attendees up its burgundy-carpeted stairs to encounter performance vignettes staged within its ten rooms. Viewers were ushered through each doorway to find Estonian Americans of all ages cast as "living sculptures"—such as a woman speaking incoherently and pouring an impossibly long-running stream of water into a flowerpot—in ambiguous scenes construed from club members' accounts of their lives. In Kasearu's sketches, characters' reconciliations were equal parts playful and poignant: From behind a counter in the basement, one woman shared newspaper clippings featuring the art gallery she once opened in a fish market after immigrating to the United States, adding that all the while she had dreamed of owning a Corvette. Down the hall, a young singer in a sequined dress leaned into a microphone onstage, staring vacantly ahead in prolonged silence, as though waiting for a signal to begin. From the building's roof, visitors opened a skylight and peered downward to discover the club's housekeeper—who once voiced to Kasearu that she felt unseen within the house—lying on the floor below, her body bound in Christmas lights in an instance of exaggerated visibility.

Flipping convention on its head, Kasearu's performances suggested that the Estonian House's role in instilling a collective identity is evolving, as some traditions become superseded by new conceptions of community. In an upstairs office where the club publishes its weekly newspaper, visitors gathered and listened as a man recited short, autobiographical poems Kasearu had stitched together from posts she found on an Estonian American community Facebook page, an online platform which is progressively supplanting the newspaper in its role of connecting Estonians in the U.S. In the choir room, strewn haphazardly with empty chairs, a woman seated at the bench of a closed piano played the notes of an Estonian patriotic song on an electronic switchboard that only made exaggerated kissing noises, abstracted stand-ins for the sentiments of national pride and longing.

At each stopping point on the tour, Kasearu adhered colorful stickers—which the artist calls "badges"—to visitors' shirts in an ironic gesture of validation and inclusion. The tour ended in the club's bar area, where guests exchanged one of these badges for a shot of vodka and a cube of meat jelly. Exposing the arbitrariness of membership as a concept, and equating the bureaucratic process of demarcating national inclusion with that of any other members-only club, Kasearu's work might call into question the role a broader scope of institutions plays in reinforcing perceptions of difference. The work's envisioning of "membership" or collective subjectivity as a plastic space where nostalgia and heterogeneity can coincide also proposes a timely alternative to Estonia's own exclusionary immigration policies. CAMILA NICHOLS

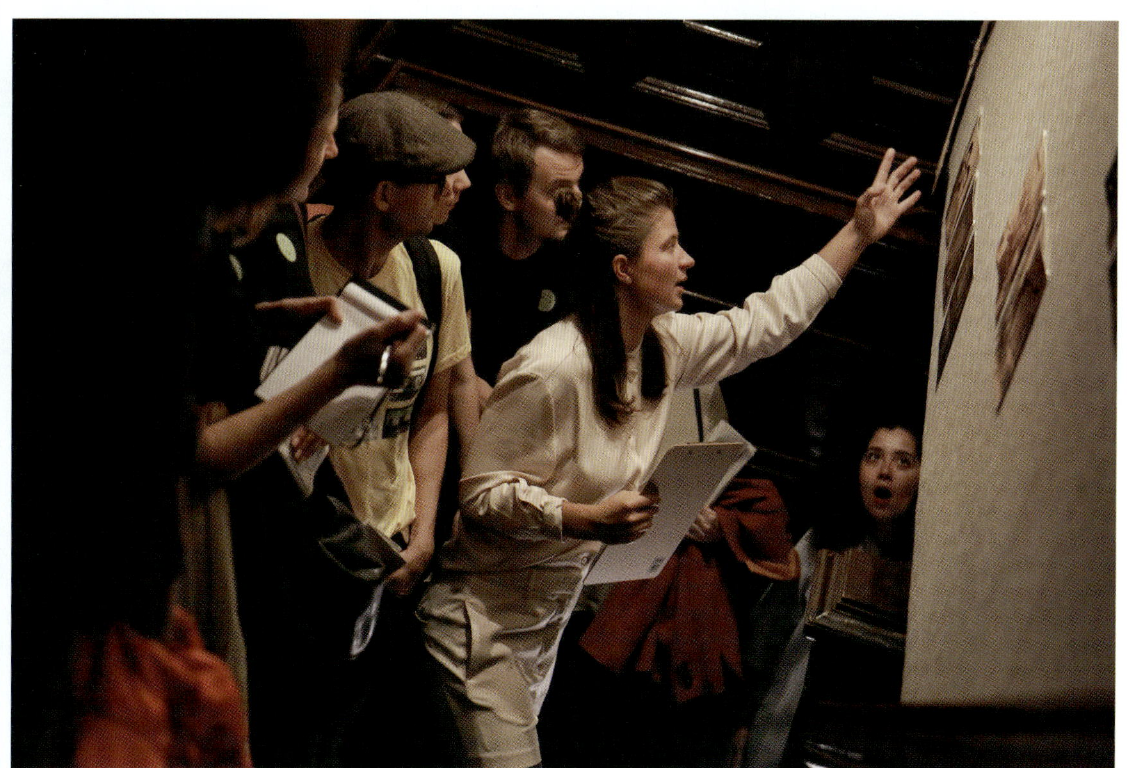

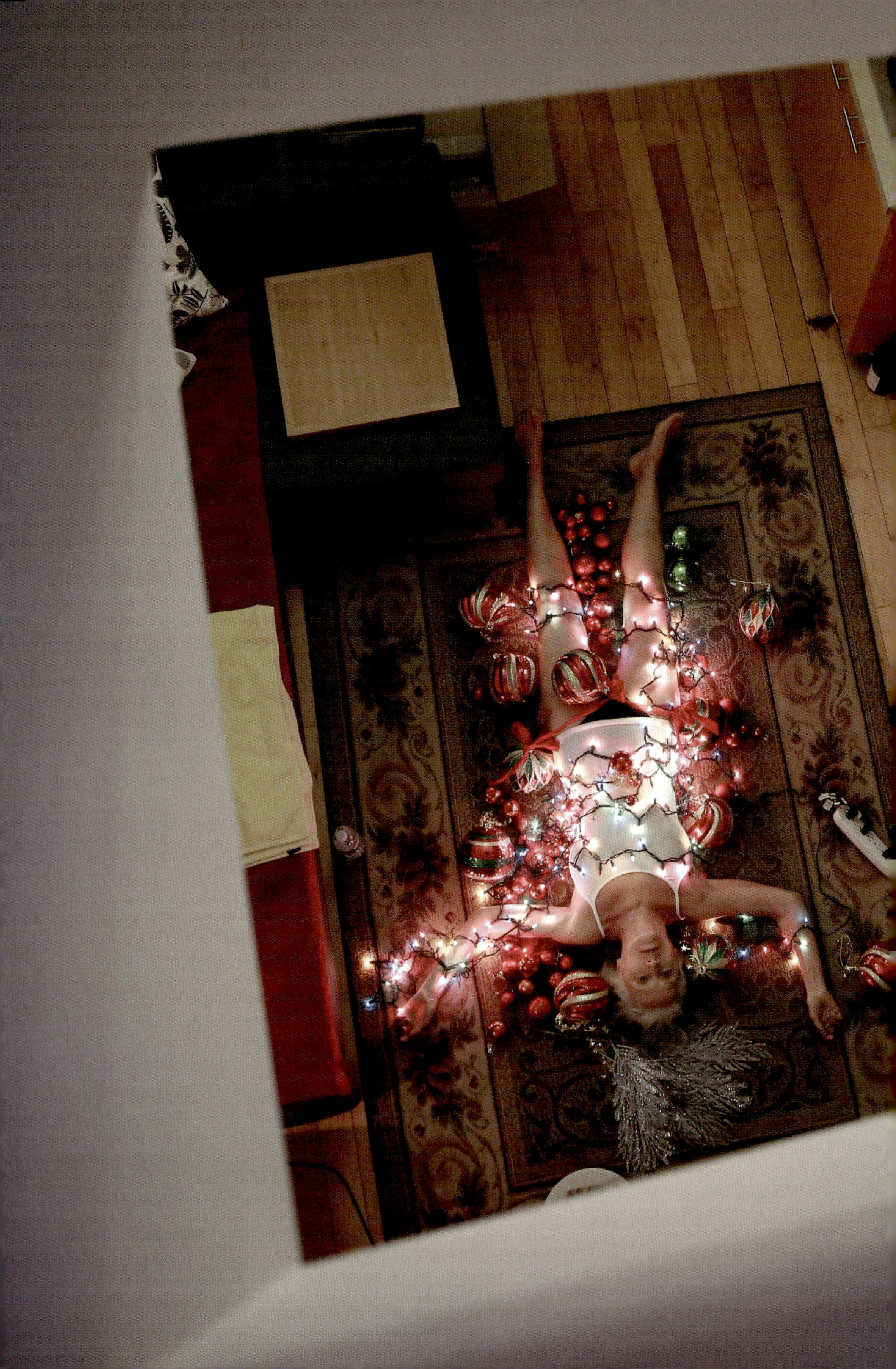

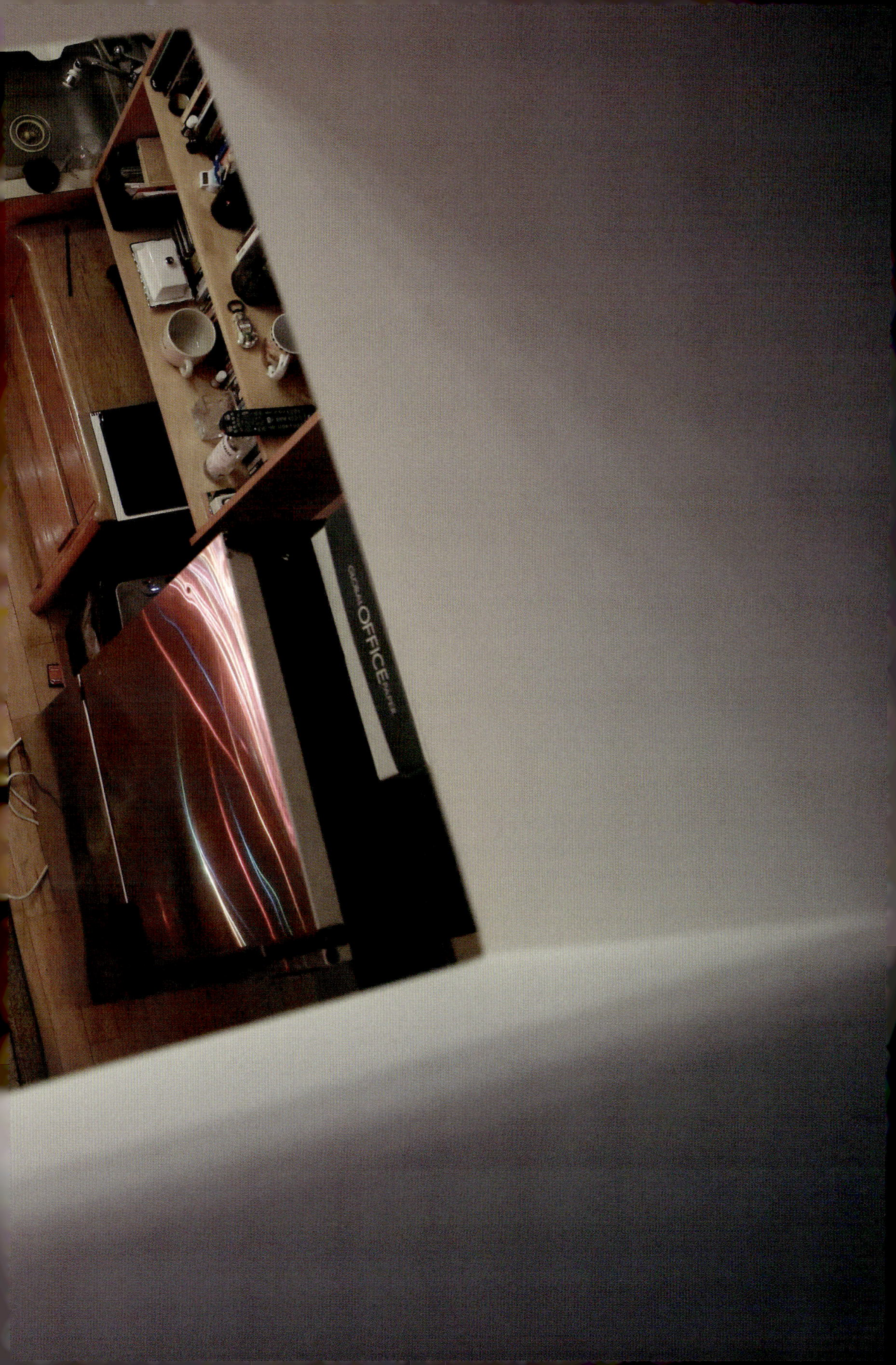
OFFICE

ANU VAHTRA

Open House Closing. A Walk

Organized by
Esa Nickle

SoHo

November 15–17, 2017

Since the 1960s, when artists first moved into its derelict cast iron factories in search of cheap housing and workspace, SoHo has been known as an artist's neighborhood. In the five decades that followed, it has transformed into a high-priced commercial district, an archetype of gentrification: First, a neighborhood brims with industrial production; then the factories close; artists, and, later, galleries move in; artists are priced out, and boutiques, cafés, and condominiums arrive to cater to the global elite. Anu Vahtra's *Open House Closing. A Walk* reflected on the long aftermath of SoHo's gentrification, a place where even chain stores cannot survive the current real estate boom, and temporary pop-up shops outnumber long-term commercial tenants.

On three evenings, the Estonian artist took audiences on an expedition through SoHo, joining past and present by delivering tour guide-style lectures in front of nearly thirty distinct locations situated in a five-square-block grid. Participants shone flashlights on specific sites, while the artist detailed high-priced rents and confronted the neighborhood's real estate frenzy with its bohemian past. She summoned some of the ghosts of a SoHo past, a time that Lucy Lippard described as "a refuge, a real live/work artists' community where artists, dancers, musicians, and politicos played and rabble-roused in apartments, lofts, rooftops ("tar beaches"), galleries and streets." Among them artist Gordon Matta-Clark—himself trained in architecture—whose work has been a key influence on Vahtra's large-scale spatial interventions.[1] Vahtra traced Matta-Clark's steps during the performance, particularly his "anarchitecture" ideas, which rethought existing spaces and sought an alternative approach to architecture unencumbered by money and power.

Following her script, as a walking guide, Vahtra highlighted relevant buildings along her chosen route, and attracted the attention of passersby who would often approach the group out of curiosity and follow along. Citing the owner for some of them, pointing out empty lots, vacancies, or current retail occupancies for many, she led the audience down the streets with her frequent direction "Follow me, let's continue." Tellingly, Vahtra's research found 100 vacant retail spaces along the route. All of the unoccupied spaces the artist stopped at were marked with a blue X in painter's tape, signifying that the building is both for rent and under renovation at the same time, something prevalent across the city.

At 63 Greene Street, Vahtra recited broker speak: "This building presents a rare opportunity to occupy space in one of the most sought-after retail neighborhoods in Manhattan. Retail locations in this area are in very high demand and rarely become

1
Lucy Lippard, "Time Capsule," in *Art and Social Change: A Critical Reader*, eds. Will Bradley and Charles Esche. (London: Tate Publishing, 2007), 416.

available. The space is available on appearhere.nyc for $3,000 per day." Pausing to look at nearby construction waste, she comically referred to it as a readymade monument titled *Work in Progress: Retail*.

Not focusing on commerce alone, Vahtra also pointed out several locations now cemented into art history: 101 Spring Street, a five-story cast-iron building bought by Donald Judd for $68,000 in 1968 and now the site of the Judd Foundation, and 127 Prince Street, the location of FOOD, a restaurant run by artists Carol Goodden, Tina Girouard, and Matta-Clark. FOOD merged social and architectural space and, as one of the first places to eat in SoHo, was an epicenter of the artist community that resided there. Vahtra projected an image of the restaurant onto the sidewalk in front of 127 Prince while recounting its 1972 day-to-day workings, which were recorded as "Family Fiscal Facts"—sixteen thousand oranges squeezed, 379 pounds of rabbits stewed, 3,082 free dinners given out.

The last address on the performance-tour was 32 Howard Street, site of the Putnam Rolling Ladder Company—a family-owned business for three generations—which was in the process of being packed up and moved out due to the skyrocketing rent increases. Before the company would leave the neighborhood for good, the audience had a rare opportunity to experience the essential character of a vintage SoHo building. After Vahtra gave a short introduction, the group was free to wander around the vacated lofts at their own pace, absorbing the layers of time made visible in the remnants of a once lively manufacturing company. Here, it was easy to imagine the SoHo of the sixties and its appeal for the artists who would come to live there. KARI CONTE

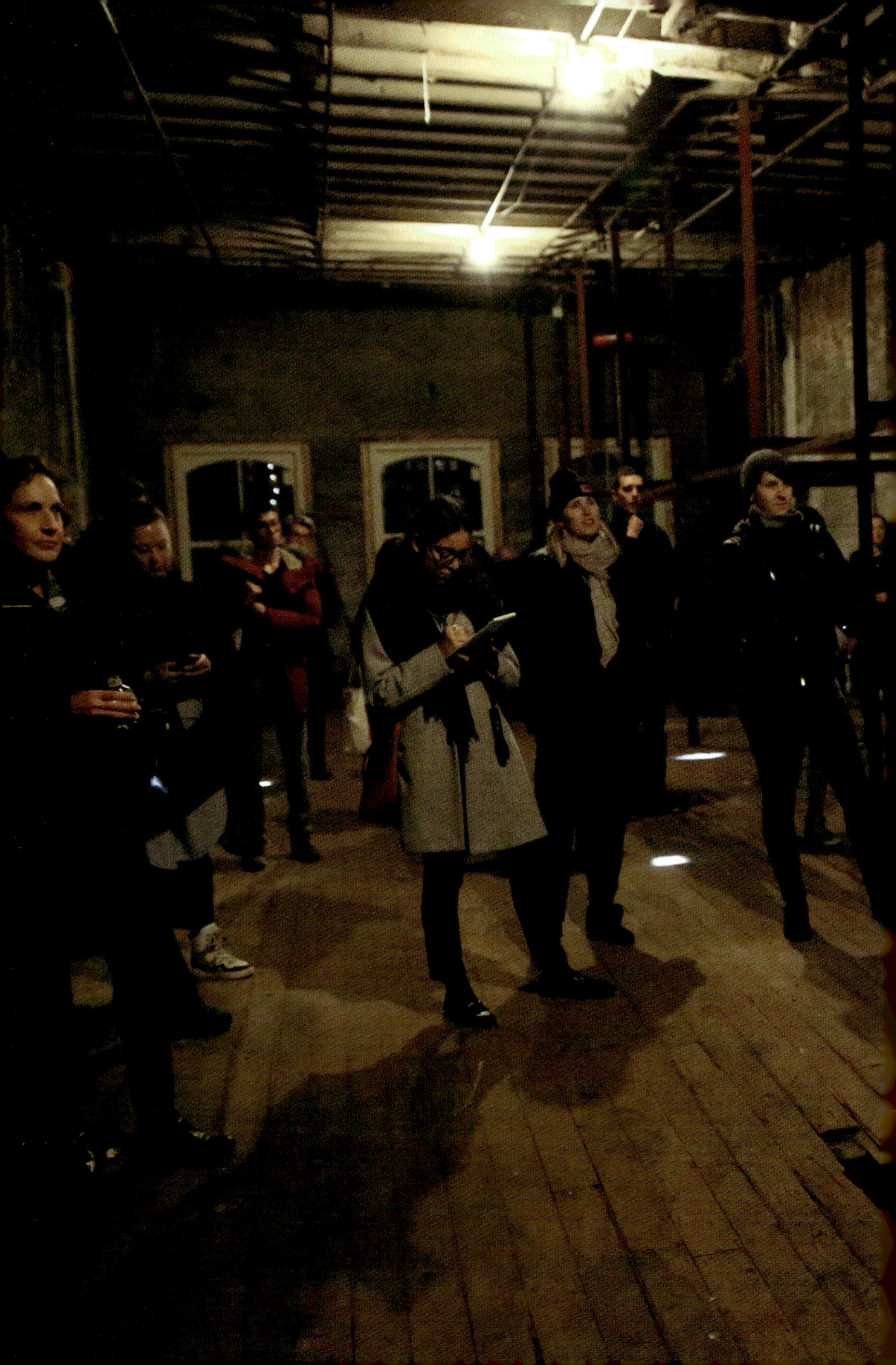

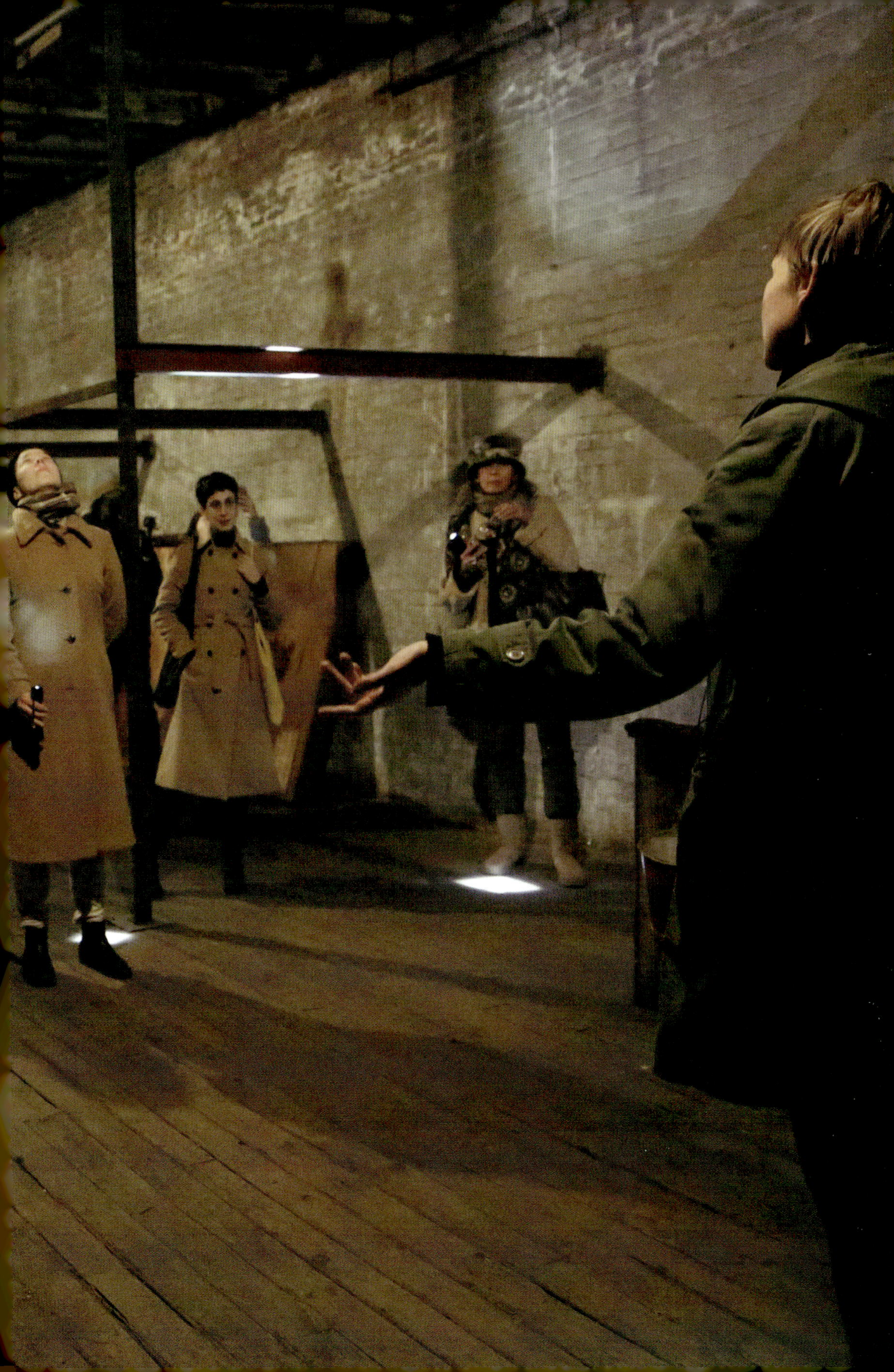

KRIS LEMSALU & KYP MALONE

Going Going

Organized by
Maaike Gouwenberg
with Evelyn Raudsepp

Harlem Parish

November 11–12, 2017

"We're all going, going, going, but where are we going?" asks the floating, disembodied head of Downtown punk icon Philly Abe, projected onto the soaring walls of the Harlem Parish. "Are we going to places we know about? Are we going to places that don't even exist?" A collaboration between Estonian visual artist Kris Lemsalu and American indie multi-instrumentalist Kyp Malone, *Going Going* riffed on their friend Abe's poetry and took the form of an otherworldly procession within the empty neo-Gothic church. The duo appeared on a large, wheeled bed draped with gaudy and flowery red blankets and winged by ten sinewy prosthetic arms, all sheathed in denim and extending beyond the bed, giving to the makeshift float an air of the many-armed Hindu goddess Durgā. Malone knelt on the bed, played a haunting, trickling composition by using a portable synthesizer and an electric kalimba mixed with his own vocals. Standing behind him and the headboard, Lemsalu, caked in white makeup and rouge and donning a petaled aviator helmet, inspected the scattered viewers all around them.

When Malone rang his golden bell, Lemsalu operated a makeshift crank attached to the bed. The hands beside her began to wave slowly, rippling back and forth, gesturing at the audience or trying to make space and clear a path through the crowd. The vessel drifted forward in a slow, circular motion, evoking a rite of passage that seemed to take the duo from life to death to rebirth. As they reached the end, a pulsating, psychedelic video beamed against the towering interior, its animation merging line drawings, glitchy photographs, emojis, and kaleidoscopic screensavers. "I often want to fly," said the projected face of Abe at the performance's finale, her likeness dotted with a constellation of small pale orbs. "And my wings—my wings are already there." QUINN SCHOEN

In memoriam Philly Abe (1949–2018)

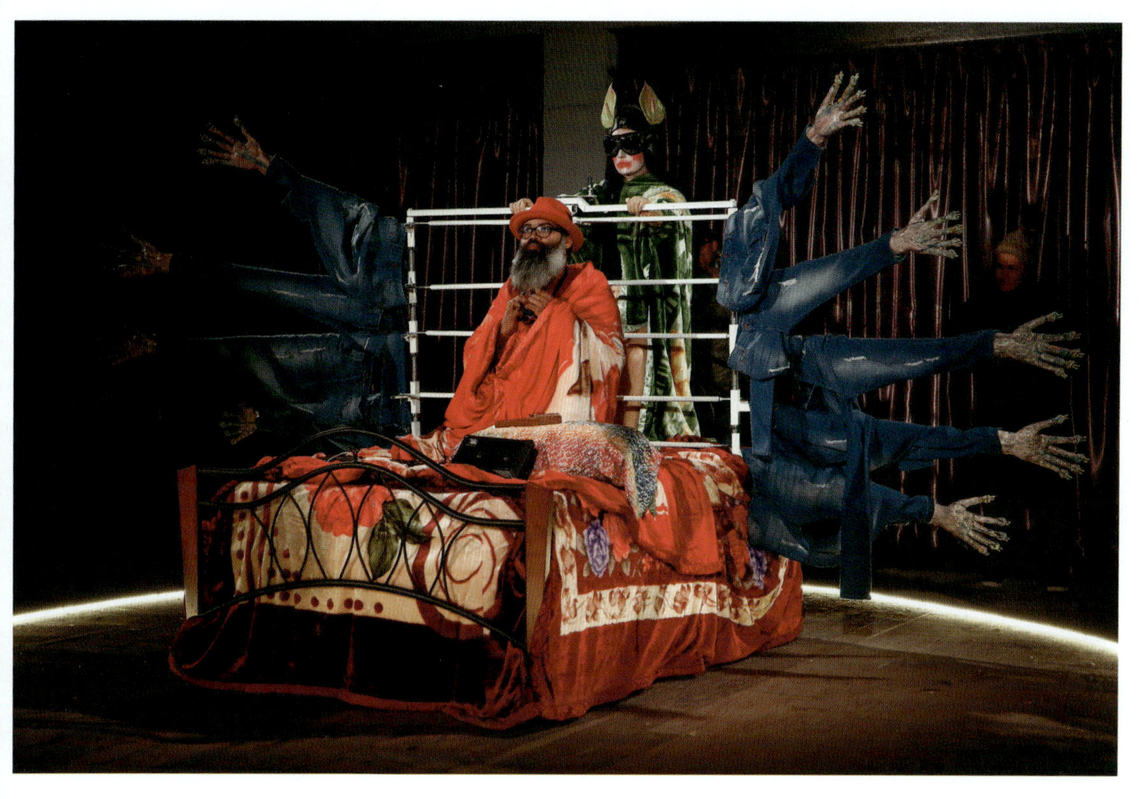

Since its very first edition in 2005, the Performa Biennial was conceived of as a form of radical urbanism. It spans and embraces New York City, drawing routes for visitors to discover unexpected venues and create new memories of performances in situ. The transient nature of the three-week-long program allows for hybrid works to be set up in unusual contexts, such as a deconsecrated church, an empty storefront, or a disused post office. The Performa Biennial engages with the fabric of the city and attempts to remold, even only ephemerally, its cityscape and physical and mental space. With each edition, Performa also returns to key partners—such as Abrons Arts Center, the Brooklyn Academy of Music, Danspace Project, and PARTICIPANT INC—to build on enduring friendships and co-conceive or co-present new works of live art for the twenty-first century. Taking new forms every two years, these ongoing artistic conversations strengthen each Biennial as a platform that showcases the wide range of viewpoints and sensibilities that constitute contemporary performance.

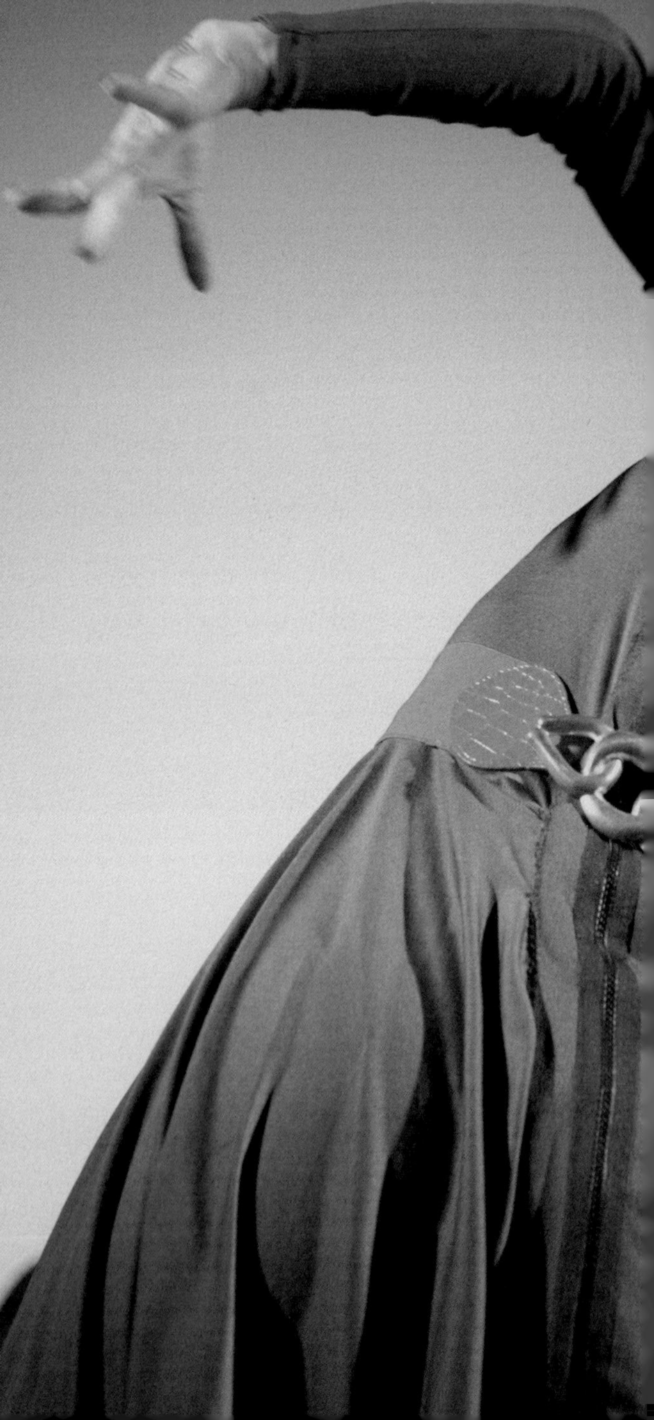

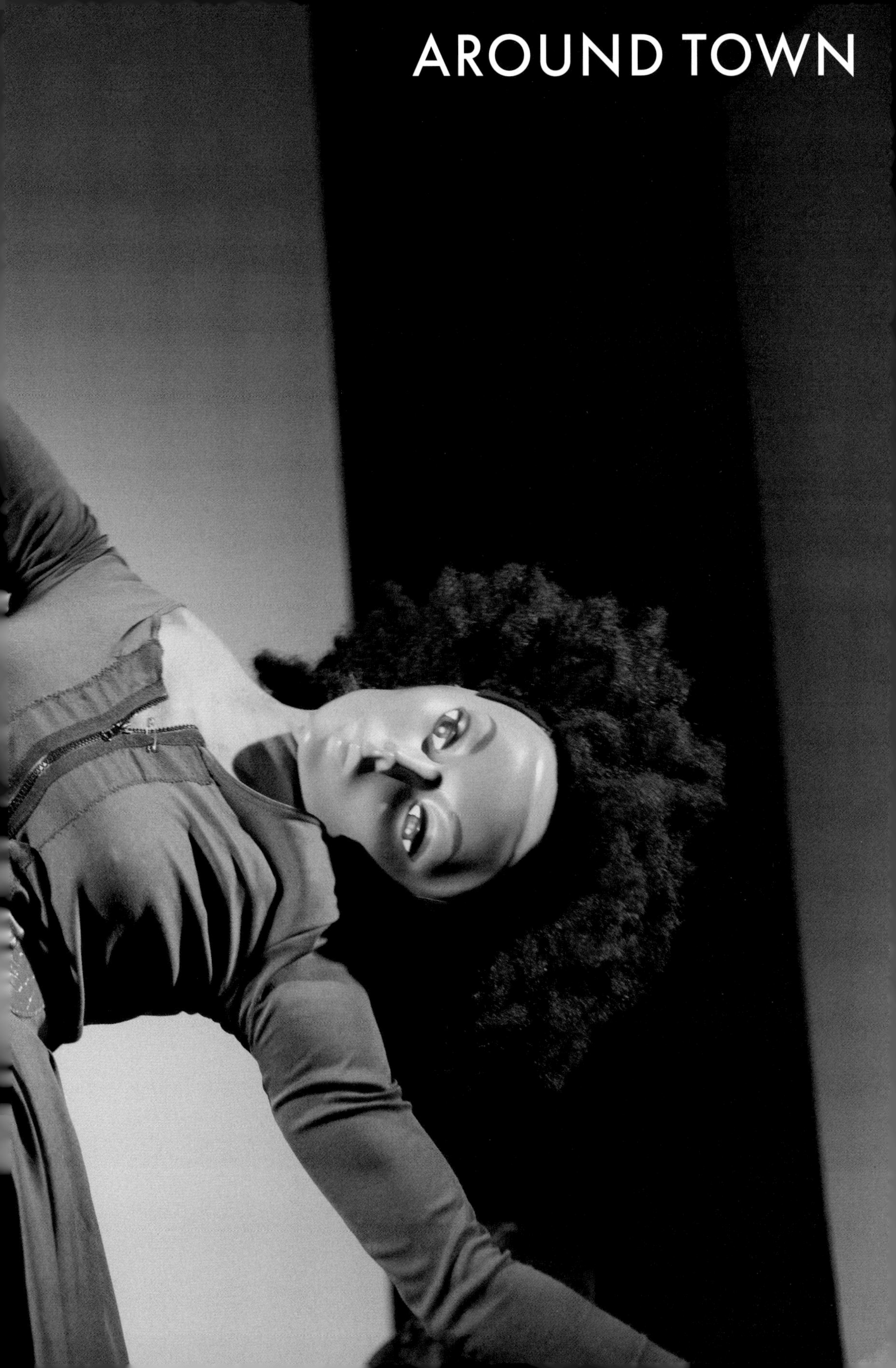

AROUND TOWN

BRIAN BELOTT
People Pie Pool

Curated by
Jens Hoffmann

Abrons Arts Center

November 10–11, 2017

In a nod to Dada's anarchic legacy, New York artist and prankster Brian Belott (known for his frozen paintings at the 2019 Whitney Biennial) staged a raucous, frenetic comedy of simultaneity at Abrons Arts Center. The production featured a property lawyer, yoga teacher, sword swallower, SAT tutor, and acting troupe among its cast. Ricocheting between the mundane and the prophetic, *People Pie Pool* offered a series of entirely unpredictable events that eschewed narrative or logic; instead, it relished in a joyous parade of confusion.

To assemble *People Pie Pool*, Belott immersed himself in an eclectic theatrical lineage. From American stand-up and slapstick comedy to the absurdist tendencies of the early twentieth-century European avant-garde, the performance resisted simple categorization. With fantastical costumery and gleeful disarray, the artist looked to the rowdy, singular anti-structure of Dada, updated with decidedly contemporary quotidian materials and motions. All actions were fair game over the course of the evening, including a lecture on proton characteristics; a round of basketball practice; improv games with the audience; the sacral, euphoric cries of a glittering masked figure; and dozens of bouncy white balls thrown across the stage. Performers ripped paper in front of a slideshow on real estate investments and paintings rolled across the floor on wheels, all resulting in exuberant pandemonium, Belott's signature.

The performance pushed the limits of language, with characters' speech overlapping shouting and intersecting with abandon. Together, they forged unexpected collaborations, producing interactions that mimicked the jumble of society. Many performed themselves—basketball players dribbled and professors lectured; some wore illustrations of their likeness hanging from their necks. As the artist said when he commenced the piece, "acting is so much more real than life."

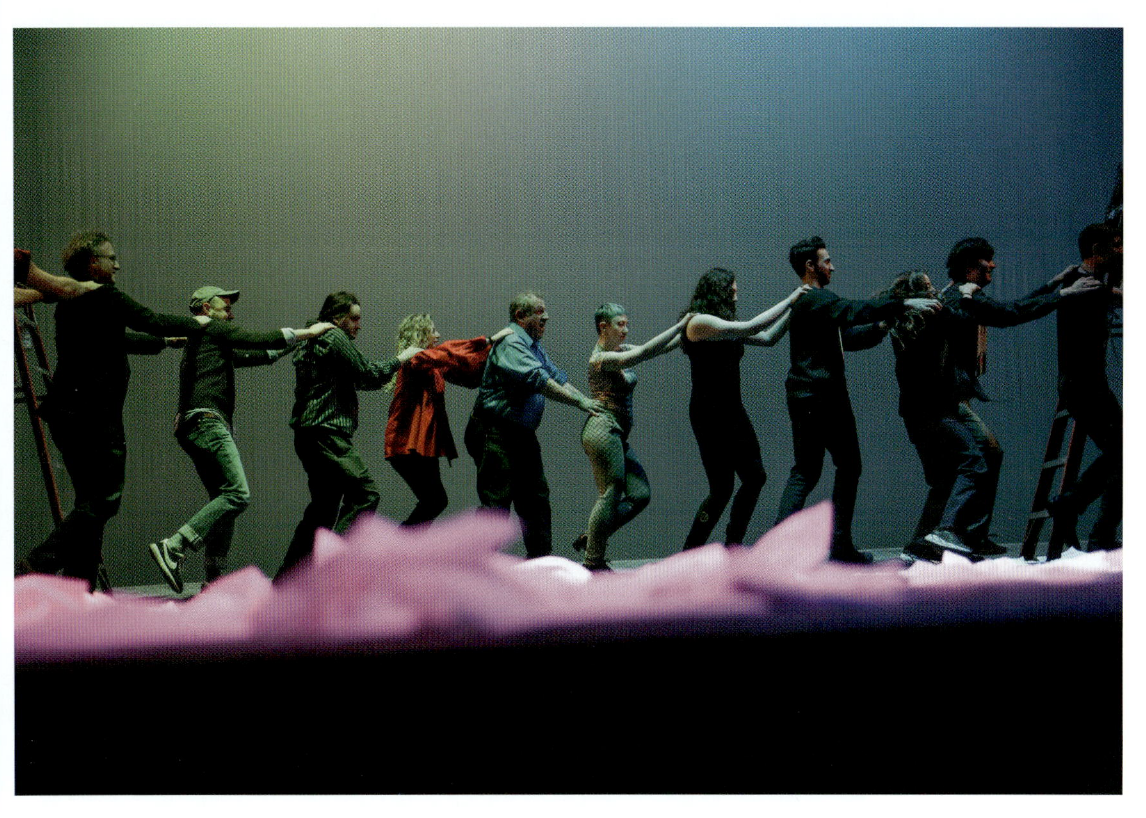

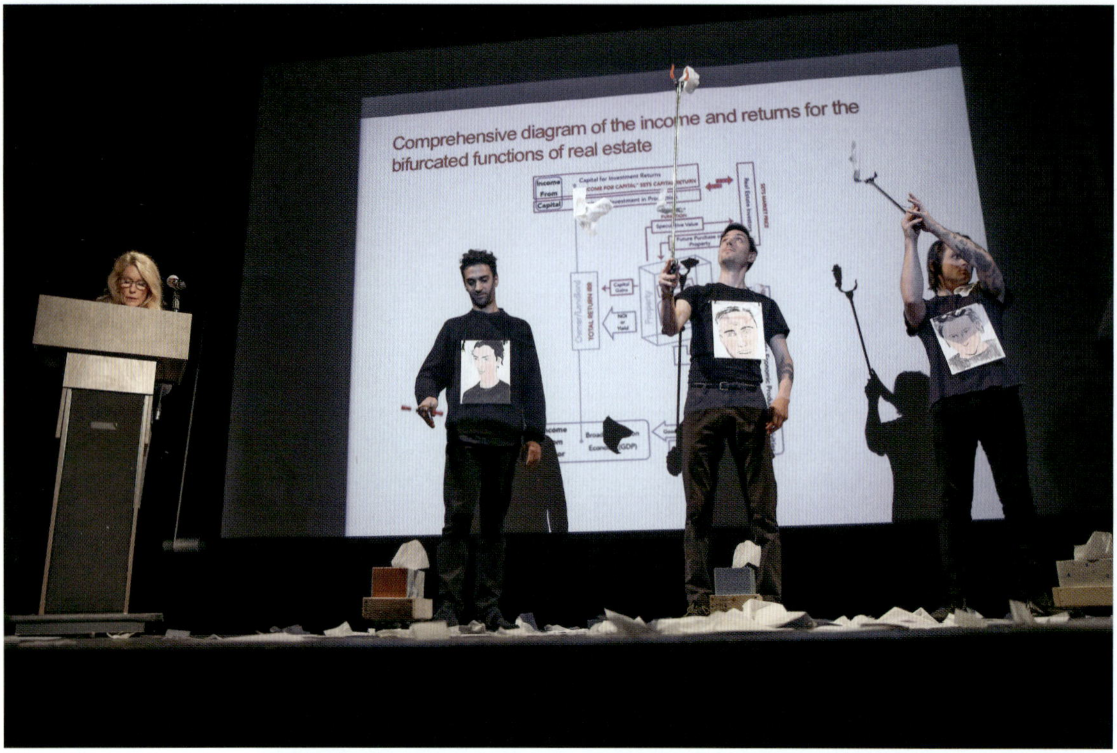

Comprehensive diagram of the income and returns for the bifurcated functions of real estate

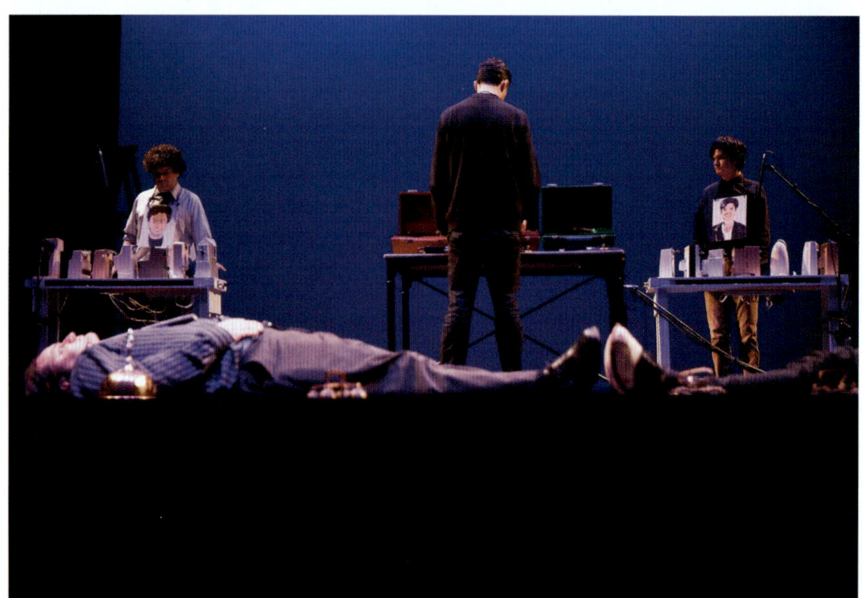

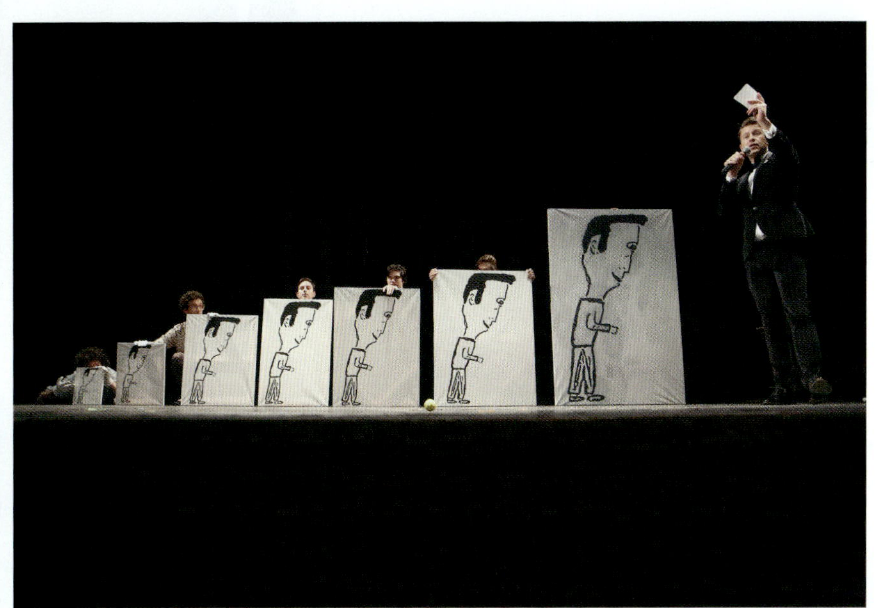

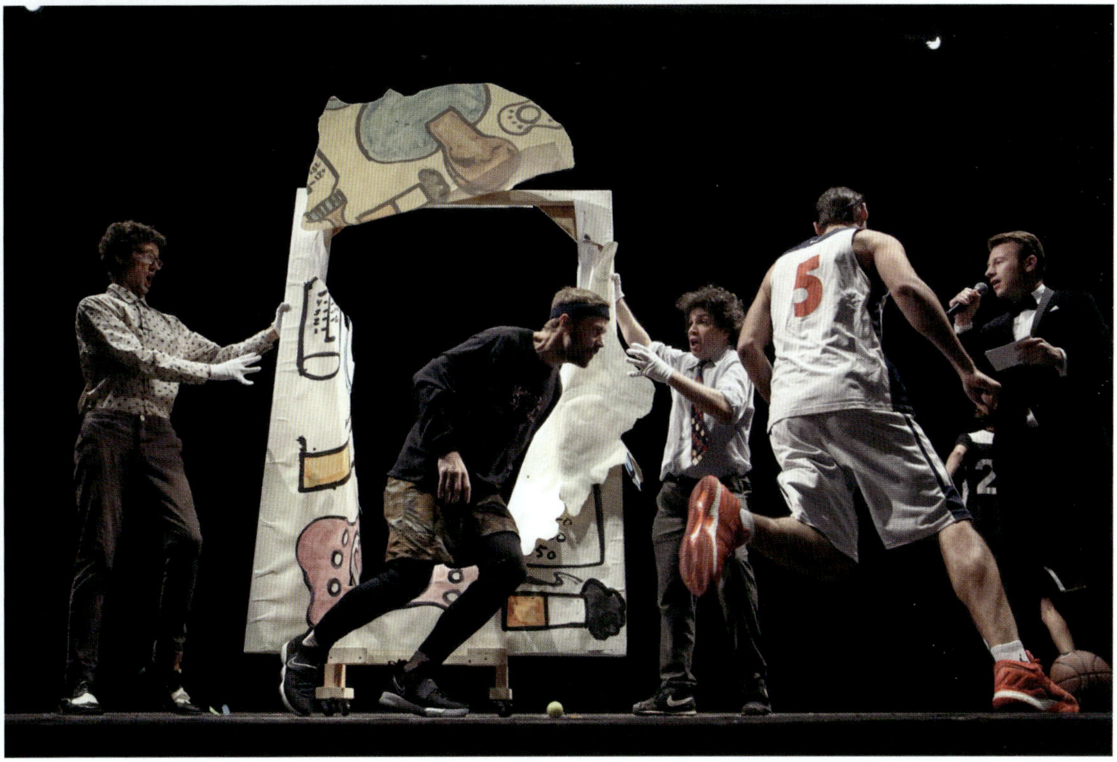

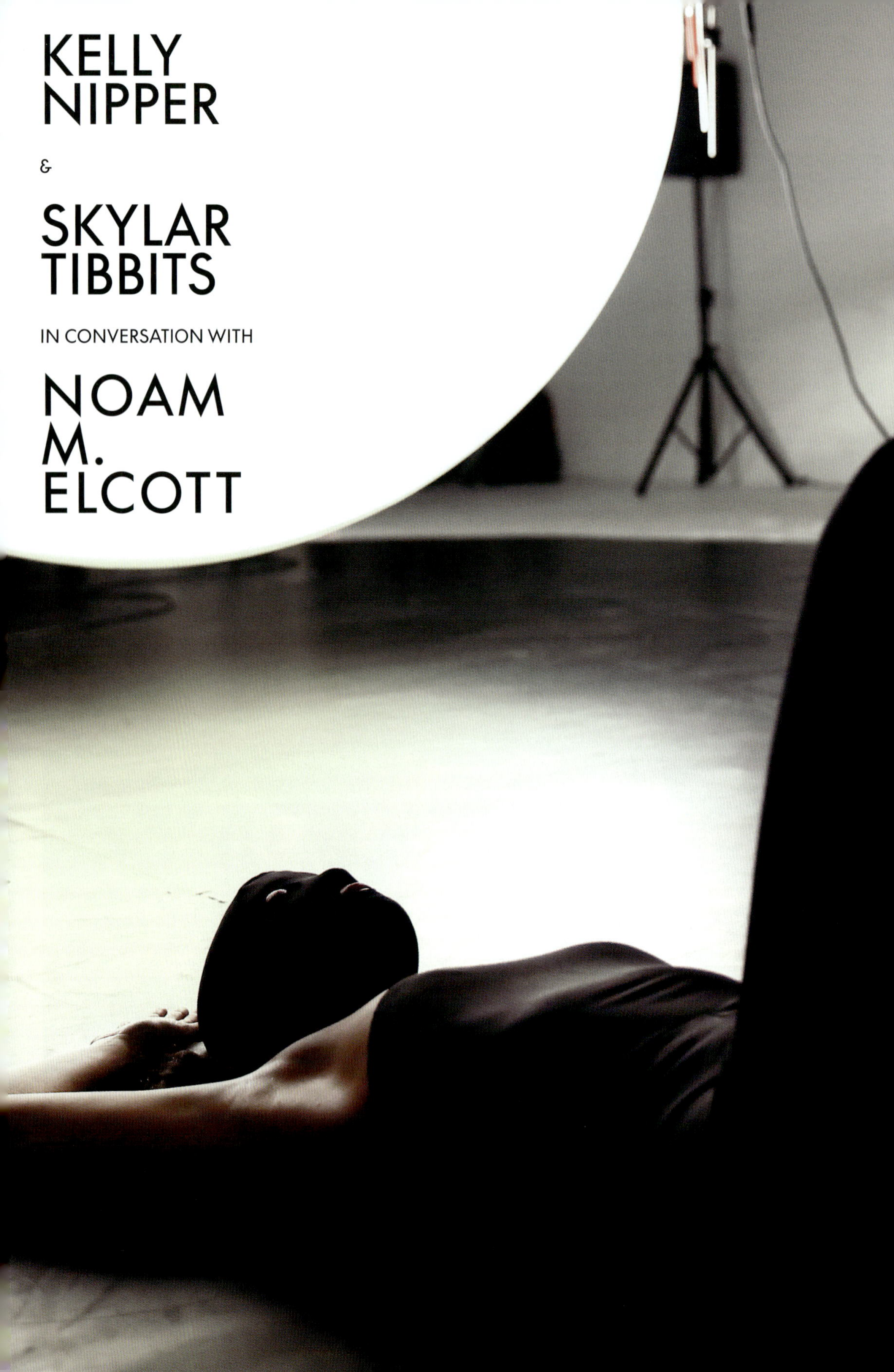

KELLY NIPPER

&

SKYLAR TIBBITS

IN CONVERSATION WITH

NOAM M. ELCOTT

Terre Mécanique

Organized by
Esa Nickle

371 Broadway

November 9–11, 2017

Visual artist Kelly Nipper and designer and computer scientist Skylar Tibbits discuss the intersection of technology and choreography with art historian Noam M. Elcott. The collaborators examine their shared interest in robotic innovation and 4D printing, which prompted Terre Mécanique, *Nipper's Performa 17 Commission.*

NOAM M. ELCOTT

I'd like to start by asking you, Kelly and Skylar, to give us a sense of your respective practices up until this performance and how you two came to work together.

KELLY NIPPER

I come out of photography, film, and video. I started working with dancers and live performance in 1998, out of my interest in exploring time and space in three dimensions. I taught at MIT for a couple of years, where I was introduced to Skylar's work.

SKYLAR TIBBITS

I run a research lab at MIT called the Self-Assembly Lab. By *self-assembly*, we mean where physical components come together on their own. We run a whole series of projects where we look at self-assembly in different environments, like water and air. It's more than just a manufacturing or fabrication discussion. It's more like a generator, where design and functionality emerge through the process of building. One topic that we look at is how to program physical materials to assemble themselves or transform themselves. For instance, in one project, we tried to print robots. We called it 4D printing because you add the element of time, and you print something that transforms over time.

NME

I know this project had been incubated for a while, and it's gone through massive growth just in the last weeks. Step us through, from your perspective, what this project is about, and how it evolved.

KN

When I was at MIT and learned about Skylar's work, especially with 4D printing, I was thinking about my relationship to photography, and the production of images in the dark room. When I started working with dancers, in fact, I wasn't interested in dance per se, but I was more looking at the anatomy of the human body and the body moving in space. Back then, I worked with a system called Laban Movement Analysis. When I approached Skylar, I had a similar impulse, thinking more about the built environment or the construction of a material, of matter, of things coming together, and their fluctuations in time and space. So, I reached out to him and suggested we talk.

NME

So, at this point, did you have specific objectives in mind? Was there some end product that you were envisioning?

ST

In the beginning, we started to look at what we were *not* going to do. We listed the cliché collaborations we wanted to avoid. We were not going to have robots dictating what the dancers should do or dancers mimicking robots in some awkward ways. To be frank, I was kind of hoping that Kelly would be like, "Can you just make this?" and then we'd respond, "Yeah, sure, we'll figure out how to make that thing." That would have been much easier. But Kelly made it very clear from the beginning she didn't want that to happen, she wanted us to—

KN

Get on board.

ST

—continue to do our research and be a part of the process of figuring it out together.

NME

That's superb! So, can you tell us what this performance is?

KN

There are three dancers in the piece, and there is a researcher, Bjørn Sparrman, from the lab. There's a large tank. The technology we use in the performance hadn't been developed yet when Skylar and I started talking, so a lot of this happened along the way. There's a photographic tool, which is very abstracted in the space.

ST

There's a cylinder.

KN

There's a mirrored cube. And a big wash bin.

ST

And then there's a cable system that moves around and prints inside the jaw. So, these pieces are printing while Bjørn operates the cable robot. He takes the prints out, washes them, runs the machine, and produces these objects throughout the performance.

KN

It was important that Bjørn could stick to what he would usually do in the lab, although he wears a mask during the performance, which he doesn't do otherwise. The tank had to work on an architectural scale, and we had to think about the cable system and how these different lines are being pulled through space, through the human body, and what's resonating around those vibrating cables or internal parts of the body.

ST

One aspect of the piece that our lab developed was a new process of printing in gel. For the performance, we were interested in making the system much more spatial. Could we print at the size of a room? Can you create objects by drawing in 3D, where the room is part of the printing process? The tank we use is eight feet in diameter, and the cable can be up to eighty feet long. You can print really large things, and the things that we're printing are referencing some of these geometries: We are always printing in cylinders and circles and in nets and mines.

NME

So, in the performance, we've got what you call 4D printing, which is very much drawing in space, almost in the most literal sense. Choreography is another form of drawing in space. How does drawing in space inform your own practice?

KN

Sometimes this gets a little complicated, because we can say *drawing in space*, but I don't really think about drawing in space so much as pulling lines through space and how the pulling goes through multiple dimensions. That also has to do with the movement work that I've been interested in, which is very subtle, and will look very different in different bodies.

ST

In terms of drawing in space—normally, when you print something in three dimensions, it's layer by layer. You're slicing something, and you typically have to build support structures. But once we were able to print into a gel, we didn't need to slice anymore and, as a consequence, there wasn't any need for the supporting structures. Instead, you can literally draw as you're moving, like in calligraphy; you're drawing in three dimensions.

KN

There's also a big underlying notion here about time and duration. We can talk about linear time, but it's also about the "stacking" of time.

ST

If you notice, in a way, the performance is reversed. First, Bjørn takes out the print from the previous day. You don't want people to sit there and just watch a boring print come out. So, everything that is removed in the beginning of the performance is something that Bjørn experimented with the day before. He takes it out, washes it, and then starts a new print.

But this thing is gross—the process of taking it out looks like an alien birth or something. And when we were working on the piece, I was like, "You don't want to show that part of it. This is nasty." But Kelly was really adamant that Bjørn should be doing what he normally does. We're not adding anything and we're not hiding anything.

NME

Both of you have very physical, material practices at a moment when so much is turned toward the virtual, where there's no alien birth thing happening. There aren't bodies. There aren't dancers in masks that may or may not look like thieves or S&M enthusiasts. And I'm sure this is a question that we're all asking in some form or another, in relationship to the live performance but also well outside the confines of art: Why insist on the material, on this embodied material realm, when all of the money, all of the fame, seems to be going toward the virtual, the digital?

KN

Well, yeah, but we're losing touch. Where is the contact? In my opinion, nobody really knows or understands anything anymore. Everything is so removed.

NME

I'm going to push the point, because it's a serious one. We all exist in the real world. We all have to touch each other. There's a certain "metaphysicality" that's required, but why insist on this physicality when powerful computer-generated alternatives exist? ... Why insist on this big block and this big vat of goo and these forms that initially came out and looked like roadkill? I can show you endlessly fascinating complex forms in four dimensions on a computer screen. Why insist on taking this to the physical realm?

ST

Well, one thing that we all joke about in the

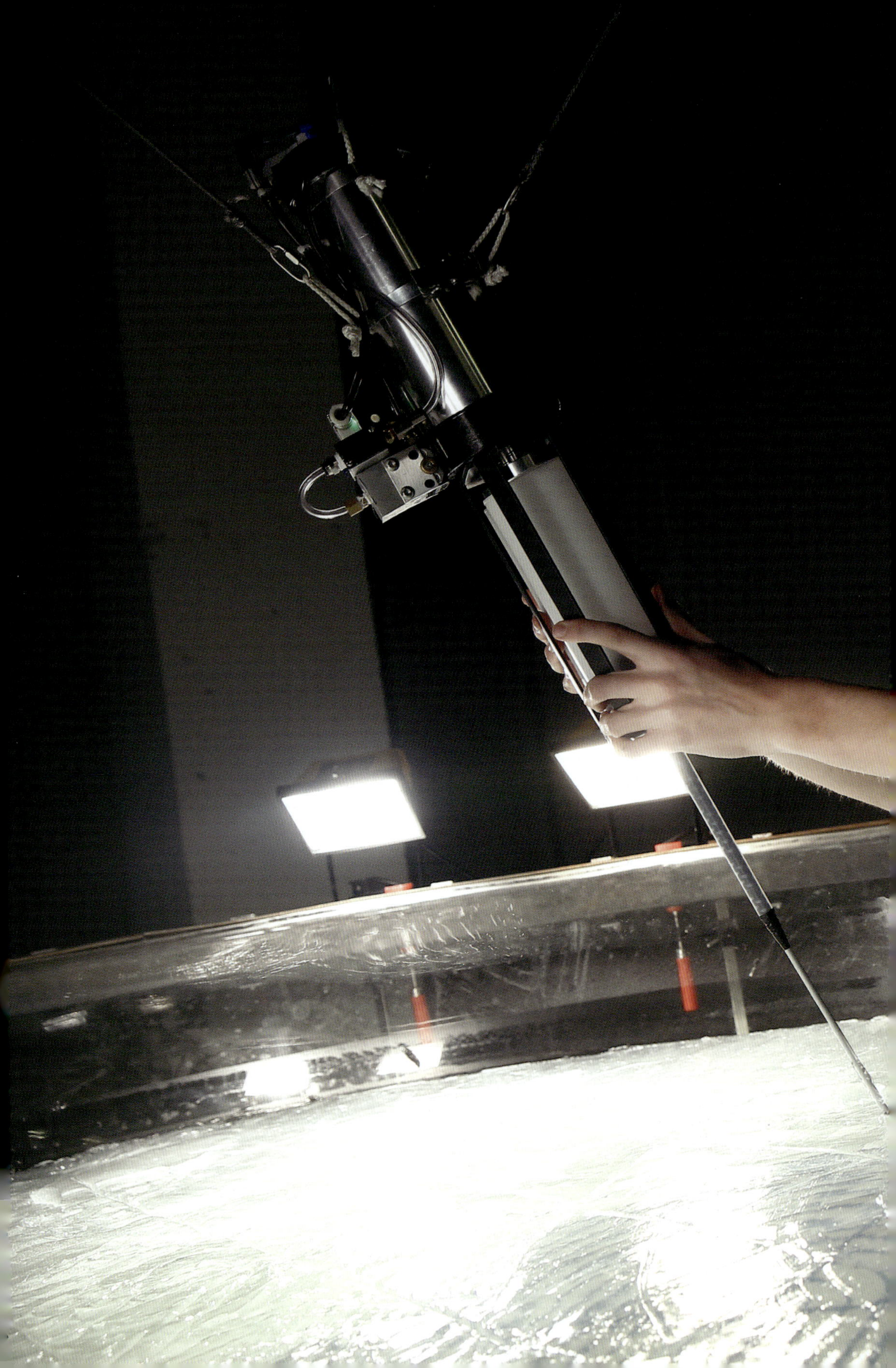

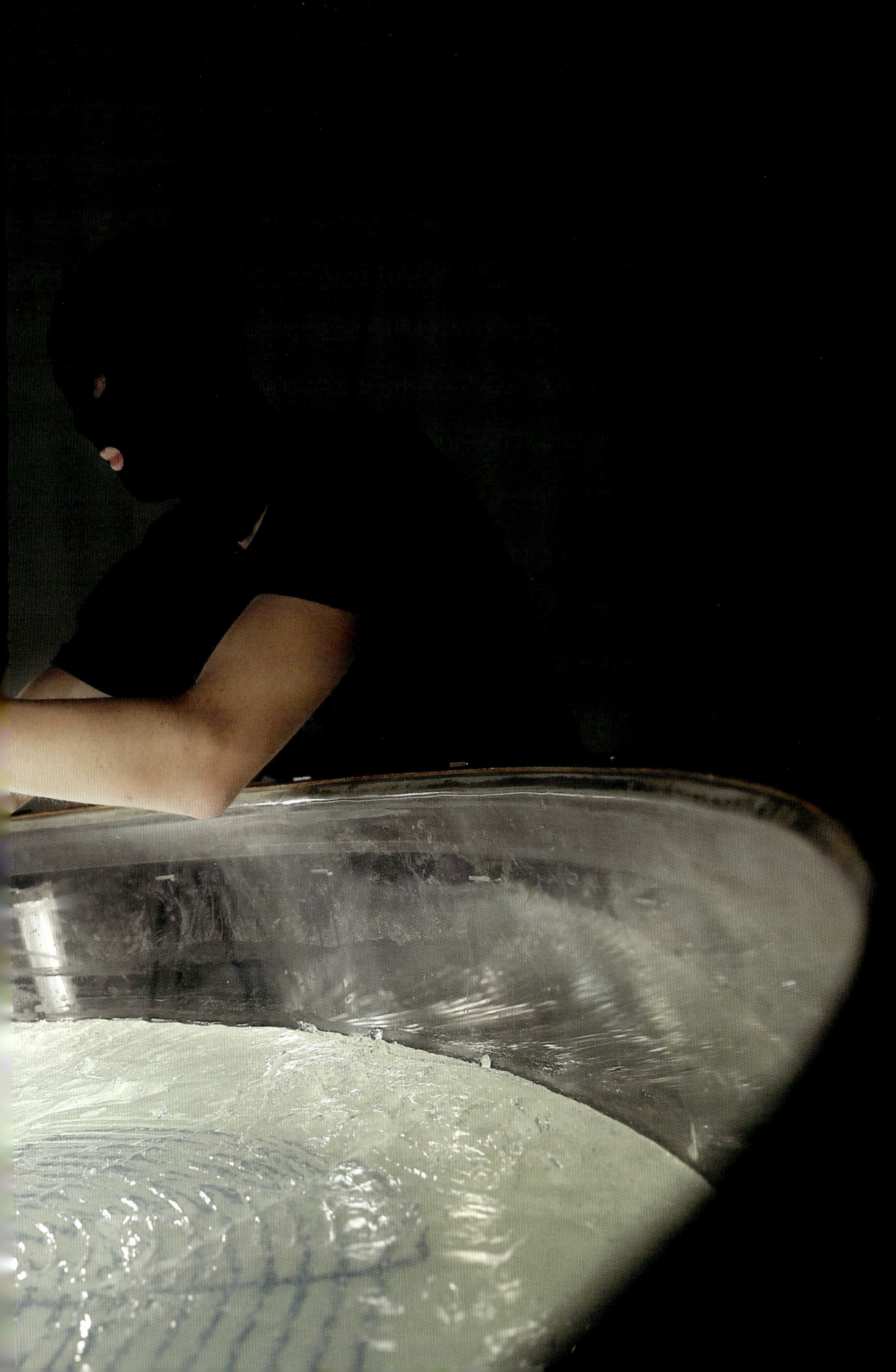

lab is that ideas are cheap—until we build it, it doesn't matter. But it's too easy to come up with some random crazy *idea*. Until you realize it, it doesn't matter. So, we don't get excited about ideas anymore until we make them happen. It has to be real, tangible.

Also, all of our work is about making the physical digital and the digital physical. We already had the computer revolution and the software revolution. Everything became digital. And in my mind, we've already had the hardware revolution, because there's digital fabrication, 3D printing, CNC routers, laser cutters, industrial robot arms, wearable robots, etc. Everything is now moving back to the physical from the digital, and we're embedding more and more capabilities into physical materials, like smarter textiles. It's synthetic biology. There's a material science boom right now.

So, in my mind, it's not strange that we're going physical. The digital's not interesting anymore. We need to push and go back to real human experience. How

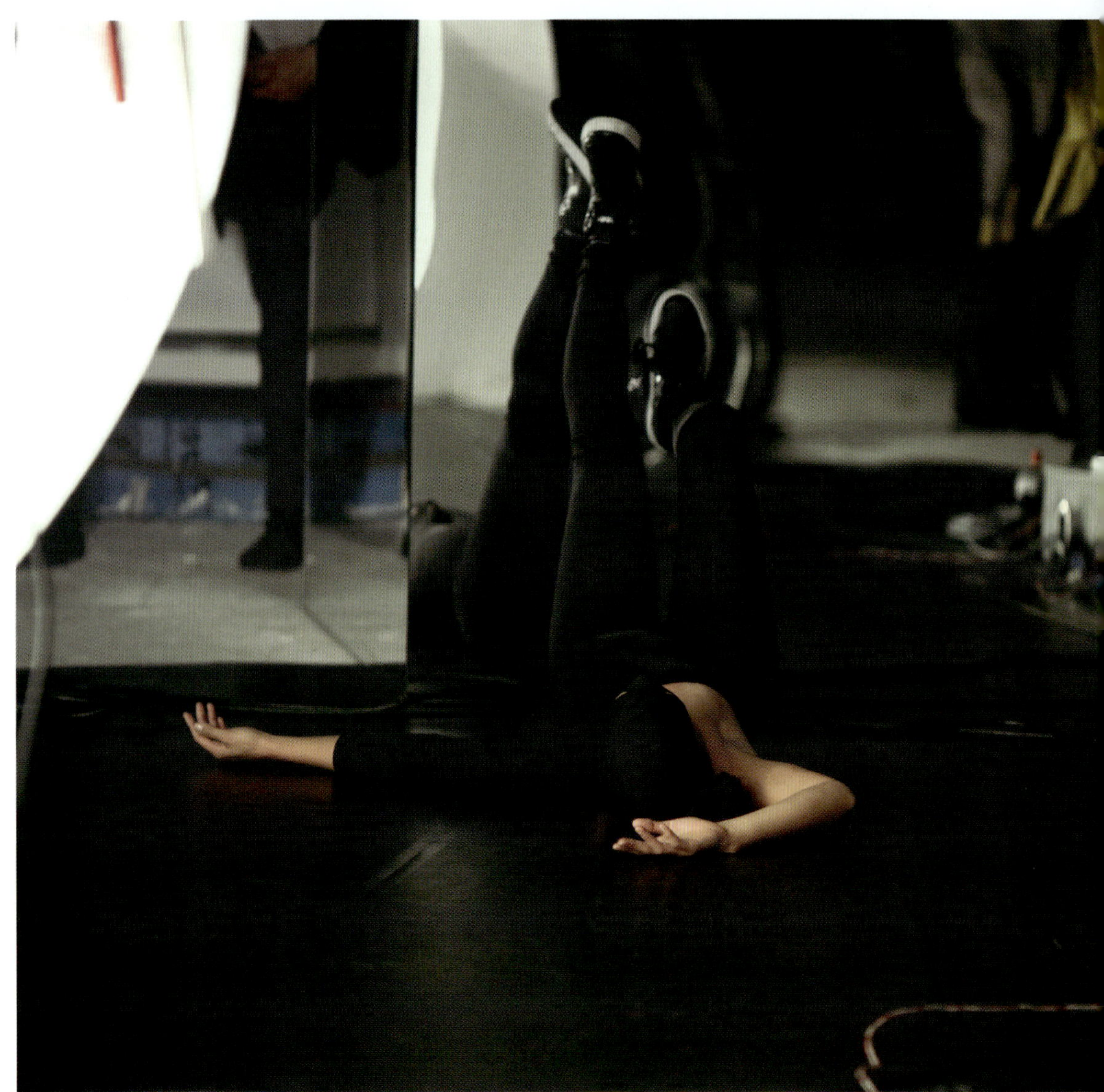

do we make things? How do we interact with products? How do we interact with our environment in a smarter way? For most people right now, the cliché is just to digitalize your physical world. Put on a headset. Put a robot in your shoe. Put a robot on your wrist. That's how they think digital meets physical, but for our lab, it's the antithesis of what we look for. We want physical materials that have new capabilities. It's not about putting robots everywhere.

NME

What I find to be the most profound investigation and experience within the performance is this very unnerving, very unexpected, chiasmus at the center of your collaboration. When you come to the performance, you experience a machine. We're looking at the apparatus around the 3D printing machine. It feels amniotic, biological, uterine. To me, it almost looks like chromosomes of some kind. It's a machine deeply shot through with biological metaphors and physiological substance.

On the flip side, we encounter these three human beings circumscribed within and around platonic solids, not mechanized, but almost even more idealized than mechanization enables. There is, over the course of the sixty minutes, this very strange relationship where the people become much more idealized and crystalline and almost mechanical, while the machine takes on more and more of a human, unctuous quality. That, to me, is a strange, unnerving, disquieting place to occupy as those two poles are inverted and eventually just confused.

How much of that emerged in your collaboration? I don't want to force a reading onto the work that you don't see, but how much of that is visible to you?

KN

In terms of movement, I usually work with repetition. I'm interested in what happens over time when there's a structure implied and you keep repeating a certain pattern in space. I look for how that form will change over time. The reason I've been working with masks—actually since my first performance, ten years ago, with Performa—is because it's about taking away information. The first thing people usually go to is the face, so I wanted to explore what happens when that's blocked and we're dealing with the body the same way we're dealing with the printing system.

I'm not sure how I feel about metaphors in general, but at the end of the day, this is gel and there's a material being injected into it and it's suspended. We could say that they could represent or be metaphors for many things.

NME
I hate metaphors.

KN
So do I. I mean, I don't believe in them, really.

NME
I'm allergic to metaphors. To me, they're just a cheap trick that excuses bad work. But in this instance, when you're pulling these forms that were injected into this fluid, when they get washed, even I, even with my severe allergy to metaphors, can't help but see biological imagery. And what about the platonic solids? I don't think they're metaphors. I see these as idealizations made material. Ironically, it's the human operations that are less human and the machinic operations that are more human in most of the ways that we've defined those terms over the last hundred years at least. I'm with you on rejecting the metaphor, but if we just talk about it as gel and acrylic, I fear we're missing something that is too pronounced, I think, to pass over.

ST
Well, with the robots, you can get into discussions of labor and automation and how we relate to robots. I guess there are two threads here. One is how, at the lab, we're really trying to go past the robotics and focus on materials. That's what I was describing before. We're trying to move away from an electromechanical vision of robots into physical materials.

The second is about automation. People think about robots becoming more and more precise and taking away jobs from workers. But hidden underneath that is all the work that we're doing, which Kelly was really interested in. Everyone gets excited about some crazy software or crazy robot that does whatever, but behind that is just a very normal process of pulling things out and sending files or hosing something off. It's very, very human. A human relationship with machines and digital technologies that is completely natural in a way. We're interested in this.

It's not about robots and software just eliminating us and becoming the designers of the future. In some ways, it's more essential that there's a collaboration between us and robots and us and materials. I think, with our piece with Kelly, we were just trying to

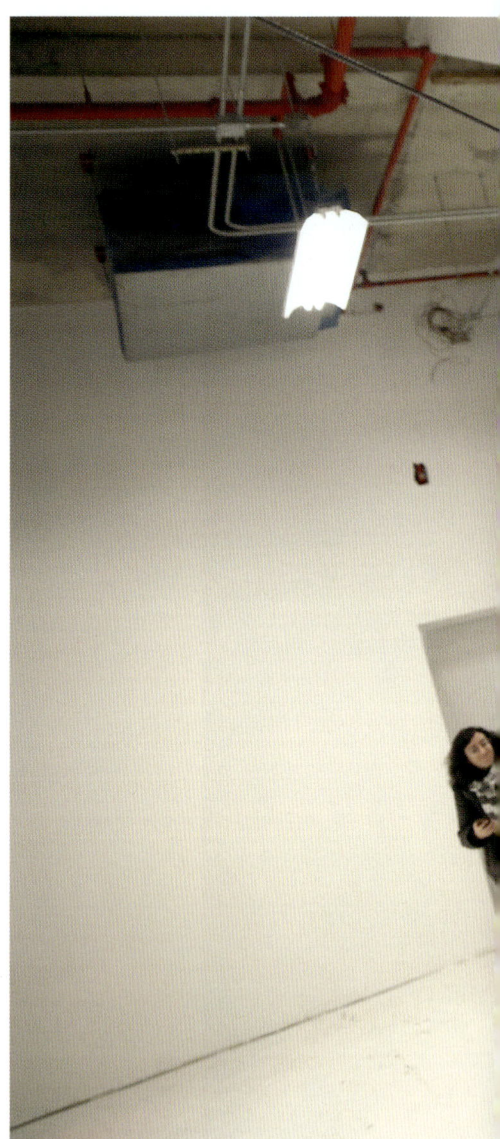

show that collaboration super bluntly and insist on the fact that it's very human, that it's just a mundane thing. That's how we can collaborate with robots. You usually don't see that when you see a robot performing.

This conversation took place in front of an audience at the Performa 17 Biennial Hub on November 12, 2017. It has been edited for clarity.

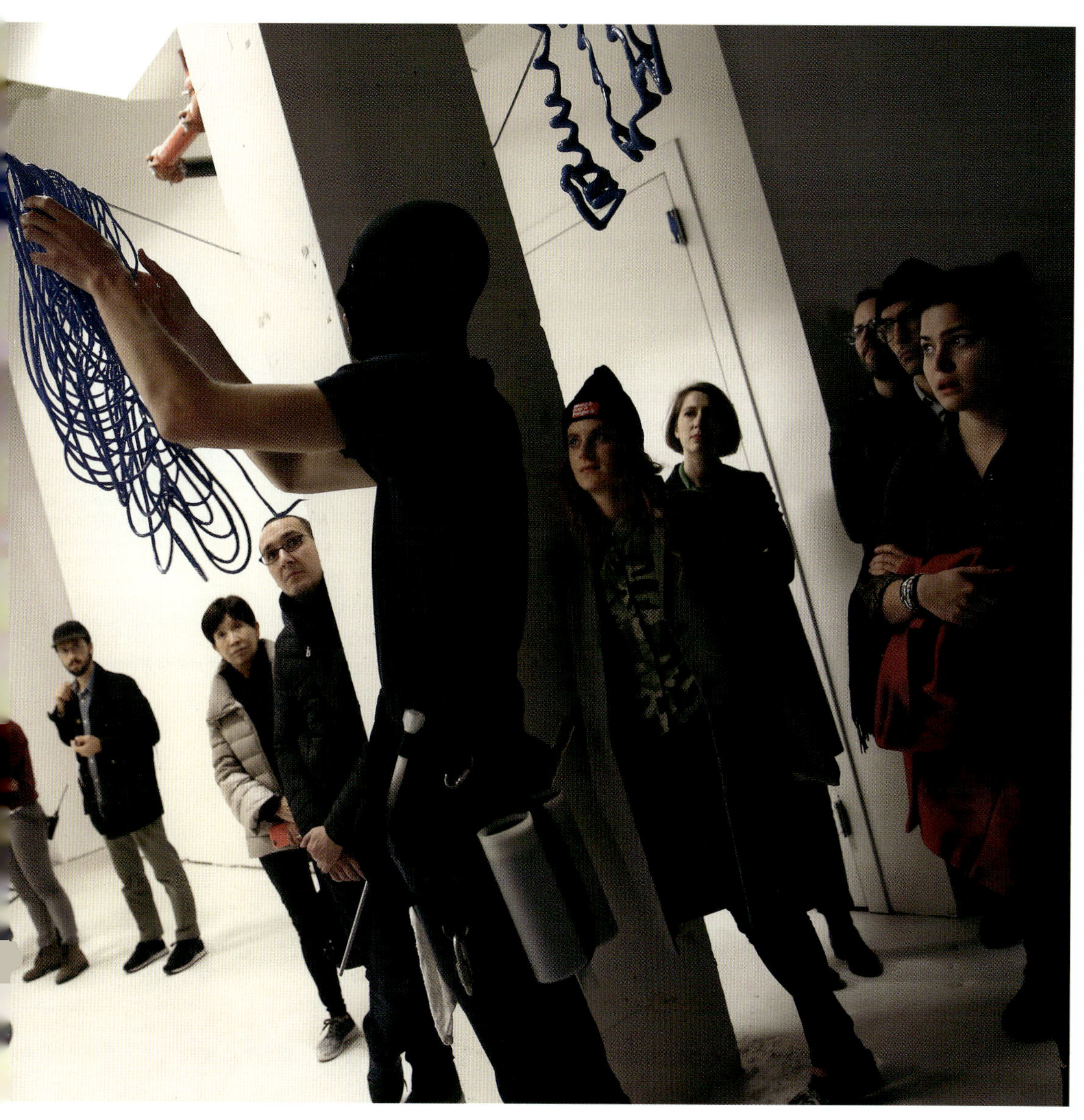

GILLIAN WALSH
Moon Fate Sin

Curated by
Judy Hussie-Taylor

Danspace Project

November 16–18, 2017

Over the course of three evenings, the American choreographer Gillian Walsh presented *Moon Fate Sin* for approximately an hour each night at St. Mark's Church in the East Village. *MFS* was composed of three forms—a book of single-line poems, a dance, and an audiotape—each one a work of collage, stolen material, deadness, and spiritualism. While the single-lined poems were anagrams sourced from Yvonne Rainer's "No Manifesto" (1965), the audiotape mixed sound clips from the reality television show *Dance Moms* with self-help-like invitations to think of dance as a vortex of "spiritual enlightenment."

The program had already begun, under a haze of white smoke, as the audience entered the church each night. The dancers looked dutiful and poised performing a dauntingly simplistic choreography in a state of near silence. Maggie Cloud, Emily Hoffman, and Justin Hyacinth occupied the ground floor, while Mickey Mahar and Walsh performed on mezzanines. The dancers were not in sync: Moving at a deadening pace, they assumed positions that signaled different modes of choreography, citing tai chi or yoga and the gestural act of "playing dead" while occasionally moving into more traditionally legible codes, like ballet. They were accompanied by pervasive smoke, four spotlights, and a low-pitch drone.

The gestures and references of the work consisted of stolen materials, slowed down and abstracted, like disaggregated content made beautiful, deceptively so. As in almost all of her previous works, Walsh included a slowed-down, practically unrecognizable, dance routine by Britney Spears. As outlined by dance scholar André Lepecki, re-performance taken as a choreographic strategy is always the reanimation of "dead" bodies—even after death, the body remains available for "body snatching."[1] Applying this logic to *MFS*, the dead body was Britney Spears's, rendered dead on account of her disintegrating relevancy in popular culture. With *MFS*, Spears was publicly abstracted and dismembered to facilitate the labor required of our collective digestive tract. Rather than emptying the *sign* Britney Spears, Walsh reinscribed the pop idol with new affects, new lines of aesthetic, and empathy throughout her liturgy.

Walsh's dances never begin or end—instead, the choreography is only resumed and paused. At St. Mark's Church, the choreographer and her four dancers moved gracefully, with a focused but lifeless affect. Walsh never abandoned Britney Spears—she dislocated and rewired her, imprisoning herself within Spears's ghostlike figure in a three-night-long feedback loop.

THOMAS RAGNAR

This text is an abridged version of the essay "Moon Fate Sin: Gillian Walsh speaking with her mouth full" by Thomas Ragnar, initially published in Women & Performance: a journal of feminist theory *(vol. 28, no. 2, 2018; 182–185). Reprinted courtesy the author and* Women & Performance: a journal of feminist theory.

1
André Lepecki, "Teleplastic Abduction: Subjectivity in the Age of ART, or Delirium for Psychoanalysis: Commentary on Simon's 'Spoken Through Desire,'" *Studies in Gender and Sexuality* no. 14 (2013): 300–308.

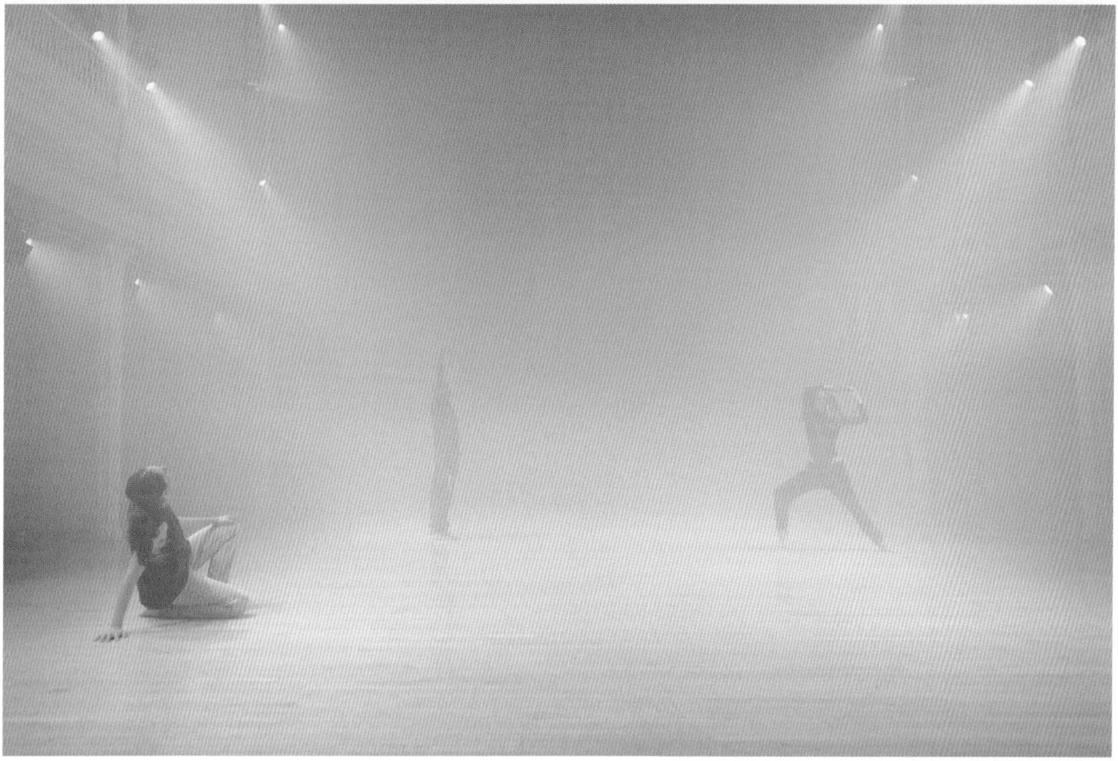

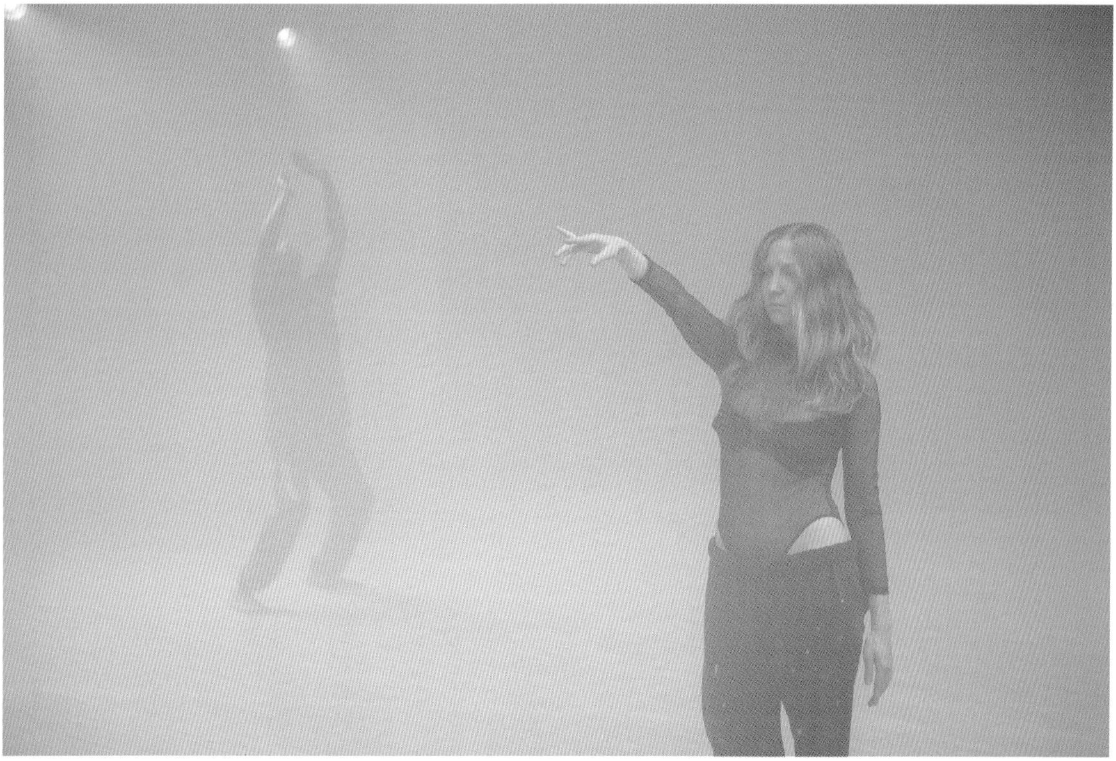

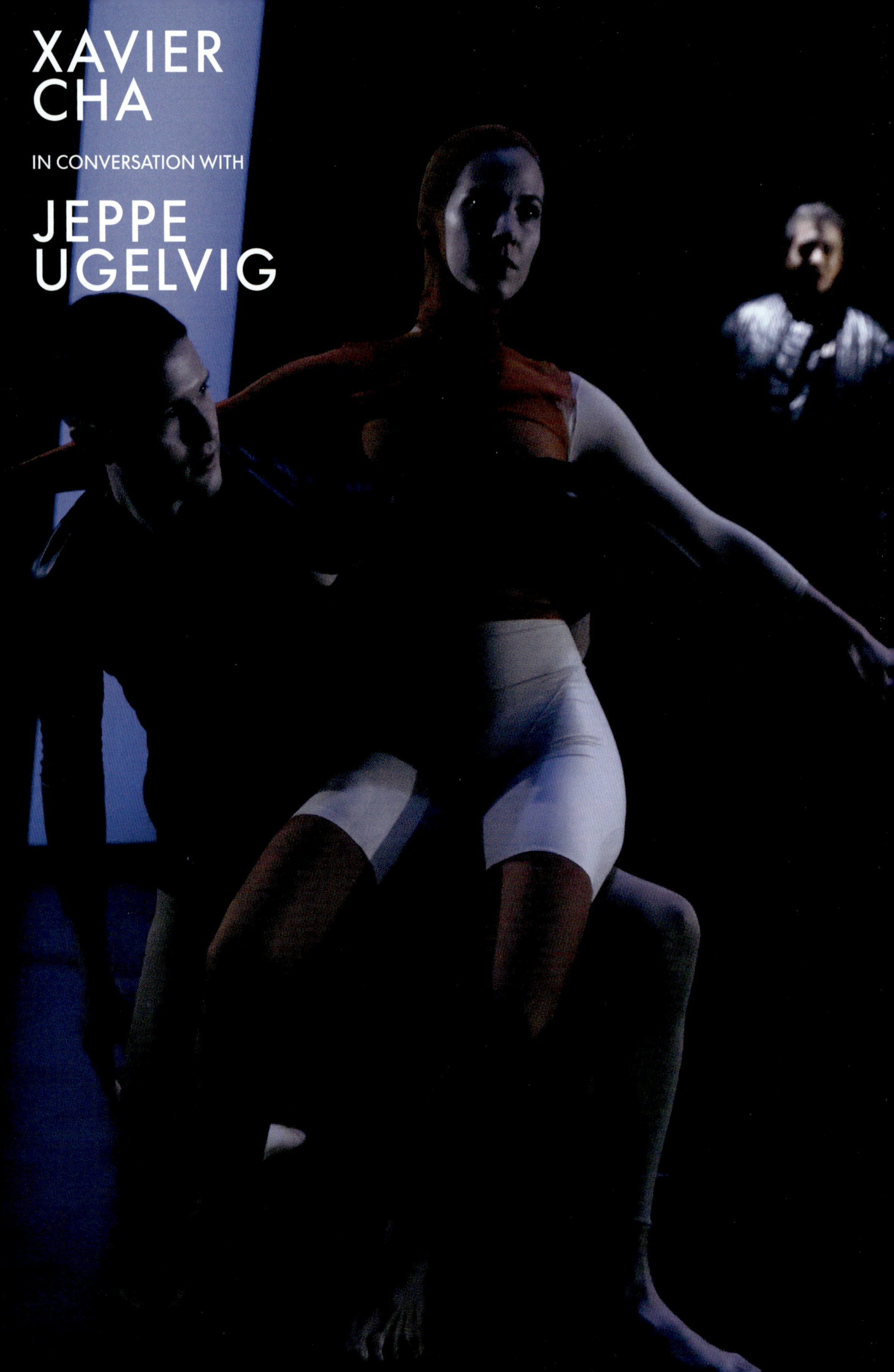

XAVIER CHA

IN CONVERSATION WITH

JEPPE UGELVIG

Buffer

Curated by
Holly Shen

Brooklyn Academy
of Music

November 1–4, 2017

Turning perception and communication into bare and abstract experiences, American visual artist Xavier Cha probes today's digitally mediated reality through both screen-based and live performances—often highlighting the uncanny theatricality and alternative temporalities of life online. Though perceived through screens and images, Cha approaches this reality with bodiliness, movement, and lived emotions. In Surveil *(2014) the artist used spyware to generate the choreography of her performance from the online behavior of various Internet users. With* Buffer, *the artist took to the theatrical stage, working with a crew of actors, dancers, and vocalists.* Buffer *set out to translate and decipher the alienating processes of digital consumption—glitching, buffering, and looping included.*

JEPPE UGELVIG
How did *Buffer* come about, and what was your starting point with the project?

XAVIER CHA
Last year, I was approached by Holly Shen, the curator of Visual Arts at BAM. She was interested in my work, we had a studio visit, and it just happened from there. Holly originally wanted me to re-stage *Surveil* (2014), but I had already done that twice and wanted to create something new. I was invited to show work in BAM's Next Wave Festival and was awarded the Harkness Dance Residency, which is given to one Next Wave artist every season. It's uncommon for Next Wave to work with individual artists, so they took a risk on me. I feel so grateful.

BAM got me thinking about the specificity of the theater format. Usually, people can enter and leave my performances as they please; the work typically exists in a non-narrative form in a museum or gallery, so I was curious to explore what it meant for the audience to be forced to sit in their seats for an hour. I was thinking about the audience's experience of theater and what they can compare it to. When people sit and view something for that amount of time, it tends to be in front of a screen. I wanted to experiment in conflating the two, testing people's modes of spectatorship as well as their patience. If you're at home waiting for something to buffer online, it's somehow okay to wait, but what happens when you put that into a live situation? I wanted to play with the expectations of the "live" and confront them with digital phenomena, like freezing. It makes us feel uncomfortable and slightly anxious. But why?

JU

There are so many parameters that are defined really drastically when you enter a theater, a space of performance that is not only historically loaded, but predates the internet, cinema, and the moving image as such. At the same time, there are some essential parameters that are very similar to elements of the online realm that you've dealt with before. In some of your previous works, such as *abduct* (2015), you specifically took on the cinematic apparatus as it relates to human expression. How did you approach the theatrical apparatus when you began *Buffer*?

XC

I wanted everything I did onstage to have a cinematic presence. I wanted to create a screen-based intimacy that's usually hard to get from a theater stage. As a result, there were three alternating scenes, like switching between channels on TV or tabs in a browser. This also speaks to the attention span—our limited capacity to follow a single narrative thread. One scene is a conversation between a man and a woman, and it's very domestic and intimate. They're not doing stage voices; they're just sharing thoughts in an almost banal way. It's not like theater... it felt like we were watching it through a screen, zooming in on this very intimate moment.

JU

You've previously explored the tension between the heightened performativity of the self versus the banal experience of being online. Your work abduct explored highly coded "theatrical" modes of feeling, such as "shocked sorrow," "ecstatic cerebral pleasure," "apologetic laughter," and "inhibited sadness," and your *Body Drama* (2011) at the Whitney Museum also lingered in the overtly "theatrical." It's interesting to try to compare performance with theatricality.

XC

That's a difficult distinction, but there is a kind of performance in the everyday. It's the minute and subtle, or the grand gestures of being and identity. Theatricality has a clearly evident filter or framing that offsets it from "real" experience. In *Buffer*, I want to multiply or layer the framing device of theater with this lived performance of viewing/consuming.

JU

Your earlier work has dealt with self-estrangement online; the feeling of being foreign to yourself. Is that extended to this project, or is it more about a sort of technical formalism of the internet?

XC

No. The formalism is definitely there as a kind of structural layer, and then, even deeper than that, I think *Buffer* fundamentally looks at the loneliness of being human: feeling a sense of distance even in the most intimate relations. With the dance scenes, there's an alien quality to the movement. Moving from the dance scene and the conversation between the couple to the love scene, there's definitely a search for human connection. In writing the script, it was about trying to understand where authentic emotion exists, particularly in an experience structured by capitalist interests, where impulses and drives, like longing or love, are manufactured for the purpose of profit and consumption.

JU

Criticism of "post-internet art" often revolves around it leaving the body behind. Much of your work talks about disembodiment, or at least, the extension of subjectivity online. At the same time, you're also a performance artist grounded in the physical body. How do you use the body? Or why is the body useful in studying experiences or phenomena that are highly digitally mediated, like the disembodied experience of surfing the Web, for example?

XC

I like to address these things through the body because I think the easiest way to express that alienation is to look at the residue of the body itself after that feeling of disembodiment, as opposed to trying to express it through the use of more screens, more digital platforms. Otherwise, you don't get thrust into that weird space where you're able to say, "oh, wait, this is what feels so weird," "this is what I'm uncomfortable with," etc. With *Buffer*, when I was applying for grants, I think a lot of people misunderstood and thought that the piece involved video projections. I had to clarify that the work is "without the use of screens" and "purely analog."

JU

That's really interesting. Can you speak more about the set design? This must be a first for you.

XC

I worked with Felix Burrichter and Michael Bullock of *PIN–UP* Magazine and the artist Paul Kopkau on the stage design. It was very minimal. Since the piece primarily revolves around the conversation between a couple in a domestic setting, the central set element is a sectional sofa, which was donated by Swiss furniture company Vitra. Felix decided that the stage should be symmetrical, so the sofa had two identical room-divider screens behind it, giving depth to the space. During the dance/opera scenes, the set pieces were turned around so the audience had the inverse view of the stage, which related to these scenes being the subconscious level of the piece. During the love scenes, the sofa was moved closer to the audience, as if we had zoomed in on the stage.

JU

How have you translated these technicalities of the Web—like the zoom or the lag or the glitch—into space or into bodies? I imagine that to be really difficult, but also very generative.

XC

Yeah, it was—in writing the script, it was almost like a rhythmic thing, or like writing a song. I suddenly felt like, "okay, now it makes sense for the scene to freeze or for this to repeat or loop." It was definitely more of a rhythmic decision.

JU

Which creates a sort of temporal layer to online activity, like surfing. It's like there's a beginning and there is an end, but with tons of loopholes and no linear time.

XC

Right. And with the dance, it was more subtle, but there were some very technical movements which then retrograded or were caught in a brief loop.

JU

Can you talk a little bit about the cast and what it was like to work with such a large group of people for an extended period of time?

XC

It was amazing. I worked with the dancers separately from the actors until the last week of the residency in August. It was the first time we put all the scenes together. I was nervous that it wouldn't work, or that nothing would make sense, but, in the end, I was really, really happy with it. The abrupt scene changes somehow energetically made sense. You came back to the actors and you picked up where you left off.

Cory Koons and Cutler X, who played the lovers, were cast by Michael and Felix; they helped me a lot in this process. Both Cutler and Cory are well-known porn actors. Their chemistry together was beautiful, right from the beginning. The two other actors were Babs Olusanmokun and Cassandra Freeman. Babs also happens to be my *jiu-jitsu* teacher—and he had a previous role as Omoro Kinte in the History channel miniseries Roots. Cassandra Freeman, who has appeared in the comedy series Atlanta, was amazing to work with. They were both very generous and emotionally curious with the piece. I've learned so much from everyone involved. It was interesting that after working separately with the dancers and the actors, which initially felt very much like switching gears, it all started to feel more related, altering the environment and manipulating emotions through physical languages.

JU

The sexual scene was between two men. Is there a political dimension to the work?

XC

Well, I just didn't think it was necessary to proliferate more heteronormative images, especially of men and women having sex—that is just not interesting to me.

JU

Buffer seems to be about desire in one way or

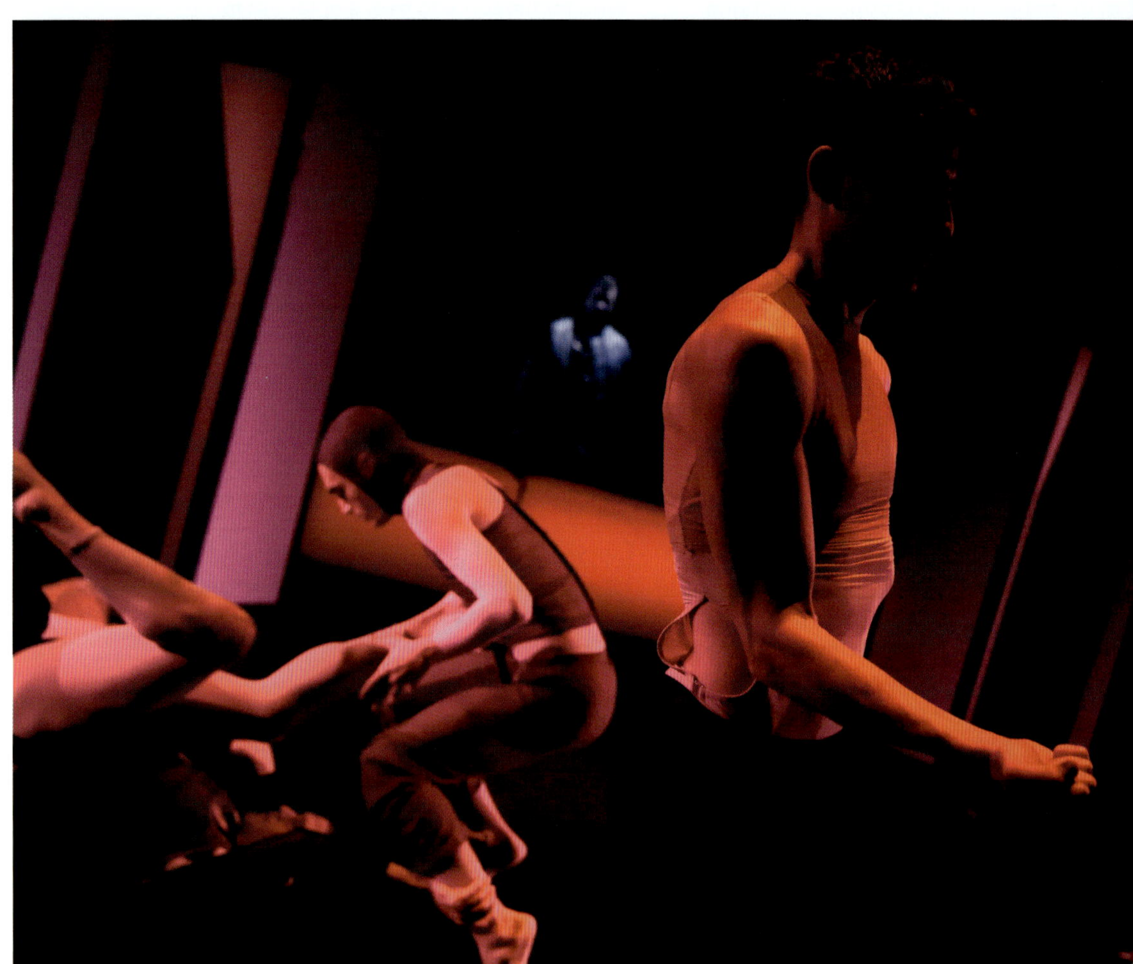

another, but particularly, the way technology and media shape it. What exactly do you think happens to desire online? How does desire exist in an age of Grindr, porn-streaming sites, algorithmic advertising, and romantic relationships that are maintained via FaceTime? What happens to desire when mediated through a screen?

XC

I guess I would not use the word desire necessarily. I think it would be more about this kind of emptiness. This longing for connection. A loneliness and a questioning of what it is that you're feeling. A feeling of being somehow disconnected from your own emotions. I guess that could be some form of desire, in a way.

JU

Do you give an answer to that? How to solve that alienation?

XC

I want to leave it pretty abstract. You might be left with a feeling of loneliness, and maybe you're left with a question of what, if any, emotions are real. Do "authentic" feelings exist when we are constantly swayed by capitalistic, hetero-patriarchal manipulation?

JU

Is this idea or fantasy of "the real" made obsolete in an online age? Or how do we continue to look for it, despite its displacement?

XC

It's been displaced so much that it's like there is no authentic thought left. Everything is pulling emotions from you, trying to trigger things from you. Everything is trying to manipulate your emotions and wants you to consume and buy... capitalism is so affective. It's a violently effective tool, a way of seeping into and modifying our behavior. It's hard to know what you'd be, who you would be without all these things pulling you. That's kind of what I'm exploring. I don't know what that means to come back to that question—if it's possible to look past the point of affective capitalism.

JU

I think it's very beautiful to say that you know the real has been displaced, yet we will always try to look for it and hunt it down. And that can also be counterproductive sometimes.

XC

By chasing it, it's pushed further away.

This conversation was initially published in Performa Magazine *on July 16, 2018.*

NARCISSISTER

The Body is a House

Curated by
Lia Gangitano

PARTICIPANT INC

November 3–5, 2017

How do we get to know Narcissister through all her swerves, inversions, and transposals? Feet replace heads, heads replace feet; front is back, back is front. Even while exposing so much flesh, her face and vagina are ever concealed with mask and merkin. As we witness her pulling clothing from her orifices during the reverse striptease *Every Woman* (2009), we find the artist both penetrable and impenetrable. What about her *can* we know? *The Body is a House* was a collection of videos and performances, including live versions of *The Basket* (2013) and *Upside Down* (2011), which highlighted an oeuvre that demands that we grapple with passive beliefs and stereotypes. In *The Basket*, the artist's women-selves are subjected to basket-holding across racial and ethnic presentations: Transitioning between a prewar Eastern European grandmother to an African American maid to a flashy, early aughts celebrity with the slip of a mask or frock. The compulsive costume changes and insistence on covering her facial expressions engage instability to perform a transgressive magic—a melancholic mash-up of her own post-soul, mixed-race feminism. What can we believe in all this/her/our code-switching? "Cake, cake, cake, cake / Cake, cake, cake, cake / Cake, cake, cake, cake / Cake, cake, cake," chants Rihanna as her song "Birthday Cake" booms, while sparklers flicker from between Narcissister's legs as she manipulates bride and groom puppets into a frenzy in *Unforgettable*. Bringing the evening to climax, ending on a high note: "I know you wanna bite this / It's so enticin' / Nothin' else like this / I'mma make you my bitch." ARIEL OSTERWEIS

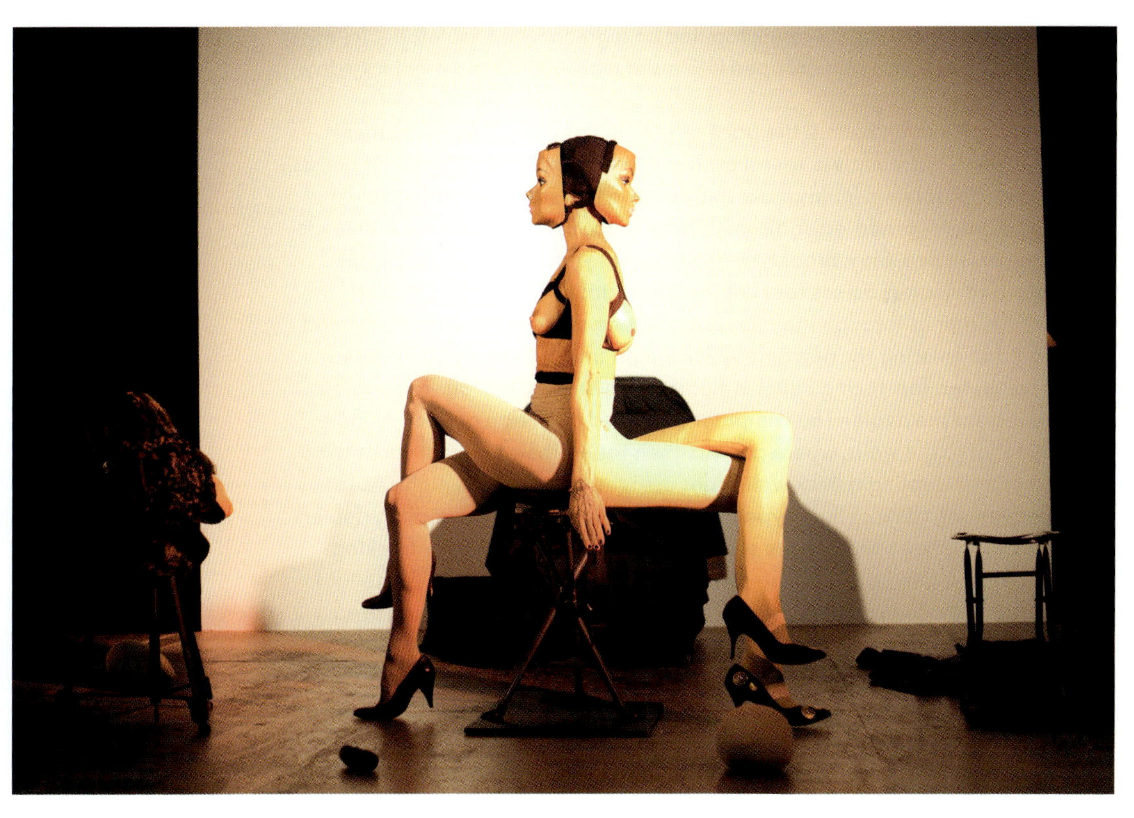

STEPHEN FAN RYAN JOHNS MEI LUN XUE

House of Cards

1.5 Rooms

November 12, 2017

"Red, next! Blue, next!" *Thud!* A drink toppled on a green felted tabletop. "Yellow, next, next!" *Clink clink!* A coin dropped into a slot machine. "This is your lucky day, pal! Green, next!"

Taking place at 1.5 Rooms, the pace of play in this blackjack tournament moved between the relentless speed of shuffling and the slow trudging of guests milling about, observing. In this makeshift gaming hall set up at 1.5 Rooms—a shared apartment-turned-episodic exhibition space by a collective of architects and designers in Bed-Stuy, Brooklyn—participants were divided into groups of players and dealers across four color-coded tables. The dealers tracked the course of the games through their keypads, hitting reset each time a new hand was dealt and entering the outcome which would then be sent to the room's central computer. Top-facing cards indicated player wins; bottom-facing ones meant a loss for the dealer. The computer projected an image of each round's final layout onto the walls, where players then taped their physical cards over the projections, creating a thick wallpaper over the course of the night. As the rounds advanced, some of the keypads began to break down, prompting dealers to instead shout their results to the scorekeeper, who was frantically tracking the news while manning the mainframe. *Whew!* Stand and stretch. Some took the opportunity to join in; others walked away. The din of the adjoining area ballooned, then dimmed. Old fashioneds melted in cocktail glasses. Rice crackers, peanuts. *Red, blue, yellow, green!* Shouts above a backdrop of film jingles evoked good luck, and the noise of restaurants and casinos.

The evening-length performance drew on both Allan Kaprow's rigorously timed Happenings at the Reuben Gallery in New York in 1959 as much as it did on film scenes of workers on the factory floor. Architects Stephen Fan, Ryan Johns, and I conceived of the piece as a collapse of labor across its spectrum, from manual assembly to automation, and addressed discursive arguments within our field positing the analog and digital, or artisanal versus mass production, as disparate and opposing forms of progress. Thus, in their off-hours, the laborers are drawn to the casino where they play an integral role in the assembly initiated by a computer's repetitive strokes so that their leisure might also be productive. Our game of chance was at once programmed and an index of human missteps, revealing fallibility as its own form of replenishment. At the end of the night, the place was shingled in playing cards, basking in the red glow of the projections. In the window, a neon light buzzed. MEI LUN XUE

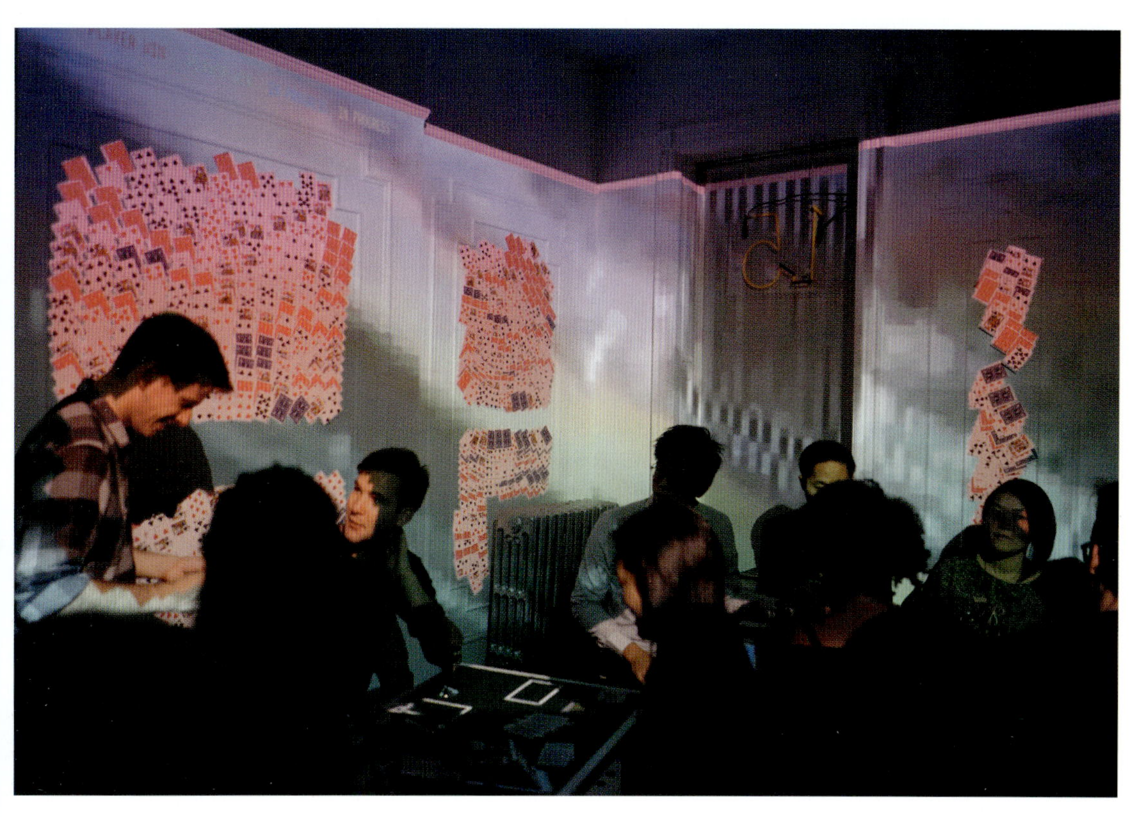

BEARCAT
DISCWOMAN
RICHARD KENNEDY
ZANELE MUHOLI
TABITA REZAIRE
SHYBOI

Afterhours

Curated by
Job Piston and
Lydia Brawner

PUBLIC Arts

November 4
and 16, 2017

Afterhours was a post-show get-together featuring a variety of emerging and established performers. The spirited late-night program brought together local and international DJs, musicians, and producers, as well as artists and nightlife favorites. Crowds joined Performa 17 artists and the biennial team for drinks, casual conversations, performances, and some dancing at the Herzog & de Meuron-designed space inside Studio 54 co-founder Ian Schrager's newest hotel. South African art star and LGBTQI activist Zanele Muholi opened *Afterhours* with a joyous night of spontaneous singing and dancing with Sisonke, the South African collective of nearly two dozen musicians, drag performers, and poets. The revelry was followed by an uncompromising, bass-heavy set by London-born, Brooklyn-based DJ and producer BEARCAT.

For its second program, organized with New York feminist DJ collective Discwoman, Johannesburg-based multimedia artist Tabita Rezaire emerged from behind the red velvet curtain wearing a playfully large pink bow and matching floor-length dress. With a gong mallet in hand, she gently guided the audience through a 45-minute-long Kemetic yoga circle—an ancient Egyptian healing practice of deep breathing, slow movements, and meditation. In sharp contrast, multidisciplinary artist SHYBOI delivered a punchy set of trap music with Caribbean inflections. American artist Richard Kennedy led us into the upbeat final portion of the evening: He appeared onstage in a neon blue glow, belting out operatic melodies with a three-piece band, while a dancer meandered through the space. The result was an entrancing blend of opera, gospel, funk, and hip-hop.

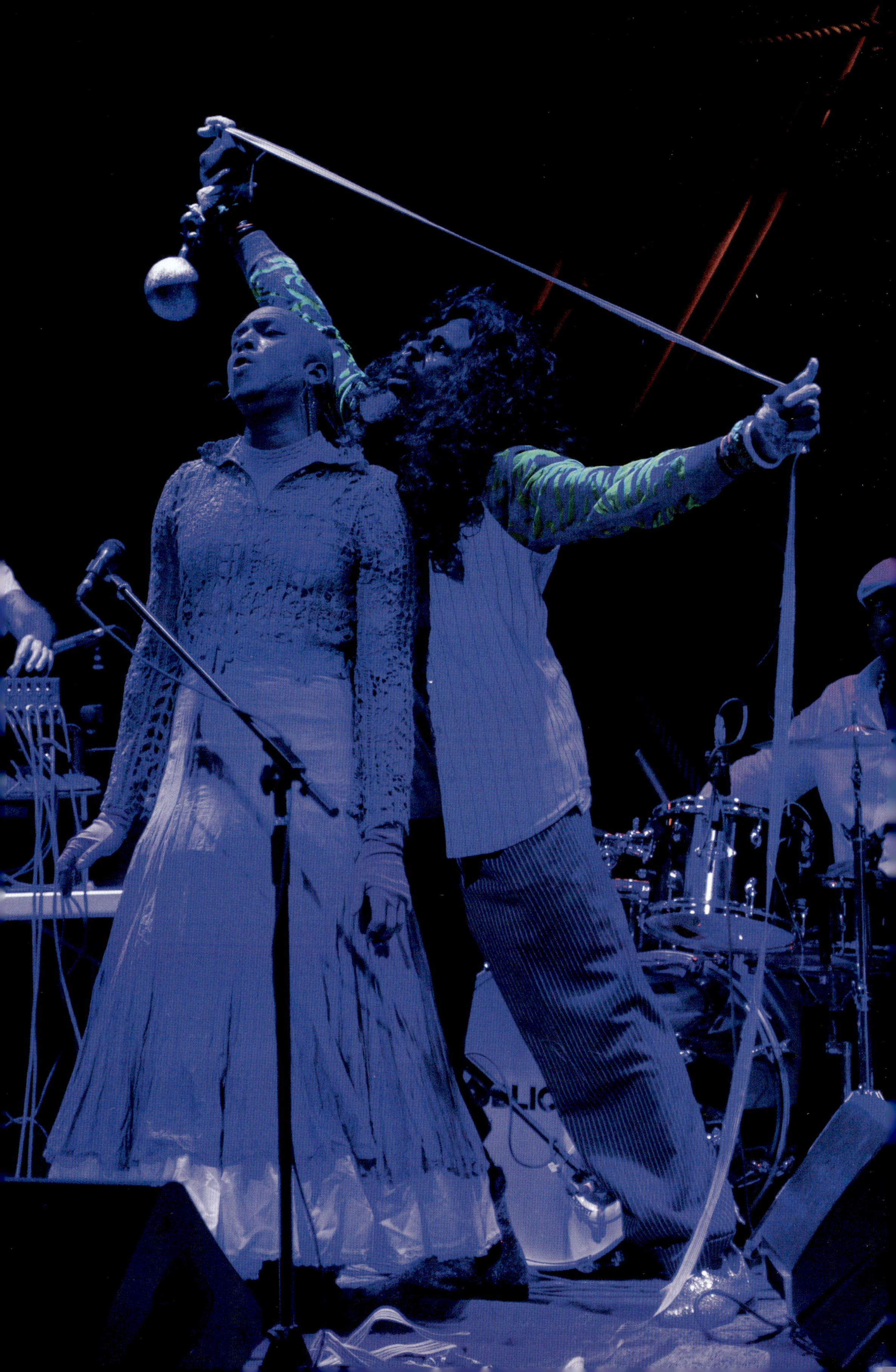

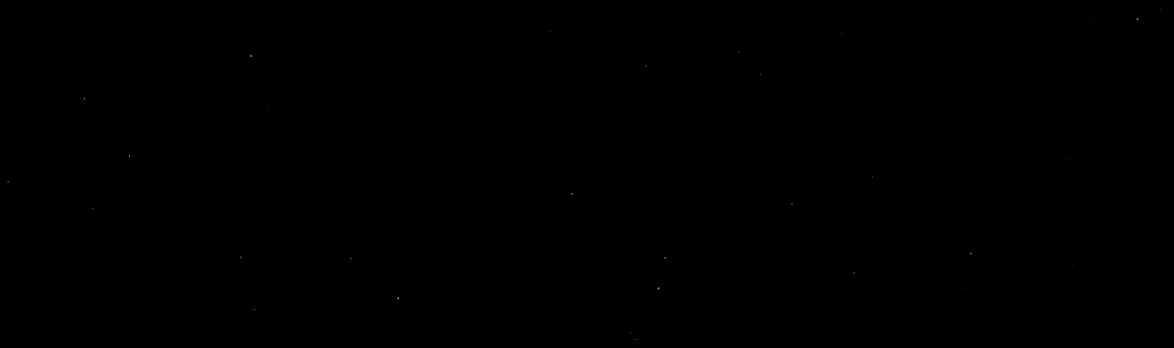

PERFORMA 19

BUILDING BRIDGES

Each Performa Biennial picks up where the last one left off, extending the ongoing threads of extraordinary propositions by artists today. Driven by an intense humanism, they respond to the immediacy of shifting political and societal tides, using the Biennial's platform to communicate complicated emotional and aesthetic histories to a broad cross section of audiences.

Initiated in 2013, Performa's Pavilion Without Walls program has showcased vibrant creative practices from Norway and Poland in 2013 and Australia in 2015. Following extensive exploration, dialogue, and engagement with curators, historians, artists, and educators in those nations, the Pavilions aim to reflect the social, geographical, and political landscapes of each country, and to present the work of emerging and established artists to the New York arts community and public at large.

While Performa 17's Estonian and South African Pavilions were conceived as individual entities, Biennial themes and the Bauhaus historical anchor were integrated into the Swedish and Taiwanese Pavilions for Performa 19. The 2019 program took place at a time of upheaval in every imaginable category of society, with the complex politics of identity, race, class, environmental catastrophe, and economic inequality igniting protests around the globe. Performa staff made exploratory visits to both places to soak up histories, working closely with local experts and guides. Through a schedule of studio visits, conversations with curators, tours of art spaces, and many shared meals, Performa developed powerful projects with four artists from Sweden (Tarik Kiswanson, Lap-See Lam, Éva Mag, and Ylva Snöfrid) and six artists from Taiwan (Yahon Chang, Shu Lea Cheang, Chou Yu-Cheng, Huang Po-Chih, Su Hui-Yu, and Yu Cheng-Ta). The enlivening and fruitful exchanges continued as they took up residency in New York City to plan their projects, cultivate links, share knowledge, and expand networks.

By partnering with institutions including Bonniers Konsthall, Hallands Konstmuseum, ICIA—Institute for Contemporary Ideas and Art, and the Royal Institute of Art in Stockholm, as well as the Taipei Museum of Fine Arts and Taiwan Contemporary Culture Lab (C-Lab), the curatorial teams fostered meaningful connections and bridged the distance between cultures, organizing their co-commissioned programs collaboratively. The Swedish and Taiwanese Pavilions Without Walls reflected these aims, building relationships and generating alliances
for years to come.

Illustrating media theorist Marshall McLuhan's dictum "the medium is the message," early video art of the 1960s and 1970s comprised performed actions in front of the camera, with the equipment functioning simultaneously as a tool for broadcasting and a mirror for self-representation. Today, the lineage of these artistic experiments extends to include the use of social media platforms as transmission mechanisms for both personal and professional lives. The artists working within this realm—Paul Pfeiffer, Su Hui-Yu, and Samson Young—embraced the intersections between experimental theater and the digital present in their Performa 19 commissions, reflecting the close affinity that the avant-garde maintains with new technologies. Ephemeral by design, theatrical performance and digital worlds were enmeshed in their dynamic presentations, incorporating innovative projections or taking cues from the internet age to tell their stories.

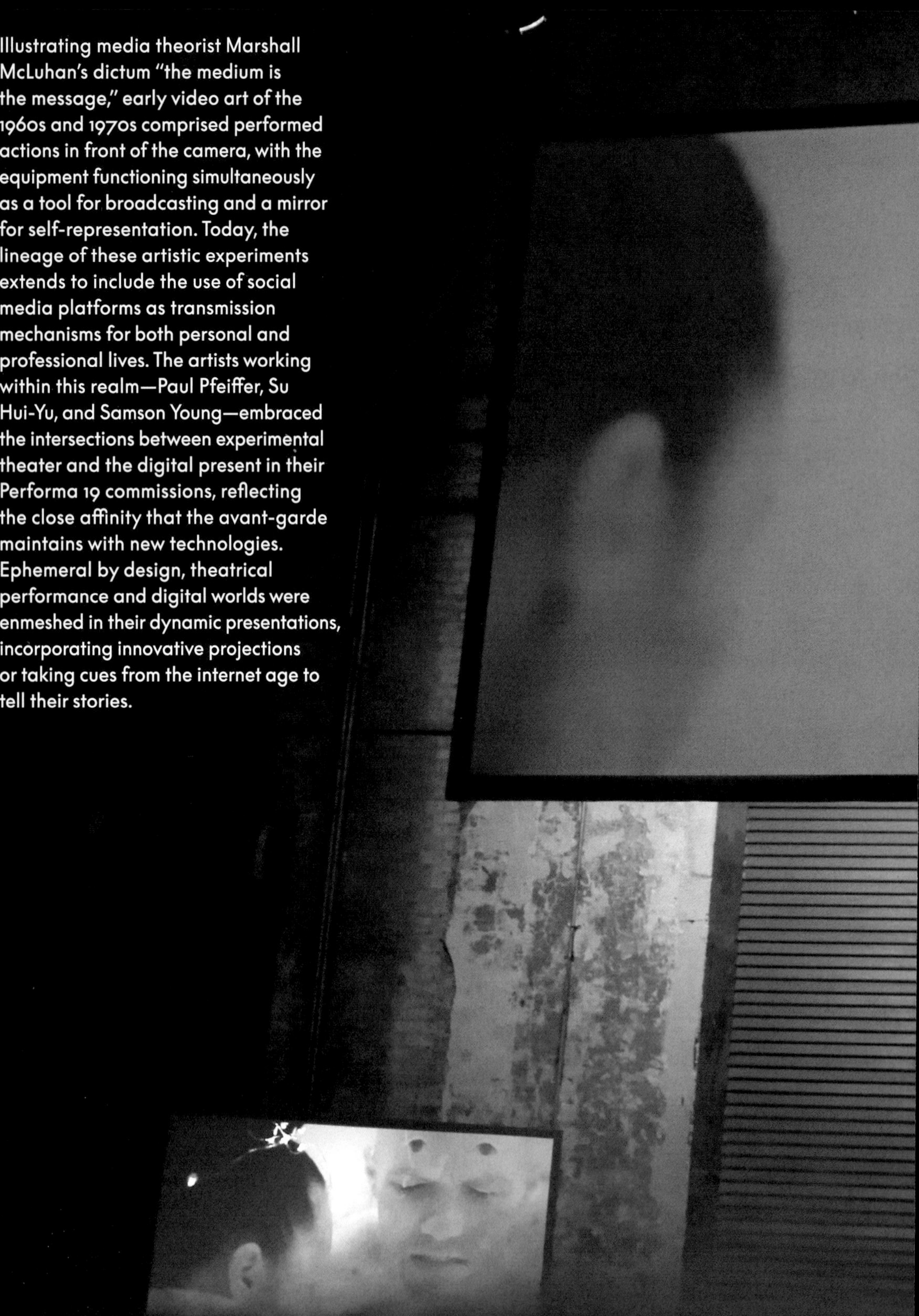

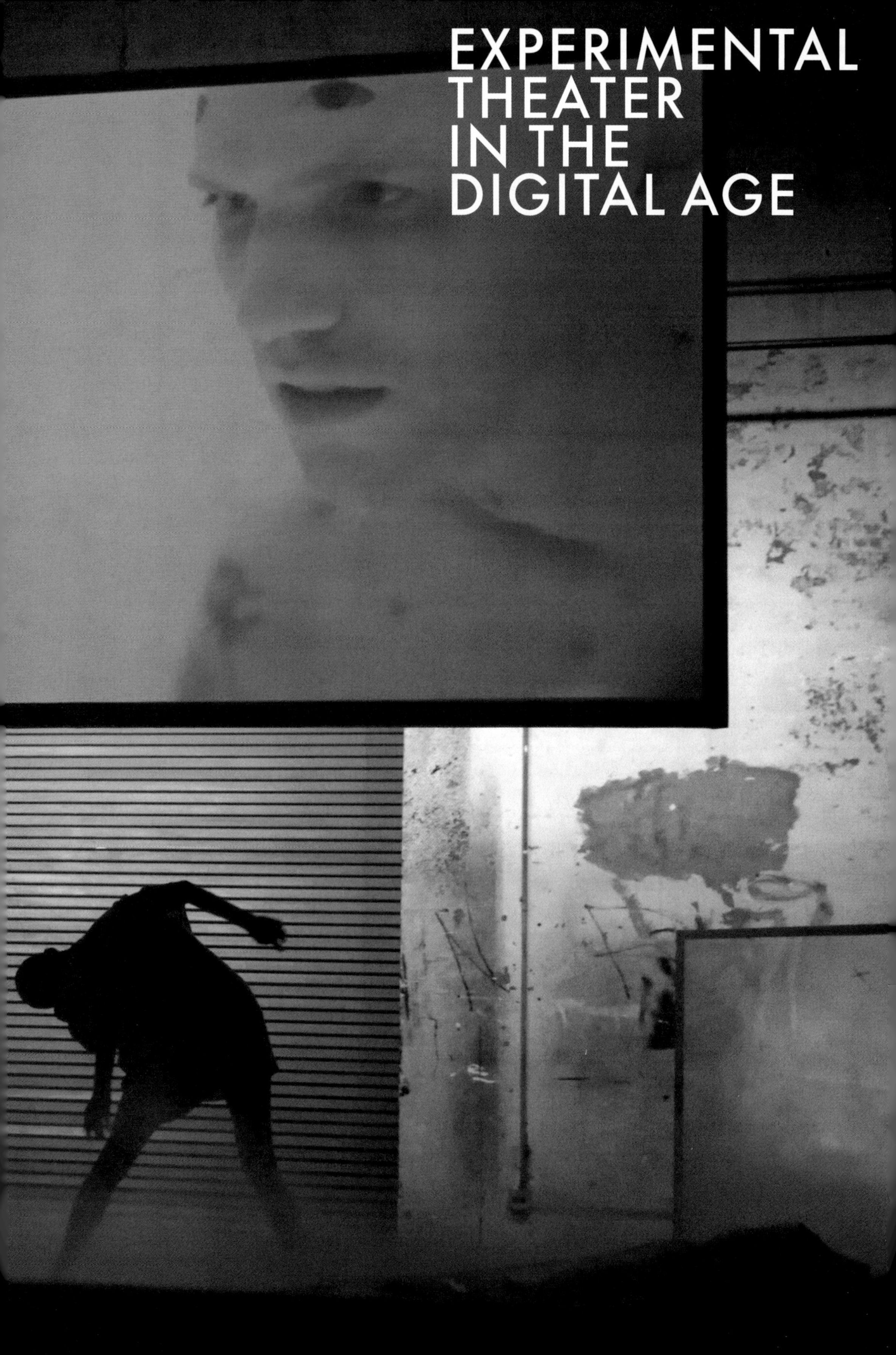
EXPERIMENTAL
THEATER
IN THE
DIGITAL AGE

PAUL PFEIFFER

University of Georgia Redcoat Band Live

Curated by Kathy Noble assisted by Uchenna Itam

Apollo Theater

November 11, 2019

Paul Pfeiffer's first live performance, *University of Georgia Redcoat Band Live*—the first chapter of a two-part Performa Commission titled *Amazing Grace/ RGB*—was presented at The Apollo Theater in Harlem in collaboration with The Georgia Redcoat Marching Band from the University of Georgia. Fifty Redcoat members—who normally perform during breaks in the Georgia Bulldogs' matches—recreated a musical score from a typical American college football game, using both front and back of house of the iconic theater in Harlem, New York. Simultaneously, the rest of the 400-strong ensemble played the exact same musical score inside the empty Sanford Stadium on campus in Athens, Georgia, which was livestreamed into the Apollo; it brought together and contrasted the architectures of stadium and theater.

University of Georgia Redcoat Band Live was the culmination of several years of research and filming undertaken by Pfeiffer during his tenure as the Lamar Dodd Chair of Art at the school from 2016 to 2018. During this time, Pfeiffer focused his cameras on the details and underlying structures of the orchestra's performances, observing the way the band punctuates the game with starts and stops, determined by the pauses in game play and the conductor's cues. Playing hundreds of times each season around the country, the Redcoats are a ritualistic sonic amplifier of crowd affects: The dramatic arcs of the play on the field are fueled by powerful bursts of music, hyping the crowd, heightening its emotional response to the game. In this peculiar, fragmented rhythm, no song is ever completed; the instruments are continually starting, stopping, and starting again, mirroring the action of the competition.

The architecture of the theater and of the stadium originated as sites of public performance and gathering in ancient Greece. Both were designed to house the collective emotional experiences of art, culture, and sport, by releasing the passions of the audiences that filled them, allowing individuals to watch both the action and each other. Today, sports and music are still two of the most popular, and therefore economically rewarding, sites of contemporary culture; as such, they are also some of the most widely broadcast forms of mass-media events. Watching along on our TVs and telephone screens, rather than physically attending, is a dilemma of the digital age: Can the intense experience of assimilating and participating in these social rituals be transmitted through the broadcast mediation of its sounds and images? By divorcing the Redcoats' performance from the hometown crowd of UGA fans, and interweaving live music with live broadcast, the audience's sensory experience was denaturalized

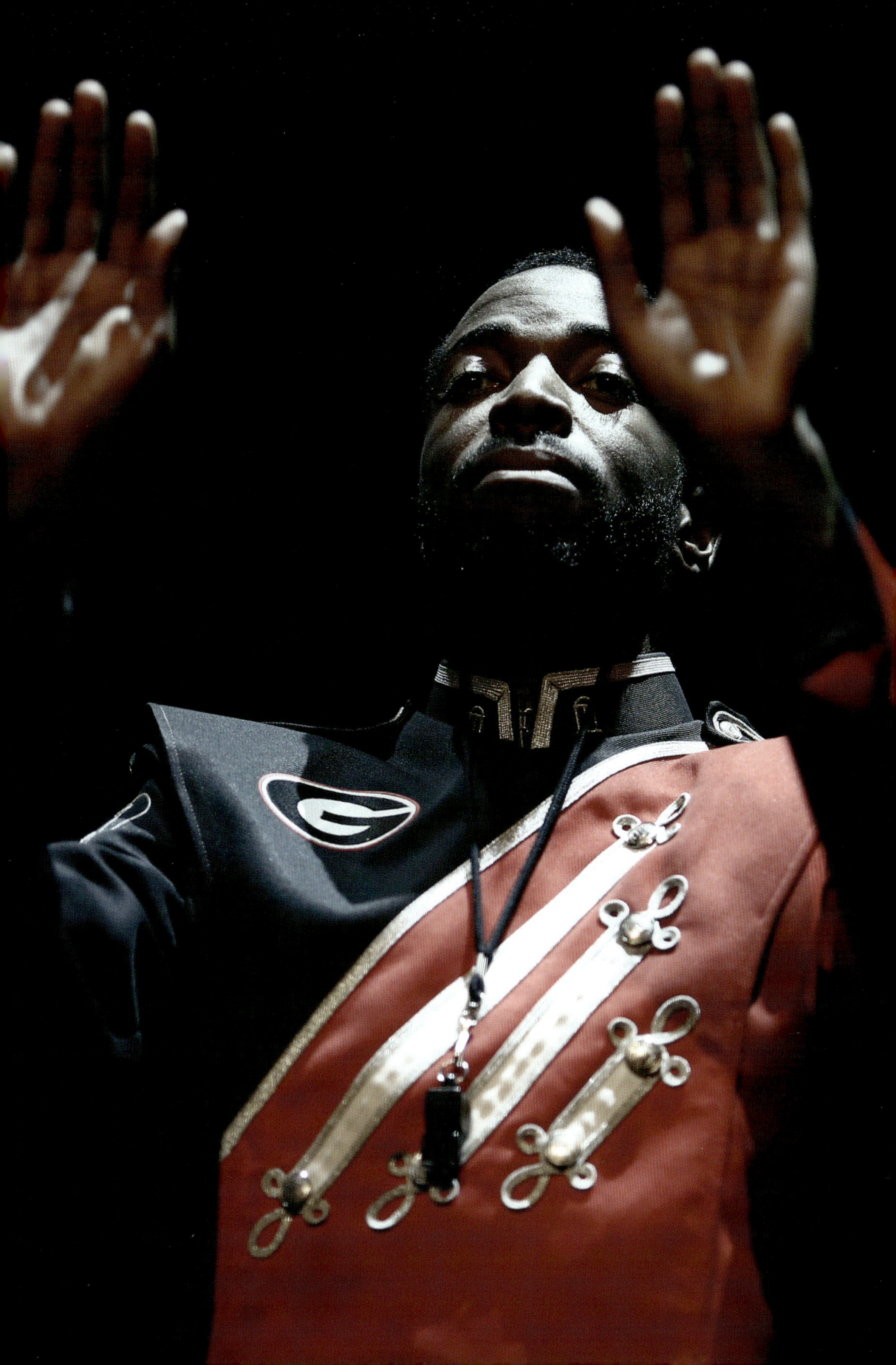

and the focus shifted to the manufacturing of a group identity. Alongside this, by exploring the Redcoats role as the emotional soundtrack to one of America's most popular pastimes, *University of Georgia Redcoat Band Live* considered the affective impact of live music, the constructed nature of collective feedback, and the blurring of mediatized and in-person experience.

This was an extremely ambitious production involving hundreds of people working together to present a technically complex operation performed across two sites—it was both Performa's and Pfeiffer's largest production to date. The production process was an exciting journey that took the artist, musicians, curatorial, production, and university teams into unchartered territory, where we experimented with modes of live theatrical and broadcast performance, alongside audience management and participation. The project tested methods of artistic collaboration with people working outside of the field of visual arts from various different backgrounds, uniting staff from music and sports departments at the University of Georgia.

The commission was also an exercise in the fabrication of group identity that explored the use of music and sport as popular contemporary mechanisms for the production and experience of mass emotion. It became a self-reflective experiment in group-working and collaboration that fundamentally addressed these ideas in its structures and its realization. Producing and staging two simultaneous live performances, in a theater and sports stadium, with 400 performers and a production and front of house team of over 80 people from three institutions—Performa, The University of Georgia, and The Apollo Theater—created a temporary community in which the individuals from each institution, and each group within these institutions, had to temporarily unite to interweave their usual behaviors and actions together, in order to enact Pfeiffer's vision. Yet what became quickly apparent during the process was how modes of behavior and performance, alongside ritualistic and relational acts, are deeply ingrained within groups that work together regularly.

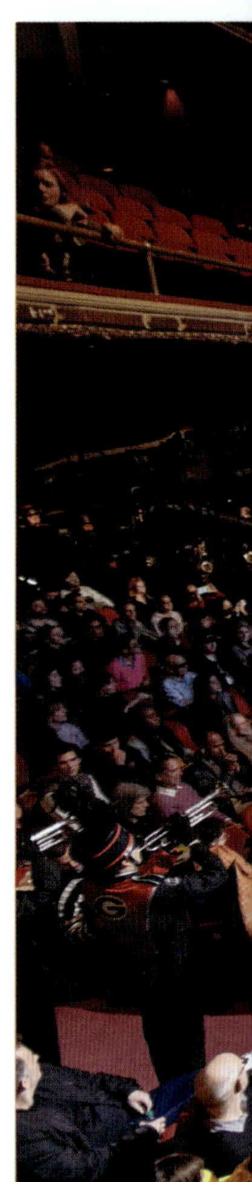

The Redcoat Band have a strict format to their performance: although largely improvised in response to the game, there are numerous rituals and staging methods used by the group that were complicated to transpose to another venue, let alone rework. Pfeiffer's original wish to take the band as a "readymade" entity and present the musical performance of an entire football game in the theatrical setting of the Apollo—and to rethink and deconstruct elements of it, by moving the musicians through the building, fragmenting the band and displacing the audience from their usual seated position—was far more of a challenge than either the band, Pfeiffer, or the Performa team imagined. Rather than following the artist's scripted instructions, the performance became entirely collaborative in every aspect, from artistic musical decisions to technical and relational necessities. The band responded to the site (which they visited for the first time on the day of) and Director Dr. Brett Bawcum and Associate Director Rob Akridge responded to Pfeiffer's wishes with their own understanding of what was acoustically possible. Alongside this, the technical requirements to stage dual simultaneous performances—and for both band directors to work simultaneously from the same score in two sites using livestream—were far more complex than anyone originally imagined.

As such, every single person involved became part of the final performance—the artist, curator, producers, operations crews, two band directors, 400 musicians,

Apollo theater ushers, front of house and operations staff— became one, creating an intensely moving, wildly joyful and affecting, politically and socially complicated work in which nothing was concealed. The back of house became the stage; the complex—and sometimes failing—technical process was on view for everyone to see; the ushers held up signs to get the crowds moving; the live musicians improvised their response to the scene that unfolded in the theater, as their streamed counterparts played on, unaware of the deconstructed reality of the Apollo performance. KATHY NOBLE

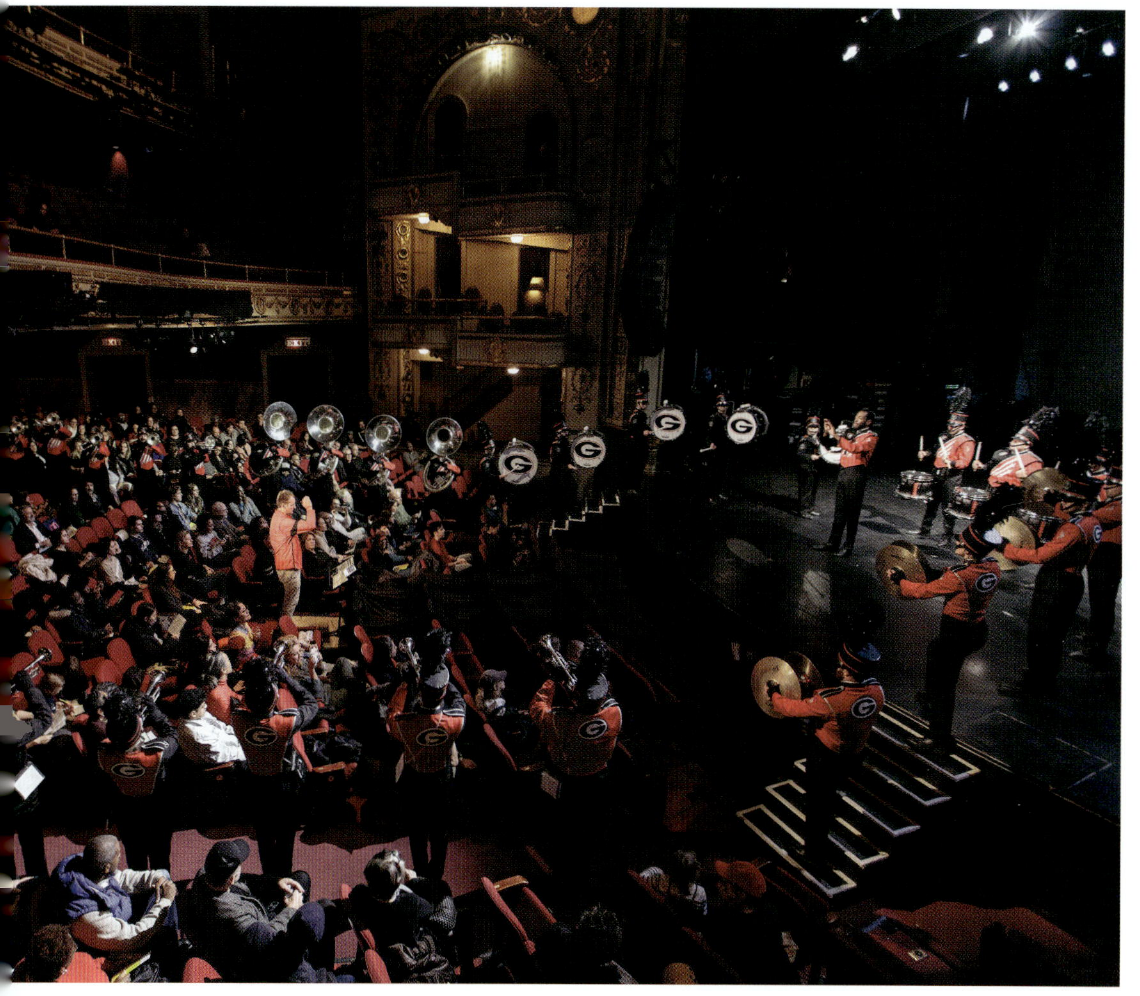

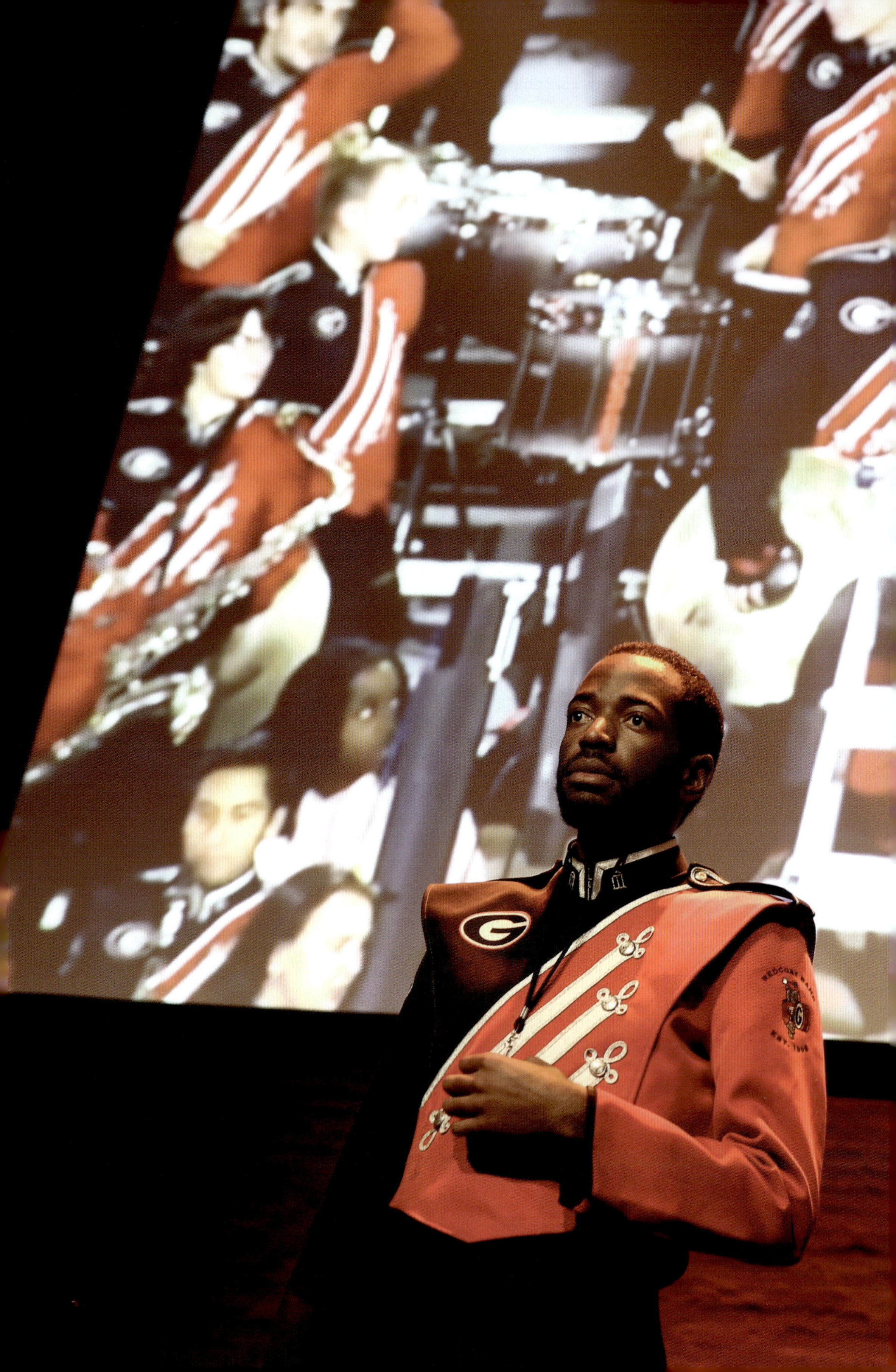
G

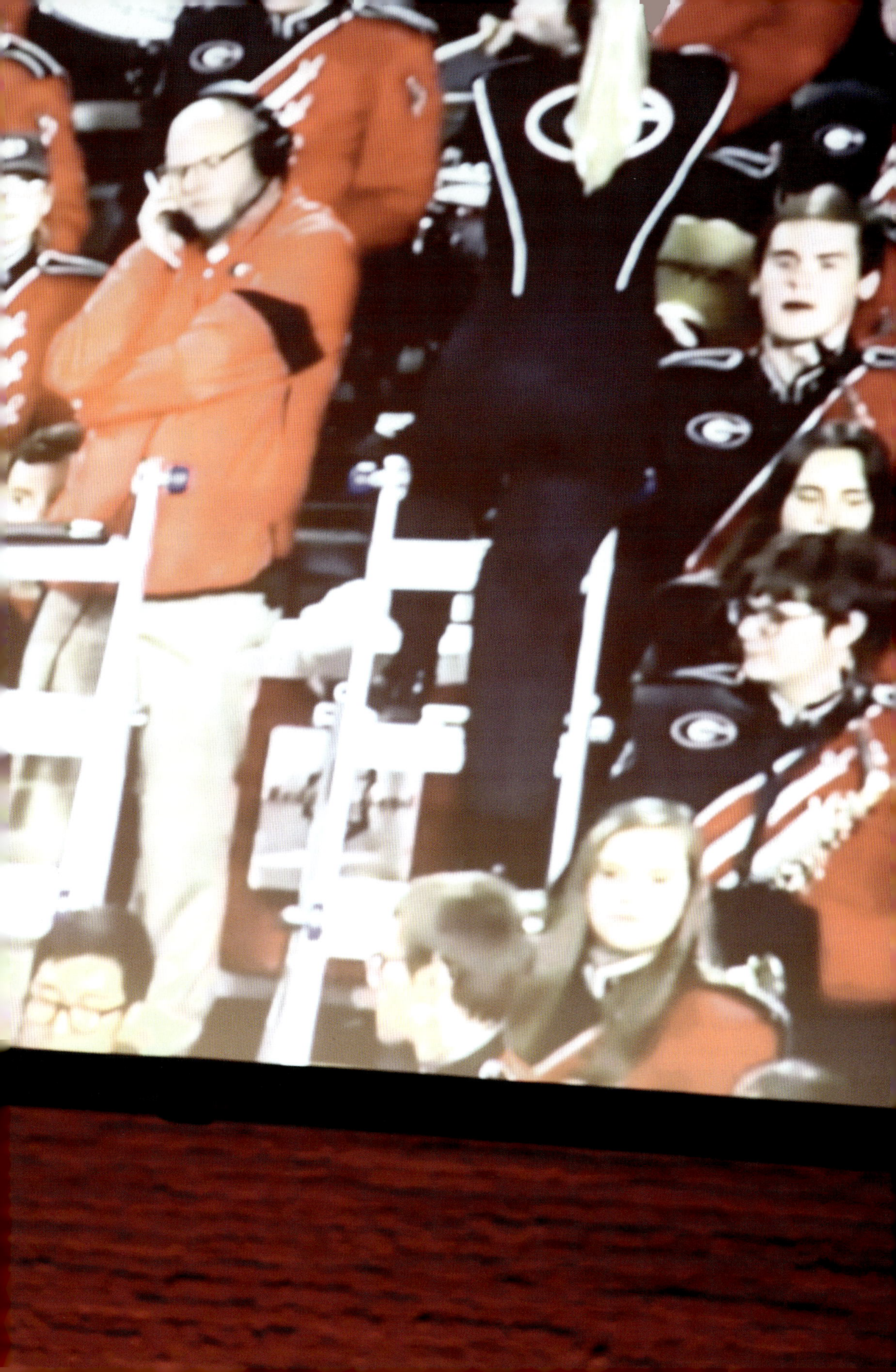

Get your rah-rahs out: Paul Pfeiffer marches to a political tune at the Apollo

What's more American than baseball and apple pie? Football, that's what.

This is not the game known as football everywhere else in the world, called soccer in the U.S. Every high school and college student in the fifty states grows up with this aggressive sport, where male athletes in crash helmets and bulging, protective padding compete for control of a pigskin ball in stadiums roaring with partisan spectators.

As public spectacle, it is a defiant, ritually enforced expression of fealty to both God and country. At college games, spectators are subject to emphatic cheerleading and the patriotic music of a disciplined marching band, making their response to the action on the field less spontaneous than calculated and undemocratic.

This irony was the heart and soul of Paul Pfeiffer's collaboration with the University of Georgia's Redcoat Marching Band, a commission for the Performa 19 Biennial in New York. Like the game itself, it was a troubling experience that was also somehow liberating and joyful.

The date for this one-night-only event was as significant as the location: November 11, Veteran's Day, at an historic African American music venue, the Apollo Theater in Harlem. It didn't take anyone present long to note that white faces far outnumbered Black, both in the audience, on the home team (seen on video), and in the uniformed band, which is 400 players strong. Their job is to play music that will keep up the energy and induce a frenzy in the stadium crowd during the frequent lulls in the action. "It's a 60-minute game played over two hours," noted the Art Basel director Marc Spiegler, one of a number of art-world figures present.

Fifty uniformed band members played live at the Apollo, drawing from a repertoire of patriotic and spiritual tunes that included the national anthem, the college's theme song, and a repeated Battle Hymn of the Republic.

The drum corps that began the show took the stage while the blaring horn sections filled the aisles. (Thankfully, provided earplugs were not needed.) Though directed by a conductor, the pace of the performance actually was set by the other 350 musicians, livestreamed to a projection screen above the stage from their school's empty stadium in Athens, Georgia. Their conductor timed each musical intrusion to a recently recorded game that she watched on a video monitor barely visible to the audience.

Sometimes, the audience heard the live music or the ambient sounds of an actual game; at other times Pfeiffer took out the sound to produce a silence filled by the band in the theater.

This text was initially published online by The Art Newspaper *on November 19, 2019. Reprinted courtesy the author and* The Art Newspaper*.*

As the concert progressed, the musicians moved backstage, to the dressing rooms, the green room, the lobby, and the balconies. Ushers carrying placards that read "FOLLOW," "STAND," or "MOVE" encouraged the audience to explore these usually off-limit spaces, as well as the stage. I have to admit that standing where so many music legends have played was a special and unexpected thrill. But it made me queasy to see many in the audience stand, unbidden, for the Star-Spangled Banner, when no game was actually being played. I'm as American as they come, but I have never understood all the flag-waving at domestic sports events, especially when attacks on this country since 9/11 have come mostly from within.

"They totally flipped the script on me!" Pfeiffer exclaimed, during a reception at Red Rooster that followed the show. The band, he said, was supposed to play the anthem outside the theater and then march into the aisles to begin the "game," which played to the imagination as the Redcoats stuck to their own, internal plan. They left out the Confederate song "Dixie," banned since 1971 (when the word was also dropped from the marching band's name), as well as the theme from *Gone with the Wind*, their usual finale, deemed inappropriate for the Apollo, Pfeiffer said.

At the same time, the tug of war that Pfeiffer set in motion—between commanded and elected movement, the freely vocal and the forcibly silenced, patriotic fervor and propaganda, the virtual and the actual—made a powerful and inescapable metaphor for the destabilizing forces at work in the country today. It also underscored historic and ongoing differences between north and south, and emphasized the control various media exercise over society as a whole.

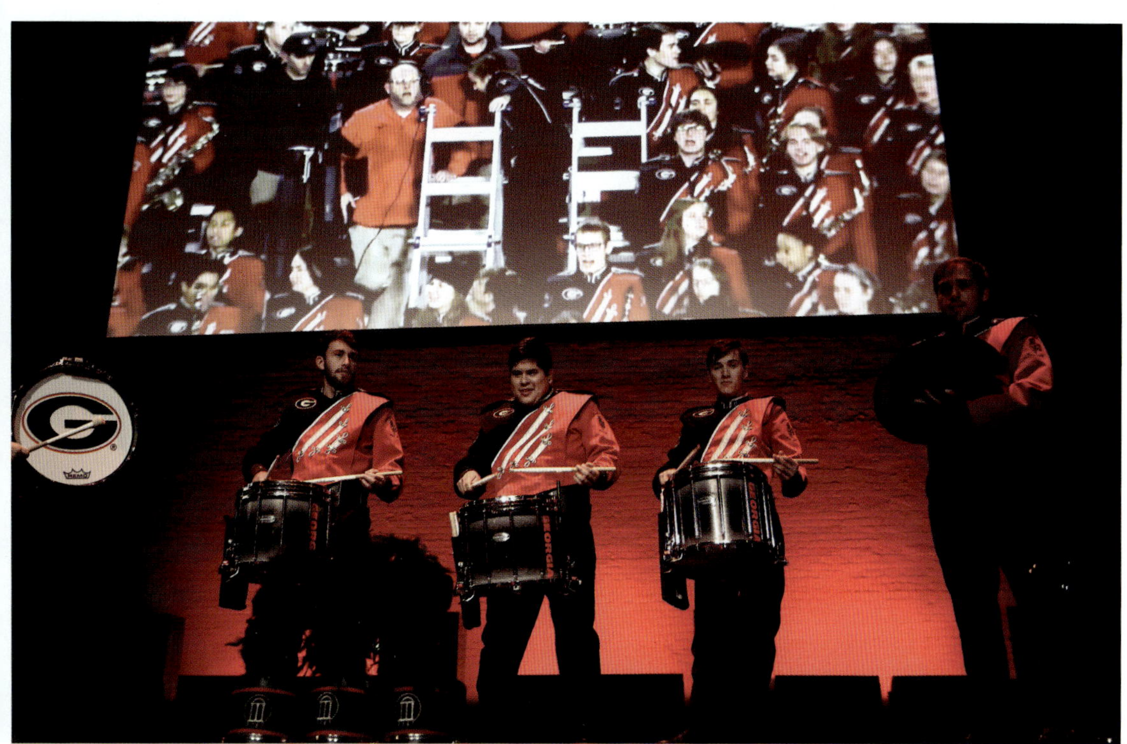

In other words, it wasn't just about a game. Politics and poetry were on the docket.

At the halftime point, I spotted Matthew Barney seated at the rear of the theater. Because Barney has wrested visceral metaphors from football training methods and shot the first of his *Cremaster* films in a stadium, I was curious to know what he made of Pfeiffer's show. "I love it!" he said, with unqualified enthusiasm. "And it keeps getting stronger."

That was true. It did, culminating in a choreographed rendition of the Battle Hymn of the Republic that featured a chorus line of supercharged bowing by band members, who suggested mechanized toy soldiers at a religious revival.

"The issues Paul deals with are so *disturbing*," said Paula Cooper, Pfeiffer's longtime dealer and the reception's host. "His work is deeply philosophical and troubling, but this was brilliant. Just brilliant."

Pfeiffer is well known for his manipulations of broadcast videos from professional basketball games and other sports, for which he employs sophisticated editing and selective erasures to point up social inequities that such spectacles mask. The performance, his first live work, was developed during a two-year visiting professorship at the University of Georgia in Athens, and will result in a new video installation.

"I loved every minute," said Jack Pierson, another artist at the performance, which also attracted such disparate sensibilities as David Byrne, Ingar Dragset, Josh Kline, Lucy Raven, the Whitney Museum curators Donna DeSalvo and Adrienne Edwards, the incoming Tate Modern curator Polly Staple, and the independent curators Defne Ayas and Linda Norden.

"Best Performa ever!" exclaimed the dealer Jeanne Greenberg Rohatyn, a board member of the organization. But, as RoseLee Goldberg, Performa's founder, told me, "We just did our usual thing." LINDA YABLONSKY

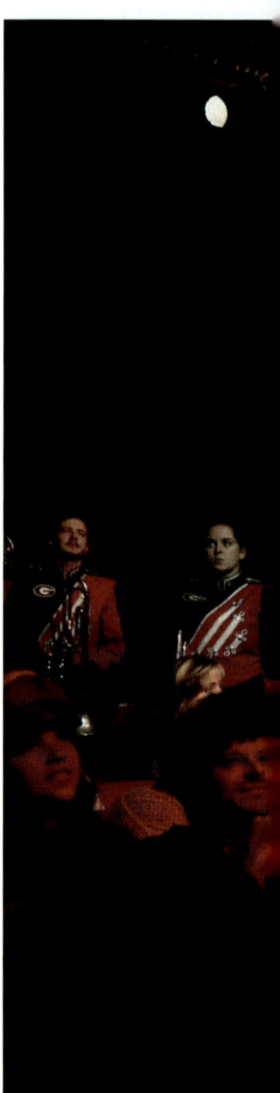

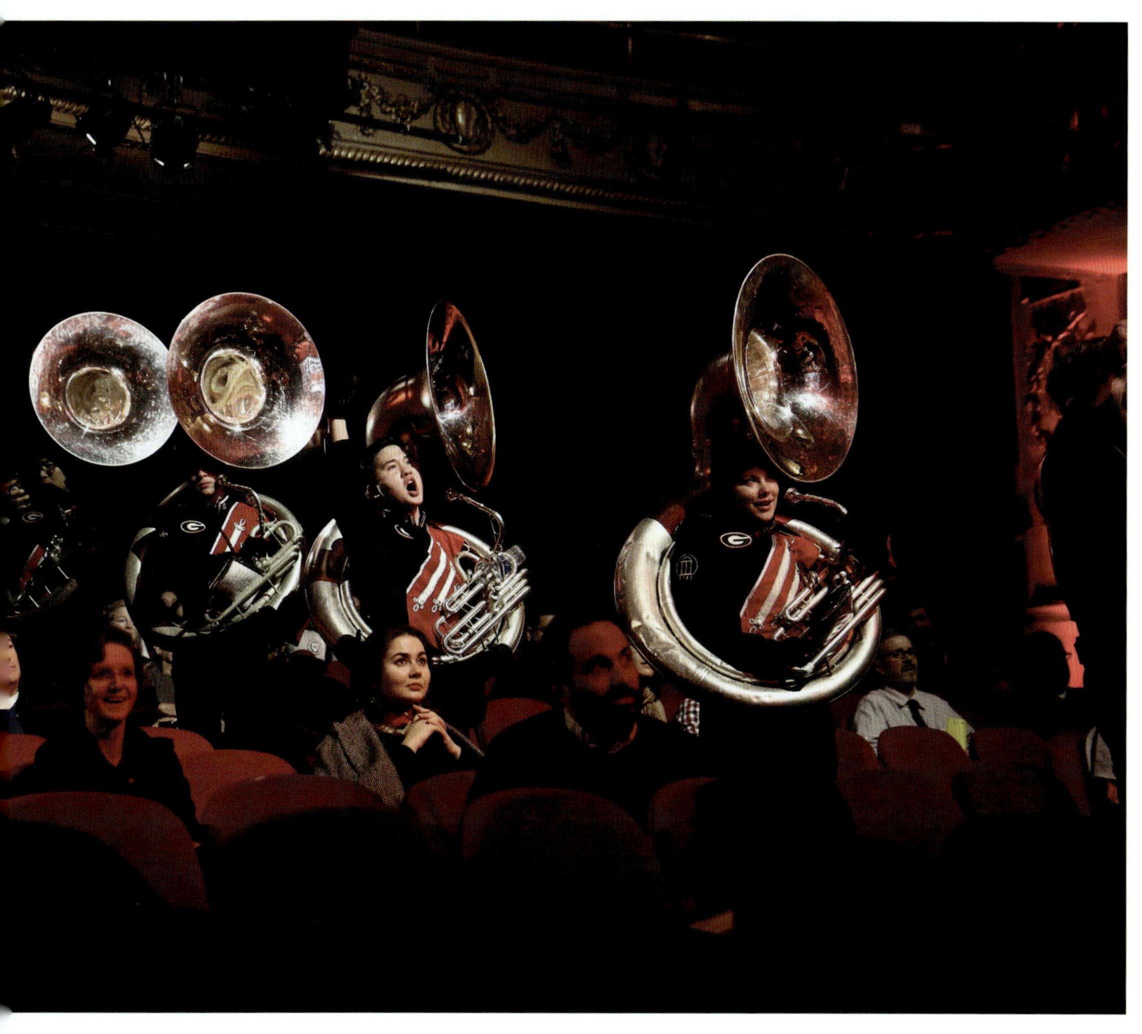

SU HUI-YU *The White Waters*

Organized by Maaike Gouwenberg

Abrons Arts Center

November 15–16, 2019

It began as many stories do: slowly and quietly. Taiwanese artist Su Hui-Yu's meditative performance reimagined the Legend of the White Snake, a fable which dates back to the Ming Dynasty (1368–1644). As one of the four great folktales of classic Chinese mythology, the story is a familiar one: An ancient spirit, Lady White Snake, is transformed into a beautiful woman. She falls in love with a mortal man and finds an enemy in a zealous monk who opposes their trans-spiritual union. In more recent history, the narrative has taken on new resonance as a metaphor for repressed or persecuted desires. In 1993, in the midst of the AIDS crisis, Taiwanese theater director Tian Qiyuan (1964–96) reimagined the legend in an all-male adaptation. Titled *White Water*, the work touched on themes of violence and intimacy within the Taiwanese queer community. It called into question the collective pressure often imposed on individuals and their privacy, as Tian himself was outed as HIV positive against his will while enrolled at the National Taiwan Normal University in Taipei.

With *The White Waters,* Su Hui-Yu paid homage to Tian's precedent. Onstage, Su juxtaposed his signature minimal futurist aesthetics with the traditional theater setting of Abrons's playhouse, pairing a multichannel video installation on moveable screens with live dance. It began with a lone performer sitting under a spotlight near center stage, surrounded by a sea of smoke. She wore a translucent smock over a white gown, her head shaved close to the scalp. Her body and behavior were hard to decipher. She conveyed multiple layers of ambiguity and concealment—of gender and illness—and resembled both an ethereal being and a patient in need of care.

Atmospheric music was offset by pounding drums as two additional characters appeared onscreen behind the lead. Like Tian's *White Water*, Su's video component focused on two oppositional figures: Lady White Snake and the monk, Fa Hai. Each looked otherworldly, draped in pristine white clothing. The monk wore a string of pearls and two additional sets of eyes painted on his forehead, while Lady White Snake, in a long dress and with an exaggerated beehive hairstyle, was covered in bright lights. The screens on which they appeared shifted throughout the performance, either descending from above the stage or manipulated by the dancer. A different color of light tinted each sequence of the performance, corresponding in mood to the onscreen narrative. A warm, pale pink washed over Lady White Snake and Fa Hai as they were first introduced; the delicate color was then supplanted by a deep crimson horizon, reflecting the imminent conflict and underlying fear between the new acquaintances. As they navigated this encounter, onscreen images of Lady White Snake and Fa Hai started to break up and duplicate until they were nearly unrecognizable. Blue then washed over them, and the monk slowly fell to the ground as if injured by Lady White Snake's penetrating gaze.

All along, the onstage dancer channeled this celestial encounter, where each progression saw a new layer of emotion unfolding. The dancer responded to each sequence with both grace and self-inflicted violence. She reconfigured the screens while jerking and convulsing, flagellating herself in a manner that seemed both disciplinary and sexual. In the end, Lady White Snake and the monk merged into a singular body onscreen. A horizon of yellow light enveloped the stage as an elegiac score played. The dancer collapsed to the floor, gently writhing alongside her counterparts.

Through moments of apprehension, revulsion, attraction, and empathy, a delicate balance was eventually struck between the dancer, the monk, and Lady White Snake. Their solemn acceptance of one another produced a peculiar catharsis, an emotional reckoning that ended by coming to terms with interpersonal trauma. In evoking Tian's life and work as an HIV-positive artist and a queer person of color, Su offered a nuanced portrayal of stigmatized existence. *The White Waters* meditated on the violence of repression, and what it could mean to live free from assumption, denial, and erasure. RE'AL CHRISTIAN

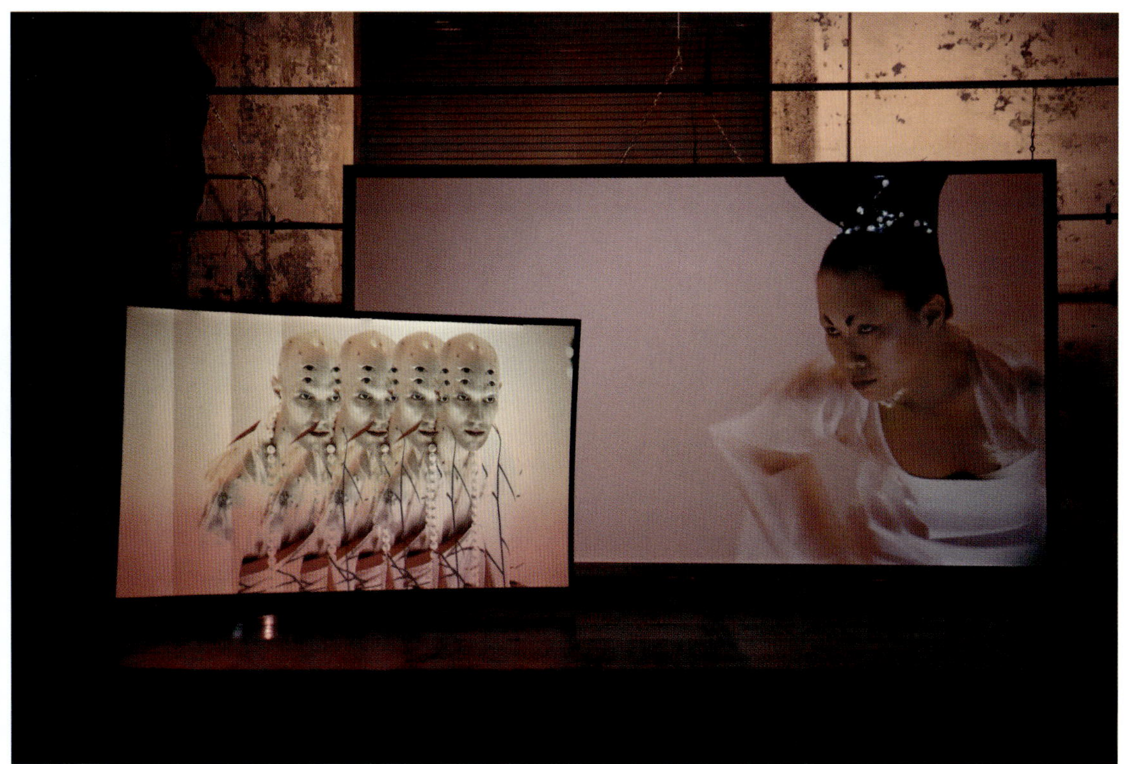

SAMSON YOUNG
The Immortals

Curated by RoseLee Goldberg and Kathy Noble

Castle Williams, Governors Island

November 2, 2019

Hong Kong artist and composer Samson Young created a contemporary interpretation of the popular Chinese folkloric myth *The Eight Immortals*—a centuries-old legend that has numerous iterations in Chinese mythology and culture, ranging from opera to children's cartoons. This popular fairy tale recounts the story of eight deities, each with their own special power represented by a magical tool (a fan, a flower basket, a sword), as they cross the ocean from an island in the Bohai Sea to attend the birthday banquet of a higher deity, the Queen Mother, in mainland China. New York-based experimental guitar quartet DITHER, Cantonese opera singer Eliza Li, and German jazz vocalist Michael Schiefel played the lead characters, performing music and lyrics composed and written by Young. Set up at Castle Williams on Governors Island, a twenty-minute boat ride from Manhattan, they were accompanied by other protagonists moving on cranes and interacting with digital animations projected onto the fortification's circular walls. The cranes—giant locomotives to power the Immortals across the sea—slowly rotated through the space creating a mechanical ballet, while also forming a ambulatory sound system that fragmented the music's journey throughout the sandstone architecture.

These figures, revered by Taoists and considered signs of prosperity and longevity, have appeared in different guises in Chinese art and popular culture since the Yuan dynasty in the thirteenth century. Historically, wealthy families would hire Cantonese opera troupes to perform at private celebrations, a tradition that continues today in mainland China and in Hong Kong, where Young was born and still lives. During these public performances the narrative of the opera is over-simplified—the eight characters appear and introduce themselves with their magical weapons and celebrate the birthday of the honoree. For Young, the higher deity of the Queen Mother symbolizes a grand patron of the arts, and he equates the singing troupe that performs at these private parties to the "artist for hire," existing to entertain the privileged. Cantonese opera, however, has traditionally been a cultural repository for the icons of defiance and revolution: The sword, for instance, symbolizes the passage to a new world and is often accompanied by destruction. Through the lens of these contrasting positions, Young repurposed *The Eight Immortals* as an allegory that offered a latent critique of the institutions and systems of contemporary artistic and cultural production in late capitalist societies.

In Young's own lyrics, the fortune teller He Xiangu presented the artist as soothsayer: a psychic being, a human whose prophecies occur either too early or too late, but never on time—misunderstood while alive, only to be comprehended much later on, when the urgency of their message has passed, exalted when no longer relevant. Young's *Immortals* commented on the schizophrenic role of artists in society today, positioning them as people who see and hear things inaccessible to others, as individuals whose role is to fracture and disrupt the systems of power. Each of the *Immortals* was an oracle, and an outcast, a speaker of truth to power, a deity who could ride a gigantic legendary animal through the air, one that elevated them to great heights and then lowered them to the ground to meet the audience on their own terms.

Taking shape through sound sketches and audio recordings, Young's music encompassed diverse sources, including the avant-garde compositional traditions of aleatory, or chance, music; *musique concrète*; and graphic notation. For his *Immortals*, the artist accumulated references—materials and images, from Chinese and Western histories of art, literature, music, culture, and politics—that created a collage of symbols and a constellation of ideas, that offered Young's own alternative system. KATHY NOBLE

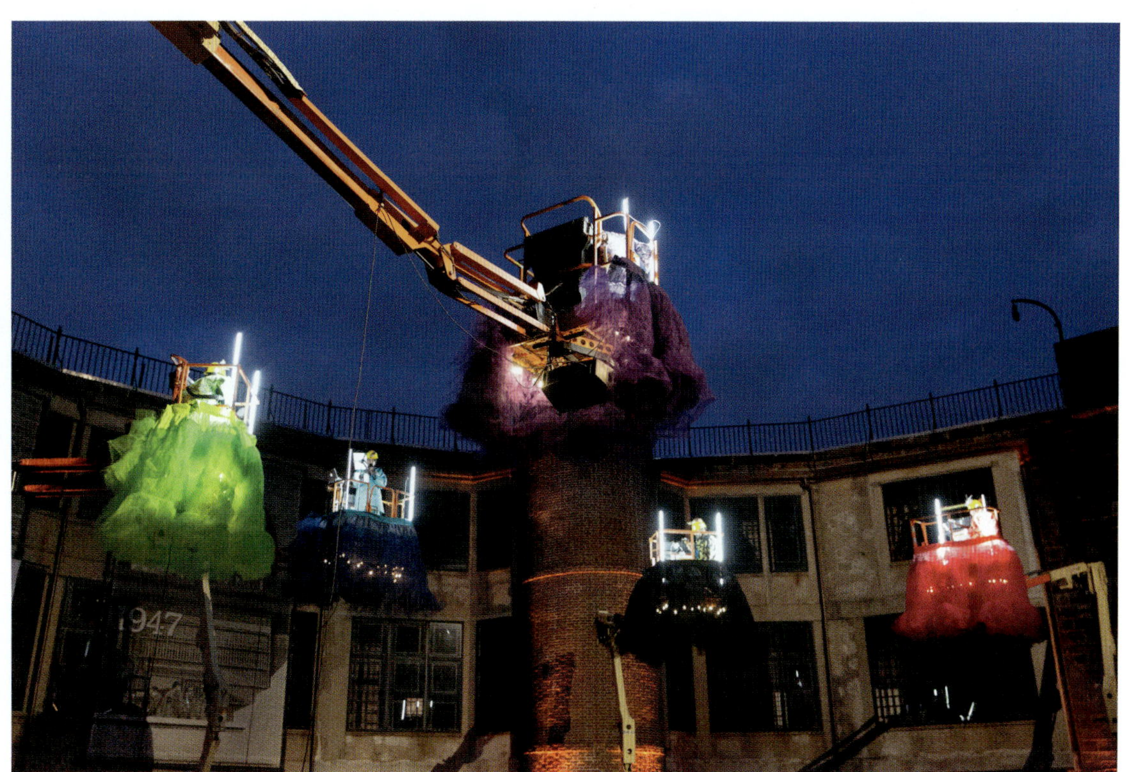

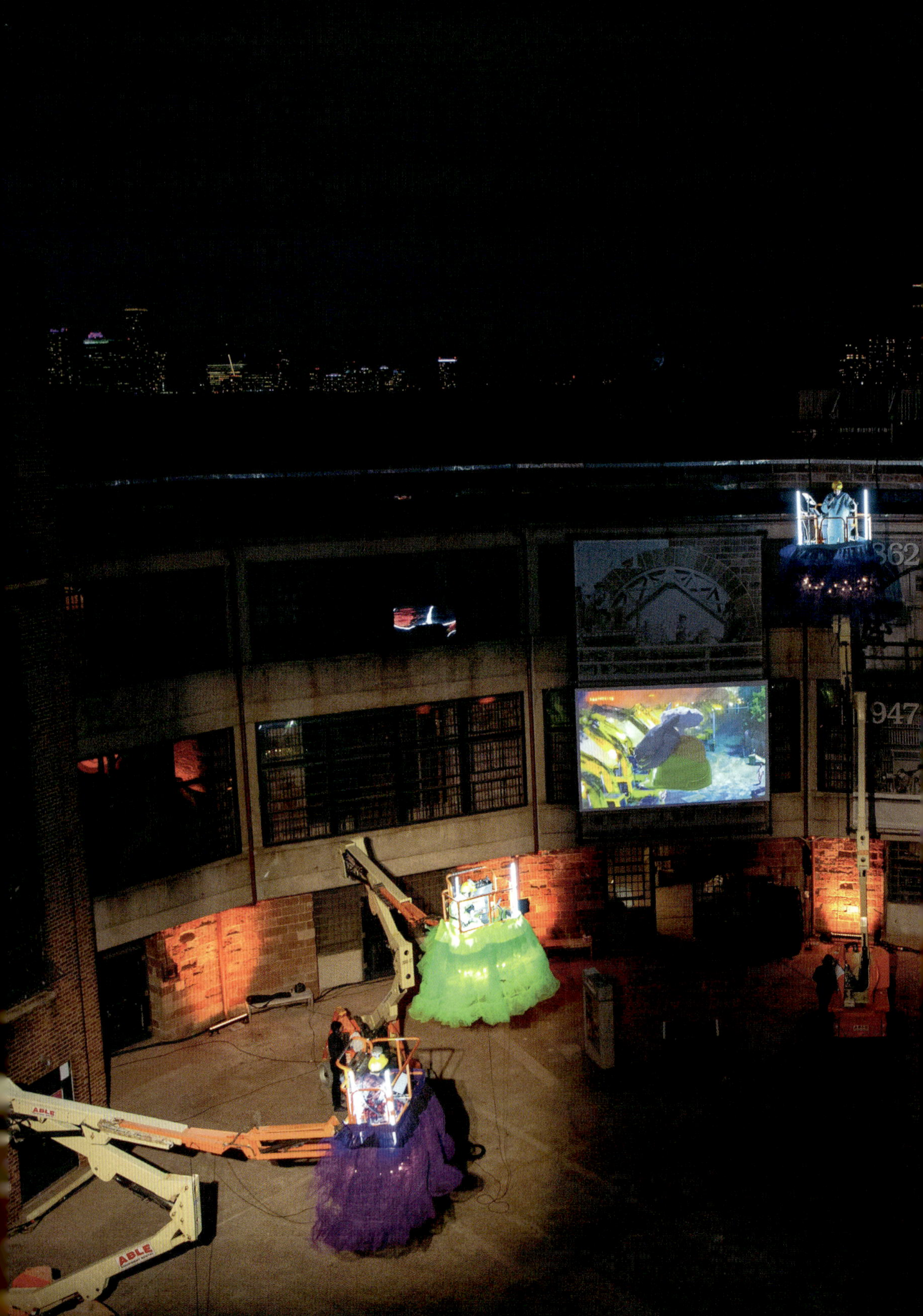
ABLE
ABLE

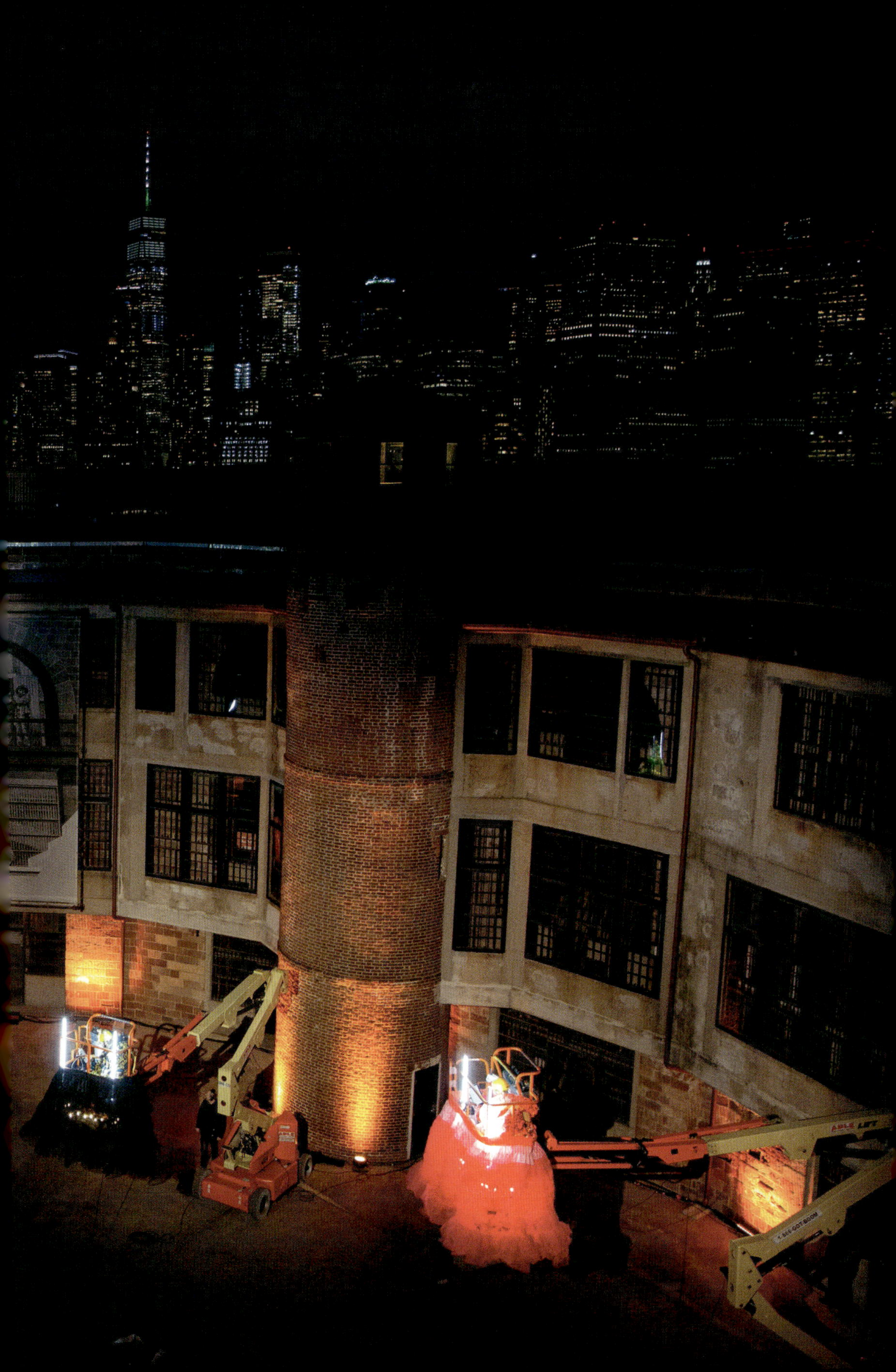
ABLE LIFT

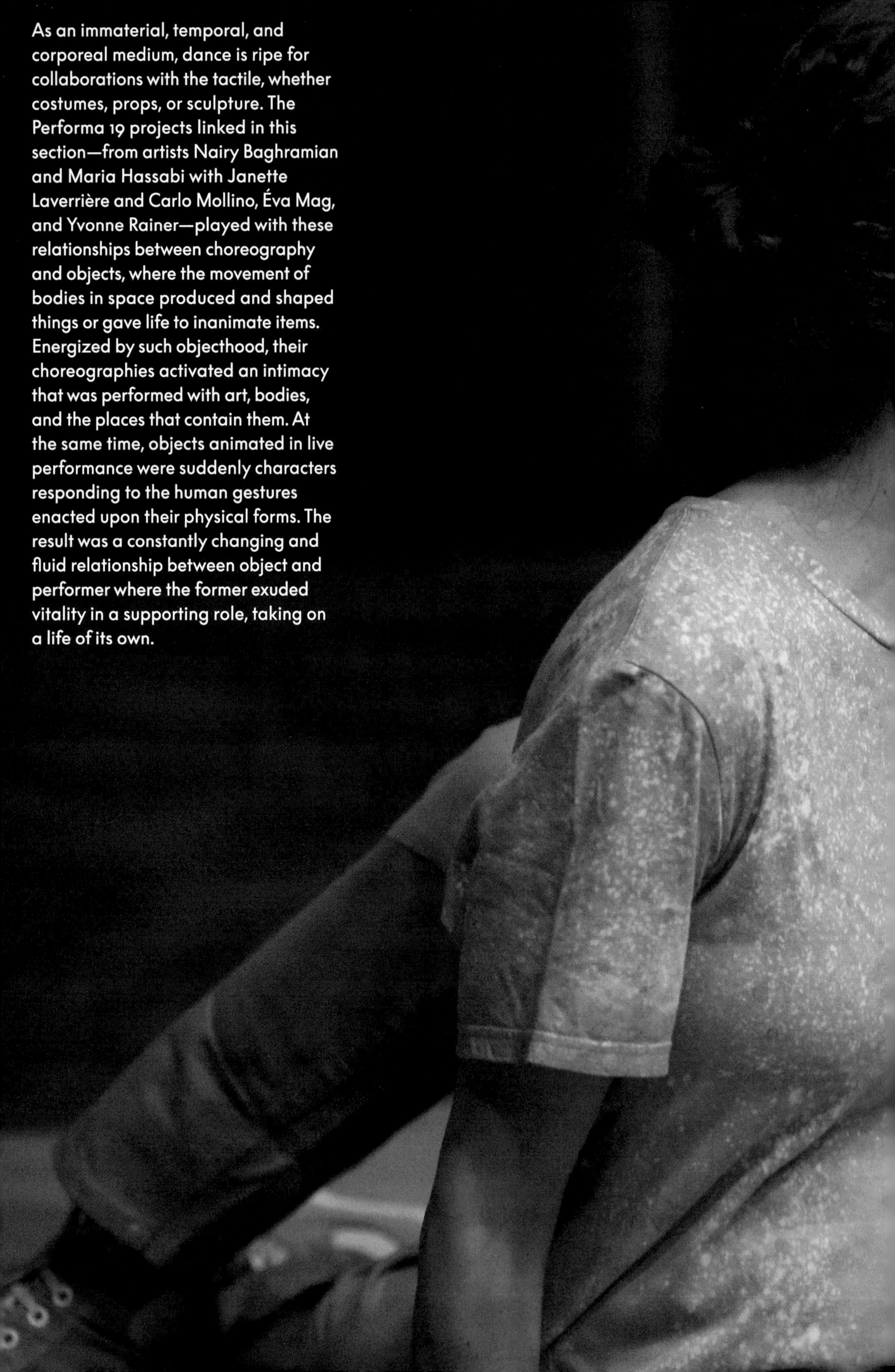

As an immaterial, temporal, and corporeal medium, dance is ripe for collaborations with the tactile, whether costumes, props, or sculpture. The Performa 19 projects linked in this section—from artists Nairy Baghramian and Maria Hassabi with Janette Laverrière and Carlo Mollino, Éva Mag, and Yvonne Rainer—played with these relationships between choreography and objects, where the movement of bodies in space produced and shaped things or gave life to inanimate items. Energized by such objecthood, their choreographies activated an intimacy that was performed with art, bodies, and the places that contain them. At the same time, objects animated in live performance were suddenly characters responding to the human gestures enacted upon their physical forms. The result was a constantly changing and fluid relationship between object and performer where the former exuded vitality in a supporting role, taking on a life of its own.

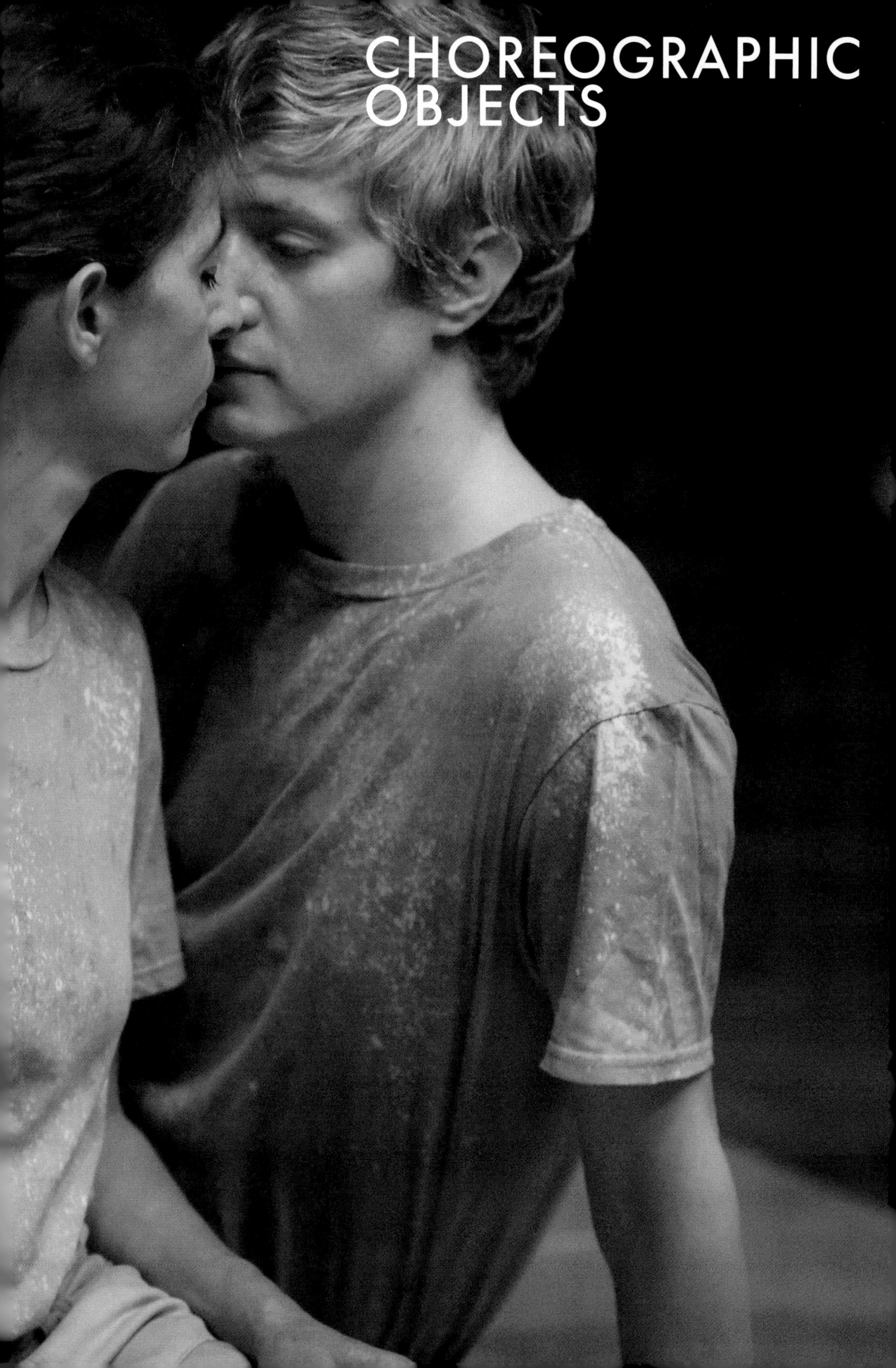
CHOREOGRAPHIC
OBJECTS

ÉVA MAG

DEAD MATTER MOVES

Curated by Kathy Noble with Uchenna Itam, in collaboration with Yuvinka Medina

The gym at Judson Memorial Church

November 19–24, 2019

This text is an abridged version of the essay "Learning to Stand Up" by Kathy Noble, initially published in Éva Mag: There Is a Plan for This *(Bonniers Konsthall, Stockholm, 2020). Reprinted courtesy the author and Bonniers Konsthall.*

Éva Mag's work changed radically after the birth of her second child. Her experience of retaining an intimate sexual relationship with her husband during the nursing period transformed the way she viewed the function of her body and its role and relationship to other bodies: Hers did not exist autonomously, it was physically interconnected to other bodies that needed one another to survive. This experience inspired a desire to work with raw clay—a malleable, yet densely heavy material—in order to consider how we "stand up." After several sculptural and performance experiments using rudimentary body-like clay forms, Mag understood that these figures would never stand up alone, as they had no skeleton nor armature inside to hold them up. As such, the Romanian-born Swedish artist began to make life-size, hand-sewn, multicolored costumes, which she stuffed with clay. These form textile "skins" enabled her to move the "bodies" more easily—dragging, manipulating, carrying them, and hoisting the heavy, awkward forms into the air, in a laborious exercise of contact improvisation dance with an entirely dead weight.

DEAD MATTERS MOVES is the title of Éva Mag's Performa 19 Commission which took place in the storied basement gym of the Judson Memorial Church, in New York's Greenwich Village. Mag envisioned what she originally described as a factory for the production of clay bodies, to create a space in which to test the question of how we, as humans, "stand up," both psychologically and physically, by working with a group of ten performers to create ten clay bodies. The performance began simply when the performers arrived and dressed in uniforms designed and made by Mag from simple cloth. When the two tons of dry clay were delivered on the sidewalk outside the church, the ten performers—who had never worked together before—formed a bucket line to transport the material inside. The clay was passed along in buckets, down the stairs, and along the corridor, eventually arriving in the gym, where it was dumped into large sacks. This hard, physical, collaborative exertion set the tone for the week. Over the course of six days, the performers followed Mag's instructions—beginning with adding water to the clay and mixing it—to fill their working days from 11am and 6pm.

The first time I walked into the gym, the smell of wet clay made me leave; it was a hot, intense, dirty situation. When I returned, the performers were mostly sitting or crouching down on the floor, working with the clay. The scene struck me as a kind of perverse, underground factory where humans massaged, caressed, and cared for inanimate objects for an hourly wage. The crude limbs were crafted from clay and then stuffed into their "skins"—colored textile suits sewn by Mag. The artist asked the performers to "charge" the skins, in order to imbue them with some kind of life, or emotion, before they were filled with the clay. Throughout the week the performers met each morning with Mag—prior to the public opening—to discuss the previous day, and to decide the routine and tasks for that day.

What unfolded in the space was existential. Firstly the process asked a great deal from the participants, both psychologically and physically. Their days were filled with relentless repetition, as they undertook the same tasks over and over again. For the most part, they were also learning something new: how to sculpt and maneuver extremely heavy wet clay. For some, tasks were drawn out over hours. Others completed them immediately and moved through fast cycles, finding inventive ways to spend their time, such as hanging in the material hammocks suspended from the ceiling—originally made to hang the clay bodies—dancing, chipping clay from the floor, or cleaning up. This was survival: In order to make it through the week, the performers had to make tiny decisions about their activities, in order to endure their time in the gym. The space, the clay, the bodies, the people, and the tasks were in a constant state of flux, as energies, moods, and physical capacities ebbed and flowed through the group as they enacted a form of labor. All tasks were equally important—cleaning, sewing, sculpting, carrying, stuffing—as one needed the other to continue the cycle. At times, as they expressed in our daily meetings, performers felt a sense of futility, some were consumed with anger, others became extremely emotional. Yet after it finished, each of them described having their expectations confounded, experiencing a form of transcendence through the process.

The structures and system Mag envisioned for her ten performers, or "workers," created a container for an array of behaviors and emotions, a micro social system in which the clay bodies became stand-ins—these objects absorbed, carried, and transmitted the emotions of their makers. In a conversation held on the final day of the project, the performers described how their relationships with the objects, with Mag, and with each other developed and evolved. As one of the performers stated: "I think I expected it to feel more anthropomorphic than it did. I expected to feel more empathy with the figure. We were not prepared for the full extent of the weight that these skins could hold. I felt we became desperate at times in trying to move them. Amidst that desperation, it became acceptable to destroy them... Of course, we all have some destructive impulses. But I think I ended up enacting violence on the figure through a frustration, or desperation, to move the thing that was so against being moved through the weight of its materiality." Another spoke at the performers' discussion about the idea of the "factory," and how people behave in a group, how emotions ran between them, invisibly, while they managed their own needs and attempted to stay in the moment. All the performers felt that rather than focusing on the relationship to their inanimate clay body, the labor forced them to focus on their selves, their mood, their feelings, their state of being, in order to carry on working. At times they enacted violence, smashing sculptures, beating the clay with a shovel, throwing it around and creating eruptions of more threatening energy within the room.

In psychoanalytic theory the concept of *transference*—originally developed by Sigmund Freud—is considered by many psychotherapists and analysts as essential to the therapeutic process, a key part of the psychological transformation that, with the right therapeutic relationship, can occur. During transference, the patient projects their unconscious feelings for others—often for their parents, or other formative emotional relationships from childhood—

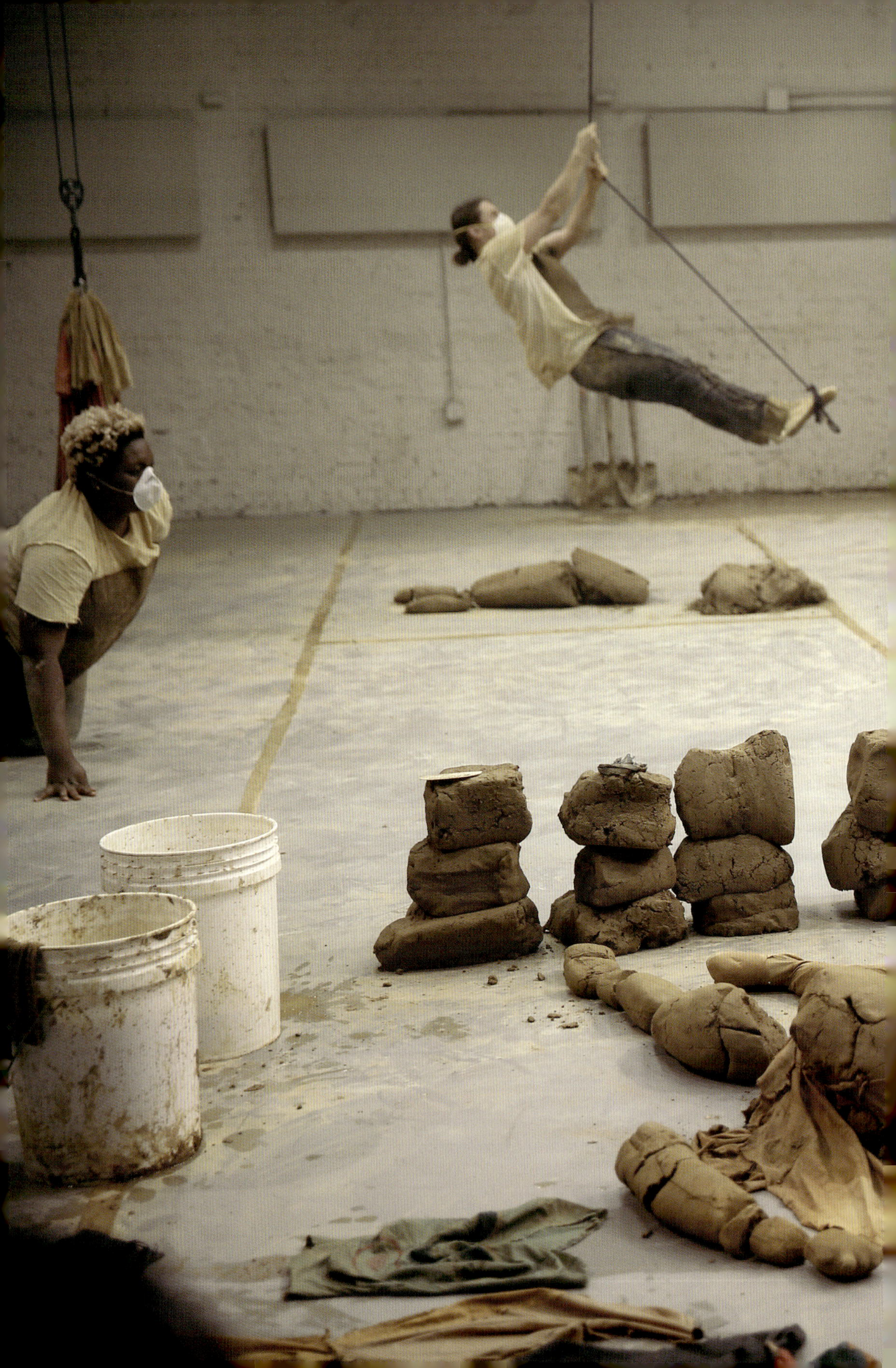

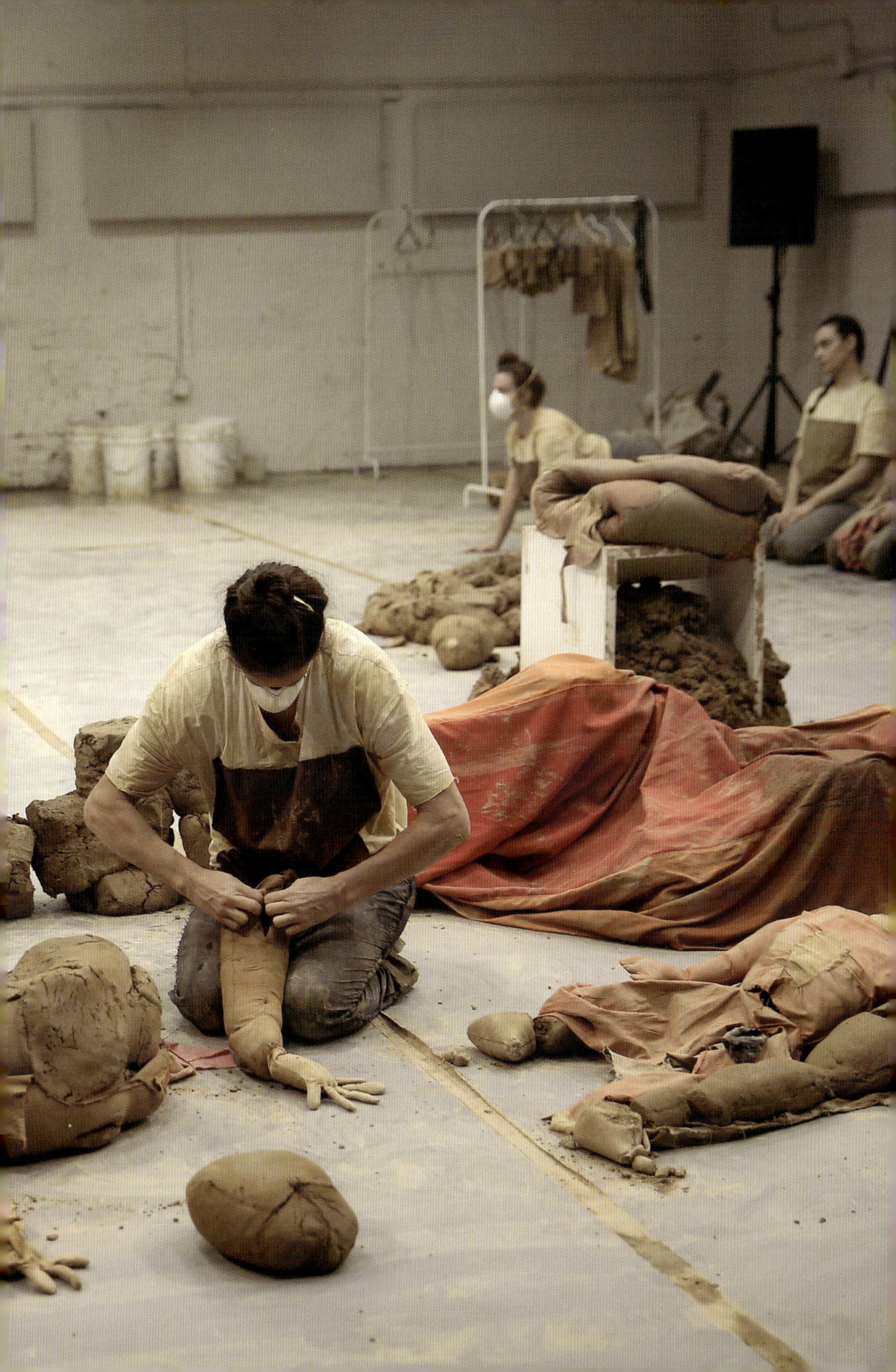

onto the therapist. The therapist simultaneously becomes a stand-in for the parent. Carl Jung later elaborated on this concept to describe the process of transformation as successful if the patient learns how to hold the opposing dynamics that occur between them and the therapist. Then, they can transform through the process. For Jacques Lacan, the transference exists in the dialectics of the relationship, which occurs in the speech between the patient and therapist. Regardless of its origins, or interpretation, transference, in its simplest sense, is the displacement of a feeling onto another action, or thing. During *DEAD MATTER MOVES*, a web of relationships—and the transference of emotions—occurred between the artist and the performers, their objects and spectators, in surprising and unpredictable ways, reinforcing the fact that although they worked individually, they were an inextricable part of a temporary micro social system in which they needed one another to survive.

The history of the Judson Church gym, located in the basement of the building, is important to consider in the context of Mag's work. The gym was home to the Judson Church Dance Theater in the early 1960s—a moment in which New York dance and art history coalesced in the collaborative work of artists, choreographers, and filmmakers, including Simone Forti, Steve Paxton, Robert Morris, Yvonne Rainer, and Carolee Schneemann. Their performances evolved from experimental workshops in which they used unconventional methods to develop choreography, adopting movements from everyday gestures and social occasions, resisting the tropes of theatrical staging to recalibrate the fundamental nature of what a dance might be. Their work also drew on the language of post-minimalist sculpture, dismissing the notion of the untouchable artwork to explore the direct relationship between body and object, exuding a latent anti-capitalist inclination in their rejection of the commodification of either the self or the object.

Yvonne Rainer, specifically, developed a choreographic language of anti-spectacle. She formed complex sequences via a process of "radical juxtaposition," a term coined by critic Susan Sontag, that Rainer applied to her dances (and later films) that combined pedestrian gestures with political and sociological references alongside bursts of more intuitive, sometimes humorously animalistic, movements. Rainer's assemblages position viewers as untrained anthropologists watching something equally recognizable and baffling, pushing them to draw from their own experiences in their interpretation. Rainer dissected the overly easy relationship that critics made between minimalist sculpture and dance in her 1968 essay "A Quasi Survey of Some 'Minimalist' Tendencies in the Quantitatively Minimal Dance Activity Midst the Plethora, or an Analysis of *Trio A*," in which she stated: "Repetition can serve to enforce the discreteness of a movement, objectify it, make it more object-like. It also offers an alternative way of ordering material, literally making the material easier to see."[1]

This question of repetition, and of using repetition to allow us to reorder material in order to make it easier to see, as Rainer describes it, is fundamental to Mag's *DEAD MATTER MOVES*. The repetition of tasks enacted by the performers was a revelatory process, allowing them and the audience to observe minute details in their behavior, actions, and emotions that they would not have noticed otherwise. Ultimately, even though clay was moved around the space, objects were formed, and rudimentary bodies were sculpted, Mag created a primitive factory whose real product was emotion.

1
Yvonne Rainer, "A Quasi Survey of Some 'Minimalist' Tendencies in the Quantitatively Minimal Dance Activity Midst the Plethora, or an Analysis of Trio A" in Work 1961-73 (Halifax, Nova Scotia: The Press of the Nova Scotia College of Art and Design), 63-69. Written in 1966, first published in 1968 in *Minimal Art: A Critical Anthology*, ed. Gregory Battcock. (Berkeley. University of California Press, 1995).

Retaining one's individuality in a group while remaining a part of the group or the social system—without imposing one's belief systems or emotions on others—is a difficult, often painful, task. Sometimes the systems fail. Sometimes the network cracks; the web breaks; the family, the institution, the society crumble. Hands are no longer held, hair is no longer stroked, the unspoken bonds of psychological connection evaporate, leaving the individual to exist in isolation. Incarcerated humans are often put in solitary confinement as a punishment. The act of isolation is an act of torture. Yet, even in moments of genocide, massacre, or totalitarianism—at times where the Darwinian "survival of the fittest" instinct should surely have kicked in—humans have come together, have protected one another, have joined forces, have risen up against the system. Under the great weight, the enormous pressure, they have stood up, and they continue to stand up. KATHY NOBLE

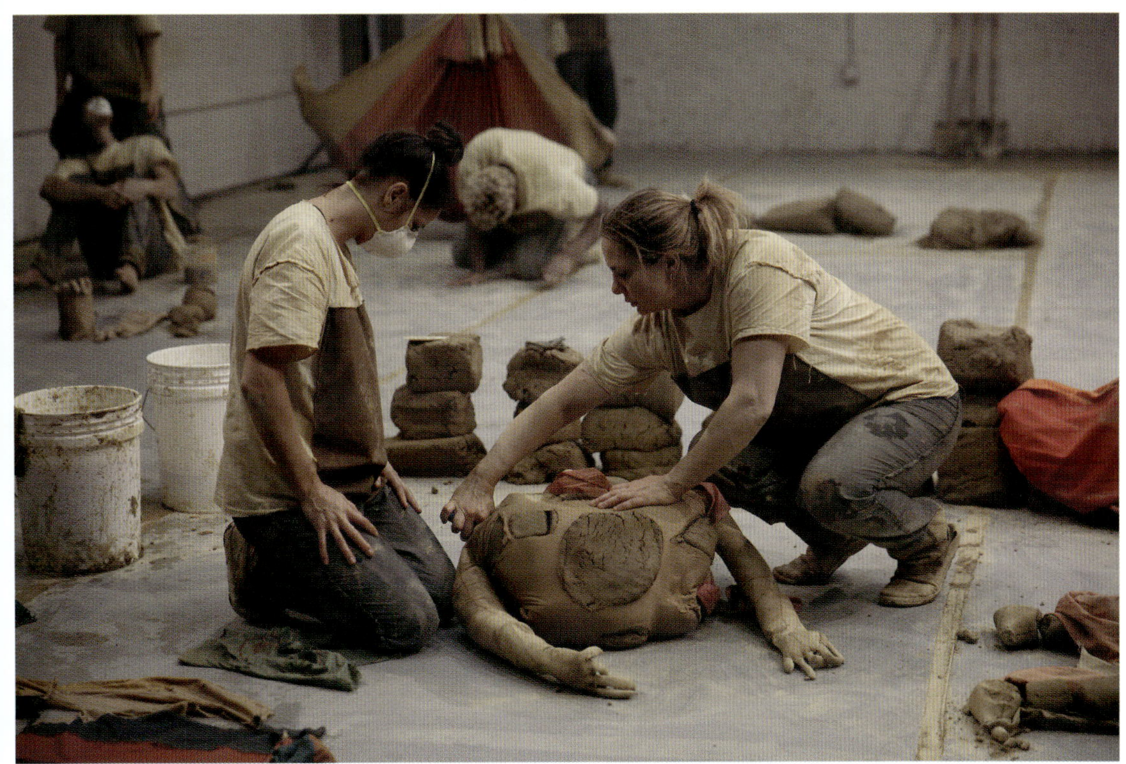

NAIRY BAGHRAMIAN & MARIA HASSABI WITH JANETTE LAVERRIÈRE & CARLO MOLLINO

Entre Deux Actes (Ménage à Quatre)

Curated by
Charles Aubin

1014

November 6–10, 2019

For more than a decade, in total secret, the architect and designer Carlo Mollino used an apartment on the Po river in Turin to stage a private theater of his own fantasies. Throughout the 1960s, the eccentric Italian invited streetwalkers for one-night-only modeling sessions behind closed doors, posing for him in extravagant clothing, wigs, lingerie, and various accessories. Created for the eye of the camera, these staged portraits were "fairytales for grown-ups," in Mollino's own words.[1] They exude an atmosphere of intense sensuality and genuine adoration. We can sense the polarities of control and abandon between Mollino and his guests shifting over each series: Models looked away to offer their bare legs or the curves of their lower back to the photographer, and then switched to staring straight into the camera's lens. Mollino shot with a Polaroid camera, and although he shared the task of choreography with his models, he alone retained control over the resulting prints. He never exhibited them during his lifetime. Only at his death, in 1973, did more than two thousand of these private erotic performances surface.

In an essay on Mollino, the architecture theorist Beatriz Colomina reminds us that *camera*, in Italian, also means *room*.[2] The angles of a doorway, the lines of the jalousie blinds, the surface of a bed: all of these frame Mollino's models as much as the models, in return, imbue his walls with the frisson of erotic play. Colomina elaborates: "For Mollino, the camera is not simply inseparable from the architectural space; it is inseparable from the space of the deepest fantasies. The camera is connected to that which cannot normally show itself, the 'fantasies of an impossible daily life.'"[3]

It was with flashes of light that the artists Maria Hassabi and Nairy Baghramian invited the audience into their own domestic theater of fantasies. Performers emerged in glimpses as we made our way through a succession of adjoining rooms on the ground floor of a grand townhouse on Fifth Avenue on Manhattan's Upper East Side. The choreography of neon lights played with our sight, revealing only gradually the four dancers before us, as Hassabi's recorded voice provided an irregular count: "Twenty-two, twenty-three, twenty-four, twenty-five, fifty-one, fifty-two, fifty-three…" The gravelly voice of the Cyprus-

1
Carlo Mollino gave the title "Fiabe per i grandi" (Fairy tales for grown-ups) to a first series of erotic portraits he took between 1936 and 1942.

2
Beatriz Colomina, "A Slight Nausea: Carlo Mollino," *Thresholds*, no. 43 (Cambridge, Massachusetts: MIT Press Journal, 2015), 59.

3
Colomina, 60.

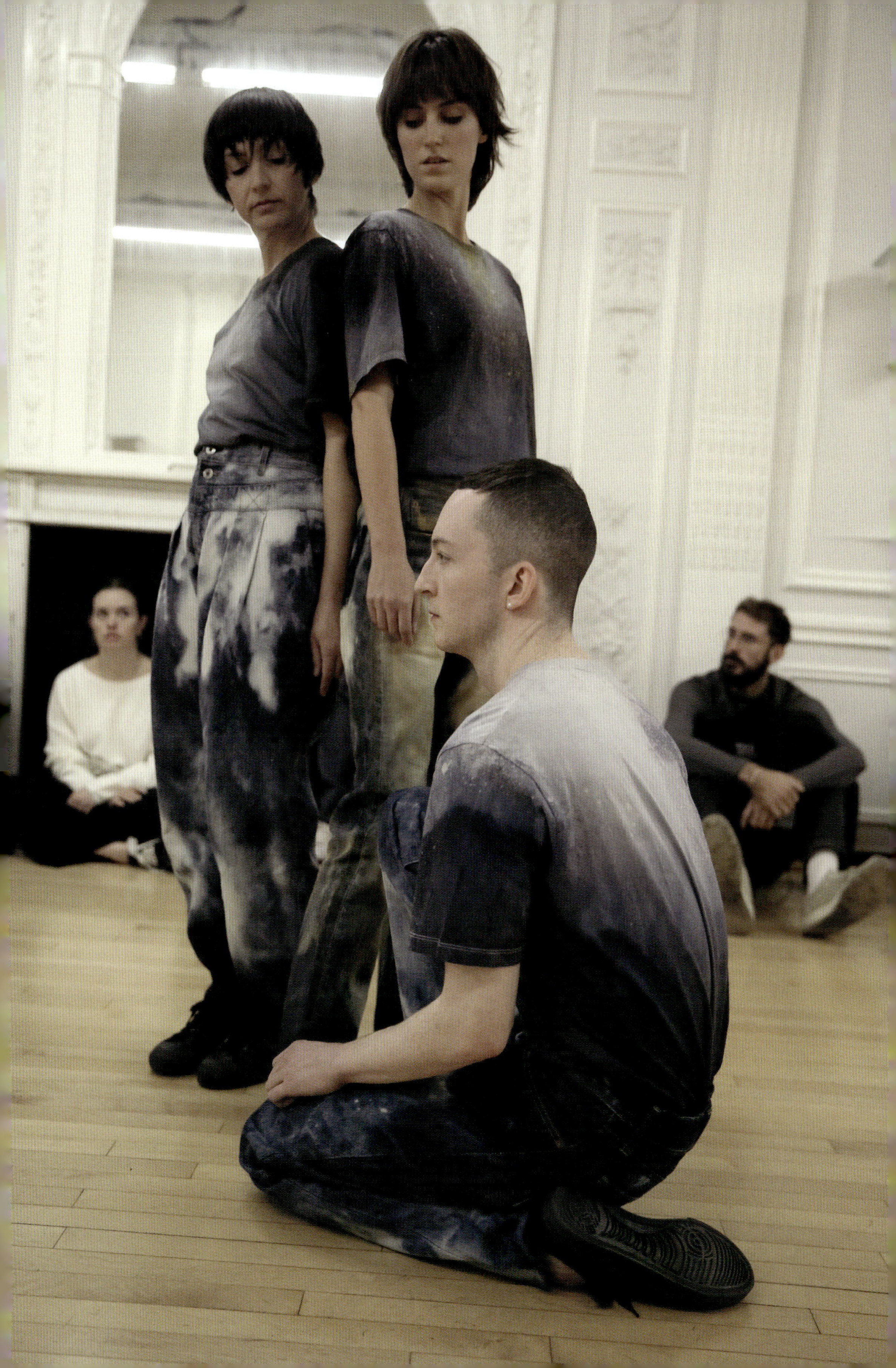

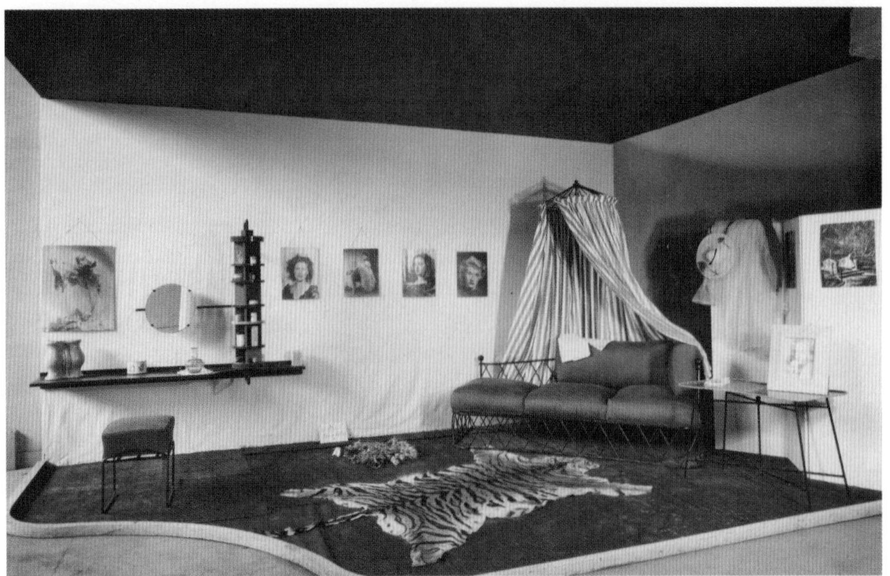

born New Yorker at first seemed to be steadily clocking the passing seconds, but soon became its own rhythm.

Dancers held poses for prolonged periods: Alice Heyward standing with her legs open wide and deeply anchored, scrutinizing the floor; Mickey Mahar in contrapposto, as if staring at a horizon far beyond the mansion's wall. While Hristoula Harakas stood stock-still, Oisín Monaghan laid on the floor, impassive, detached. All four wore tie-dyed deep blue ensembles by Victoria Bartlett, subtly sparkling with flecks of muted gold. As the dancers slowly hunkered down and spread themselves on the floor, a ballet of restraint began. Moving at a slow pace—what Hassabi calls a "velocity of deceleration"—the four created abstract formations on the worn-out parquet, alternating between elongated and contorted postures, and passing into and out of registration with one another.[4] At times, we could even hear Monaghan counting the seconds as he passed from one pose to another, a counterpoint to Hassabi's ambient enumeration. Recurrent pings and a few floating musical accords thickened the air. At last, the performers progressively stood up and regrouped—Heyward carefully placed herself between Mahar and Harakas, prompting the latter to leave the room, followed in turn by each of the other dancers. Had twenty minutes passed, or was it an hour? In this atmosphere of suspension, flashes of light magnified these open-ended formations. The imprint on the retina remained ambiguous; the outlines of live dancers, images, and sculptures indeterminate.

The performers' cautious motions served as implicit cues for the audience to follow. We made our way back through the ground floor toward the entrance and went up the townhouse's grand main staircase to the home's piano nobile. There, a fifth dancer awaited us: Leslie Cuyjet, lying on the ground, performed a subtle routine of loops of legs constantly moving between wall and floor. The audience was left to wander the house's worn aristocratic rooms, and we eventually discovered the parlor, converted by Baghramian into a stylized dressing room. The installation, titled *Entre deux actes II (Loge des comédiennes)*, has its origin in

Janette Laverrière, *Entre Deux Actes—Loge De Comédienne*, 1947.

4
Maria Hassabi in conversation with Victoria Marks, The Herb Alpert Awards in the Arts, March–April 2015, accessed April 18, 2020, https://herbalpertawards.org/artist/chapter-one-0.

5
Nairy Baghramian created *Entre deux actes II (loge des comédiennes)* in 2009 at the Staatliche Kunsthalle Baden Baden, where, for the first time, she brought together works by Janette Laverrière and Carlo Mollino.

6
In a conversation with the author featured in the playbill for *Entre Deux Actes (Ménage à Quatre)* (November 2019). Unpaginated.

7
Idem.

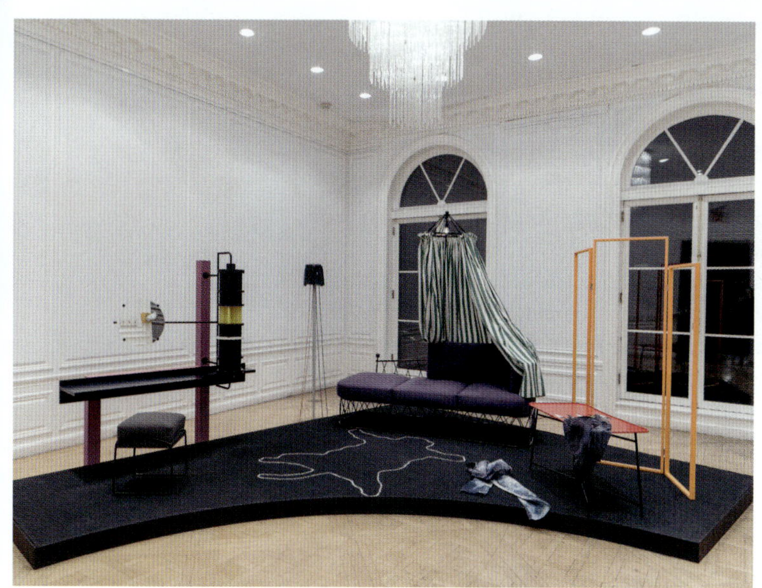

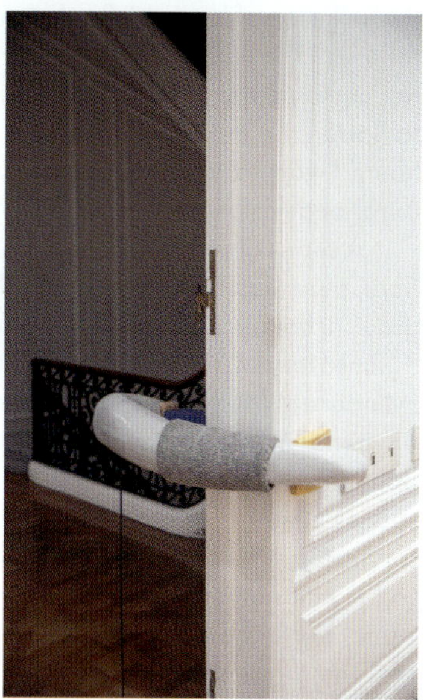

an actual green room that the Swiss-French modernist designer Janette Laverrière submitted to the 1947 Salon des artistes décorateurs in Paris, which her (mostly male) peers criticized for being too "feminine." Learning about its rough reception first triggered Baghramian's desire to revisit Laverrière's room over a decade ago, for her exhibition at the Staatliche Kunsthalle Baden Baden.[5] In this installation, placed on a conspicuous black platform, the artist and designer joined forces to playfully engage the gendered assumptions that attend architecture and interior design. Here, the audience found a vanity and a comfortable stool, a purple sofa snugly fitting under a white and green striped curtain, a gangly floor lamp, and the simple armature of a folding screen. By situating this dressing room in the parlor, Baghramian took delight in upending the initial function of the room. The parlor, a place where we talk (*parler* in French) and entertain people, became here a place of retreat, a refuge. In Baghramian's words: "To me, Janette's boudoir, or changing room, functions as a moment of self-indulgence, a pause... It is an antechamber where one collects one's thoughts and prepares before entering the theater of the world."[6] The blue outfit of one of the dancers, left nonchalantly on the platform, alluded to the use of the room in accordance with its title: *Entre deux actes*, in between two acts, in a moment of suspension.

In the adjacent hallway, Baghramian included her personal collection of Mollino's erotic portraits, which appeared in frames of her own design and hung under Laverrière's lighting fixtures. This imbrication of artworks—identifiable on their own but now placed within this network—was at the heart of *Entre Deux Actes (Ménage à Quatre)*. As Baghramian explained: "Combining and examining different artistic positions is a *Leitmotif* of my thinking, and a parallel strand of my practice. For me, it's always about understanding how artistic attitudes can coexist, and thereby create a respectful dialogue, without mutual or one-sided appropriation."[7] Baghramian deployed this modus operandi to produce a benevolent aggregation, and at Performa, her initial *ménage à trois* with Laverrière and Mollino morphed into a sympathetic *ménage à quatre* with the inclusion of Hassabi. Baghramian summarizes the resulting constellation as follows: "This was one reason I invited Maria Hassabi to work with me: to have her perform alongside the installation, not over or under it. I was also trying to flatten the hierarchy of different mediums. By limiting the venue's opening hours, I wanted to allow sculpture, drawing, painting, and performance the same durational visibility."[8]

A series of discreet sculptures by Baghramian, distributed across the second floor, punctuated the audience's perambulation. Most of them took the form of grayish, bulging, biomorphic arches, between whose ends the artist suspended rudimentary assemblages of yellow or blue discs or blocks of cork; some even had cylinders of fabric wrapped around them, like the fur muffs worn by Fifth Avenue doyennes in winter. Positioned at the threshold of each room, these fixtures held open the doors of the mansion and permitted a free circulation throughout its spaces. Baghramian affectuously named these sculptures *Repos*, the French word for *repose*, or state of rest, in an undisguised nod to their physical invitation. In soft touches across the floor, they conjured moments of potential rest for the weary performers.

The climax of *Entre Deux Actes (Ménage à Quatre)* was a *pas de deux* of intense intimacy, choreographed by Hassabi and titled *TOGETHER*. In a hidden ballroom at the back of the parlor floor, Hassabi and Monaghan, wearing subdued ochre and ash gray outfits that clashed with the ballroom's dark wood paneling, at first stood firm next to each other, looking off into different directions. The duo gradually enmeshed into a succession of poses that, slowly, conjured affection, reserve, tenderness, distance, and desire. They got closer, then progressively turned away; they rejoined, then separated again. Despite the slowness of their *tête à tête*, the dancers' relationship remained volatile, and the two imbued each gesture with an extreme athletic precision. Halfway through the duet, Hassabi rested on Monaghan's back. Then, in a twist of roles, both slowly pivoted, and Monaghan placed the weight of his head on Hassabi's shoulder while she held him by the waist. They crouched, with Monaghan looming over Hassabi in a lustful manner before the two sat peacefully, looking at one another from a distance, as if pondering the ebbs and flows of their relationship. Having journeyed through this slow dance for nearly an hour, the audience shared the performers' intense cascade of emotions, emphasized by the disjunctive soundtrack of crackling, a sporadic flute, otherworldly voices, and snippets of melodies composed by Stavros Gasparatos.

The building was a co-conspirator in all of this. While it framed the dramas of this fragmented chamber play, it also took up a leading role in the installation-performance. At once enclosed and on display inside the mansion, the performers operated in a realm of fantasies not unlike Mollino's Turin apartment, inviting all manners of interpretive possibilities. In this contained architecture, Baghramian and Hassabi's *ménage à quatre* with Laverrière and Mollino was an open system of encounters and complicities, one in which sculpture and architecture, design and photography, enmeshed with performance yet never receded into a backdrop. Enlivened with new potential from their extended cohabitation, each medium became a player in a romantic game of hide and seek. CHARLES AUBIN

8
"Nairy Baghramian on Janette Laverrière and the politics of space," interviewed by Amelia Stein, *Artforum*, November 26, 2019, accessed April 18, 2020, https://www.artforum.com/interviews/nairy-baghramian-81407.

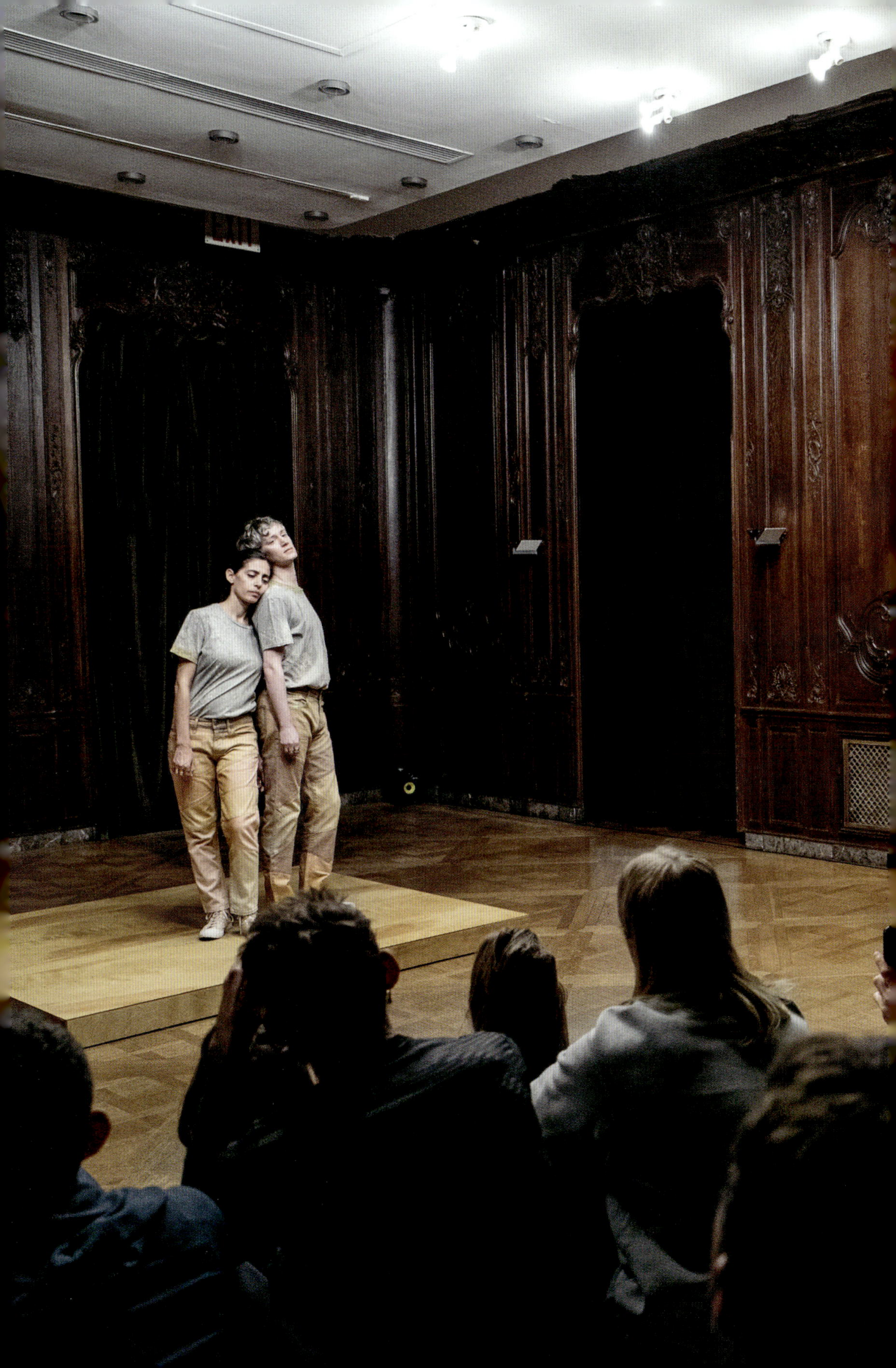

YVONNE RAINER

Parts of Some Sextets, 1965/2019

Curated by Kathy Noble assisted by Brittany Richmond

Gelsey Kirkland Arts Center

November 15–17, 2019

Like many people, I first encountered Yvonne Rainer's *Parts of Some Sextets* (1965), via two iconic images: the first of ten dancers, including Rainer, perched atop of a pile of twelve thin, soft mattresses; the second of artist Robert Morris flying toward the pile. They sit alongside images of the experiments by Rainer's Judson Dancer Theater collaborators, such as Simone Forti and Robert Morris, in which performers partnered with simple, static wooden constructions and ropes. Yet in their vivid staging of movement and stillness, these images conjured a scene, and a type of choreography, that was unlike any other produced at this time. The original images of *PoSS* position the mattresses as malleable entities, equal performers in the choreography that unfolds in partnership with them. In hindsight, my reading of these images offers merely a glimpse into *PoSS*, among Rainer's most complex works, and one that uses time as both a structuring mechanism as well as its subject.

PoSS was brought to life once again in 2019 through an accumulation of parts, as both a reconstruction and a special new commission for the Performa 19 Biennial. When dancer and choreographer—and longtime member of Rainer's current group, which she affectionately calls the Raindears—Emily Coates approached Rainer about attempting a reconstruction, she was at first skeptical that this long-ago work could be reconstructed based on such scant documentation (a small number of photographs and a score she had not seen since the late 1960s). But Coates persisted, and was soon on her way to the Getty Institute in Los Angeles to begin her research. Guided by Coates's determination, Rainer, Coates, eleven dancers, the Getty Institute, the Rauschenberg Foundation, the Peter Moore Photography Archive, and Performa—and a little miraculous serendipity along the way—led to a dance that is both a recreation of the past and an entirely new work for the present.

The 1965 version of *PoSS* was a pivotal moment in Rainer's career; a monumental composition of a constellation of parts—influenced by all her work prior to 1965—that formed a dance that, in hindsight, has shadow traces throughout the film and choreographic works she has created since. The 1965 cast comprised a remarkable group of dancers who were referred to as the Judson Dance Theater—Lucinda Childs, Judith Dunn, Sally Gross, Deborah Hay, Tony Holder, Steve Paxton, Yvonne Rainer, and Joseph Schlichter—as well as two visual artists, Robert Morris and Robert Rauschenberg. The matrix of movement is accompanied, and the changes cued, by Rainer reading from *The Diary of William Bentley, D.D.*, by the eighteenth-century American Unitarian minister of

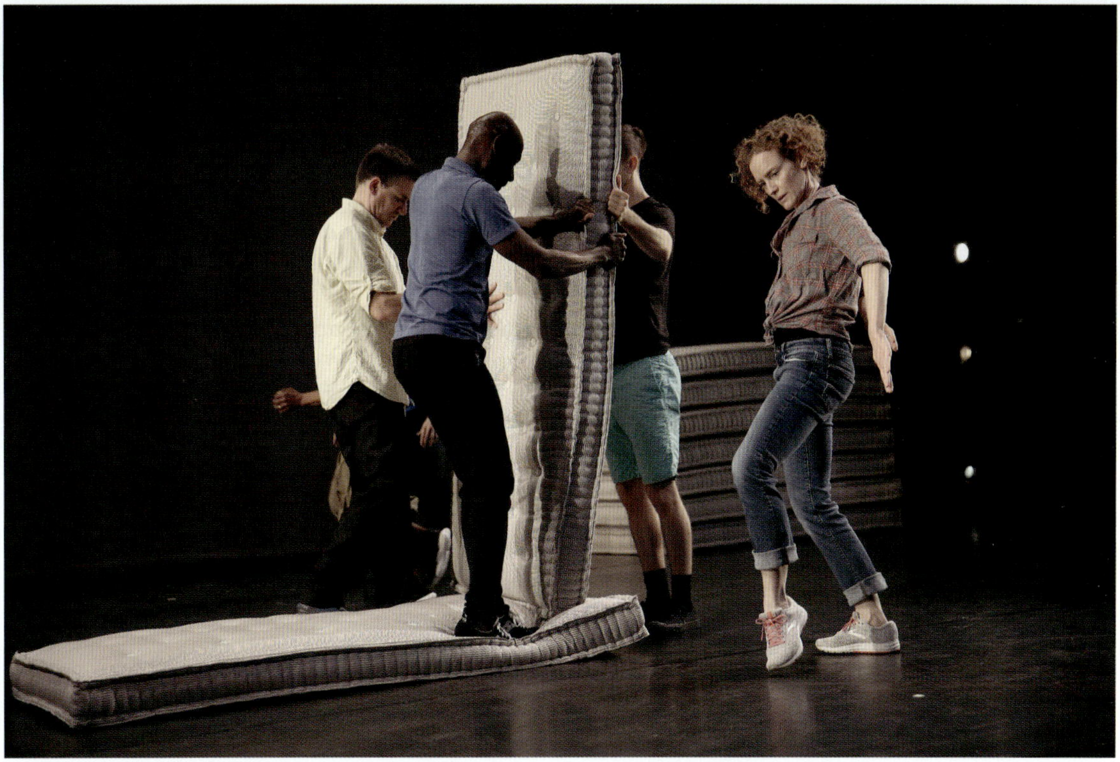

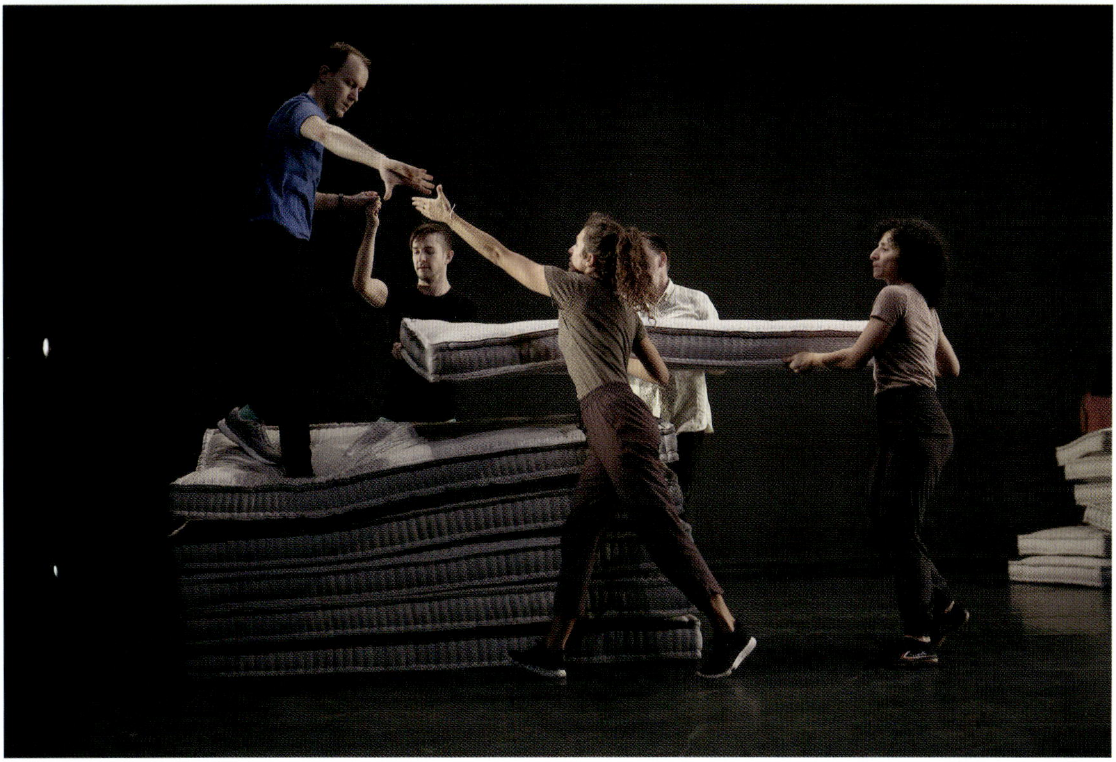

the East Church in Salem, Massachusetts from 1783 to 1819 in post-independence America. Bentley's text, humorous and harrowing, chronicled the social situation and politics of his era via the characters and *mise-en-scène* depicted in visceral, evocative prose.[1]

PoSS is composed from thirty-one pedestrian moves, such as "race-walk" and "through-run" as well as more whimsical instructions, such as "bird run" and "Swedish werewolf." This mix of straightforward movements and phrases is interspersed with more athletic, task-like directives. "Crawl through below top mattress," dancers are told. The performers unexpectedly switch in and out of each instruction every thirty seconds, creating an irregular and seemingly random choreography, forming a constantly evolving sequence of stage images that would influence generations of dancers to come. For Rainer, the mechanics of the 1965 production, its irregularity, interruption, and change, were essential to her ethos of dance. She described her overview in a 1965 essay published in *The Tulane Drama Review*: "Continuous simultaneous actions changing abruptly at perhaps thirty-second intervals, sometimes the whole field changing at the same time, sometimes only a portion of it, but every thirty seconds something changing."[2]

One year after *PoSS*, Rainer produced *Trio A* (1966), a dance constructed from one seamless motion, the polar opposite of *Parts of Some Sextets* in its relationship to time and in its montage of phrases of movement. The "mattress dance," as Rainer sometimes calls *PoSS*, also deepened her exploration of the relationship between mind and body, and the "object-like" quality that the body takes on through repetition of seemingly ordinary steps, a style that she further developed in *Continuous Project—Altered Daily* and dances such as *Chair Pillow* (both 1969). Rainer went on to dissect the relationship that critics drew between minimalist sculpture and dance, writing that "repetition can serve to enforce the discreteness of a movement, objectify it, make it more object-like. It also offers an alternative way of ordering material, literally making the material easier to see."[3]

The 2019 cast of *Parts of Some Sextets* brought together a mix of known Downtown dancers—Rachel Berman, Brittany Engel-Adams, Patrick Gallagher, Shayla-Vie Jenkins, Jon Kinzel, Mary Kate Sheehan, David Thomson, and Timothy Ward, as well as Emily Coates—with visual artists Liz Magic Laser and Nick Mauss cast in the roles of Rauschenberg and Morris. As only three quarters of the score exists, the last section of choreography was newly created by Rainer for the 2019 version. Before Rainer and the dancers entered the rehearsal studio, I had a conceptual and structural understanding of what *PoSS* would entail: a rhythmic flow of images depicting the artist's everyday gestures, coupled with more stylized sequences of movement, flowed through my imagination. I did not, and could not, have predicted how the combination of these almost arbitrary elements—the juxtapositions of which are equally structured by chance and Rainer's direction—would create such a powerful emotional experience. As Rainer's choreography played out to the sound of her voice flatly intoning the blunt, matter-of-fact descriptions of eighteenth-century Salem life, the athletic, energetic, playful movements of the dancer's bodies contrasted starkly with a world in which casual racism and sexism slipped all too easily from the tongue of a man considered a pillar of the community.

The 2019 cast of eleven dancers came together to form their own village onstage; a community working in unison helping one another safely fling

1
Excerpts from *The Diary of William Bentley, D.D., pastor of the East Church in Salem, Massachusetts: 1783 to 1819*, extracted by Yvonne Rainer in 1964 from four volumes (out of the original thirty-two) in the New York Public Library.

2
Yvonne Rainer, "Some Retrospective Notes on a Dance for 10 People and 12 Mattresses Called "Parts of Some Sextets," Performed at the Wadsworth Atheneum, Hartford, Connecticut, and Judson Memorial Church, New York, in March 1965," *The Tulane Drama Review*, vol. 10, no. 2 (winter 1965), 173.

3
Yvonne Rainer, "A Quasi Survey of Some "Minimalist" Tendencies in the Quantitatively Minimal Dance Activity Midst the Plethora, or an Analysis of Trio A," in Work 1961-73 (Halifax, Nova Scotia: The Press of the Nova Scotia College of Art and Design), 63–69. Written in 1966, first published in 1968 in *Minimal Art: A Critical Anthology*, ed. Gregory Battcock. (Berkeley: University of California Press, 1995).

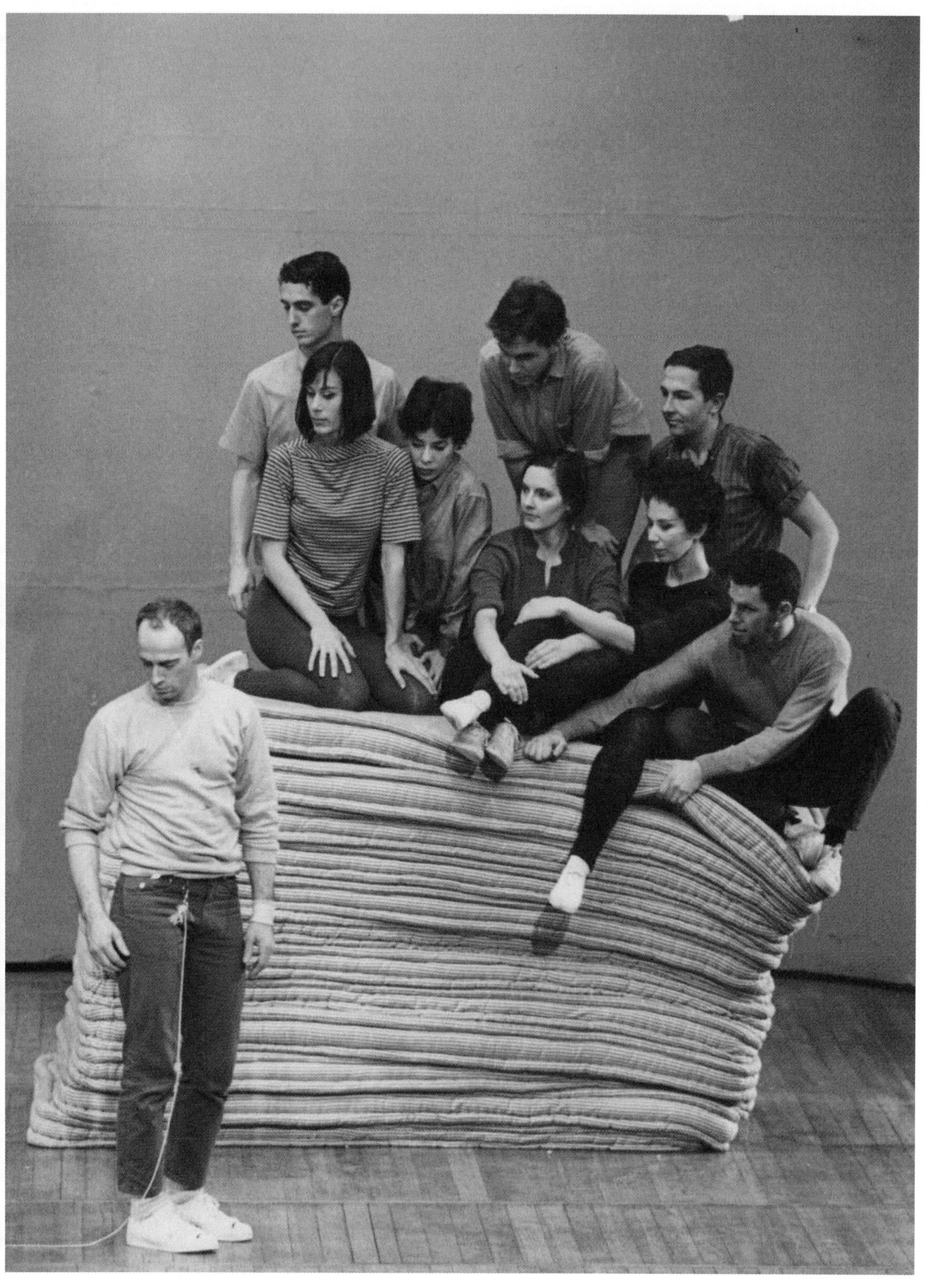

themselves over the mattresses, crawl through them, or pose on top of them. At times the dancers coexisted as individuals, flowing in and out of one another, a flock that momentarily united in small group formations as couples and threesomes, and at other times scattered across the stage. When the original audio recording from 1965 was fortuitously rediscovered in the Rauschenberg Foundation's archive, just in time for the biennial, Rainer edited the reel-to-reel tape of her thirty-year-old voice with newly recorded excerpts of her eighty-four-year-old voice, also inserting new phrases of angry expletives into the existing text. Past and present Rainer's timbre and tone of voice are distinct, yet their intonation is similar, forming an uncanny aural thread that spans over half a century of time. Thus, *PoSS* is an exercise in how the full spectrum of human life—in its gestures, behaviors, movements, and sounds—are seen, chronicled, enacted, performed, and remembered.

The refusal of spectacle set forth in Rainer's now ubiquitous *No Manifesto* (written in 1964, a year before *PoSS*) is often quoted as the key to understanding her early choreographies—yet this citation is repeated so often, and with so little thought or context, that Rainer herself now rejects it. As I watched the series of images created by the dancers on the sparsely lit black stage, I couldn't help but read these as spectacle. We, the audience and I, were positioned as voyeurs looking down on the inhabitants of a surreal village, watching the routines of their daily lives unfold as their intimate relations coalesced with communal action. *PoSS* ends when the dancers, slowly, one by one, climb onto the pile of mattresses in the middle of the stage to pose, statue-like in their stillness, to create a consciously iconic image. If this isn't spectacle, what is? KATHY NOBLE

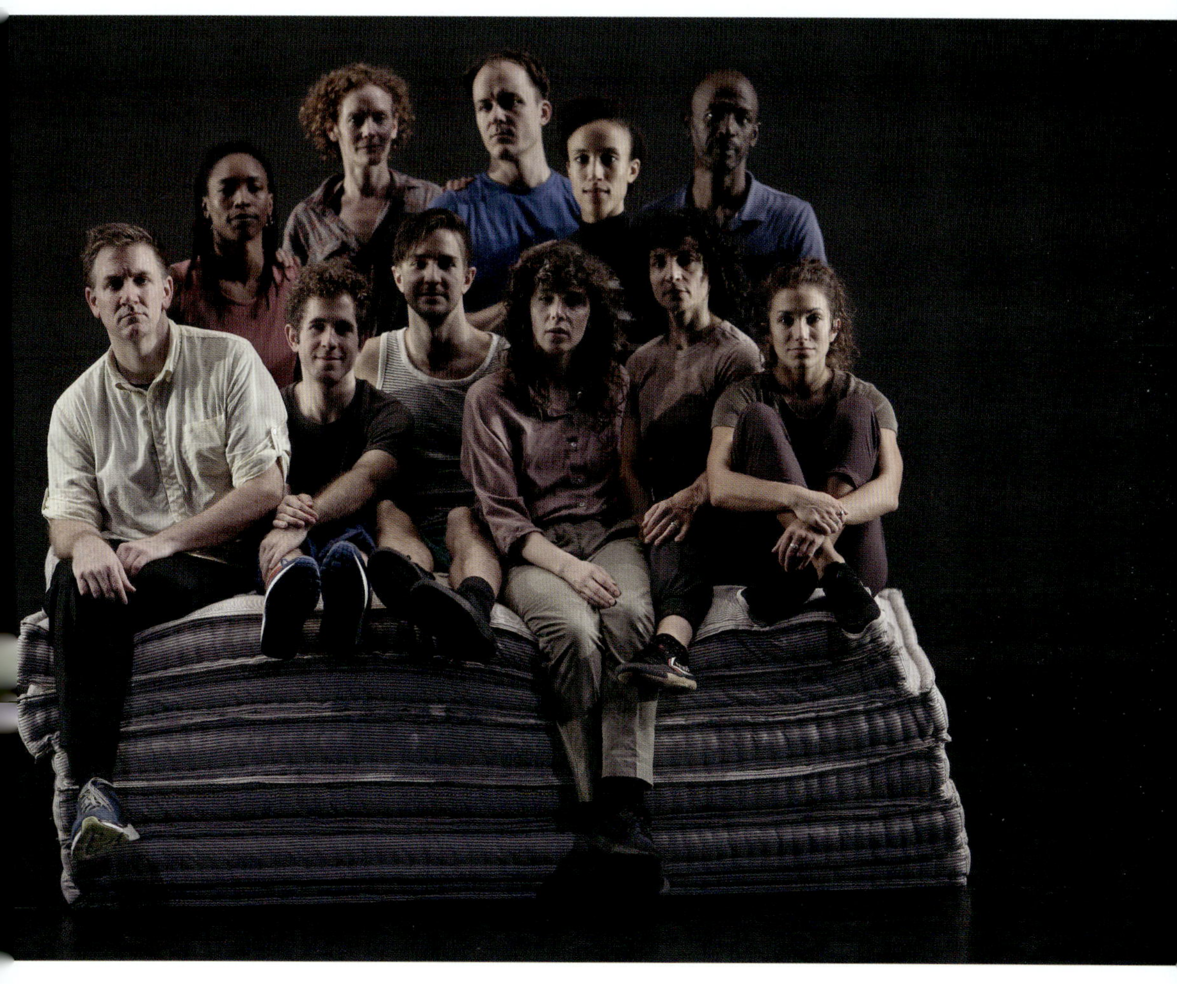

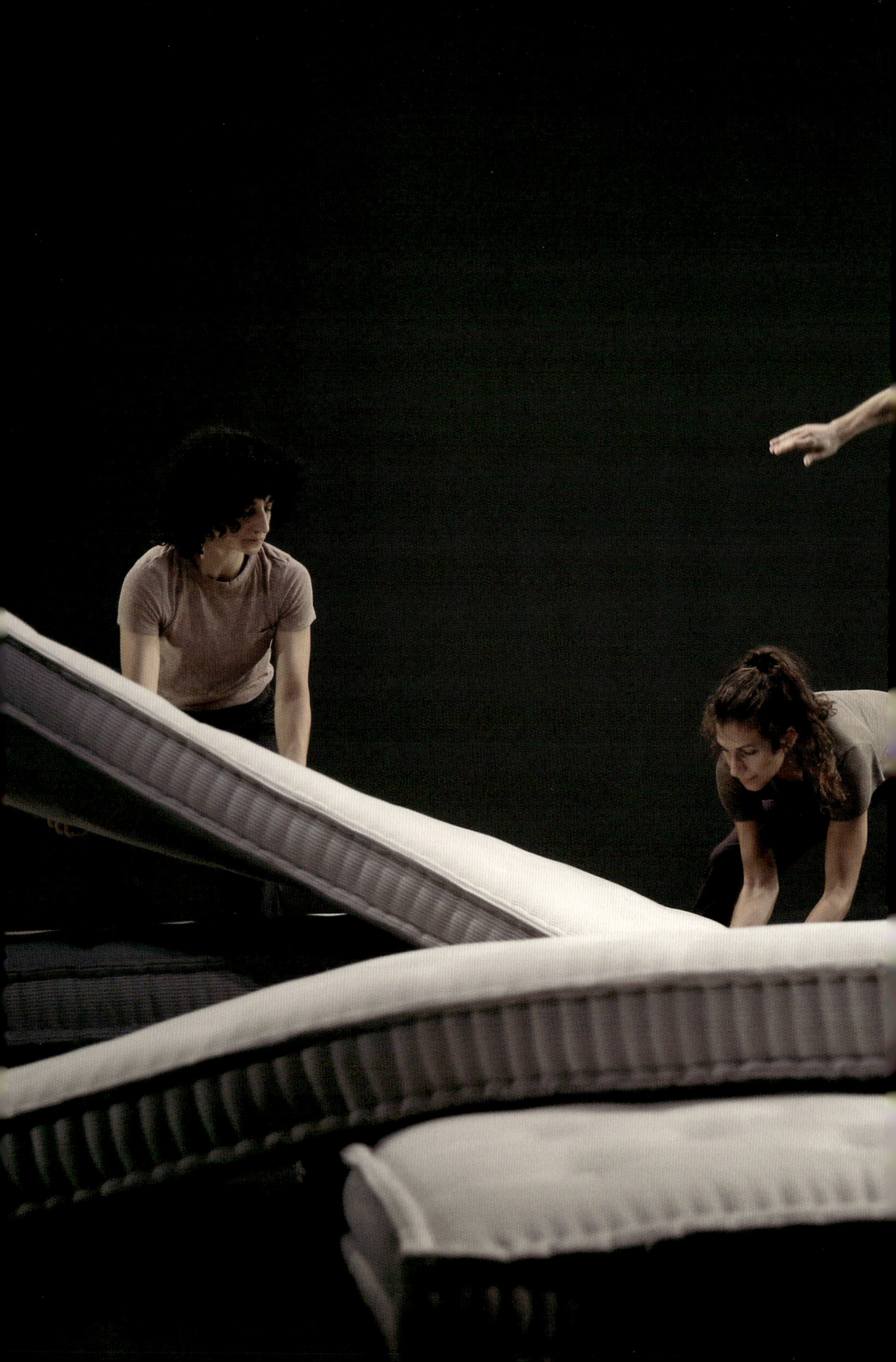

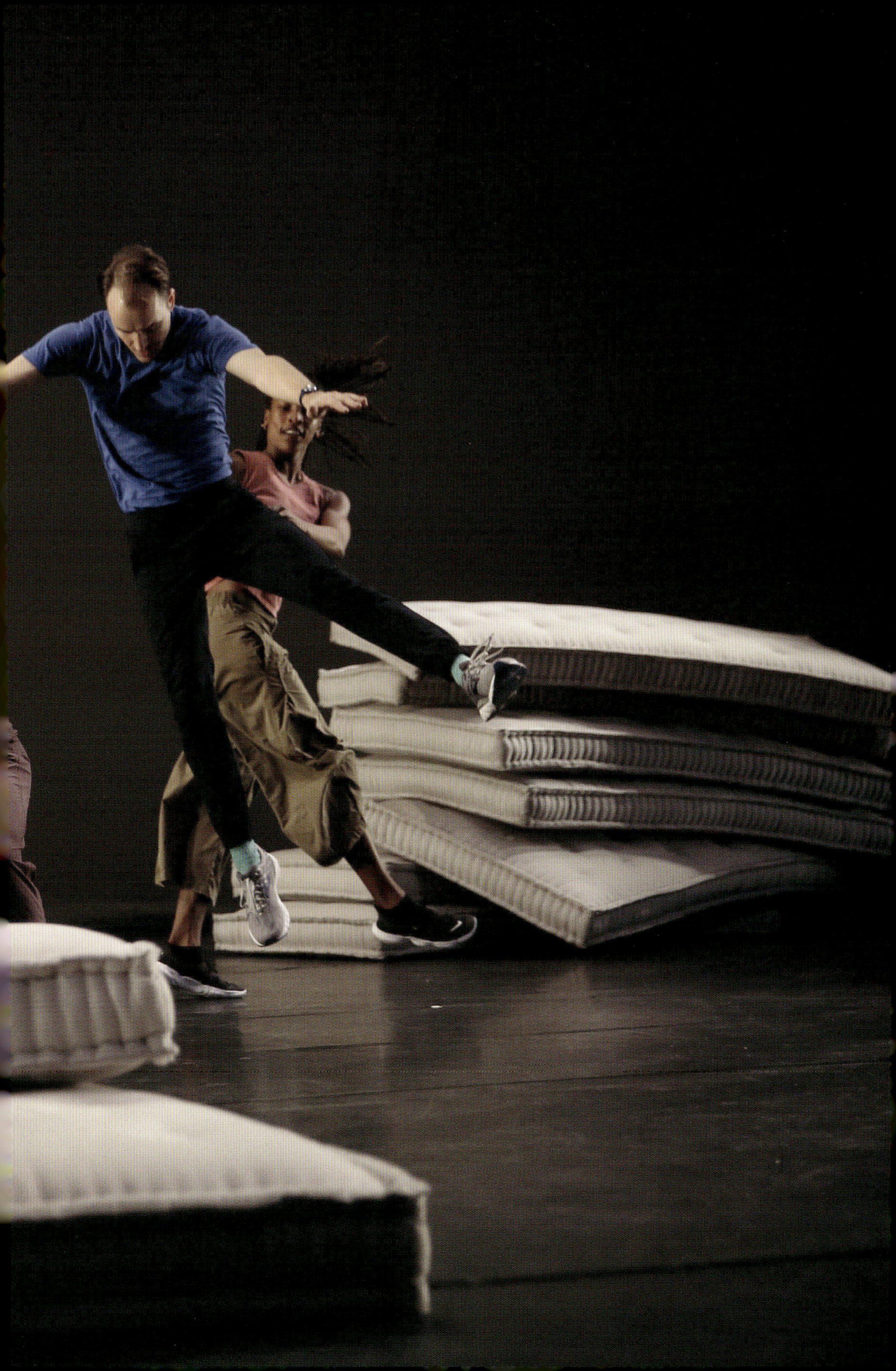

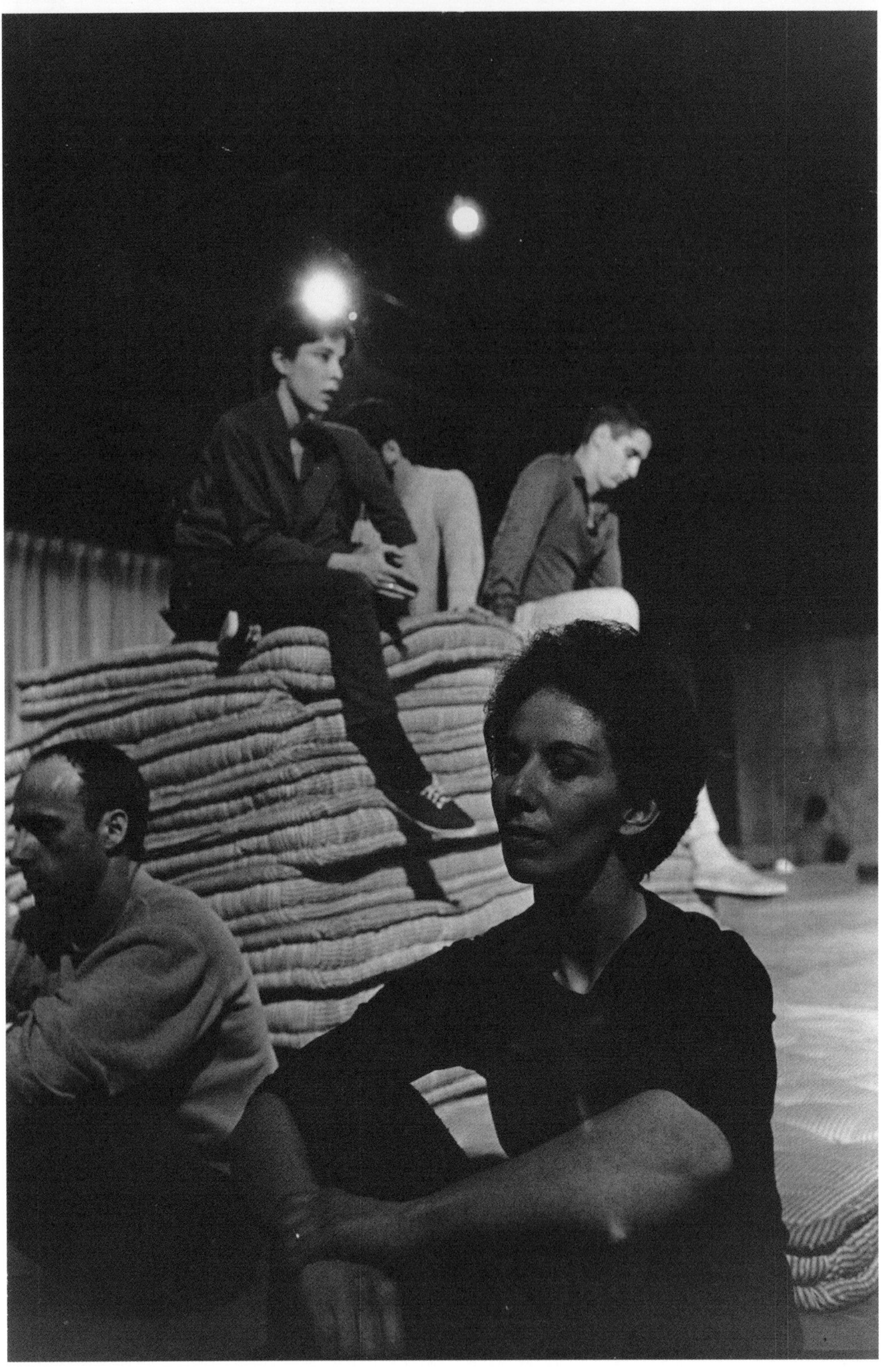

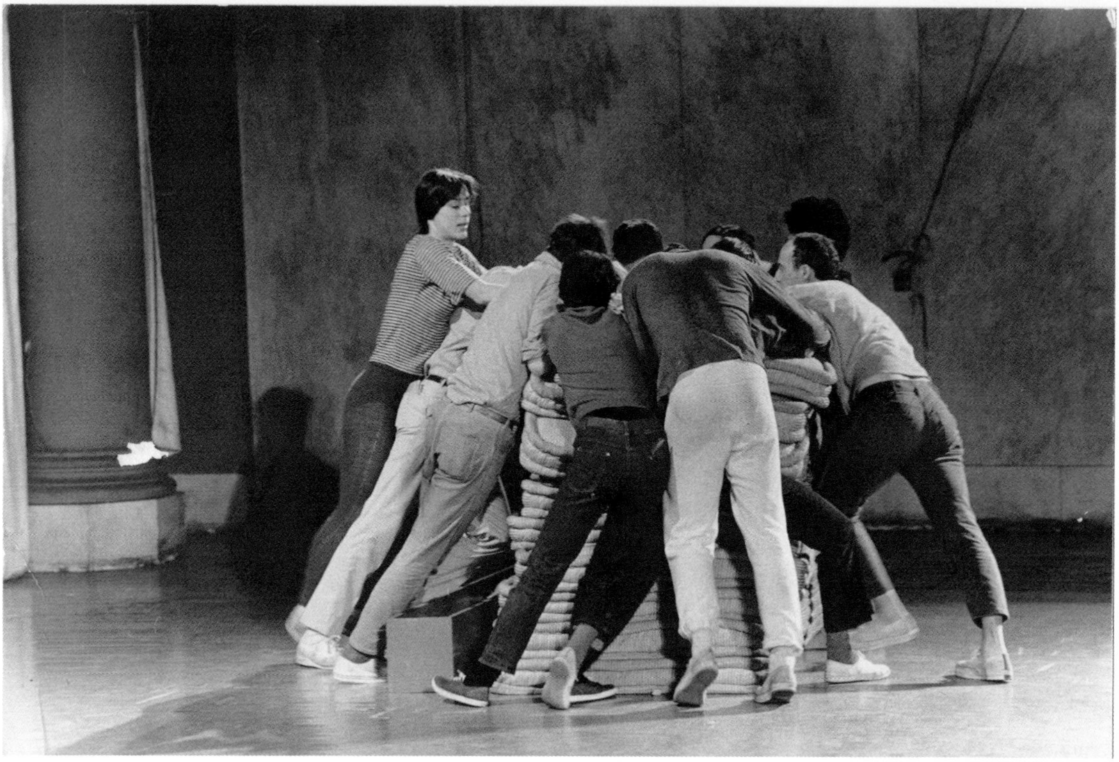

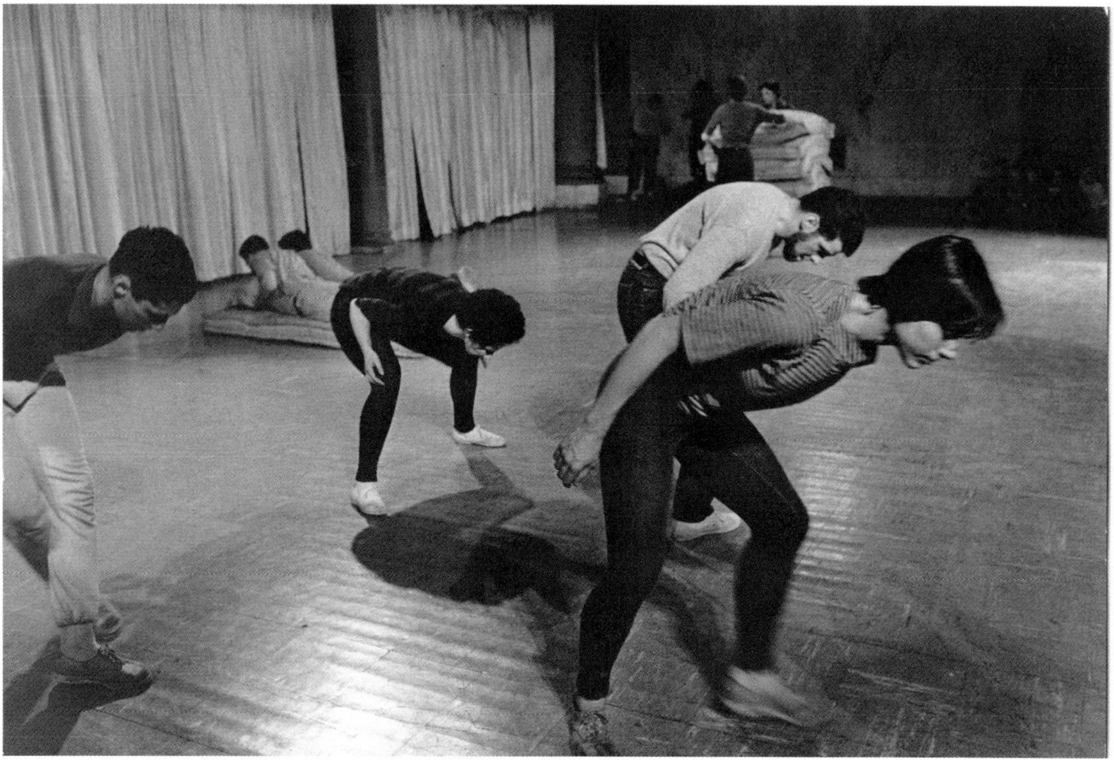

A NOTE FROM YVONNE RAINER

Parts of Some Sextets is both a reconstruction and reconfiguration of a dance of the same name, initially performed by ten people with twelve mattresses and presented at the Wadsworth Atheneum of Music and Art and Judson Memorial Church in 1965. The original ten performers were Lucinda Childs, Judith Dunn, Sally Gross, Deborah Hay, Tony Holder, Robert Morris, Steve Paxton, Yvonne Rainer, Robert Rauschenberg, and Joseph Schlichter.

At that time, after we had learned all of the dance moves and tasks, I created an elaborate score, then joined my fellow performers to begin building the dance. The process required that we continually consult two sheets of graph paper pinned to a wall of my studio that contained a timeline plus words and initials assigning specific movements and tasks to individual performers. We rehearsed three or four times a week for at least eight weeks. I rarely, if at all, stood apart from the goings-on as a detached observer.

During the 2019 rehearsals, now in the role of director rather than performer, I found myself once again acknowledging the influence of Alain Robbe-Grillet's *For a New Novel*, a tract that I and many of my contemporaries were absorbing in the early 1960s. Back then, its critique of nineteenth-century romanticism and narrative conventions was launching a number of artists' ships, *Parts of Some Sextets* among them. The present rendition owes much to the initiative and persuasiveness of Emily Coates.

A NOTE FROM EMILY COATES

When I arrived at the Rauschenberg Foundation on August 29, 2019, I discovered that Yvonne had beaten me by fifteen minutes. I found her sitting tall at a computer in their library, her ears encased in large black headphones, her glasses glowing from the light of the screen. She was listening intently to her thirty-year-old self reading the text by William Bentley that accompanies *Parts of Some Sextets*. She had recorded the voiceover in her living room on East 25th Street on a Wollensak reel-to-reel tape recorder around 1am in January 1965. Traffic hums in the background. Until that day in August, we thought the recording had vanished.

I had hoped to catch her first reaction, a moment of reckoning with her past, but she had already been listening for a while. "Yeah, that seems to be it," she simply said. Behind her on a long table lay the original ¼-inch reel to reel. On the front of the plastic case, Rauschenberg had written on a piece of masking tape, now brown with age, "CH 1: RAINER: PARTS FROM SOME SEXTETS." He then stored the recording in his basement for decades. The tape's survival felt like a small miracle.

Parts of Some Sextets is a missing puzzle piece in Yvonne's oeuvre: Its excesses—ten performers, twelve mattresses, her voiceover reading from a minister's late eighteenth-century diaries, a systematic score in which she plays with disjunctive continuity and duration—predate by

Many months prior to our first rehearsal, she had traveled to the Getty Research Institute in Los Angeles to dig out traces of *PoSS* in my archive. Despite the fact that she was not yet born in 1965, she continually reassured me that the entire enterprise would require less time to complete than it had previously and would be well worth the effort. Her intuitions proved to be correct. It took ten days in June to sketch out the dance and ten more to polish it in August. Without Emily's initial confidence, I would never have touched the "mattress monster!" And without her unflagging optimism and assistance, it might never have seen the light of the present day.

I must also applaud the current eleven performers for their goodwill and patience as they hung in there with the arduous process and my occasional befuddlement, as there was no film or video documentation of the earlier version to guide us, only Peter Moore's photographs, a brief essay by me, and the first half of the original score (the other half long vanished). The performers not only learned all the moves (some of which needed reinvention), they had to listen for word phrases in the William Bentley texts that in my voiceover reading signaled total or partial changes in the field of vision every thirty seconds! I am filled with gratitude and admiration for all who have been involved in this project.

one year the economy and flow of her seminal dance *Trio A*. And yet only a handful of people living today saw *PoSS* when it was performed in March 1965—and never again.

The research for this revival began with a trip I took in August 2018 to the Getty Research Institute, where Yvonne's papers are housed, and culminated in our visit to the Rauschenberg Foundation one year later. My role in this process has been that of instigator, information sleuth, memory jogger, pep-talker, co-puzzle decipherer, kinesthetic conjurer, and overall Rainer tracker.

One thing is clear: Yvonne Rainer is difficult to track. If she headed into this process with some trepidation, she flew through it as we went along, with each archival detail put before her getting whisked up and either definitively established or speedily reinvented. Throughout this work, Yvonne encountered her youthful self almost as if she were another artist and this was a new dance. The scene at the Rauschenberg Foundation suggests a provocative revival: The passing of time changes the technology and the materials of art-making no less than the perspective of the artist as she ages. But the art endures. As Yvonne wrote to me recently, "Life is short. Art is forever." Reborn from 1965 notes and photographs, this evening's dance began in February 1786 and came to a second fruition 233 years later, in November 2019.

In his 1966 *Manifesto*, Allan Kaprow famously coined the phrase "the blurring of art and life" to explain the concept of the "Happening," describing the move from creating objects in the studio to staging actions out in the world. Today, this amalgamation of art into life and vice versa has extended to seamlessly integrating physical and virtual realities as well. The Performa 19 Commissions by Shu Lea Cheang and Matthew Fuller, Lap-See Lam, Bunny Rogers, Ylva Snöfrid, Yu Cheng-Ta, and Andros Zins-Browne with Karthik Pandian all took this approach, collapsing boundaries between public and private and weaving imagined and live elements into all-encompassing works that enveloped viewers into their spheres of invention.

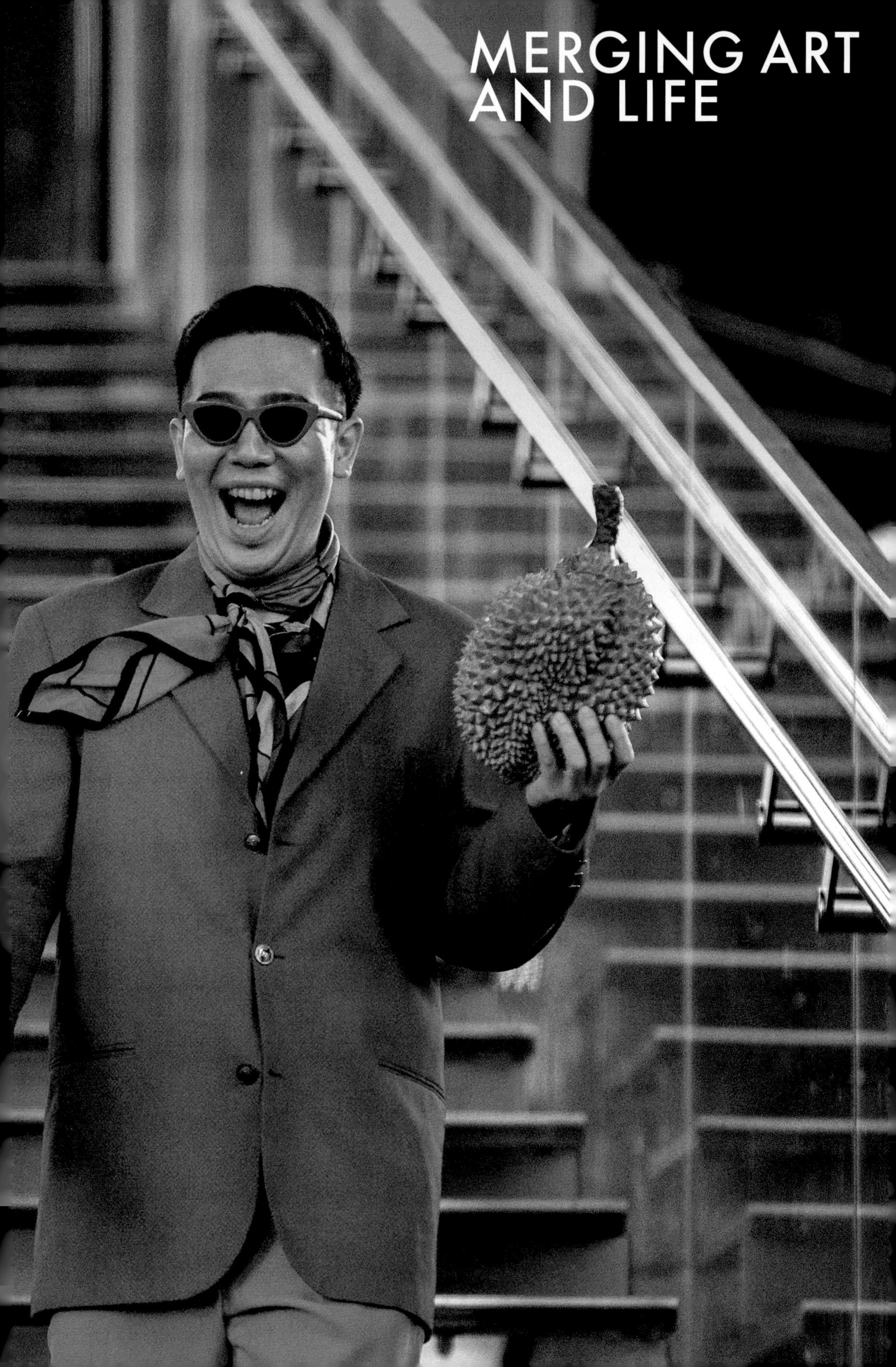

MERGING ART AND LIFE

YU CHENG-TA *FAMEME*

Organized by Esa Nickle and Jo Hsiao

The Museum of Durian and Times Square

November 2–24, 2019

Welcome to the Museum of Durian, where the rotten stench of the fabled fruit pumps through the air filtration system, aggressively neon-orange merchandise scales the walls, and the clock ticks with each flashing light from a glitzy photobooth. Located on busy Canal Street in Downtown New York, the museum was the brick-and-mortar manifestation of Taiwanese artist Yu Cheng-Ta's Performa 19 Commission. A giant garish inflatable of the export and a ball pit (filled with faux fruits) were among the highlights of this made-for-Instagram display. Yu's presentation riffed on the success of the Museum of Ice Cream, an experience which opened in 2016 just a few blocks away in SoHo, and continued to attract more than 500,000 annual visitors and thirty corporate sponsors for years after its debut. A serving of the crop, considered the stinkiest fruit in the world (public consumption and transport of the plant are banned throughout Southeast Asia), would finally be as coveted a treat as a scoop of ice cream.

This was all thanks to the fictional character of *FAMEME*, the Museum of Durian's poster boy brought to life by Yu Cheng-Ta for the occasion. *FAMEME*'s backstory was that of an Asian billionaire farmer who had come to New York City with a mission of promoting the regional delicacy as a "superfood," the trendy buzzword applied by marketers to boost undervalued vegetables like kale by overpromising on their health benefits. Dubious marketing strategies have been the subject of Yu's work before, most notably in his film project *Tell Me What You Want* (2015–17), which followed local panhandlers who made money by offering suspicious night-time services, such as motorcycle rides through the red-light district of Malate in Manila to vacationers. The artist explored these clandestine transactions between East and West and exposed the inherent sexual undertone of modern capitalism's exchanges.

Yu Cheng-Ta is to *FAMEME* as Clark Kent is to Superman: a thinly veiled alter ego enacted by just the slightest change of costume. Once dressed in his flashy red suit, "I♥NY" t-shirt, high-top Converse sneakers, and red cat-eye sunglasses, Yu Cheng-Ta embodies his new identity, a flamboyant and gregarious celebrity, playing in the crosscurrents between persona and artist, fantasy and reality.

FAMEME, whose name combines the words *fame* and *meme*, shamelessly touted durian around town, soliciting social media followers and rattling off viral hashtags such as *#bigapplebigdurian* and *#mesothorny*, posing with anyone who crossed his path. Yu's work often involves playful interactions with audience members and passers-by, creating what the artist calls *life theater*, mockumentary style.

FAMEME's charade related to another provocateur: the iconic Hong Kong-born, East Village photographer Tseng Kwong Chi of the 1980s. Posted to Instagram, FAMEME's slew of selfies channeled the only emotionally charged portrait in Chi's *East Meets West* black-and-white photo series, in which he staged himself as a visitor donning a "Mao suit" and jumping in jubilation in front of the Brooklyn Bridge. With this comparison in mind, the glee of *FAMEME*'s images begins to spoil and the sarcastic consumerist undertones come to the surface. Has the power of branding led to our mindless acceptance of cultural stereotypes? *FAMEME*'s over-the-top showmanship ultimately revealed identities to be easily reduced to packaged performances, bought and consumed, for better or for worse.

In a final climax of fame-chasing, *FAMEME* took us on a jaunt to Times Square, the most popular tourist site in NYC, for his "big reveal." His music-video streamed across the massive digital billboards at Father Duffy Square. Then, in real time, one of his songs boomed from surround-sound speakers while a flash mob broke out, with the character leading an army of pom pom-waving cheerleaders. A bewildered crowd gathered and succumbed to *FAMEME*'s frenzy: New fans and followers were easily won over by the impersonator-influencer. BRITTANY RICHMOND

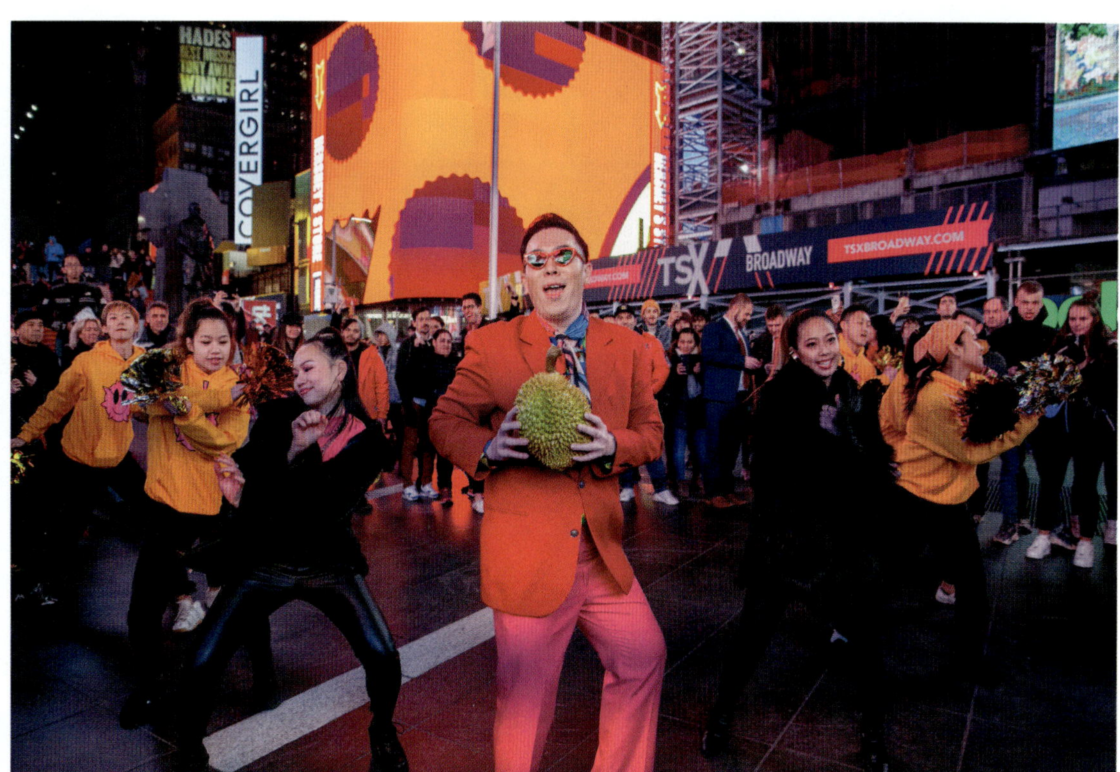

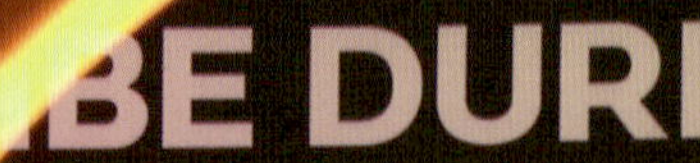
BE DURI

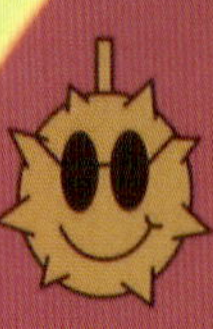
→PERFORMA 19
NOVEMBER 1→24, 2019
NEW YORK CITY

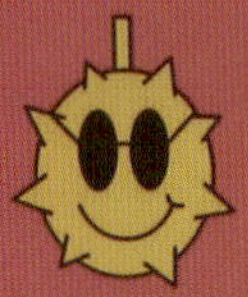
MUSEUM
OF
DURIAN

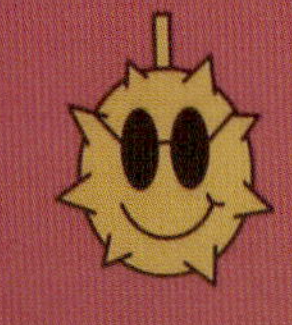
→PERFORMA 19
NOVEMBER 1→24, 2019
NEW YORK CITY

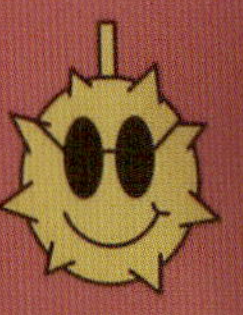
MUSEUM
OF
DURIAN

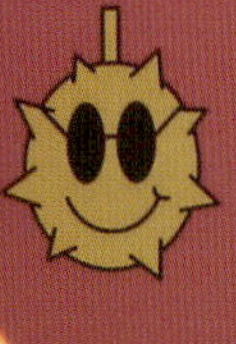
→PERFORMA 19
NOVEMBER 1→24, 2019
NEW YORK CITY

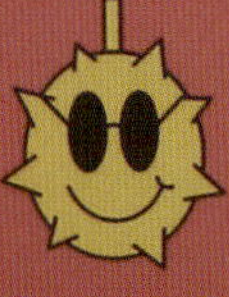

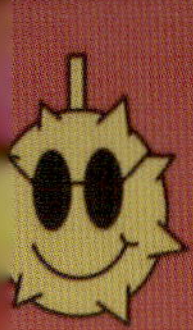
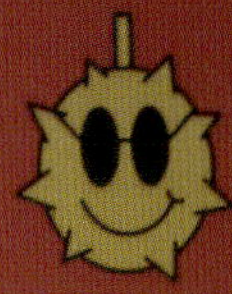
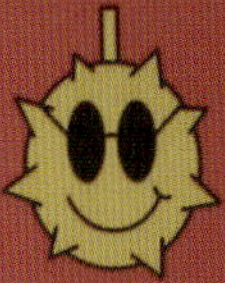
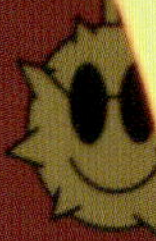
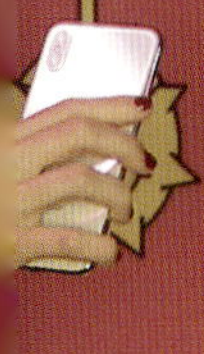
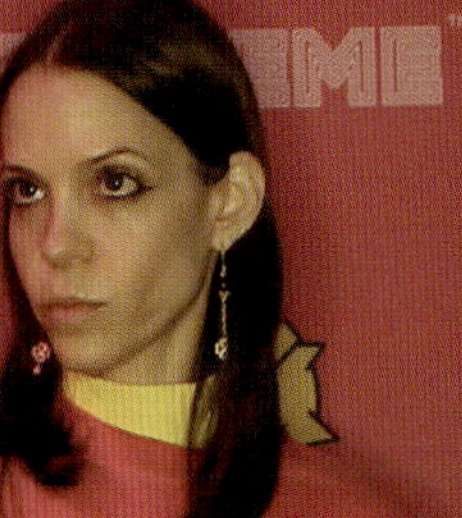
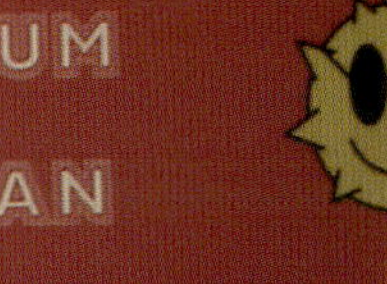
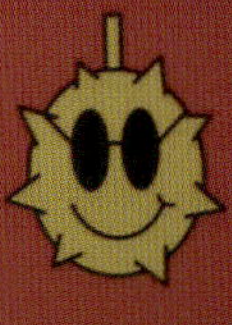

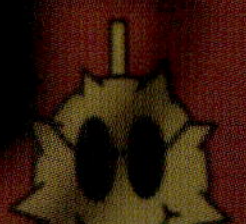

YLVA SNÖFRID

Nostalgia—Acts of Vanitas

Curated by Kathy Noble and Anna van der Vliet with Uchenna Itam

147 Spring Street, fifth floor loft

November 2–24, 2019

Nostalgia—Acts of Vanitas by Ylva Snöfrid began on a street of SoHo, with the simple press of an unmarked apartment buzzer. After entering and embarking on a six-floor climb, the front door opened to a traditional Downtown, sky-lit loft temporarily occupied by the Swedish artist. An attendant was reading *The Odyssey*, the eighth-century BCE tale of Greek mythological hero Odysseus's decade-long expedition home after the Trojan War. It was required reading for each guardian shift of Snöfrid's installation during visiting hours: The epic poem offered something of a gateway to the artist's larger body of work. *Nostalgia* was a culmination of Snöfrid's own journey to dissolve the boundaries between her art and life, initiated in 2009, when she moved parts of her household and its daily activities into Brändström Stockholm gallery for her exhibition "Snöfrid at Her Mirrors, an Odyssey." For Performa 19, the artist voyaged from her home in Greece to create this live/work space in New York City for the course of the three-week biennial.

The room was sparsely furnished with wall radiators, a stovetop, mirrors, a few tables, and an unmade twin-size bed on a stilted platform. Candlesticks, palette knives, lobster tails, and lamb shank bones were laid out on a skinny-legged white table. Nearby still lifes, made in blood reds, fleshy pinks, bile greens, and chalky whites, doubled the presence of these objects. Many of these images were laden with esoteric diagrams and symbols, recalling the spiritual works of Swedish mystic Hilma af Klint (1862–1944). What was once an empty, skeletal space—a blank canvas—had evolved over time with layers of habitual mark-making, both painterly and domestic. Walking toward the middle of the dark hardwood floor, you encountered the artist dressed all in black, sitting on her knees, her long icy-blonde hair grazing her heels while painting a canvas that was propped up against a chair. Her back was turned to visitors as she glanced upward into a handheld mirror and quickly returned brush to canvas. She was painting an enlarged and menacing image of the back of her throat in washed-out gray tones of gouache.

For the most part, Snöfrid proceeded with the painting, undisturbed by onlookers and continued to go about her day, alternating mundane acts of cleaning, cooking, sleeping, or eating with making artworks—all equal "acts of vanitas" for the artist, a reference to the seventeenth-century Dutch artform that symbolizes the transience of life. Depending on the time of your visit, you might get the chance to partake in a ritual directed by Snöfrid, at which point the artist would usher you to come closer into her personal orbit and take a seat at a nearby table. There she would would hand you a coupe glass filled with a concoction of champagne and her own "elixir" to perform what she called a "Transmutation." These séances revolved around incantations, summoning past times and places of her own life to imbue her artworks. Or she could invite you to dine with her and literally eat off of the surface of one of her paintings, subjecting the vulnerable picture to the assault of human voracity.

These intimate encounters transcended into spiritual manifestations. Guided by the otherworldly artist, we were not only reminded that life isn't just about the destination, but rather an epic Odyssey of living, and that art reveals itself in the transient exchange of making. BRITTANY RICHMOND

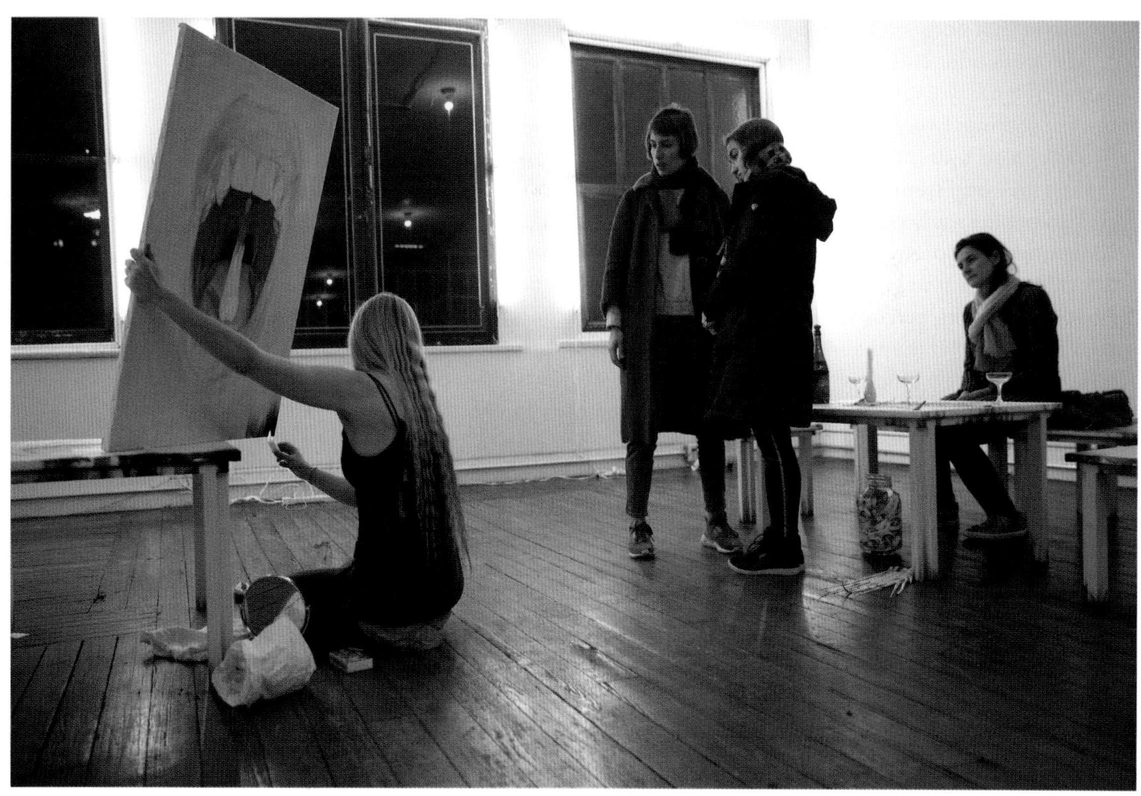

BUNNY ROGERS
Sanctuary

Curated by
Kathy Noble

Essex Street Academy

November 16, 2019

Bunny Rogers—a New York-based artist working with animation, sculpture, installation, and performance to explore how emotion is evoked via the things, spaces, sounds, and ephemeral conditions of the environments we inhabit—transformed the ground floor of Essex Street Academy, its hallways, gyms, and auditorium, into a live installation of sculpture, light, special effects, and performers. Upon entering the building through the front doors, fake snow fell on visitors' heads, and they found bodies slumped on the floor or leaned up against walls of the darkened hallways, illuminated only by a green light coming from under closed doors. Some seemed to be barely hanging on for their lives, others played dead. The horror of this mise-en-scène evoked *Silent Hill*, the popular survival video game of the late 1990s, or the zombie apocalypse television show *The Walking Dead* (2010–). It also, tragically, echoed elements of the mass shootings that occur all too frequently in U.S. schools.

Minutes after entering, music from the school's auditorium, situated at the center of the building, directly opposite the front doors, drew visitors into its rows of seating. Two young women, standing center stage, sang cover songs accompanied by a pianist, just as they would if performing in a talent show, or as though they had stepped out of *Clone High* (2002), the popular MTV animated series from the early aughts. Dressed to mimic the main characters of the show, Cleopatra, Joan of Arc, JFK, and Catherine the Great, the live performers in *Sanctuary* were also in the imagined afterlife of the apparent zombie massacre. Performing on the quintessential auditorium stage, the heart of high-school life, their presence in this unnerving setting was a total contrast to the often-touted idea of school as a place of refuge. Mixing the aesthetics of animated television shows and video games, Rogers created an uncanny environment that was at once familiar and magically surreal.

Haunted objects and visceral effects extended the artist's intense and dramatic iconography: Symbolic twines of flowers and ribbons were woven onto the railings at the main entrance; a funeral wreath of dark purple and black flowers stood at the auditorium doors; plastic snow falling in the halls; dense fog in the two adjacent gyms; and one hundred bodies in jeans, t-shirts, and goth makeup were both horrific memento mori of real events and re-enactments from low-budget B-movies. Taken together, everything clashed in a disturbing inspirational quote hanging on a classroom door: "Everything will be okay in the end. If it's not okay, then it's not the end." The artifice of it all was an overt simulation, yet the haunting affect of the sensations and the emotions it evoked in the viewers was very real.

Rogers dissects precisely how her worldview was shaped by her media consumption of the late 1990s and 2000s and explores the contemporary adolescent experience in today's digital world to analyze how individual and collective memories are shaped. Her previous work has explored the media's representation of being a teenager, including the violent school shootings in America—such as the 1999 Columbine High School massacre, in which fifteen students and teachers died and another twenty-four were injured, ending with the two teenage shooters committing suicide together after their killing spree. The crime was subsequently glamorized via copycat murders and online fangirls who expressed their love for these destructive young men. Alongside ruminating on the formation of memory, Rogers's work addresses the way that images of trauma are instantly consumed, and on the same visual plane, as any other image on the internet.

Sanctuary was preceded by a trilogy of exhibitions addressing this tragedy: "Columbine Library" (2014), "Columbine Cafeteria" (2016), and "Brig Und Ladder" (2017). Each installation evoked the aesthetics of the communal spaces in the school—the cafeteria, the library, and the auditorium. Each exhibition recalled symbolic details of the scene of the massacre via color, image, sculpture, light, architecture, and gestures. In addition, Rogers created a prelude titled *A Very Special Holiday Performance in Columbine Auditorium* (2017), in which a similar

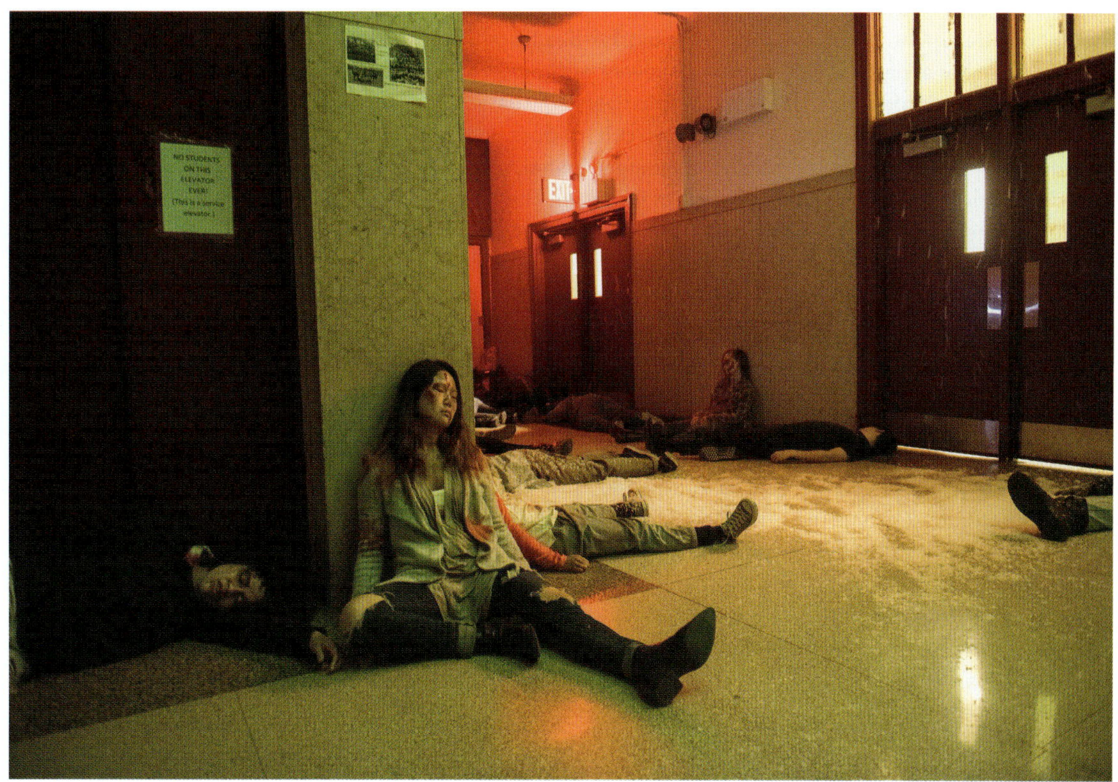

performance is presented in animated form; she also staged a fictional funeral for herself the following year that included a self-portrait in the style of Victorian memorial photography, hung between dark purple and black funeral wreaths, to allude to the part of Rogers that has already died. Columbine occurred during the artist's teenage years, and her online consumption of its details was deeply formative in her own understanding of trauma, both personal and collective, making it a lynchpin in her artistic exploration of societal trauma.

Sanctuary is perhaps her most viscerally affective exploration of this massacre to date. Staged in a large complex housing five public high schools on Manhattan's Lower East Side, it merged fiction with reality in an uncomfortably confrontational way. One of the school's Deputy Heads worked closely with the artist, curator, and producer to facilitate the performance; fully aware of its content and intentions and the possible effects of this reconstruction on the students, the school was supportive of the open address of this ongoing, terrifying issue. The duty of protecting their students from gun violence, or any violence, is a frightening reality for teachers across the country: Due to the widespread availability of guns throughout the U.S., there is no way to predict when and where something like this may occur. Nevertheless, this form of mass murder is almost always committed by young white males who display a lethal combination of privilege and violently misanthropic feelings toward society and themselves, often displaying traits of mental illnesses and personality disorders caused by childhood trauma. Sociopaths disguised as average white teenage boys are all too real in the history of trauma— political, racial, sexual, and social—and its continued manifestation in America.

It is too easy to describe Rogers's fascination with the massacre as a romanticization of the death of youth or the martyr-like tragedy or spectacle of suicide. Yet her series of exhibitions on the event addresses how the mass media has disseminated these scenes to be passively consumed, its aesthetics permeating our lives in the same way that pop culture does. In turn, her own experience of this trauma was a formative moment for her, rooting itself in her own chronic depression and teenage suicidal fantasies. The personal and the public became inextricably intertwined as she came of age during the evolution of the internet, a time when horrific events began to be experienced in isolation on one's own small glowing screen—causing the viewer to experience them in a more intimate way than ever before.

Sanctuary recreated one of the worst moments in recent American history, yet it also appeared as a macabre spectacle. Which leads us to the question: How can we come together to face collective horror, especially when we watch it alone? Beyond the trauma of the initial event, its second, third and fourth iterations, ad infinitum—online, as a set of still and moving images in a Möbius loop of repetition—become the primary mode in which most of us experience this tragedy. This type of documentation circulates freely online, often appearing on our screens without warning. Therefore, the trauma of viewing it secondhand is, in its own right, another genuine experience. The flattened nature of the image, the mimicry, the allusion, the fake becoming real and the real becoming fake, the blurring of the digital and the physical— is all interwoven here in a performance both evocative and provocative. Rogers uncannily conjures the internet's role as a communal repository for every aspect of existence today, as well as its online performance and re-performance, with *Sanctuary*; the architecture of the real high school combined with the spectacle of nearly dead bodies and the amateur nature of the talent show invoked both the spectacle of the mediatization of this event online and the emotional fragility we felt at the shock of aspects of this massacre being brought to life. KATHY NOBLE

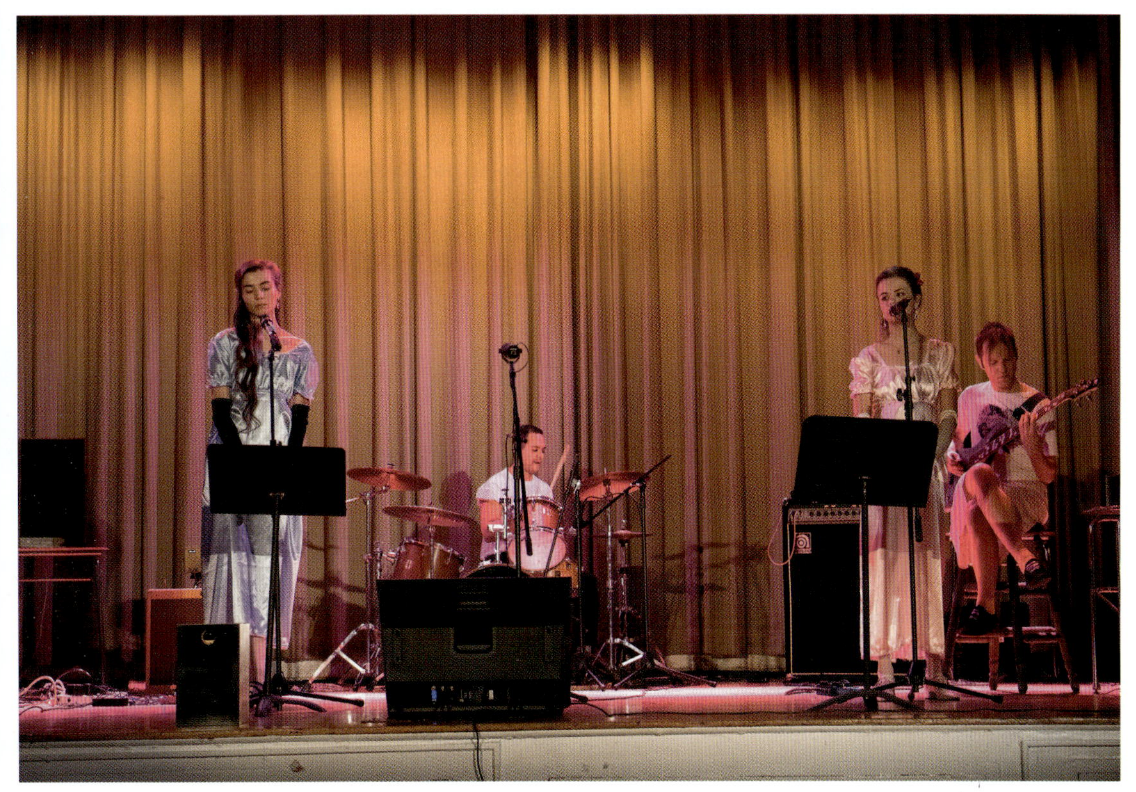

LAP-SEE LAM

Phantom Banquet

Curated by
Sara Arrhenius

Performa 19 Hub
(18 Wooster)

November 12–16, 2019

In an ongoing process of digital preservation, Lap-See Lam documents and exhibits Stockholm's endangered traditional Chinese restaurants, archiving the material, spatial, and cultural legacies of the Hong Kong and Chinese diasporas in her hometown. Lam grew up in these restaurants; in the 1970s, her grandmother and grand-uncle opened Bamboo Garden in Stockholm's Södermalm district and passed ownership to Lam's parents before closing in 2015. In an attempt to recall her family's restaurant, the artist began collecting and archiving similar eating houses as "emotional souvenirs," preserving them through 3D scanning, cartography, installation, virtual reality scenarios, and storytelling.

Each night of *Phantom Banquet* gathered an intimate group of ten guests, the event interweaving live performance with virtual reality. In her installation of three small, connected rooms, Lam replicated the rituals and hospitalities of a Chinese restaurant, with a performer acting as its host. Visitors became restaurant patrons, and were escorted into a dark, curtained room to find edible miniature banquet chairs prepared by Mission Chinese Food, a beloved Downtown destination for Sichuan cuisine. While the audience snacked, Lam narrated the tale of Ying, a young girl who, while cleaning her parents' restaurant, pricked her finger and found, suddenly, that the restaurant around her was vanishing. We were beckoned further into the kitsch decor of Lam's makeshift banquet room, where we sat at a pearl-white table and, fitted with VR headsets, entered a similarly unsettling, virtual space: a restaurant or, rather, the digital remains of it.

In creating her index of Chinese restaurants in Stockholm, Lam spends hours producing multiple color scans and 360-degree images, usually at the restaurant's emptiest moments. At first striving for complete accuracy, Lam soon relished the imprecisions and frictions that the technological process may incur. For the artist, the digital translations of these spaces can produce "the feeling of a ruin, like a shipwreck." With Lam, tools for architectural preservation are put to better use when evoking memory and its slippages.

Indeed, in *Phantom Banquet*, renderings at first appeared stable, like a fly in amber; but quickly, rooms began to twitch in our headsets' fields of vision. Walls started to vibrate around us and interior objects such as cushioned booths, high chairs for infants, and intricate carvings and woodwork began to shake and warp, producing the feeling of a volatile, shifting architecture. As we moved throughout the restaurant's interior, our vision of it was pulled away to reveal its exoskeleton; we were floating in the undefined space of a borderless digital realm.

A ghostly figure appeared and began to wander this virtual space with us. The figure was, in part, a glitch: While documenting the restaurants, anybody caught in front of the lens—patrons, workers, passersby—would be momentarily captured by the scanner, leaving behind a fuzzy, near-human form. Lam treats these specter-like figures as welcome guests.

A joyous, high-pitched melody erupted and, with it, reality pierced VR. We removed our headsets to encounter a live quartet playing traditional Chinese music in the adjoining room, where the same haunting figure was now sitting in a cherry-red neon banquet chair in between two of the musicians. The luminous sculpture filled the room with an ember glow. Seated among the living, it reflected for Lam the lives within these restaurants, the people who worked or dined there, and the traces they left behind. For the artist, people, and their spiritual presence, define space as much as aesthetics and objects do. All linger, and distort, in memory. QUINN SCHOEN

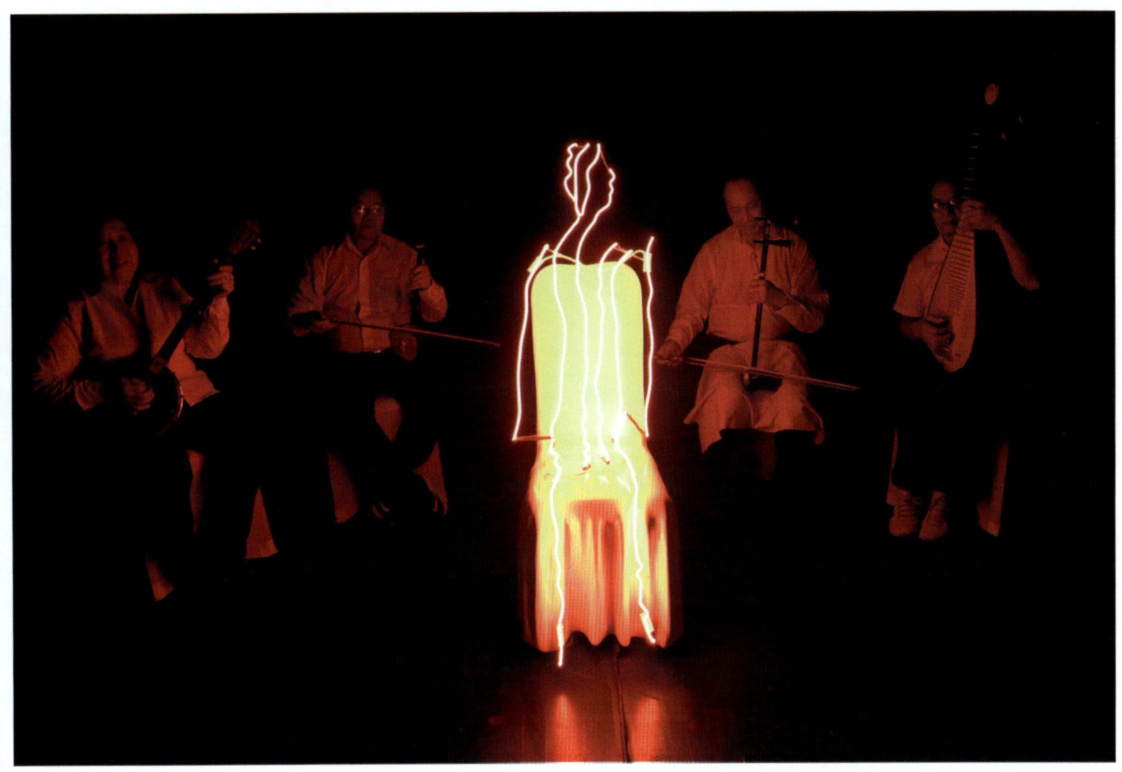

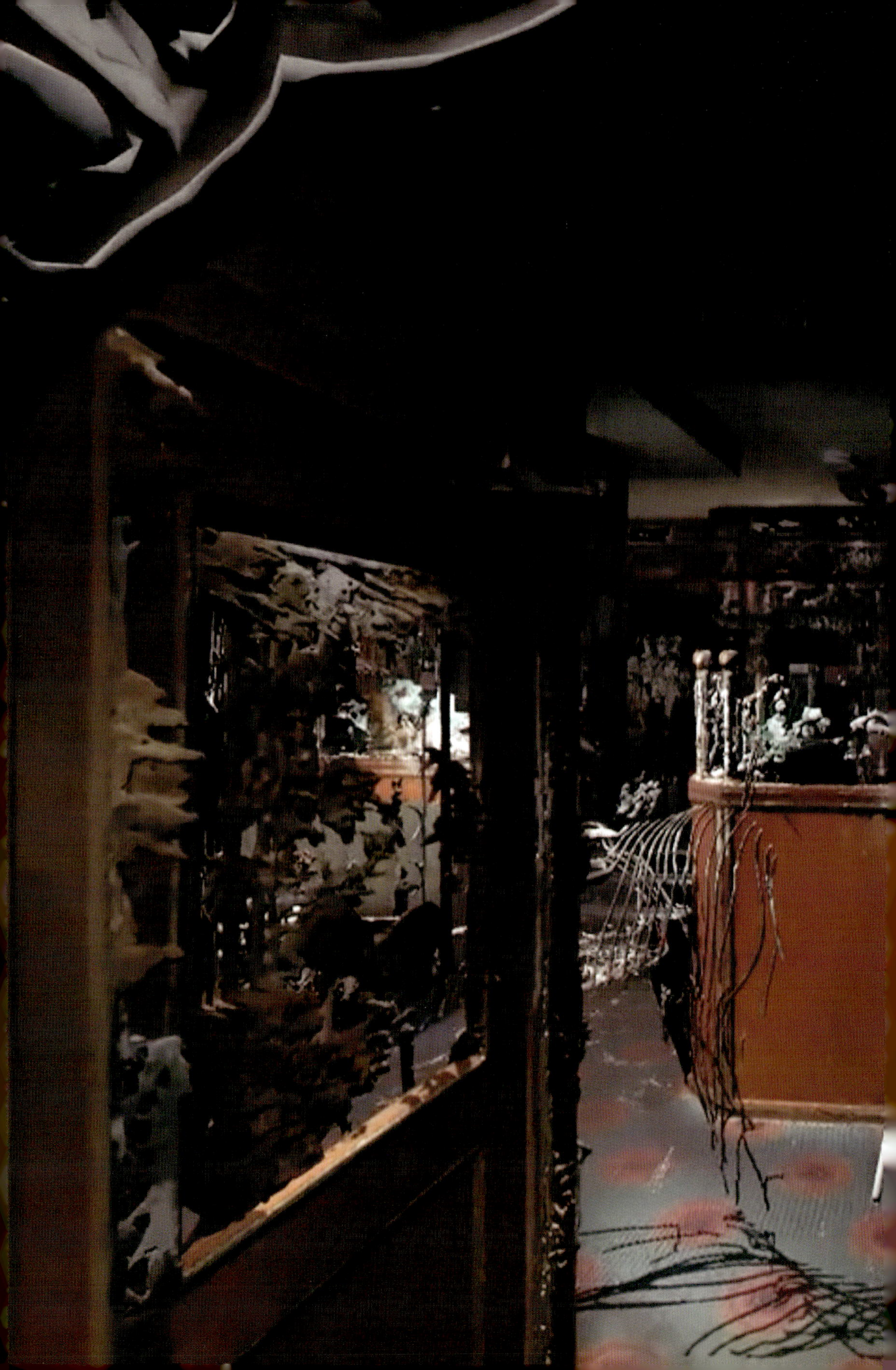

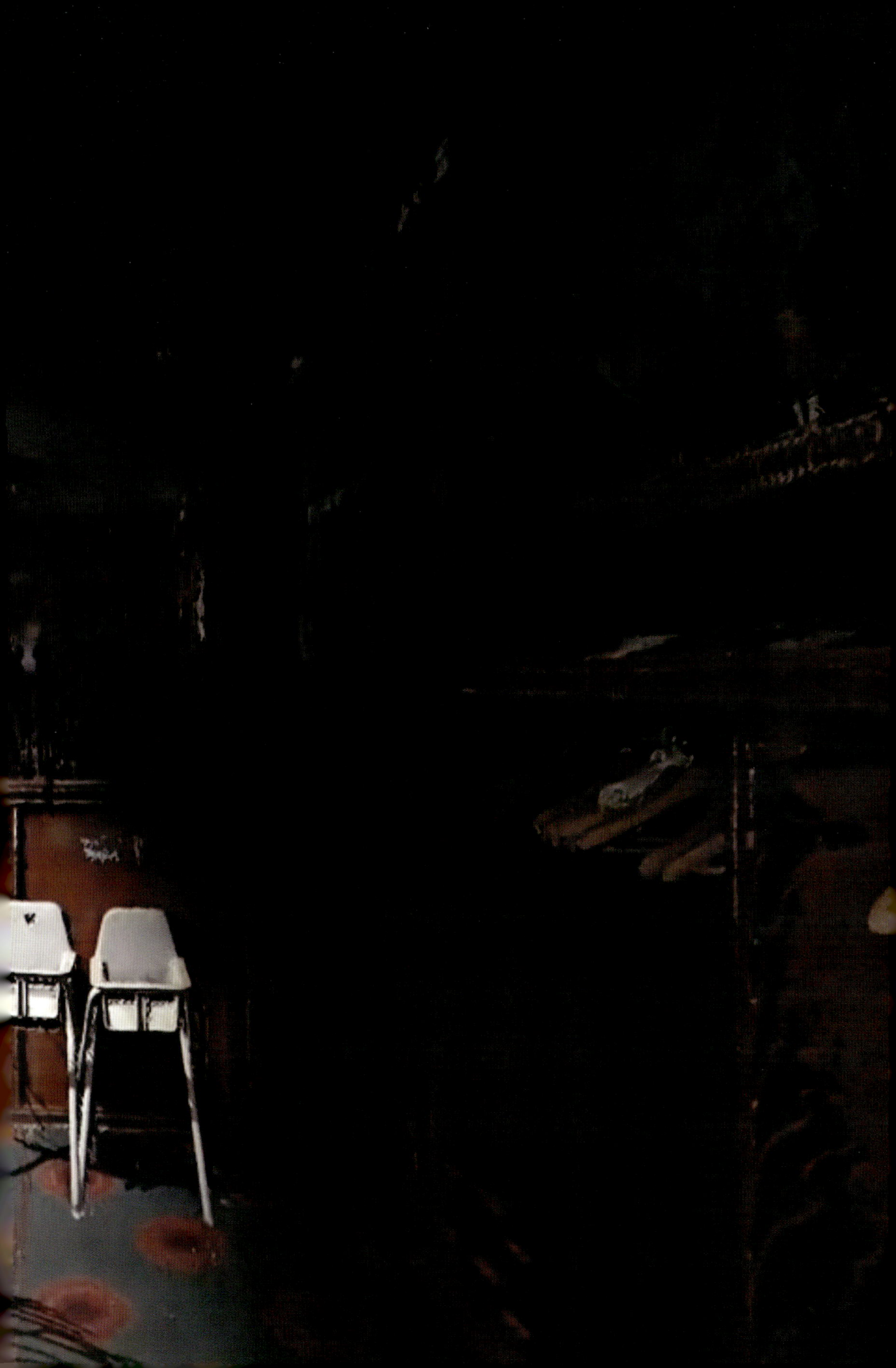

SHU LEA CHEANG

SLEEP1237

Strolling by the Performa 19 Hub at 47 Wooster Street, one couldn't help but notice the piles of heavy machinery, plywood tool sheds, and tarpaulins, as well as stacks of scaffolding strewn along the street outside, so ubiquitous is road construction in the city these days. Inside the clean white cube of the Hub, behind the big plate glass facing the street, the interior scene was not dissimilar. Tall scaffolding towers loomed over poured concrete; sleeping mats and garbage bags randomly littered the floor. In the center, a red upholstered neoclassical-style *chaise longue* and a reading lamp awaited activation.

At sundown on November 2, 2019, Taiwanese-born media artist, filmmaker, and cyberfeminist Shu Lea Cheang and cultural studies theorist Matthew Fuller's *SLEEP1237* took over the space with an overnight reading that lasted until sunrise. Broadcast live on the arts organization Wave Farm's net radio station and WGXC-90.7 FM in New York's Upper Hudson Valley, the title of the event was named for its length—twelve hours and thirty-seven minutes—and accounted for daylight savings time, which fell back one hour that night. Thirteen readers, made up of artists, performers, scholars, and writers each spent an hour and five minutes lulling the audience to sleep with their readings of so-called "grey" literature, complicated technical texts not usually considered ideal for bedtime reading. Conceptual artist Martha Rosler, lying comfortably on the chaise, read legal briefs from a court-case battle to keep the free-speech radio station WBAI-99.5 FM running. She would change places with investigative data journalist Surya Mattu, who began a monotonous reading of Facebook Inc.'s patent documents, while new media scholar McKenzie Wark later read instructions for hormone replacement therapy. Particularly effective at inducing sleep in audience members, who lounged on bunched-up blankets and mats on the floor, were the instances in which numbers were read aloud; actress Phumzile Sitole rhymed on Pantone color codes and artist-writer Larissa Pham calmly delivered prime numbers, the latter recalling On Kawara's many-days-long readings of *One Million Years*. As the performers droned on, listeners dozed off, aided by sleep-inducing food and drink, including wild rice salad loaded with melatonin, soothing tisanes, and a custom-brewed ale infused with calming herbs.

Departing from previous iterations of their "sleep" projects hosted by C-LAB in Taipei, Taiwan and by STWST in Linz, Austria (both 2018)—which offered cozy beds fashioned to look like luxurious rickshaws and no-nonsense army cots, respectively—Cheang and Fuller relinquished any remaining smidge of comfort in New York City. Here, there were no beds, only scratchy olive-green army blankets,

Curated by Charlene K. Lau with Taiwan Contemporary Culture Lab (C-LAB)

Performa 19 Hub (47 Wooster)

November 2, 2019

1 Matthew Fuller, *How to Sleep: The Art, Biology and Culture of Unconsciousness* (London: Bloomsbury, 2018), 19.

2 Ibid., 19.

thin foam sleeping mats, and a mess of dusty garbage bags scattered on the cold, hard floor. But anyhow, what use is a bed? As Fuller reflects in his book *How to Sleep: The Art, Biology and Culture of Unconsciousness* (2018), "The bed is not a refuge but a place to be beset by problems in a different mode."[1] Like a discomfiting slumber party, *SLEEP1237* knew no real restfulness, no sweet dreams, only ratcheting boredom as the hours passed by. But its success was precisely in this peculiar boredom, like a strange spectacle of anti-entertainment whereby surrendering to the mundane generated interest.

While the performance's aesthetics of rough sleeping point generally to economic inequality, it more incisively troubles the relationship of the art world to commodification and labor, where exploitation is in service to the art market. Staged in what was once a designer footwear store, contemporary art squats at the literal site of luxury consumerism, lapping up the leftovers in a city and country where buying things is the ultimate expression of selfhood and success. Simultaneously, *SLEEP1237* faced off with art's complex entanglement with gentrification and global capitalism, as seen in the transformation of SoHo from an industrial area in the late nineteenth century into affordable housing for artists in the 1960s, and onward to the "world-class" shopping destination that it is today. In its antidote to boredom, sleep is the death of capitalism, a respite in the face of labor and commerce. For Cheang's own reading at 3:03am, a computer-generated recording read code that designer and coder Jason Lee wrote for *3x3x6*, her exhibition for the Taiwanese Pavilion at the 58th Venice Biennale held earlier that year. The artist also slept, slouching on the chaise, her eyes covered by dark, futuristic sunglasses. A mark of refusal, Cheang did not perform her work for her audience. Instead, it worked for her. Befuddlingly, while sleep was the (art) work, it was also against work.

On the other hand, maybe repose comes as a means of avoidance and a chance to disappear from the world, if only for a moment. Perhaps being awake is too awful, reality too horrible, and, as Fuller says, "Sleep is a merciful chance to escape the treadmill of your own subjectivity."[2] We sleep to forget. But even then, it's difficult to commit to sleep. Dozens upon dozens of audience members drifted in and out of sleep, and in and out of the space over the course of the night. Their transience echoed the rhythms of city life, with most of them not being able to stay awake till dawn. And yet, some stalwarts remained as the sun rose over the East River at 6:28am. CHARLENE K. LAU

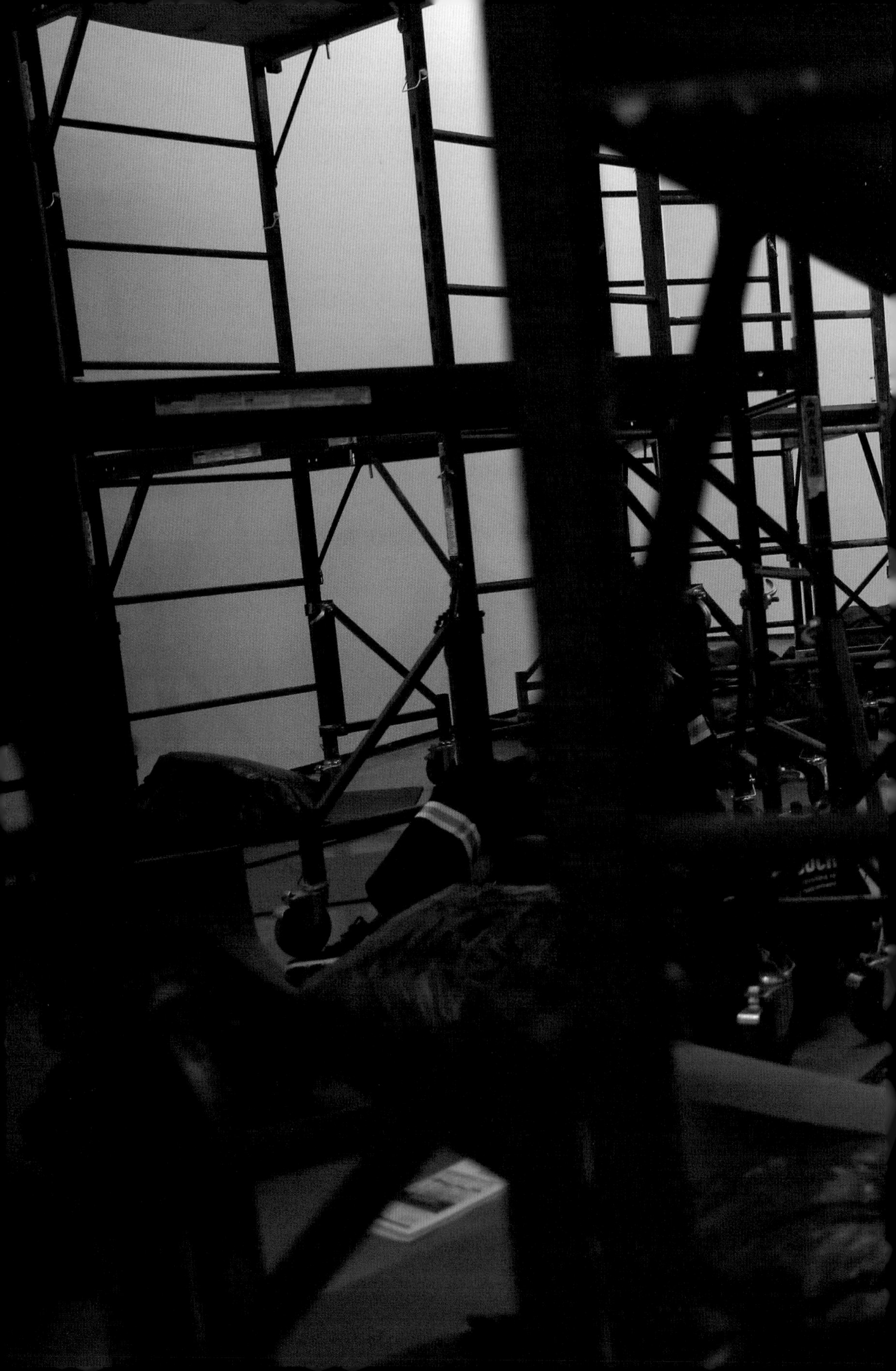

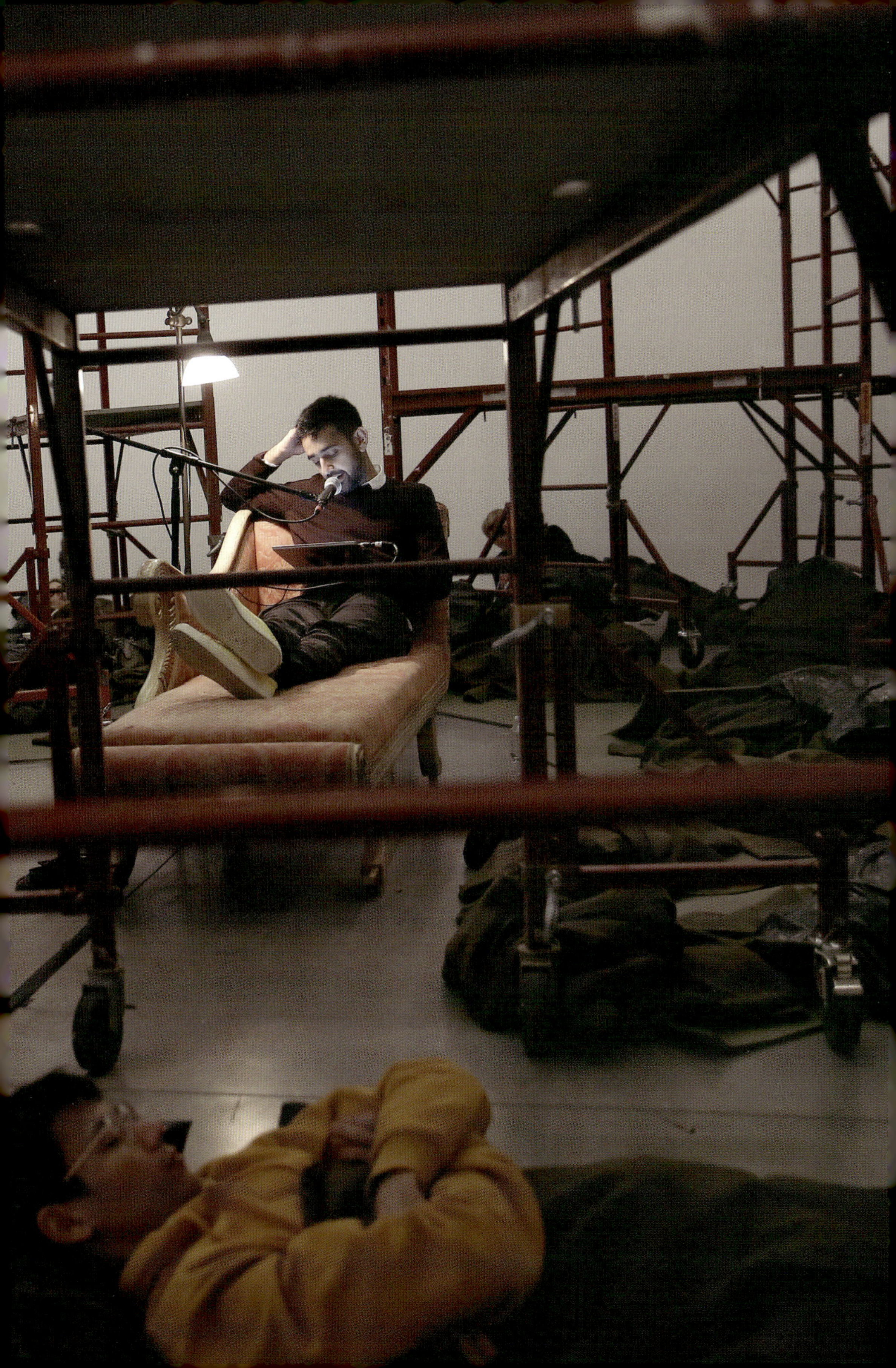

KARTHIK PANDIAN & ANDROS ZINS-BROWNE

Atlas Unlimited Acts VII-X

Curated by
Nicola Lees

80WSE Gallery

October 10–
November 3,
2019

I caught the show on the afternoon of its final Sunday. Speeding southwest off of FDR Drive straight into a snarl of East Village traffic, the crawl to Washington Square took almost the same time as the hundred miles of preceding highway. Like the digital latency of local communications networks, it is always the last mile that takes the longest. But for American visual artist Karthik Pandian and American choreographer Andros Zins-Browne's *Atlas Unlimited*, an ongoing series of interrelated exhibitions and performances, the spectator necessarily arrives late, and always enters into the middle of the act(ion). Their collaboration began in the wake of the Arab Spring in 2011, and early *Atlas* iterations centered on the mass circulation of images from those revolts. In their installation/performance at 80WSE Gallery, their wider range of actions were instantiated by the stories, related in absentia, of their friend and collaborator Zakaria Almoutlak.

That Almoutlak is a sculptor whose life trajectory would be radically altered by the events that sprang from the nascent days of the Syrian revolution, and just how radically; that he'd made counterfeit ancient sculptures displayed in prominent museums and had made and destroyed some of the work shown in this exhibition; that he'd met Pandian and Zins-Browne by chance, developing a long-lasting friendship and collaboration with the pair, I would only learn later. When I did, these details and all their attendant dramas seemed to resonate less as information and more as reverberation, the stories bouncing literally and figuratively off the gallery's walls, off the bodies of the performers and visitors alike, off the objects (playing the roles of both sculpture and resonator) placed within the exhibition.

80WSE is not only familiar to me because of its vernacular "gallery" architecture—the series of domestically scaled rooms that flow front to back behind a nineteenth-century façade—but because my collaborators and I worked so deliberately against such associations in our own show here,[1] which was presented right before this one. Whereas we immersed the rooms in the reddish-gray pallor of lost time common to the edit suite, the cinema and the casino, *Atlas Unlimited* enhanced, rather than concealed, the gallery architecture. Instead of losing track of time, this exhibition sought to still it and then to deliberately point to its capture.

The first room greeted me with the light that filtered through the window's sculpted *mashrabiya*, a design feature typical in Islamic architecture. The wooden screen, equal parts devotional and carceral, projected such a perfectly constructed image of museological affect that it simultaneously signaled contemplation and conquest, as if an object was swiped from elsewhere and forced (lovingly) into this new architectural context. Such plays on the slipperiness

1
13BC: Fatal Act, 80 Washington Square East, New York University, June 21–September 7, 2019.

2
Nina Sun Eidsheim, *The Race of Sound: Listening, Timbre, and Vocality in African American Music* (Durham, North Carolina: Duke University Press, 2019), 50.

of cultural imperialism and ideological staging are typical of Pandian and Zins-Browne's collaborations, which engage us in a bait-and-switch between persuasion and coercion, using the seduction of theatrical and exhibitionary aesthetics to prod at their uncomfortable consequences.

A grotesquely large hoof bore down on a fragment of a cartoonish camel head in the central gallery. Drawn toward it by singing voices, an exchange of stories reverberating through the flimsy walls, I turned to the room next door. Two singers knelt on a canvas mat of fragmented images: The scenic backdrop stitched the Roman Theatre at Palmyra to Cairo's Tahrir Square to the desolate space of a refugee encampment, each set against a collage of sky. In front of this photorealistic backdrop that stretched from the wall down and across the floor like a broken cyclorama, I sat on one corner of it to listen.

"Sound is produced by the listener," writes musicologist Nina Sun Eidsheim, "[and] the evidence is planted."[2] Her reading of sonic subjectivity came immediately to mind as I self-consciously switched registers between aesthetic and perceptual appreciation of the expertly trained voices of Ganavya Doraiswamy and Aliana de la Guardia, their physical presence in the gallery, and the work I had to do to decipher Zakaria Almoutlak's story channeled by the genre-shifting libretto they were performing. Melodic fragments from sources as varied as Solange; Peter, Paul and Mary; and *The Sound of Music* traced the borders of musical recognition, while the lyrics, co-authored by Pandian and Zins-Browne along with Almoutlak, narrated stories from Almoutlak's life—from his time imprisoned by the Syrian regime for his media activism; a wedding in his war-torn hometown of Homs; receiving his refugee status in Belgium; to his devastating visit to the U.S. consulate in Brussels, when his visa to come to New York to participate in this exhibition was denied. As the voices danced a *pas de deux*, they switched seamlessly from the repetition of vocal rehearsal into choral harmonics and recitative speech act. When one took over and the other manifested a supporting rhythm, each singer's timbre and technique imprinted subtle aural differences. It was no accident that my untrained ears could notice this, as Pandian and Zins-Browne cast these two singers for their specialized backgrounds: de la Guardia in the Italian operatic style, Doraiswamy in the Hindu devotional practice of *Abhang*, two distinct traditions that require equal vocal skill in dynamic dramaturgy and tonal resonance. A discrete polyphony emerged from the playful grammar of the libretto: "When the mu-usic begin, that's when I said, we lost the game."

I felt glaringly aware of my own body, the behavior of my face in proximity to the performers', my knowledge of the gallery, and of how, here, sounds usually work against us. Performed as much by the architecture and its staging as by the voices of the singers, this work reached us through the sonic waves of secondary reflections. It projected Almoutlak's travails through Pandian and Zins-Browne's *mise-en-scène*. The songs literally interacted with the materiality of that which surrounds them, vibrating from the vocal cords of the singers to be absorbed by the bodies of the spectators and the weave of the canvas backdrop. The exposed studs and gaps between the drywall joined the textured foam and limestone surfaces of the sculptures to generate a gentle diffusion, such that the Syrian artist's journey resonated softly through the spaces, as intimate as a radio transmission that enters your living room. I was suddenly struck by how good it all sounded, how intimately profound in all its a cappella high frequencies. It felt strange that in this gallery—

with all its hard, parallel surfaces, where sound reverberates into flutters of echo that should render voices unintelligible—that I should understand or feel anything so clearly. But this artwork is both speech and song, both critique and fiction; it wants resonance for its music and clarity for its narrative.

In a tight space at the back of 80WSE and adjacent to the room where we listened, someone was excavating a sculptural relief, working upon a small scaffold tucked against the wall. It was a succinct operation that communicated how both the past and future were concealed in each object, refrain, and action. This itinerant work took shape from the ruins of a sculpture produced and then destroyed by Almoutlak during *Act III* in Belgium in 2018. The stone fragments from this statue were subsequently transported to Chicago to be conserved by others in *Acts V–VI*, only to be displaced here, destroyed, ground into rubble, and reconstituted again as the fresco that was being revealed on the wall before us.

"As a spectator, I always come late,"[3] said Ariella Aïsha Azoulay, mulling the simultaneous capture of past lives and the perceptual encounter with photography. Earlier *Acts* of *Atlas Unlimited* reverberated throughout the gallery, radically extending the same latency and tension Azoulay identified. A single sound wave hit the eardrum, containing every spatial, material, and perceptual characteristic of its surroundings, an acoustic fingerprint that we unconsciously absorbed as we tried to piece Almoutlak's life together. VIC BROOKS

3
Leslie Hewitt in conversation with Ariella Aïsha Azoulay, Pratt Institute, Brooklyn, New York, October 30, 2020. See also Ariella Aïsha Azoulay, *Potential History: Unlearning Imperialism* (Brooklyn; London: Verso, 2019).

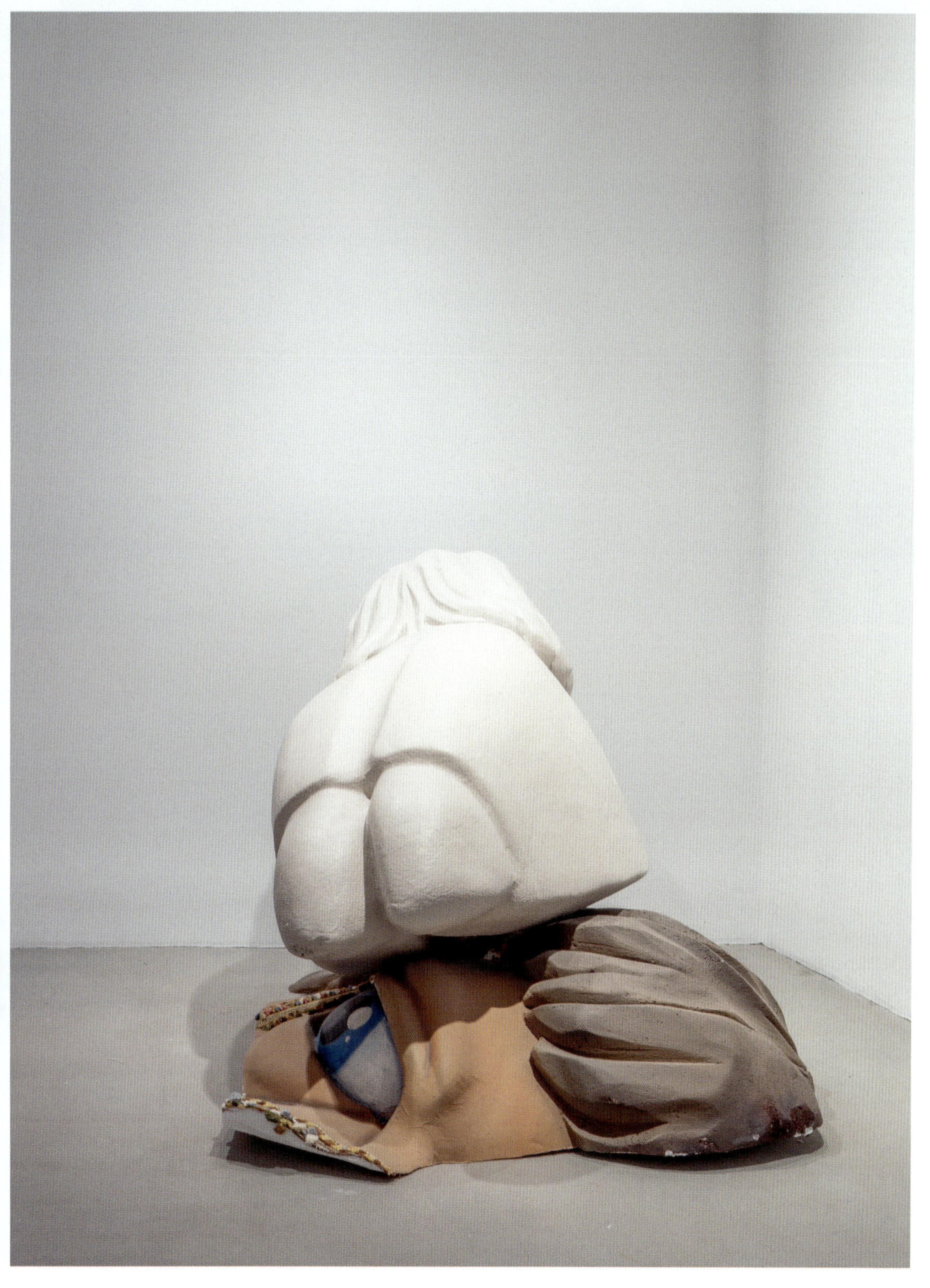

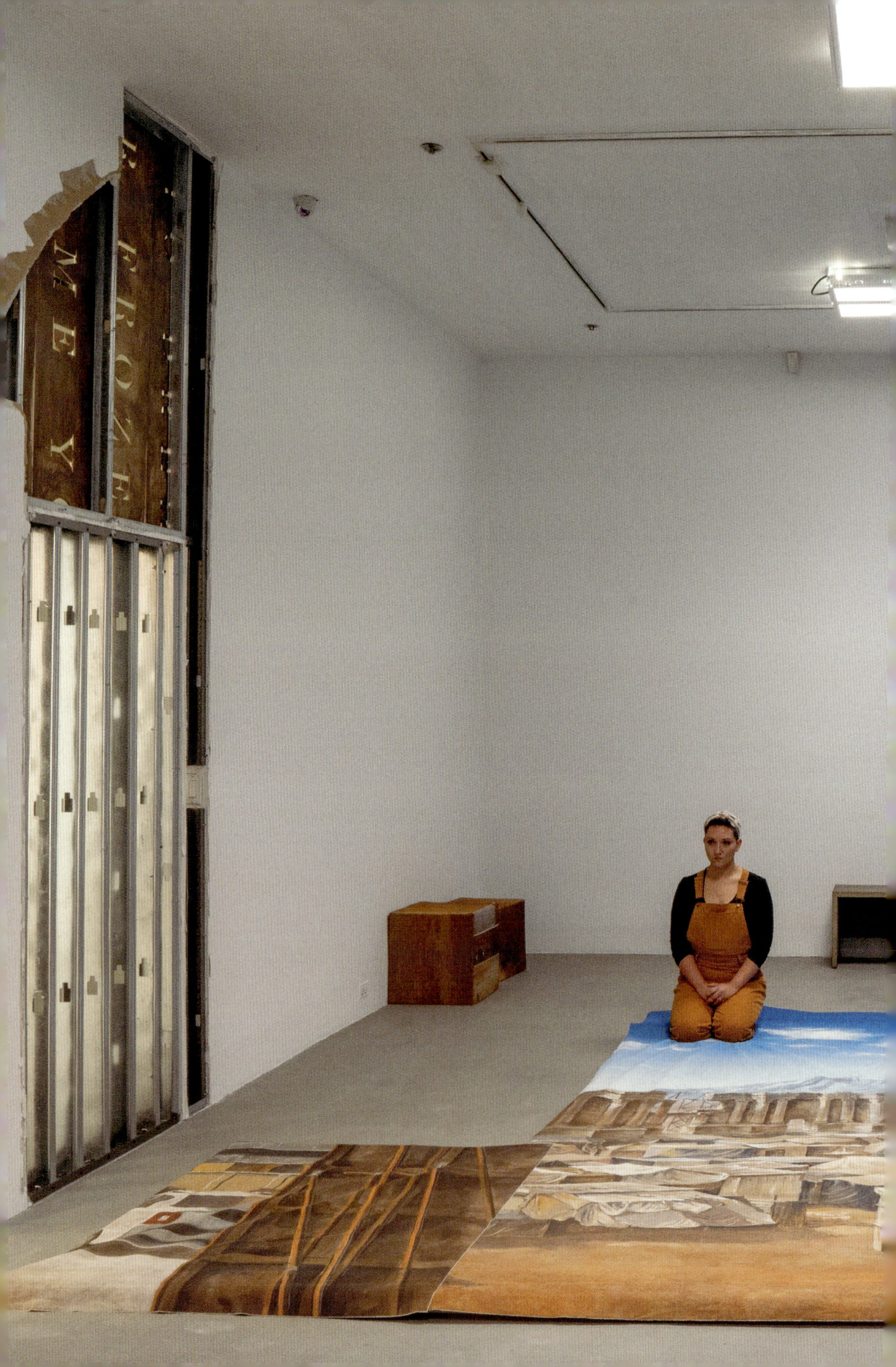

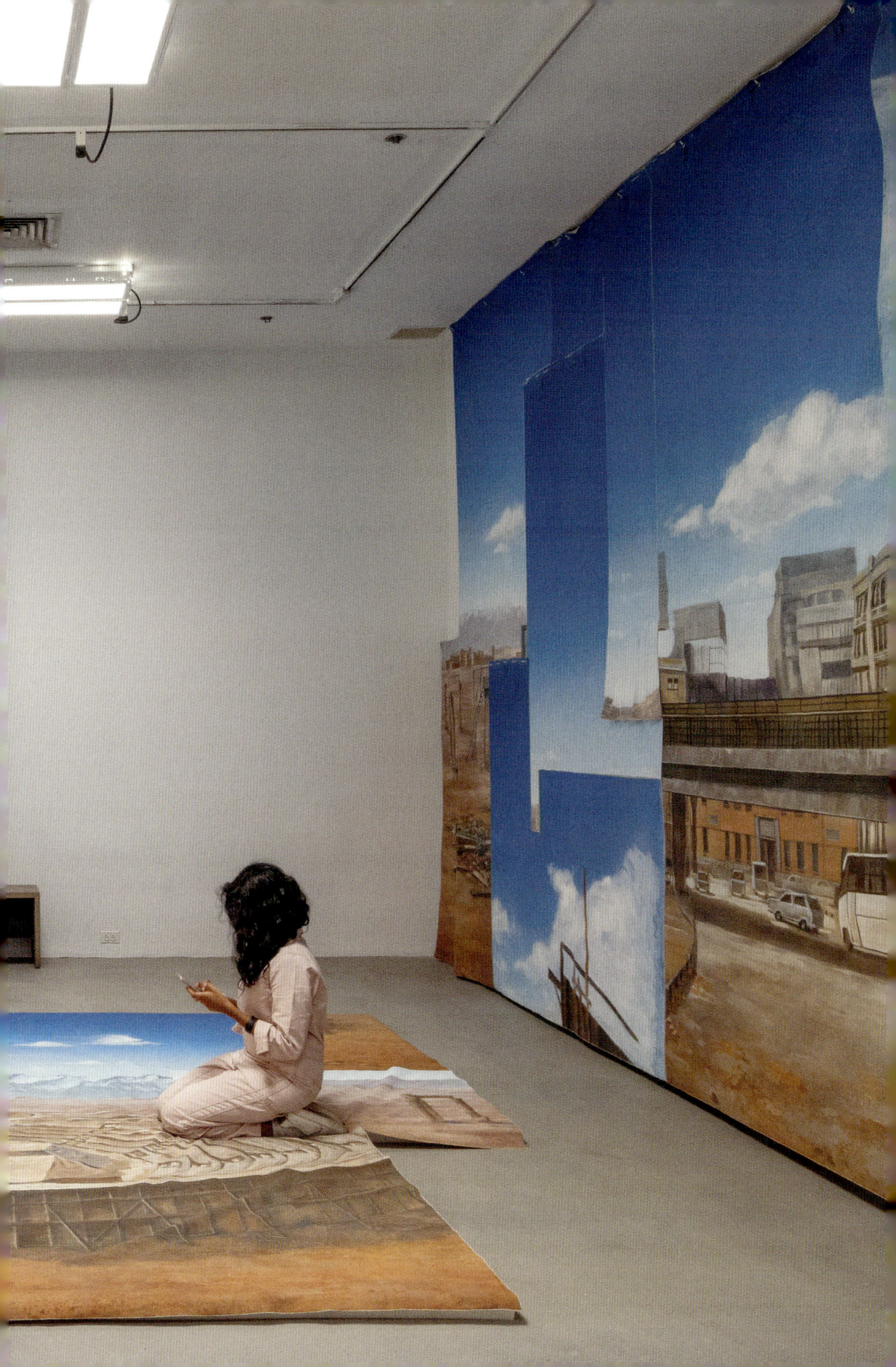

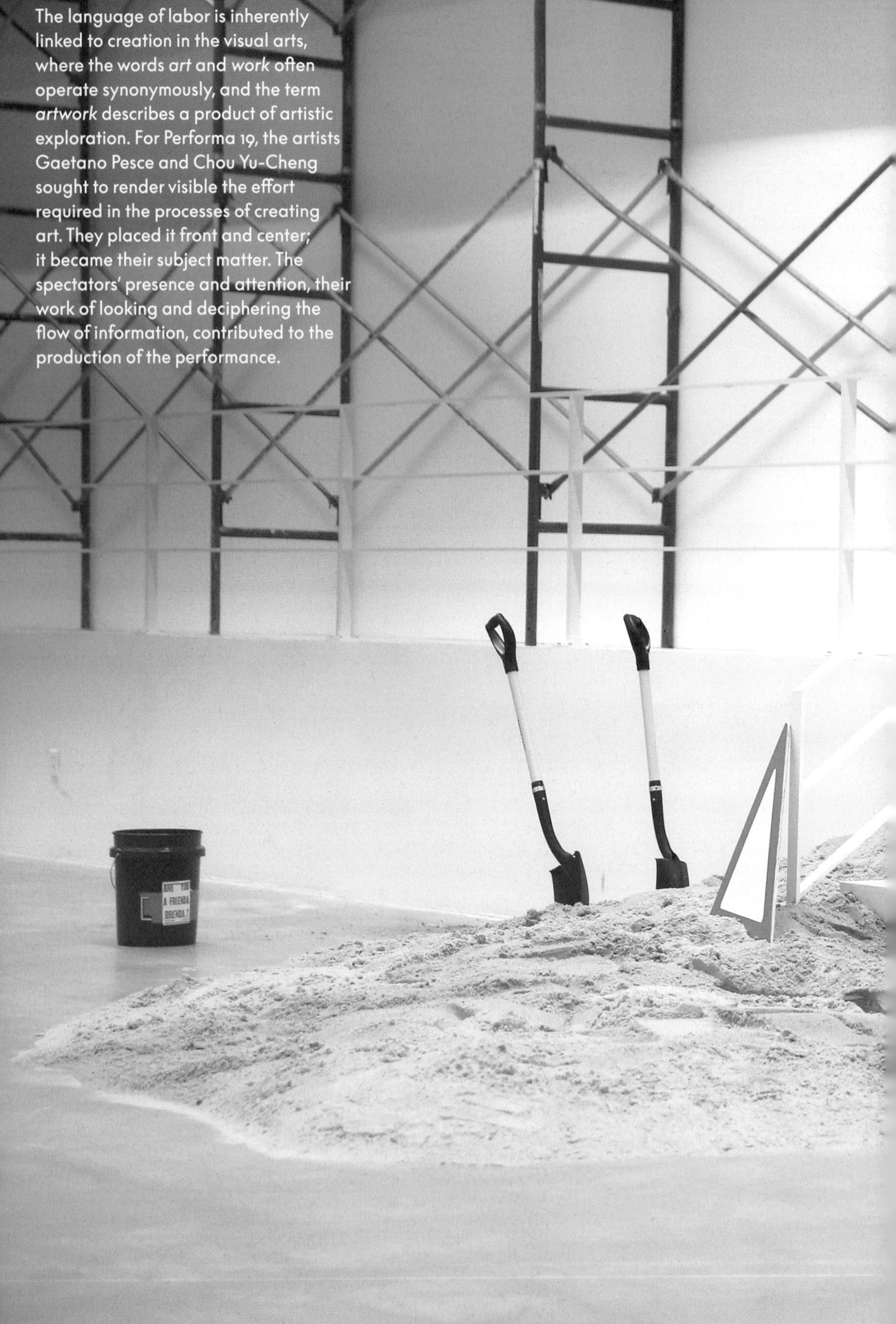

The language of labor is inherently linked to creation in the visual arts, where the words *art* and *work* often operate synonymously, and the term *artwork* describes a product of artistic exploration. For Performa 19, the artists Gaetano Pesce and Chou Yu-Cheng sought to render visible the effort required in the processes of creating art. They placed it front and center; it became their subject matter. The spectators' presence and attention, their work of looking and deciphering the flow of information, contributed to the production of the performance.

LABOR AS PERFORMANCE

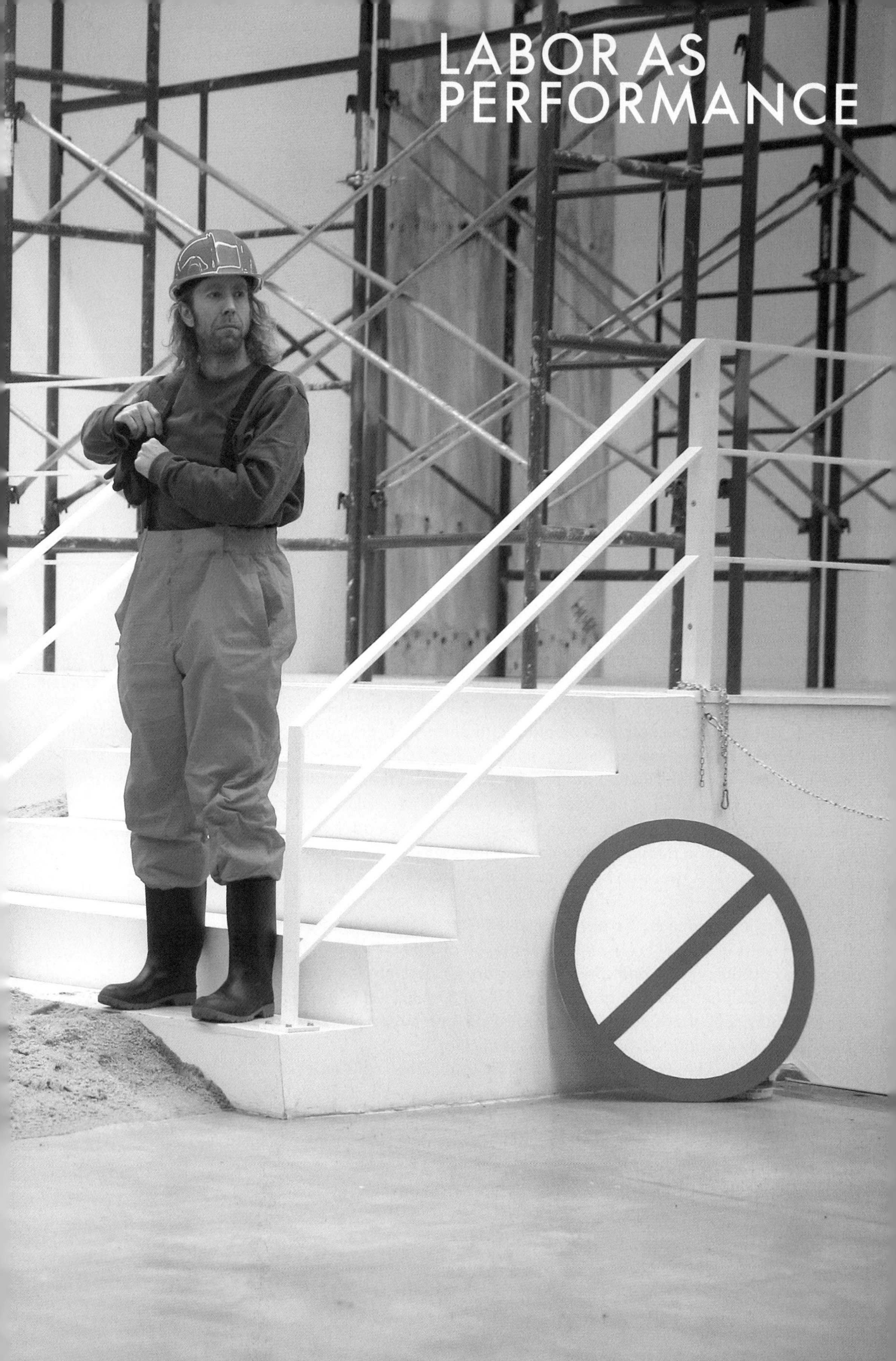

CHOU YU-CHENG

Chemical Gilding, Keep Calm, Galvanize, Pray, Ashes, Manifestation, Unequal, Dissatisfaction, Capitalize, Incense Burner, Survival, Agitation, Hit

Curated by Charlene K. Lau and Wu Dar Kuen

Performa 19 Hub (18 Wooster)

November 20–21, 2019

"The work is never done; sanctuary always needed." Choreographer Steve Paxton's axiom comes to mind when seeing Taipei-based artist Chou Yu-Cheng's industrious performance. Chou's sanctuary took the form of a lumber warehouse-turned-gallery in SoHo. There, on a chilly day, Chou transformed the space into a construction site, complete with performers dressed as LEGO Minifigures-inspired workers in a mix of brightly colored gear. Massive scaffolding took up two walls of the gallery, with the epic title of the performance stenciled upon its upper edges in white letters. Like a curtain rising, the performance officially began when the gallery's garage door opened, with each "worker" posing throughout the construction zone, waiting to be given further instruction. A two-man band—bassist Schuyler Maehl and drummer/vocalist Ian Vanek—played experimental post-rock anthems commissioned by Chou at maximum volume. The distorted sound echoed off the bare walls of the large white-cube gallery. As the band played on, the crew continued their seemingly arbitrary tasks and curious spectators trickled into the space. The audience huddled together in observation, trying our best not to get in the way. For two hours, they shoveled sand, stacked bricks, and hurled bags of cement. Their actions were scripted, but their motives unclear.

Chou's addition to Performa 19 was the fifth installment in his series of "Chemical Gilding" performances and installations initiated in 2015. With each chapter, Chou seeks to replicate commonly seen but often overlooked workplaces and reveal the choreographies of labor that underpin them. In blurring the division between reality and fiction, the artist shows the edges and tears off the simulation through imperfect facsimiles. Here, as in previous iterations of these performances, Chou collaborated with actual manual workers—foremen, machinists, and builders—who authenticated the labor practices at play.

Everything about the scene seemed out of place in a Downtown art gallery. Co-opting the aesthetics of manufacturing, Chou alluded to the uncanniness of a simulated reality, showing how specialized forms of labor are often absorbed by institutional systems. The workers rested only occasionally before being called back to work by a supervisor, establishing a clear hierarchy of authority. They navigated the space with limited mobility, like pawns in a game of chess. But as the performance drew to an end, it became clear that there was no endgame to this calculated effort.

After two hours of exertion, all of the pieces—the bricks, the sand, and the cement—had been moved by the workers, but by the following night's performance, they were back to where they started. There was something comforting about this cyclicality, yet unsettling. It forced all of us to contemplate the centrality of labor in the production of art. In Chou's well-oiled routines, the body becomes a commodity and the use value of the worker is measured by output, not progress. RE'AL CHRISTIAN

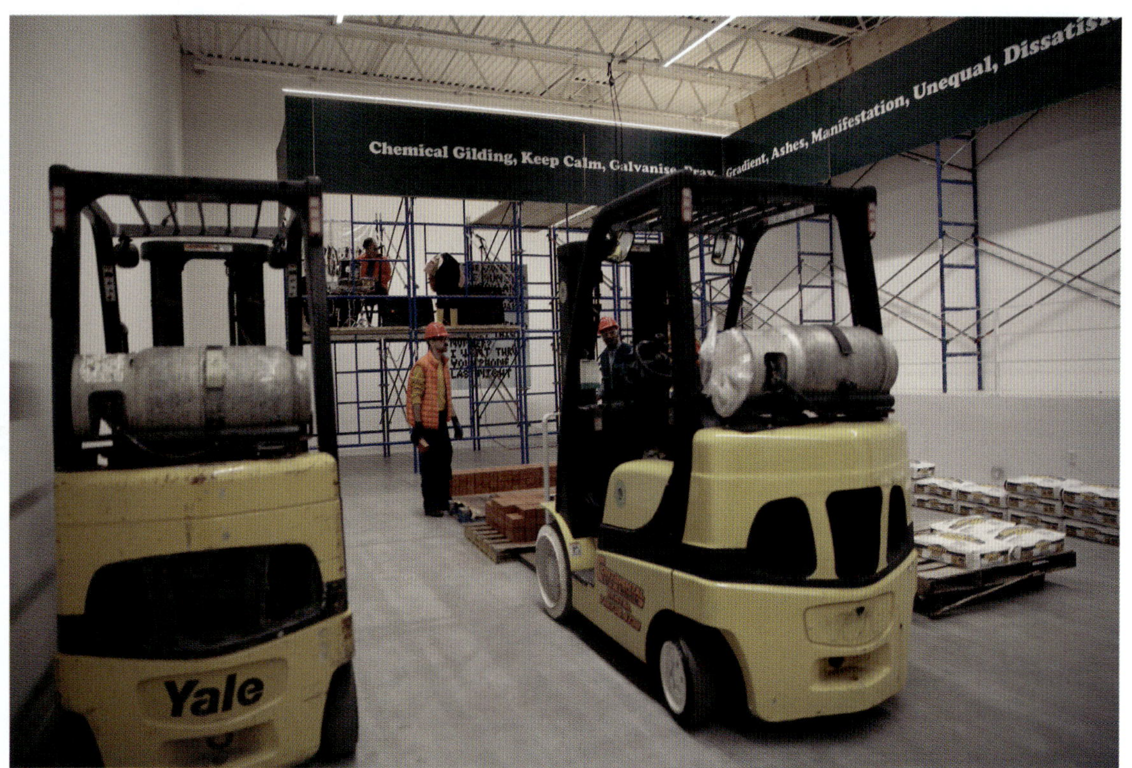

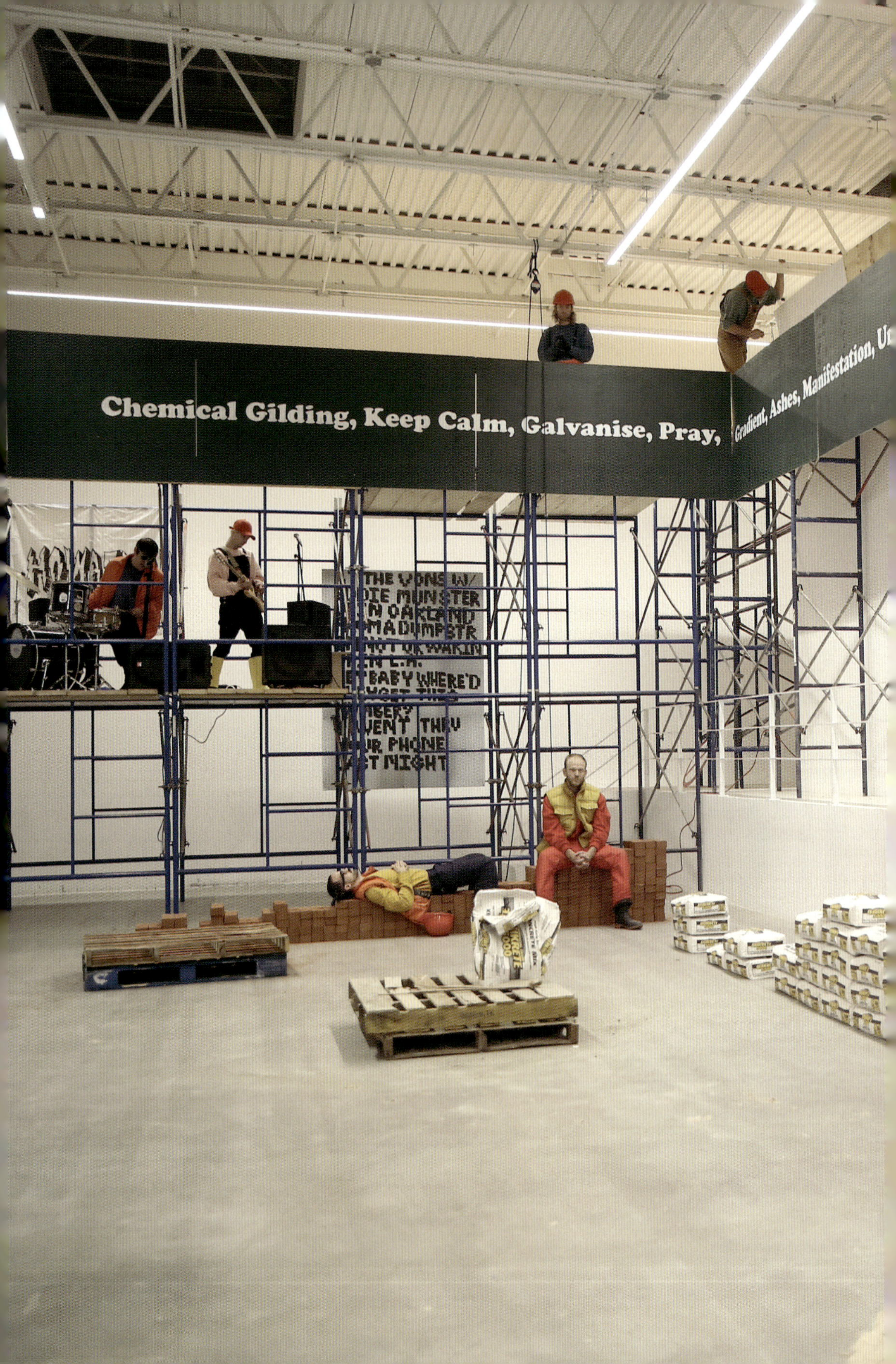
Chemical Gilding, Keep Calm, Galvanise, Pray,
Gradient, Ashes, Manifestation,
THE VONS W/

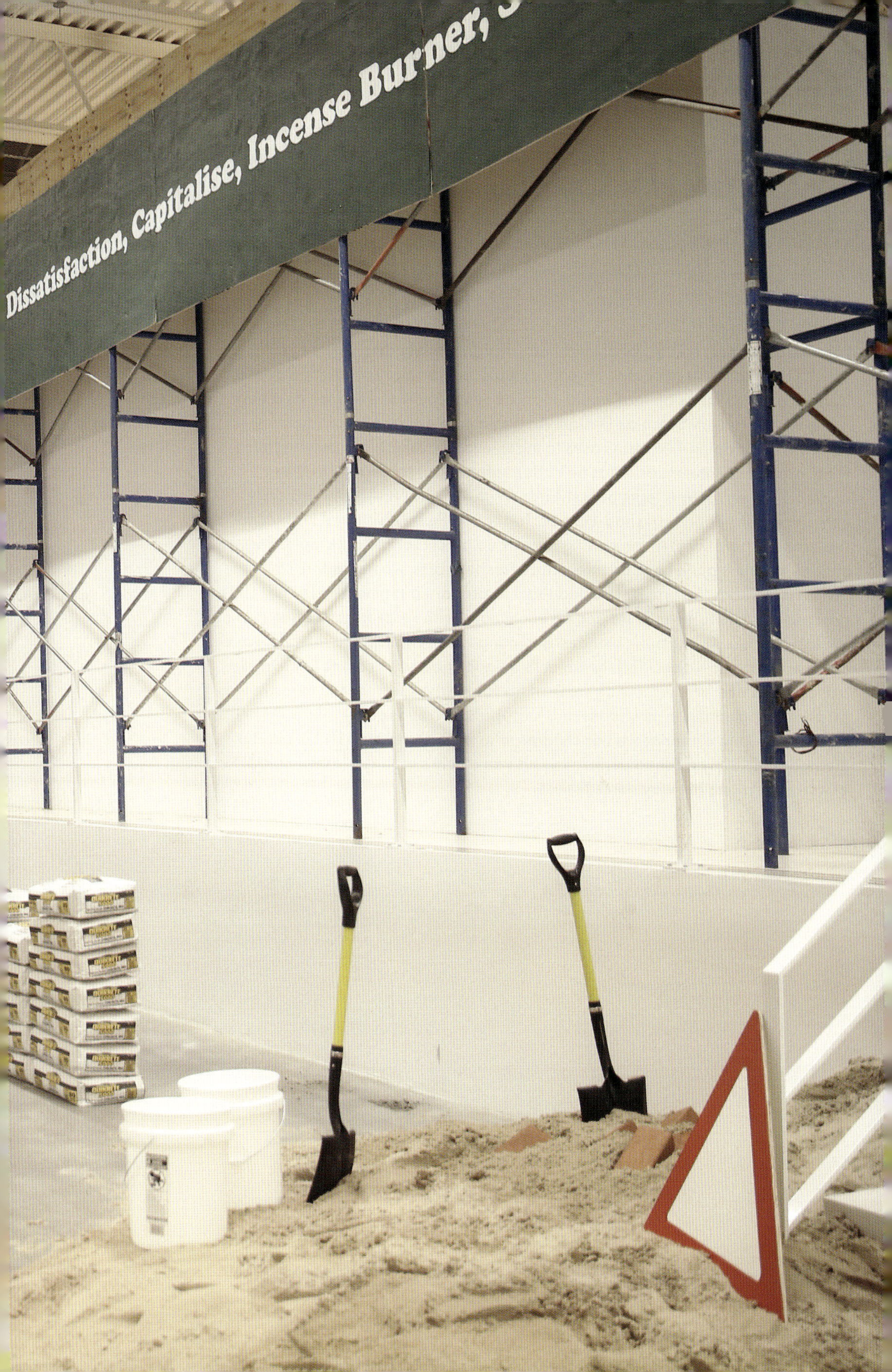
Dissatisfaction, Capitalise, Incense Burner,

GAETANO PESCE

WORKINGALLERY

Salon 94 Design

October 25–November 2, 2019

For nine days, the radical Italian architect, design pioneer, and avant-garde artist Gaetano Pesce relocated his entire studio to the empty rooms of a derelict Upper East Side mansion that would undergo renovation and reopen as a new home for the gallery Salon 94 Design. Among a scattering of his productions—from brash, dripping-like resin vases to mischievously voluptuous polyurethane foam armchairs—the *maestro* (as he's often referred to) sat regally in the audience, supervising a team of assistants. With *WORKINGALLERY*, his daily exhibition-cum-open workshop-cum-performance, Pesce displayed his behind-the-scenes operations. At the closing, the group placed bright pink molds for making coasters and chairs on three large trestle tables, where visitors could gather around as the artist instructed them to prepare a pigment-resin mix. They proceeded to pour the mixture and fill each mold, with Pesce himself often adding the last touches. As the brew blended and congealed, chance had the final word in these creations—it decided the object's unique lines, color composition, and accidental blobs. While showing some of his fabrication secrets, the maestro was again experimenting in new forms and materials. Surrounded by friends from his six-decade-long career as well as children who were captivated by his playful methods, he visibly relished performing his workroom's routines, revealing a little of its magic along the way. CHARLES AUBIN

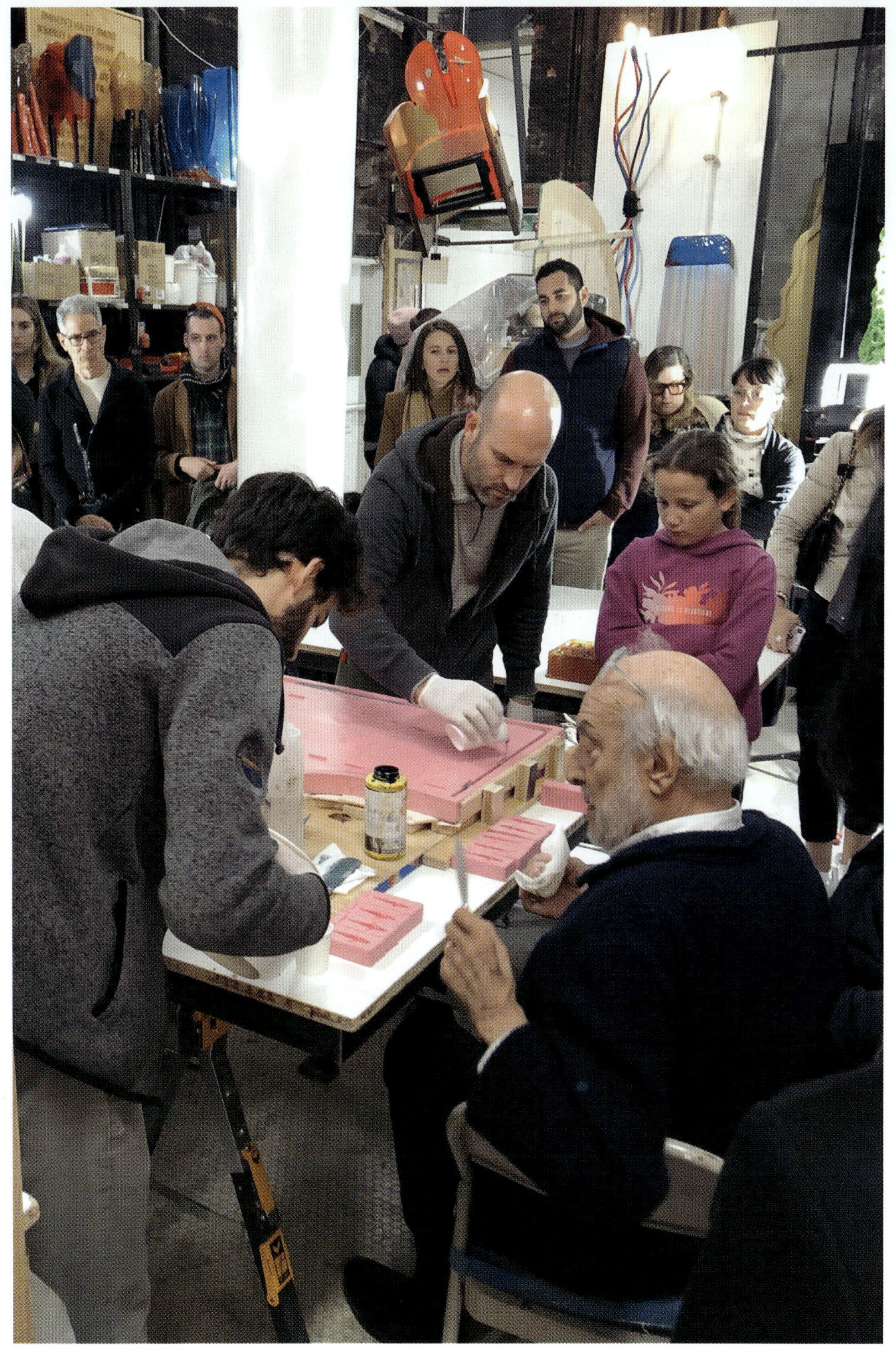

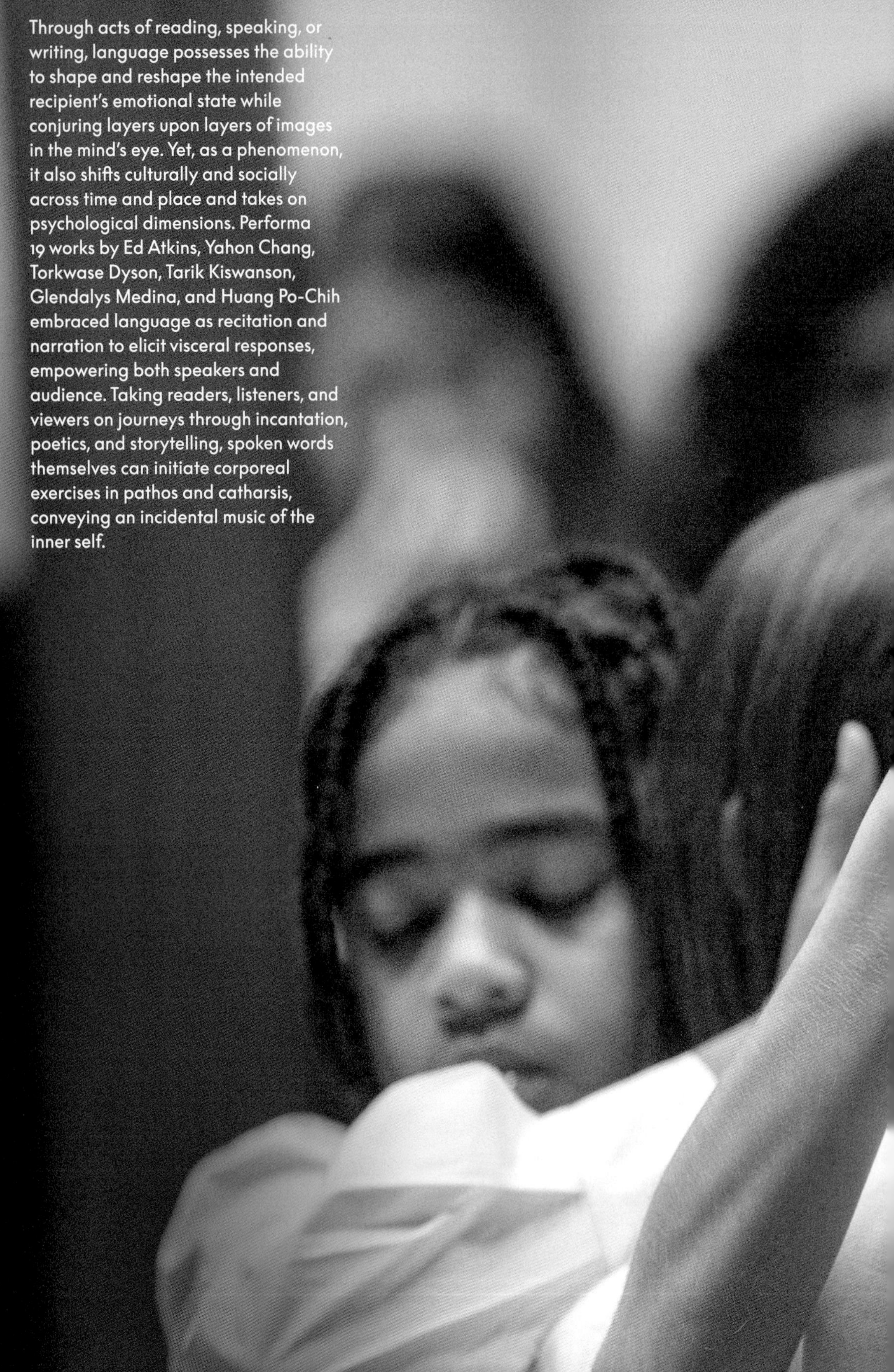

Through acts of reading, speaking, or writing, language possesses the ability to shape and reshape the intended recipient's emotional state while conjuring layers upon layers of images in the mind's eye. Yet, as a phenomenon, it also shifts culturally and socially across time and place and takes on psychological dimensions. Performa 19 works by Ed Atkins, Yahon Chang, Torkwase Dyson, Tarik Kiswanson, Glendalys Medina, and Huang Po-Chih embraced language as recitation and narration to elicit visceral responses, empowering both speakers and audience. Taking readers, listeners, and viewers on journeys through incantation, poetics, and storytelling, spoken words themselves can initiate corporeal exercises in pathos and catharsis, conveying an incidental music of the inner self.

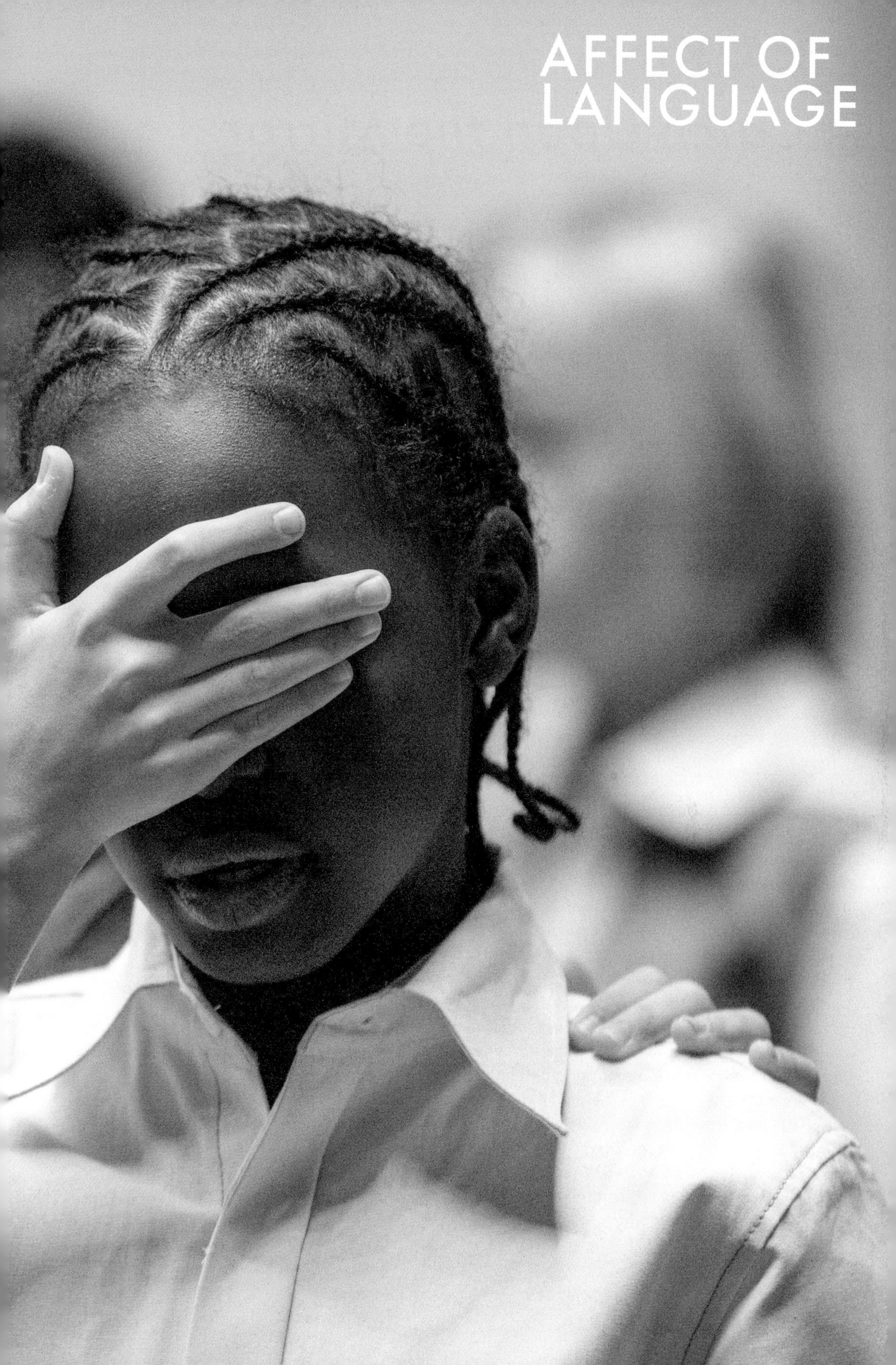
AFFECT OF
LANGUAGE

ED ATKINS
A Catch Upon the Mirror

Curated by
Kathy Noble

Abrons Arts Center

November 8–9, 2019

If insanity is repeating the same action over and over again and expecting a different result, then spectators of British artist Ed Atkins's performance *A Catch Upon the Mirror* were most certainly pushed to the brink of it. As viewers were comfortably installed in their seats, they watched a lone figure spotlit on the proscenium playhouse stage. It was the artist, reciting "The Morning Roundup" (1971), a short poem by New York writer Gilbert Sorrentino (1929–2006),[1] over and over again:

I don't want to hear any news on the radio
about the weather on the weekend. Talk about that.

Once upon a time
a couple of people were alive
who were friends of mine.

The weathers, the weathers they lived in!
Christ, the sun on those Saturdays.

Wearing a calf-length black pleated skirt, a baggy black knitted sweater, and a white shirt buttoned up to the collar, he recited each line in numerous ways, toying with pace, rhythm, tone, intonation, pronunciation, and volume, reverberating in a standing microphone, commanding the space with his relentless yet rhythmic speech.

The crowd sat in low light. Atkins paused each time he reached the last phrase, which built up a strange energy across the room: Each fleeting silence created a sense of dread mixed with anticipation and expectation. Bewildered looks were exchanged between spectators, as if to ask: When would this performance of repetition end? Had it even started? What's the catch? And just as this feeling became palpable, the artist began again.

Occasionally, the artist would punctuate the rounds of repetitious recitations with a brief musical interlude. He sang Old English nursery rhyme-like tunes, a cappella and in full histrionics, before he returned to Sorrentino's words. The text morphed into a mantra, one akin to "Oh this is a happy day" in Irish playwright Samuel Beckett's play *Happy Days* (1961), in which the expression is repeated ad nauseam by the main character, Winnie, as a failed self-fulfilling prophecy. Buried to her waist and next to her taciturn husband, she uses her daily mundane routine

1
Gilbert Sorrentino, "The Morning Roundup," *Corrosive Sublimate* (Los Angeles: Black Sparrow Press, 1971).

2
Stanley E. Gontarski, *Beckett's Happy Days: A Manuscript Study* (Columbus, Ohio: The Ohio State University Libraries, 1977)

to distract herself from existential doubt. "Language generally in Beckett's world is not a means of conveying meaning, but a balm for the sores of existence," writes scholar Stanley E. Gontarski.[2] Likewise, in Atkins's performance, language creates the illusion of a narrative built around prosaic references to the news on the radio and conversations about the weather, but the artist exhausts the words to a point of incomprehension and befuddlement until the metaphysical cycle of life and death emerges from it.

This terse poem has accompanied him for nearly a decade, first appearing in the artist's video *Warm, Warm, Warm Spring Mouths* (2013)—an unidentified male avatar's soliloquy, part of a series of uncanny works using advanced technology software and digital alter egos who perform existential crises and loneliness. In his live rendering here, the artist embodied the type of melancholy he typically bestows on his CGI protagonists.

The final twist came from the audience, when members of a choir, who had been covertly seated among the spectators, began to sing rounds of English composer Henry Purcell's tavern song "Under this Stone Lies Gabriel John" (1686). Like Sorrentino's composition, Purcell's tune is three melodic stanzas long. Again, even though the lyrics were repeated, it was difficult to grasp the message behind the words that washed over you. In retrospect, the title of the final song calls to mind the idiom "no stone left unturned." After a thorough search for a different result to the same formula, there was finally a release—a generous reprieve from the obstinate exercise in catharsis that we had been subjected to. What is insanity, anyway? BRITTANY RICHMOND

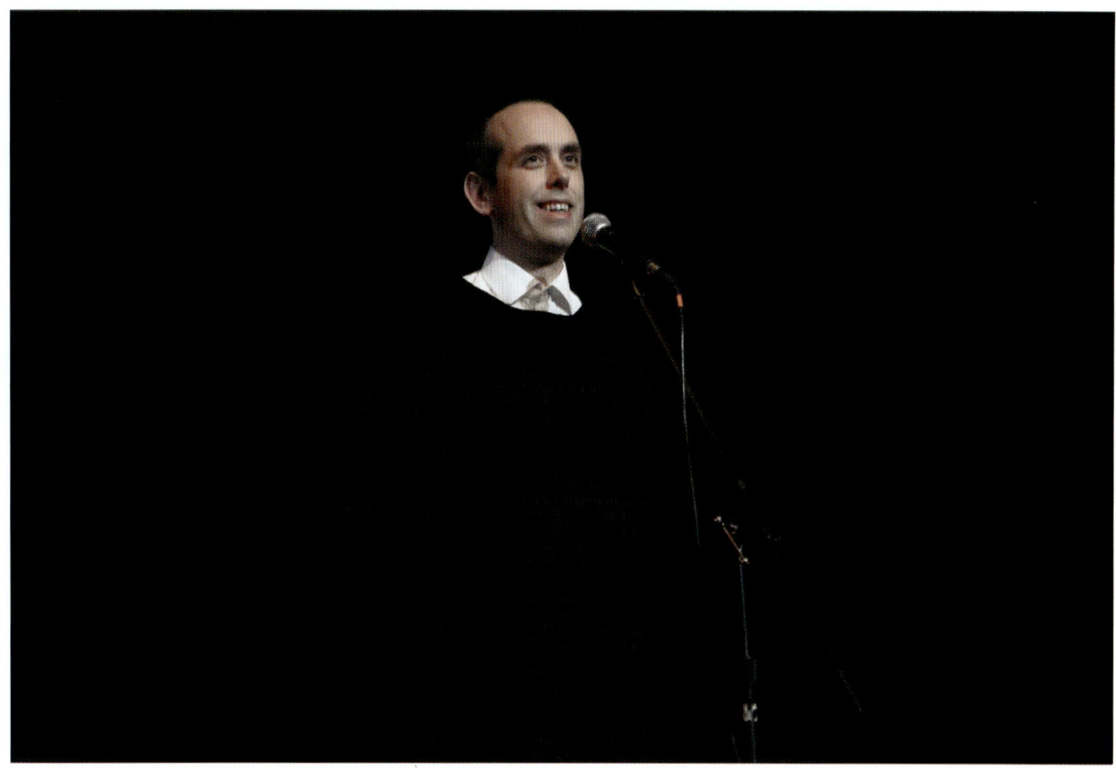

TARIK KISWANSON

AS DEEP AS I COULD REMEMBER, AS FAR AS I COULD SEE

Curated by
Charles Aubin

Alexander Hamilton
U.S. Custom House

November 21, 23, 24, 2019

When Ziad Kiswani moved to the small southern Swedish town of Halmstad in 1979 to pursue his career as a glassblower—a trade he learned in his native Palestine—immigration services advised him to add a *-son* to his patronym to make it more Swedish, and so his family name became *Kiswanson*. His wife, Hanan, joined him a few years later, and the couple settled in and went on to have three children, among them Tarik, all born and raised in Halmstad.

S, *o*, and *n*: the three letters offer a trenchant metaphor on the politics of assimilation for the Kiswansons. This new spelling was meant to "facilitate integration," but the appendix resulted in a surname that is disconnected from lineages in both Palestine and Sweden. It encapsulates the challenges of negotiating one's ancestry while partaking in a new community, a leitmotif in Tarik Kiswanson's oeuvre. This three-letter supplement also sheds a bright light on the role of the son, a figure the artist has returned to often; and perhaps, more obliquely, when read in Kiswanson's adopted language of French, *son* (or *sound* in English), alludes to his talent for chiseled and textured soundscapes.

"I see life as a cluster of endless connections, windows constantly opening and closing, letting in and letting go of things. The weave is sometimes linear and physical, but, most often, it's a body endlessly displacing itself, constantly connecting and disconnecting, continually being shaped and transformed by the rhythm of time," explains the artist.[1] Leaving Halmstad at seventeen to study in London, the artist then began his career in Rome. In 2011, Kiswanson moved to Paris, where he still resides, although he regularly visits his mother in Amman, Jordan, where she has relocated. These are the conditions by which his work is formed: in motion, crossing borders, and living in different languages—Swedish, Arabic, English, and French, so far.

Initially planned for Performa 17, Kiswanson's performance was postponed due to his visa restrictions. It seemed apt then, two years later, once having overcome the intricacies of the U.S. Department of State, to stage it at the Alexander Hamilton U.S. Custom House. Located at the southernmost tip of the island of Manhattan, the federal site, a Beaux-Arts landmark inaugurated in 1907, is a monument to the might of the port, and of the city. The five shows took place under the same vaulted ceilings where, decades prior, clerks reviewed tariffs on global goods entering the United States.

AS DEEP AS I COULD REMEMBER, AS FAR AS I COULD SEE stems from Kiswanson's book of poetry of the same title: A volume composed of eleven interior monologues which serve as scripts for the performance. Each entry—with

1
In conversation with the author featured in the playbill for *AS DEEP AS I COULD REMEMBER, AS FAR AS I COULD SEE* (November 2019). Unpaginated.

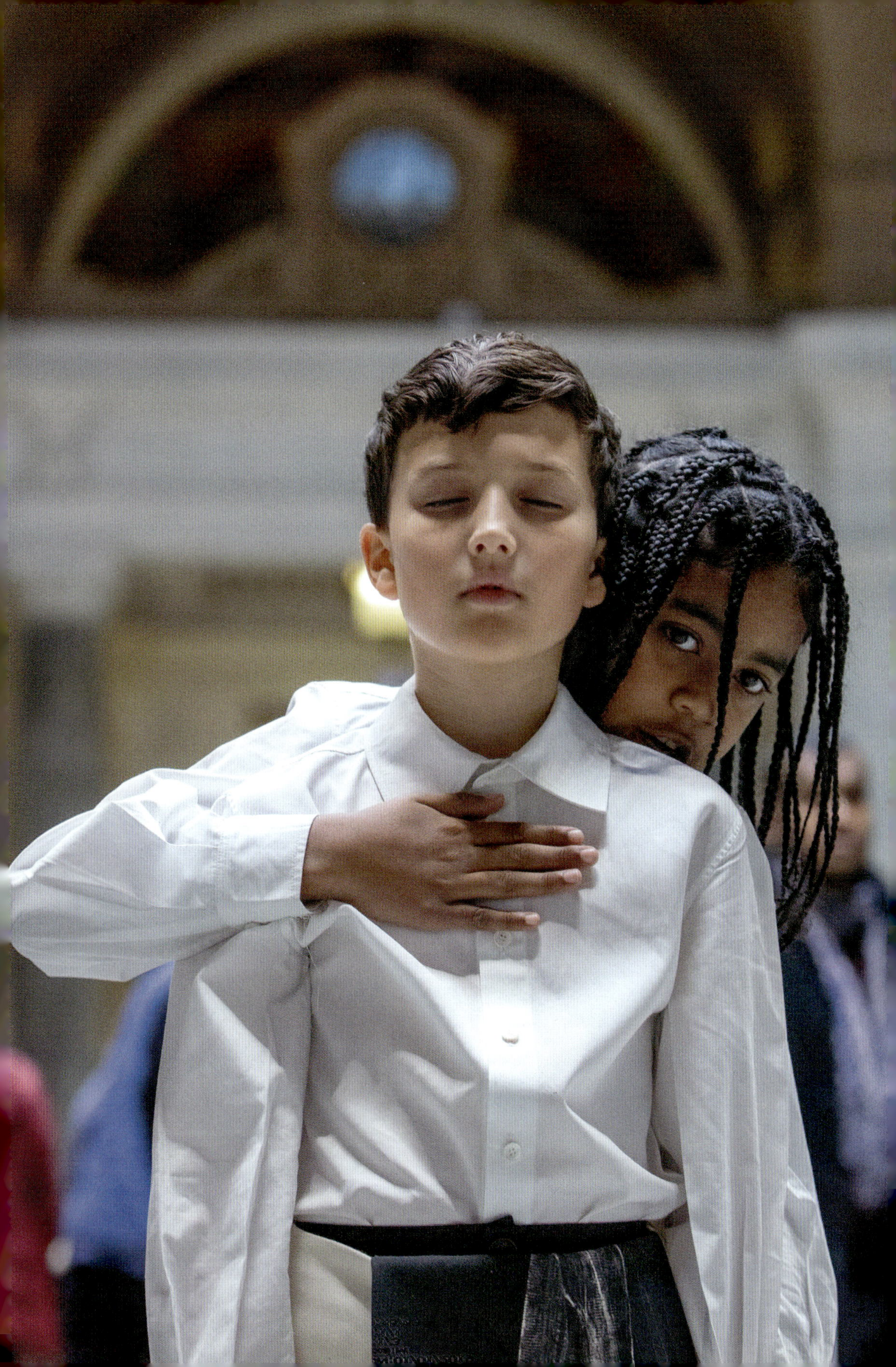

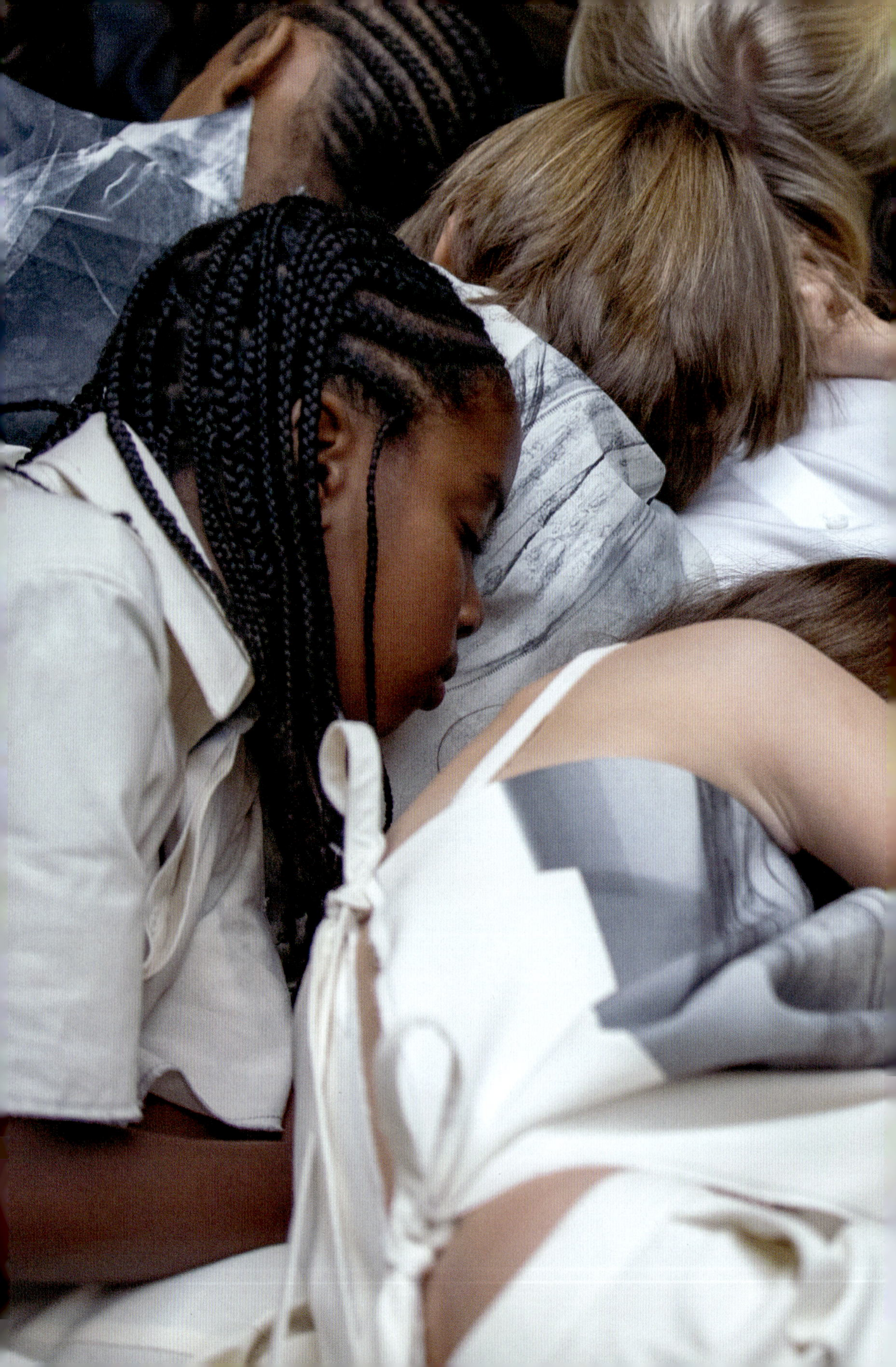

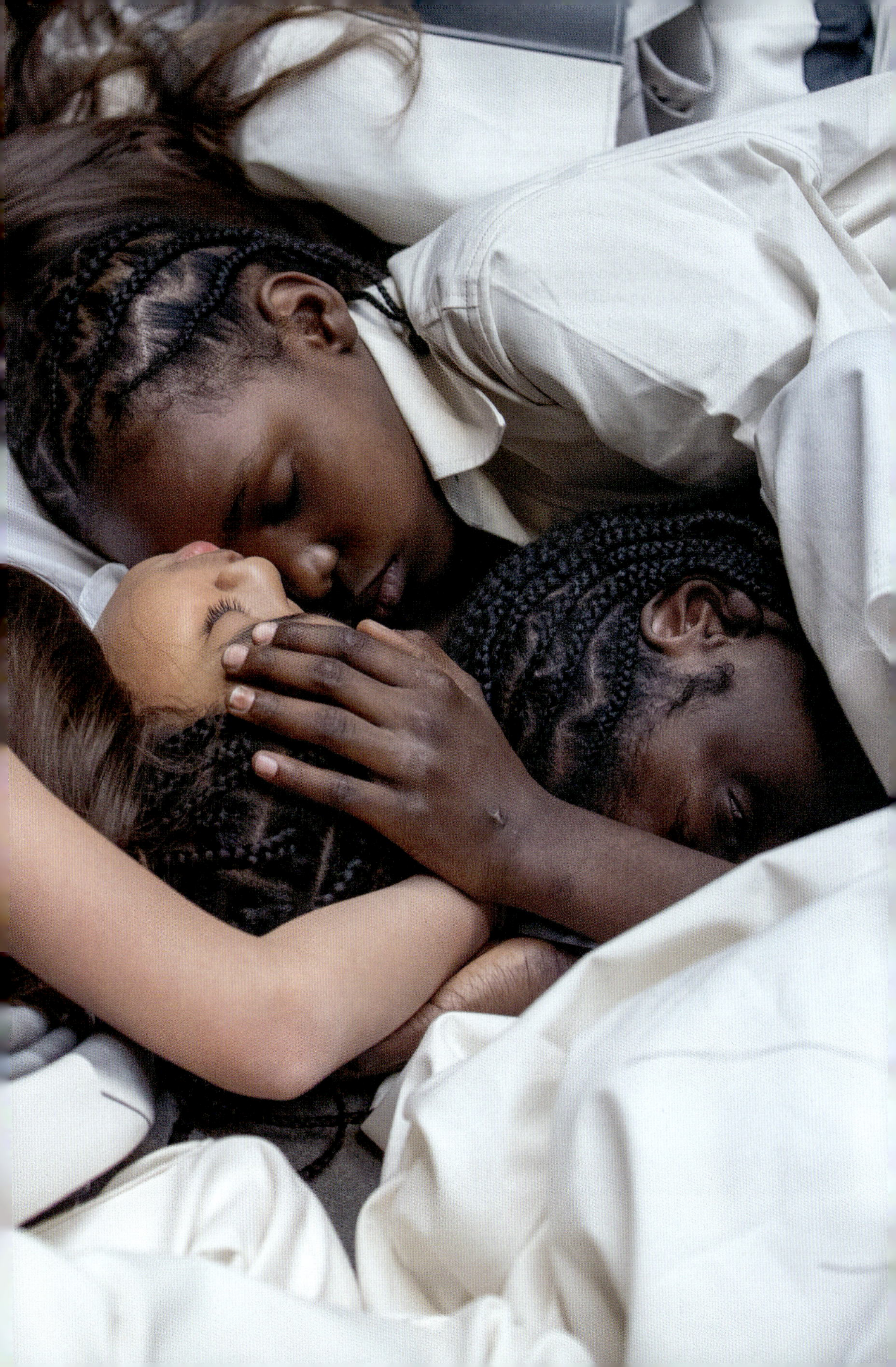

titles such as "The Welder," "The Whisperer," "Healer," "Seeker," "Holder," "Their Eyes," and "This Floor"— meander across geographies and temporalities. Scientific statements ("A force is any interaction that, when unopposed, will change the motion of an object. Force equals mass times acceleration") are interspersed with enigmatic prose ("We are momentary vessels. Floating where these waters lead") and casual comments ("You look borderline ridiculous dressed like that"). These soliloquies allude to the experience of exile, the desert, and boundaries mixed with children's emerging anxieties and desires around these concepts. Written specifically for a cast of eleven-year-olds, they express this moment of in-between, of blossoming out of childhood but not quite yet embodying their teenage selves. They are sons (and daughters) on the brink of entering the world.

Alone in the large expanse of the rotunda's inner ellipse, the young Akiro Thomas opened with a slow and solemn dance solo before his companions began to move around with him in the space. At first the audience kept their distance, staying outside of the central arena, as if in a theater in-the-round, then eventually began to creep into the stage area and walk among the cast. The performers' soft recitations demanded that spectators slow down, prick their ears, and pay close attention as they softly brushed up against them, occasionally choosing to deliver their lines to someone individually while delicately brushing aside others who were more interested in snapping photos than listening. Using the entire room, Kiswanson choreographed a succession of solos, duos, and cluster formations that conjured tableaux of true friendship, care, and tenderness.

These young New Yorkers of wildly diverse backgrounds (African American, American Ukrainian, American Sudanese, French, Haitian, Italian Ethiopian, Maldivian Nigerian) wore costumes created by the artist in collaboration with

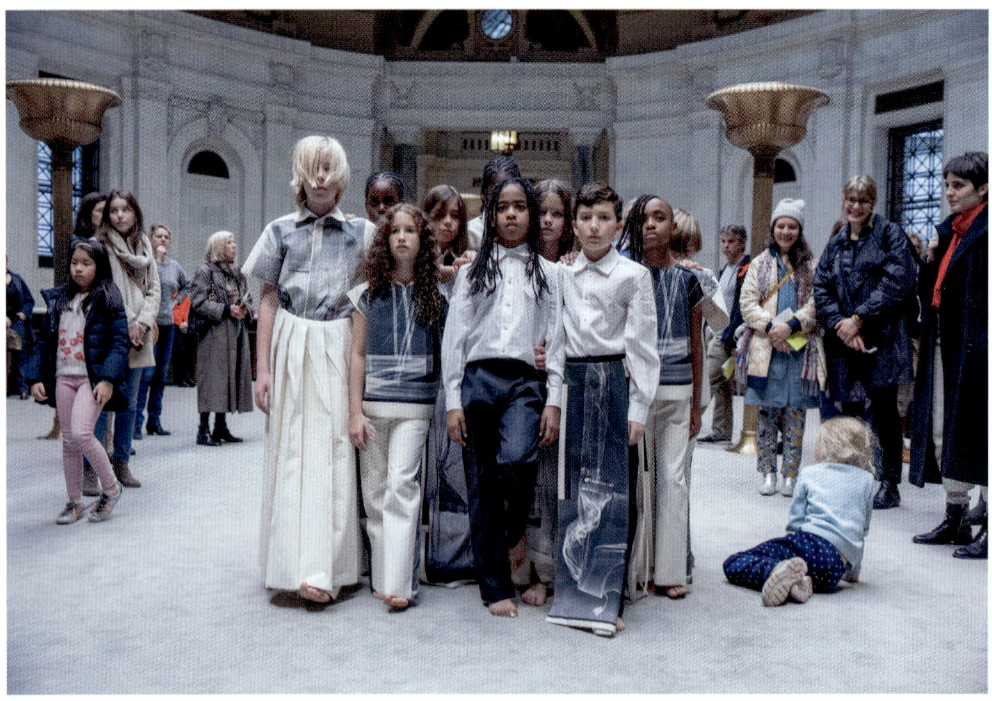

the Tiraz Centre in Amman—one of the largest collections of Middle Eastern clothing, spanning two centuries of Arab craft heritage. For *AS DEEP*, Kiswanson X-rayed traditional embroidered tunics and dresses from the foundation's collection and superimposed them with teenagers' hoodies and t-shirts, resulting in a fabric of ghost-like images that carries centuries of cultural history. He cut and tailored it into his actors' costumes of formal button-down shirts and suits, and oversized capes and romantic draped skirts.

Bathed in the sunlight from the rotunda's oculus, the crowd was plunged into a layered acoustic environment. Though each monolog was given separately, the individual recitations generated a wavelength of words and phrases drifting across the room. The kids' unamplified voices created a soft polyphonic mesh knit together by a discreet system of keywords like *breaths*, *index*, *filthy*, *border*, *resistance*, and *welcome*, all of which featured in each soliloquy. When the work premiered at Lafayette Anticipations in Paris, the ambient noise of the streets of Jerusalem (the artist's parents' hometown) piped in; here, the sounds had been abstracted. Conceived with composer Luciano Chessa, it unfolded by lofty notes of piano and short melodic motifs, alternating between prerecorded music and live improvisation by pianist Gaspar Souchard.

The children had all found each other again and huddled by the time a second group—who had been circulating in plain clothes, unnoticed—accompanied them in the round. They gently placed their hands on the bodies of costumed performers and started singing: "Switch your phone to silent mode, we are going deeper, it's time to move further." The audience gasped. Quietly, yet epically, *AS DEEP* revealed a generation of young adults effortlessly commanding a crowd, leading us to a brotherly, poetic realm. CHARLES AUBIN

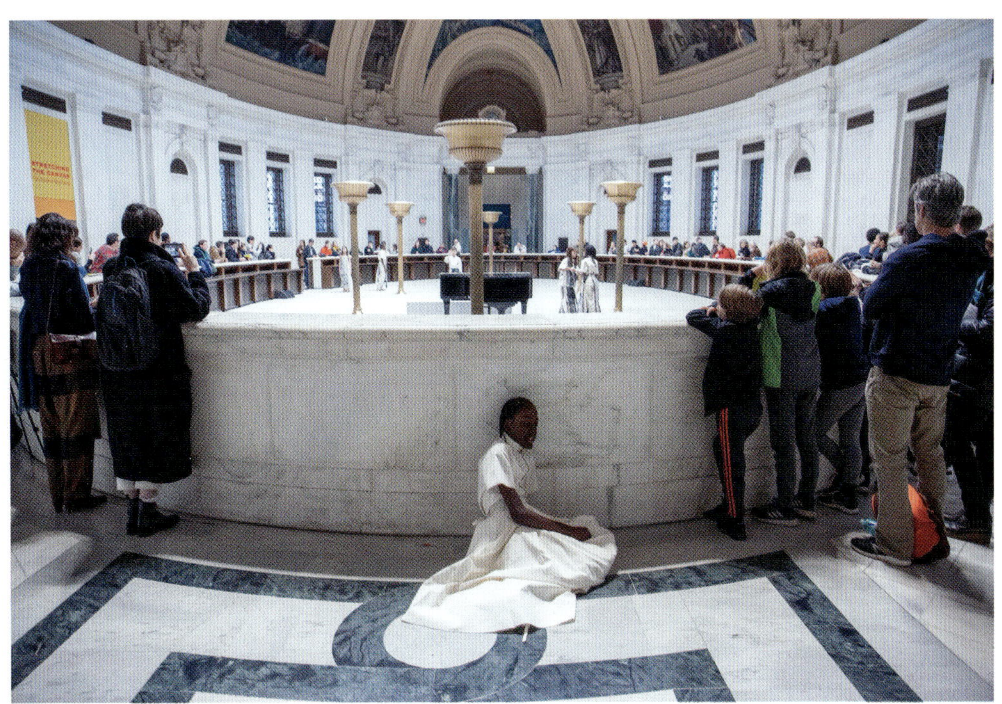

GLENDALYS MEDINA

Dear Me

Curated by
Lia Gangitano

PARTICIPANT INC

November 12 and 19, 2019

A small room built within PARTICIPANT INC gallery served as a space of encounters between Glendalys Medina and solitary guests. Dear Me, *a two-minute lyric, was sung continuously for one visitor at a time for six hours each performance day. Medina performed in total darkness, leaving no documentation behind. A dim light shone from under the doorway to guide everyone out of the chamber when they heard a "thank you" and the moment was over. Upon exiting, they were given a literal token of affection, which bore el coquí, a frog endemic to Puerto Rico that sings its mating call from sunset to sunrise. The co is believed to repel males, while the quí attracts the females. Like the auditory systems of the responsive male and female amphibians, sensuous attractions were heightened by the darkness inside* Dear Me.

It was a freezing autumn evening. My appointment was one of the last that day, and both the streets and gallery were empty when I arrived. I was familiar with Glendalys Medina's graphic abstractions, imbued with Taíno cultural references, but I hadn't attended any of their performances, nor had I seen such explicitly figurative pieces as their self-portrait, titled *Mx. Nuyorican,* exhibited alongside two other large-scale images of their parents: *Ms. Puerto Rico* and *Mr. Borikén.*[1] As I entered the structure, the door closed behind me, and Medina's visage stared right at me.

Once in the shadows, I expected my eyes to adjust, but they never did. I was enveloped in a palpable void, hesitant of my orientation, or how far I should move in any direction. A voice breached the silence. "Dear Me," began Medina, yet despite this self-referential title, I could not help but wonder whether I was an interloper in an internal monologue, or the intended witness. As their phrases and cadence moved between descriptions of the self and offerings to "you" (me?), I tried to find the source of the sound. My position was further unfixed when I thought Medina suggested that I reach out a hand, which I did, unsure of whether I was supposed to do so, or if my touch would be reciprocated. It was not. Finally, I got my cue —"thank you"—though I lingered a moment, uncertain. As I exited, a ceramic amulet with the glyph of a coquí inscribed in gold was pressed into my palm. I still have this in my home, a token of our exchange.

SUSANNA TEMKIN

1
The artist uses they/them pronouns.

I didn't know what to expect. I only knew I wanted to be one of the first to experience *Dear Me*, a work inspired by the mating call of Puerto Rico's indigenous frog. I signed up for the second slot, not wanting to seem overeager. When I walked into the pitch-black room, I began floating, except for the soft touch of my feet on the floor. After who knows how long, I experienced (more sensorially than simply *heard*) the raspy, deep, melodic voice of Medina reciting the poem "Dear Me." The artist's voice traveled around me.

Sometimes I would feel the artist in my ear—was that whiff of air their breath? Other times, they were distant. They and I, two accomplices tangled in the *me*'s and *you*'s of the verse. I was absorbed into a nothingness that was pregnant with everything. That realm of sweet words—was that our "colony by the sea?" I was handed a keepsake on my way out—tiny and brown, just like a coquí—that I keep in my coat's left pocket. MARCELA GUERRERO

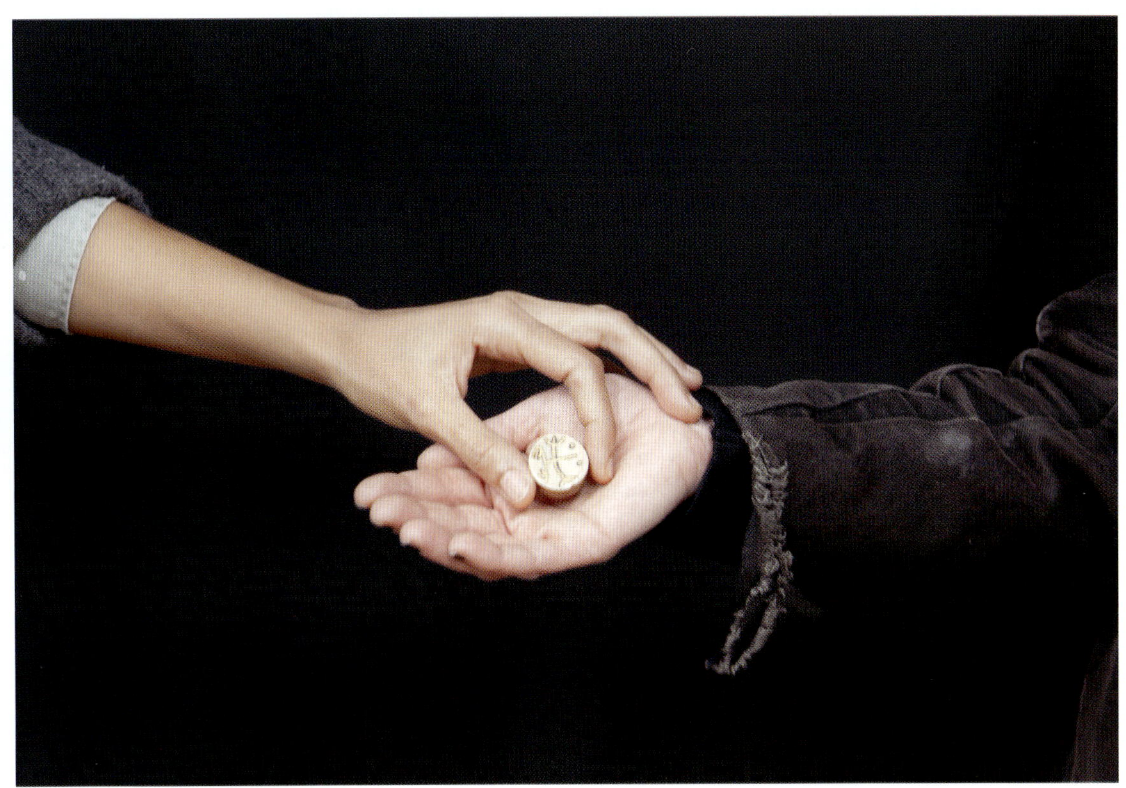

HUANG PO-CHIH

Heaven on Fourth

Curated by
Jo Hsiao, Esa Nickle,
and Charlene K. Lau

Performa 19 Hub
(47 Wooster)

November 14–16
and 21–23, 2019

A requiem, a soul song, a ritual for the spirit of the dead. Upon entering the atrium of *Heaven on Fourth*, a projector clicked on, displaying news articles about a Queens sex worker who died while fleeing a police sting. Her police case number and the words *Jane Doe Ponytail* glowed in red neon inside the darkened room. Her name was Song Yang, and she was an undocumented Chinese immigrant who fell from a fourth-floor balcony in Flushing, Queens, dying from her injuries while in custody at New York Presbyterian Hospital in 2017.

Following a short introduction describing Song's death, we followed Taiwanese artist Huang Po-Chih around the corner to a dimly lit speakeasy, where our bodies, packed into the small space, generated both warmth and a feeling of intimacy. The proceeding night of readings, punctuated by a series of made-to-order cocktails infused with Taiwanese mountain pepper moonshine, functioned as a vigil on the second anniversary of Song's death. The tradition of oral history, with stories written by five writers of Chinese and Taiwanese descent—Huang Po-Chih, Karen Gu, Yen-Chiao Huang, Jenny Xie, and myself—carried us solemnly through the evening's program.

Huang erected a loft above the speakeasy's long bar. Perched on the steps leading up to the loft, a performer read a text commissioned for the evening, while a bartender lined up shot glasses filled with moonshine in front of a row of unmarked glass bottles containing the high-proof spirit. As we imbibed and listened to the readings, some themes emerged: limbo, immigration, the ethics of prosecuting sex workers, violence against women, hunger, surveillance. Their intrinsic intertwinements were revealed progressively over the course of the evening.

Song's death has been contested by activists and her family, who both dispute the police report stating that she leapt to her death that night, committing suicide in a desperate attempt to escape a vice squad targeting Chinese sex workers in the neighborhood. Her supporters claim that after refusing to become an informant for the NYPD, Song was the victim of the police officers' repeated sexual assaults and harassment. The police pushed her off that balcony, they claim—it was murder, not suicide.

As the bartender mixed drinks, a performer descended from the loft to invite a couple of audience members upstairs. There, a young woman gave them massages while the performer whispered a story in their ears. The scene replicated the illicit nature of illegal massage parlors where sex workers labor, often hidden behind or above another business, as well as the living and working conditions of undocumented immigrants, who are often constrained to live in the shadows of society. Their existence in the country is often only materialized through the act of arrest and subsequent criminalization. Jane Doe Ponytail, the fetishizing moniker given to Song in police records, contains one defining feature in its mantle of anonymity, of namelessness: the hairstyle she wore when she died.

In Chinese culture, paying respect to the dead is an important act, often ritualistic, involving prayers carried out by monks to guide the deceased's soul in finding peace, avoiding the fate of becoming a restless ghost. Huang's performance used the homonyms of *spirit*—the spirit of liquor, the spirit of the deceased—to transgress a reality defined by police brutality, gendered violence, and the abjection of an underclass in threefold: woman, sex worker, undocumented immigrant. Through its commissioned texts and by inviting Red Canary Song, a grassroots organization advocating for the rights of sex workers formed in New York after Song's death, to contribute to the program, Huang formed an ad hoc collective of immigrants, cultural producers, activists, and artists to enact a remembrance where multiple narratives merged to form a new experience—one that commemorated and celebrated Song's life. SARAH WANG

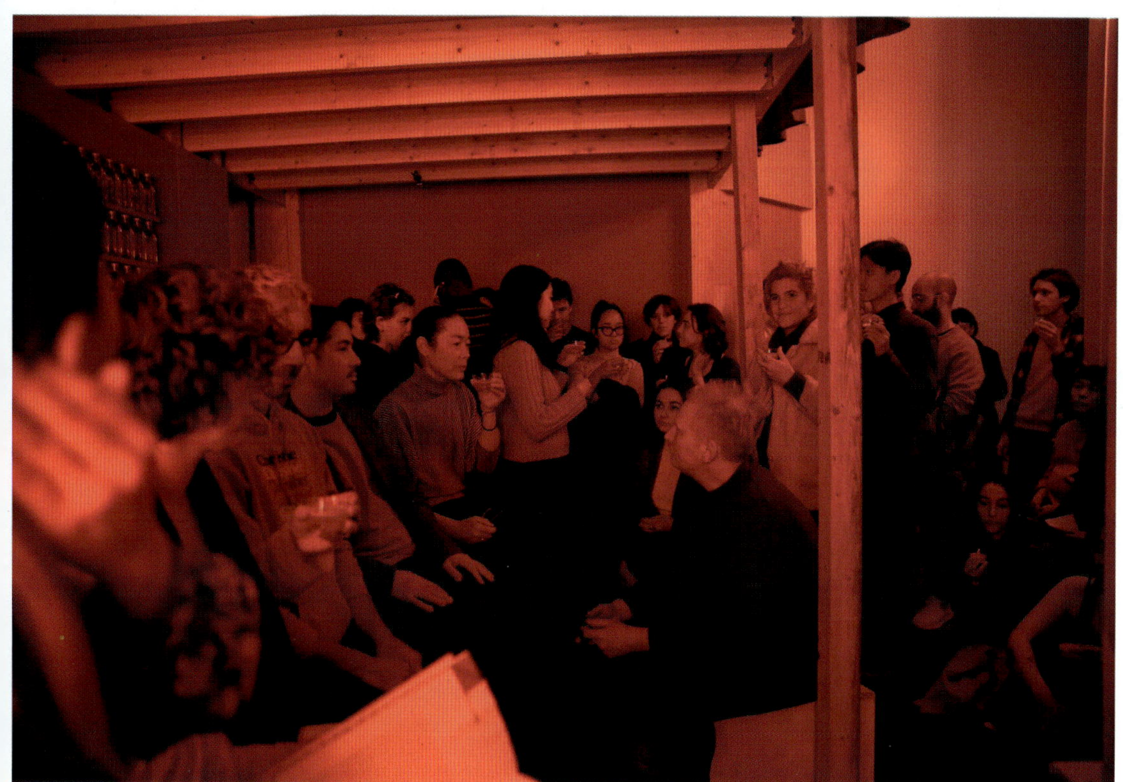

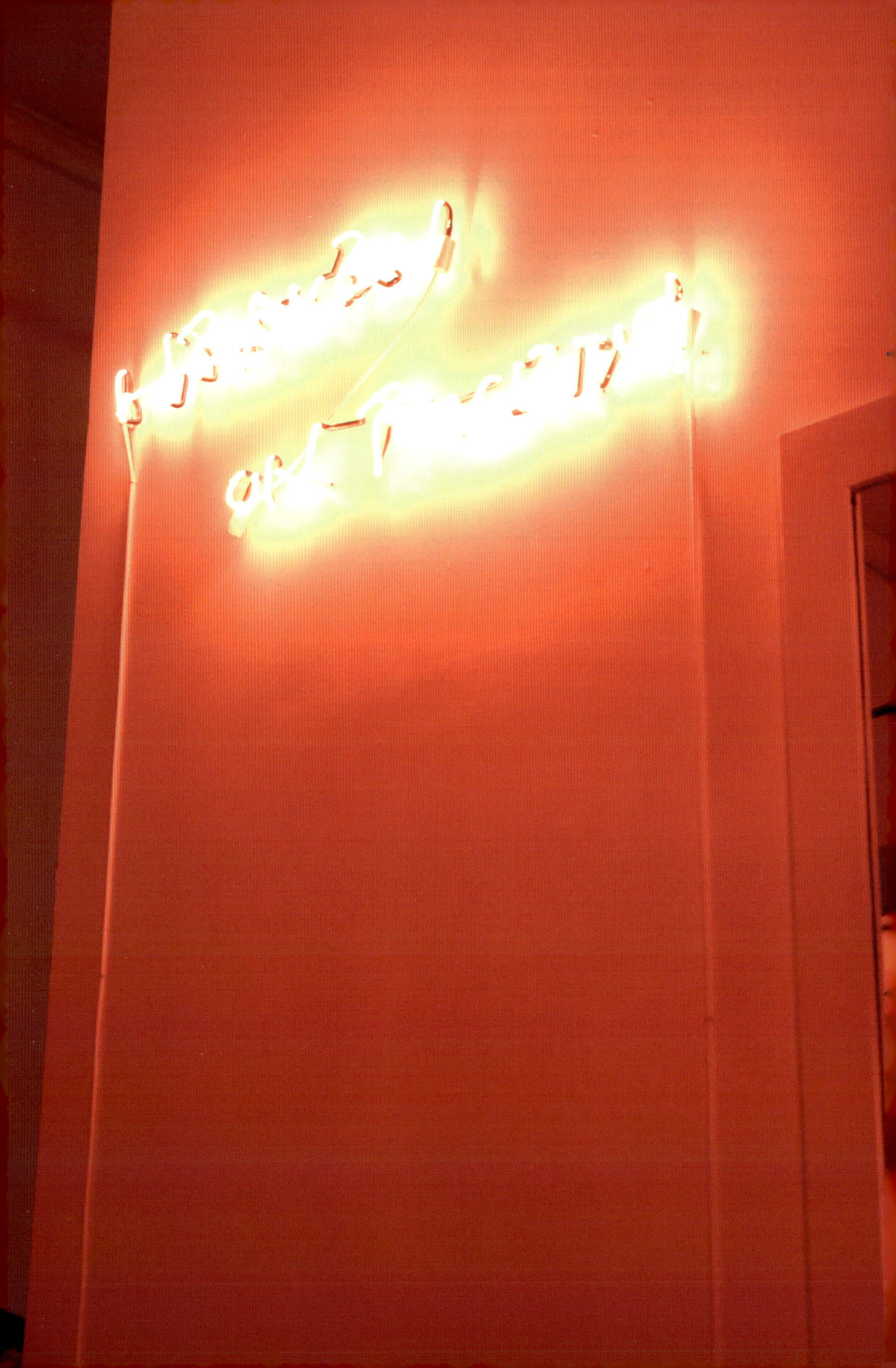

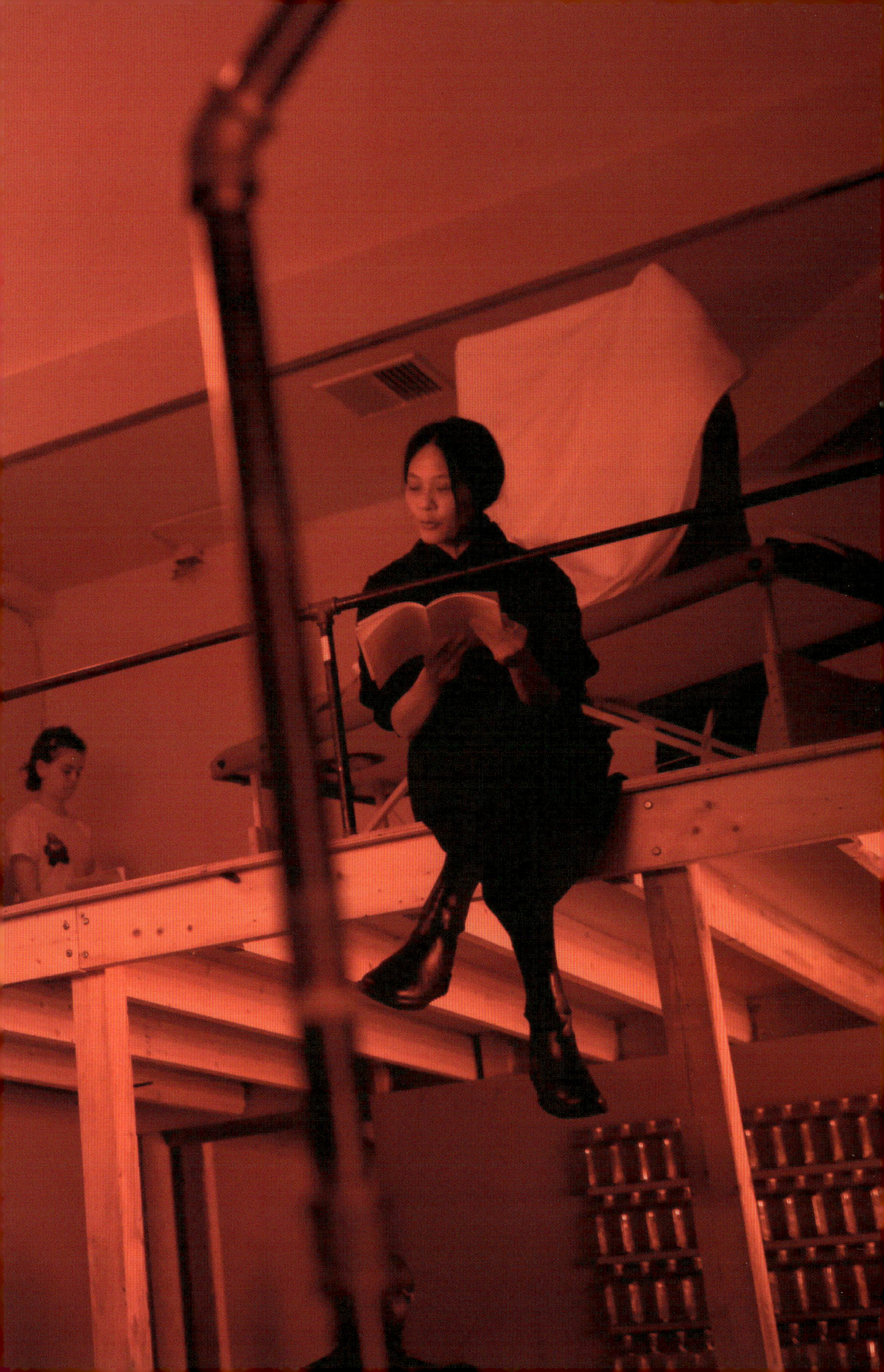

YAHON CHANG

Untitled

Performa 19 Hub (18 Wooster)

November 7, 2019

"Before I paint, I want to be very peaceful and quiet, and flexible. When you see me wield the brush, the movement is the same as in tai chi. Tai chi is performed slowly, and appears to be gentle, but in fact it is very powerful. The Chinese way is to softly maintain inner balance while sustaining inner strength. The sudden release of force can be explosive. Therefore, when I splash ink with my brush, the audience can feel the difference, as I am releasing the energy within my whole body."[1] Exploring painting as performance, the contemporary Taiwanese ink artist combines classical Chinese techniques and gestural Western expressionism in a highly physical manner.

For his first presentation in New York, Chang referenced the biennial's Bauhaus theme. In his own words: "I incorporated this in my work using simple materials and simple brushes. These silk drapes, eight of them, can be interpreted as buildings. Bauhaus architecture has very simple forms, and it feels hard, so I respond with softness in my calligraphy; the reaction of the two is a new transformation. It's a new clash… A clash of when East and West meet. That's what I paint." The angular structure of the set was interrupted by the fluidity of Chang's vigorous strokes on canvas in echoes of tai chi: "overcoming hardness with softness" and "combining hardness with softness."

1 "Yahon Chang: 'The Bird Looks Beautiful, but It Is Very Strong,'" *frieze*, December 9, 2019, https://www.frieze.com/video/yahon-chang-bird-looks-beautiful-it-very-strong

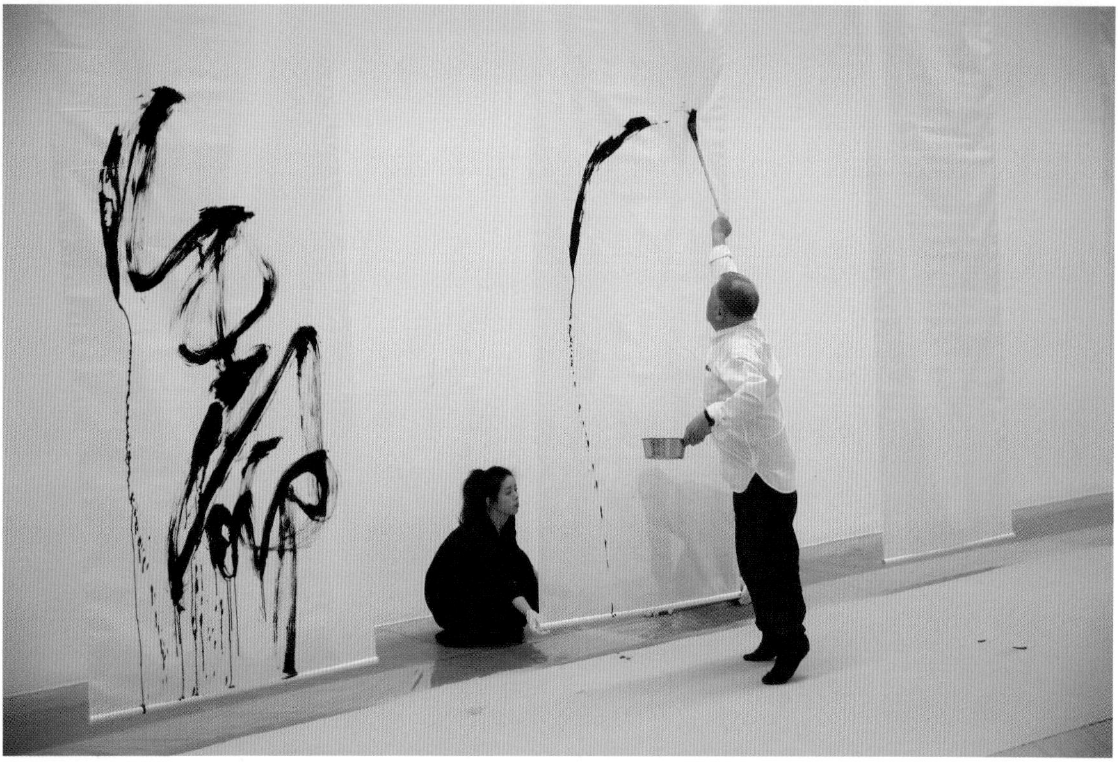

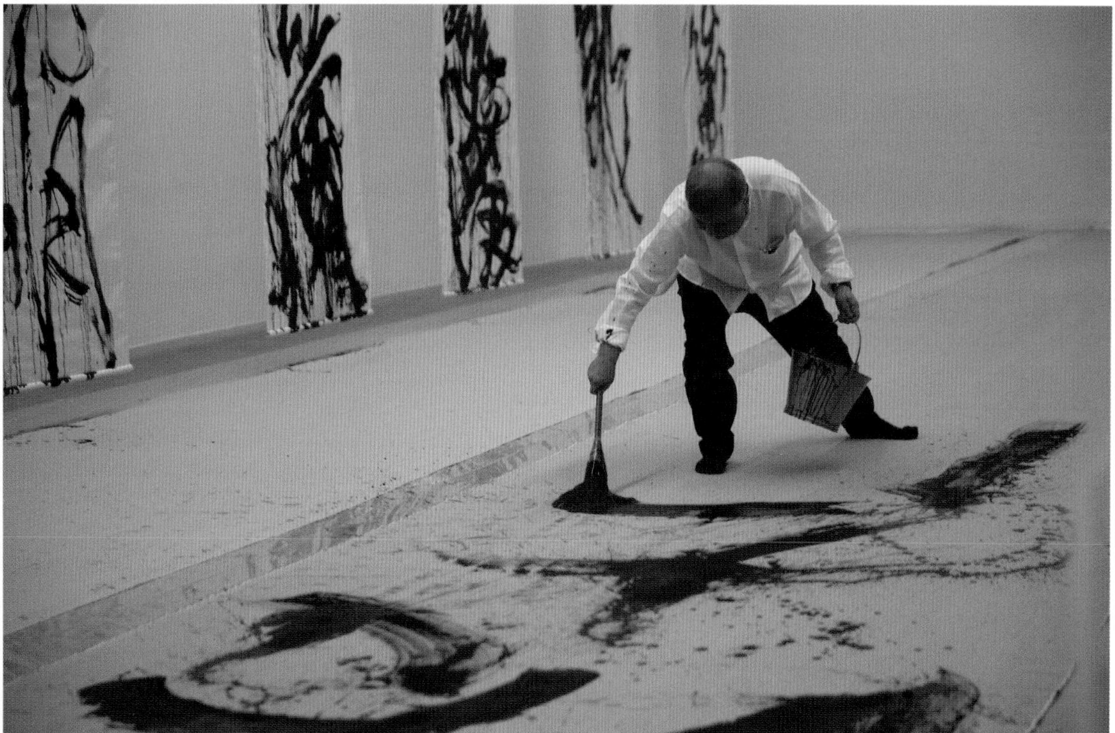

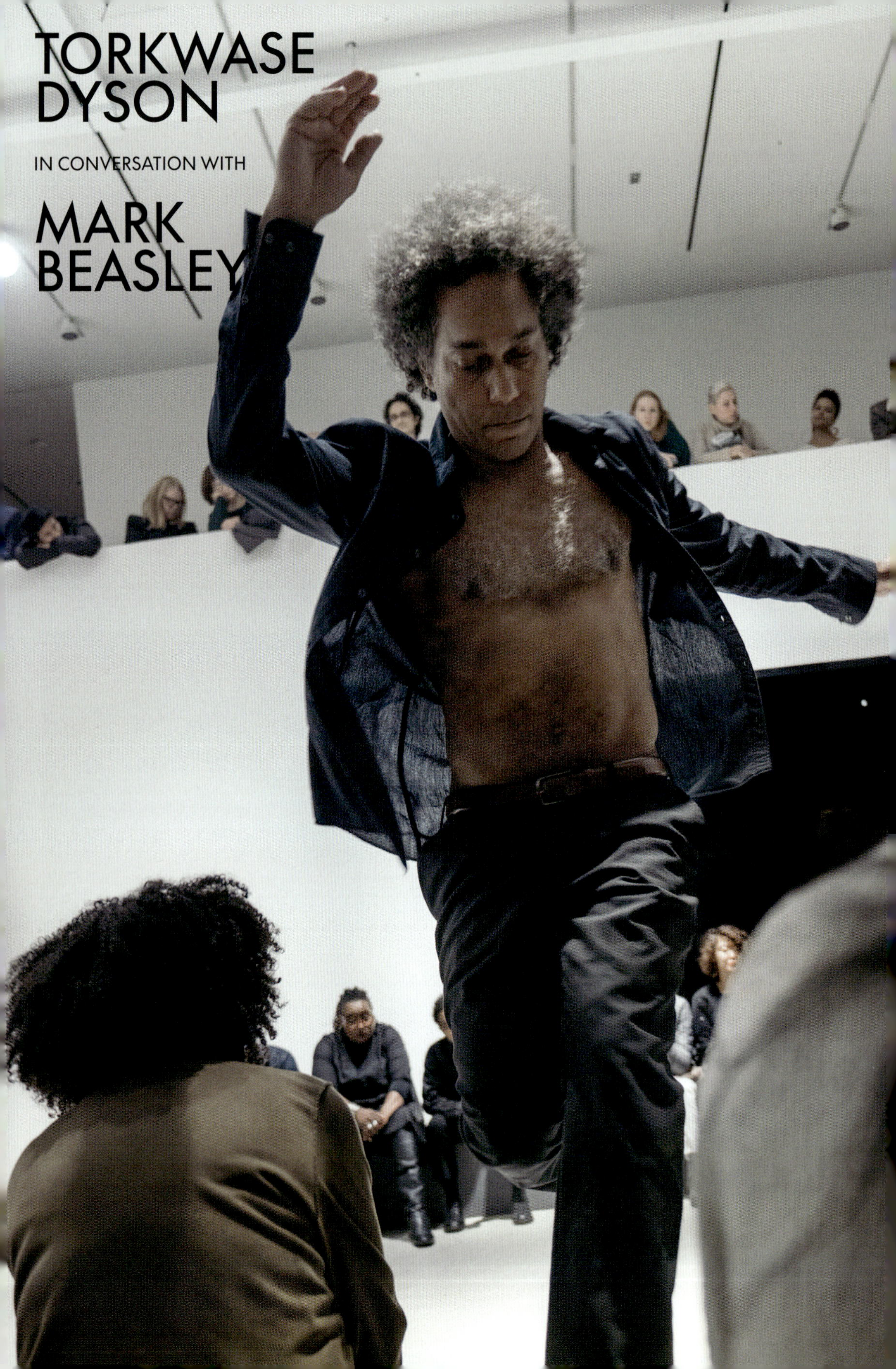
TORKWASE
DYSON
IN CONVERSATION WITH
MARK
BEASLEY

I Can Drink the Distance: Plantationocene in 2 Acts

Curated by Mark Beasley

Pace Live

November 19 and 22, 2019

Drawing on her theory of "Black compositional thought," Torkwase Dyson's two-act performance and sculptural installation I Can Drink the Distance *was a platform for artists, writers, and musicians to consider contemporary Black spatial and ecological relations. For Dyson, one of the most pressing issues of today is human-induced climate change, a defining phenomenon of the Anthropocene. For this project, Dyson considered the Anthropocene's relationship to racism, plantation slavery, and the white supremacy that informed much of industrialization—a matrix of relations referred to as the Plantationocene. Staged over two evenings, Dyson's spatial practice became a means through which to navigate shared environmental precarities, hauntology, architecture, and unfixed geographies composed by Black bodies. She explored the properties of movement, narrative, scale, and sound that can provide networks of liberation.* I Can Drink the Distance, Act I: Way Over There Inside Me *featured Autumn Knight, Christina Sharpe, Dionne Brand, and Dark Adaptive.* Act II: I See You Across That Water *featured Deja Smith, Arthur Jafa, and Gaika.*

MARK BEASLEY

We met in 2019 at Columbia University, when you were installing an exhibition titled "1919: Blackwater." We talked about many things—literary and social connections, mutual icons, what we'd been reading—and slowly built a thread between people, ideas, and thoughts together. We discussed the group that you'd been working with, Dark Adaptive (Zachary Fabri and Andres L. Hernandez). As someone who has a clear studio practice, what is it about performance and its collaborative aspect that appeals to you?

TORKWASE DYSON

Performance is a lot of things. But most important is its ability to produce real-time sensoria. The medium can absorb, answer, or open up questions that are at once corporeal and can instantly become phenomenal. The ability to make a multisensory condition over time and distance means that it has power, right? Dark Adaptive allows for experimentation, instinct, habits, imagination, and creativity in ways in which objects are limited, but invites potential for the multiverse that is performance. Skills, quotidian or not, have the immediacy of motion, and the wonder of improvisation is simply thrilling. And I want to feel alive in my own body. It also forces me to confront ideas of the interstitial. The otherwise space. I think about Dorothy Donegan on piano or Meredith Monk, watching them play, or McCoy Tyner, or imagine Mary Lou Williams—I'm mesmerized by the wrist. Not always the fingers, but the wrists—the space between the hand and the arm, the hinge. Performance can allow for a space to express that moment as a beginning, then move to the rest of the body.

My work is fundamentally built upon human need and lived experience. The need to be in the body. To be deeply into my own humanity, and how that humanity is related to creative potential. Dark Adaptive was, and is, an opportunity for me to organize and direct how these exchanges and happenings occur. I want the work to sort of envelop, for artists that I admire to play out that hinge moment. The invitation from Pace was an opportunity to consider the history of Black liberation, its methodologies, theologies, embodiments, and spatial practices with creatives who are also in tune with these ideas.

MB

You've spoken often about Black compositional thought. Is it a mode of operation, a "mode of solidarity," as Antonio Negri might term it?

TD

What I call Black Compositional Thought is an infrastructure I use for constructing movement. It has never-ending potential in that it's completely based on the histories of Black liberation strategies. Dark Adaptive and other forms of communing and collaborating allow me to say, "here are the issues and topics and here is a subject that I'm dealing with." What do we do with this information? What do we do with the histories of emancipation? What do we do with the histories of abolition? What do we do with the histories of creating Liberations while in a moment of degradation and enforced isolation? These are the many ways our ancestors have done this.

It has the potential for collective knowledges, but it also operates for the loner inside me. It's a simple compact theory that I'm developing in my studio to use as a lens to create new form. It provides a foundation/equation. I need structure in order to invent configurations that speak to world formations, space, reality, distance, place, geography, environment, and ecologies.

I needed something to set me up to be aware of perspectives and cognitive transformations inside the global field of spatial resistance. Enough dispossession. For me, Black and brown spatial composition is the challenge for new world-building, so I need to keep making visual fields which speak to that. The theory can be used in deep silence as well.

MB

This reminds me of another compositional form and a piece of literature that you mentioned early in our conversations: *The Blue Clerk* by the Canadian poet and author Dionne Brand. The book takes the form of a conversation between two parties. It's a reckoning of sorts, between a bookkeeper-cum-clerk and the author-cum-artist. It became a template of sorts for "I Can Drink the Distance." Throughout the progression of *The Blue Clerk*, we are introduced to key figures and key thoughts that figure in the mind of the author, from Jacob Lawrence to Walter Benjamin. I wonder what the text meant to you and how you took inspiration from it?

TD

The Blue Clerk, yes. For me, it works on multiple levels. Primarily, Brand's narrative structure was the starting point. It's a nonlinear story, layering the conditions of history, memory, and time like beautiful scaffolding. The clerk's statements appear on the left-hand pages, and the author's on the right. It represents a kind of indeterminacy while also containing the absolute determinants of the constant adjudicator that is the clerk. The tension between the writer and the clerk is absolute potential.

And again, this is my conflict here. The clerk, as an entity in the story, is revealed to us as someone who does not *use tracing paper*. That makes the clerk acute. Acute in a fearful, obvious way— in an unapologetic way that understands what it means to be and articulate things that are horrific and horrible. And unbelievable and miraculous. I'm always asking, where is my *Blue Clerk*? Where is my left-hand page? The layout of the book is acrobatic. It helped me sharpen my own possibilities. I have read and listened to it again and again to understand its poetics, calmness, and the unique layers of expression in it. When you invited me to make a new work for Pace Live, I had the book in my head; it suggested ways in which to accept the compositional challenge of the space.

MB

In terms of your design for the Pace Live space, you inserted a series of structures and sculptures, from a sculptural line that moved from the balcony to the stage to a wall mirror that reflected the buildings of Downtown Manhattan and Chelsea as well as the audience, alongside a plinth and screen for Dionne and Arthur Jafa, and soft, sculptural seating (designed by Shani Ha) for Christina Sharpe. In essence, a series of stages for language, for music, for dance, for readings. Can you describe these choices?

TD

On my first visit, there were several beautiful Fred Wilson chandeliers hanging from the ceiling. The gravity was palpable. I sat under the chandeliers; I sat on the stairs; I sat on the balcony. I walked through it several times. I looked outside and through the double-height windows toward the surrounding architecture and felt the density of the city, but also its light, throughways, and refractions. I wanted to pull those layers into the space as an invitation and add my own sense of infrastructure. So, my use of the space was in part an acknowledgement of Wilson's work, an arrangement with three different elevations and the city. This was a hinge for me, and I understood the installation had to be a spatial solution to meet the forms of expression that the collaboration would present. Agility. I needed an environment that was adaptable to variables, and, with Dionne's text and the continual prodding of *The Blue Clerk*, I wanted to address the space with ambition, to improvise and respond to the envelope. In the tradition of Black liberation, I sought to invent something else within a found architecture, you know, redefining how people might move through space. I looked to fabricate both a cantilevered and a sitting space, both mirrored and projecting different geometries. I wanted an instantaneous compositional tension that considered scale, distance, and play. I didn't want to make something that was overwhelming, but I did want to scale up the generosity.

MB

I love the idea of an installation that borrows its structure from a poem. The gallery became a page of sorts. The performance was broken into two acts, with two distinct moods. Can you take me through that decision?

TD

Yes, primarily a regard for human life or regard for the politics of things and the abstraction that comes as a productive mode of expression that then makes

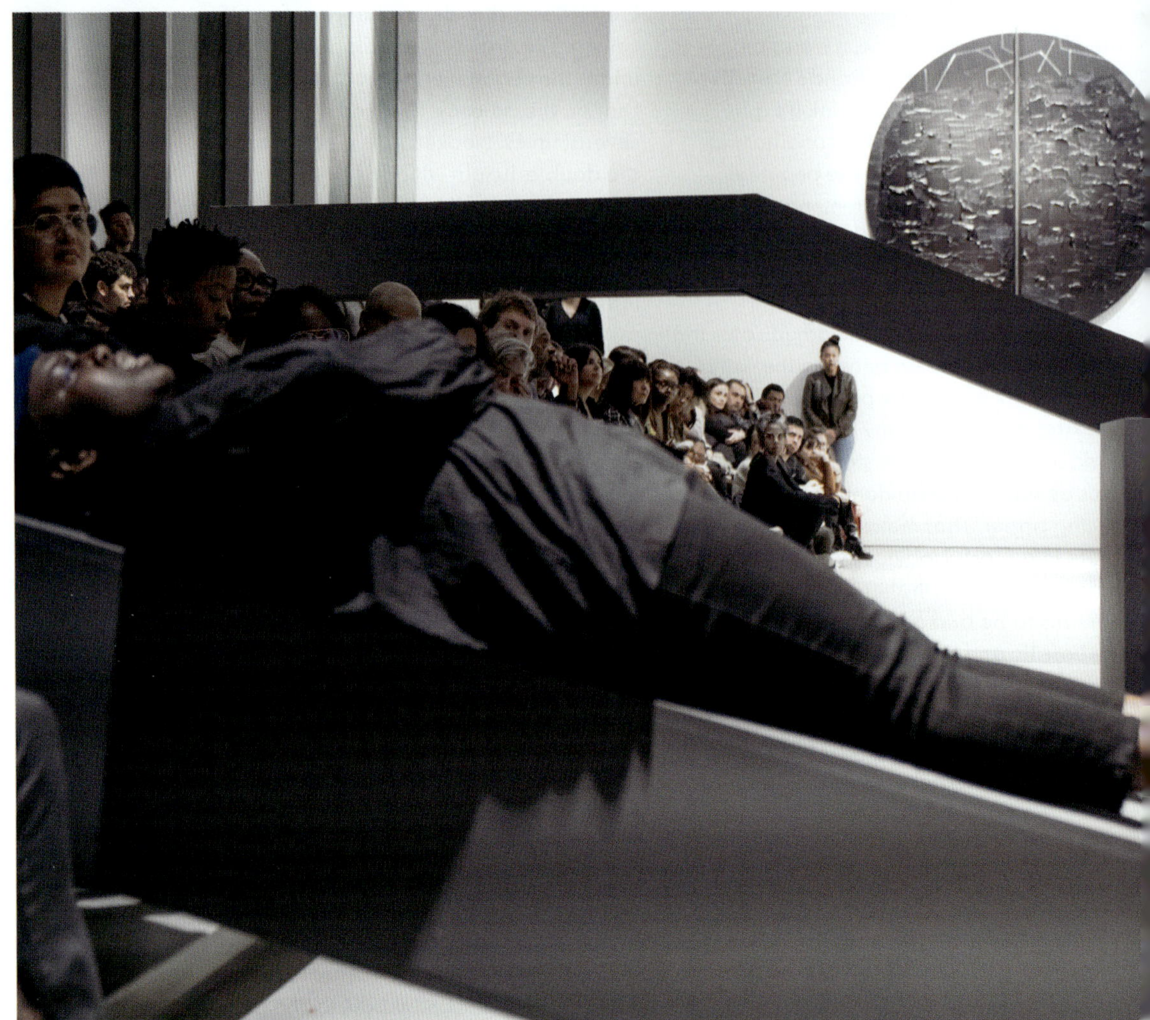

all these accounts and realities. That experiences are shared and connected—connection, sociality, culture, demography as radical forms of existing and moving and lasting, while all operating in these systems. Each participant decided what they wished to contribute. I did ask Dionne to read from *The Blue Clerk,* as this was central to this and stemmed from a former project we'd worked on together in Chicago.

MB

You began the second act by reading from your text "Blackness will swallow the whole of terror to be free." Can you repeat it for us now? It spoke to so much of what the performance was about.

TD

Yes, I recall you telling me to introduce the second act. At first, I resisted, but then recognized and realized that it needed to be that way. It begins with, "I think Blackness will swallow the whole of terror to be free. It will move across separations, molecules, units—through architecture, atmospheres, and concrete, in magic and bloodstreams to self-liberate. To image and imagine movements and geographies of freedom, known and unknown, is to regard

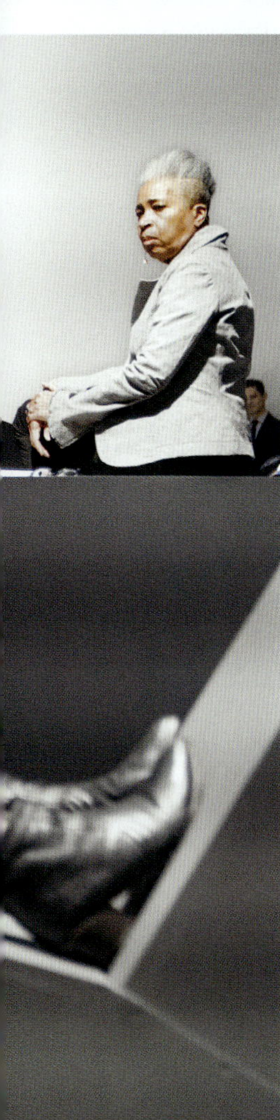

this space as irreducible, or to regard Black spatial movement as irreducible."

MB

The reading held space and quieted a very busy room. And from there, we moved on to Autumn Knight. A voice and an approach that again changed the emotional architecture of the room. We'd had some time for some rehearsals, but not a lot. It was a case of good ingredients and fast cooking.

TD

Right. Deep skill and improvisation. Her introduction, her cry into the space, also had a sense of ceremony, of setting the room. I didn't know what she was going to do either; I didn't ask. I just trusted her energy, her brilliance, to know what the moment called for.

MB

It reminded me of a gospel meeting, like a gospel singer setting the scene, before the message that Christina read.

TD

I'd read Christina's contribution and Dionne's. In a beautiful way, Christina's reading of the list was embedded in the doings of the clerk, the grandfather, the cab drivers, and the small girl in Brand's text. All the characters were taking account of their world; ledgers of ships, counting of barrels, accounts of rain, memories of color, water, and movement. I thought one piece of writing informed the other. It was a duality that I knew Zack and Andres would understand. Christina began to read, and, a few minutes after, Zach delivered Andres's moment score. The brief overlapping was important, and I wanted the audience to feel a cadence of the count in their own bodies from Zach's moves. As Christina concluded, Zack continued in silence and Dionne started to read from *The Blue Clerk*. The pitch was exactly right. The resonance was clear. Zack moved like liquid and sometimes like a mountain. He made full use of the architecture and the audience, telling a story with his motion that pointed to ideas of transition, continuance, and indeterminacy as embodied politics. I directed Zach to finish and wanted Dionne to close the performance.

MB

And to the second act, which had a contrasting mood and approach.

TD

When I was thinking about the second night, we discussed music and a number of musicians, and, after much discussion, you introduced me to Gaika, whose aesthetic and character were that of the monster—a monstrous being that's both beautiful and magical—who could bring a reckoning to injustice. The artist brought a melody and energy that connected global music and liberatory sound. There was another cadence to that night because of Gaika, because of Deja, and because of AJ [Arthur Jafa].

I invited AJ to bring *La Scala*, a former work of his that only existed as a photograph. It was informed by the story of Mary Jones, a pickpocket and sex worker in Manhattan in the 1830s. She was also possibly the first known trans woman in the United States. Grace Wales Bonner designed the garb Arthur wore in that photo. It was transcendental: AJ held the spirit of non-colonized bodies, a possessed body. It was powerful. Deja introduced the trans voice into the room, speaking aloud the thirty-seven trans bodies who had been murdered in America that year. This was the furthest from my own lived experience. The environment for unfamiliar Black trans

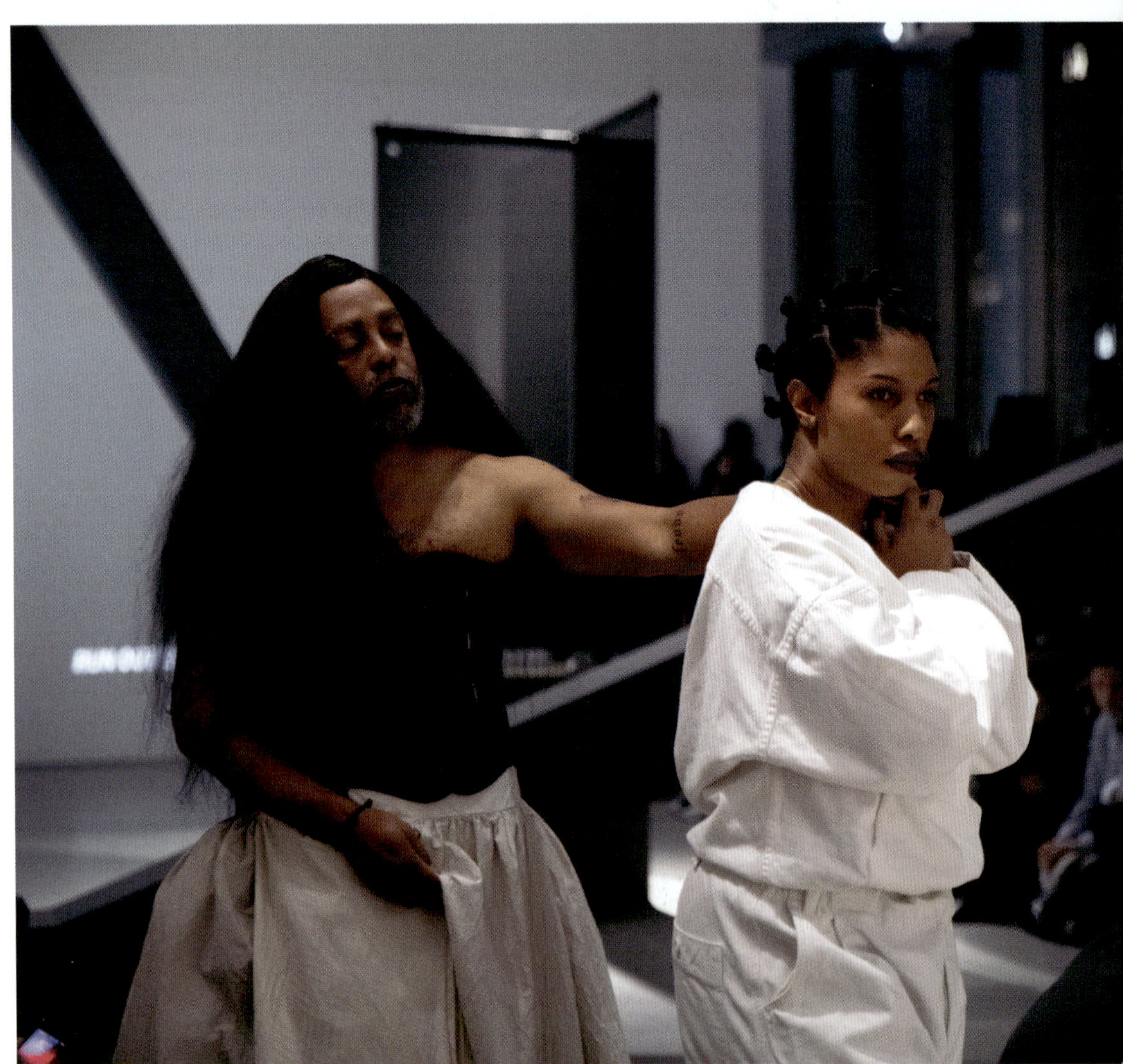

lives is most critical, and Deja brought in the humanity of it all at once. She pre-recorded the names, and we played it out loud. As a trained dancer, she moves in the space and brought the ancestors in with her. That was completely unexplainable. It was so Black. Perfect and nonconforming.

Lastly, Gaika performed, calling everyone to stand in awareness and recognition and certain histories.

Both performances were about Black systems. Systems that induce improvisation and encourage invention. I find it inspiring and encouraging to witness performance that happens in and recognizes the now. So, the second night was off the cliff. I'm from Chicago and followed the early house scene there. That's what I keyed into, late night—nothing but bass, nothing but bodies: gospel mixed with disco. It had a distinct vibe from the first night. The contrast—or, should I say, the arch—was productive.

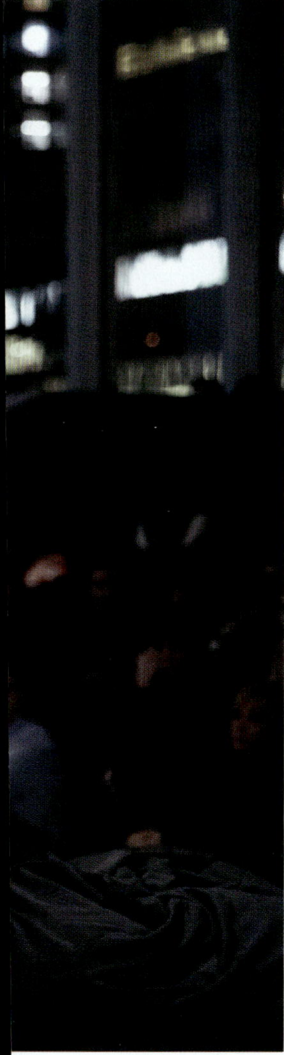

MB

They all carried the evening. There was something about Gaika calling everyone to stand, to recognize the names and history that was being expressed. It felt evangelical, a ritual evocation. It was a very simple action and very effective.

TD

Gaika came in, open, creative, inventive, charged, ready, generous. Here's a person, an artist, who's already dealing with liberation, a liberation he's living right now, and all I wanted to do is to provide a platform for that. A small crew of us went upstate the day before the show and shot footage in an abandoned building I own. It was a massive place, and he commanded it. I directed, he improvised, and, the next day, he added a bit of the footage I shot to a video he was working on. Along with his performance, I brought in three projectors to make a kind of kaleidoscope of moving images. How do you set up a system where the best improvisational notes and tones can ring true, like the free jazz of Cecil Taylor? How do you create the situation and the conditions for improvisation?

Both performances used the architecture completely differently. It felt lucid.

This conversation between Torkwase Dyson and Mark Beasley took place in New York in September 2020. It has been edited for clarity.

The romantic German concept of *Gesamtkunstwerk*, or "a total work of art," proposes a synthesis of artistic forms. While the original idea referred to the borderless-ness between libretto, theater, and music in opera, contemporary examples of the unitary artwork often extend to spectacular cultural productions that consider sound, movement, costume, light, and scenography in equal parts, immersing viewers in fantastical displays and sometimes removing the boundaries separating the viewer and viewed. For Performa 19, Kia LaBeija, Korakrit Arunanondchai with boychild and Alex Gvojic, Cecilia Bengolea and Michèle Lamy, and Paul Maheke with Nkisi and Ariel Efraim Ashbel crafted multisensorial environments that championed collaboration as a mode of working to bring to life multifaceted worlds.

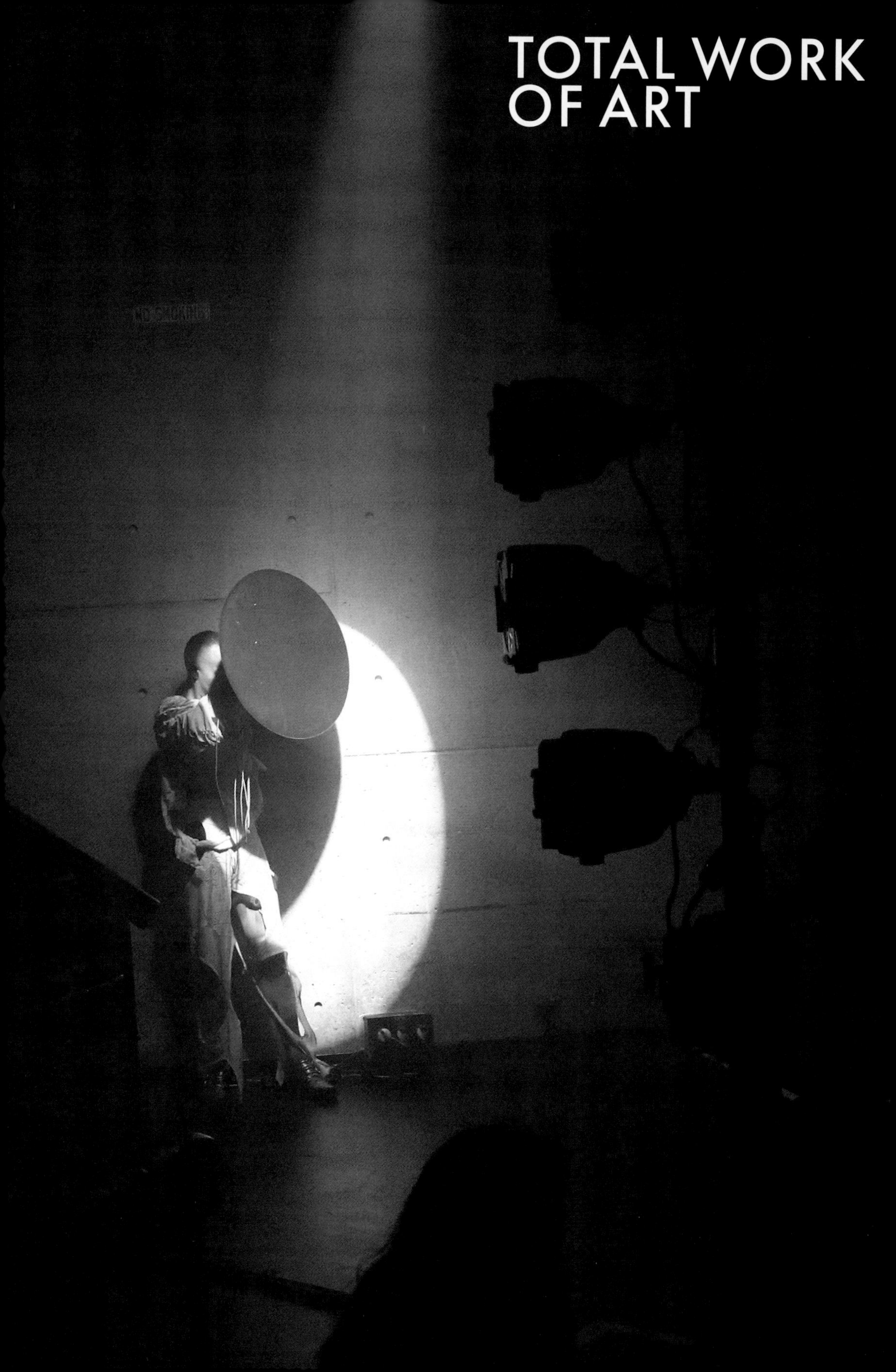

TOTAL WORK OF ART

CECILIA BENGOLEA & MICHÈLE LAMY

before we die

Curated by
Kathy Noble

Performa 19 Hub
(18 Wooster)

November 23, 2019

Ten dancers wearing an archive of Comme de Garçons sculptural dresses lay on the floor in a tableau of slumbering, genderless, animal-esque creatures frozen in time. Fashion icon, artist, and designer Michèle Lamy wandered onto the stage area and laughed into a microphone, beginning with a light giggle and ending with raucous howls as thumping music by Nico Vascellari began to play. As the beats grew louder, Cecilia Bengolea took the stage and moved into a headstand against the wall, legs spread, ass shaking. The sleeping bodies slowly unfurled and rose to scatter to the walls and pick up placards of mythical hybrid animals created by Bengolea for Desert X 2019—where she installed them in the highly polluted Salton Sea in Southern California.

Holding these wooden figures, the performers walked in a procession over the shiny concrete ground, posing, walking, running a little, part reluctant models lolling on a circular catwalk, on display, part shamanic entities enacting a ceremonial ritual. Calm came before chaos, as each one set down their critter companion and began to spin on the spot, scattering across the room without formation. As their pace increased incrementally, the ten whirling dervishes whipped the heavy costumes around their bodies, the gravity of which slowed them as they sped up, almost bumping into each other in the dizzying frenzy.

One after another, the performers dropped to the floor when they reached a breaking point and could no longer cope, leaving a final dancer spinning manically, as fast as they could, simultaneously in and out of control, edging in and out of climax until they collapsed. The animals rested momentarily, their heavy breathing audible, until one rose to perform a solo. One after the other, they performed individual styles of dance—interweaving disparate languages of movement including dancehall, vogue, and ballet—before the group jumped up to end with a triumphant mass choreography composed by Bengolea. Suddenly the metal shutter to the gallery rose and the dancers pushed wildly through the crowd on their way out of the building. The shutter descended behind them, imprisoning the audience inside. KATHY NOBLE

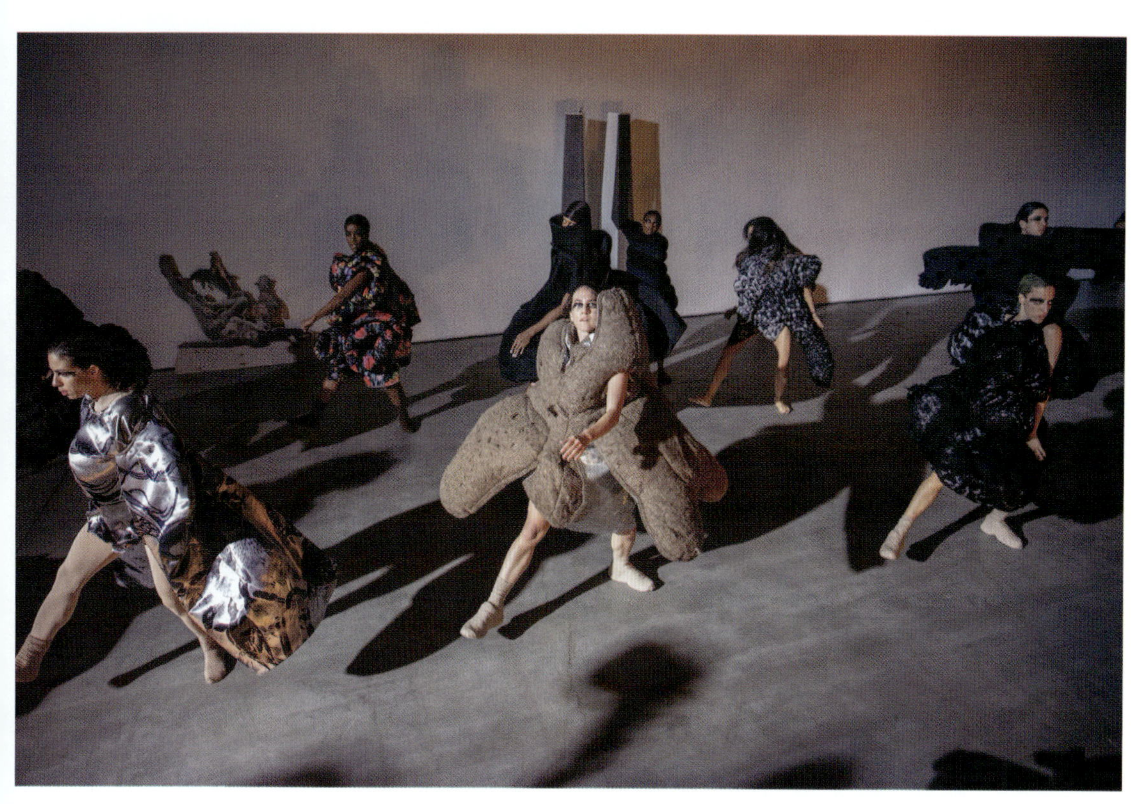

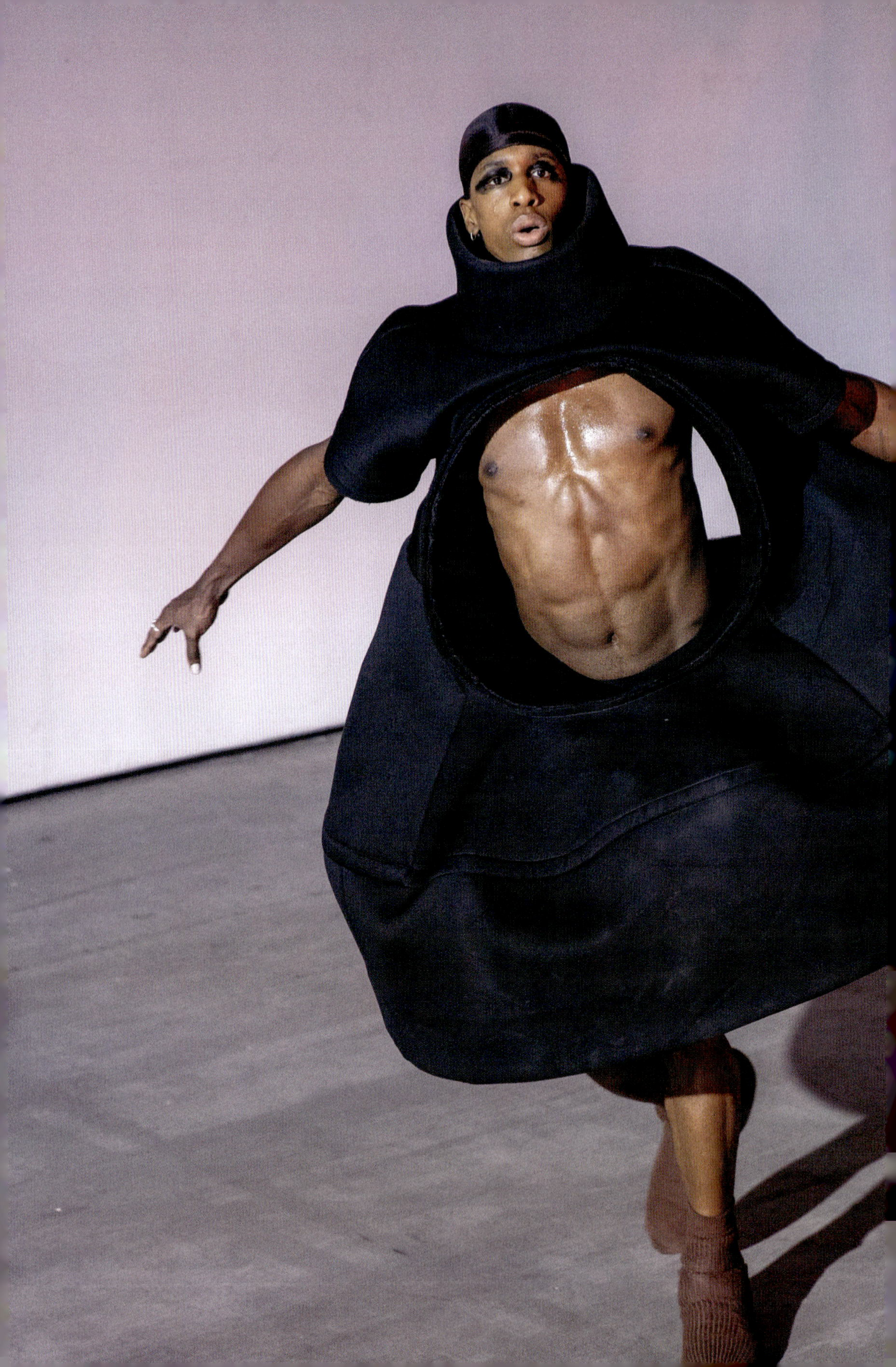

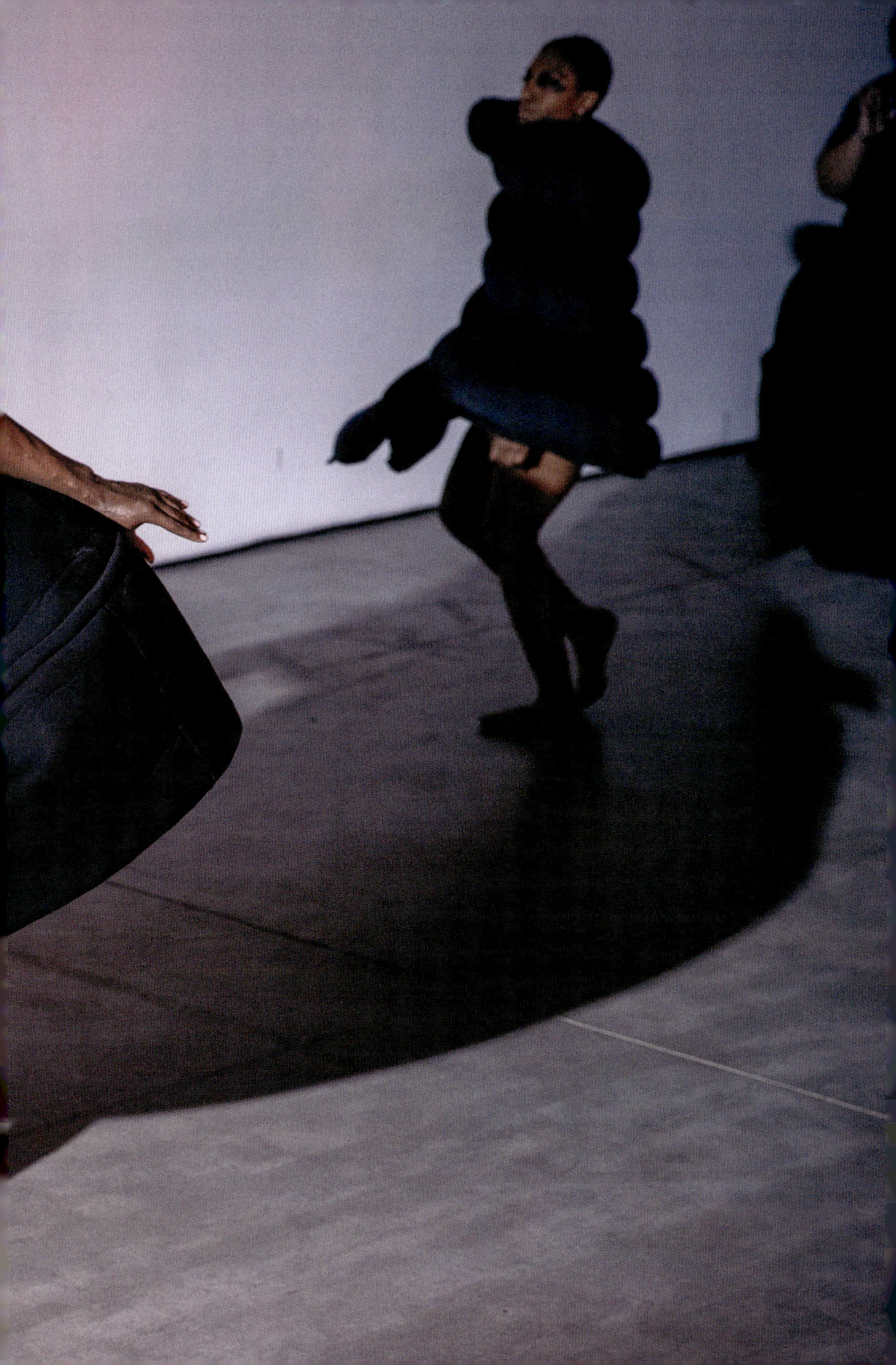

KIA LABEIJA

(Untitled) The Black Act

Curated by
Kathy Noble
and Job Piston

Performance Space
New York

November 7–9, 2019

"I have, at many times, been a spiral.

An abyss of obscurity, falling deeper into the same patterns; over and over. And somewhere amidst the twisting, turning and reaching that happens when one falls, I find that I am breathing backwards..."

— Kia LaBeija, Part 1.

Kia LaBeija's *(Untitled) The Black Act* offered a contemporary interpretation of the third act of Oskar Schlemmer's 1922 *Triadische Ballett* (Triadic Ballet). The performance's "black act" refers to the fantasy, mysticism, and infinite void of the black stage. From a historical and linguistic viewpoint, the first incarnation of *Triadische Ballett* was created prior to Schlemmer's time on the Bauhaus faculty, and he did not call the three parts "acts" (*Akt* in German), but *Reihe*, literally translating to *row*, or *series*. LaBeija's interpretation expands Schlemmer's original vision by inserting her own narrative and inviting five artists—Daniella Agosto, Selena Ettienne, Khristina Cayetano, Taína Larot, and Terry Lovette, all of whom have played a crucial role in the artist's life—as representations of herself.

(Untitled) The Black Act was conceived while in residence at Performance Space New York in August 2019. Together with Taína Larot, her creative producing partner, LaBeija led a series of movement workshops in order to develop a score organically. By straying away from traditional choreography, she allowed the performance to unfold differently each night, using tasks that were executed in real time. Each performer took a unique journey through a geography that recalls Schlemmer's geometric markings and the grid of New York City's streets.

Working collaboratively as a community was one of the founding principles of the Bauhaus: It was the first art school to have a stage school at its core, and envisioned social utopia through multi-disciplinary collaborations between art, dance, theater, music, and utilitarian craft. Collaborators include fashion stylist and designer Kyle Luu, who created transformative, architectural costumes that both provoked and restricted movement, while simultaneously masking and exposing elements of the performers' physiques. Music was composed with artist and producer Kenn Michael, who is LaBeija's brother. RESHI, the software instrument that utilizes healing frequencies—and Michael's brainchild—made its world premiere, with accompaniment on percussion by Warren Benbow, the artist's father. KATHY NOBLE

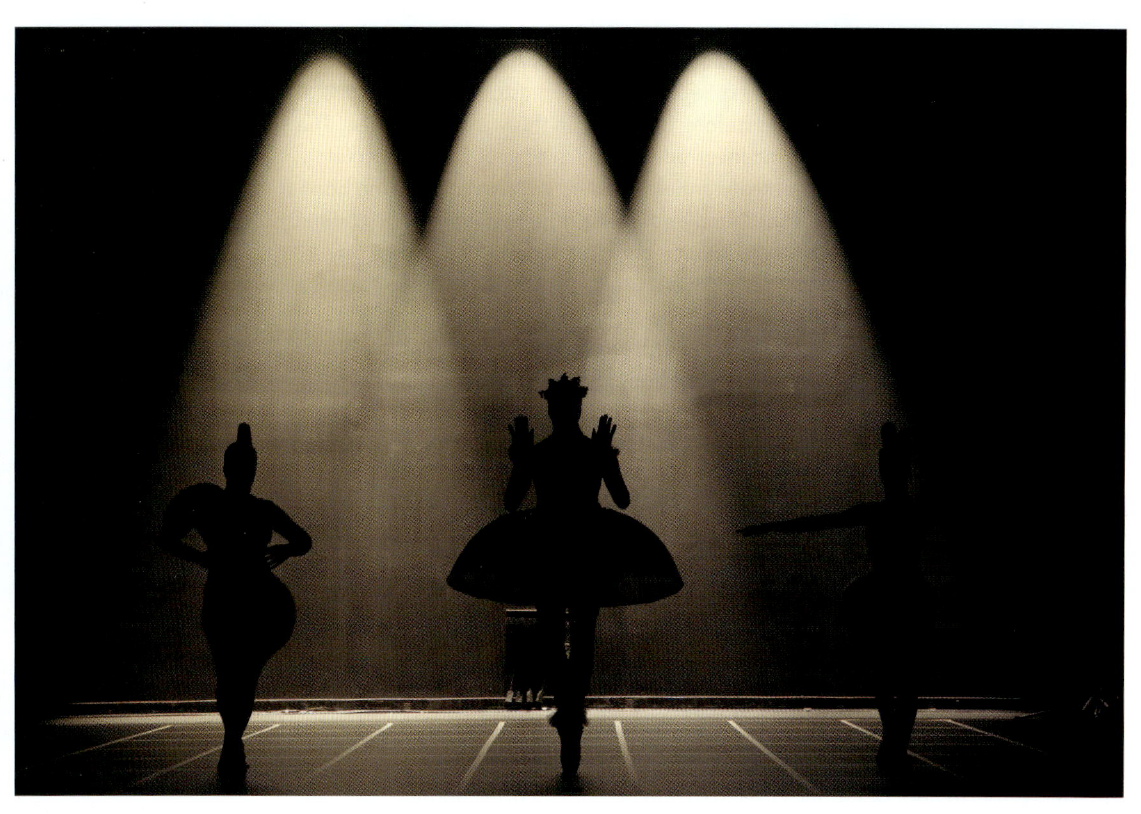

Abstract/Black/Bodies: Kia LaBeija's (Untitled) The Black Act

A dance of rigorous geometries; primary shapes: circle, square, triangle; primary colors: red, yellow, blue. Dancers costumed as abstract forms. A dance of solos, duets, trios. Spirals, disks, grids. A total artwork of dance, music, scenography, lighting, costumes. We have seen this before, but never in this way. In *(Untitled) The Black Act*, Kia LaBeija reinvented and inverted Oskar Schlemmer's *Triadic Ballet* (1922), the singular touchstone of early twentieth-century abstract dance, the banner achievement of Bauhaus performance, and enduring riddle of modern art. *(Untitled) The Black Act* is in a long line of *Triadic Ballet* reconstructions, reinterpreted, say, through the drag ballroom scene where LaBeija literally made her name—the former Mother of the Royal House of LaBeija entered the scene at the age of nineteen. *(Untitled) The Black Act* is not an interpretation of *Triadic Ballet* so much as its dialectical sublation: at once a preservation and a negation. Schlemmer aspired to abstraction; LaBeija foregrounded personal narrative. Schlemmer dematerialized bodies; LaBeija concretized them in specific identities, relations, and skins. Schlemmer's strict rules were countered by LaBeija's queer improvisations. And where Schlemmer marshalled technologized darkness to construct universal forms that abide by the laws of the abstract stage, LaBeija co-created a work through the relations between intimately linked Black, queer, female bodies and subjects.

Crucial to LaBeija's relation to space is an engagement with personal narratives: "Whenever I come into a space, I imagine what stories it has to tell. It's vital that the locations I choose for my portraits have a strong history."[1] *(Untitled) The Black Act* was co-commissioned by and first performed at Performance Space New York (formerly PS 122) in the East Village. In the past, LaBeija has situated and photographed herself in deeply personal locations, such as her bedroom on the twenty-fourth floor of Manhattan Plaza, the legendary artist housing complex where she grew up; her doctor's office, where she has her blood drawn regularly to manage her HIV symptoms, a condition with which she was born; the fashion photography set where she constructed eighties-inflected self-portraits for *W Magazine*;[2] or the entrance to the building where she visited her great-aunts, who sojourned north as part of the Great Migration. LaBeija had no previous personal connection to Performance Space New York, but, in any event, *(Untitled)* would have begun in the same space no matter where it would have been performed. It began in a pitch-black theater. It is this dark space whose history she mined and whose story she told with unrivaled urgency and beauty.

Her interlocutor is Oskar Schlemmer, the Bauhaus master most famous for his abstract dances and otherworldly costumes. LaBeija reinvented Schlemmer's

1
LaBeija in Kia LaBeija and Alex Fialho, "Kia LaBeija," *Artforum International* 56, no. 5 (2018).

2
See Horacio Silva, "Kia LaBeija Is Remodeling One of Ballroom's Legendary Houses For the Future," *W* magazine (2018). https://www.wmagazine.com/story/house-of-kia-labeija-ballroom-voguing.

3
My discussion of Schlemmer's *Triadic Ballet* draws on "Spaceless Play: Oskar Schlemmer's Dance against Enlightenment" in Noam M. Elcott, *Artificial Darkness: An Obscure History of Modern Art and Media* (Chicago: University of Chicago Press, 2016), 165–228. For further reflections on the intersections of contemporary art and artificial darkness, see "A Brief History of Artificial Darkness and Race," in *Rethinking Darkness: Borders, Landscapes, Practices*, ed. Nick Dunn and Tim Edensor (London: Routledge, 2021), 61–76.

4
Oskar Schlemmer, "Das Triadische Ballett," ed. Gesellschaft der Musikfreunde zu Donaueschingen (Donaueschingen1926), no pagination. Translation mine.

Triadic Ballet, among the most sustained, rigorous, and inscrutable attempts at defining abstract space and dance in the early twentieth century. Performa 19 was organized around the centennial of the founding of the Bauhaus as the biennial's historical anchor; in the history of performance art, no Bauhaus work looms larger than *Triadic Ballet*. In order to grasp the magnitude of LaBeija's intervention into this legacy, we must venture a deep if brief dive into Schlemmer's magnum opus. Between their shared and divergent dances with darkness, *(Untitled) The Black Act* is a *pas de deux* with *Triadic Ballet* above all.

After several years of preparation, Schlemmer and several collaborators premiered *Triadic Ballet* on September 30, 1922, on the small stage of the Württemberg Landestheater in Stuttgart.[3] For Schlemmer, *triadic* connoted a range of references: the musical triad; the threefold qualities of form, color, and space. Primary forms: circle, square, triangle; primary colors: red, blue, yellow; and primary spatial dimensions: height, depth, width. Additionally, there would be three when "the monomaniacal ego and the dualistic opposition are surmounted and the collective begins."[4] For all the textual and visual documentation of *Triadic Ballet*, however, its choreography remains a mystery—the notation has been lost, save for the trio finale. The ballet languished for a generation after Schlemmer's death. LaBeija's primary access to the ballet was the 1968 film directed by Margarete Hasting, with artistic guidance by Bauhaus affiliates Ludwig Grote, Xanti Schawinsky, and Tut Schlemmer, Oskar's widow. In the most patently triadic invocation, Schlemmer divided the ballet into three movements, series, or acts,

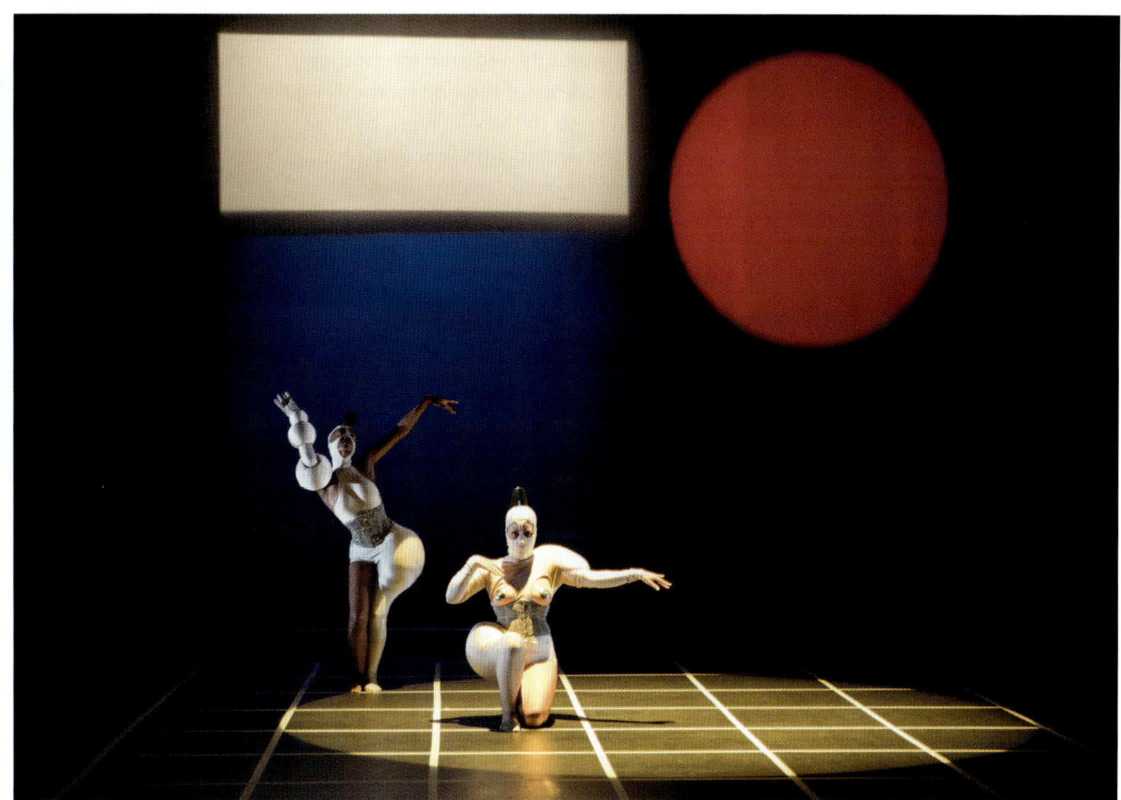

each with its own color and atmosphere. As Schlemmer elaborated: "The first is a gay burlesque with lemon-yellow curtains. The second, ceremonious and solemn, is on a rose-colored stage. And the third is a mystical fantasy on a black stage."[5] Soon after the premiere, Schlemmer reconstituted *Triadic Ballet* as an extended version of its third act; he abandoned the yellow and pink sets and embraced the black stage as the exclusive backdrop against which his costumes came to life. Even as the third, black act served as the basis for LaBeija's new work, in which she extended what Schlemmer called the "gay burlesque" of his original first act in ways he never could have envisioned.

With its black costumes and black sets, the third act, more than any other, realized Schlemmer's aspiration to "dematerialize the body."[6] Following a long line of scientists, magicians, charlatans, photographers, cabaret performers, filmmakers, and directors of all stripes—most or all of whom were unknown to him—Schlemmer discovered that black costumes worn on a black stage could make the bodies of his dancers effectively disappear. Performers were given abstract names—*Spiral, Wire Costume, Disk Dancer, Abstract Dancer*—and were transformed into life-size marionettes controlled from inside the costumes. Other than the occasional unmasked face or naked hand, their bodies, enshrouded in black materials, were absorbed into the darkness of the black backdrops and yielded to their abstract costumes.

Schlemmer's choreography echoed or amplified the wardrobe, even as it obscured the bodies. At the premiere, *Spiral* traced a corkscrew path to a *toccata* by the eighteenth-century Italian composer Pietro Domenico Paradisi. But her body—clad in black leather over a black unitard—vanished, or "dematerialized," in favor of a blue, green, and silver overlay and a coiled spiral of transparent celluloid. Similarly, the duet for two *Disk Dancers* violently negated the bodies of its dancers. Costumed identically except for the colors of their disks, they wore black unitards and robotlike masks (later likened to the one worn by the robot in Fritz Lang's 1927 film *Metropolis*) and were armed with lance tips for hands. Viewed frontally, they were reduced to vacant masks, weaponized fists, and invisible bodies bifurcated by metallic lines that ran from their pelvises up the center of their masks and extended well over their helmed heads. A swivel in either direction revealed the flamboyant disks and an absence where one might expect their bodies, which were occluded by the black-on-black effect. Over and over again, Schlemmer's *Triadic Ballet* transformed the bodies of dancers—including his own, as Schlemmer always took on the all-important role of *Abstract Dancer*—into abstract shapes moving in geometric patterns amidst "the invisible linear network of planimetric and stereometric relationships" of the abstract stage.[7]

For Schlemmer, the battle came down to a fundamental opposition between humans and space:

> The human organism stands in the cubical, abstract space of the stage. Human and Space. Each has different laws of order. Whose shall prevail? Either abstract space is adapted in deference to the natural human and transformed back into nature or the imitation of nature. This happens in the theater of illusionistic realism.
> Or the natural human, in deference to abstract space, is recast to fit its mold. This happens on the abstract stage.[8]

Oskar Schlemmer, overview of *Triadisches Ballett*, ca. 1924-1926.

Oskar Schlemmer, *Triadisches Ballett* costumes: spiral and disk, 1926.

5
"Man and Art Figure," in *The Theater of the Bauhaus*, eds. Oskar Schlemmer, László Moholy-Nagy, and Farkas Molnár (Middletown, Connecticut: Wesleyan University Press, 1961), 34.

6
"Ballett?," in *Staatliches Bauhaus Weimar 1919–1923* (Münich: Kraus Reprint, 1923; reprint, 1980), no pagination. Schlemmer published these notes in the program for the 1922 premiere and republished them repeatedly throughout the decade.

7
"Man and Art Figure," 23.

8
Ibid., 22–23; Oskar Schlemmer, "Mensch und Kunstfigur," in Die Bühne im Bauhaus, eds. Oskar Schlemmer, László Moholy-Nagy, and Farkas Molnár (Berlin: Gebr. Mann Verlag, 1925; reprint, 2003), 13. Translation modified. The English translation, now patently patriarchal, erroneously translates "Der Organismus Mensch" as "Man, the human organism." For the sake of bibliographic usability I left the English title of the essay uncorrected in the notes.

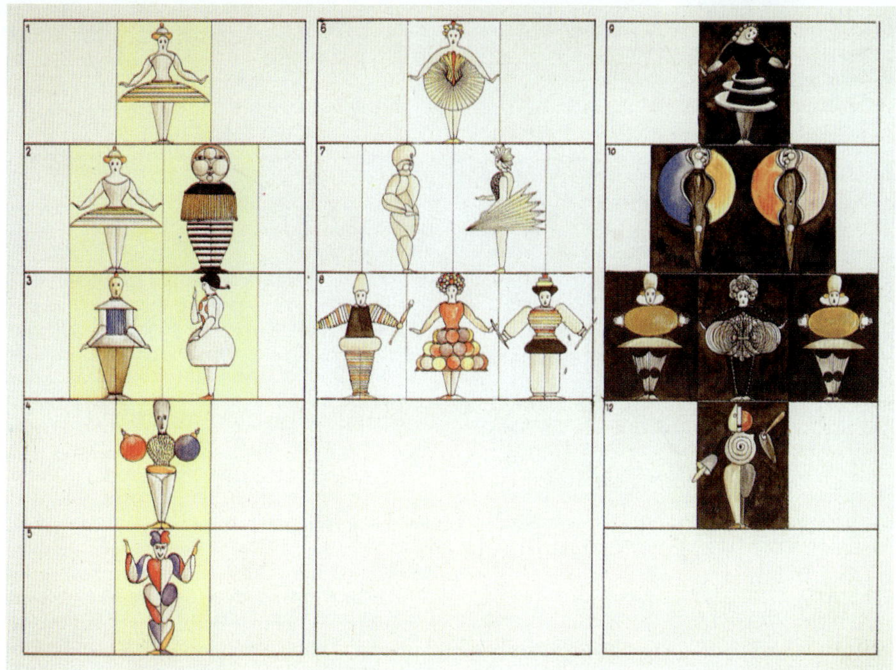
1
2
3
4
5
6
7
8
9
10
12

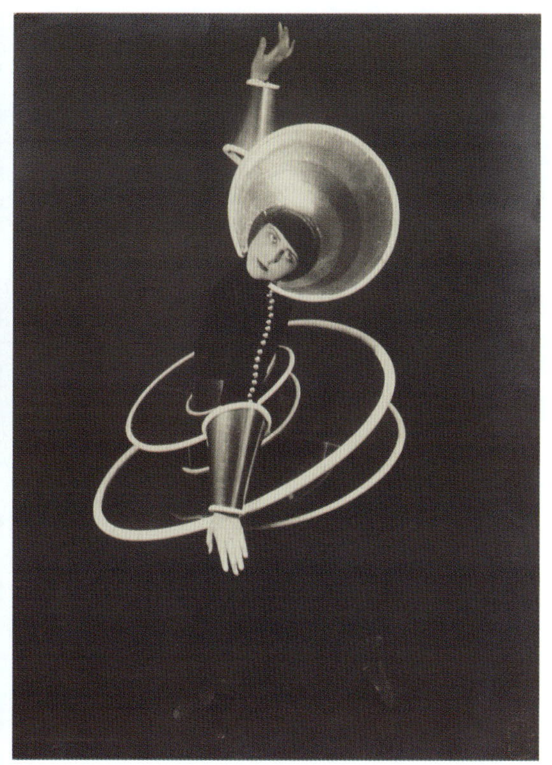

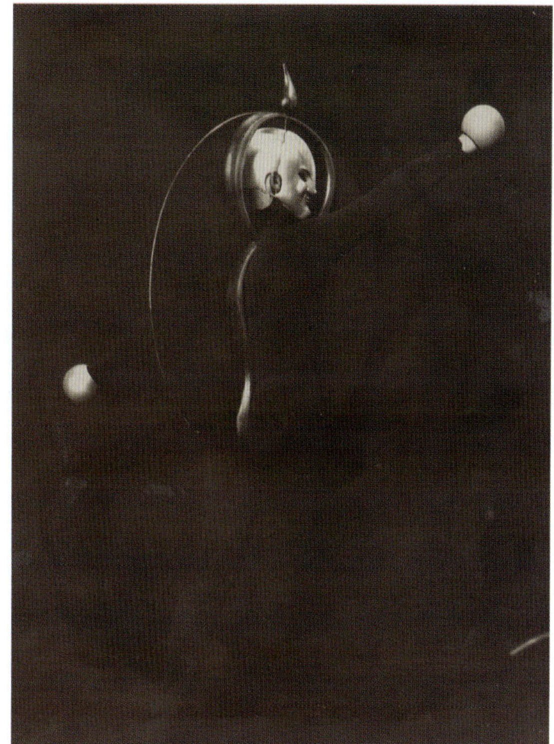

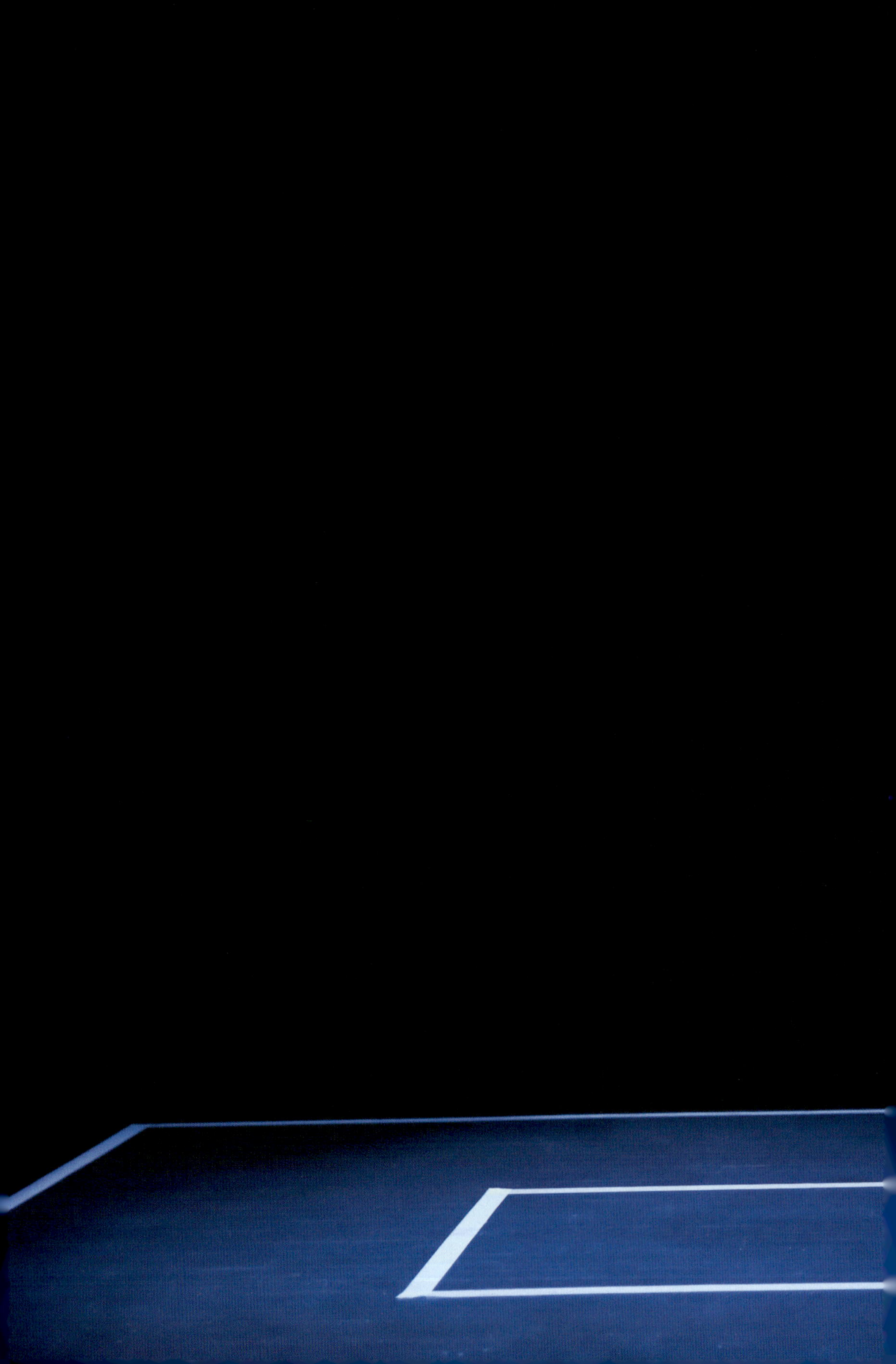

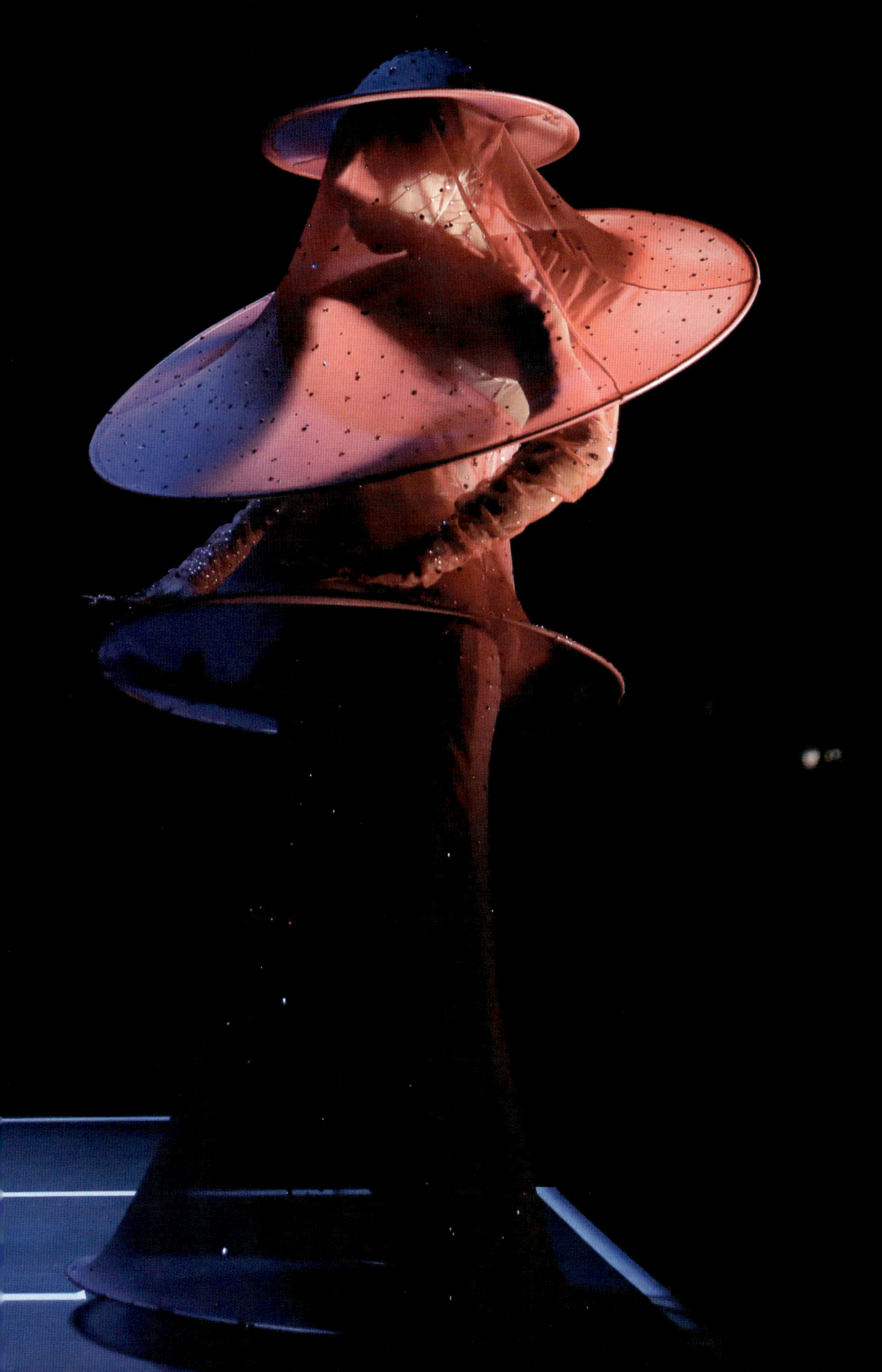

Schlemmer staged a choice between the human organism and abstract space—and recast the human accordingly. Yet even as he unequivocally prioritized abstract space, he endorsed universal biological laws, which "reside in the invisible functions of his inner self: heartbeat, circulation, respiration, the activities of the brain and nervous system."[9] What Schlemmer excluded absolutely was the personal and historical—as well as, to the degree possible, human attributes like sex/gender, race, or sexual orientation. Schlemmer's were abstract bodies, freed from the vagaries of human difference.[10]

LaBeija's *(Untitled) The Black Act* opened with a spiral: an undulating, costumed figure bathed in blue light, alone in the darkness. Slowly, white footlights augmented the blue overheads to reveal a dancer in a sheer pink sequined ballroom dress with matching flamboyant hat and opera gloves. LaBeija occupied Schlemmer's original *Spiral* as "Camp."[11] Just as the overhead lights slowly revealed a geometric maze on the floor, white footlights revealed the silhouette of LaBeija's body within the glamorous spiral costume in a double striptease of abstract staging and individual body. LaBeija's sinuous movements, however, contrasted starkly with the rigid geometry of the labyrinth from which she escaped. In forceful yet tender opposition to Schlemmer, LaBeija chose the human: not the human recast to fit the mold of abstract space, nor the human reduced to biological and universal laws, nor the dematerialized human whose body gives way to technologized darkness. Instead, LaBeija inhabited that very thing discounted in advance by Schlemmer's abstract ballet: a queer, gendered, Black body.

> *Interviewer*
> Where do you move furthest away from Schlemmer?
>
> *LaBeija:*
> Life experience. We've both created works looking at the world we live in, but we have lived in different and separate worlds.[12]

Through program notes, interviews, and other avenues, LaBeija announced that the spiral is less a geometric form than a position with which she regularly identifies:

> I have, at many times, been a spiral.
> An abyss of obscurity, falling deeper into the same patterns; over and over. And somewhere amidst the twisting, turning, and reaching that happens when one falls, I find that I am breathing backward ...[13]

(Untitled) The Black Act is a deeply personal narrative for LaBeija and a personal journey for her and her collaborators. LaBeija performed the first and last of the four dances herself. Both her solos are performances of escape: In the first one, she spiraled out of a geometric labyrinth; in the final one, she pulled the gridded tape off of the floor and lay down a line of flight out of the dark space of the theater.

The second dance featured Daniella Agosto and Selena Ettienne, LaBeija's "gay kids," young adults she has nurtured as the mother of the Royal House of LaBeija, the birthplace of house culture within the ballroom scene and an

9
"Man and Art Figure," 25.

10
Like most but not all of his Bauhaus associates, Schlemmer appears to have had no interest in engaging the "queer Bauhaus" recently excavated by art historian Elizabeth Otto. See Elizabeth Otto, *Haunted Bauhaus: Occult Spirituality, Gender Fluidity, Queer Identities, and Radical Politics* (Cambridge, Massachusetts: MIT Press, 2019), 132–69.

11
Susan Sontag, "Notes on 'Camp,'" republished in *Against Interpretation* (New York: originally published by Farrar, Straus and Giroux in 1966; Picador, 2001), 275–92. As Sontag writes: "Time liberates the work of art from moral relevance, delivering it over to the Camp sensibility" (285). If *(Untitled) The Black Act* delivers Schlemmer's *Triadic Ballet* over to Camp, then it does so precisely to enhance its moral relevance. LaBeija—along with artists such as Kehinde Wiley—may have reinvented Camp as political commitment. Committed Camp, as an alternative to Sontag's still-brilliant exposition, could be a category for further inquiry.

12
LaBeija in Emma McCormick-Goodhart, "Kia LaBeija: Attenuated Iconographie," *Flash Art* (2019). https://flash--art.com/2019/11/kia-labeija-attenuated-iconographies/.

13
LaBeija in the program notes for *(Untitled) The Black Act*, Performance Space, November 7, 2019.

14
LaBeija quoted in Maximilíano Durón, "For Performa Biennial, Kia LaBeija Reinvents a Bauhaus Classic—With a Ball Culture Twist," *ARTnews* (November 7, 2019).

enduring alternate family structure for gay and gender-nonconforming youth. The dance of *Disk*—a highly abstract battle in Schlemmer's ballet—was, for LaBeija, a psychological and spiritual duel of the self, a struggle toward inner peace. The two performers mirrored each other's movements seamlessly, the result not of predetermined choreography but rather of intensive rehearsals spent in mutual recognition and anticipation. LaBeija instructed them: "If you keep your eyes together, you'll automatically know what the other is doing because you can feel it. It's not an easy thing to do, but if you can, you'll see things you could never see before."[14] LaBeija rejected rigid choreography and instead jointly created, with her collaborators, the framework in which movement could unfold, which it did differently every night of the performance's run. Her performance practice aims equally at theatrical presentations and the real-world healing of an ever-widening circle of participants. Most immediately, Agosto and Ettienne were not on speaking terms when rehearsals began; LaBeija's collaborative, introspective performance practice restored their real-life relationship.

The third scene unfolded on a seven-by-seven-foot grid and featured Taína Larot, LaBeija's producing and life partner, as well as Khristina Cayetano and Terry Lovette, close friends and collaborators. Whereas the first two sequences reimagined specific moments from *Triadic Ballet*, this dance cast a far wider net of allusions. The choreography hinted at ballroom culture (specifically voguing) as well as classical ballet (particularly dancing *en pointe*), without adhering to either sets of conventions. The costumes intimated a range of sources and interlocutors: the first two acts of Schlemmer's ballet; the 1997 Comme des Garçons "Body Meets Dress, Dress Meets Body," or "lumps and bumps," collection

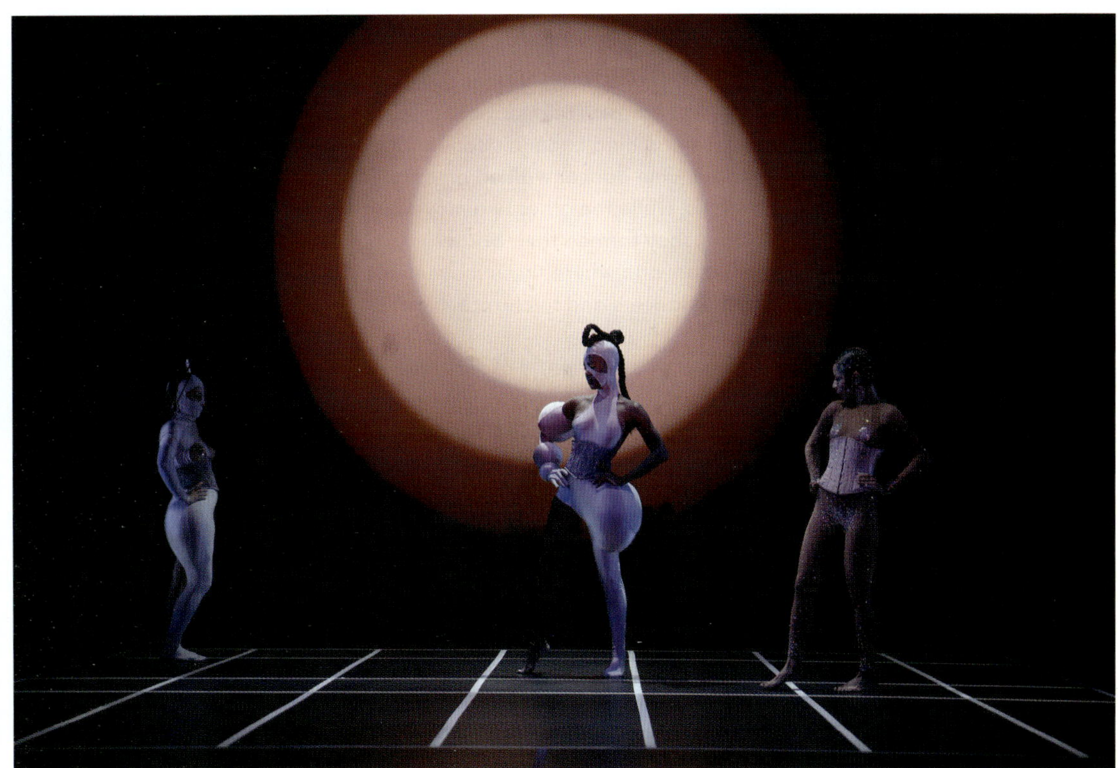

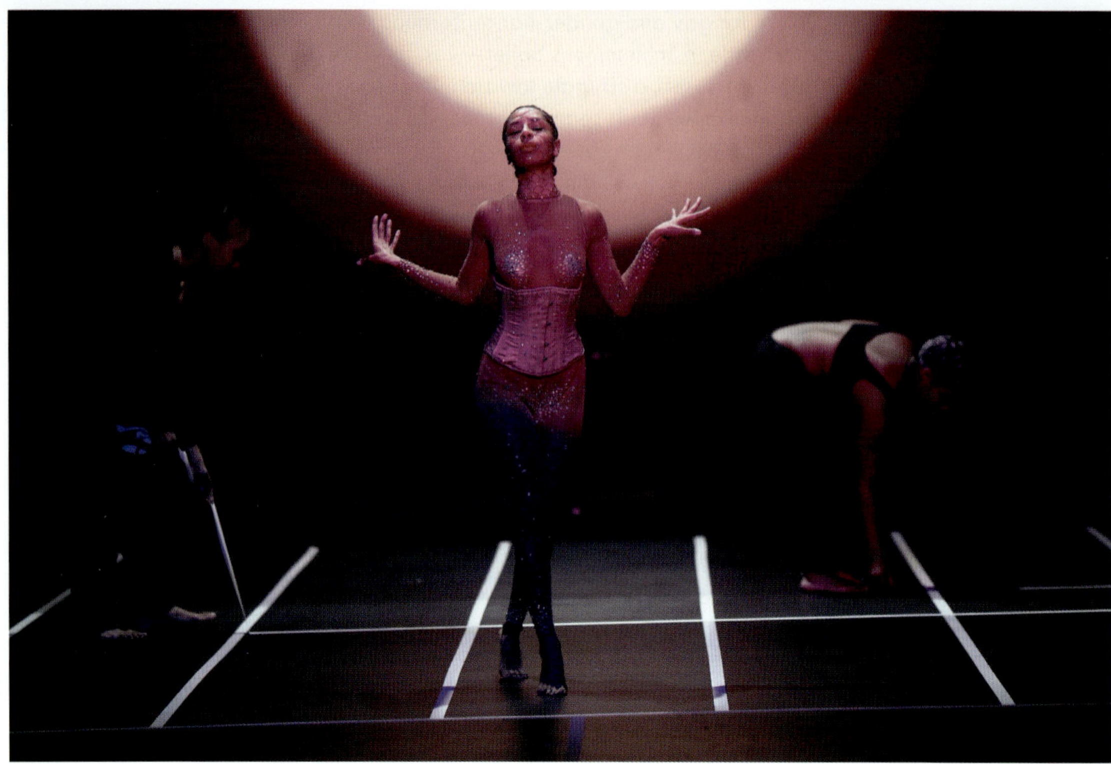

by Rei Kawakubo, fashion which was adapted for the performers in Merce Cunningham's *Scenario* later that year; fetish suits, replete with circular cutouts for breasts and thighs, as well as hooded sex masks; and elaborate African hair braiding styles. The choreography exemplified LaBeija's combination of strict parameters and individual freedom: One dancer walked *en pointe* along the edges and down the center of the grid, while the other two moved about the interior of the square; when they met, they formed their bodies into human sculptures. These were the rules. How, when, and where these movements and interactions unfolded was left to the dancers and to chance. No two performances were alike.

LaBeija entered the fray and began to clear the stage of the other dancers and of the tape that demarcated the grid (from this dance) and the geometric labyrinth (from the first dance). For LaBeija, the gridded tape echoed the lattice of Manhattan's streets, perhaps mediated by the tape Piet Mondrian employed to sketch his final paintings, not least (and still visible in) the unfinished versions of *New York City* (1941) and *Victory Boogie Woogie* (1944). The grid—delineated in white lines on a black stage—must also refer to the linear network of planimetric and stereometric relationships Schlemmer made visible in his Bauhaus books and demonstrations. The removal of this grid is the most explicit and violent rejection of Schlemmer's abstraction and the suppression of human difference it entailed. The grid and labyrinth signified psychological confinement, and the dancers returned—now in outfits that are not quite street attire, costumes, or stagehand clothing—and assisted LaBeija in removing them

Werner Siedhoff performing Oskar Schlemmer's Bauhaus demonstration "Raumlineatur mit Figur" ("Spatial delineation with figure"), 1927.

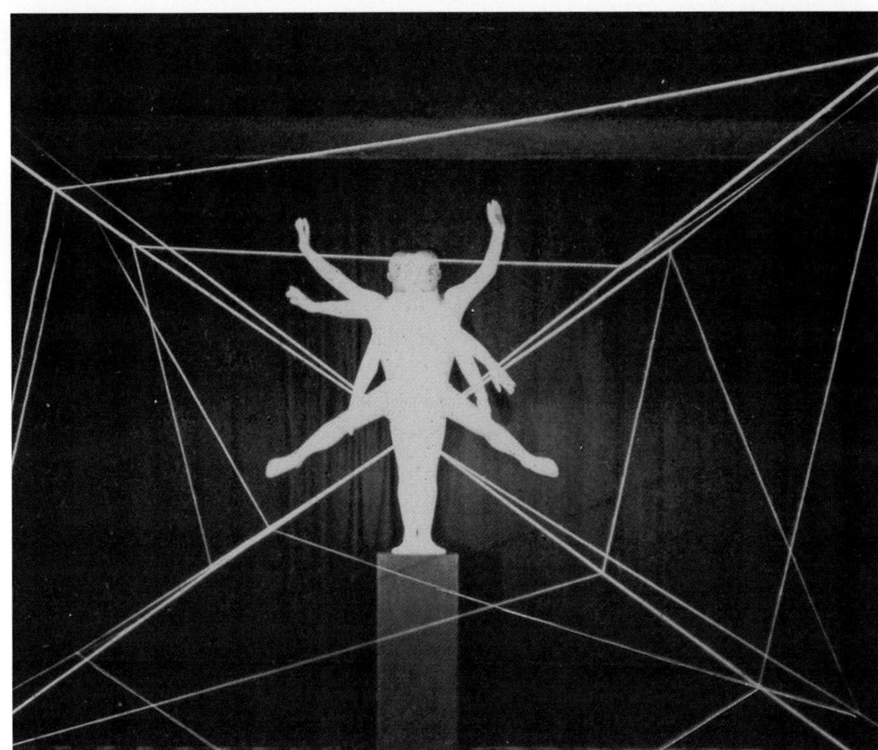

from the stage. The final dance was a solo but was executed in the company of her collaborators. When the old gridded and labyrinthine world had been crumpled up into a ball, LaBeija—once again a solitary figure in the dark—taped down a line of flight out of the theater. Her troupe followed. She closed the door. Empty darkness. The end.

Each of her five dancers represent a facet of LaBeija. The moves embody her struggles, passions, and aspirations in forms blatant and latent. For LaBeija, self-discovery is always an incomplete journey and never one ventured alone. Accompanied by the electronic music of her brother, Kenn Michael, and the percussions of her father, Warren Benbow, LaBeija constructed *(Untitled) The Black Act* as a family affair that adhered to an expanded definition of family. LaBeija is—and redefines what it means to be—daughter, sister, mother, partner. In *(Untitled) The Black Act*, the world is not limited to geometric relations.

The most vital arc of *(Untitled)* was traced by the potent and intricate presentation of bodies—bodies that were purposely obfuscated in Schlemmer's *Triadic Ballet*. Where Schlemmer's *Spiral* dematerialized the body into artificial darkness, LaBeija's *Spiral* brought her body into visibility—or at least hinted at it through silhouette and attire. With vacant, black holes where we would expect eyes and dark voids where we would anticipate torsos, the disks yielded their bodies to exuberantly abstract metal shapes. LaBeija's forms inverted these operations. Agosto and Ettienne were not transformed into disks; rather, they sported them as highly reflective ornaments: oversize earrings, forearm flares, and reflective surfaces woven onto balaclavas and along the arms, legs, and waists. LaBeija's ensembles, designed by Kyle Luu, also revealed the wearers' midriffs. LaBeija shared: "I wanted to show skin."[15] Black bodies were not acknowledged in Schlemmer's black act; only white bodies were visible in the darkness. LaBeija's *(Untitled) The Black Act* insisted on shades of black that traversed theatrical darkness, costume materials, skin tones, and the complex histories—painful and jubilant—that imbricate and disaggregate through her lived experience.

In the third act, the figure was no longer presented as a physiological given. And it was there that LaBeija most directly took up Schlemmer's notion of abstracting bodies. In Luu's costumes, hips, shoulders, elbows, and wrists bulged to elephantine proportions. Breasts and legs were exposed, but still retained an otherworldly quality. Extended hair braids nearly brushed the floor. There was no recourse to a "natural" body before the impositions of culture and politics. "Schlemmer abstracted these bodies," LaBeija has said. "In a way, that's what we're doing now. We're getting so much work done to mimic the bodies of women of color—bodies that used to be shamed."[16] Finally, there is Kia LaBeija's concluding solo. She first entered the stage alongside the trio of performers from the third dance, dressed in a silver, sequined corset over a bodysuit (adorned with rhinestones to "veil" her breasts and crotch) and a sequined fishnet head covering. Her hands and feet were bare. Dazzling costume, dark attire, and human flesh were no longer in strict opposition. After removing the gridded tape from the floor, the other dancers collapsed to the floor and effectively disappeared. LaBeija was alone, nearly without costume yet entirely covered. One astute reading of *(Untitled) The Black Act* sees in this final dance the revelation of the artist:

> With no mediating costume, and with unrestrained movement, the figure of the performer emerges. This is not the abstract figure but the specific, individual figure of LaBeija herself. [...] The controlled abstract gestures of the Bauhaus are replaced with organic, improvised movements. The spring and the spiral are no longer studies of bodies in space, but represent the artist finding her path through life. The Bauhaus's study of impersonal unification is replaced by a preoccupation with the individual. This is in fact the 'pathos and heroism' Schlemmer once hoped to avoid. The finale is not the brink of abstraction but LaBeija herself, in glittering glory.[17]

This reading speaks the truth, even as it is incomplete. For as much as LaBeija was herself, she was not only herself. Many spectators immediately perceived an allusion to the Jazz Age icon Josephine Baker, a citation confirmed by LaBeija herself.[18] Who is Josephine Baker to Kia LaBeija? The answer seems to align with Anne Anlin Cheng's perspicacious reading of the woman variously dubbed the "Black Venus," the "Bronze Venus," and the "Creole Goddess."

> What is this thing called race? It is both more and less than biology or ideology. It wields its claim most forcefully and destructively in the realm of the visible, yet it designates and relies on the unseen. [Josephine] Baker, precisely as an apparent racial symbol, counterintuitively and significantly reveals the ellipses and the suspensions preconditioning the stability of that sign.[19]

15
Interview with the author, December 16, 2019.

16
LaBeija in Durón, "For Performa Biennial, Kia LaBeija Reinvents a Bauhaus Classic—With a Ball Culture Twist."

17
George Kan, "Voguing Bauhaus," *The Brooklyn Rail* (2019–2020).

18
See, for example, Brian Seibert, "Two Vogue Shows Strike Art-World Poses," *The New York Times*, November 12, 2019, C6. Confirmed in conversation with the author, December 16, 2019.

19
Anne Anlin Cheng, *Second Skin: Josephine Baker & the Modern Surface*. (Oxford, United Kingdom: Oxford University Press, 2010), 13.

20
Uri McMillan, *Embodied Avatars: Genealogies of Black Feminist Art and Performance* (New York: New York University Press, 2015), 7.

LaBeija was at once herself and—to borrow Uri McMillan's potent concept—an avatar, a Black subject that has performed objecthood to become an art object: "Wielding their bodies as pliable matter, [...] Black women performers [...] repeatedly become objects, often in the form of simulated beings. [...] Put differently, performing objecthood becomes an adroit method of circumventing prescribed limitations on Black women in the public sphere while staging art and alterity in unforeseen places."[20]

Kia LaBeija's *(Untitled) The Black Act* was nothing if not a staging of alterity. It began with the reality and visibility of Black bodies; then explored their abstraction through annexation, as bodies and braids once shamed become cosmetic ideals; and, finally, it revealed a Black, queer, female body at once wholly itself—wholly herself—and yet forever interlaced with the ellipses and suspensions of those seemingly stable categories. NOAM M. ELCOTT

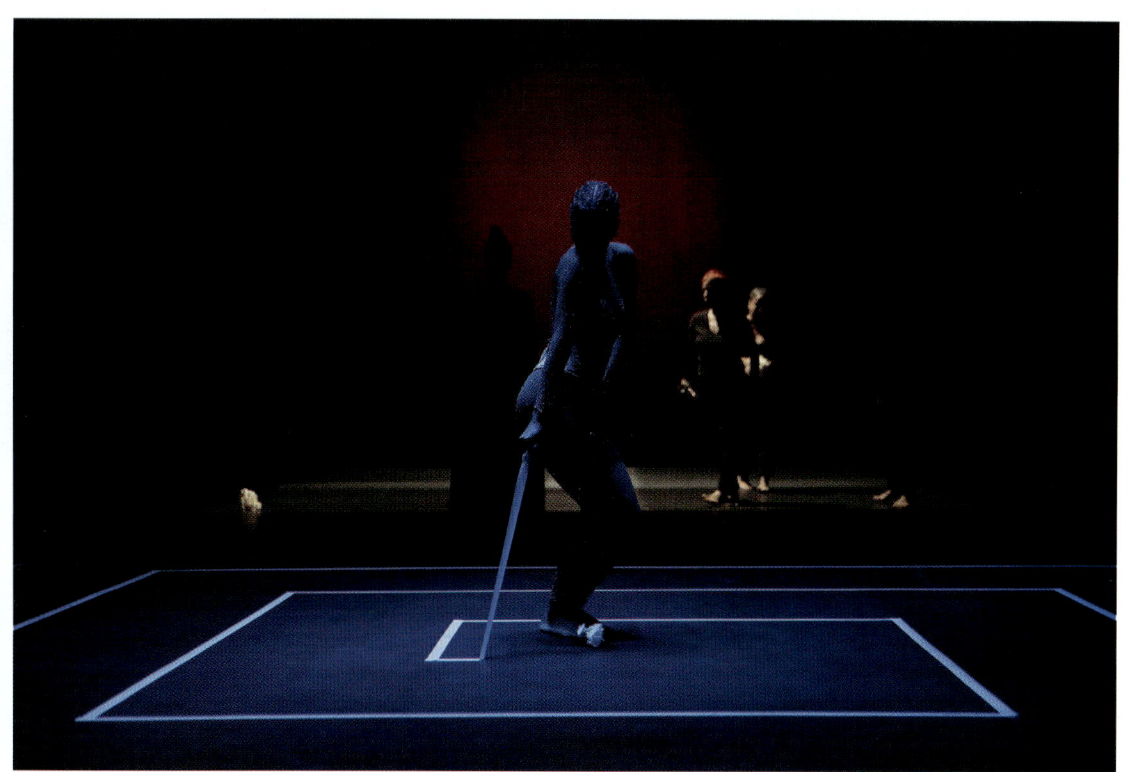

KORAKRIT ARUNANONDCHAI WITH BOYCHILD & ALEX GVOJIC

Together

Curated by
RoseLee Goldberg
and Job Piston

Harlem Parish

November 12–13, 2019

The atmospherics started twenty minutes before the audience entered, and the performance ramped up gradually. Korakrit Arunanondchai sat still in front of a large screen pulsing a green light that cast the tall room in its hue. The artist, known to his friends as Krit, has used the same color in other works, often in the form of laser-like beams or mesmerizing geometric daubs. It offers a leitmotif across his art, although its meaning seems to be fleeting. In *Together,* though, green explicitly represented both the military of Thailand, the artist's homeland, and the skin of a mythical Southeast Asian serpent spirit called the *naga*, a water deity and another recurring image in his work. A deep drone sound that recalled the noise from a low-flying helicopter, rumbled heavily. Both light and sound evolved, becoming more present and enveloping, until Krit walked to the front of the room and resolutely stopped them. This opening gesture announced the centrality of the artist's body in the work.

The next phase entailed Krit, his body dramatically bathed in green light, manipulating a single concentrated beam of it, which now shone from beneath him. He pressed his palm on the light beam, causing it to rise and fall. And yet, the first words of the piece (spoken in Thai but translated onscreen in English) were "dear ghost, welcome to my body." If Krit's first appearance, and his authoritative silencing of the crowd, suggested control over nature, the artist quickly made clear that the light, and the ghost that it implied, was the true sovereign, and was the entity that the entire work addressed.

Krit then delivered a framing monologue in which he invited the ghost (whose avatar appeared onscreen as a green snake) to "make kin with my unconscious." His speech evoked the tones as well as the concepts of Thai Buddhist worship, and the other performers repeated after him as though he were a monk. His sermon refused distinctions between the material and spiritual dimensions of existence in a manner inflected by Buddhist notions of ephemerality. The pervasive green color we saw was not the signature green of corporate environmentalism, but of a nature made up of "bodies greater than our own," in the artist's own words.

All of this had a distinctly political context. Following the monologue, the screen showed news footage of the 2018 Tham Luang cave rescue, where a group of Thai Navy Seals rescued twelve members of the Wild Boars, a junior national soccer team, from a flooded cave in northern Thailand. Three of the young players were stateless, as it turned out, and after their rescue, the Thai government granted them citizenship. The story, which was celebrated internationally, was made unsettling here. Laser beams shot at the projection screen; were these searchlights or ghosts? Citizenship, Krit suggests, fills us like a spirit, and controls us.

The green, so far, seemed to shine from the uniforms of the Thai soldiers. But there is another story here, which calls back to the era of the Vietnam War, when hundreds of thousands of American soldiers were stationed or took leave in Thailand, transforming the country both economically and culturally. In particular, Thais and Americans built a complex relationship through sound and music. GIs brought over vinyl records of American rock and roll, which would later circulate throughout Thailand and transform the country's musical landscape. The Americans, however, perceived the sounds of Thailand as threatening noise. The sounds in *Together* channel this thorny relationship.

This era and its effects are present in Krit's work, and recall a vintage shade of military green: Krit thus pulled back further to situate the hue of army green as possessive. American soldiers were afraid of the forest during the Vietnam War, he said, and they used lights to trick Vietnamese locals into believing that ghosts were in their midst; in effect, they seized the power of implied possession or omnipresence. After the war, they left these projectors with local monks, who continued to treat these lights as performances for ghosts. Material, spirit, and knowledge can combine in strange ways.

As the stories paused for a bit, the otherworldly dancer boychild entered the performance area to provide a different kind of interpretation of the political material in the background. She led, sometimes in solo fashion and sometimes as the key figure in a circle of dancers, wearing jeans (the garment was a highly

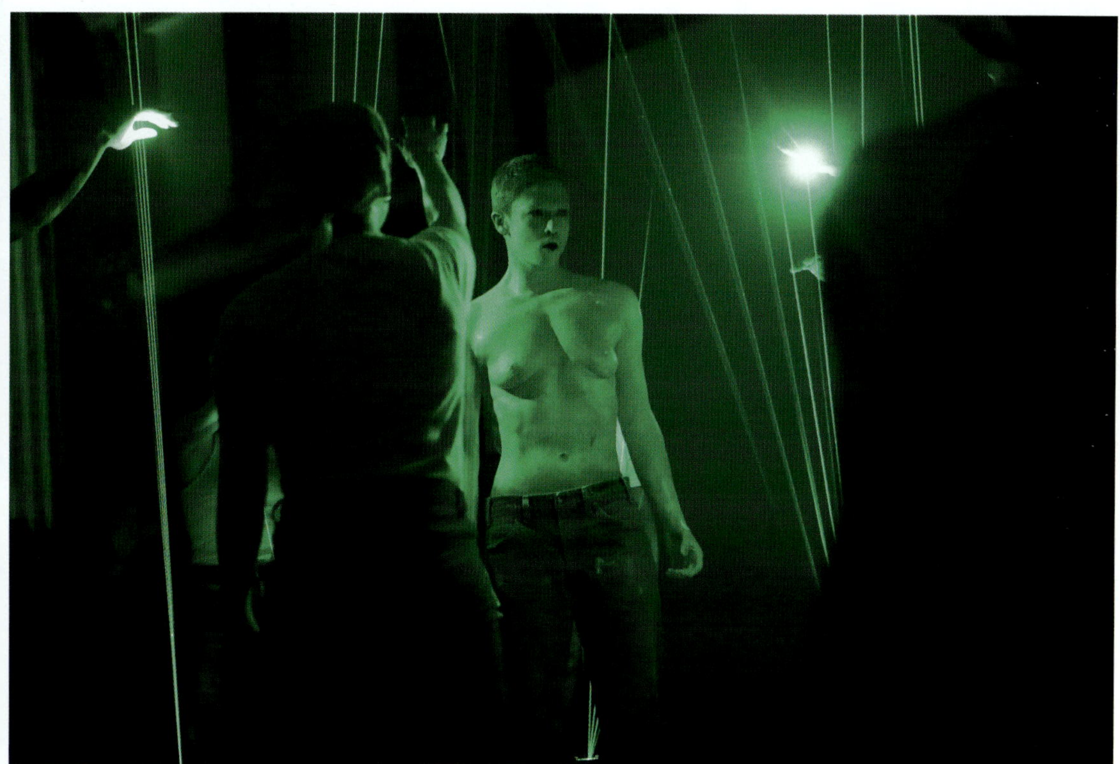

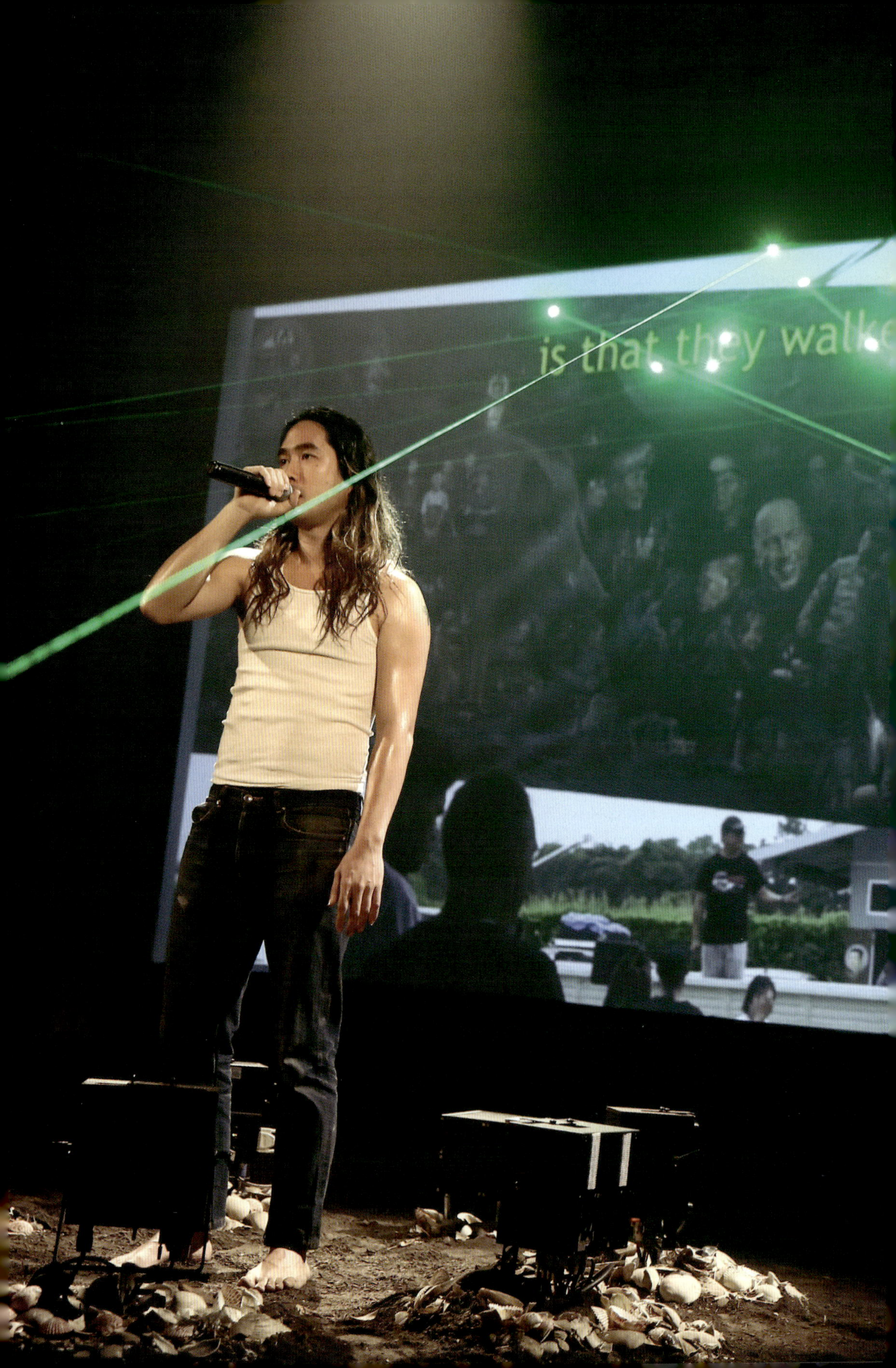
is that they walke

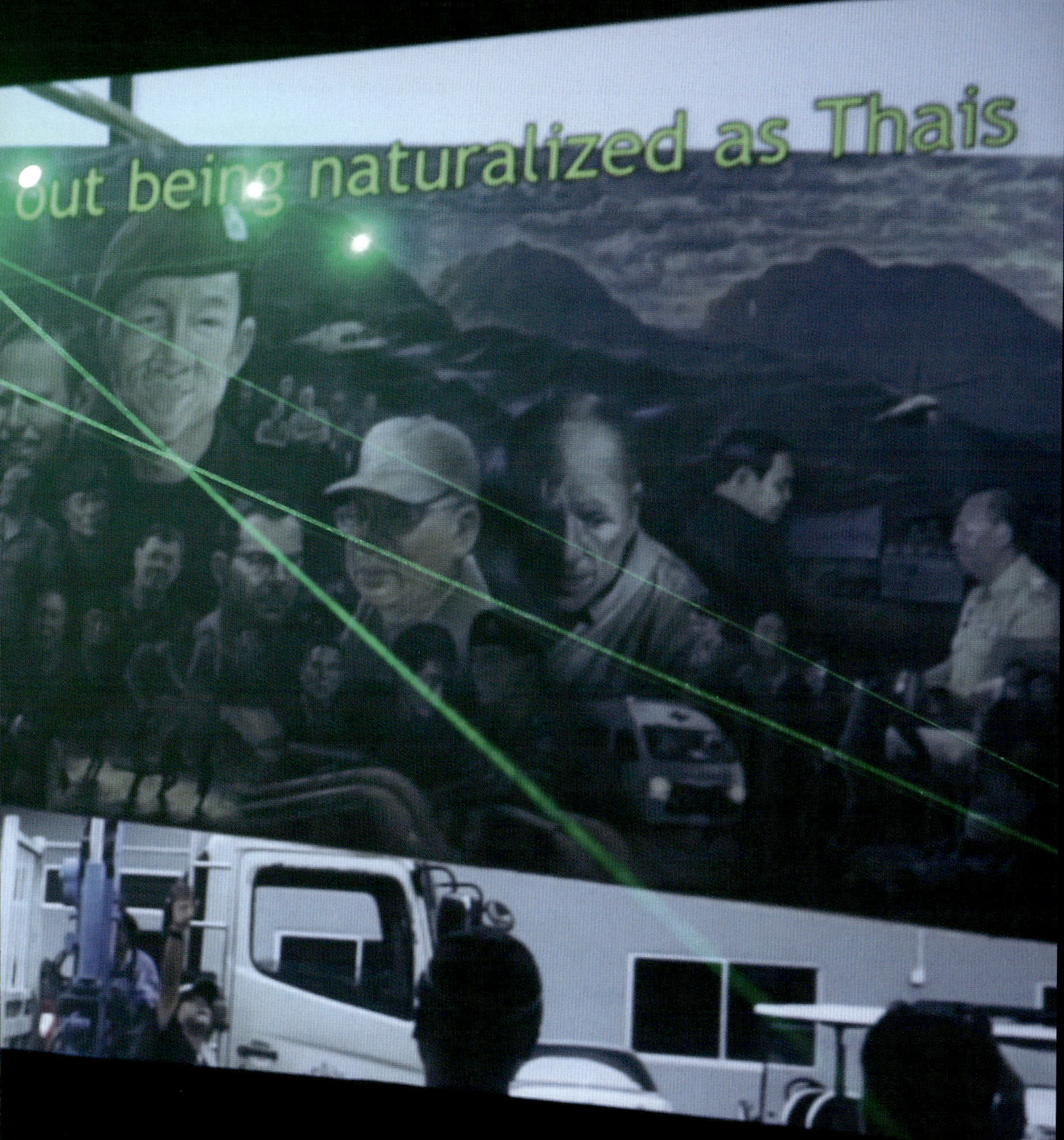
out being naturalized as Thais

valued commodity in Southeast Asia during the Vietnam War era) without a shirt. In the background, images and sounds alluded to a historical relationship between Thailand and the U.S. that had been dark, coercive, and secret, including the CIA's establishment of a "black ops" torture site in the northeastern province of Udon Thani. The dancers evoked *ram wong* gestures, spinning with ghastly speed. The music seemed an eerie amalgam of American soul, *mor lam* traditional singing, and industrial techno. All the while, blinking green lights shone as, perhaps, ghosts of Americans past.

"In a place as dark as a cave, where you couldn't tell the difference between a Thai soldier and the CIA, the soldiers abstract themselves into a green light," intoned Krit in a monologue around halfway through the performance, bringing the piece's major elements together. "This green light transforms itself into a

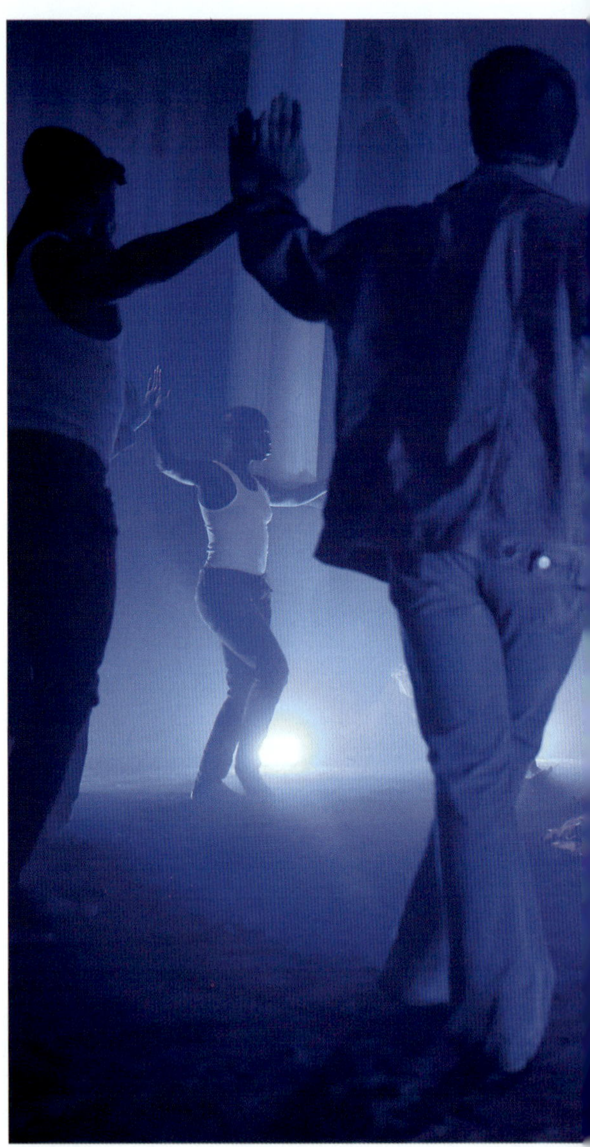

naga. The naga possesses a human spirit medium, who turns into a ghost. The ghost has the ability to give citizenship to a body of people who prove that they can be transformed into a good story."

A precisely choreographed performance, *Together* pondered Korakrit's "bodies greater than our own"—the hauntings and histories that inhabit people, and which we/they cannot escape. All the while, it scrutinized the entanglement of the Thai state with an imperial American government that has often granted itself the naga-like power to possess others in its neocolonial network. And yet, as Krit offered near the end, "the essence of the caretaker and the care-receiver end up in the same place."

For the last ten minutes, the other dancers walked off slowly, and only Korakrit remained in front of the glowing green screen, as if at an altar. BENJAMIN TAUSIG

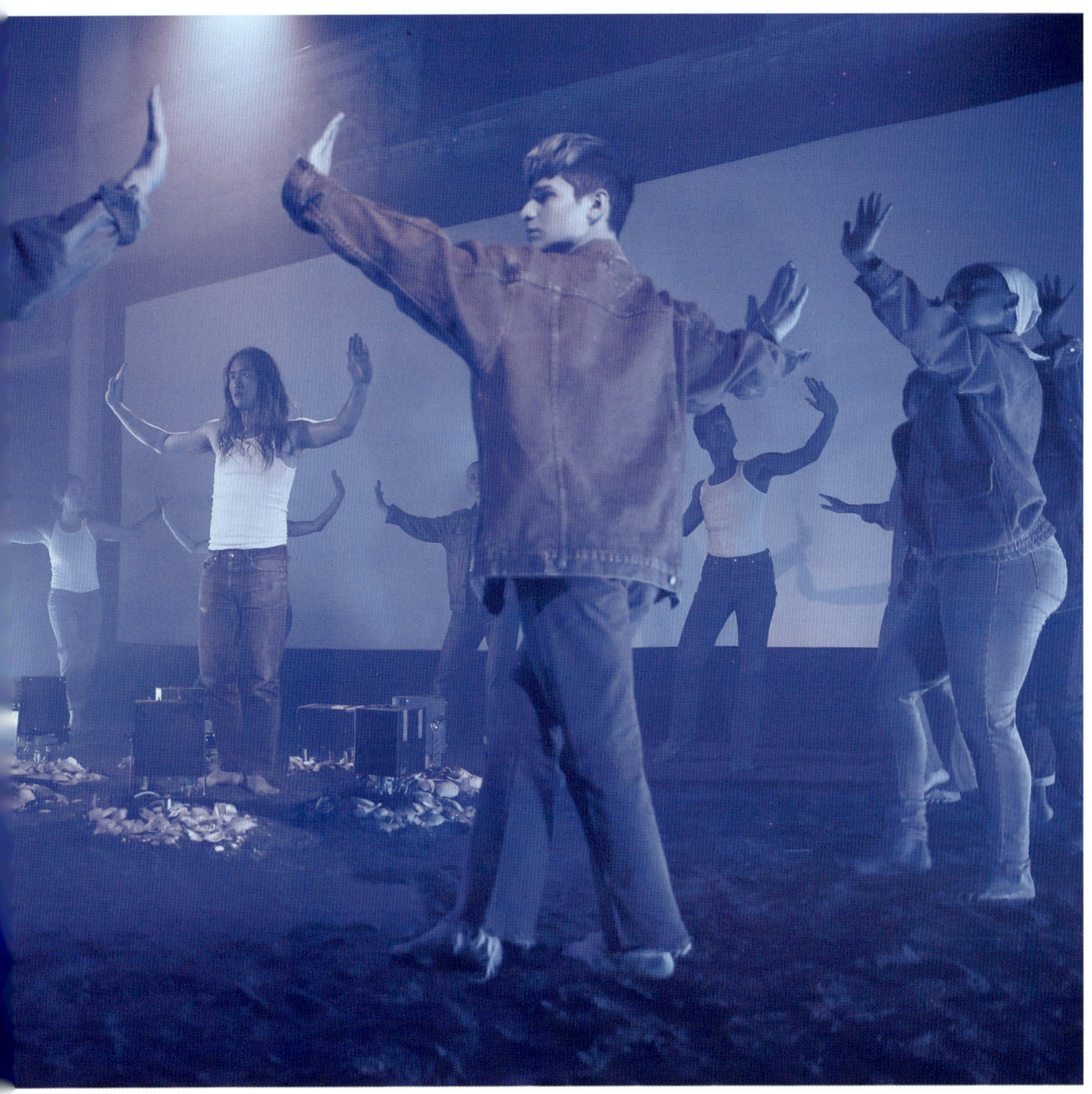

PAUL MAHEKE WITH NKISI & ARIEL EFRAIM ASHBEL

Sènsa

Curated by
Charles Aubin
and Ali Rosa-Salas

Abrons Arts Center

November 7–9, 2019

In the Bantu language of Lingala, the word *sènsa* describes a transmutable act: "to come to visibility," "to reveal," or "to appear from far away." It was in the darkness of an underground theater that *Sènsa* began. The performance took place in an intimate room filled with fog; spotlights on a mezzanine bounced off of clouds of smoke and illuminated the dance space below. The lights dimmed just before the action started, and Paul Maheke entered the room by descending a set of stairs backward on his hands and knees. He had a tattered mix of fabrics wrapped around his body; black athletic shorts and metallic alligator dress shoes completed his look conceived by fashion designer Firpal Jawanda in collaboration with Curtly Thomas—a combination of bespoke and readymade garments. At first, we could hardly see him, but by the time he reached the floor, we knew where to look. He crawled throughout the room, among the audience, seemingly directionless. The space was nearly silent, aside from the small beads dangling from Maheke's sleeves that clacked against the floor. Musician Nkisi's live soundscape slowly ruptured the stillness: Atmospheric water sounds with a metallic ring started to cascade over the room, with sequences of deep pulses layered over a steady African techno beat.

Combining choreography by Maheke, sound by Nkisi, and lighting design by Ariel Efraim Ashbel, *Sènsa* navigated the threshold between being seen and unseen. The performance defied regimes of visibility and classification imposed on bodies of color as a lingering symptom of colonial rule. As Maheke appeared and disappeared on his own terms, he enacted Martinican writer Édouard Glissant's claim to the "right to opacity," a demand to escape systems of racial domination and to live wholly in one own's complexities. With all the glamour and exploration of classic ballroom culture, we saw a performance of an authentic self at a site of defiance, agency, and freedom.

Nkisi's base rhythm vibrated through the floor like a steady heartbeat, while her electronic dance music ebbed between soft- and hardcore intensities, as if gasping for air. Maheke's improvisational dance took him throughout the room, spinning, swaying, and reacting to both the music and the movements of the audience. He seemed uninhibited by the presence of eager spectators surrounding him. At times, the room plunged into total darkness, and we had to rely on our other senses to move across the space. Maheke slipped in and out of shadows to musical pulses, cutting through the crowd as if parting waters. In those moments of obscurity, the music slowed and Maheke could hardly be seen or heard. He then used mirrors to refract beams of light, suddenly redefining the space and, like a beacon, they called our attention back to him as he reclaimed his visibility and continued to dance. There was something affirming about seeing Maheke move so freely and exist so ubiquitously in this space. His gaze became a symbol of power as he sashayed his way through the space, locking eyes with viewers, subverting their spectatorship.

As a viewer, to be unseen and unheard in a space in which a singular body holds all the power is perhaps an unsettling experience—for racialized, gendered, and queered communities, this experience can be one of violence and urgency. With Maheke, Nkisi, and Ashbel, the word *sènsa* might now describe the process of confronting the systems that seek to surveil or stigmatize individual bodies. By challenging tacit modes of visibility, the artists inverted the privilege of the seer as we, the audience, were left to find our way through darkness, light, sound, and silence. RE'AL CHRISTIAN

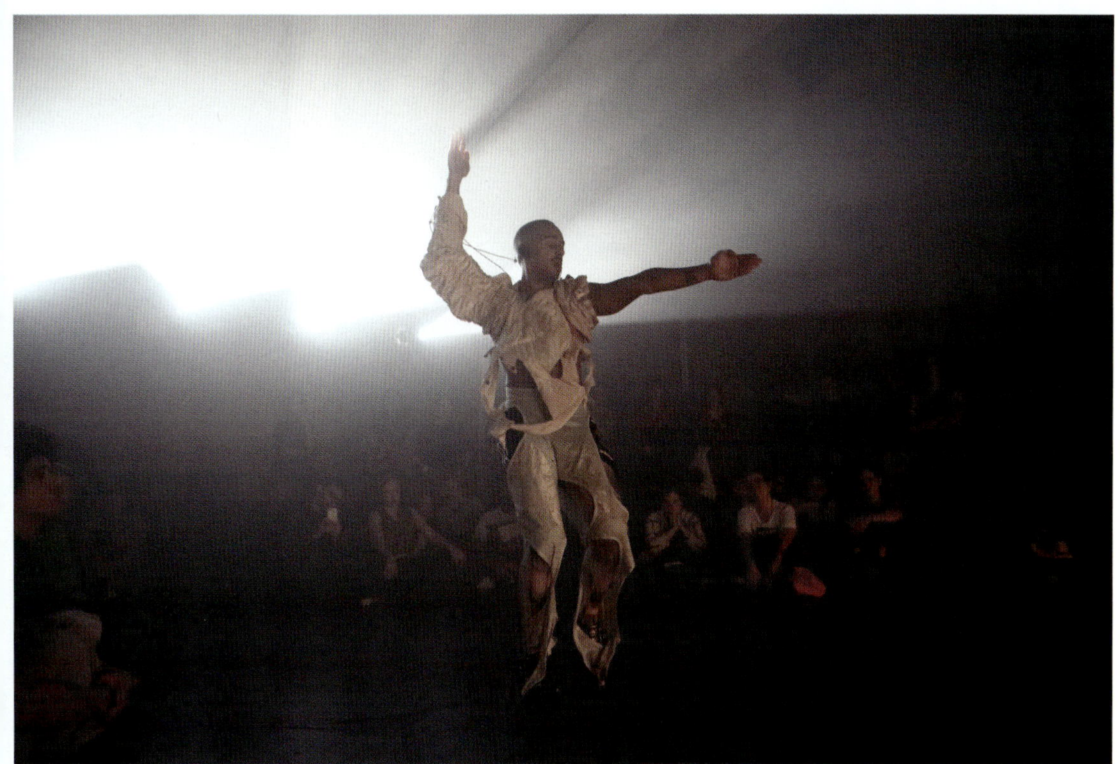

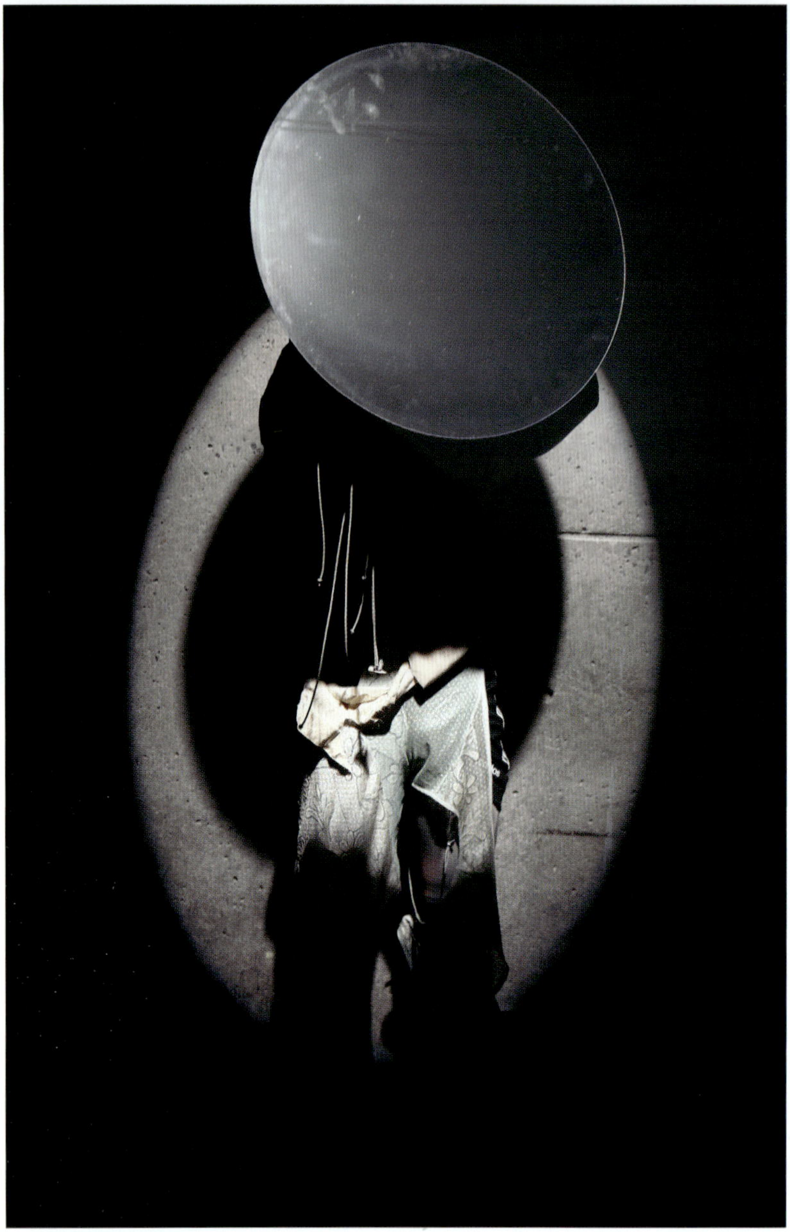

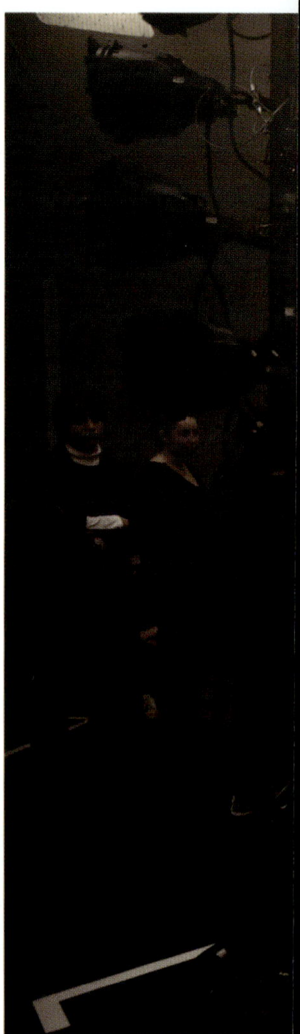

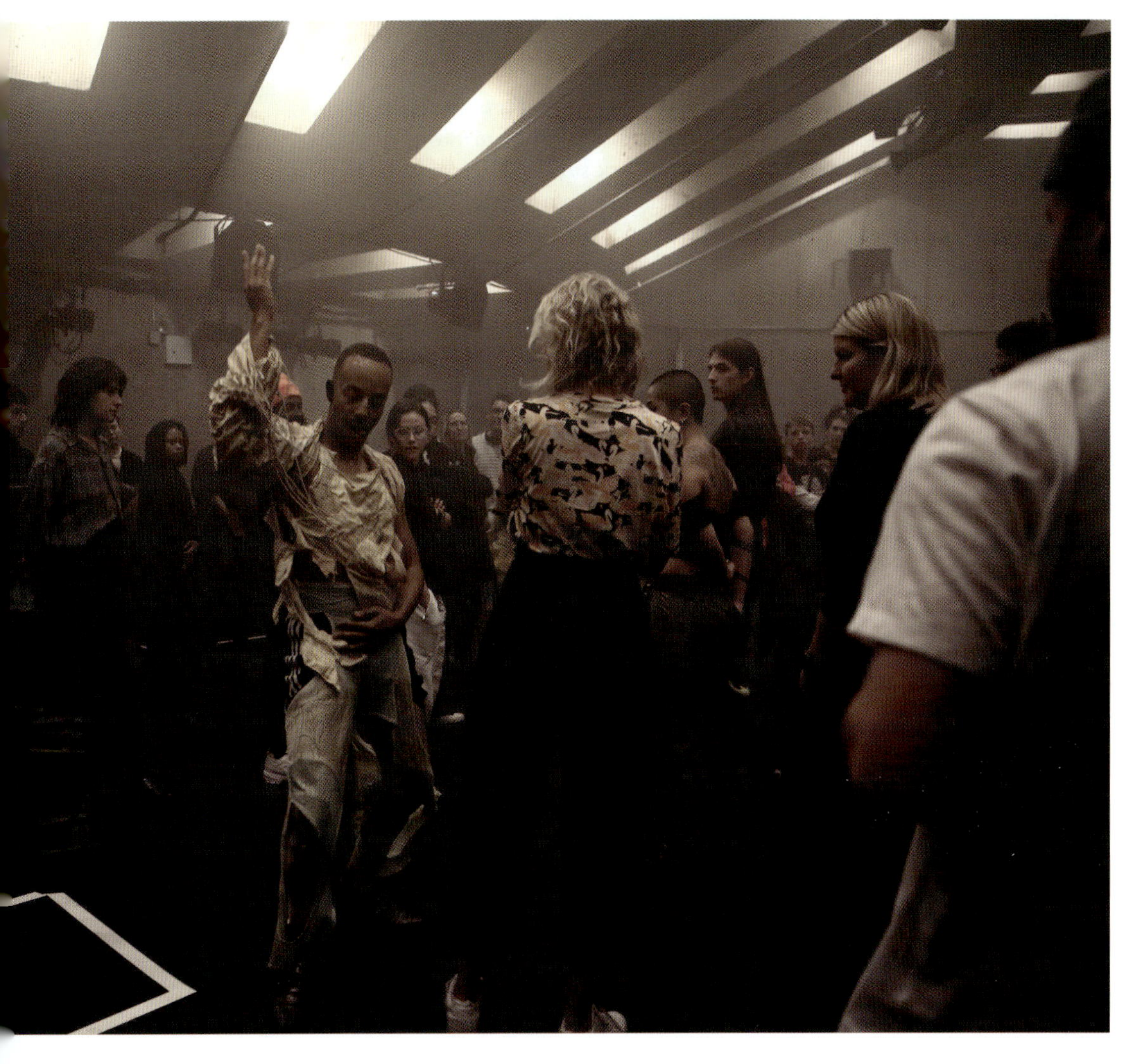

PAUL MAHEKE WITH LIGIA LEWIS & NKISI

Levant

Curated by Franziska Sophie Wildförster

Ludlow 38—MINI/ Goethe Curatorial Residencies

November 13–December 15, 2019

Paul Maheke's video installation *Levant* (2018) was in direct dialogue with *Sènsa*, his live performance at Abrons Arts Center conceived with musician Nkisi and lighting designer Ariel Efraim Ashbel. Both onscreen and onstage, the French artist of Congolese descent blurred our field of vision, refusing to flatten bodies into mere images. In his own words: "Deeper meaning always lies beneath the representation, in the shadow image."[1]

For *Levant*, Maheke collaborated with American choreographer Ligia Lewis, and together they created an hour-long black-and-white film revolving around a sequence of dance movements for an atmospheric soundtrack composed by Nkisi. Fleeting light and smoke billows make it impossible to see Lewis's body in its entirety, but behind these visual obstructions, her quick, repetitive gestures produce some ambiguous shapes. Here, the artist and his collaborators sought ways to evade the constraints of visibility, creating a poetic, opaque space instead.

1
Paul Maheke in "Standing Still, roundtable with Charles Aubin, Aruna D'Souza, Brendan Fernandes, Ligia Lewis, and Paul Maheke," *Frieze* no. 213, September 2020.

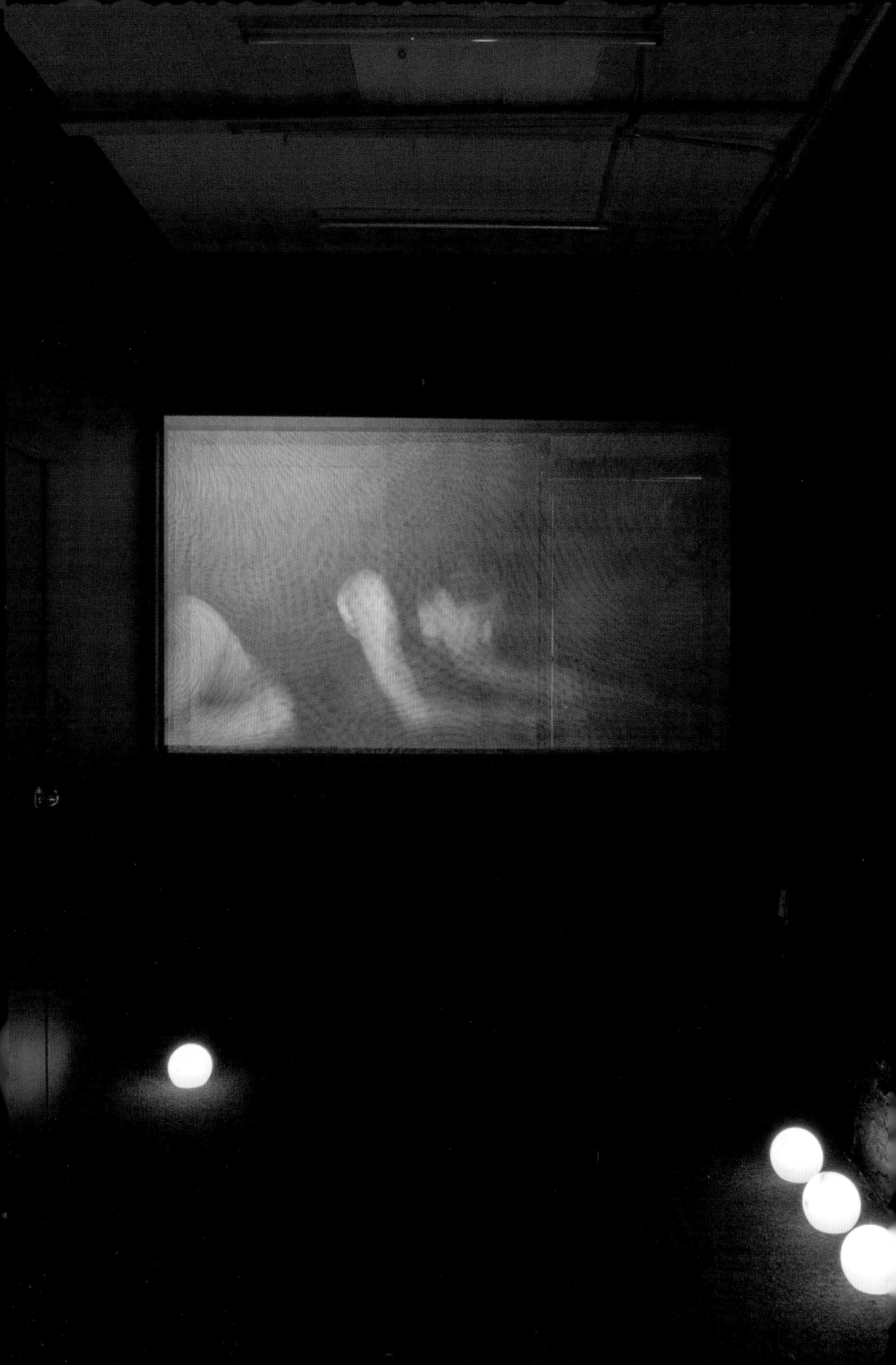

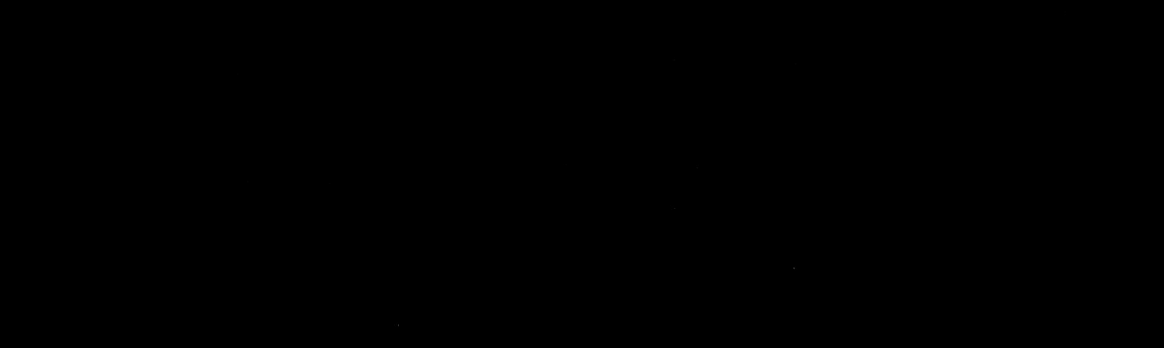

PERFORMA AT LARGE

PERFORMA AT LARGE

PERFORMA ARCHIVE

Whitechapel Gallery
September 6, 2017–March 4, 2018

Copenhagen Contemporary
June 20–October 11, 2019

As a time-based artform, performance creates multiple future lives for itself through documentation. Actions and gestures are preserved for as long as recording technology and formats will allow, with still and moving images serving as surrogates for live art. The exhibition "Performa Archive" took the form of revolving video highlights shown daily in a hybrid screening and reading space at the Whitechapel Gallery in London (2017–18), and as a weekly film program at Copenhagen Contemporary (2019). Featuring Biennial Commissions from more than twenty-five artists, it provided a retrospective

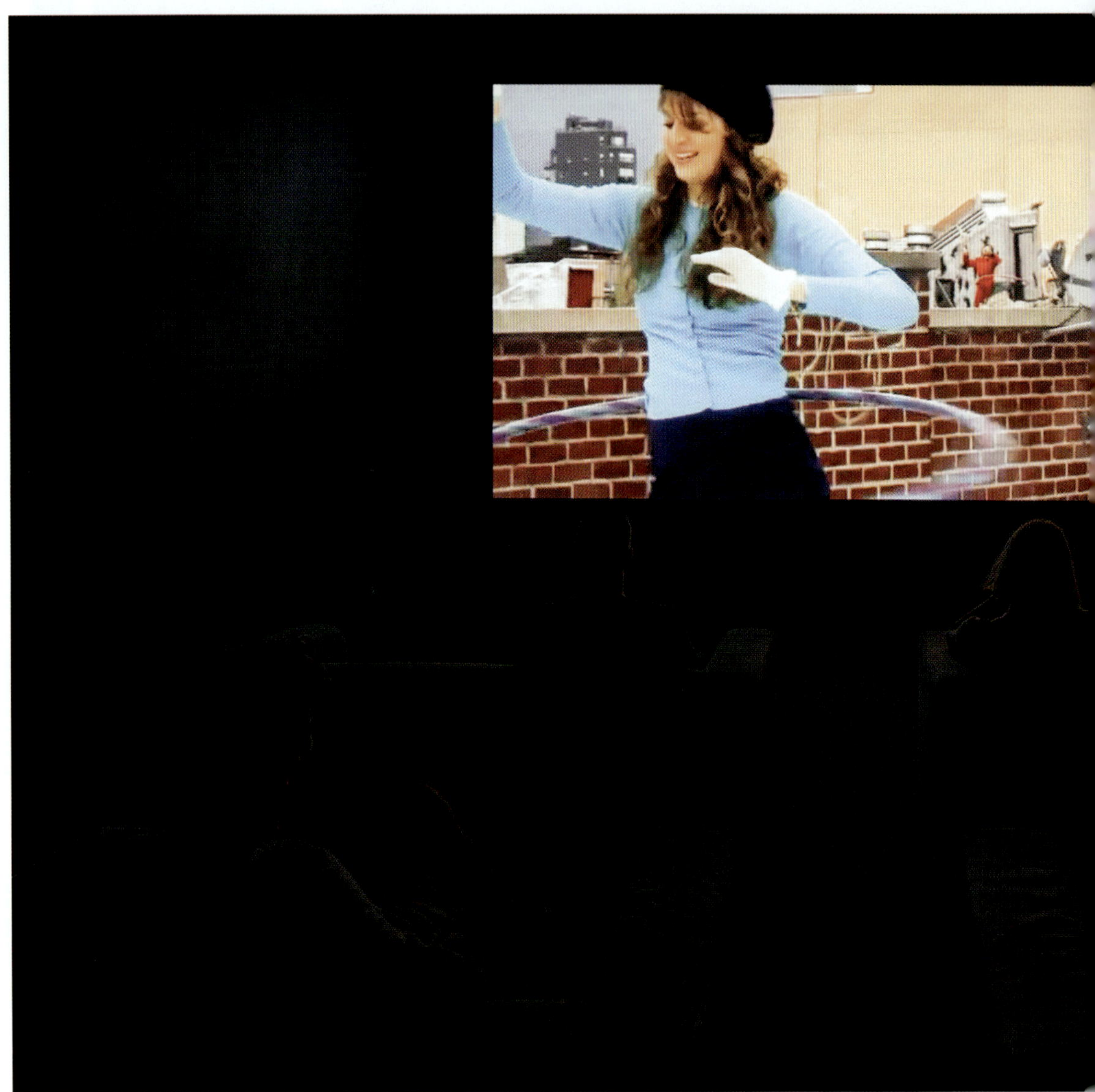

look at Performa's breadth of experimentation and innovation between 2005 and 2017.

For Performa 07, Yvonne Rainer's dance *RoS Indexical* presented what she described as an "imagined approximation" of composer Igor Stravinsky and choreographer Vaslav Nijinsky's divisive ballet *The Rite of Spring* (1913), turning it into an absurdist production at the Baryshnikov Arts Center in Manhattan. The four women dancers—Pat Catterson, Emily Coates, Patricia Hoffbauer, and Sally Silvers—were all in softball team-esque costumes, scored not to Stravinsky's original music, but *Riot at the Rite*, the BBC's 2005 dramatization of events based on *The Rite of Spring*'s riotous opening night. Four years later, the painter Rozeal gave us *battle of yestermore* for Performa 11, combining Japanese theater traditions, including kabuki and noh, with kung-fu, hip-hop, and Harlem ballroom culture. As the title suggests, Rozeal's work encompassed "battles" of breakdancing and vogueing to martial arts, featuring performers such as Javier and Benny of the ballroom House of Ninja and New York hip-hop dancers Rokafella, Beasty, GI Jane, Lady Beast, SnowBunny, and Mona Lisa. Dancing in Adidas tracksuits and streetwear and wearing traditionally African American hairstyles, *yestermore* mixed and melded global cultures and references between Black America and Asia. At Performa 15, Edgar Arceneaux's *Until, Until, Until...* delved into the racist history of Blackface and minstrelsy via a redux of actor and entertainer Ben Vereen's infamous 1981 production celebrating Black vaudeville comedian Bert Williams for Ronald Reagan's inauguration. The re-enactment by actor Frank Lawson as Vereen incorporated clips from the original gala's broadcast as well as live video feeds from Arceneaux's iteration, layering past and present on top of one another. Its effect generated a chilling merge of art and life, a stark reminder of the systemic inequalities that Black individuals continue to face today.

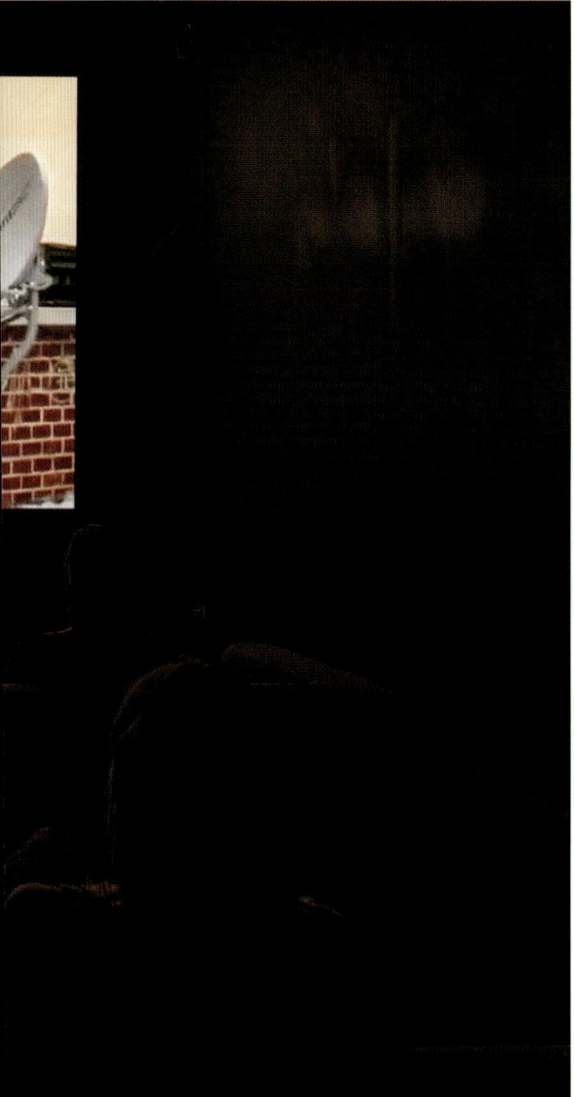

With video documentation of Performa commissions by Edgar Arceneaux, Yto Barrada, Jérôme Bel, Brian Belott, Sanford Biggers, Candice Breitz, Elmgreen and Dragset, Omer Fast, David Hallberg, Christian Jankowski, Isaac Julien, Jesper Just, Wyatt Kahn, Mike Kelley, William Kentridge, Jon Kessler, Ragnar Kjartansson, Kris Lemsalu, Arto Lindsay, Liz Magic Laser, Russell Maliphant, Kyp Malone, Mohau Modisakeng, Oscar Murillo, Kelly Nipper, Adam Pendleton, Yvonne Rainer, Raqs Media Collective, Robin Rhode, Jimmy Robert, Mika Rottenberg, Rozeal (formerly iona rozeal brown), Francesco Vezzoli, Kemang Wa Lehulere, and Tori Wrånes.

Christian Jankowski, Rooftop Routine, a Performa 07 Commission, 2007. Installation view. Copenhagen Contemporary.

TOURING YVONNE RAINER

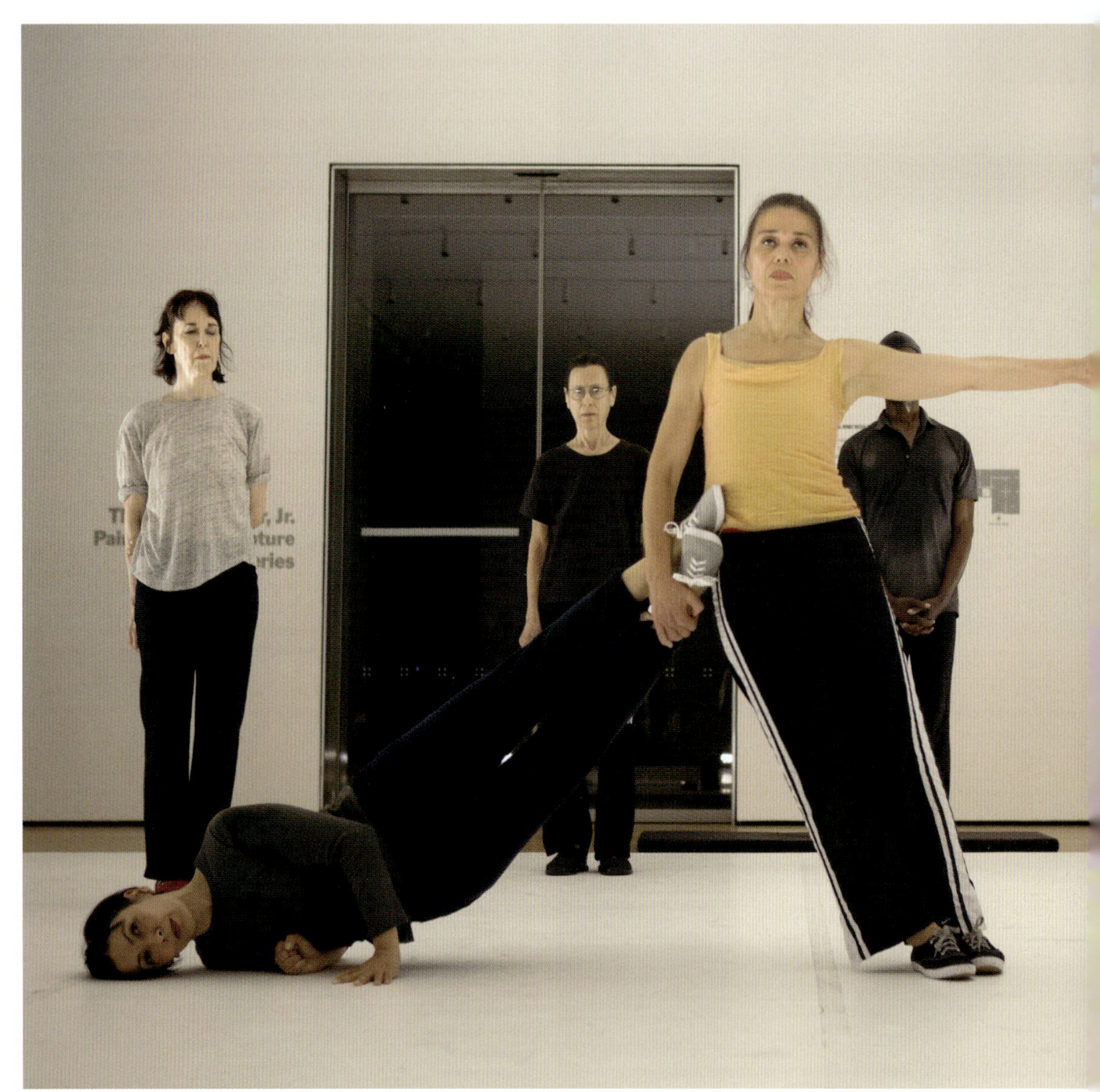

When Yvonne Rainer premiered *After Many a Summer Dies the Swan* in 2000, she returned to dance after a quarter-century-long hiatus during which she made seven feature-length films. Since then, she has created seven new works in collaboration with the Raindears, the informal company she built around herself that includes Pat Catterson, Emily Coates, Patricia Hoffbauer, Emmanuèle Phuon, Keith Sabado, and David Thomson.

For *Summer*, the artist combined texts by Viennese *fin-de-siècle* figures Oskar Kokoschka, Adolf Loos, Arnold Schoenberg, and Ludwig Wittgenstein, read aloud over a remix of her own postmodern choreography. She sought to examine the very idea of "avant-garde" and probe its relevance in the nascent new century.

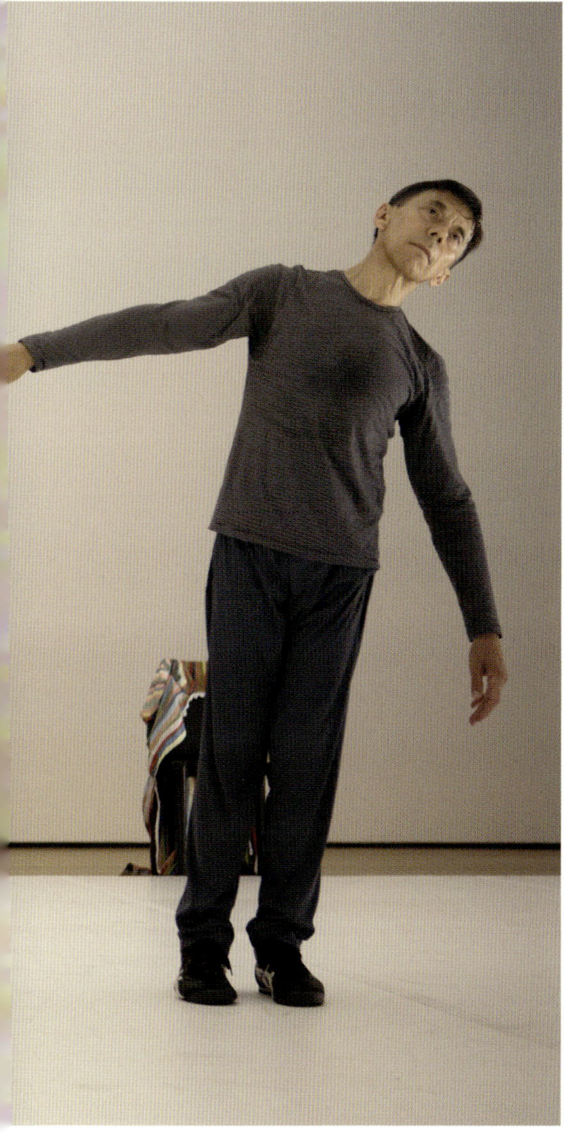

In her subsequent compositions, she borrowed postures and movements from historical modern choreography, popular culture, and sports. In *AG Indexical, with a Little Help from H.M.* (2006), she drew on her memory and documentary footage of *Agon* (1957), a famous neoclassical ballet by George Balanchine and composer Igor Stravinsky. Initially conceived for eight male and four female dancers, Rainer reconfigured it for a group of four female dancers, reusing some of the steps and replacing part of Stravinsky's score with Henry Mancini's theme song for *Pink Panther*.

Soon after, Performa invited her to conceive a new work for its 2007 biennial. The choreographer responded to the prompt with *RoS Indexical*, a reimagining of Stravinsky's *Rite of Spring*, which reflected on the ballet's controversial 1913 premiere in Paris. It drew material from diverse sources, such as the BBC's dramatization of the event, *Riot at the Rite*, and the gestures of Sarah Bernhardt, Groucho Marx, and Robin Williams. Co-commissioned with Documenta, *RoS Indexical* debuted in Kassel, Germany, in August 2007 and was presented in New York in November of that year at the Hudson Theatre on Broadway.

Since then, Performa has produced and toured all her new works, including *Spiraling Down* (2008), *Assisted Living: Good Sports 2* (2010), *Assisted Living: Do You Have Any Money?* (2013), and *The Concept of Dust, or How do you look when there's nothing left to move?* (2015).

In *The Concept of Dust*, the performers are given the freedom to initiate and abort movement phrases as they wish, making spontaneous decisions and exercising options throughout its forty-five-minute duration. Rainer reads onstage from ancient Middle Eastern dynasties, paleontological findings, and assorted literary quotations that together depict a portrait—both melancholic and tongue-in-cheek—of the changes, aches, and pains experienced by the aging body. The result is a structure that is seemingly random with unpredictable moments of unison, humor, and startling convergences with the spoken texts. *Dust* premiered at the Museum of Modern Art (MoMA) in June 2015.

The following year, *Dust* became *The Concept of Dust: Continuous Project—Altered Annually*, a revised title which affords the artist the freedom to revisit a performance that touches on personal themes while also channeling the memory of her iconic 1970 piece *Continuous Project—Altered Daily*, which established the foundations of The Grand Union, a collaborative improvisatory group which featured Rainer and other dancers.

In the past five years, Performa presented *The Concept of Dust* at the Kitchen in New York for the American Dance Institute, and at the University of California, Santa Barbara. It also toured internationally to Marseille Objectif Danse in France; MACBA in Barcelona, Spain; and Fundação de Serralves in Porto, Portugal. These shows were often accompanied by her early works as well as a lecture, such as "Doing Nothing / Nothin' Doin'!: Revisiting a Minimalist Approach to Dance," a meditation on the ends of minimalism in postmodern performance from the position of an elderly dancer.

In 2018, the choreographer's earlier work was on view at MoMA in New York as part of "Judson Dance Theater: The Work Is Never Done," an exhibition examining the trajectory and legacy of the Downtown experimental scene that gathered at the Judson Memorial Church in the early 1960s. For the occasion, Performa produced an extensive program of Rainer's early pieces: *Three Seascapes* (1961), *Three Satie Spoons* (1961), *We Shall Run* (1963), *Talking Solo* and *Diagonal* (both from *Terrain*, 1963), *Trio A* (1966), and *Chair-Pillow* (1969) were staged in the museum's atrium.

International invitations have kept Yvonne Rainer busy rethinking the appropriate format to show her historical works while offering new perspectives on them. With the Swedish organization Weld Company, she made *Again? What now?* (2019), an amalgamation of excerpts of previous presentations remixed with spoken word, music, and new movement configurations. At Remai Modern in Saskatoon, Saskatchewan, Canada, she constructed *Continuous Project: Sixty Years*, where she disinterred and re-combined ideas from her long career in the field.

In New York, she returned to the Performa Biennial in 2019 with a contemporary version of her seminal *Parts of Some Sextets* (1965), originally made for ten people and twelve mattresses (see page 188).

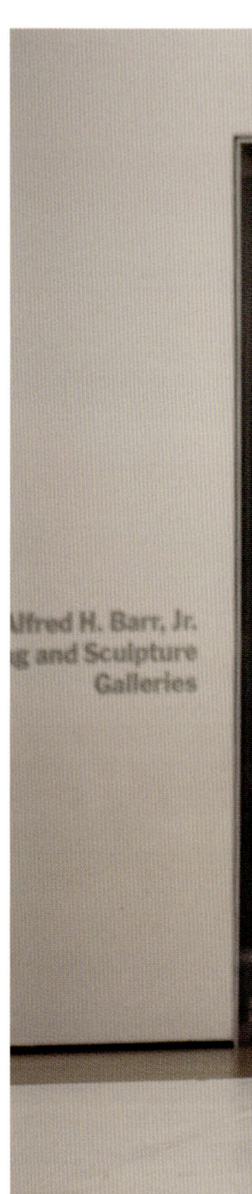

Yvonne Rainer, *The Concept of Dust, or How do you look when there's nothing left to move?*, 2015. Performance view. Museum of Modern Art, New York.

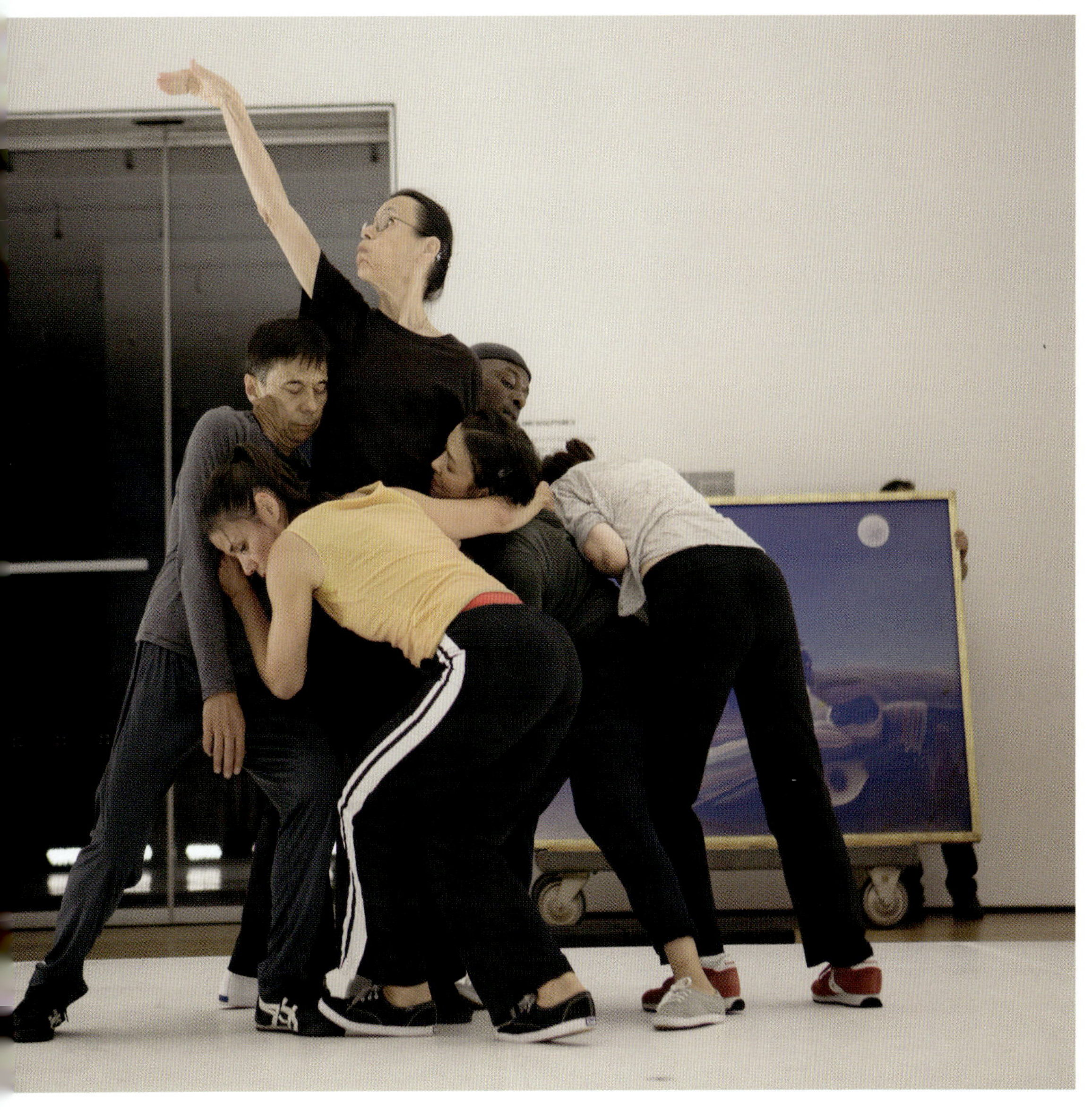

RADICAL BROADCAST

As television became a key part of American life in the mid-twentieth century, artists took to it as well—as both a medium and a place to exhibit. By the 1960s, New York art dealer Howard Wise was championing hybrids of art and technology at his gallery on West 57th Street, ushering in unconventional forms such as kinetic art and new media as well as the seminal exhibition "TV as a

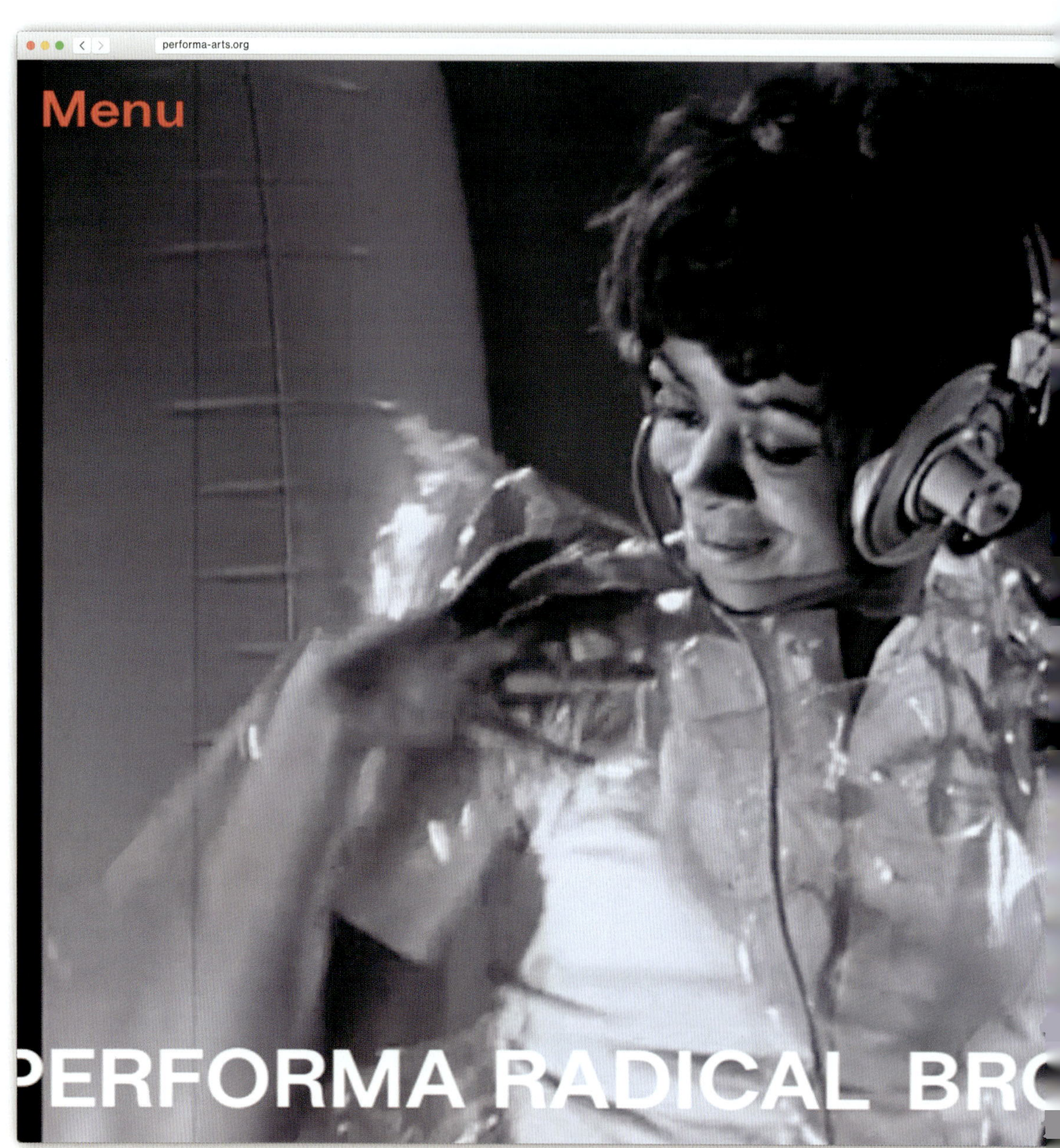

Creative Medium" (1969). Soon after, Wise closed the gallery in order to found Electronic Arts Intermix, a nonprofit organization dedicated to video and media art with which Performa continues to collaborate today.

Artists further incorporated the form and elements of television broadcasting throughout the 1970s, sometimes showing these clips on public access television. As the curator for the multidisciplinary New York space the Kitchen, RoseLee Goldberg organized "MADE FOR TV?" (1978), a video program that featured works by artists including Nancy Holt, Anthony Ramos, Vito Acconci, Bill Viola, Richard Wilson, and Lawrence Weiner. Probing what differentiated artists' videos from material produced for network TV, Goldberg questioned the irony of why it remained so difficult for artists to break into the commercial market.

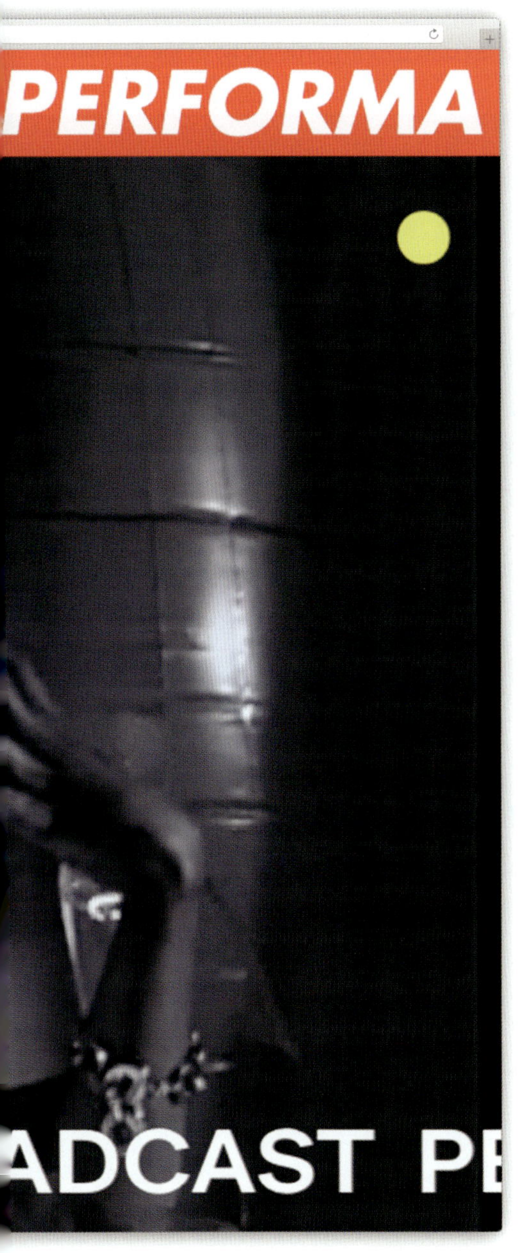

This interest resurfaced in 2007 with Performa TV, a program originally conceived of and developed by artist-musician Ronnie Bass and Performa curator Tairone Bastien to feature artists and curators involved in the Performa 07 Biennial. With Bass taking on the role of talk show host, Performa TV evoked the mood of late-night community-television variety shows, only now they had the global reach of the Web.

In this spirit, Performa launched Radical Broadcast in March 2019, reimagining the tradition of working on the small screen while sticking to a bold vision for the internet age, inspired by visionary artist Nam June Paik's playful experiments with television. His live broadcast *Good Morning, Mr. Orwell* (1984)—which featured performances by Laurie Anderson, John Cage, Merce Cunningham, Peter Gabriel, Charlotte Moorman, and Thompson Twins—foretold the way we connect today by broadcasting on WNET TV in New York and FR3 in Paris, with local partners across the globe. Performa paid homage to this historic event with its first ever telethon on November 18, 2020 (see page 338).

Today, Radical Broadcast presents curated screening programs of both documentation from the Performa archives and new, livestreamed performances, free for all on the organization's homepage. Designed in partnership with Los Angeles-based creative studio SPECIAL OFFER, the striking Radical Broadcast banner greets each visitor with moving images twenty-four hours a day, seven days a week, engaging audiences in contemporary visual art performance regardless of time zone or geographic location.

Michael Pilz, *Kultur Aktuell: Himmelblau im TV*, 1970, on Radical Broadcast. Screenshot, 2020.

RADICAL BROADCAST: MUSICAL CHAIRS

Curated by Kathy Noble
March 7–May 7, 2019

"In the nineteenth century, with the invention of the machine, Noise was born," stated Italian Futurist painter and composer Luigi Russolo in his 1913 manifesto *The Art of Noises*. The Futurists' exploration of noise as both a material phenomenon and a sensory form radically framed art music in the decades that followed. Artist Mike Kelley and curator Mark Beasley honored this lineage in Performa 09's *A Fantastic World Superimposed on Reality: A Select History of Experimental Music*, a two-day mini-festival of sound art and avant-garde music at the Gramercy

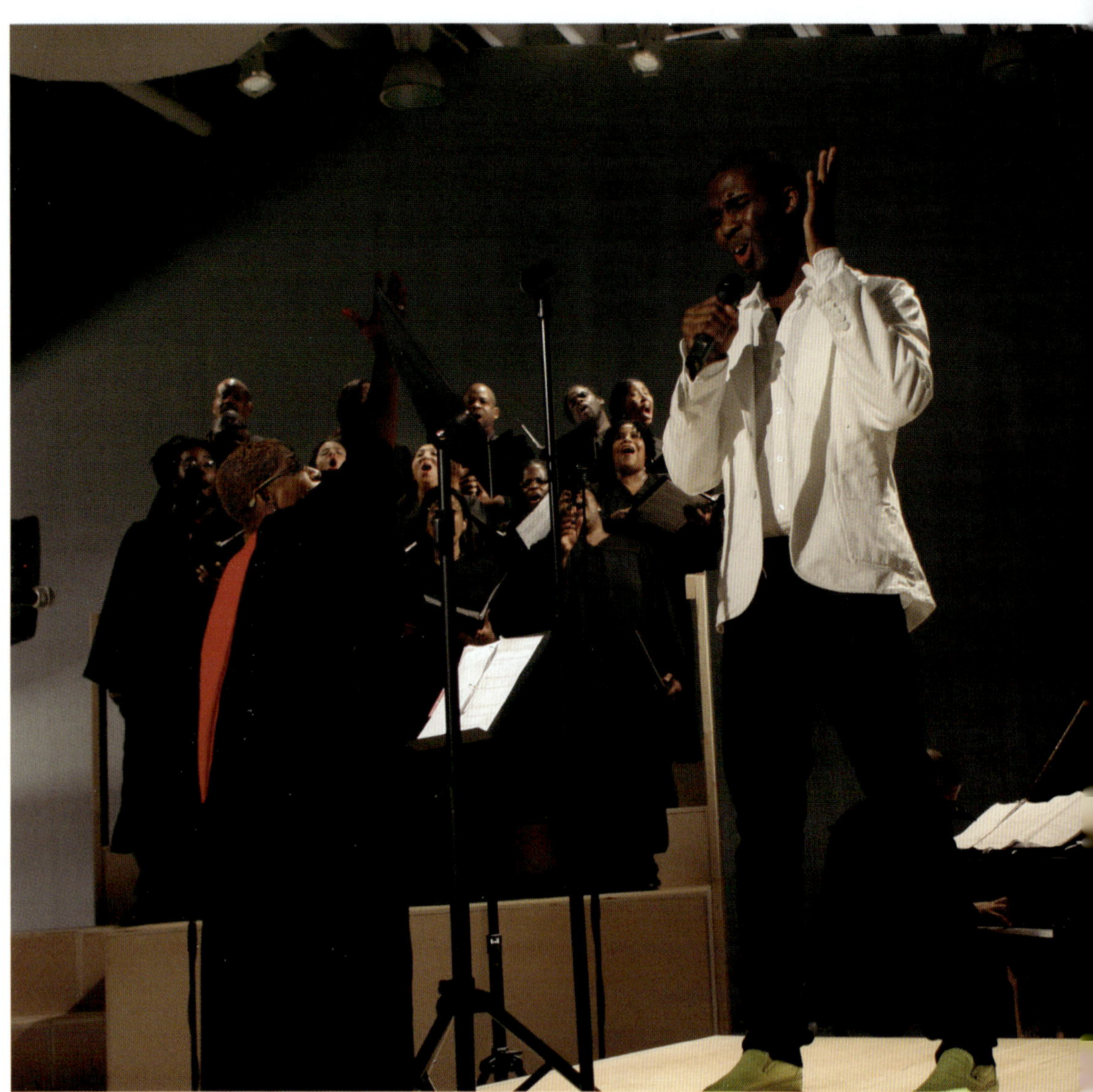

Theatre in Manhattan. Presenting two excerpts from *A Fantastic World*—a set from Genesis P-Orridge and one by Mike Kelley and Jim Shaw's "anti-rock" band Destroy All Monsters—the Radical Broadcast program *Musical Chairs* compiled biennial documentation of performances that have engaged various aural traditions by using a revolving carousel of videos, recalling the party game of the same name.

In a work of unparalleled vocal affect, the X-Patsys—an ensemble whose founding members include actress Barbara Sukowa and artists Robert Longo and Jon Kessler—delivered a powerful version of country singer Patsy Cline's song "I Fall to Pieces" (1961). Sukowa sang the lyrics "I fall to pieces / each time I see you again" over and over, beginning softly and working up to a crescendo of cracking and bellowing, then slowly retreating and ending the line in a whisper.

Based on her 1976 album *Voice is the Original Instrument,* vocalist and composer Joan La Barbara also tested the range of the voice during Performa 13, where she presented her own works along with those of Meredith Monk's and other performers. Rapturous vocals by Shadi Yousefian, accompanied by *setar* player Mohsen Namjoo, were essential to Shirin Neshat's Performa 11 Commission *OverRuled*, which explored the dynamics of censorship and creativity in a politically unstable and repressive Iranian society. *OverRuled* touched upon moments throughout Persian history, from the 921–22 CE trial of Sufist Mansur Al-Hallaj to the nation's present theocratic rule.

The power of collective versus individual vocal expression was addressed in Adam Pendleton's Performa 07 Commission *The Revival*, a work that incorporated a gospel choir and Pendleton himself as the church preacher. Collaboratively creating improvisational jazz and painting were key to Julie Mehretu's and Jason Moran's Performa 17 Commission *MASS (HOWL, eon)*: While Mehretu created two monumental and turbulent paintings—a form of mourning the United States' political landscape in 2017 as well as the extra-judicial killings of young Black men—Moran joined her in the studio to improvise a score of fast-paced, melancholic songs on electric piano synonymous with the music of New Orleans jazz funerals.

With video documentation of live performances by Destroy All Monsters, Joan La Barbara, Julie Mehretu and Jason Moran, Meredith Monk, Shirin Neshat, Adam Pendleton, Genesis P-Orridge, and The X-Patsys.

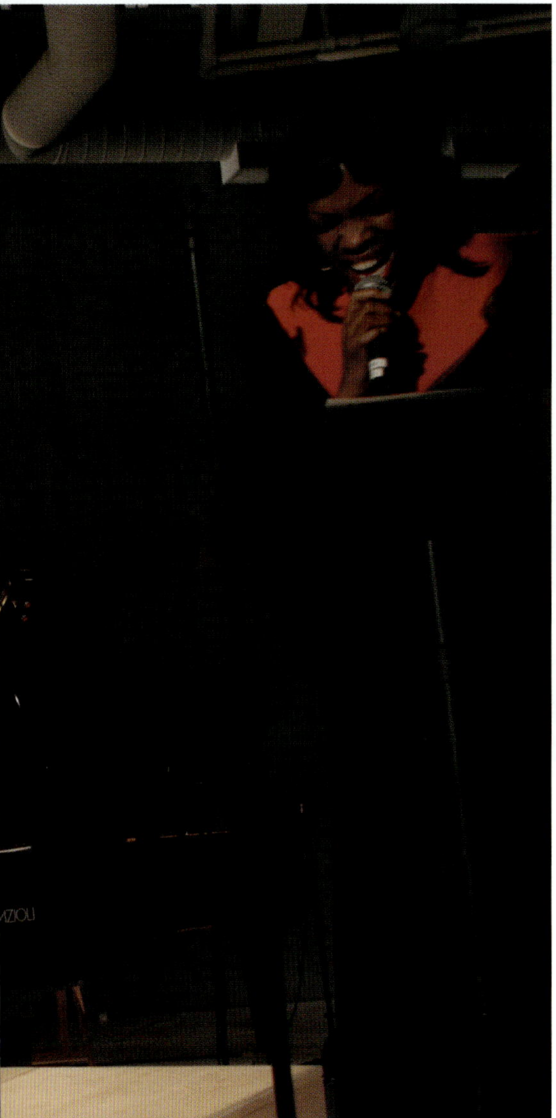

Adam Pendleton, *The Revival*, a Performa 07 Commission, 2007. Performance view.

RADICAL BROADCAST: FASHION TELEVISION

Curated by Charlene K. Lau
September 19–October 31, 2019

In the fall/winter 1995 runway show for art and fashion collective Bernadette Corporation, self-assured models sported a variety of off-trend and DIY looks that included a cropped double-breasted blazer, puffy vest, sneakers, tight mini dresses and skirts, all accessorized in pearls, gold chains, and statement earrings. They strutted down a makeshift runway at CB's 313 Gallery on the Bowery in New York, the art annex of the famed punk venue CBGB's space next door. They smoked, chewed and blew bubble gum, and smirked at the audience as if being intruded upon. Who was looking at who?

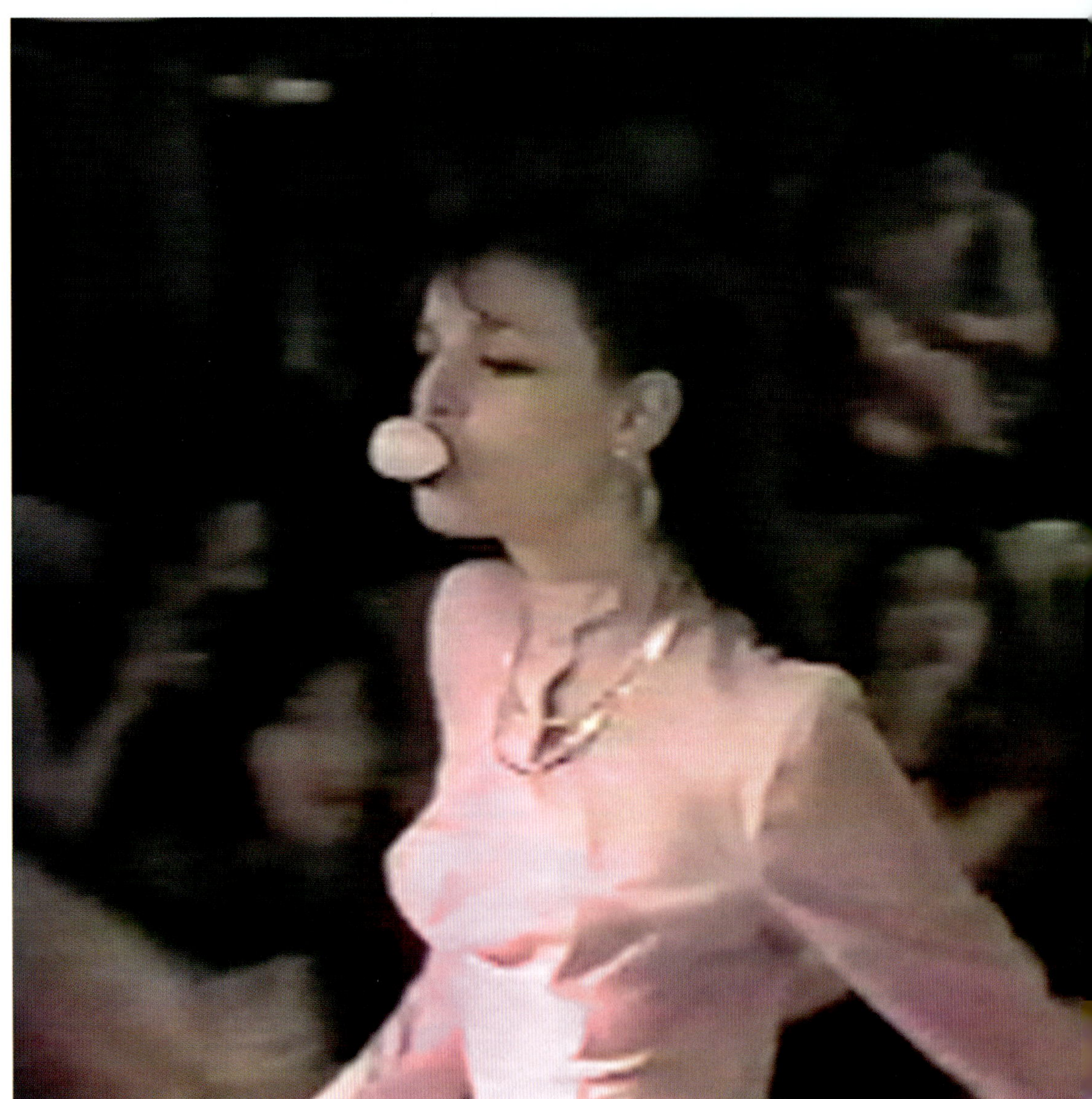

Named in honor of the pioneering Canadian program *Fashion Television*—which covered international runway shows and seasonal collections between 1985 and 2007—this Radical Broadcast online exhibition harkened back to a time when television was one of the few accessible ways of consuming fashion if you were not on the guest list. Together, these videos parlayed goofy authenticity stripped of the industry's glamor that typically glosses over imperfection and difference, instead upending capitalism, beauty, and power with a healthy dose of devil-may-care attitude and self-conscious mockery. These humorous takes unmasked the deep awkwardness of being human below the cool sheen of fashion, oscillating between a submissive obsession with current style and anti-fashion. As historical documents themselves, the videos also spoke to the ways in which clothing can be mediated and experienced beyond its ephemeral appearance on runways.

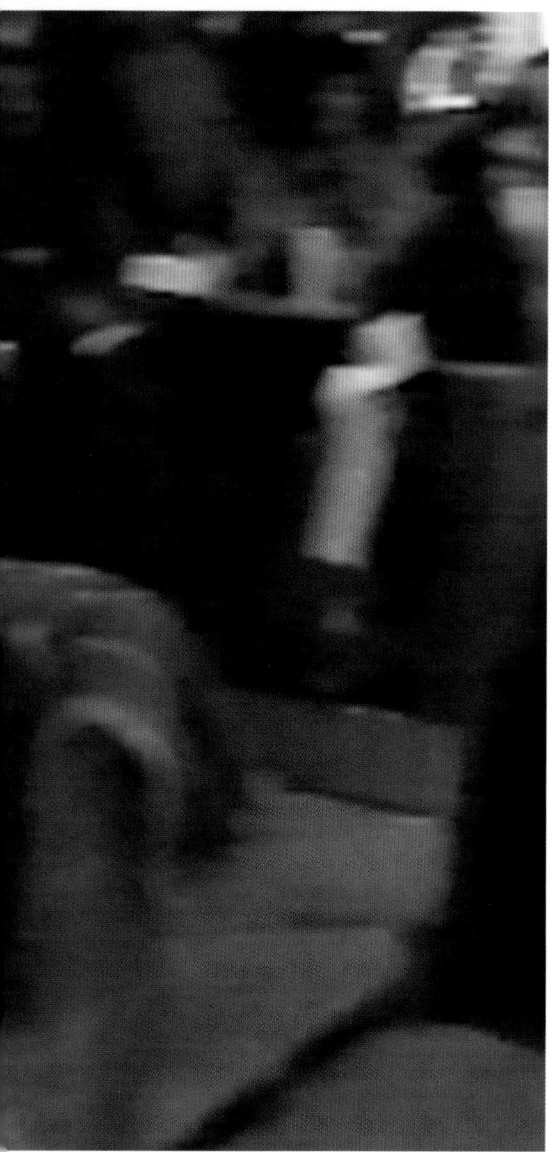

Through campy display and pointed critique of fashion as a world with its own rules, the featured video performances blurred the lines between couture and goofy costuming. Playful dressing and undressing—against conventional standards of beauty and socially acceptable ways of appearing—rebuffed the viewer's expectations. For instance, Canadian art collective General Idea's *Blocking* (1974) documented rehearsals for their *1984 Miss General Idea Pageant*, a satirical beauty pageant that poked fun at the conflation of glamor and celebrity in the art world. In an interplay of surfaces, the performance seemed to serve as a stand-in for the pageant itself, leading the viewer to question what is constructed in the situation and if records of the event can be trusted. On the other hand, *The Way Underpants Really Are* (1975) by Cynthia Maughan featured the American video artist slowly rotating in front of the camera to demonstrate the disintegrating condition of her pair of white, hole-ridden briefs held together at the waistband by a single safety pin. By emphasizing the underpants' banality, Maughan sought to mount a small rebellion against the ideas of a femininity exclusively entangled with sexy lingerie, taunting the audience with the underwear's bedraggled state.

Two videos by Bernadette Corporation offered a glimpse into their operations as an avant-garde brand in New York in the late 1990s. Using the language of (anti)fashion, the Downtown collective showed how capitalism, power, and spectacle happily converge in the industry. *Bernadette Corporation: Fashion Shows* (1995–97) compiled documentation of their runway presentations, while the work *Hell Frozen Over* (2000) contained a montage constituting what Bernadette Corporation calls a "fashion film about the poetry of Stéphane Mallarmé and the color white." Footage from a photo shoot is paired with snippets of French semiologist Sylvère Lotringer on a frozen lake lecturing on French poet Mallarmé, contrasting notions of the superficial with the depth that may lie beneath.

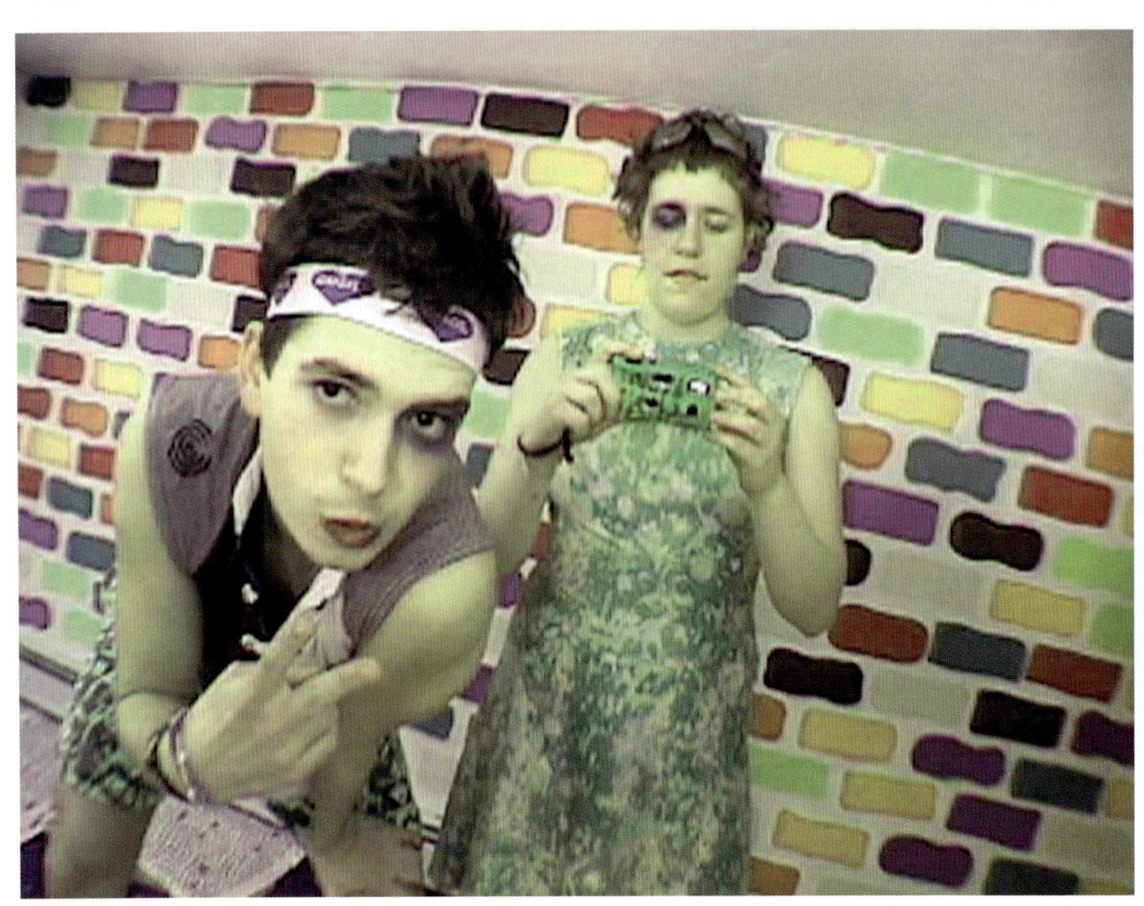

Bernadette Corporation, *Fashion Shows*, 1995–97. Video still.

Ryan Trecartin and Lizzie Fitch in *Wayne's World*, 2003. Video still.

Bernadette Corporation's restraint and cool aesthetic—as in "aloof," but also as in "ice cold"—slanted toward the minimal when compared to Trecartin's maximal offering *Wayne's World* (2003), another video in the program. Titled after the American comedy film of the same name from 1992 starring *Saturday Night Live* comedians Mike Myers and Dana Carvey, *Wayne's World* featured Trecartin and collaborator/co-star Lizzie Fitch in an intentionally awkward, variety show-like satire of conversation, song, and dance. The bombastic visual and aural components assaulted the viewer in its eight minutes of making strange. Frenetic patterns in lurid hues flashed on the screen, accompanied by a dense electronic harpsichord soundtrack and interspersed with Trecartin and Fitch's brightly sneakered feet dancing on a floor tiled with textiles. Their offbeat costumes and garish makeup visually computed as anti-fashion or even literal garbage: At one point, Fitch sports a brown paper bag "dress" held together with silver duct tape. With their jumble of avant-pop music references and mass media tropes—featuring a soap opera romance dialogue—the host-performers presented their fictional worlds while questioning the constructed surface.

Looking back on the autumn of 2019, Radical Broadcast strangely anticipated how much we would rely on personal devices during the pandemic for so many facets of our lives. In some cases, online life has become an entire world, a home of sorts. While many spent countless hours in front of screens pre-pandemic, the primary mode of viewing fashion today has shifted even more so toward online consumption, subsuming the lives of those who are isolated and/or working from home. Looking at fashion has returned exclusively to the screen, coming full circle from the early to mid-twentieth century when runway shows were occasionally inserted into the narratives of "women's films" in movie theaters. Now, smaller, palm-sized screens can be carried anywhere, and so can the access to style.

In an episode of "4 Nights at the Museum" (2020), German artist Hito Steyerl's self-professed "weird-ass visual podcast," the artist quipped: "I don't care about fashion, I don't have clothes. I barely wear clothes, especially during lockdown." Why bother wearing clothes if no one will see us? What is fashion if not both visual and social markers? The phenomenon of getting dressed for the public constantly necessitates new and different ways of seeing and being seen, a response to our interior selves reflecting back to ourselves and upon others. With so much of life lived online in the pandemic moment, fashion centers on the public performance of people wearing clothes on the Internet. "Virtual" interactions—following, liking, commenting, tagging, sharing, browsing, buying—are made very real by our total absorption into a glowing rectangle, a tiny on-demand theater in our hands.

After photography, film, television, and the internet, fashion adapted to another prevailing imaging technology in 2020: gaming. Georgian Creative Director Demna Gvasalia presented his Balenciaga fall 2021 ready-to-wear collection in a video game titled *Afterworld: The Age of Tomorrow*, inviting "players" to navigate around virtual environs to view models-as-characters wearing the season's hybrid Medieval-armor-meets-contemporary-Balenciaga-blasé-cool looks. In it, the player moved between zones: a bunker-like flagship store, a midtown New York streetscape circa 2031, a rave in a forest, caves. In an Excalibur moment near the end, the game revealed the "hero" as a Joan of Arc figure played by artist-model Eliza Douglas. After a Caspar David Friedrich-like contemplation scene atop a crag, a directed breathing exercise appeared onscreen, and the game ended with the message, "Congratulations, you have reached the highest level of digital enlightenment." For the more traditionally inclined viewer—industry insiders were provided VR headsets for this, but all others could watch via YouTube—an option existed to "attend" a runway show from the perspective of a VIP, complete with a front-row seat, an unlikely achievement for any fashion-week outsider. While the internet is no great equalizer, it afforded a visual trip through an otherwise inaccessible realm, albeit still suspending its visitors between poles of exclusion and belonging. And, in a way, fashion belongs online: consumed, performed, purchased, disseminated, and critiqued. Today, as a necessary escape from harsh daily realities, we can at the very least glance at the looking screen and into a universe of fantasy, imagining a time when we will dress for others again.

CHARLENE K. LAU

With moving-image works by General Idea, Cynthia Maughan, Bernadette Corporation, and Ryan Trecartin.

RADICAL BROADCAST: TIME SHARE

Curated by Job Piston
April 2–May 14, 2020

1

At some point, in those early, frightful days of the coronavirus pandemic, I found myself rereading Susan Sontag's twinned essays "Illness as Metaphor" (1978) and "AIDS and Its Metaphors" (1989). I remember clearly the impetus for doing so came during a "press briefing" President Trump gave on March 19, 2020. In his opening remarks, the president declared that the administration was doing everything it could "to defeat the Chinese

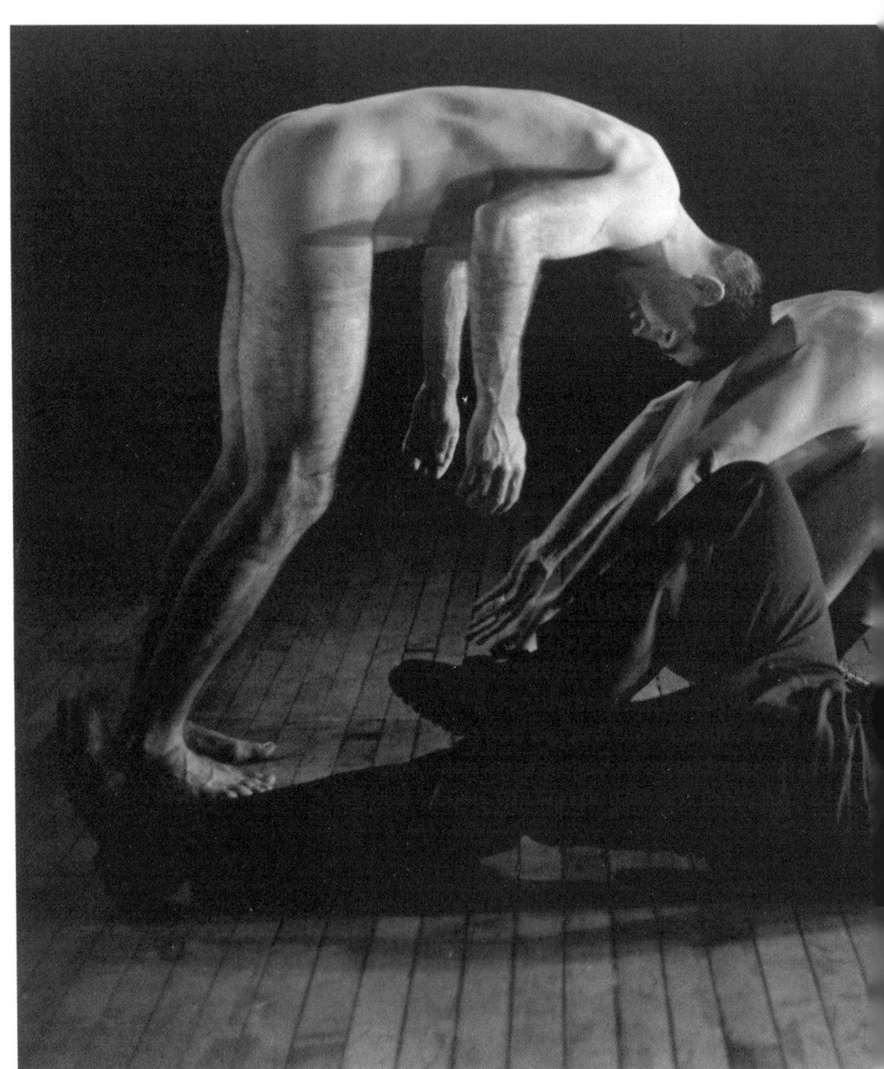

Keith Hennessy, Patrick Scully, and Ishmael Houston-Jones in *Unsafe Unsuited* by Patrick Scully, 1995. Performance view. PS 122, New York.

Virus." Trump, of course, had already been bandying about his xenophobic appellation for the coronavirus as early as January, and, just the day before, defended his use of the term, stating that it wasn't racist "because it [the novel coronavirus] comes from China."

That day, as I watched our president doubling down on his racist rhetoric, a line from "Illness as Metaphor" came to me in a flash of recall. "One feature of the usual script for plague," Sontag noted, was the belief that "disease invariably comes from somewhere else." That "somewhere," Sontag pointed out, was anywhere *but* white or European. "There is a link between imagining disease and imagining foreignness," she noted, that associates "illness with the foreign: with an exotic, often primitive place."

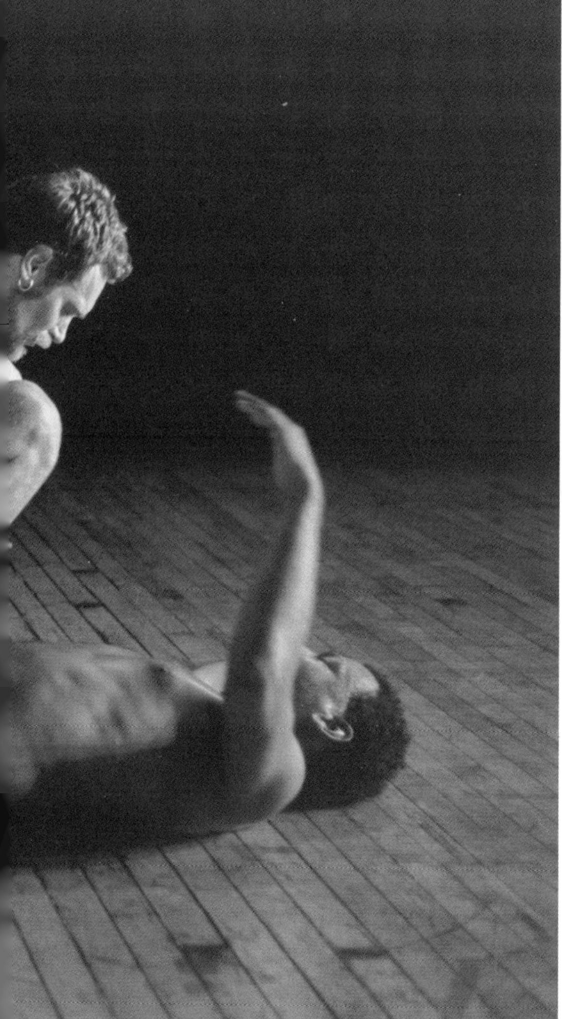

Underpinning that truth was, of course, economic inequality. "The fact that illness is associated with the poor," Sontag posited, further adds to the perception that those who get sick are alien to "Us" — "they," the sick, are seen as the "Other."

It was a distressing pattern Sontag saw evident in the early years of the AIDS pandemic—a political and ideological response which sought to situate the virus's origin within marginalized communities. Once AIDS could be confined to communities defined by their "Otherness"—race, sexual preference, socio-economic markers—the initial alarm amongst the "general public" was abated, deploying an "Us" versus "Them" logic that always tallies up to the same insidious sum: isolation and marginalization.

2

To be sure, the "Othering" of a community, its isolation (whether socially, economically, culturally), is a power-based ideological process that ensures its marginalization. In times of plague, owing to the acute characteristics of the conditions they provoke, the visibility of techniques deployed to marginalize communities comes to the fore. Recognizing these oppressive techniques presents an opportunity to develop and deploy strategies of resistance, applicable not only to the current crises, but also in addressing entrenched—and thus more "hidden"—mechanisms of inequality.

One such strategy of resistance is founded in *community-focused performativity* and its emphasis upon *making visible* the "Other." During the AIDS crisis, artists such as Ron Athey, Tim Miller, David Wojnarowicz, Karen Finley, and Patrick Scully, among others, created performances that sought to highlight and make visible the marginalization of those afflicted by AIDS. As Gwyneth Shanks, curator of the 2018 exhibition "A Different Kind of Intimacy: Radical Performance at the Walker,

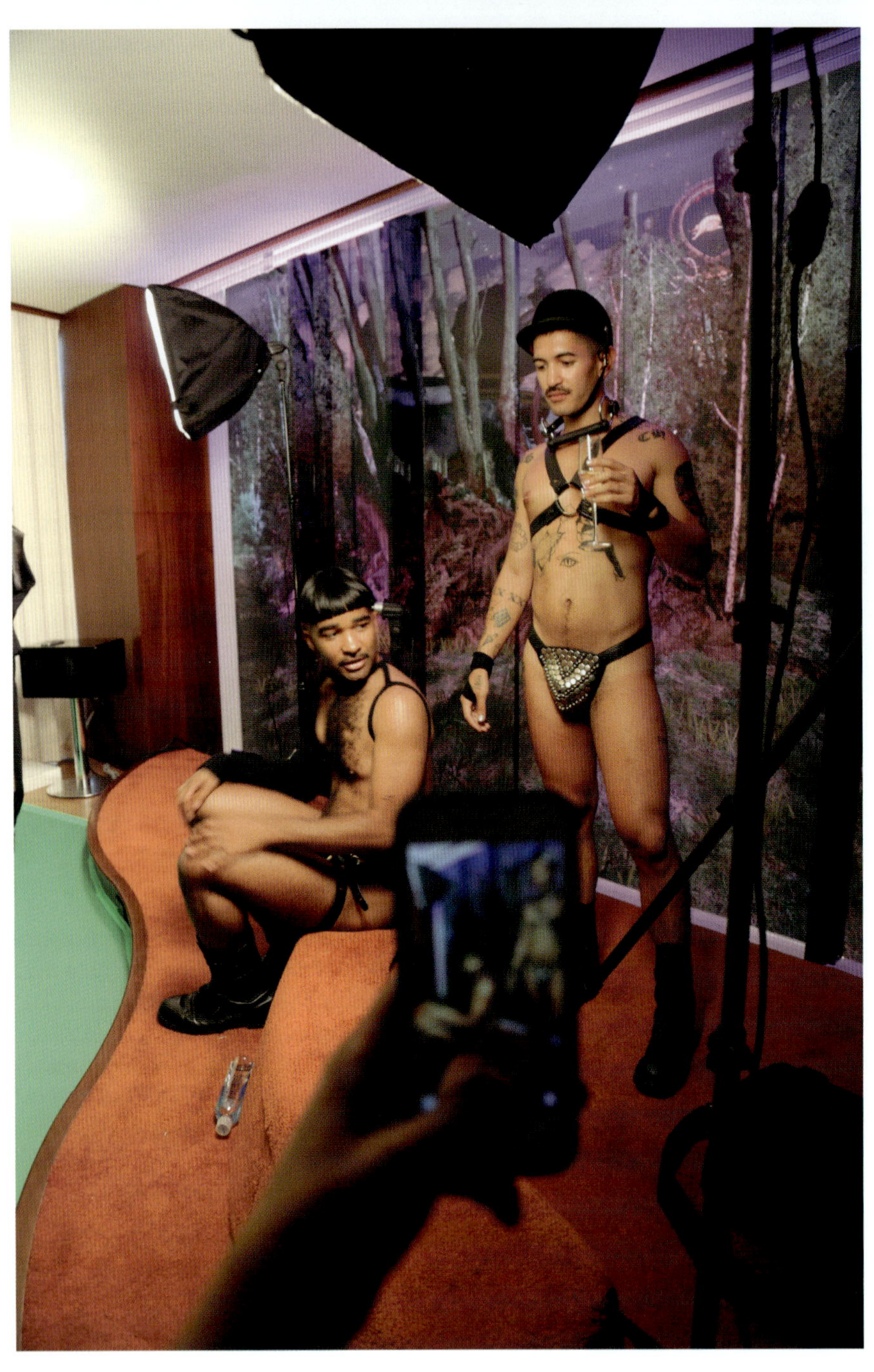

Jacolby Satterwhite,
Grindr for Visionaire, 2016.
Performance view.

1990–1995," noted, "such performances proclaimed the embodied importance of being in communal and collective co-presence." Indeed, for Shanks,

> to be in embodied co-presence was never only about the particular definitional valence of "performance"; rather, it asserted the political imperative of proclaiming one's life—one's *liveness*—as valid in the face of political inaction, homophobia, and national vitriol.

Meanwhile, for others at the time, the creative animus was framed in more stark terms. As Sean Metzger, a queer and performance studies scholar, noted in an interview for the Walker exhibition, "You weren't sure you were going to make it to 40," noting that art produced in response to the AIDS crisis was "a way of creating some kind of sign of life."

3

That same sense of urgency Metzger spoke of, informed by a fear both of death and the marginalizing forces that would bring it about, once again staked a claim in our lives as the twin specters of pandemic and racial injustices were made manifest across America in 2020. And, as it was during the AIDS crisis, artists and the institutions that support them came together to embody the "collective co-presence" that Shanks speaks of.

"Time Share" featured a selection of archival video works documenting performances by artists, many of whom addressed, whether indirectly or in response to, the very same structures of marginalization that Sontag observed and which Shanks saw at play during the AIDS crisis. And while, as Metzger contends, being "radical is always relational," a state dependent on a "set of specific conditions," for all of the artists included in "Time Share," the confluence of pandemic and racial tensions provided a new retrospective lens through which to consider their works.

Jacolby Satterwhite's *Grindr* (2016) takes aim at the censoring and restraining of queer bodies of color and discourses of queer sexual expression. Performers clad in BDSM and fetish gear enact erotically suggestive poses before a green screen in which a CGI projection of Central Park is applied, a "virtual" restaging of cruising in the park's famed Ramble section. Satterwhite's reference to cruising—a queer sexual practice which developed as a result of cultural oppression—underscores the very physical ways in which marginalization can manifest itself, pushing the "Other" into liminal public spaces with the hopes of fulfilling sexual desire.

Meanwhile, in the video clip *The Inaugural Ballroom Throwbacks Awards Ball Alpha Omega* (2020), dancer and movement artist Honey Balenciaga's voguing performance in New York's contemporary ballroom scene represents a direct through line to the city's historic Harlem-based venues, forums for the expression of LGBTQ culture which, since the 1960s, have provided safe spaces for marginalized—largely Black and Latino—individuals. Whereas Satterwhite's piece gestures toward the oppressive push of the "Other" into the liminal public space of cruising, Balenciaga's video demonstrates how marginalized communities—constituted here through ballroom culture—can embody the "collective co-presence" Shanks refers to. With Balenciaga, voguing becomes the expression of the very political imperative of "proclaiming one's life." It is a retooling of dance as "performative resistance"—a subversion of oppressive prescriptions of gender expression.

Performative resistance can also take the form of documentation on the part of the viewer, of bearing witness to acts of non-conformity, a gesture in which the artist can actively unite audience and performer in a "collective co-presence." Such is the case with Shigeko Kubota's *Europe on ½ Inch A Day* (1972), a video diary created by the late Japanese-born New York Fluxus artist. Shot on a handheld Sony Portapak, Kubota's travelogue captures her encounters with liminal communities—a gay theater troupe in Brussels and a Parisian "sex cabaret" among them. Documenting these "subversive" performances, Kubota made visible the "Other" through the sharing of her film with communities who otherwise would have no firsthand exposure to them.

This gesture of making the "Other" visible as an act of performative resistance can also be a lens through which to understand Judy Chicago's live installation series, "Women and Smoke" (1971–72). Part of her larger "Atmosphere" series, "Women

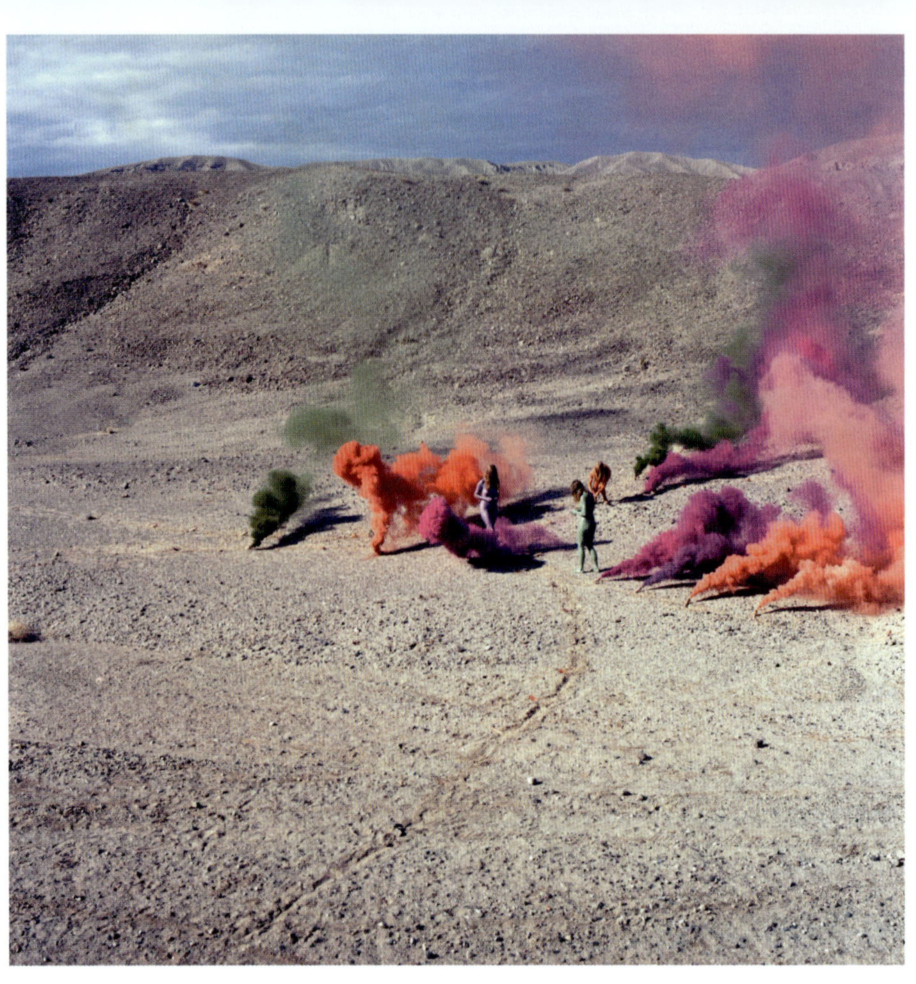

Judy Chicago, *Women and Smoke*, California, 1971-72. Film still.

1 Alexxa Gotthardt, "When Judy Chicago Rejected a Male-Centric Art World with a Puff of Smoke," Artsy.com, July 26, 2017, https://www.artsy.net/article/artsy-editorial-judy-chicago-rejected-male-centric-art-puff-smoke

2 Alex Fialho, Viva Ruiz talks about *Thank God for Abortion*, Artforum, June 22, 2018, https://www.artforum.com/interviews/viva-ruiz-talks-about-thank-god-for-abortion-75854

and Smoke," as Chicago notes, was created with the aim of "making images of female power." Enacting ritual-like scenes of fire-starting and self-immolation, nude female performers covered in vividly colored body paint move about the arid landscapes of California's desert as nebulous plumes of color rise from smoke bombs while fireworks are set off. "There was a moment when the smoke began to clear, but a haze lingered," she noted in a 2017 interview, "and the whole world was feminized—if only for a moment."[1] In the case of Chicago, making visible the oppressed female body requires nothing short of symbolically exploding the power structures that serve to subjugate it.

Dismantling the power systems that seek to suppress women's reproductive rights strikes is at the heart of artist Viva Ruiz's ongoing performance series, "Thank God For Abortion" (2015–). In her 2018 sculptural and performance-based iteration of the series, a "Thank God for Abortion" float included in that year's New York Pride Parade, Ruiz sought to underscore the need for collective co-presence in the face of marginalization. "Linking this project to Pride is important to me because I've started to articulate that abortion rights are queer rights," Ruiz noted in a 2018 interview with *Artforum*.[2] Featuring choreography by Megan Curet, in addition to musical performances by members of her fellow artistic community including Sigrid Lauren and Monica Mirabile of artistic duo FlucT, the aim of Ruiz's performative float is clear: "I want us to be on the same side," she contends, adding, "we do have a common enemy, [one] who dictates a religious, fundamentalist, hetero-normative structure of the family that no one at Pride conforms to."

4

To be sure, the realities of enacting and staging performative resistance in the age of the coronavirus present very real challenges in achieving the collective co-presence that Shanks speaks of. However, the "virtual communities" which exist today have, in the climate of the pandemic, rapidly become the venue for communal expressions and connectivity. For better or worse, social media is the dominant form of expression until the day returns when we can gather in public without fear. How artists respond to the difficulties this crisis poses while utilizing the virtual realm to address the power-based mechanisms of marginalization is still playing out before us. "All rapid epidemics," Sontag noted, "give rise to roughly similar practices of avoidance and exclusion." The question is, how can we learn from these experiences, observe the systems of inequality and marginalization it has laid bare, and adopt acts of resistance that transform the isolation it renders into gestures of communal empowerment? JOSEPH AKEL

With moving-image works by Korakrit Arunanondchai and Alex Gvojic, Honey Balenciaga, Sam Banks, Vanessa Beecroft, Xavier Cha, Judy Chicago, Sara Cwynar, FlucT (Monica Mirabile and Sigrid Lauren), Christian Jankowski, Jane Jin Kaisen, Farrah Karapetian, Richard Kennedy, Shigeko Kubota, Zanele Muholi, Oscar Nñ, Robert Rauschenberg, Robin Rhode, Viva Ruiz, Jamilah Sabur, Jacolby Satterwhite, Nick Sethi, Ryan Trecartin, and Tori Wrånes.

This essay was initially published in Performa Magazine *on October 19, 2020.*

RADICAL BROADCAST: BODYBUILDING

Curated by Charles Aubin
and Carlos Mínguez Carrasco
May 15–September 7, 2020

In 1979 and 1980, Aldo Rossi docked an enormous floating theater off Punta della Dogana. Commissioned by the Venice Biennale, the fantastical structure joined the stunning cityscape before setting sail on the Adriatic Sea, harboring in Dubrovnik and other territories that were once under Venice's control. Designed by the Italian architect and theorist, *Il Teatro del Mondo* (Theater of the World) was a temporary stage, hosting chamber music concerts and *commedia dell'arte*. The ship comprised a central octagonal tower topped by a steel ball and flag, flanked by two towers with

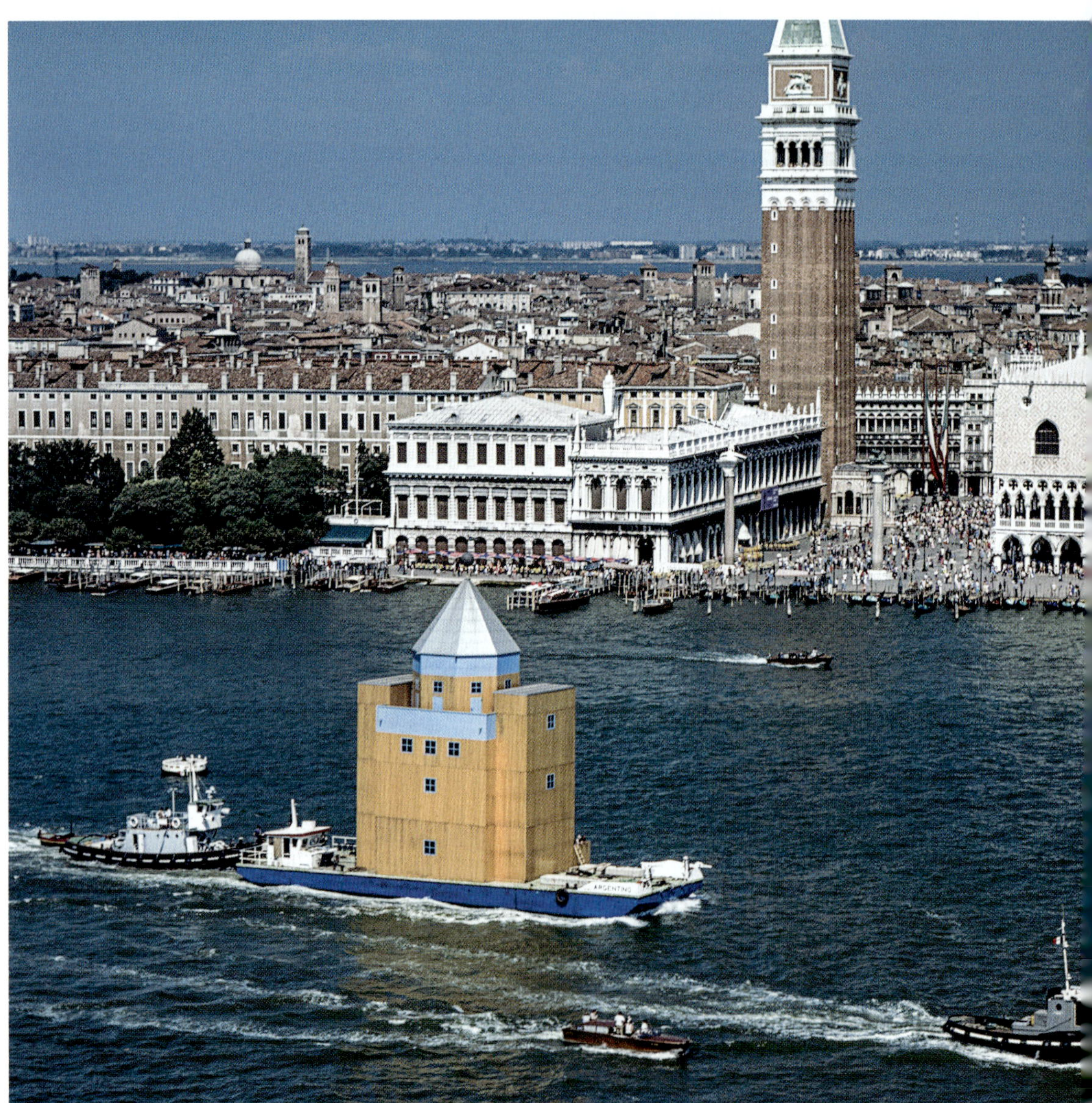

interior stairs, all set upon a barge. This maritime arena—with its boxy, simplified forms, bright gold and blue hues, and exterior wood covering—gestured toward the city's historical precedent of floating pavilions in the sixteenth century as well as architectural traditions as varied as lighthouses, baptisteries, and Shakespeare's Globe. According to Rossi, the ephemeral framework was buoyed at "a place where architecture ended and the world of the imagination or even the irrational began." Rare Super 8 film footage, transferred to video for the online exhibition "Bodybuilding," showed the ethereal *Teatro* peacefully making its way to La Serenissima.

In films and event documentation, "Bodybuilding" brought to life and prolonged Performa's 2019 book of the same name. Along with Rossi's *Il Teatro*, it featured the work of nearly forty other architects and studios, examining their use of performance throughout the twentieth and twenty-first centuries: They proposed radical new approaches to the theory and practice of their discipline by using performance as a method of invention, a tool to transform user experience, and an instrument of critique. Highlighting the social and political impact of planning and construction, the exhibition included documentation from a series of *Design-A-Thons,* run by the American firm Moore Grover Harper between 1976 and 1984. The charrettes, broadcast live on local television, had viewers call in and brainstorm solutions for regenerating neglected cities while architects sketched illustrations of these proposals in real time. It also featured Anna and Lawrence Halprin's *Sensory Walk* (1971), in which they explored the Californian coast on foot as a preface to creating the landscape design for Sea Ranch, the progressive residential community on the Pacific Ocean; and Haus-Rucker-Co's *Ballon für Zwei* (Balloon for Two), the Austrian collective's 1967 PVC bubble with bench seating, a weightless and mind-expanding construction for the future. Along with Rossi's rare footage, "Bodybuilding" also shared rich archival material such as Arata Isozaki's gigantic dancing robot-buildings at Osaka's Expo '70. The program positioned these iconic works in an alternative historical lineage, one now available to be revisited by architects such as Andrés Jaque and the creative duos Cooking Sections and New Affiliates, who have, like visionaries before them, turned to performance in the face of economic and environmental challenges.

CHARLES AUBIN

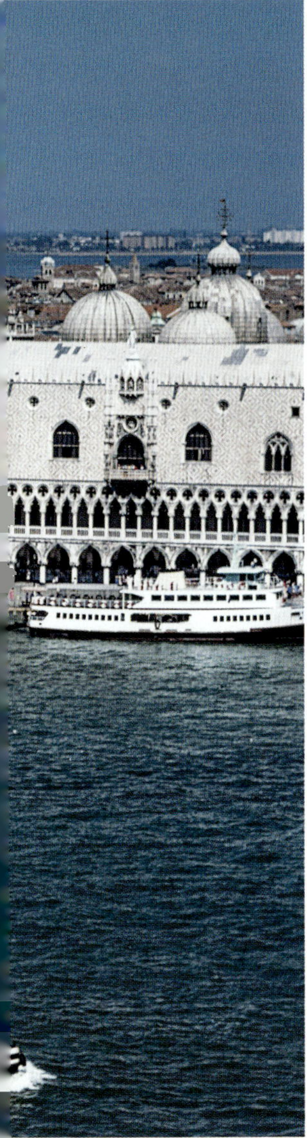

Aldo Rossi, *Il Teatro del Mondo*, 1979–80. Venice, Italy. Performance view.

With works by Ant Farm, Basurama + Area Ciega, Ricardo Bofill, Cooking Sections, Coop Himmelblau, Decolonizing Architecture Art Residency, Diller Scofidio + Renfro and David Lang, Estudio Teddy Cruz + Fonna Forman, Fake Industries Architectural Agonism, Didier Fiúza Faustino, Anna and Lawrence Halprin, Haus-Rucker-Co, Hans Hollein, Arata Isozaki and Associates, Andrés Jaque / Office for Political Innovation, Francis Kéré and Christoph Schlingensief, Ugo La Pietra, Moore Grover Harper, New Affiliates, NLÉ, Office for Metropolitan Architecture, Gaetano Pesce, Julieanna Preston, raumlabor, visual artist Jimmy Robert, Bryony Roberts and Mabel O. Wilson with the Marching Cobras of New York, Aldo Rossi, Alex Schweder and Ward Shelley, SO – IL with Ana Prvački, Bernard Tschumi, Nomeda and Gediminas Urbonas, and Wolff Architects.

RADICAL BROADCAST: THRESHOLD: ART IN TIMES OF CRISIS

Curated by RoseLee Goldberg, Kathy Noble, Charles Aubin, Job Piston, and Brittany Richmond
September 11–November 30, 2020

To reach a threshold is to hit a limit, to come to a boundary or a place where you can no longer carry on or move forward. In scientific terms, a threshold is a magnitude or intensity which must be exceeded for a chemical reaction to take place. A threshold is also a catalyst for moments of change, when social or political situations reach the point of being intolerable. How we get to that threshold—be it a personal or collective one—is often hastened by trauma or great difficulty. Although painful, shocking, and sometimes unbearable, these experiences can lead to profound transformations.

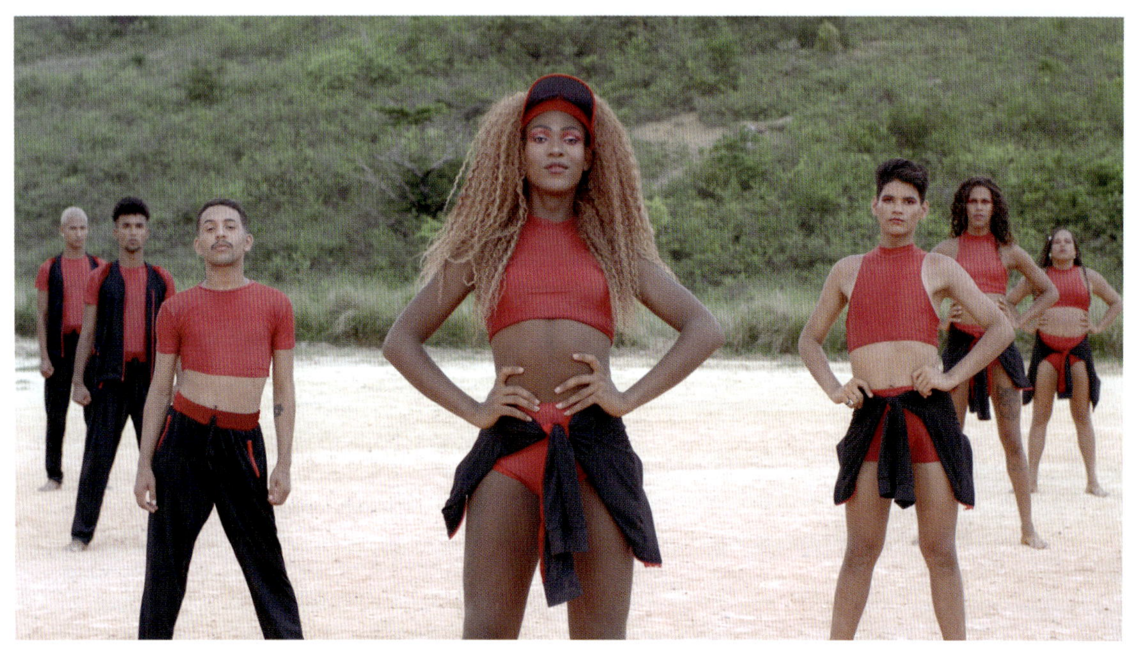

"Threshold: Art in Times of Crisis" featured art from critical turning points of the past five decades, when crises resulted in major cultural shifts and societal transitions. It also reflected on 2020's unprecedented global upheaval, when a worldwide pandemic destroyed enormous numbers of human lives—and livelihoods—across the globe. In the U.S. in particular, the virus has been addressed through a political lens at the expense of following medical best practices, leading to vastly differing regional results as well as disproportionately affecting Black and Latino populations. In addition, police brutality was brought into focus in parallel, leading to widespread protests of the institutional racism and inequity that pervades America.

ALL IMAGES
Bárbara Wagner and Benjamin de Burca, *Swinguerra*, 2019. Film stills.

The perceptions of this turbulence raised the question, how does one make art now? Whether faced with war, genocide, displacement, civil unrest, political oppression, environmental disasters, or racial, ethnic, sexual, and gender-based violence, artists have responded to our eras of catastrophe in thoughtful and powerful ways, creating work that critiques the horror of it all, explores the environments that give rise to it, and reveals the forces at play, while also offering a place of reflection, mourning, and healing.

As part of "Threshold: Art in Times of Crisis," the Brazilian duo Bárbara Wagner and Benjamin de Burca presented *Swinguerra*, a work they premiered in 2019 as a two-channel video installation at the Brazilian Pavilion of the Venice Biennale. Since 2013, the duo has collaborated on a series of films that track the political and social upheavals in Brazil through the country's popular music and dance scenes: From the end of the fifteen years of the Workers' Party in power, to the surge of conservative evangelism, a political coup, and the election of a far-right populist government. *Swinguerra* is the final chapter in this series of works. It draws its title from *swingueira*, a popular dance movement that originated in the state of Bahia, in the Northeast region of Brazil, fused with *guerra*, the Portuguese word for war. In this recent cultural phenomenon, dance groups consisting of ten to up to fifty performers, predominantly Black Brazilian dancers of various gender expressions, train weekly to perform in popular annual competitions. With *Swinguerra* Wagner and de Burca reveal the nuances and complexities of contemporary Brazil.

With moving-image works by ACT UP, Yael Bartana, Mykki Blanco/Zoe Leonard, Lee Bul, Kota Ezawa, William Greaves, Gran Fury, Lynn Hershman Leeson, William Kentridge, Glenn Ligon, Nicole Miller, Rabih Mroué, Shirin Neshat, Yoko Ono, Walid Raad and Souheil Bachar, Martha Rosler, Studios Kabako (Faustin Linyekula), Kara Walker, Carrie Mae Weems, David Wojnarowicz, and Artur Żmijewski.

"Threshold: Art in Times of Crisis" was intimately linked to the syllabus of RoseLee Goldberg's fall 2020 graduate seminar at NYU Steinhardt.

BÁRBARA WAGNER & BENJAMIN DE BURCA IN CONVERSATION WITH CHARLES AUBIN

CHARLES AUBIN

I'd like to start by asking you to give some context for *Swinguerra*. Can you explain how you came to these dance battles?

BÁRBARA WAGNER

Living in Recife since 2013, we've been following the emergence of different music genres rooted in traditional expressions of the Northeast of Brazil but, in short, everything starts with the *trios elétricos*—

BENJAMIN DE BURCA

—They're mobile sound systems, trucks with speakers that you mostly see in music parades during carnivals. They originated in the city of Salvador in the 1950s. The tops of the trucks would be used as stages for bands who played to the crowds on the street.

BW

Trios elétricos made *frevo* very popular. Frevo comes out of *capoeira*: It's an Afro-Brazilian dance too, but it's less of a martial art here; it's more exuberant. In the 1990s, TV shows picked up these concerts and showcased bands from Salvador. It influenced dancers everywhere in the Northeast, and they started to make their own groups. That's when swingueira appeared—in the beginning of the 2000s—with competitions often taking place in public sports courts. They're based on precise choreographies that follow and illustrate lyrics that often carry a sexual undertone and are delivered in a light and humorous way. The important thing here is that the dances were never really made for the camera. That's the big difference compared to what comes afterward: the *brega* music that started five years ago. Brega draws influences mostly from *baile funk* in Rio de Janeiro and São Paulo. But today, when you can make music videos yourself, there is a third-generation genre called *Passinho dos Malokas*. They radicalize the image of the body

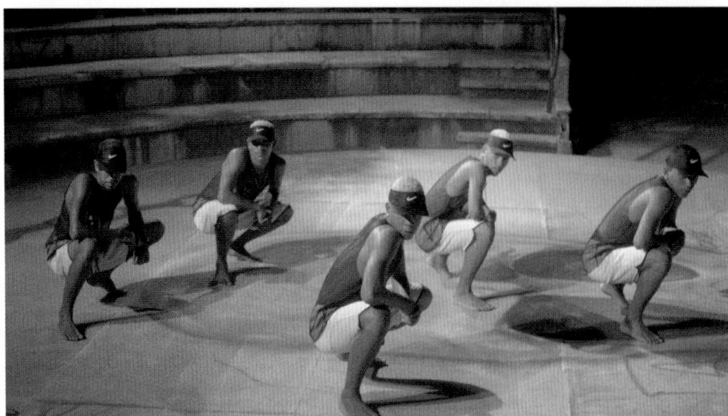

by dancing not only onstage but also anywhere: in the favelas, in the streets, in the schools. It's really due to the impact of the mobile phone.

BDB

Because the camera is in their hands and they have total control of image dissemination.

BW

In *Swinguerra*, the main troupe, called Extremo, is the group that is a bit more, let's say, "old school." They're like the first generation that performs the swingueira on sports courts. The lyrics are more naïve. Then comes *brega funk*, represented in the film by a group called La Máfia. They perform in an outdoor amphitheater with a more dramatic, Gothic look. And then, at the end, you see the Passinho dos Malokas, on the football pitch. This is performed by a much younger generation. They're super familiar with technology and make videos for social media, Instagram mostly.

CA

You've been tracking these evolutions.

BW

Swinguerra is the fourth and last chapter of a body of works we started in 2013, a crucial moment in Brazilian politics. Back then, people were taking to the streets, initially to protest the increase of the cost of public transportation and then, more generally, corruption. The Workers' Party had been in power since 2003, first with Lula [Luiz Inácio Lula da Silva], then with Dilma [Rousseff], who was reelected in 2014; 2014 was also the year of the World Cup in Brazil. Shortly after that, in 2017, we had a coup, which paved the way for Jair Bolsonaro to be elected the following year. Clearly, in the previous decade, the Workers' Party succeeded in creating a new middle class and, with that, came a generation of artists who began developing their own music industries. So, it's true that the four works we developed during those years brought us to look at these changes very closely. *Faz que vai* (*Set to Go*, 2015) focuses on contemporary frevo as a rather hybrid form of resistance. *Estás vendo coisas* (*You Are Seeing Things*, 2016) approaches the brega scene by its relationship to labor. *Terremoto Santo* (*Holy Tremor*, 2017) looks at the growth of a new gospel scene as evangelism surged across the country. With *Swinguerra* (2019), we turned to the dance competitions as a phenomenon of community and participation.

CA

A lot has changed in Brazil between 2013 and 2019.

BW

When we felt the urgency to make films on cultural production by a new, rising middle class, we understood that this new generation of popular artists was assuming the means of their own representation.

BDB

It might be helpful here to clarify what is meant by *middle class* in a Brazilian context, as the parameters are different from what you may expect in, let's say, the U.S. or Europe. In Brazil, quite simply, it's related to an index of ownership and quality of life, like having a car or a television, or access to running water. Employment too. Not going hungry and the availability of credit. It's really the result of a decade of the PT [Workers' Party] in power.

CA

You mentioned technology and the importance of new music industries. In these four works, your starting point is music. Where does it take you?

BDB

Music is always a fantastic inroad into what is happening in terms of social dynamics. It touches upon social and political phenomena of the present. For instance, when we started with *Faz que vai*, frevo had just been recognized as "intangible cultural heritage" by UNESCO in 2012. It became a capital currency for tourism, and schools dedicated to it formalized its dance steps. The dance form itself became much more "stageworthy," no longer performed on the street only. It was somehow marketed to travel around the world and represent a form of culture from Brazil.

CA

Being deemed "intangible cultural heritage" by UNESCO crystallized it.

BDB

Yeah. It became associated with an idea of tradition.

BW

You know, I come from a background in journalism and Benjamin studied Fine Arts. When working in journalism, I was particularly interested in the self-representation of the Afro-Brazilian community and was constantly looking at the idea of tradition, trying to make sense of it. What underlies what Benjamin says about the new value attributed to frevo by the state is that, actually, the people who practice those traditions are constantly working to make them survive. And the only way to do that is by making them open to change. So, I'd say that our interest lies in how dance and music unveil the labor that's behind this idea of tradition.

BDB

In fact, I should add, people who dance frevo sometimes simultaneously get involved in other forums and other dance forms. This is what happened with Eduarda [Lemos], one of the dancers in *Faz que vai*. She dances frevo while also taking part in swingueira contests. She's the lead performer in *Swinguerra*.

CA

I saw that. So, I understand that you've remained in touch with her over the years. Can you talk about your collaborations with your performers?

BW

We met dancers Eduarda and Bhrunno [Henryque] when filming *Faz que vai* in 2014, and they brought us to the sports courts where swingueira competitions were taking place. Back then, we already understood the importance of it—there were thousands of young dancers there, from the whole city of Recife. They were all, I don't know, something between, like, seventeen and twenty-five years old—

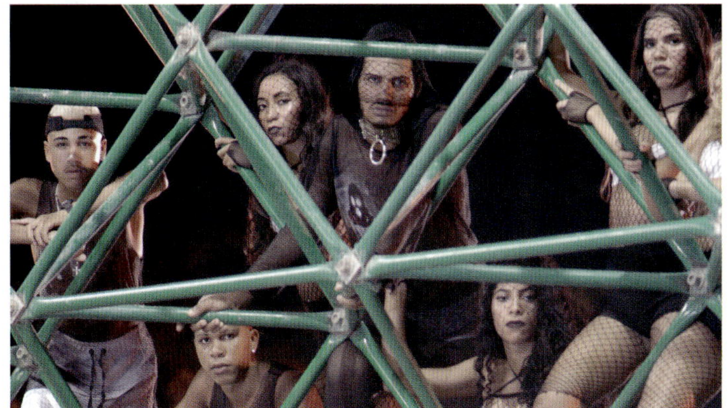

BDB
—at twenty-five, you become a little too old to dance swingueira because it's—

CA
—very physical.

BDB
Yeah.

BW
They have a very sophisticated relationship to space and architecture. What I mean by that is the way they perform the choreographies on the sports courts: As much as swingueira derives from frevo steps in Recife and from trios elétricos bands in Salvador, it's also very influenced by the aesthetics of samba schools' rehearsals or parades in Rio de Janeiro. In a way, I'd say it synthesizes many aspects of Black Brazilian culture. And because the competitions happen only once a year, they force the groups to rehearse for an entire year.

CA
To excel.

BW
It's highly competitive.

BDB
There's also a very interesting aspect of the competition format: Performances only last fifteen minutes; each one is organized in three parts, although those three acts aren't necessarily five minutes each. At the beginning of the performance, the dancers present a press release to the jury. In fact, the theme of the competition gets represented in many different ways, from the outfits to the banners or what they may shout in unison as much as the actual choreography itself. It's the moment when they bring urgent social issues to the court.

CA
Sounds like a very specific script.

BDB
Yes, it may seem a bit strict, but a lot of freedom is still left, for instance, with gender expression. In *Swinguerra*, we followed the usual structure of three movements: The dance of the girls, dance of the boys, and then the entire group formation. But the dance for the girls isn't necessarily only for cis female performers—it's what the person feels like dancing.

CA
It remains fluid.

BW
They rehearse in order to spend time together. Differently from the other music genres we've worked with before, which are often based on the promise of making a living from them, in swingueira competitions, you don't see a potential financial return. I mean, when they win, they do get a prize, a trophy, and eventually a bit of money that might cover aspects of the production, like costume fabrication. But in no way is it for money that these dancers get together and rehearse three times a week, throughout a whole year, at night, after work, after school, sometimes crossing the whole periphery of the city, from north to south or east to west, which is not at all an easy thing to do by bus in the city of Recife. We quickly realized it had to do with a sense of community and belonging. Most of them are young people who live under conditions that make them feel unsafe in the streets.

BDB
That said, the swingueira groups also really vary. You find different mindsets and politics; some with more conservative leanings, to put it simply, who would be in favor of a greater presence of military police, for example. In any case, discipline and order are key. In most cases, if a dancer is ten or fifteen minutes late, even though they had to cross the whole city to attend the rehearsal, they will have to sit out the entire session. It can be very strict.

CA
Yes. There's this moment in the video in which Eduarda is dancing for the camera, filmed by her friend, and the dance instructor scolds them. He tells them: "Enough of this anarchy, come over here and get in formation." Can you talk about that reference to a military-style organization?

BW
This is Brazil. I mean, it's not always legible, but, you

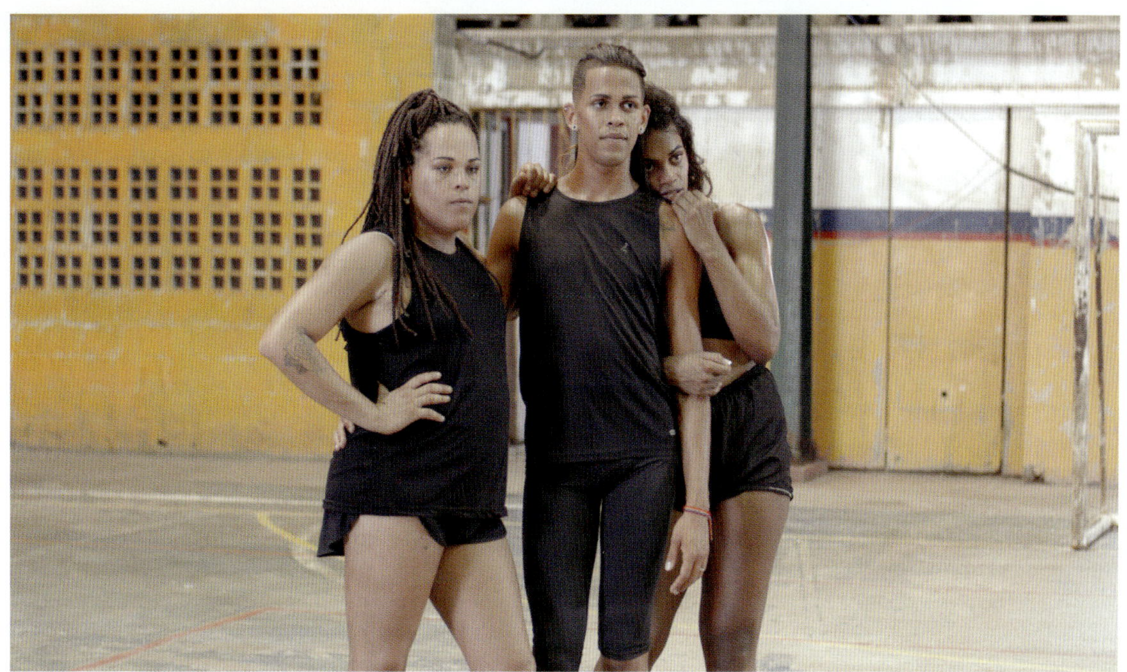

know, most of these dancers, who are Black and live in the peripheries, often go down military police trajectories themselves. Most of them go into the army at a very young age to make a living. Many of them have served. The final scene was filmed at a location very important to Brazilian military history: As you might know, Recife was a Dutch colony, but the Dutch were defeated by the Portuguese here during the Second Battle of Guararapes in the 1600s. Many consider it the birthplace of the Brazilian army.

BDB

During filming, several dancers were already familiar with the base. They knew many of the soldiers stationed there, and, would even all sit together and chat at the canteen, where we set up catering services. You had the transgender dancers who had been in the army several years before talking to their friends who were still there, all eating together at the same table.

CA

I want to hear you talk more about that. I mean, the military history of Brazil is so dark—more than twenty years of military dictatorship is still now very present in the public discourse. I have in mind Bolsonaro dedicating his vote to Colonel Carlos Alberto Ustra, who ran a torture camp in the 1970s, when he voted in favor of Dilma's impeachment in 2016. She herself was a victim of torture in the 1970s for her political activities. And yet, for all of that traumatic history, *Swinguerra* is still structured around military-style organizations of bodies in space. Can you articulate it?

BDB

Yes, this can come across as our subversion of what a representation of Brazil, especially in a national pavilion in Venice, could be. But just to clarify, *Swinguerra* is based exclusively on already existing choreography. We worked with what the dancers were rehearsing at the time for their annual competition, which took place shortly after we filmed. The whole project came about at an opportune moment, let's say, for the notion of a national representation of Brazil.

BW

I'd say that this comes very much from our documentary background. In terms of method, we always deal with the content that comes from the people we portray. It's where the complexity comes from. The same happened in *Estás vendo coisas,* when we were working with groups of dancers and MCs who were very much part of an industry that celebrates ostentation and the power of consuming. It was the mark of Brazil in the first years of the 2010s, which is also quite connected to the evangelical church. While they sang songs with super-explicit lyrics, many of them would still go to church.

Going to the evangelical church also meant investing in social ascension. Believe it or not, it wasn't antithetic. The same goes for swingueira, where bodies are extremely fluid in terms of gender, yet dancers are still super-willing to follow a strict discipline in the sense of ordering their lives. This is the complexity of today's Brazil. And I'd say this is the beautiful challenge we face when we try to portray Brazilian culture or popular Brazilian expressions. It's beyond our control, the picture is never complete, and there's a kind of opacity that makes the work bring up questions that we don't always know how to answer. I think this is very much the place where we want to stand.

CA

I'm curious about the salute to the Brazilian flag. You've shot it in a specific way; it has this kind of propaganda style, with close-ups of the performers filmed from below. It's pretty dramatic.

BW

You know what—that scene is the very first sequence of the actual presentation that they prepared for the dance competition.

CA

I see. You didn't stage it. It predated the film shoot.

BW

Always. Everything. And I should add that it took us maybe four or five visits to their rehearsals at the community center in the neighborhood of Ibura to properly understand what was being said during the salute. It comes from a local song from Salvador, which I didn't know then. Extremo appropriated it for the beginning of their presentation: "Brazil / such a wonderful country / Indeed / We must honor what is written on our flag / Order and Progress." And regarding the camera work, we started with the situation on the court. Normally, the performers are facing the jury. It's always frontal. We decided to take advantage of that but also challenge ourselves to not always be where the jury would be positioned. We developed a kind of choreography with the cinematographer to make their synchronicity and the perfection of their gestures even more perceptible in the film. Their original choreography wanted the jury to pay attention to each performer saluting the flag. We stuck to this attention. It's like an apotheosis, a celebration of Brazilian-ness.

CA

I mean, the camera work is very loaded.

BW

It is. And that comes with a purpose. Let's take, for example, the title of your show, "Threshold: Art in Times of Crisis," and this word—*crisis*. Right now, with the pandemic and the economic collapse, under Bolsonaro, millions of people fell back below the poverty line. We shot *Swinguerra* before this current crisis, but its other matters of representation are still important today: We wanted to look at the emergence of a working class and how it intersects with race representation. With *Swinguerra*, the performers reinvent their representation in the public realm. I think this is the crisis that we've been following throughout all the works we've made in Brazil. We want to register how these bodies subvert the ways in which they are seen—

BDB

—and heard.

CA

What is the situation right now in Recife for the performers you've worked with?

BW

I was on the phone with Eduarda yesterday to prepare for this conversation. It's beyond fragile.

Brazil is now back to what we lived through in the 1980s. Inflation is through the roof—a pack of beans is now ten *reals* (it was four last year). She told me that, even though not much seems to have changed in daily life in the favelas—very few people can afford to quarantine or wear masks; many are unemployed. It's a huge crisis, which will have an enduring impact in Brazil.

BDB

Although she did say the competitions are back. Next month.

BW

It's the discipline, right. Incredible. The groups understand very well how to be economically self-sufficient. The performers were always finding ways to finance their own costumes and help each other with transport, etc. It's a very sophisticated form of a "non-hegemonic" economic system that they've invented for themselves.

BDB

Social media again! Instagram is a very interesting dynamic for this economy, you know. Some brands and services, like pizza deliveries, decided to sponsor some of the dancers. There's a kind of payment in return for advertising.

CA

Product placement. I want to go back to something we talked about earlier—the relationship between, let's say, live performances and what is done for the phone camera and is meant to live online, on social media. I mentioned this moment when Eduarda dances for the camera, but we can also think of the beginning of the video, when you show the group all together, waiting for the rehearsal to start, and everyone is using that downtime to check their phones. How do these two realities cohabitate?

BDB

That's definitely something we came to recognize progressively during the making of *Swinguerra*. First, we concentrated our attention on the public competitions, but, over the years, swingueira became more versatile as dancers would infiltrate other scenes like brega, which is much more intertwined with nightlife. You go out to a club or party and the MCs always have two, three, sometimes even four, dancers on the stage around them. This is how dancers start their careers. To be honest, even when we were shooting back in 2018, swingueira was starting to feel old or passé. To me, that was related to changes in technology. The choreography itself became more clearly influenced by social media, even including scripted movements of the cell phone camera that were incorporated into the dance. For example, throwing the camera's perspective to the side or throwing it up in the air as in a pan or tilt up to reveal other dancers. They're recurrent motifs in the passinho dos malokas. It's the most recent, and, in fact, an entirely new phenomenon that started while we were researching for *Swinguerra*.

CA

It's the last group we see in the video, right? The younger dancers?

BDB

Yes. There's a slight age difference.

BW

Passinho means *little step*, and *maloka* can generally refer to a kind of precarious architecture, a precarious house.

BDB

Maloka is also a bit pejorative. If you're called a maloka, you're a bit crazy. It's an interesting dynamic because using the phrase *passinho dos malokas* is basically reclaiming the term; it's turning it into something positive for yourself.

BW

Passinho dos malokas as a form is coded with representations of the Black male body in Brazil. Their dance addresses both the way in which violence is historically inflicted on these bodies as well as the fear that is constructed around their image by white elites. And this is why the performance is super-subversive. The dance can be very blunt; performers mimic acts of violence with guns or knives—

BDB

—or being handcuffed. You know, in Brazil, these bodies are in constant danger, often stopped on the street by the police for no reason, pushed against a wall and searched. All of these images are present in the dance but are turned into more humorous forms. It can look like a strange dynamic, but passinho dos malokas have a direct, often comedic, sense to them by how stories play out.

BW

They confront the violence projected onto them. They're the malokas, and, when they dance, they touch the nerve of this history of oppression.

This conversation was initially published in Performa Magazine *on November 2, 2020.*

RADICAL BROADCAST: *LEAN*

Curated by Legacy Russell
December 1, 2020–February 28, 2021

Subsequently presented at Kunsthall Stavanger in Norway, March 4–April 25, 2021

"I prefer no curves at all, unless they be the // : This angle the cryptographic slant into figurative space is toward a poetics of internal excess[.]"

RONALDO V. WILSON[1]

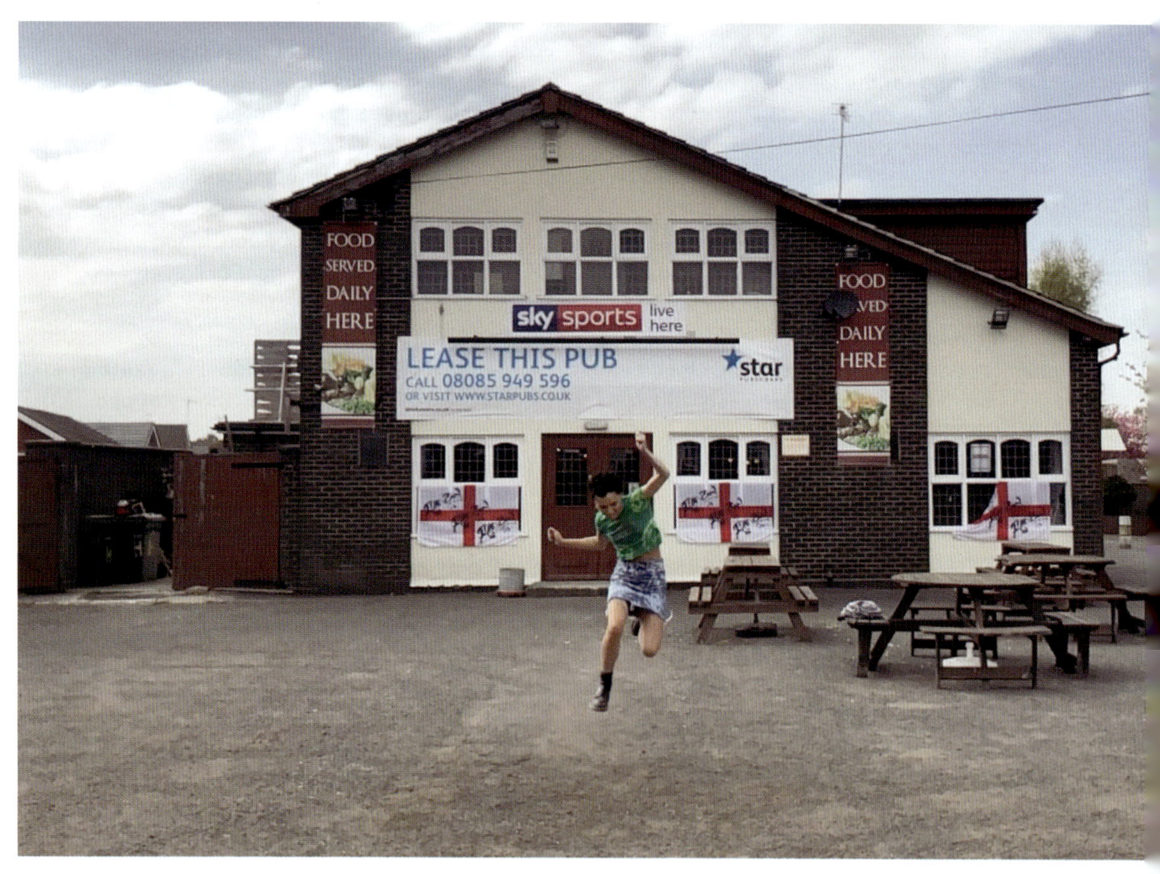

LEAN brought together seven artists—Justin Allen, Jen Everett, Devin Kenny, Kalup Linzy, Rene Matić, Sadé Mica, and Leilah Weinraub—who, through movement, sound, and film, collectively congregated and conferred toward *lean* as a Black vernacular and queer poetic proposition. Across these seven artists and their work shown as part of Performa's Radical Broadcast, *lean* was intimacy, collaboration, intergenerational conviviality.

Kemi Adeyemi observed: "[A] white ruling class [is] obsessed with the verticality and perpendicularity of the 90° angle."[2] Thus, expansiveness of the *lean* across these pages extended far beyond its definition of origin, an active refusal of a ninety degrees that is, as Adeyemi notes, "distinctly gendered and racialized." As a lexicon, *lean* is a suture, and a song; it throws shade, and makes it. Its constellation is far-reaching and galactic while still somehow dense, sensual, and sticky. It is a visual axis and a line break. Spiritual, it is what our hands do when they pray.

Lean holds us and holds us up, and as a 1972 Bill Withers song reminds us, "we all need somebody to lean on ..." // *Lean* is the bounce, dissent, and sway of Dem Franchize Boyz on bass, an entire club on a mid-aughts dance floor snapping back to their "Lean Wit It, Rock Wit It." (2006) // *Lean* is the very essence and energy of the *contrapposto*, a classicized angularity made whole and holy by the blend, blur, and limens of a luminous Blackness and queerness. // *Lean* is the birth of drag ballroom competitions in 1920s Harlem and the 1990s genesis of Atlanta trap, bound in decadent conversation and entanglement across dance floors and decades // *Lean* is the exact radical repatriation that emancipates these canonized slants back into the world where they belong and, beyond the freeze of Carrara marble, makes them move. // *Lean* is the sonic re/negotiation of sound in what is chopped and screwed as a hall-haunting alongside of, and in remix with, the innovations and technologies found in the notes and lines of Julius Eastman, Alice Coltrane, and Nina Simone. // *Lean* is all at once a complex interdependence, codependency, community, and kinship, a rhizomatic set of mathematical possibilities that break from the static and pose in lyrical abstraction.

Thus, to *lean* represents a gesture that forces an impossibility of physics: a falling without collapse; an epic draping that never meets the floor but instead floats. It is an image that defies imagination. When the sites we travel through are designed to surveil us, dictating how our bodies should move and feel, we who *lean* enact essential spatial and emotional labor, protective enclosures that break and remake space, decolonize time, remix memory, reformat care. As Harmony Holiday notes: "Now we have to thank the catastrophe for imbuing us with the stamina to reach ourselves at these endless slants[.]"[3] *Leaning* scores and slants with urgency, a performative and political proposal for new worlds to be dreamt up and built, and new ways of reading, listening, becoming, being.

Forever reaching somewhere between the horizon and the sky, this *LEAN* here and the artists therein offered windows into a networked architecture, an endless form of communication, a call awaiting a response, gorgeous glyphs of desire. LEGACY RUSSELL

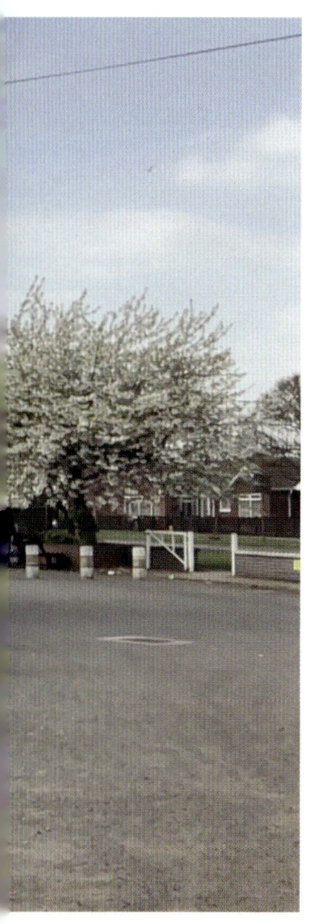

1 Ronaldo V. Wilson, "VERGELIOIAN SPACE V: CALIBAN X," *Poems of the Black Object* (New York: Futurepoem Books, 2009), 49.

2 Kemi Adeyemi, "Beyond 90°: The Angularities of Black/Queer/Women/Lean: Kemi Adeyemi (29.1)," *Women & Performance*, February 26, 2019. www.womenandperformance.org/bonus-articles-1/29-1/adeyemi

3 Holiday, Harmony, "The Black Catatonic Scream," *Triple Canopy*, 2020. www.canopycanopycanopy.com/contents/the-black-catatonic-scream

Rene Matić, *Brown Girl in the Art World III*, 2019. Video still.

FLUCT
UPWARD FACING CONTROL TABLE TOPS

Lever House
May 3, 2017

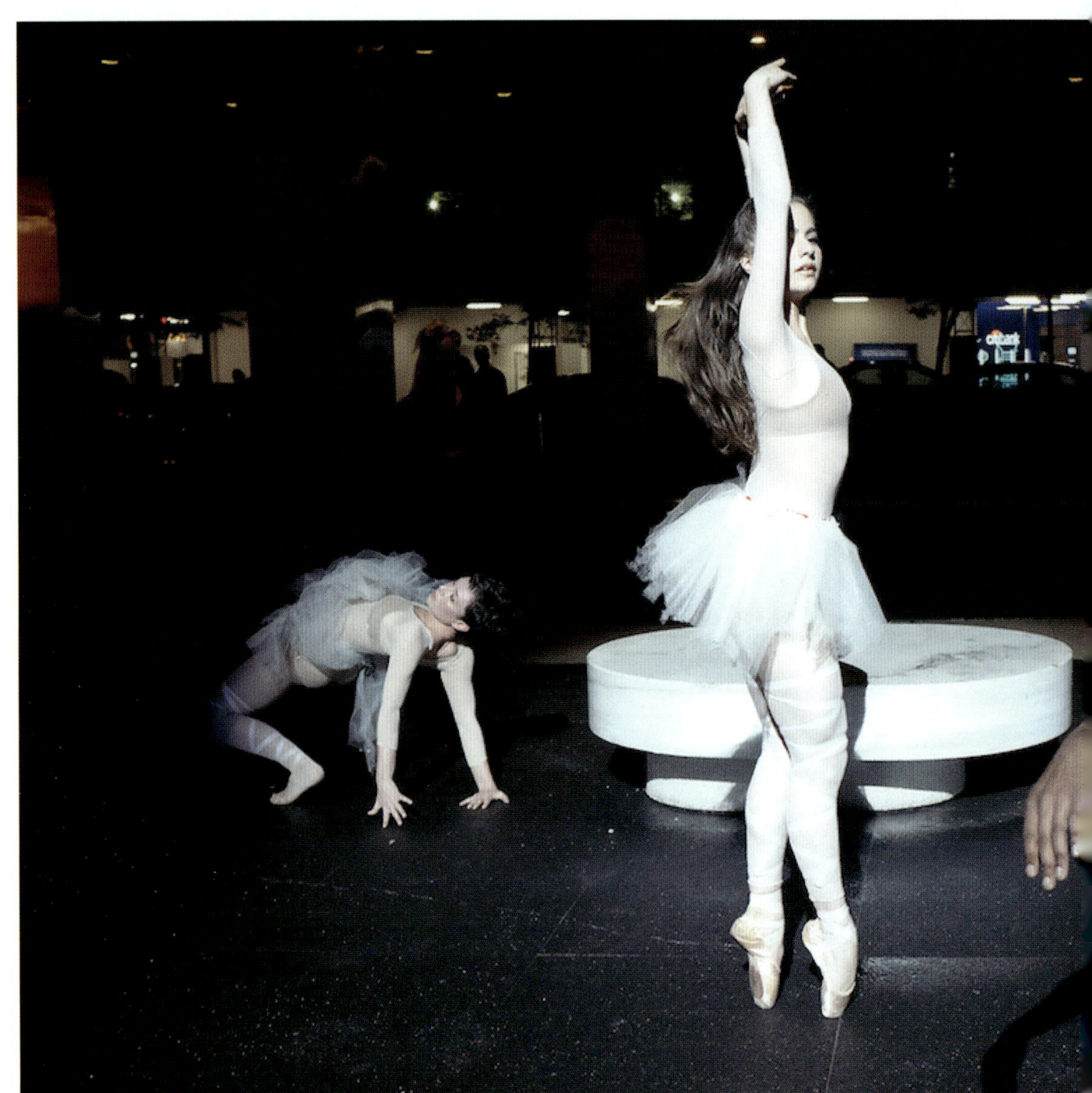

FlucT is the collaboration of Monica Mirabile and Sigrid Lauren, two American artists and choreographers, who often assemble a diverse cast of both trained and self-taught dancers from their Brooklyn artistic community to rowdy and visceral effects. Whether touring with the late avant-garde pop star SOPHIE or performing a "freak out" during Miami's art week, they manipulate modern ballet techniques and enact acrobatic feats, disrupted by human interferences or "glitches," to create an idiosyncratic vocabulary of gestures that feel both playful and distressed. *Upward Facing Control Table Tops*, their performance for "MIDTOWN," an exhibition of visual art and experimental design, filled the gutted areas of Lever House, an iconic modernist glass building in Midtown. The electrifying cast took complete control of the place, from its galleries and windows to its balcony and outdoor plaza.

A spotlight shone on a *Swan Lake* music box-like recital by ballerina Violetta Komyshan and Quentin Stuckey on the central courtyard, drawing hundreds of attendees and passersby into a circle around them. As Mirabile and Lauren joined in, they theatrically overcorrected the pair's moves and asserted themselves over the pas de deux. Suddenly, eighteen performers appeared, moving in unison across the three levels of the building with an athletic choreography of lifts, flips, and strikes before splitting up the dense crowds and sculpting out space to perform by firmly backing viewers up into the dead zones of the exhibition layout. With their exuberant spirit, the defiant group confronted head-on the grand architecture of the site and its style of intimidation and power.

JOB PISTON

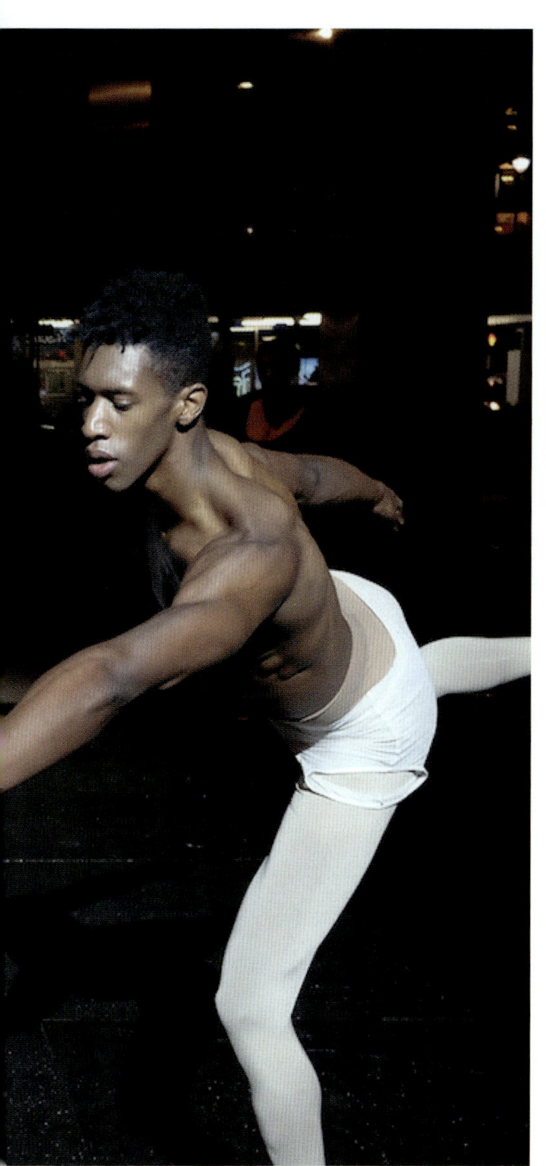

FlucT, *Upward Facing Control Table Tops*, 2017. Performance view.Lever House, New York.

PERFORMA 2016 GALA

Altman Building
November 1, 2016

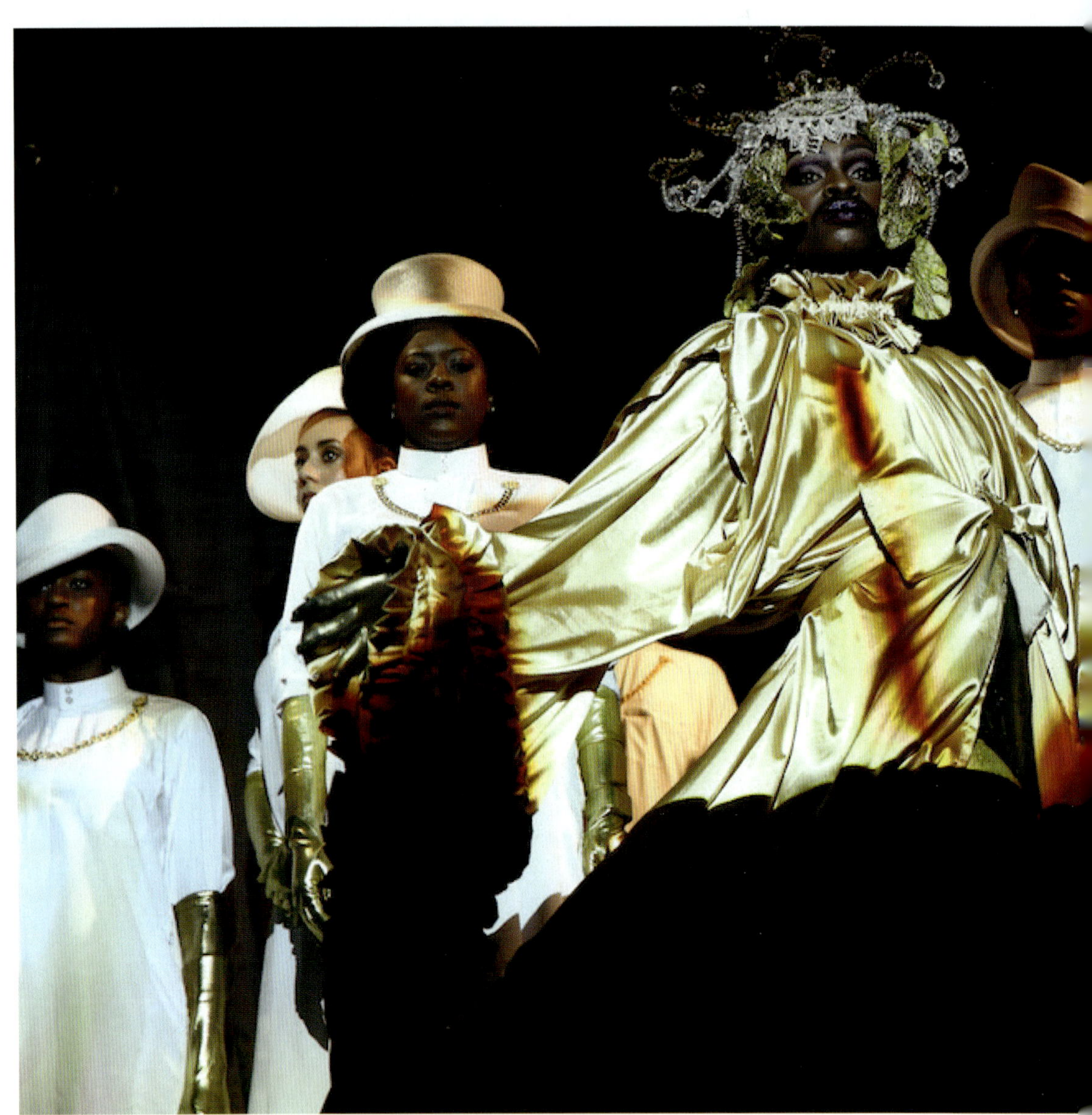

A dazzling evening of performance and South African culinary delights celebrated the renowned Nigerian-born curator and writer Okwui Enwezor, whose untimely death three years later saddened many in the art world and reverberated across the globe. Anchored in a tribute to South Africa with an homage to artist William Kentridge, the gathering had moving contributions from filmmaker Steve McQueen, art historian and artist Chika Okeke-Agulu, and artist Carrie Mae Weems, who read from Enwezor's stirring text "Middle Passage" (1990). The curator shifted centers and peripheries in the art world to spotlight art from Africa and its diaspora, championing a truly global perspective while strengthening focus on women, emerging artists, and interdisciplinary programming. In 1993, he founded *Nka: Journal of Contemporary African Art*; in 1997, he was the artistic director of the second—and last—Johannesburg Biennale; and in 2002, he was the first non-European curator to direct Kassel's Documenta. His groundbreaking postcolonial edition featured events in locations from Vienna and Berlin to New Delhi, Saint Lucia, and Lagos over the span of a year. South African artist Athi-Patra Ruga's Performa Gala Commission *Over the Rainbow*—a play on the term *Rainbow Nation*, coined by Archbishop Desmond Tutu for describing post-apartheid South Africa—invoked stereotypes of nationalist pageantry and optimism since apartheid ended there in 1994. Dressed in a resplendent golden satin gown inspired by Sergei Diaghilev's Ballet Russes, Ruga, playing the role of his alter ego Versatile Queen Ivy, and his choir referenced *The Wizard of Oz*, Xhosa culture, and traditions of drag while singing a take on "Nkosi sikelel' iAfrika," the country's national anthem, composed by Enoch Sontonga. The work critiqued continuing racial tensions and inequalities that have been "sugar-coated" and obscured by the propaganda of "rainbowism" in lieu of true and meaningful societal transformation while acknowledging historical influences and the nation's key cultural and musical movements, such as *kwaito* and *guz* music, Shangaan electro, *gqom*, and the participatory politics of *Umzabalazo* (Freedom Songs) from the apartheid era.

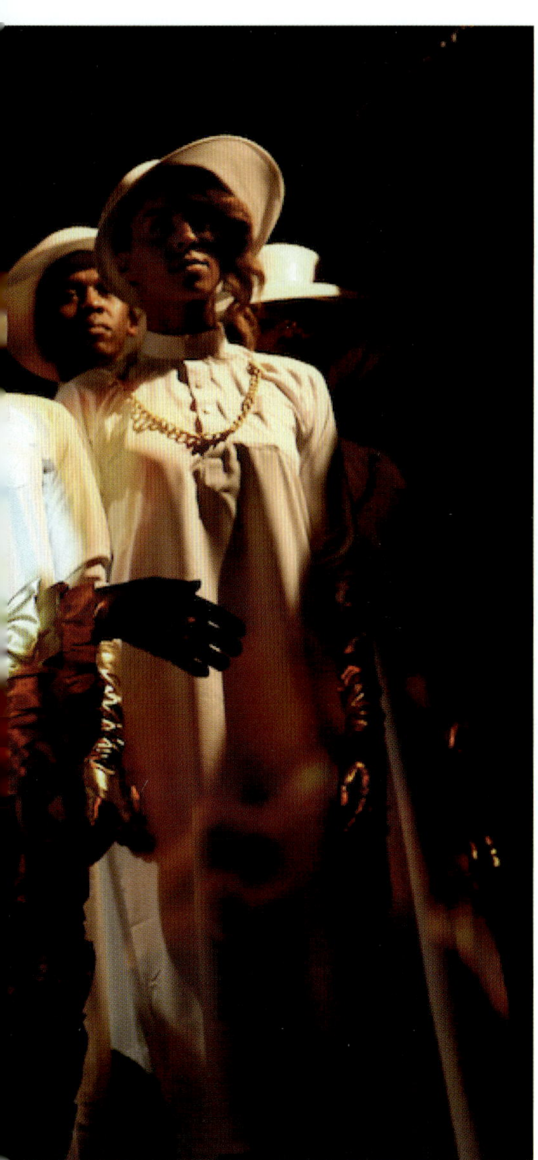

Athi-Patra Ruga, *Over the Rainbow*, 2016. Performance view.

PERFORMA 17 OPENING NIGHT

Harlem Parish
November 1, 2017

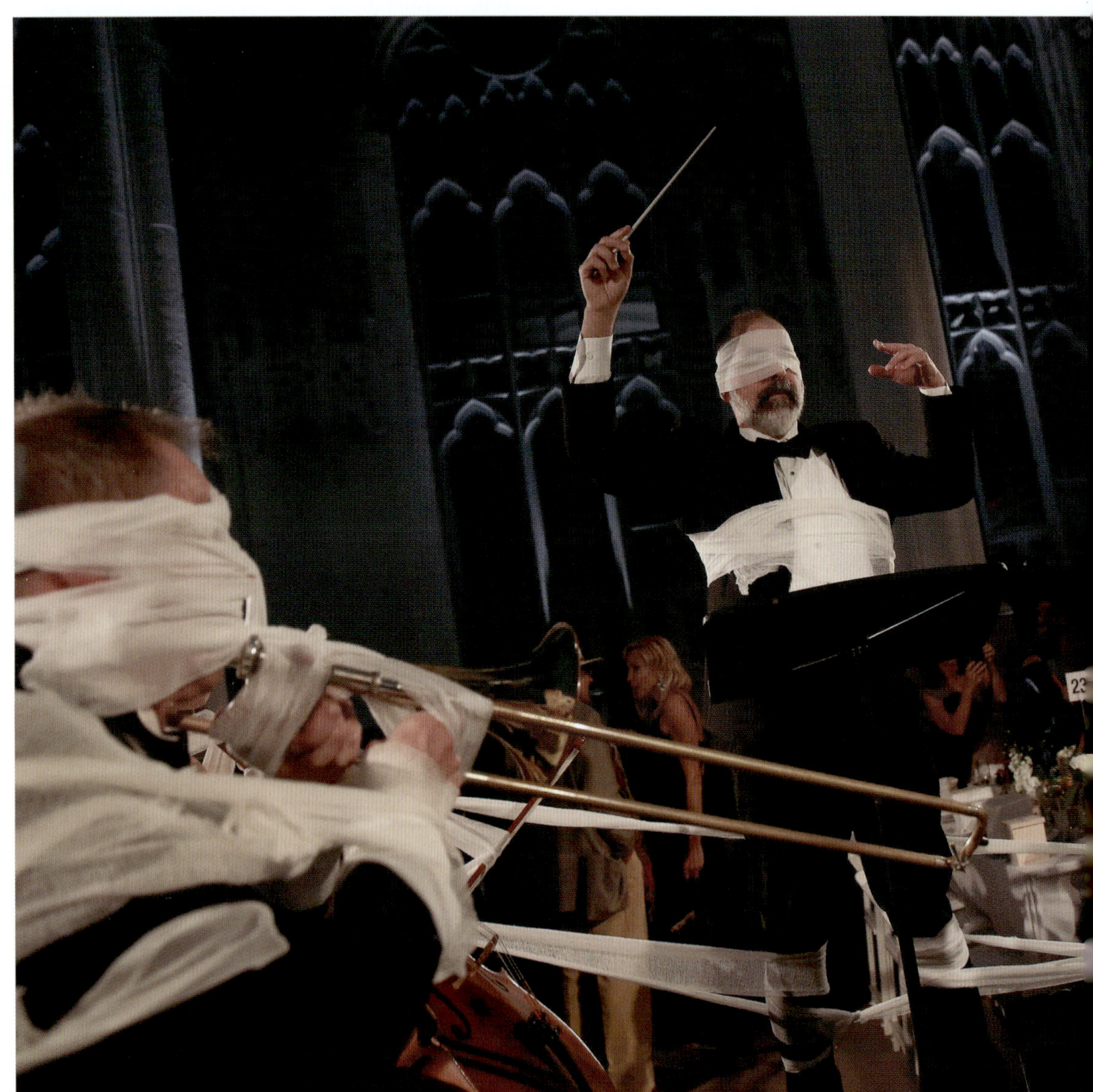

Ever the enigmatic and polymathic Fluxus artist, Yoko Ono emboldened generations of artists with her seminal early performances *Cut Piece* (1964) and *Bed In* (1969), with John Lennon.

The Performa 17 Opening Night Gala honored the singular Ono as well as Performa Board member and Chair of the South African Pavilion Committee Wendy Fisher, all under the biennial's historical anchor of Dada. Conceived as a "live retrospective" of Ono's oeuvre, the evening featured several of her iconic works, including *Touch Poem for Group of People* (1963), the instructions for which simply state, "Touch each other"; *Now or Never* (1971), performed by musician Lizzi Bougatsos with Brian DeGraw and Josh Diamond of the experimental band Gang Gang Dance; and *Lighting Piece* (1955), which involves lighting a match and watching it until it extinguishes, performed by choreographer-writer Will Rawls, in addition to installations, films, and iconic interactive artworks such as *Painting to Be Stepped On* (1960). Musician and visual artist Laurie Anderson paid tribute to Ono with an emotional speech and a rendition of the artist's "instruction painting" *Voice Piece for Soprano* (1961), which contains the directives "Scream. 1. against the wind 2. against the wall 3. against the sky." Conjuring all of the voices in the room, Anderson guided guests through the cathartic release of a thirty-second-long scream. "Put everything you've ever felt into this scream: All the rage, all the sadness in your life, all the ecstasy and all the love for this incredible artist, Yoko Ono," Anderson instructed, striking a gong before bringing the house down with screams of anger, anguish, fear, weariness, and everything in between.

Renowned chef Peter Hoffman conceived of dinner by drawing inspiration from the century-long legacy of Dada. Honoring the movement's radical energy, guests were directed to create their own "poem salad" with scissors and fresh vegetables in a tribute to poet Tristan Tzara's cut-up verses, followed by a "collage main course" after Berlin Dadaists Raoul Hausmann and George Grosz, and then a "floating" dessert in the manner of Hans Arp's amorphous compositions. The night ended with a rousing performance of John Lennon's "Imagine" (1971), arranged by composer Luciano Chessa and accompanied by the Ono Orchestra, led by South African jazz vocalist Vuyo (Vuyolwethu) Sotashe singing in both English and Zulu.

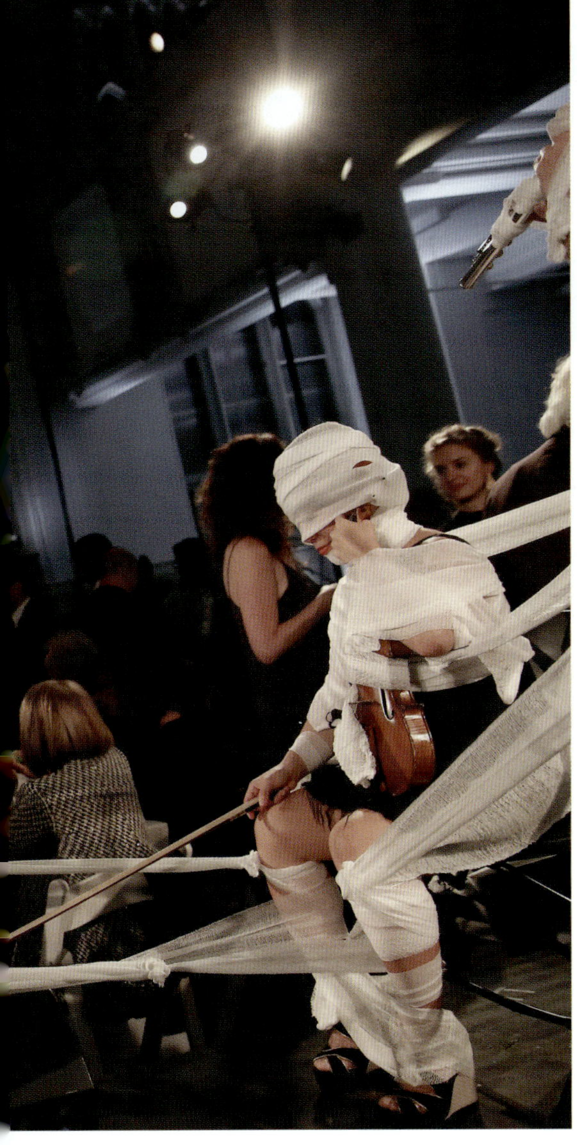

Yoko Ono, *Sky Piece to J.C.* (1965) directed by Luciano Chessa, 2017. Performance view.

PERFORMA 2018 GALA

SIR Stage 37
November 1, 2018

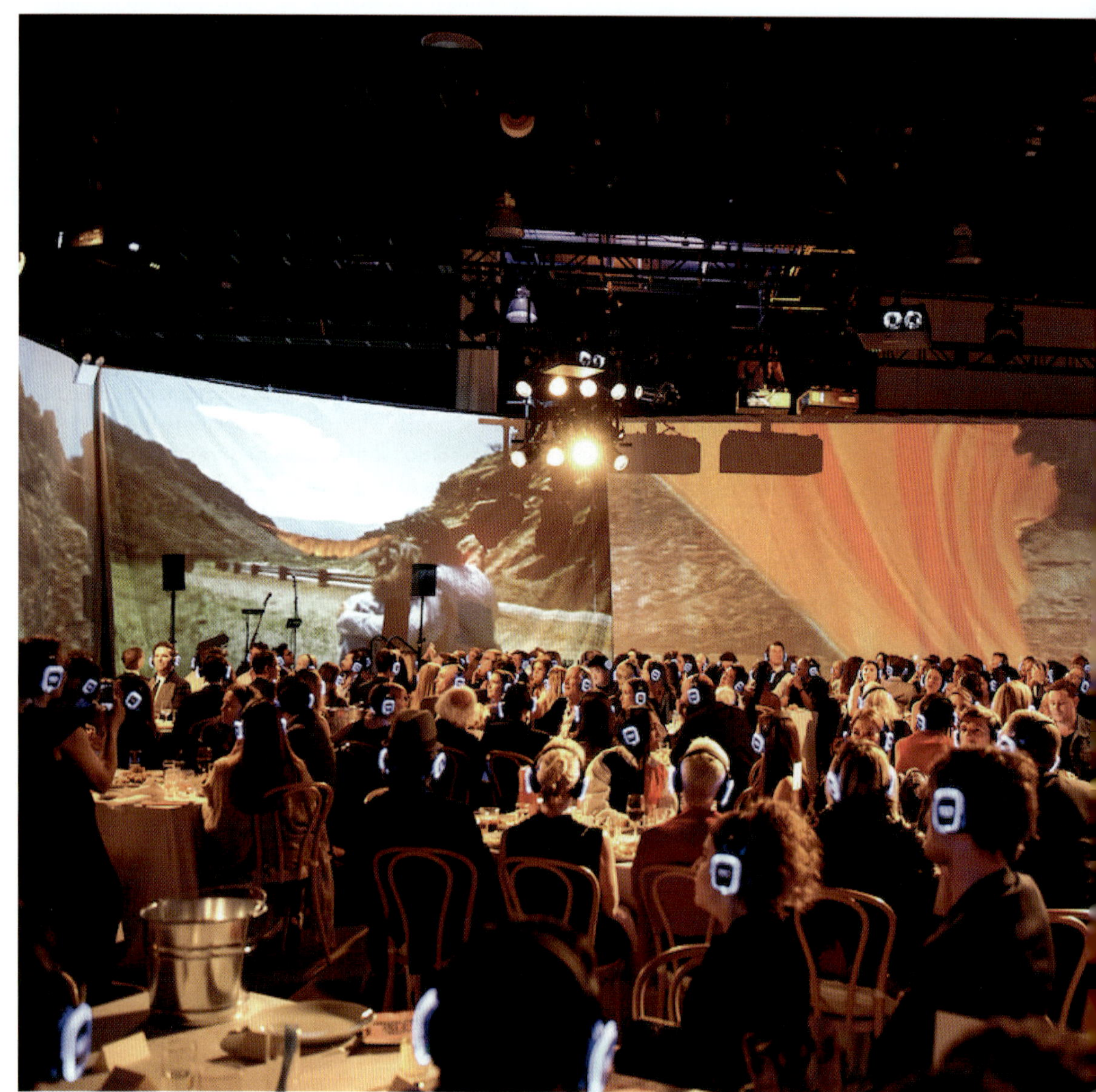

Performa fêted the wholly collaborative, everlasting, and incomparable career of artist duo and lifelong partners Christo (1935–2020) and Jeanne-Claude (1935–2009) with a night of immersive performance, installation, and film. Since meeting in Paris in 1958, the two went on to create massive-scale land and architectural works, tremendous undertakings that were gestures of their ingenuity and resolve: encircling whole islands in bubble gum pink (*Surrounded Islands* (1980–83) in Biscayne Bay, Miami), enrobing Paris's oldest bridge in Grecian folds for *The Pont Neuf Wrapped* (1975–85), or sending over 7,000 mauve, red, and blue barrels stacked in the shape of a mastaba tomb to float on the Serpentine lake (2016–18) in London's Hyde Park. Their project *The Gates* (2005) in New York's Central Park—consisting of 7,503 tangerine-saffron-colored steel and vinyl curtain structures lining the park's pathways—was twenty-six years in the making, solidifying the legacy of Christo and Jeanne-Claude as visionaries beyond the art world. The pair's work made the spaces of everyday life sublime.

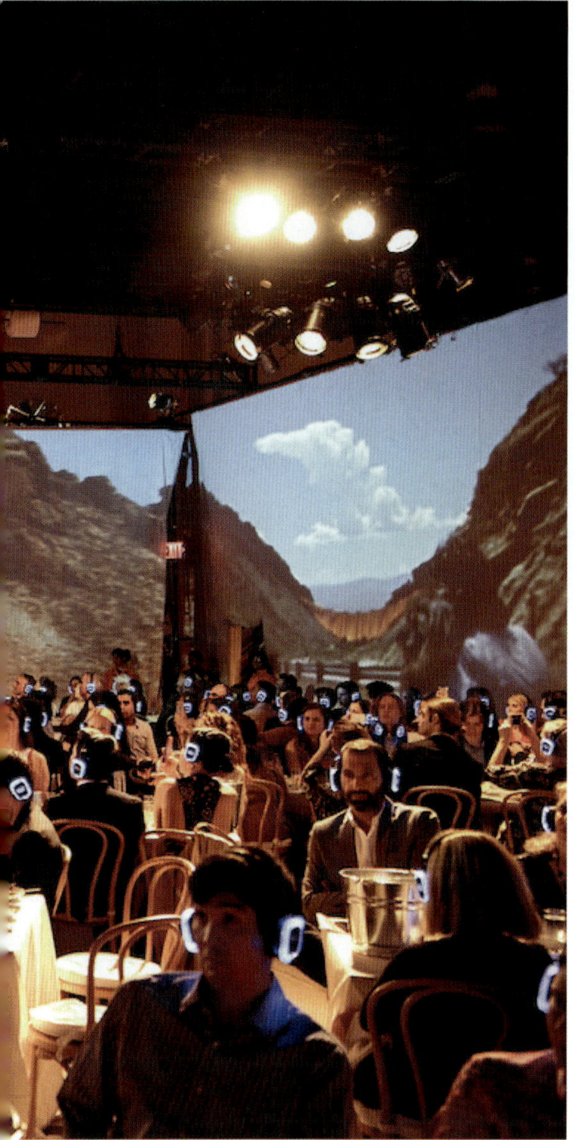

LEIMAY—artistic duo Ximena Garnica and Shige Moriya—carried out a series of choreographed actions during cocktail hour that evening: Performers outfitted in construction-zone orange coveralls and safety harnesses scaled various parts of the venue, hanging from railings and climbing in the same way a worker might install one of Christo and Jeanne-Claude's wrappings. Guests dined onstage surrounded by a set of lofty scaffolding bound in off-white canvas. Diners put on headsets and watched footage by filmmakers Albert and David Maysles that was projected onto the fabric screens—documentary scenes from the making of Christo and Jeanne-Claude's various works. Taiko drummer Kaoru Watanabe and experimental pop violinist and vocalist Sudan Archives performed sets interspersed throughout the evening, with Watanabe drumming from platforms on scaffolding high above dining tables. Toward the end of the night, buckets of colorful confetti rained down on attendees, thousands of little slips of paper each marked with the name of all the individuals who have worked with Christo and Jeanne-Claude on their monumental feats over more than six decades. Revelers departed for the afterparty, hosted by artist Marilyn Minter and DJ Venus X at the Freehand hotel in Gramercy Park, leaving with commemorative bone china plates designed by food artist Antoni Miralda.

Christo & Jeanne-Claude, *Valley Curtain*, Rifle Canyon, Colorado, 1972.

PERFORMA 19 OPENING NIGHT

SIR Stage 37
November 1, 2019

A century after the opening of the radical Bauhaus school, Performa honored two long-standing friends, collaborators, and supporters: visual artist and filmmaker Rashid Johnson and trailblazing philanthropist Dasha Zhukova. A Performa 13 Commission artist, Johnson's first live performance was his exceptional *Dutchman*, a reimagining of Amiri Baraka's Obie Award-winning theatrical play (1964) staged in the Russian and Turkish Baths on 10th Street in the East Village. This directorial debut inspired his interest in film, leading to the artist's critically acclaimed, feature-length adaptation of

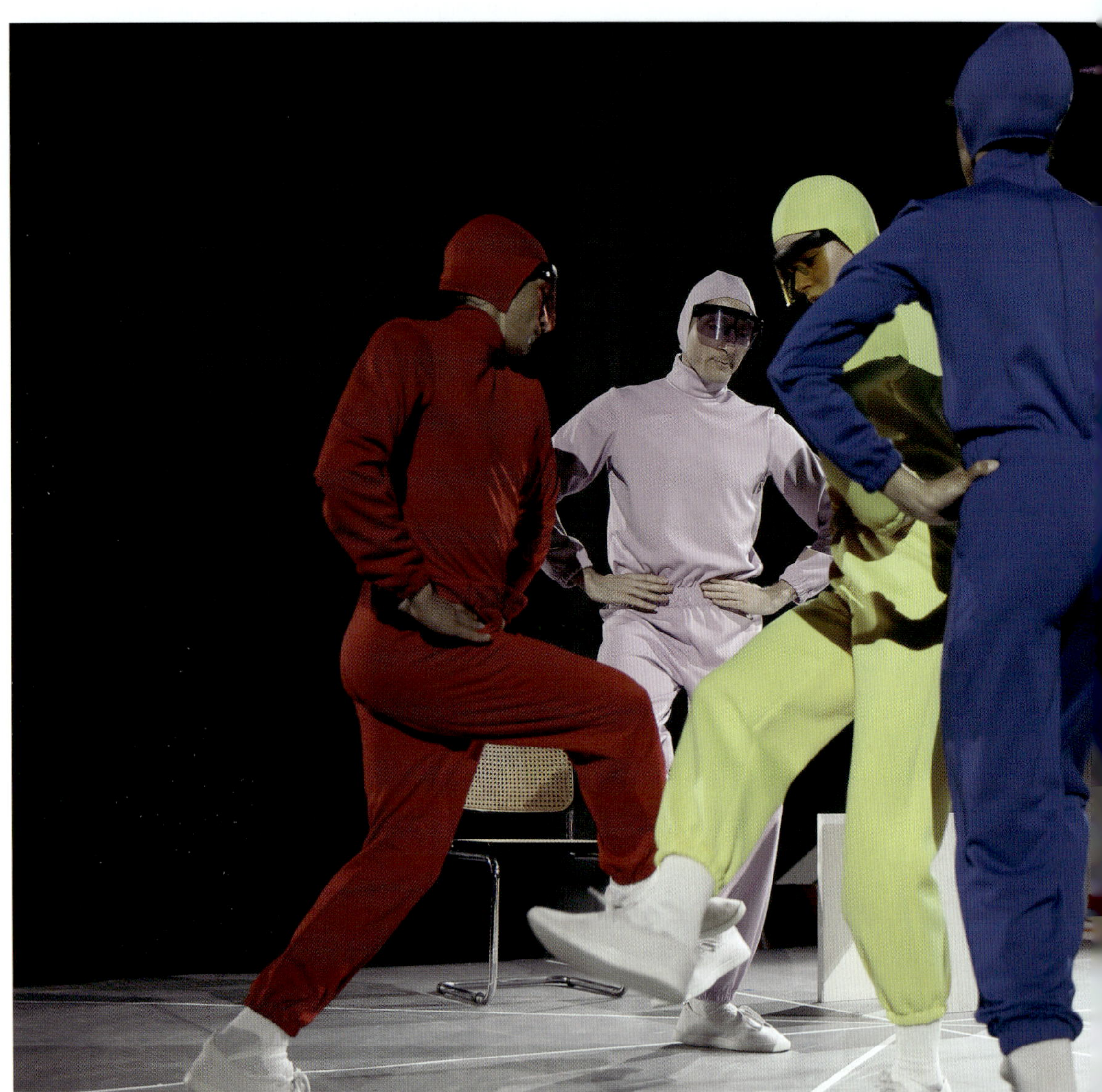

Richard Wright's novel *Native Son* (1940) in 2019. As Vice Chair of Performa's Board since 2014, Johnson has also brought his vital voice, energy, and generosity to the organization. Zhukova is a longtime supporter of Performa's exhibition and publication projects—she brought "100 Years: A History of Performance Art," an exhibition curated by RoseLee Goldberg with MoMA PS1 Director Klaus Biesenbach, to the Garage Museum of Contemporary Art in Moscow in 2010 and collaborated on the Performa 11 exhibition "33 Fragments of Russian Performance."

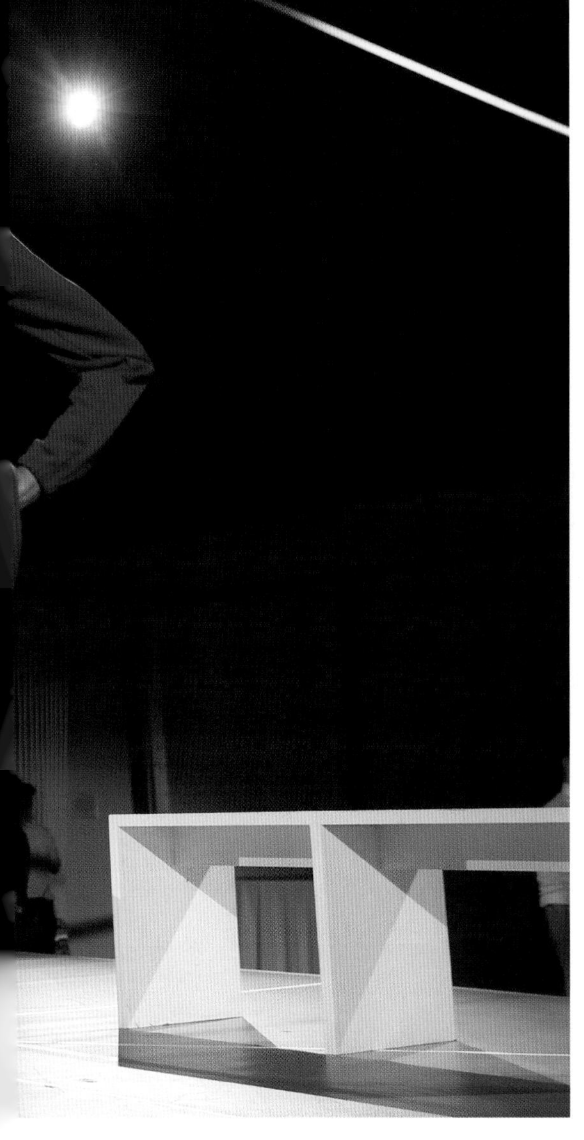

Emily Coates,
Schlemmer Loops, 2019.
Performance view.

Named the "Performa 19 Workshop," the Gala celebrated Bauhaus—the legendary institution that shaped art education across the globe, as well as the first interdisciplinary art school to hold performance within its curriculum—and the legacy of Bauhaus Master and performance pioneer Oskar Schlemmer. The evening's guests were cast as students, dressed in color-blocked primary colors evocative of the groundbreaking German school's predilection for bright hues, and were treated to classroom activities including drawing lessons led by performer and writer Morgan Bassichis and taking turns working on a giant loom that recalled the Bauhaus's iconic weaving workshop. Choreographer Emily Coates's three-part performance *Schlemmer Loops: 1, 2, 3*, with dancers Megan Wright, Brittany Engel-Adams, Miguel Anaya, and Reid Bartelme, filtered the movement and design elements of three of Schlemmer's dances through contemporary bodies and imaginations. Wearing brightly colored jumpsuits, performers enacted gestures that stemmed from Schlemmer's world: social and sculptural, theatrical and abstract, dark and light. A music program led by artist Thuthuka Sibisi complemented these choreographed movements, featuring the sounds of trumpeter Lesedi Ntsane, bassist and composer Benjamin Jephta, saxophonist and composer Immanuel Wilkins, and the NYC-based instrumental duo Nelson Patton.

Playing with food was encouraged at the dinner table: The second course consisted of plate decorating and sculpture, with brightly colored purée "paints" of red raspberry and cranberry gastrique, yellow carrot curry, green basil pistou, blue spirulina, black activated charcoal, and white parmesan cream. The celebration carried on as a giant Baked Alaska was served for dessert, accompanied by DJ Ariel Zetina spinning tracks into the night.

PERFORMA TELETHON

Pace Live
November 18, 2020

Asked, in an interview with the *Montreal Gazette*, what he would offer to Saint Peter to be let into the gates of heaven, Nam June Paik replied: "I will tell him that I made a show called *Good Morning, Mr. Orwell* and it was transmitted on New Year's Day, 1984, simultaneously on two channels from New York, San Francisco, and Paris and received simultaneously in five countries and that it has been seen by some 25 million people. I'll say that's my direct contribution to human survival and he'll let me in."[1] Paik, who first picked up a Sony portable camera in 1965 and turned video into an artistic medium, then went on to revolutionize television and its technology. It was on January 1, 1984 that he launched the first international satellite installation—an exuberant and frantic hourlong program filled with the time's most resolutely experimental artists and sensibilities.

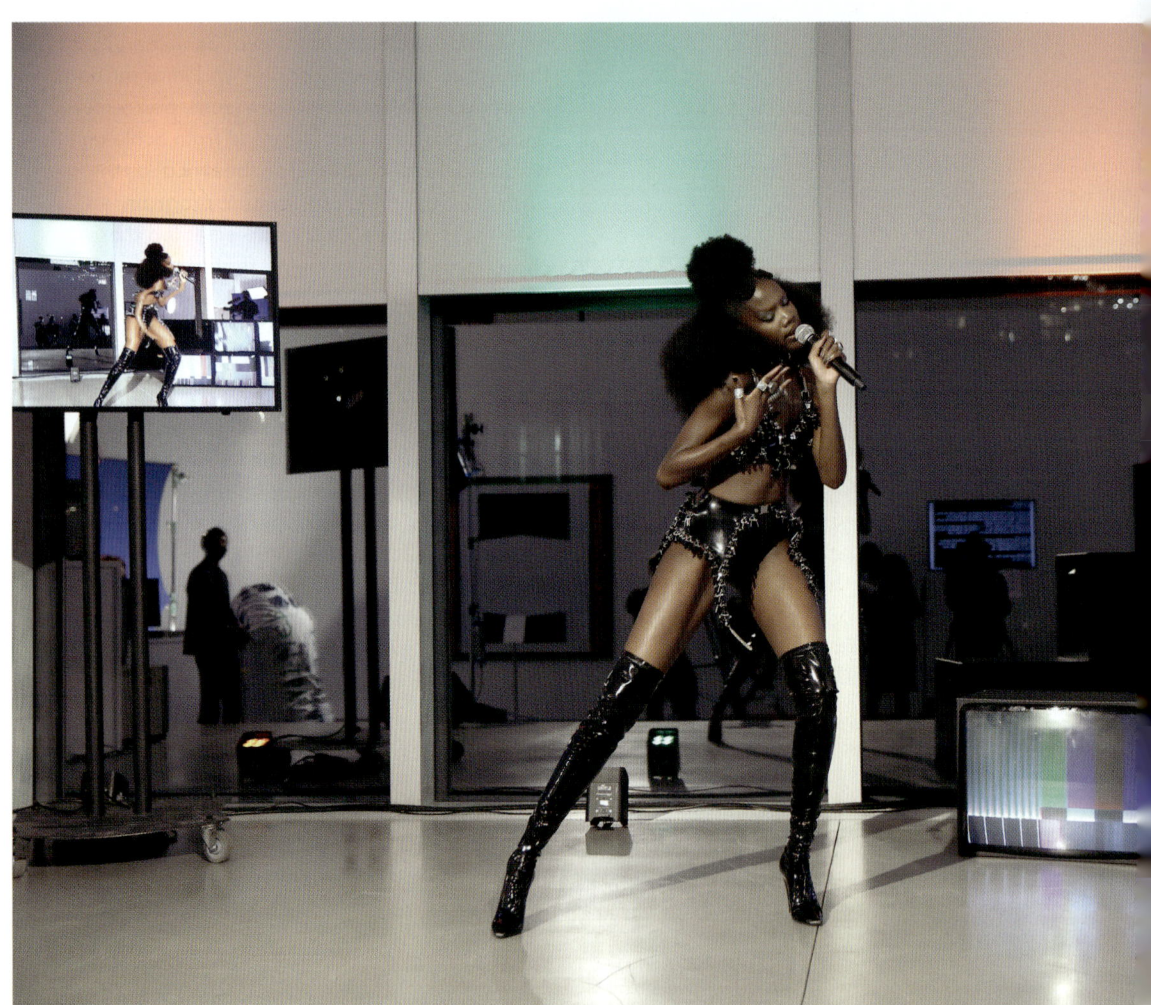

Screens, transmitters, and broadcasting were his instruments for democratic revolution.

The show oscillated between ubiquitous gallery space, concert venue, stage, and disco created from an iconic, art-star cast of Paik's peers and mentors. Musicians Laurie Anderson and Peter Gabriel, dressed in cream-colored suits and singing "Excellent Birds," floated around dreamy electronic clouds. Merce Cunningham danced against a backdrop projection of Argentine composer Ástor Piazzolla playing the bandoneon for him, with filmmaker Charles Atlas intervening in the production to delay and manipulate pixels of the choreographer's movements. There were blues-tinged yodels from the Texas plains, fireworks over the Paris cityscape, and animated cubes and geometric forms colliding and spilling through New York's skyline. Charlotte Moorman, a radical cellist and frequent collaborator, slapped and clawed the artist's three-television cello. In the segment "Cavalcade of Intellectuals," two former *Saturday Night Live* cast members, Leslie Fuller and Mitchell Kriegman, had a lovers' quarrel amidst a philosophical forum. Entertainment ricocheted from popular culture, the esoteric practices of Paik's avant-garde circle—many of them undoubtedly new to the millions of at-home viewers—and pure visual overload.

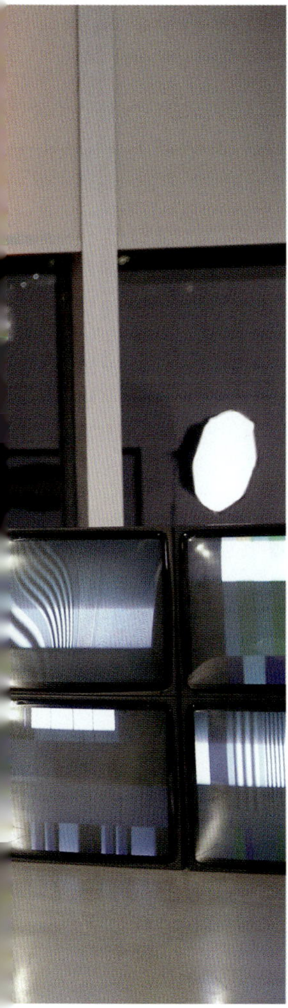

Oyinda at the Performa Telethon, 2020. Performance view.

1
"Video art's here for keeps, says pathfinder Paik" *Montreal Gazette* (October 13, 1984): B-8.

2
Douglas C. McGill, "ART PEOPLE," *The New York Times*, October 3, 1986.

Nearly four decades after *Good Morning, Mr. Orwell*'s bizarre, glitchy, limitless utopia, Performa, in collaboration with the artist-run production house E.S.P. TV, presented its own celebration of performance dedicated to the late artist. The organization's fifteenth-anniversary telethon presented an eight-hour-long amalgamation of live action, video, QVC-style home shopping, musical productions, and documentation from the biennial's archives. The Telethon aired from a makeshift TV studio set up at Pace gallery in Manhattan's Chelsea neighborhood, and featured interviews, call-ins, and clips from around the world. The evening gestured toward Paik's revelatory promise for the screen and the renewed importance of his humanist vision during the COVID-19 pandemic. "It's all your life in one," the artist said in 1986. "Our life is half natural and half technological. Half-and-half is good. You cannot deny that high-tech is progress. We need it for jobs. Yet if you make only high-tech, you make war. So, we must have a strong human element to keep modesty and natural life."[2] Ultimately, Paik understood TV as a tool for personal connection and creation.

If the title conjured the hyper-networked dystopia of George Orwell's novel *Nineteen Eighty-Four*, Paik flipped the switch, relishing in the liberation and immediacy of interfacing via screens. The 1949 book offered a searing vision of a totalitarian society where "telescreens" act as tools for surveillance, recording, and subjugation; the book's recurrent maxim is "Big Brother is watching you." The artist admitted that he had never even read the author's prophecy, but still saw the author's critique of the dangers of technological spread as only "half-true." Yes, Paik agreed, the television controls, represses, and structures our time, but it also forges heretofore impossible collaborations and connections every day. Beamed across the globe, *Good Morning, Mr. Orwell* shot 22,000 miles into space to the Bright Star satellite and returned it back to Earth via the TV set.

His program poked at the artifice of the device's façade, revealing it as both a high-tech glory and a thoroughly human instrument where the act of producing television became a performance in itself. The program was co-produced by New York's WNET/Channel 13 and Paris's FR3, which set up at the Centre Pompidou and relayed to partners in Seoul, San Francisco, Berlin, and other major cities. It mixed live and taped footage, alternating moments of play, stretches of quiet, and spontaneity as well as exposing the seams of its own production.

Performa's own evening-length marathon reveled in the unpredictable, kinetic, and joyful, recalling the 1984 psychedelic variety show. An international slate of artists, many of them past biennial participants, shared new commissions, archival videos, and personal messages. Yvonne Rainer reimagined her infamous *Trio A with Flags* fifty years after its Judson Church premiere, projecting the original documentation behind new performers. In a nod to Atlas and Cunningham's collaboration, Jacolby Satterwhite and Cunningham-trained dancer Cori Kresge staged a studio work in real time, the two moving against a backdrop of Satterwhite's elaborate digital utopias with the artist voguing and dancing in an empty nightclub. Standing on Iceland's sublime terrain, dressed in a suit and tie, Ragnar Kjartansson crooned The Louvin Brothers' "When I Stop Dreaming." There were videos from Paik and Lynda Benglis and dispatches from Tamy Ben-Tor, Sanford Biggers, and Athi-Patra Ruga. In a turn toward the material, viewers could buy Performa-commissioned artist editions by Barbara Kruger, Kia LaBeija, Cindy Sherman, and others, showcased by the evening's hostess, Angela di Carlo. Emceed by musician Nick Hallett, the fundraiser was Performa's first global broadcast, turning to the screen to relay, enliven, and produce performance.

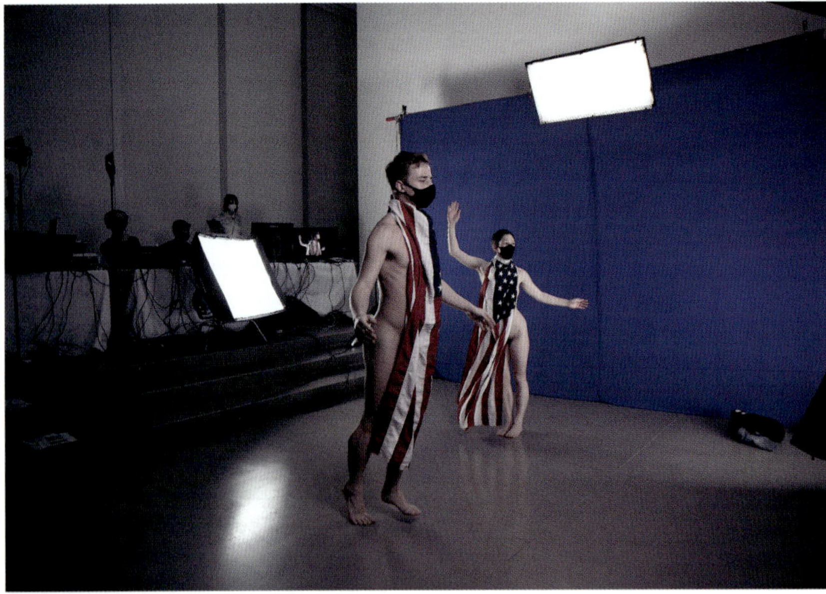

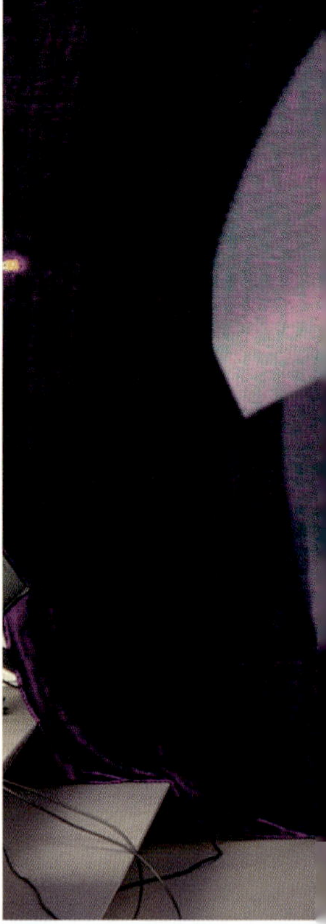

Yvonne Rainer, *Trio A with Flags*, 1970, performed by Brittany Bailey and Nick Sciscione. Performance view.

Jacolby Satterwhite with Cori Kresge, *Moments of Silence*, 2020. Broadcast still.

In *Good Morning, Mr. Orwell*, Laurie Anderson, with a modulated voice and hair styled like bolts of static electricity, tells a fantastical story of sitting next to a teenage girl before boarding a plane: "She was speaking an entirely different language: *Computerese*, a kind of high-tech lingo. Everything was circuitry, electronics, switching." Anderson, who also appeared as an interlocutor for Performa's telethon, signals not only the total newness of the twenty-first century's digitized, screen-filled era, but its potential for fundamentally new expressions of human experience. Paik's purist electronic idealism has not come to pass—he imagined that the internet would democratize the globe—but his belief in technology's ability to radically connect remains an essential aim of the medium. In 2020, as in 1984, what he and Performa indicated spoke truth: Provided that we respect Paik's call for strong "human" inputs, technology may offer a means for crossing boundaries, borders, and oceans.

QUINN SCHOEN

With performances, appearances, and contributions by Derrick Adams & Dave Guy, Korakrit Arunanondchai, Defne Ayas, Rosa Barba, Tamy Ben-Tor, Cecilia Bengolea, Jérôme Bel feat. Elisabeth Schwartz & Catherine Gallant, Omar Berrada, Sanford Biggers, Marco Brambilla, Ebony Brown, Angela di Carlo, Tommy Cash, Richard Chang, Luciano Chessa, Marching Cobras, Pauline Curnier Jardin, Keren Cytter, Torkwase Dyson, Marcel Dzama, E.S.P. TV, Elmgreen & Dragset, Omer Fast, Ryan Gander, Agatha Gothe-Snape, Ronald Guttman, David Hallberg, Barbara Hoffman, Madeline Hollander, C.T Jasper and Joanna Malinowska, Jesper Just, Kai Arts Center, Glenn Kaino, Flo Kasearu, William Kentridge, Jon Kessler, Barbara Kruger, Ragnar Kjartansson, Kia LaBeija, Michèle Lamy + Katerina Jebb, Lang Lang, Kris Lemsalu, Kalup Linzy, Éva Mag, Liz Magic Laser, Kyp Malone, Jason Moran, Shirin Neshat, Kelly Nipper, Laura Ortman, Oyinda, Paul Pfeiffer, Yvonne Rainer feat. Brittany Bailey & Nick Sciscione, Jennifer Rubell, Athi-Patra Ruga, Jamilah Sabur, Roya Sachs, Jacolby Satterwhite feat. Cori Kresge, Cindy Sherman, Laurie Simmons x David Bers Architects, Alexander Singh, Emily Sundblad & Marc Razo, Jey Van-Sharp, Ian Vanek, Francesco Vezzoli, Rufus Wainwright, Hank Willis Thomas, Chloe Wise, Tori Wrånes, Samson Young & The Chinese University of Hong Kong Chorus, and Yu Cheng-Ta.

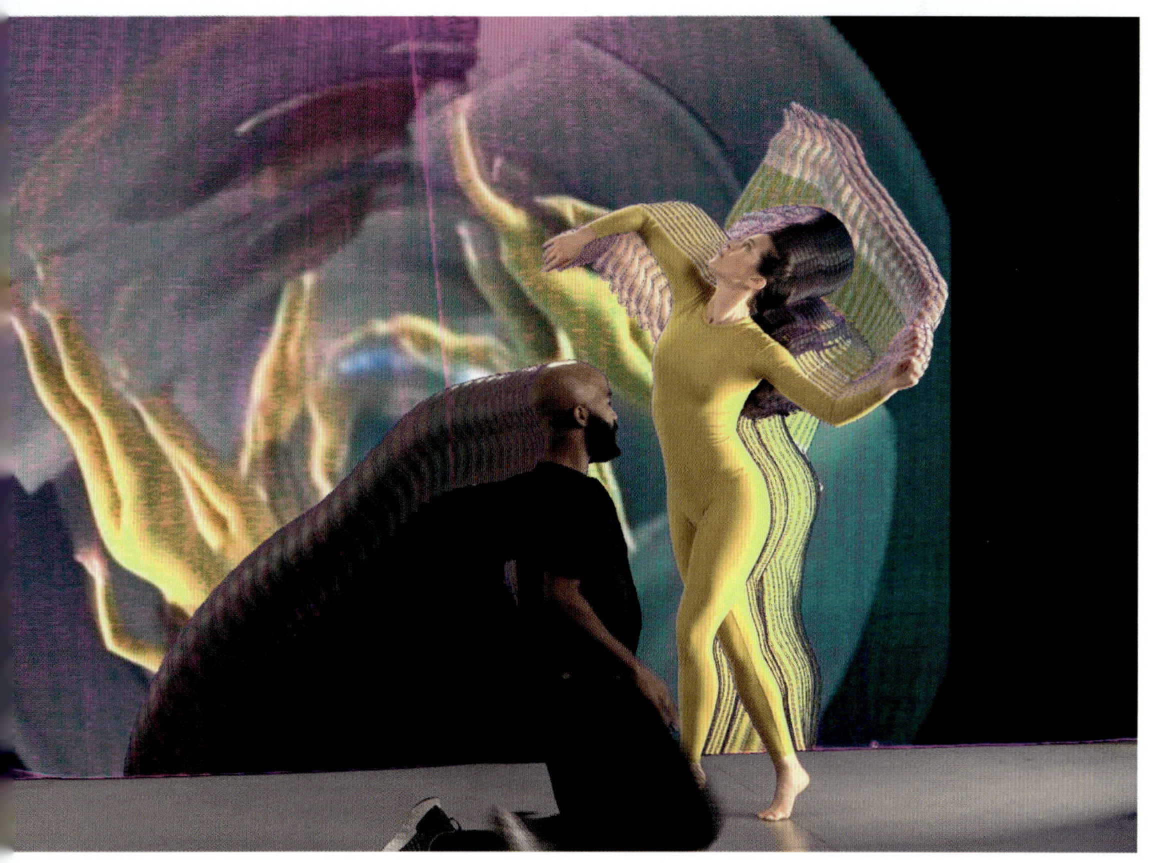

NOT FOR SALE

NOT FOR SALE

RoseLee Goldberg launched her plans for the inaugural Performa Biennial that would open on November 3, 2005, with a series of panels, ironically titled *Not for Sale*, presented in the spring of 2004 at New York University's Steinhardt School of Culture, Education, and Human Development, where Goldberg has taught since the late 1980s. Intentionally provocative, the title alluded to the exponential increase in corporate and market forces driving art, with supersized galleries in Chelsea and art fairs becoming a major social and financial force on the international art calendar. Concentrating on performance that could not be bought and sold and its significance in twentieth-century art history, these talks returned the focus to the work of artists themselves. They gathered writers, curators, and artists in fast-paced presentations to consider the live medium and its influence in the art-world ecosystem. The standing room-only crowd that attended the inaugural event, on April 19, 2004, to listen to Joan Jonas and curators Robert Storr, Chrissie Iles, and Hans Ulrich Obrist were testament to the sense amongst many that it was time to turn off conversations about record sales figures or expansive building programs and instead consider pressing art ideas and the times that shape them. The November 18 panel had artists Marina Abramović and Tania Bruguera and curators Klaus Ottmann and Debra Singer; a roundtable on the role of sound in new media assembled artist and musician Christian Marclay, philosopher Christoph Cox, sound artist Ron Kuivila, and theater director Elizabeth LeCompte in the spring of 2005. The audience for the series grew so quickly that when the first cycle of *Not for Sale* conversations concluded during Performa 05—with curators and writers Anthony Huberman, Margo Jefferson, Cay Sophie Rabinowitz, John Rockwell, Katy Siegel, Bennett Simpson, Catherine Wood, and Linda Yablonsky weighing in on writing about performance—a much larger venue was secured to accommodate the crowd.

Following the first Biennial, regular *Not for Sale* programs would become key markers of critical conversations, not only about performance, but also about contemporary art and the political, economic, and aesthetic concerns that drive them. At its heart were the very questions that animated the organization's regular internal curatorial meetings, to which colleagues from other institutions were also frequently invited. The organization's discursive engagements taking place both during and between biennials triggered a wide renewal of public interest in performance and led to museums creating departments and exhibitions dedicated to the artform. It also reflected on its own phenomenon with the panel "Forever Radical?," featuring curator Laura Hoptman, cultural critic Greil

Boris Charmatz, *Musée de la Danse: Expo Zéro* at the Performa 11 Hub, 2011. Performance view.

Marcus, and artists Adam Pendleton and Emily Sundblad on April 12, 2007. The group discussed whether—and how—performance could maintain its edge while becoming more and more present in commercial art galleries and fairs. "It's History Now," with art historian Alexander Alberro, art conservator Glenn Wharton, curators Chrissie Iles and Eungie Joo, and artists Martha Rosler and Adam Pendleton, looked at live art in museums (March 24, 2010). In just a couple of years, through its new productions and robust educational platforms, Performa had reshaped the discourse around performance—long considered to be on the periphery of art making—by showing how the ephemeral practice was in fact taking center stage in our hybridized and media-centered visual culture.

From the start, Performa's pedagogical offerings were lively events guided by the ethos of learning by doing. For instance, with *Dance and Conceptual Art in the Visual Arts (2007)*, a daylong seminar at Judson Memorial Church on November 17, 2007, choreographer Xavier Le Roy, artist Kelly Nipper, dancer taisha paggett, and scholar and theorist André Lepecki reflected on the increased presence of dance in museums and art centers. While the day was structured around a program of presentations and panels, it also left room for physical activities. The morning began with a warm-up session of exercises drawn from the lineage of dance (from ballet positions to Judson-style walking, standing, and sitting); later, an informal lunchtime workshop taught a twenty-minute-long excerpt of choreography from Trisha Brown's iconic 1971 *Accumulation*.

Performa 11 was headquartered in the former St. Patrick's Old Cathedral School on Prince Street in Lower Manhattan. For three weeks, beyond a packed agenda of new productions at sites across several boroughs, the Biennial made

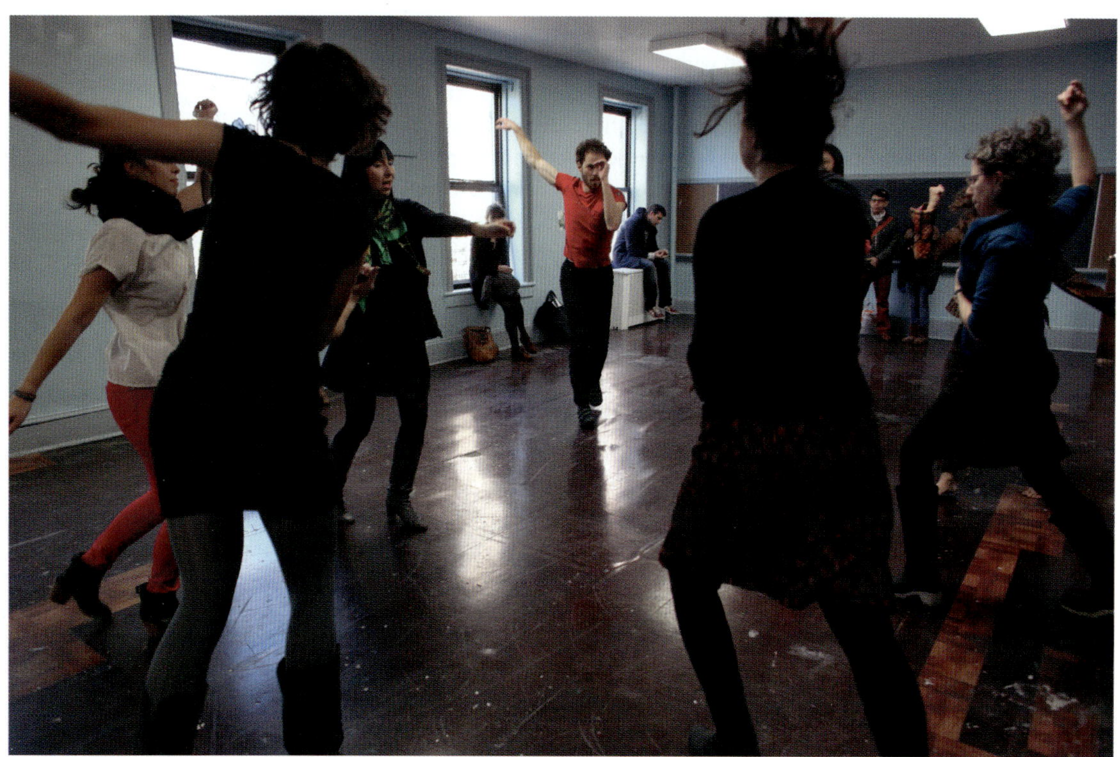

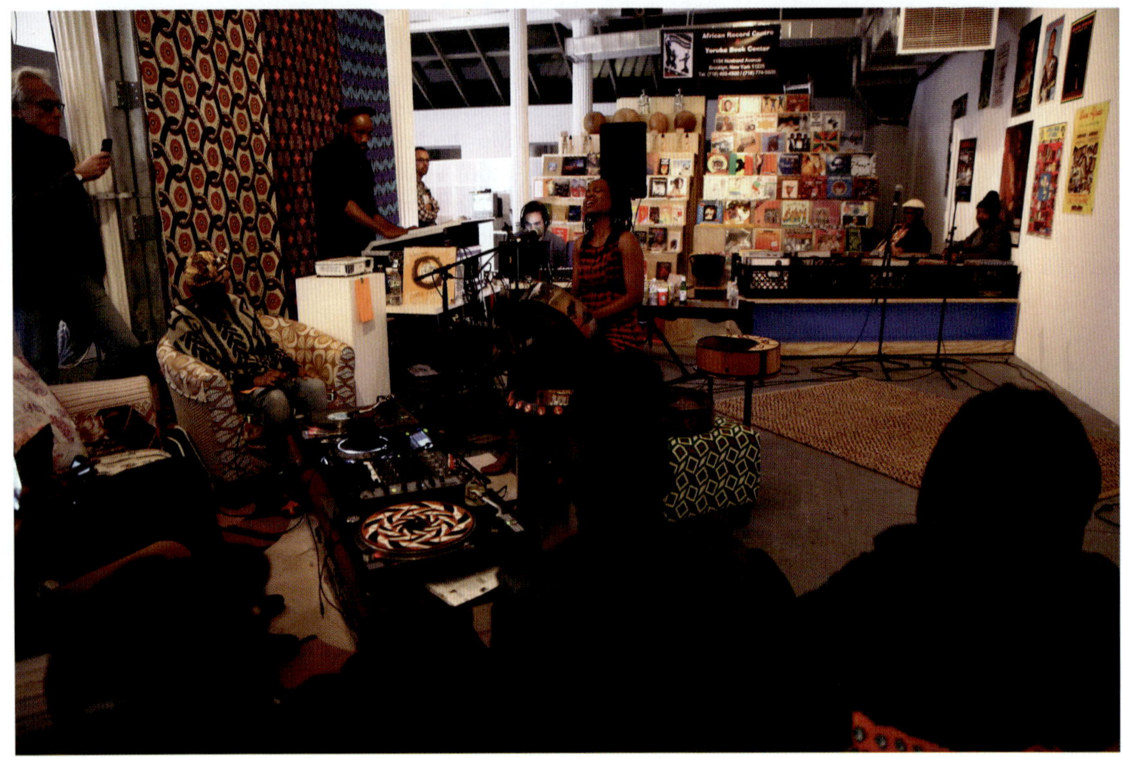

the most of its temporary Hub location with activities in the empty classrooms, including more than twenty-five classes led by artists, curators, and writers; some also staged live interventions and opened exhibitions onsite. Choreographer Boris Charmatz's *Musée de la Danse: Expo Zéro* offered impromptu workshops to visitors across five classrooms in one of the largest programs. On the top floor, the Hub featured "33 Fragments of Russian Performance," an exhibition of archives, photographs, and videos documenting Russian live art since the historical avant-garde of the 1920s. With its busy schedule of talks, masterclasses, seminars, and workshops, the organization's education initiatives were consolidated and formalized under the banner of the Performa Institute.

Since 2011, the Institute has operated as a year-round physical and virtual think tank that unites the organization's presentations, symposiums, and online and print publications, continuing to inform and expand with each biennial. *Portrait of the Artist*, for example, focuses on a seminal figure's body of work in the context of performance and has featured Lorraine O'Grady (April 2012) and Carrie Mae Weems (October 2015). In February of 2013, "Get Ready for the Marvelous," a two-day symposium exploring Surrealism in the African diaspora with voices from Dakar, Fort-de-France, and Havana to Johannesburg, New York, Paris, and Port-au-Prince, launched the planning for Performa 13's historical anchor of Surrealism.

In addition to the more than twenty artist- and curator-led classes at the Performa Hub throughout Performa 13, the Institute, under Performa Curator Adrienne Edwards's direction, offered short-term residencies and showcased its

Tanyaradzwa Tawengwa performing during the Chimurenga Library's Pan African Space Station radio broadcast at the Performa 15 Hub, 2015. Performance view.

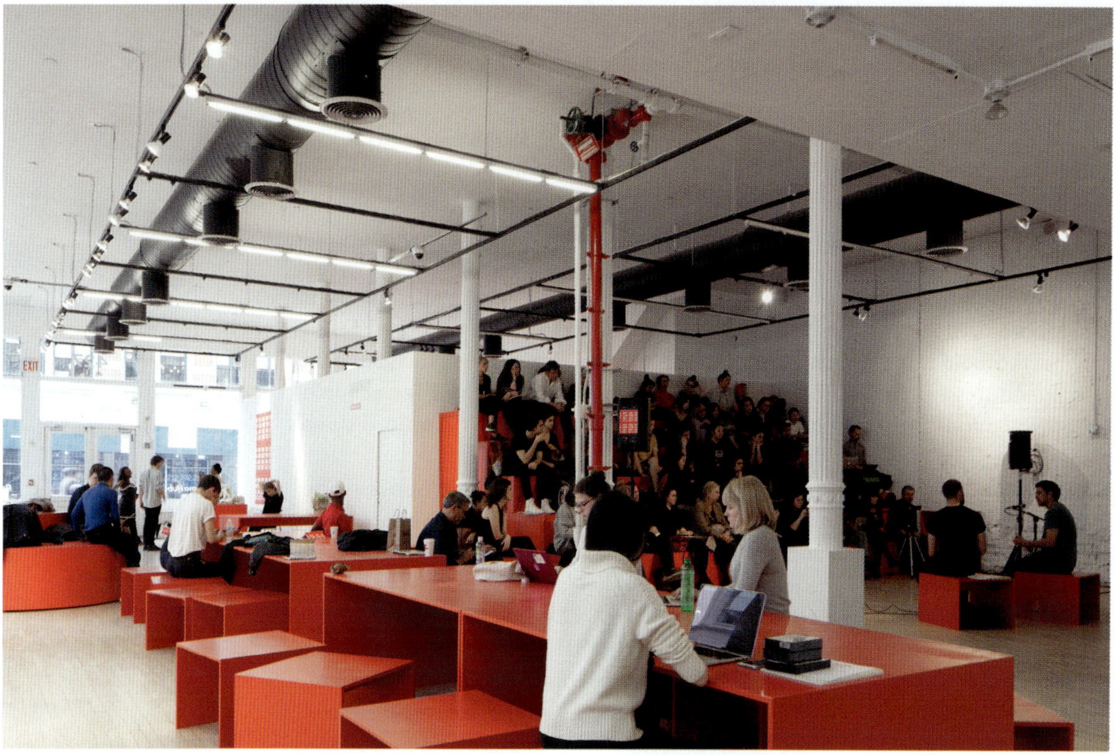

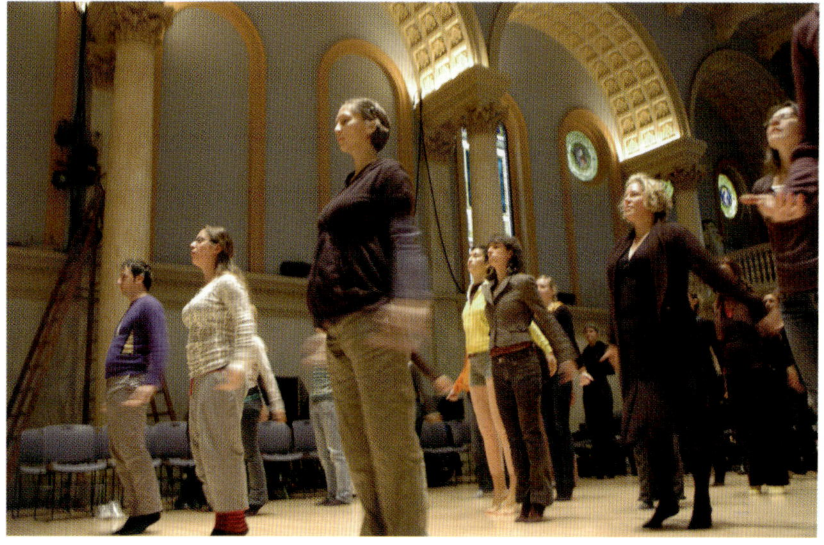

Performa 17 Hub interior view, 2017.

Participants learning Trisha Brown's *Accumulation* at "Not For Sale: Dance and Conceptual Art in the Visual Arts," 2007.

experiments with artists Jennifer Wen Ma, Derrick Adams, and Ahmet Öğüt. This new strand of programming was then amplified in 2015, with site-specific projects at the Hub by Brazilian artists Jonathas de Andrade and Eleonora Fabião, as well as Chimurenga, the pan-African collective of writers and musicians.

The Institute materializes at every Hub, a temporary arena—usually a Downtown storefront—taken over for the entirety of the biennial's three-week duration. Functioning as a meeting and ticketing office, lounge for regrouping between events, and even a co-working office, the Hub invites audiences to return often to attend its performances and screenings, daily talks, lectures, panel discussions, and symposia, all delving into the aesthetic, intellectual, and formal dimensions of the organization's commissions and projects. Designed by Berlin architects Studio Miessen in both 2017 and 2019, the Hub is a flexible space that accommodates various impromptu invitations. Established at the intersection of Broadway and Howard Street in 2017, it split into two locations in 2019, a stone's throw away from each other on Wooster Street.

For the past five years, the team has fortified the relationship between the Institute and each biennial as well as with the organization's off-year programs and publications, such as commissioning a new film by Adam Pendleton in January 2017, inviting Yvonne Rainer to explore their shared interests in conceptual strategies of juxtaposition often found in Dada. The work anticipated the November slate, which was conceived around the European avant-garde movement and its legacy. These threads of research and interests stretch out incrementally, happening in and out of the biennials. Another example here is the Performa 17 platform *Circulations*, focusing on architecture and performance, a theme that resurfaced in the following biennial with *Bodybuilding*, the first publication to survey the use of live work by architects—which itself reappeared in spring 2020, reconfigured again as an online exhibition (see page 316).

The following pages are a record of the wealth of open forums that Performa has presented since 2017, organized thematically. Most of these took place within the walls of the temporary Performa 17 and 19 Hubs, although the Institute is nomadic by nature and has also partnered with outstanding institutions such as Anthology Film Archives, NYU's Fales Library and Special Collections, The New School, and the Goethe-Institut New York.

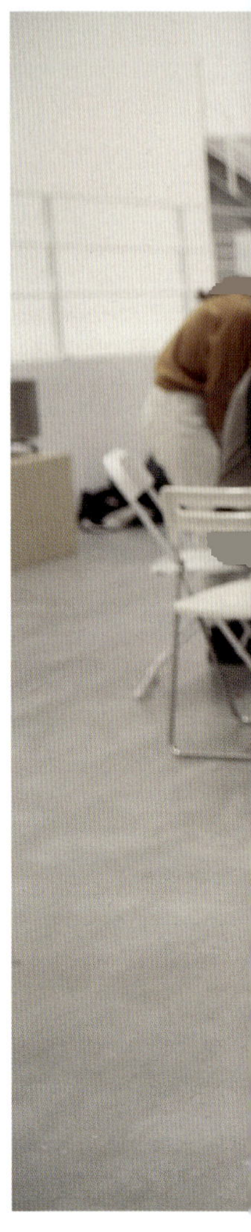

RUN HOME, *Subversive Threads: A Quilting and Dyeing Workshop* at the Performa 19 Hub (18 Wooster), 2019.

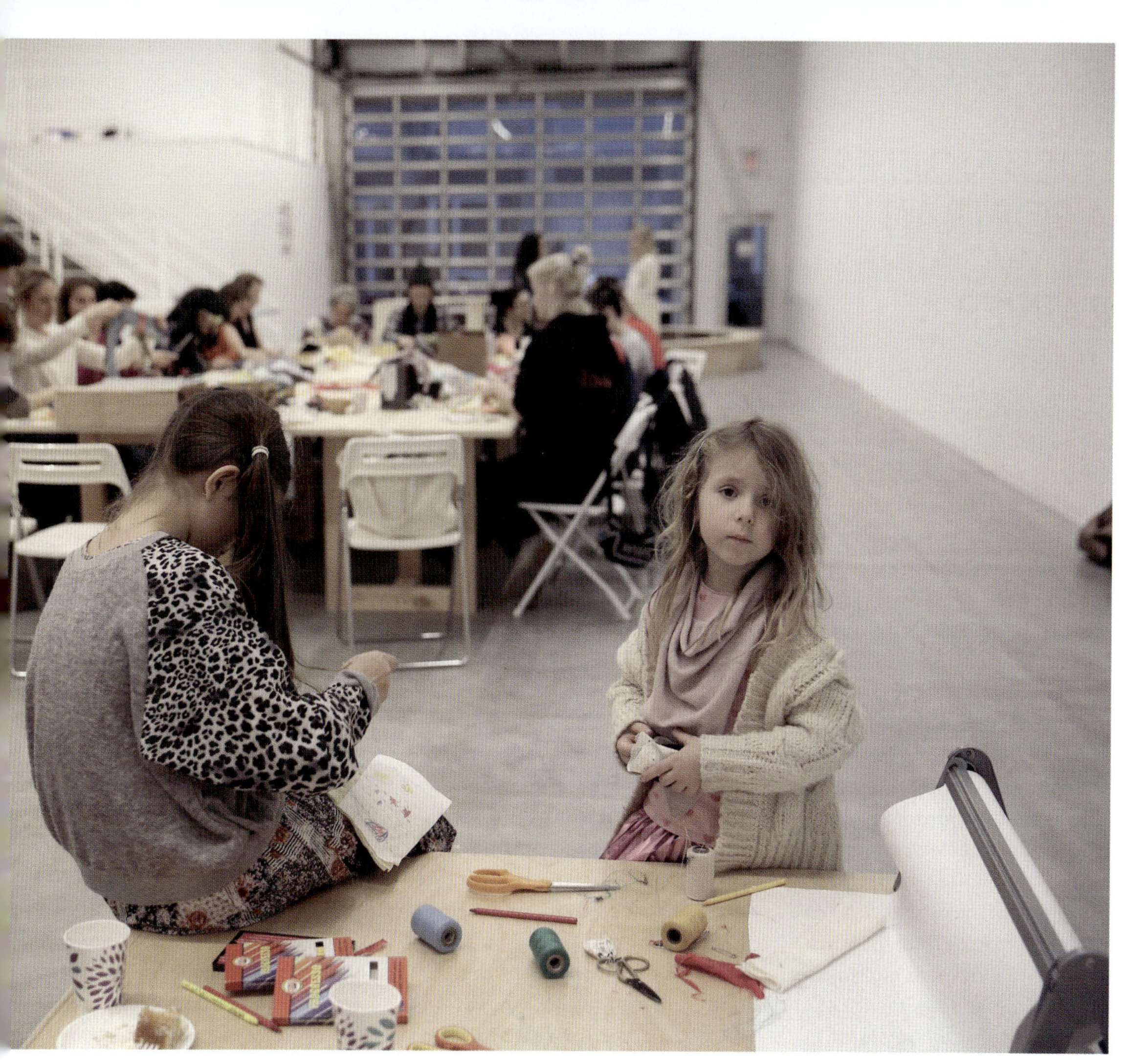

JUST BACK FROM LOS ANGELES: A PORTRAIT OF YVONNE RAINER

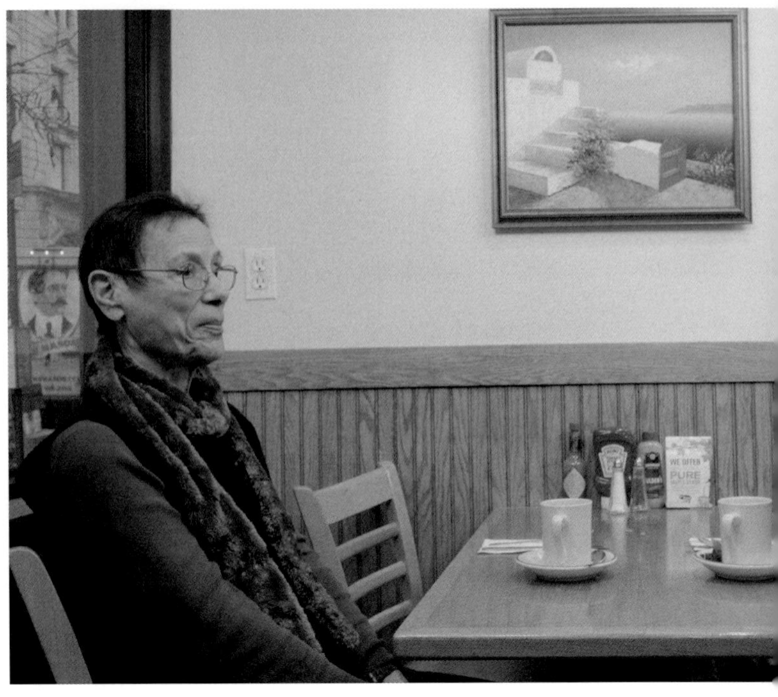

Adam Pendleton's Just Back from Los Angeles: A Portrait of Yvonne Rainer *drew on his body of work titled* Black Dada, *which began in 2008. Initially assembled as a reader of photocopied academic texts that combined thoughts from disparate sources (Hugo Ball, Gertrude Stein, Sun Ra, Adrian Piper) to disrupt easy logic and established histories,* Black Dada *expanded into many other mediums, from paintings and sculptures to wall works and videos. His conceptual paradigm has created unexpected connections between art writings from the aftermath of the First World War and seminal texts from the Black Power and Black Arts movements that addressed the violence of racism in 1960s United States.*

Commissioned on the occasion of Performa 17's Dada historical anchor, Just back from Los Angeles: A Portrait of Yvonne Rainer *premiered at Anthology Film Archives on January 9, 2017. It is Pendleton's third chapter in a series of evocative personal video portraits (following artist Lorraine O'Grady and Black Panther member David Hilliard). Together with the choreographer, filmmaker, and writer, Pendleton explored the conceptual strategy of "radical juxtapositions" (of images, texts, and sounds), a term coined by critic Susan Sontag and used by Rainer in her films and dance works to allow for new and unforeseen associations. He recorded her reading from a text he prepared that combined excerpts from her own writings from the 1968 program notes of her performance* The Mind Is a Muscle *with accounts of the killings of Trayvon Martin and Eric Garner as well as quotes from Stokely Carmichael and Malcolm X. Paired by Adrienne Edwards, Pendleton and Rainer were counterpoints to, or varying entries into, the influence of Dada in an effort to complicate its narrative and legacy.*

ADRIENNE EDWARDS

As a way to think through formal concerns in art making and the complexity of doing so in the face of conditions that impose a certain kind of ethical imperative upon the work, I wanted to start with the program for *The Mind Is a Muscle*, from its début in 1968 at the [since torn-down] Anderson Theatre here in New York. The program reads: The condition for making my stuff lies in the continuation of my interest and energy. Just as ideological issues have no bearing on the nature of the work, neither does the tenor of the current political and institutional conditions have any bearing on its execution. The world disintegrates around me. My connection to the world-in-crisis remains tenuous and remote. I can foresee a time when this remoteness must necessarily end, though I cannot foresee exactly when or how the relationship will change or what circumstances will incite me to a different kind of action. Perhaps nothing short of universal female military conscription will affect my function (the ipso facto physical fitness of dancers will make them the first victims); or a call for a worldwide cessation of individual functions, to include the termination of genocide. This statement is not an apology. It is a reflection of a state of a mind that reacts with horror and

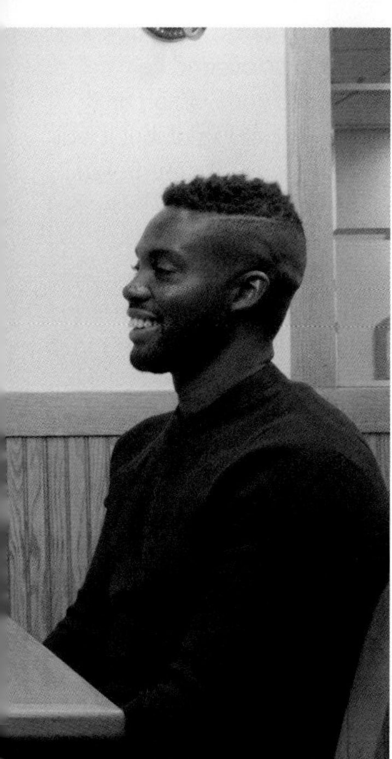

Adam Pendleton, *Just back from Los Angeles: A Portrait of Yvonne Rainer*, 2017. Film still.

disbelief upon seeing a Vietnamese shot dead on TV—not at the sight of death, however, but at the fact that the TV can be shut off afterwards as after a bad Western. My body remains the enduring reality.
—Yvonne Rainer, March 1968

Immediately after this period, you perform *Trio A with Flags*. You enter into a moment of coming to terms with an ethical imperative. I wanted to mention all this as a segue into asking what you thought about the film.

YVONNE RAINER

I thought it was great! I didn't know what to expect. We talked for a couple of hours in that diner—three hours, I believe. So, when Adam told me he was going to make a fifteen-minute piece, I was surprised. But he really distilled a great many things into this work. And I am just amazed at how he took things from his own experience, too. Some of the quotations are totally out of context and fictionalized. He did research into my work and made it personal for himself, while also quoting me. So, it is a very complex piece for me. As you saw, it almost brought me to tears at one point because it was so... I'm easily brought to tears these days, anyway. As the title suggests, I had just come back from Los Angeles after having what was, for me, an extraordinary experience with two of my contemporaries, improvising for an hour in a gallery.[1] So, it was a very gratuitous moment when we came together and had this conversation. It brought the past and the present together. Where are we now if not at a point in the history of our country that is both horrifying and energizing and demanding of us? We are seeing the kinds of resistance, protest, and demonstrations that were almost everyday occurrences during the Vietnam War and before the invasion of Iraq and in other moments in my memory—demonstrations in which I participated. So, it is amazing that Adam did all of that in fifteen minutes.

AE

Adam, there is a kind of opacity to your Black Dada paintings. There's a veneer a viewer can't quite get behind. That's a bit like the way you work, too. There were elements and aspects to how you prepared this piece that I wasn't a part of and Yvonne wasn't a part of. I wasn't there for the shoot, for example. When we had dinner together last summer to talk about what we might do together, Yvonne actually asked you to be as much a part of the piece as she was...

YR

Adam, you wouldn't have done that yourself—put yourself in the picture—if I hadn't asked you to?

ADAM PENDLETON

No. [*laughs*]

YR

Oh, thank god. I couldn't have sustained it myself.

AP

Before I say anything else, I want to say thank you to you, Yvonne, for agreeing to sit down with me and engage as another artist. As you hear in the beginning of the video, we don't know each other that well. Making art is a kind of perpetual risk, and sometimes it's an honest one. When we sat down, we had

1
New York's Judson Dance Theater members Simone Forti, Steve Paxton, and Yvonne Rainer reconvened to perform *Tea for Three* in November 2016 at The Box in Los Angeles.

an honest exchange about who we are, where we come from, and our differences in experience due simply to the gap of time that exists between us. But there was trust and empathy, and that was greatly appreciated. So, thank you.

On a more matter-of-fact note, you proposed an interesting conundrum when you said that you wanted me to be part of the piece. This is the third video portrait that I've done. The first one was of Lorraine O'Grady, who is an African American conceptual artist based in New York. The second one was of David Hilliard, who was the former chief of staff and a founding member of the Black Panther Party. I'm not in either of these portraits. You can hear my voice in the O'Grady piece, but you never see my body. So, on the one hand, I wanted to honor your wishes that I be in the piece, but I also wanted—as I often do—to disappear.

YR

But you didn't.

AP

No, I didn't. [*laughs*]

YR

I mean you could have in the editing.

AP

Yes, I could have in the editing. There was a lot of whispering going on when we were shooting the piece because the camera guys knew they had a semi-directive that I didn't want to be in any shots.

YR

There are no close-ups of you, right?

AP

Right. We actually ended up with three cameras, which was kind of a solution and a distraction, because I also didn't want you to think during the shooting that we were solely focusing on you. It's not readily apparent, but, interestingly enough, the diner became a kind of a character. It gave us this activity of sitting down, ordering tea, eating together. These rituals were played out against a backdrop—against, if you will, a stream of content or a stream of language.

YR

I'm amazed at how much juice you got out of this old warhorse of mine, *Trio A*. I keep thinking, what else can be done with this dance?

AP

It's far from an old warhorse. One of the things that interests me about how your work functions, and how my work functions, is a tendency toward radical juxtaposition. In this particular instance, I'm working within the confines of film. This is a single-channel piece, so I'm not able to have two frames at once—you can hear something, you can see something, at least in the way I'm presenting it. But I think laying the gospel music over the piece—"I'm Saved," a 1981 recording by a Detroit gospel group called the Silver Harps—gives a different geometry of attention to the movement that *Trio A* captures. It gives the piece an honesty, a radical simplicity.

YR

What about the beginning song, which is so redolent with sentiment?

AP

When I was reading your memoir, *Feelings Are Facts*, I kept dog-earing the pages where you made references to music. The book was published in 2006, and I am not sure how long you worked on it before it was published, but it was interesting to me that music was often the vehicle or the device that would drive your memory. You mention watching films when you were growing up in San Francisco and hearing [Charles Trenet's 1946 song] "La Mer" over one of them—I don't remember which one. So, in a strange way, my use of "La Mer" in the video is really a note from your own writing, from your own work.

YR

I don't remember it.

AE

You both cite other texts as sources and references in your work. Adam, would you talk about how you came up with the text that Yvonne read? You mentioned that there were elements that came from Yvonne's *Feelings Are Facts* that you subjected to another assemblage—much like you did in *Black Dada Reader*, where there's an assembly of different writers who are also seemingly incommensurable, but you put them together.

AP

Some of the texts that you hear Yvonne read are from *Black Dada Reader*, specifically Stokely Carmichael's "The Pitfalls of Liberalism," which he published in 1969. You hear "The Ballot or the Bullet," a speech written by Malcolm X in 1964 and delivered in Cleveland, Ohio; Yvonne only reads one line from this text: "They're beginning to see what they used to only look at ..." You also hear a reference to Ron Silliman. And a passage from a book about

Black Lives Matter by the scholar Keeanga-Yamahtta Taylor. You hear a letter to Yvonne from Barbara Dilley about Dilley's experience performing *Continuous Project-Altered Daily* at the University of Missouri in Columbia.

YR

Is that in there?

AP

That is in there.

YR

Do you have it here?

AP

I do have it. I brought the script with me. You actually only hear excerpts from a much longer letter—I ended up pulling those sentences that begin with "I remember."

YR

Ah, that is from the letter that was published in *Feelings Are Facts*. I thought you were making that up. [*audience laughs*]

AP

I took away a lot of the context, so it became a sort of parallel track for me.

YR

That's why I said at the beginning that it was fictionalized, but there's nothing fictionalized in the film. They're all quotations.

AP

Yes.

YR

I just don't remember my own stuff. Give me a break—wait until you guys are eighty. [*audience laughs*]

AE

I was struck by the fact that *Trio A* had its fiftieth anniversary last year. This made me think about all the things that were happening around the time that *Trio A* was made. There was the Vietnam War. In 1966, Martin Luther King Jr. was organizing the Poor People's Campaign, expanding the scope of the Civil Rights Movement. The National Organization for Women was established. The Black Panther Party was founded. There was the Supreme Court case *Loving vs. Virginia*, which overturned laws banning interracial marriage. So, it was an incredible moment. Yvonne, I sense that when you turned toward filmmaking, you were somehow trying to address all these things happening around you. You addressed complexities around identity and how certain identities are challenged in this country—in particular you addressed the complexities of being a woman. But you also talked about women of color; you talked about poor people. I

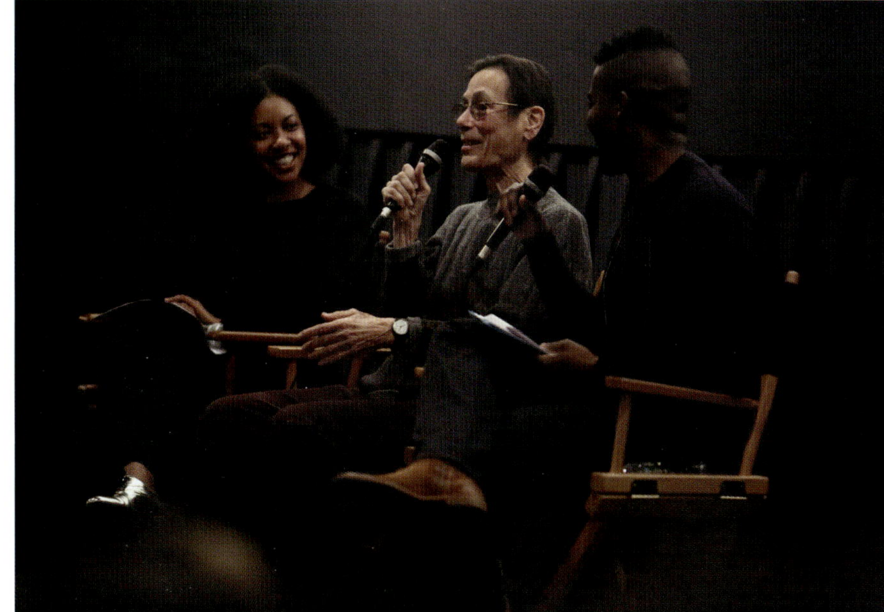

Adrienne Edwards, Yvonne Rainer, and Adam Pendleton in conversation at Anthology Film Archives, New York (2017).

would love for you to comment on that moment where you clearly felt a desire to address these issues somehow.

YR

In my work in the 1960s, there was a split between aesthetic rebellions or dialogues and my activism around the Vietnam War. Steve Paxton incorporated some of that resistance into a few of his dance pieces, but I didn't, which is why I had to move into film, where one is allowed more latitude to deal with social and political issues. Today, I can't help thinking about how this country has been involved in the so-called War on Terrorism for over a decade. It's beginning to look like another Thirty Years' War. It's being fought by young, poor people who don't have another way to make a living in this country. It's more appalling than ever.

AE

Adam, over the last year and a half, your work has turned more and more toward ethical issues, from your decision to create a Black Lives Matter flag for the Belgian Pavilion at the 2015 Venice Biennale to the new work that you debuted at Pace this summer, *Untitled (A Victim of American Democracy)*. How do you think about that evolution in your work?

AP

The simplest way to respond is to say that, as artists, I hope we are creating documents that matter. When George Zimmerman was acquitted of killing Trayvon Martin, I had to respond to the absurdity of the situation, which is to also say, to the violence of the situation. I felt an imperative to respond, less to "deal with it" or to "address it" than to bring it into a capacious space where these issues could reside with the complexity they deserve. For me, that was the space of my work. So, it's a kind of call to arms, but it's also, I would argue, a move toward abstraction, because there's something ethical about being illegible, about the human project not being something that is readily reduced to "he's a that" and "she's a this." The ethical potential is in understanding the power of collective difference in general.

AE

I was thinking about this in relation to the Dadaists. We associate them with a desire to express a certain nihilism or anarchy, to create a nonsensical language. For them, that was revolutionary. But here we are, one hundred years later, trying to revolt against systems that are nonsensical. So, what is revolutionary in the face of this? Is it a kind of measured reserve in aesthetics that allows us to be subversive, that allows us not to be so readily available? And is this particular to the U.S.? Are we living through a peculiar form of Americana right now? Or is this true of Western civilization in general?

YR

I keep thinking of the film's juxtaposition of the killings by police officers with the BLT sandwich, representing daily life in all its mundanity. I'm just amazed at how you got all of this into the same small pot, Adam.

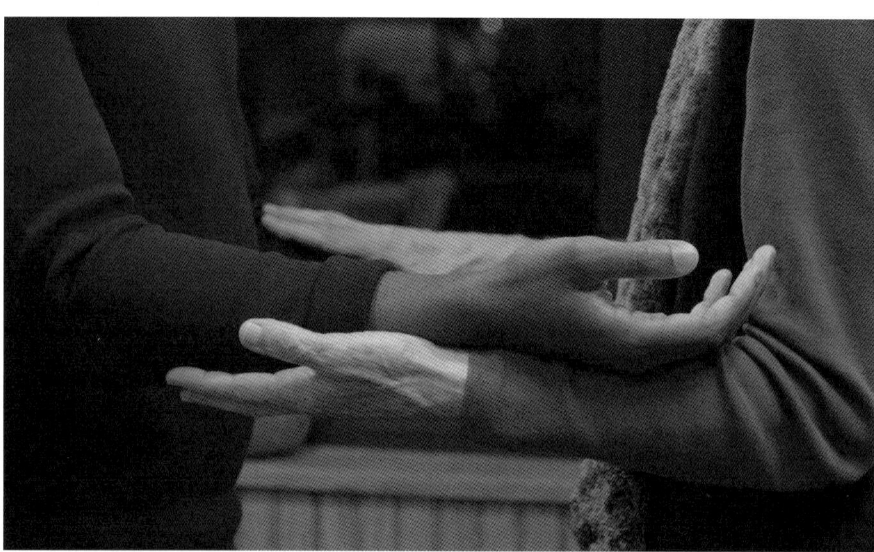

Image caption: Adam Pendleton, *Just back from Los Angeles: A Portrait of Yvonne Rainer*, 2017. Film still.

AE

But that's also true of your work, Yvonne. You also created an open container for such concerns.

YR

Well, in my current work with the so-called Raindears, they dance and I read. The reading is full of complaints and rants and humor. I stick a page in front of one of them, interrupting what they're doing, and they read. There's a real split. It's like two parallel tracks. Adam, you're working with a very different kind of strategy, right?

AP

I think of them as parallel tracks as well. That was actually something I kept underlining while reading *Feelings Are Facts* and interviews with you—I kept writing *process, process, process*, and those were the moments where I...

YR

They keep intersecting. Well, in film, you can do that.

AP

Right. You can do it in film and on a flat plane, too. There are just different kinds of resistance.

AE

Let's take questions from the audience.

AUDIENCE MEMBER

Yvonne, could you comment on the section where you do the "arm drop" and how that interweaves trust and generosity?

YR

That was invented by Steve Paxton and me in the 1960s. I hadn't done it with Steve or anyone else since then, but in the L.A. performance that preceded the conversation with Adam, Steve came over to me and offered his arms and we started to do it. He described the origin of it as we were doing it: "You invited me to dinner and made chicken, and we got stoned on pot and we just started to do the arm drop. We'd never done it before, it just sort of happened. And, as we did it, I asked you what was in that chicken, and you said, 'chicken.' And, of course, because we were stoned, we roared with laughter."

In the performance in L.A., instead of roaring with laughter, I started to cry, because I had a Proustian moment of the sensation of the arms and the reach of the others' arms and the trust and the immediate recouping when one person dropped the arms, and the memory of that evening, which I hadn't thought of for fifty years... It seems that Steve still uses it in his teachings, and I probably will too n workshops from now on. It is a very satisfying move. Do you want to demonstrate it, Adam?

AP

No, I don't do it well.

YR

Yes, you do. We just didn't do it long enough. It's in the movie. So that's the story. What was the question again?

AUDIENCE MEMBER

I think that game is about trust and generosity. When it's folded into this piece, that's what I think about. Maybe you could comment on the content that was put on the table, in terms of how it evoked this game?

AP

It wasn't as explicit as that. I brought a text for Yvonne to read and Yvonne brought this gesture. It was an exchange.

YR

We'd had about three hours, and it was the end of the conversation. I had to go off to Trader Joe's. Which again is like the BLT...

AE

The ordinary is extraordinary these days.

This conversation took place at Anthology Film Archives, New York, on January 9, 2017 after the premiere of Just Back from Los Angeles: A Portrait of Yvonne Rainer. *A transcript of this conversation was initially published in* Adam Pendleton: Our Ideas *(edited by Alec Mapes-Frances and Stephen Squibb, New York: Pace Gallery, 2019). Reprinted courtesy the authors and Pace gallery.*

FOREVER AND A DAY: ARCHIVING PERFORMA

Forever and A Day: Archiving Performa was a roundtable discussion-cum-day-long performance that brought together a think tank of archivists, artists, and scholars, all experts in addressing the unique challenges of preserving ephemeral practices within art and cultural history. Presenters included Anthony Elms, Chief Curator at ICA Philadelphia; Sur Rodney (Sur), independent curator and archivist; C. Spencer Yeh, sound artist; Nicholas Mirzoeff, Professor of Media, Culture, and Communication at NYU Steinhardt; Deena Engel, Director of Digital Humanities and Social Science in the Department of Computer Science at NYU; and Barbara Clausen, Curator and Professor at Université du Québec in Montreal. Using examples from their respective archival collections and practices, they exchanged ideas about how liveness is not only constituted through ephemera but can also exist as a collection of ideas, activities, and experiences. There was a particular focus on brainstorming new approaches to the challenges that the ephemeral quality of performance can present to traditional systems of preservation.

The participants then used media and materials from Performa's archives to draft a multi-year project to make the organization's collection available to the public while preserving its legacy. The group discussed digital platforms, designs, software, and syllabi—engaging archiving as an ideology, a creative practice, and a state of mind. One of their main concerns was to develop a system in which the archives were not valued *only* for how closely they resemble the live experience they sought to preserve, but for their ability to sustain the innovative practices employed by a range of global artists. For example, one proposal was to create an interactive website where anyone could revisit the original work via its documentation, initiate additional exchanges, and use the footage or photos to create new artworks. The event provided a model for structuring and conceptualizing Performa's archives as an expansive and always evolving collection that exists beyond its physical parameters. As a self-referential gesture to acknowledge that the options to record, store, index, and redistribute performance are manifold, a sketch artist, more regularly seen in courtrooms, was invited to attend the symposium and draw scenes from the event.

MARC ARTHUR

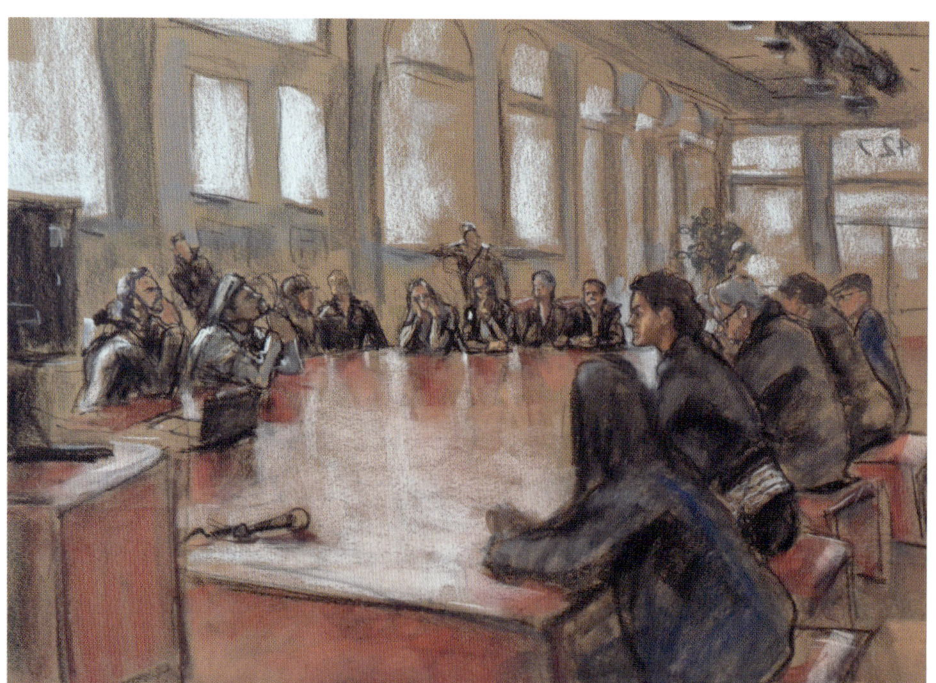

Jane Rosenberg, *Forever and a Day: Archiving Performa*, 2017. Pastel sketch.

CALL FOR ACTION: KEY MOMENTS IN ESTONIAN PERFORMANCE ART

Curators Anu Allas and Maria Arusoo led this public seminar to provide context for the Estonian Pavilion Without Walls: Mixing screenings, lectures, and conversations with audience members, the event offered a survey of significant Estonian performances since the 1960s. At the heart of the program was the complex relationship between artistic practices and their social contexts while the country shifted toward the West—from regaining its independence from the Soviet Union to becoming a modern liberal democracy and a full member of Western organizations such as the European Union and NATO.

Beginning with the emergence of politically charged happenings in communist Estonia, the program focused on the instrumental architect, visual artist, and performer Jüri Okas. Life during the dissolution of the Soviet bloc was evoked through Raoul Kurvitz's 1989 film *When Lord Zarathustra Was Young and Polite*, culminating in a scene when a dam opens up and releases waters that sweep away Kurvitz's half-naked body. The critical years of the late 1980s and early 1990s, when Estonia embraced a new economic system based on the free market—and how the national psyche reacted to these new conditions in unpredictable ways—were examined through the work of Jaan Toomik. In *Dancing Home* (1995), Toomik sways alone, alienated, on the back deck of a ferry boat to the rhythm of its engine. In *Dancing with Dad* (2003), the artist moves to Jimi Hendrix's "Voodoo Child" next to his father's grave, who passed away in 1971 and could not have anticipated the U.S.S.R.'s crumbling in 1991. Recent works by Flo Kasearu, Kris Lemsalu, Maria Metsalu, and Ene-Liis Semper completed the presentation to reveal a pluralistic contemporary creative community.

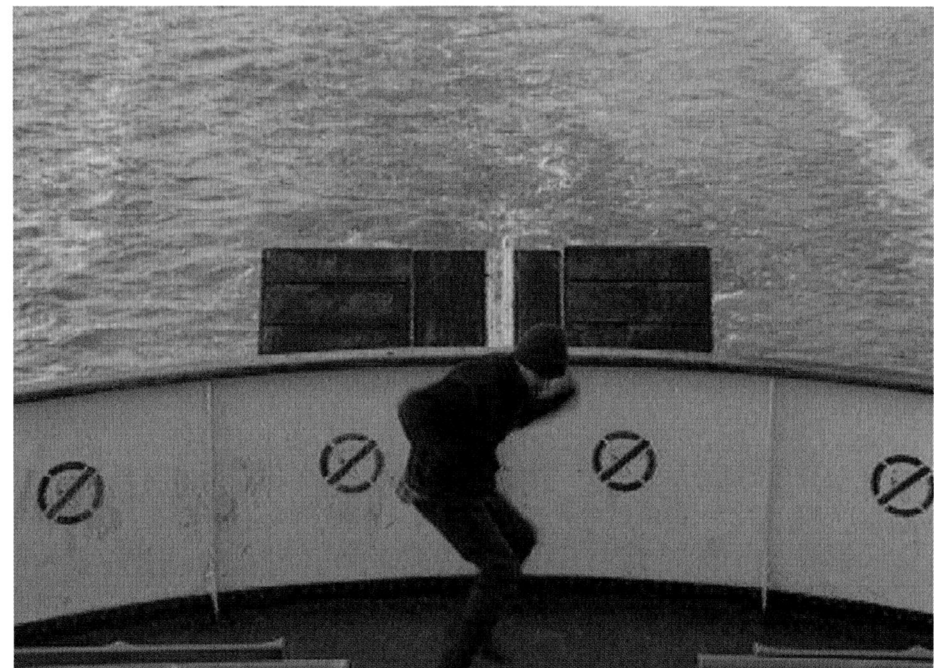

Jaan Toomik, *Dancing Home*, 1995. Video still.

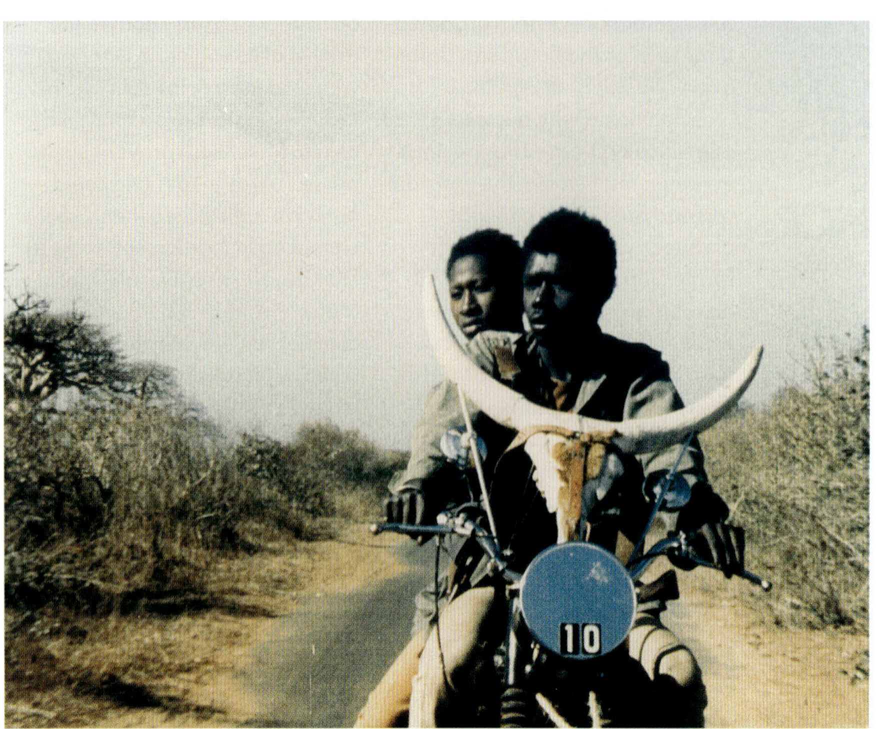

AFROGLOSSIA FILM PROGRAM AT ANTHOLOGY FILM ARCHIVES

Performa 17's program *Afroglossia* articulated diverse perspectives on experimental interdisciplinary art from various regions of the African continent into a single curatorial platform (see page 52). In their own distinct formal ways, each production, devised by artists from Ethiopia, Kenya, Morocco, Nigeria, and South Africa, touched on questions such as "What is radical?," "How do the conditions of everyday life inform creative choices?," and "What constitutes experimentation in cross-boundary performance?"

Afroglossia's set of commissions was contextualized by a special four-day film program during Performa 17, co-presented with Anthology Film Archives. Each *Afroglossia* participant was invited to present moving-image works that had shaped their aesthetic imaginations.

Teju Cole inaugurated the series with *Sans Soleil* by Chris Marker (1983), a meditation on the nature of human memory, screened alongside Victor Erice's *Lifeline* (2002), a rumination on the meaning of time, followed by *Love Is The Message, The Message Is Death* by Arthur Jafa (2016), a nuanced portrait of Black life in America. Cole concluded with *Meshes of The Afternoon*, spouses Maya Deren and Alexander Hammid's 1943 experimental film exploring desires through dreams, followed by

Djibril Diop Mambéty, *Touki Bouki*, 1973. Film still.

The Nest Collective, *To Catch a Dream*, 2015. Film still.

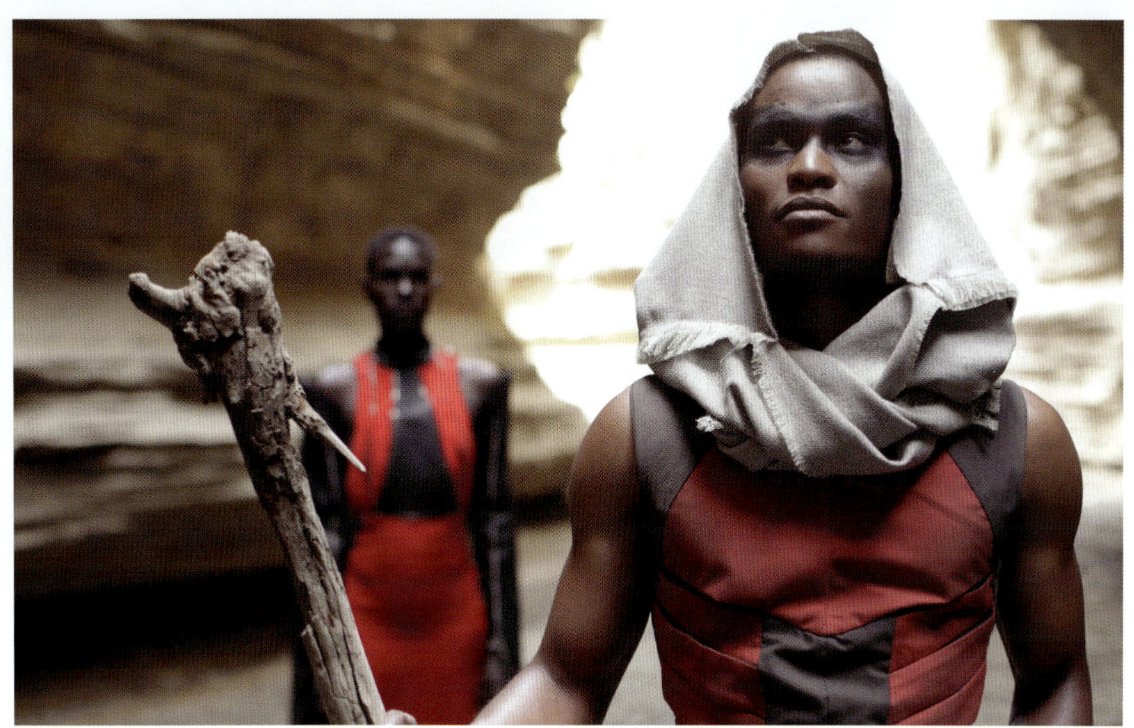

Best of Luck with the Wall by Josh Begley (2016), a voyage across the U.S.-Mexico border composed of 200,000 satellite images.

Wangechi Mutu chose to pair the 1973 picaresque and fantastical drama *Touki Bouki*, a movie depicting Senegalese filmmaker Djibril Diop Mambéty's disenchantment of his country after its independence, with Kenyan artist Mbithi Masya's *Kati Kati* (2016), a tale of a ghost seeking peace in the afterlife.

In 2006, Yto Barrada founded the Cinémathèque de Tanger to foster cinema in Morocco and bring attention to Moroccan cinema across the world. For *Afroglossia*, the New York-based Moroccan artist screened the short documentary *Sean* by Ralph Arlyck (1970), which follows a four-year-old growing up in Haight-Ashbury, the hotbed of hippie culture in San Francisco. Two cinematic classics completed the program: *Notes Towards an African Orestes* by Pier Paolo Pasolini (1970) and *Chronicle of a Summer* by Jean Rouch (1961), a study of the *cinéma verité* style's aspirations, achievements, and shortcomings.

The Nest Collective, a multidisciplinary arts group living and working in Nairobi, showed two episodes of their miniseries *We Need Prayers*, dedicated to the daily delights and challenges encountered by citizens of the Kenyan capital: *We Need Prayers: This One Went to Market* (2017, a world premiere for Performa 17) and *We Need Prayers: These Ones Stayed at Home* (2017). They also featured *When We Are/When We Are Not* (2016), a series of silent shots of Black bodies in repose; *To Catch a Dream* (2015), which follows a grieving widow plagued by recurring nightmares; and *Dinka Translation* (2013), a video lookbook by fashion designer Katungulu Mwendwa. Tracey Rose concluded the day with *The Wiz* by Sidney Lumet (1978), an African American remake of the 1939 hit *The Wizard of Oz*.

Artists Julie Mehretu and Jason Moran returned to filmmaker-anthropologist Jean Rouch and sociologist Edgar Morin's *Chronicle of a Summer*, which they shared alongside Charles Burnett's drama *Killers of Sheep* (1979), a movie that depicts the African American neighborhood of Watts in Los Angeles, and *In The Last Days of The City* by Tamer El Said (2015), a melancholic ode to the city of Cairo.

YTO BARRADA: TREE IDENTIFICATION WALK

As a complement to her film program and *Tree Identification for Beginners* (see page 66), her commissioned live work at the Connelly Theater in Manhattan's East Village, Yto Barrada organized an actual tree identification walk through Brooklyn's Prospect Park, led with environmental educator Lisa Nett. On a chilly Saturday morning, Nett guided participants through the finer points of the practice, such as pinpointing bark, buds, leaves, and trunks, while Barrada mused on the political and social complexities of human interactions with the natural world, delving into plant taxonomy as a model for the structural language within her art.

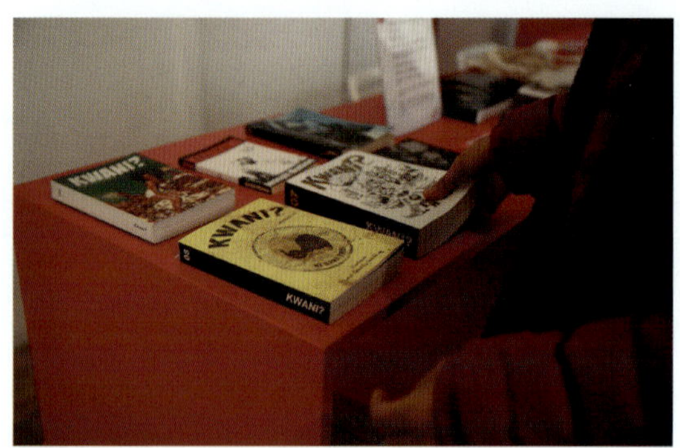

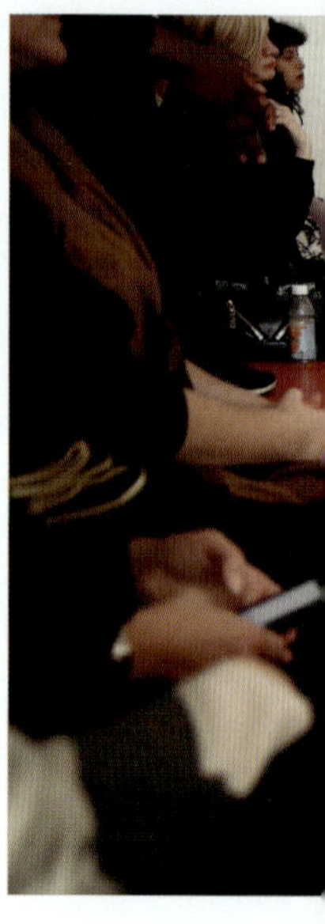

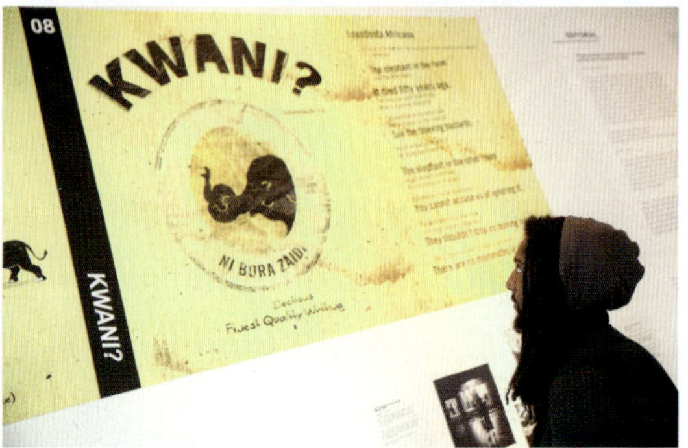

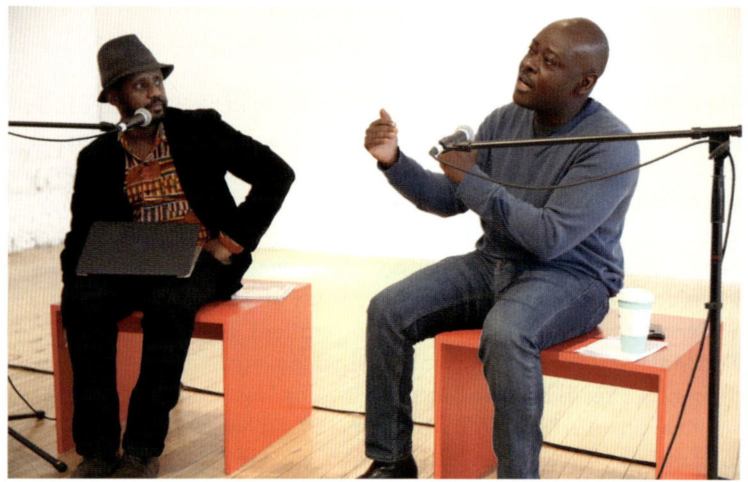

AFROGLOSSIA

Charvet typeface designed in 2013 by Kenyan graphic artist Kevin Karanja for the Nest Collective and used for the *Afroglossia* program during Performa 17.

Wangechi Mutu and Adrienne Edwards in conversation at the Performa 17 Hub

Billy Kahora and Helon Habila in conversation at the Performa 17 Hub

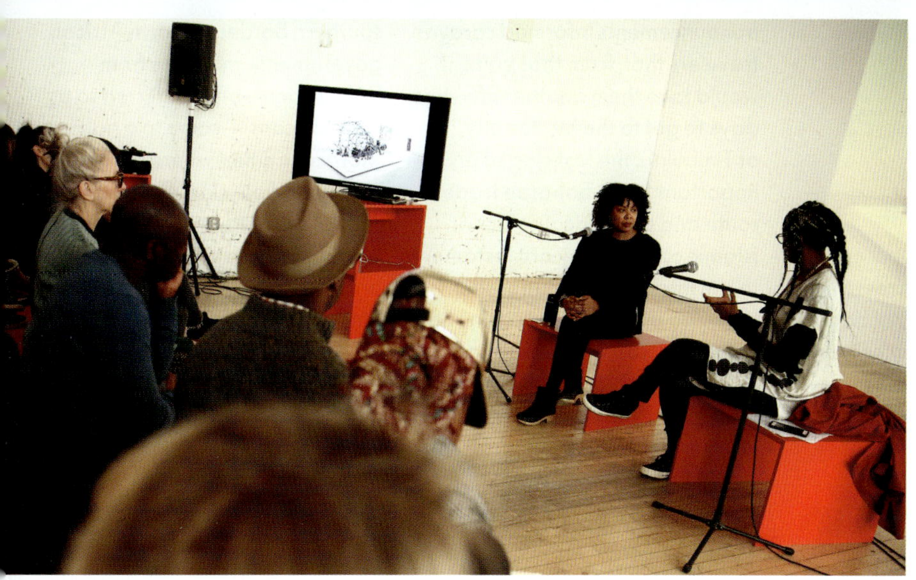

KWANI TRUST: *EVERYONE IS RADICALIZING*

The final week of Performa 17—and *Afroglossia*—concluded with a residency by the Kenyan collective Kwani Trust. Functioning primarily as a publishing house since 2003, Kwani Trust is a Nairobi-based network of publishers, writers, and editors that produces contemporary writing, offers training opportunities, and organizes literary events. In New York, the group staged everything under the title *Everyone is Radicalizing*, conceived as an experiment for an upcoming issue of their printed journal, *Kwani no. 9*. Set up at the Hub, the group created an environment for a divergent and stimulating set of oral histories, video screenings, photo essays, and a series of daily open conversations that examined words such as *terror*, *insecurity*, *violent extremism*, and *radicalization*.

Animated by writer and editor Billy Kahora, *Everyone is Radicalizing* took as its starting point the Kenyan Coast and northeastern Kenya as a nexus of cultures, religions, and politics. Kwani Trust then amplified the area's historical and cultural context beyond its nation's borders. German anthropologist and philosopher Kai Kresse shared his work on Islamic cultures along the Kenyan Coast, honing in on extremism and insecurity in the East African region. Kenyan artist and poet Neo Musangi considered contemporary photography on the continent with Nigerian writer Emmanuel Iduma and American visual artist Lyle Ashton Harris. New York-based Kenyan artist Wangechi Mutu discussed the interrelation of abstraction and performance in her work with Adrienne Edwards. Nigerian novelist and poet Helon Habila reflected on his book *The Chibok Girls: The Boko Haram Kidnappings and Islamist Militancy in Nigeria* (2016) with Kwani Trust editor Billy Kahora and filmmaker Funa Maduka. Neo Musangi examined Nairobi's queer identities and urban youth fanaticism with American scholar Tavia Nyong'o.

Each day, Kwani Trust presented a selection of moving-image works, including short and feature-length movies, to complement their talks. They included, among others, *Freddy Ilanga: Che's Swahili Translator* (Katrin Hansing, 2009), which narrated the story of a fifteen-year-old Congolese who became Che Guevara's personal Swahili teacher and translator during the seven intense months of the Marxist revolutionary's mission to train anti-Mobutu rebels in Congo; *Akounak Tedalat Taha Tazoughai* (Rain the Color of Blue with A Little Red in It, Christopher Kirkley, 2015), the first-ever Tuareg-language fictional work tied to the life of musician Mdou Moctar; and *The Revolution Won't Be Televised* (Rama Thiaw, 2016), a documentary on the resistance formed in the streets of Senegal when President Abdoulaye Wade announced he would run for a third term in 2011.

OMAR BERRADA: *TIMBUKTU 52 DAYS*

The billboards found across the southern Moroccan city of Zagora advertising *Tombouctou 52 jours* (Timbuktu 52 days) gave Omar Berrada the title for his lecture-performance for *Afroglossia*. These announcements informed caravan travelers that, from that point, it would take them another fifty-two days to get to the Malian city of Timbuktu, the last stop of an important trans-Saharan trade route and a historical center of Islamic culture. They are testaments to the intertwined relationship between the North African nation of Morocco and its sub-Saharan counterparts. Over the last decade, as the European Union has in effect subcontracted control of its southern border to North African governments, migrants from West Africa—often referred to as "the Africans"—come to a halt in Moroccan cities, where they endure verbal and physical violence. With *Timbuktu 52 days*, the New York-based Moroccan writer, translator, and curator Omar Berrada combined administrative documents, archival images of French colonial expeditions, early Moroccan cinema made after the country's 1956 independence, traditional *Gnawa*

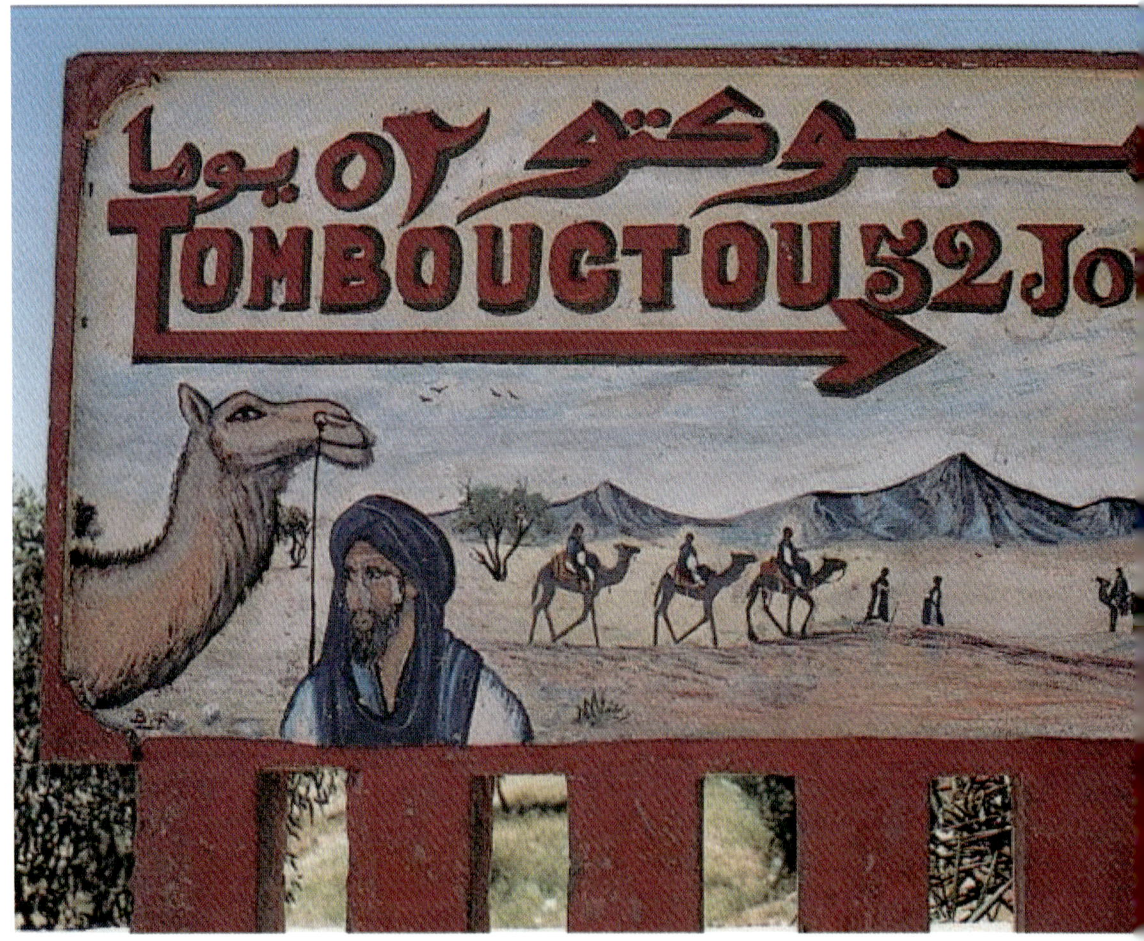

music, and personal anecdotes to unpack the vexed relationship between Morocco and the rest of the continent. At the Hub, Berrada asked, "When did the Moroccan national narrative become so racialized?," "How did the Saharan desert become a border?," "Why is 'Moroccan-ness' opposed to 'African-ness'?," and "What is the role of colonial history in these symbolic constructions?" In his hour-long presentation, Berrada gave voice to the silenced histories.

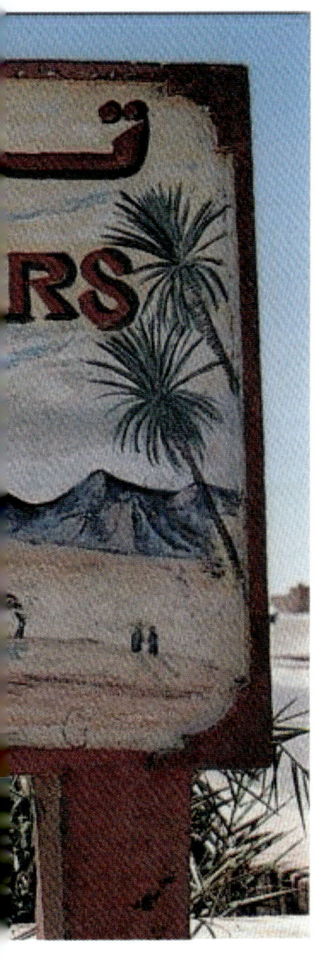

TEJU COLE: *BLACK LISTENING*

Teju Cole held a DJ lecture exploring the way music has played an essential role in shaping his personal notion of African-ness over a quarter-century spent living in the U.S. Through a rejection of national or ethnic boundaries, Cole described how he developed a sense of common cause with other Africans, in a way not possible for him as a Yoruba boy in Lagos. His talk at the Hub was accompanied by diverse musical examples from the beginning of the twentieth century to the beginning of the twenty-first, from Senegal all the way to South Africa and across the diaspora.

YVONNE RAINER: *A DANCE RANT*

A leading figure in the reinvention of dance in the 1960s, Yvonne Rainer transitioned to filmmaking in the following decade. In her seven feature-length movies produced between 1972 and 1996, she played with the possibilities that disjunctions offered her by using the montage format, incorporating and interspersing past choreography, feminist critique texts, narrative content, and photographs. In 2000, she returned to dance. In her seven live productions since then, Rainer has combined movements from performance history, images from popular culture and sporting events, and Keynesian economic theory to create unconventional, fast-paced, and witty dances. All along her career, however, writing has remained a constant activity, from publishing essays reflecting on the qualities of her "minimal" motions to poems on the rhythm of urban life to her acclaimed autobiography, *Feelings Are Facts* (2006). On the last day of Performa 17, Rainer gave her latest lecture-performance, which stemmed from her most recent foray into fiction writing.

Titled *A Truncated History of the Universe for Dummies: A Dance Rant*, her monologue drew on her anger at the year's political events channeled through an alter ego, Apollo Musagète. Apollo referenced George Balanchine's neoclassical ballet, which was choreographed to the music of Igor Stravinsky and starred the Greek god of music, *Musagète*, whose name translates to something like "leading the muses." For a full hour, Rainer embodied Apollo coming to Earth for a vacation and "ricocheting from catastrophe to absurdity, from chaos to elation, from desperation to Keystone Cops." She used the Greek god to share her ruminations on a wide spectrum of subjects, digressing from the threat of a nuclear apocalypse caused by the Trump administration's quarrel with the leader of North Korea to her rage when learning of the "ethnic cleansing" taking place against the Rohingya people in Myanmar to her thoughts on #MeToo and the disasters brought about by climate change.

JULIUS EASTMAN: *SYMPHONY NO. II*

Italian born, New York-based composer Luciano Chessa has been a close collaborator of Performa since 2009, when he directed the premiere reconstruction of Luigi Russolo's intonarumori *orchestra—a set of experimental "noise" instruments invented in the early twentieth century by the Italian Futurist to perform the new urban and industrial music called for in his 1913* Art of Noises *manifesto. Since then, Chessa has worked with the organization on many different occasions, from touring the* intonarumori *and expanding the roster of musicians composing for them (Blixa Bargeld, Joan La Barbara, Lee Ranaldo, Pauline Oliveros…) to writing new scores for Performa Commissions, such as Tarik Kiswanson's 2019* AS DEEP AS I CAN REMEMBER, AS FAR AS I COULD SEE *(see page 238).*

A musicologist, Chessa created the first edition of the score of Julius Eastman's Symphony No. II *from its only remaining existing manuscript for the music publishing company G. Schirmer and conducted its world premiere with the Mannes Orchestra at Lincoln Center's Alice Tully Hall on November 20, 2018.*

Unless other works surface in the coming years, the orchestral piece *Symphony No. II* (1983) was both American composer Julius Eastman's only symphonic composition and his last large-scale work. This piece survived thanks to poet R. Nemo Hill, Eastman's lover at the time, and the dedicatee of the work. Hill kept the manuscript in a drawer for several decades; composer Mary Jane Leach eventually published it on her website, and that is where I first saw it.

At the time that Julius Eastman (1940–1990) wrote it, there would have not been any concrete hope for this symphony to be performed publicly. The work was not a commission and none of Eastman's professional connections could have helped to land this score on a conductor's stand. Eastman turned this problem into an asset. As it was usually the case for Eastman, working on a blank canvas became the opportunity to let his imagination run unchecked.

Having effectively gained distance from Minimalism with works such as *Gay Guerrilla* (1979) and *The Holy Presence of Joan d'Arc* (1981), Eastman explored further new territory here. Yet—here is the tragic part—this moment also coincided with the point at which a combination of homophobia, racism, misfortune, and self-destruction forced the artist to essentially give up his composing career; *Symphony No. II* is followed by only a couple of small-scale works.

The work embraces the historical lessons Eastman absorbed during his training at the Curtis Institute of Music in Philadelphia while also encompassing an uncompromising modernist sensibility. It's also among the composer's few late works that show the influence of one of his early mentors, Morton Feldman, a leading figure in indeterminate and experimental music. This is particularly evident in the treatment of the timpani part—truly the spine of the piece—and, more generally, by the tectonic pace at which most of the work progresses.

Permeated by a syncretic religiosity found in several of his later works—aside from the above-mentioned, we should here include *Hail Mary* (1984) and *Our Father* (1989)—*Symphony No. II* is filled with many references, descriptive texts (eschatological, personal) and a complex labeling of recurring motifs that feel Berlioz-esque, Wagnerian, but also not far from what we find in La Monte Young. In one single movement, Eastman draws the entire arc of his relationship with Hill: From the opening statement of endless love, to the climactic fugato depicting his and Hill's sexual union, to the many loose ends of a relationship that failed, and up to the promising of a love that, despite all, transcends space and time.

While the symphony follows his biographical arc, I cannot resist reading into it the allegory of another one: that of Eastman's relationship with his own practice. The synchronicity of catastrophes, preceded by promising beginnings, followed by the teleological hope for final redemptions, is too compelling a reading to leave unmentioned. Even though this is the work of a man hitting rock bottom while still utterly undisturbed by production concerns (note the unconventional orchestral elements the piece requires), why write a symphony at all if there is no hope that one day—someday—it will be performed?

Indeed, the work had never been performed in part because

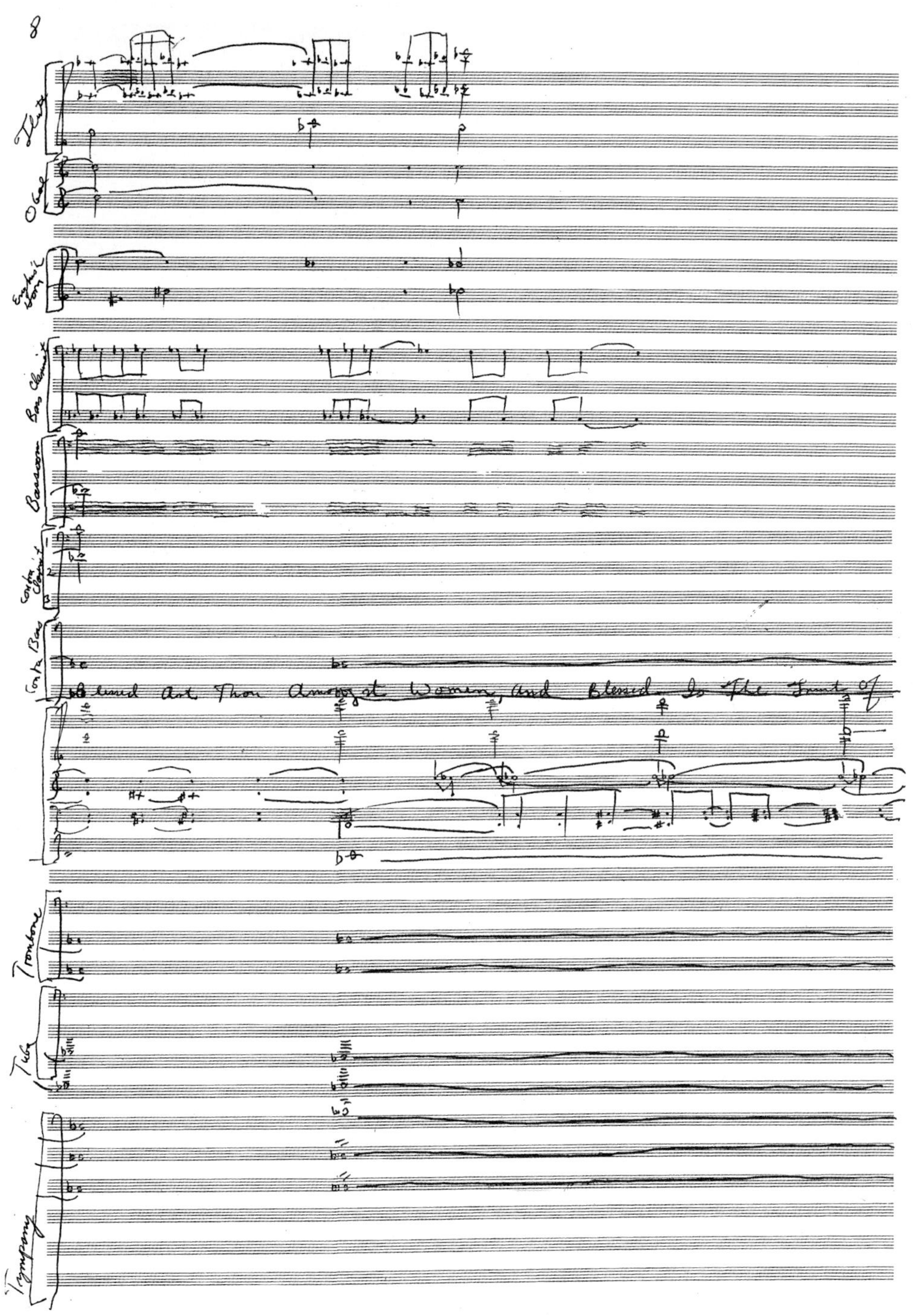

Julius Eastman, *Symphony No. II (The Faithful Friend: The Lover Friend's Love for the Beloved)*, 1983. Manuscript page 8.

it calls for rather idiosyncratic forces: three flutes, two oboes, two English horns, three bass clarinets, three contrabass clarinets, three bassoons, three contrabassoons, three trombones, three tubas, strings, and a setup of twenty-four timpani requiring six performers. And the manuscript needed a robust editorial intervention.

Eastman's manuscript bears no time signature, no tempo or metronome markings, no dynamics, and no bar lines, though all the parts were intended to be synchronized by a conventional downbeat. Naturally, many other Eastman manuscripts lack similar information (for example, in a piece like *Gay Guerrilla*, the deliberate avoidance of a *tactus* is what makes the work shimmer). Yet these pieces did not use more than a few parts at once and relied on the composer performing in the group and even taking on the role of band leader or conductor. Perhaps the sheer size of this symphony and its rehearsal complexity, first led me to join others in the belief that the work was incomplete, accidentally left unfinished, abandoned.

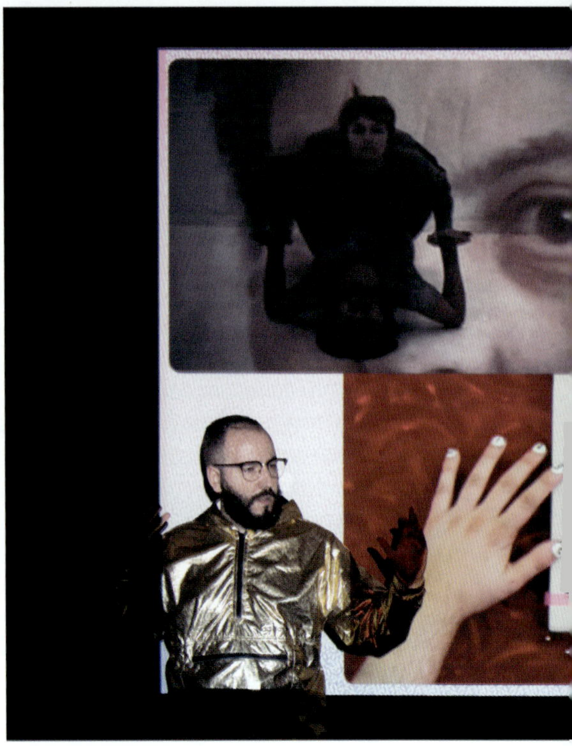

Nemo gave me a clue that led me to reexamine the situation. He told me that Eastman offered him the manuscript in a sort of ritualized ceremony that took place at the time when the two were breaking up. More important, Eastman told Nemo that the symphony was a diary of their relationship. Who would stage a signing ceremony to give an *accidentally* unfinished piece as a gift to a lover? In my mind, this rite only makes sense if the piece was *deliberately* left unfinished, mirroring how some relationships end.

Fascination for fragments aside (Heraclitus, Nietzsche, Kafka...), when I focused on what *was there* instead of *what may have been missing*, I saw a perfectly calibrated arc, with the main theme presented at the beginning and restated after the climax, as if in a promising whisper. The many loose ends of a relationship, in pieces, and then, perhaps consolation by a group of friends in a bar, helping you to pick up those pieces ... As I realized what was *there*, I was shaking, in tears.

This is what gave me the fuel to create this first edition of the score, the beginning step in getting the work performed. The editorial process alone required a considerable amount of time—adding dynamics to this work, for example, was akin to sculpting large blocks of marble. It felt like taking up the role of co-composer even though I did not add a single note to it (if an accusation can be made to me, is that I chose to be stubbornly literal, while taking great steps to avoid being what Nikolai Rimsky-Korsakov was for Modest Mussorgsky or—worse—what Franco Alfano was for Giacomo Puccini). One can say that accepting the deliberate "unfinishedness" of a work—that too is a creative act. If so, the act of conducting *Symphony No. II* completes my work on it, since a live presentation is the best way I know how to prove this composition is complete. LUCIANO CHESSA

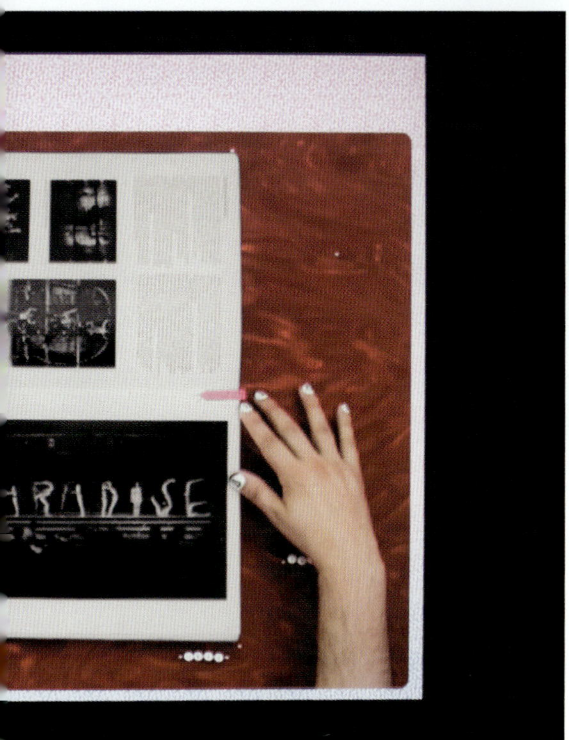

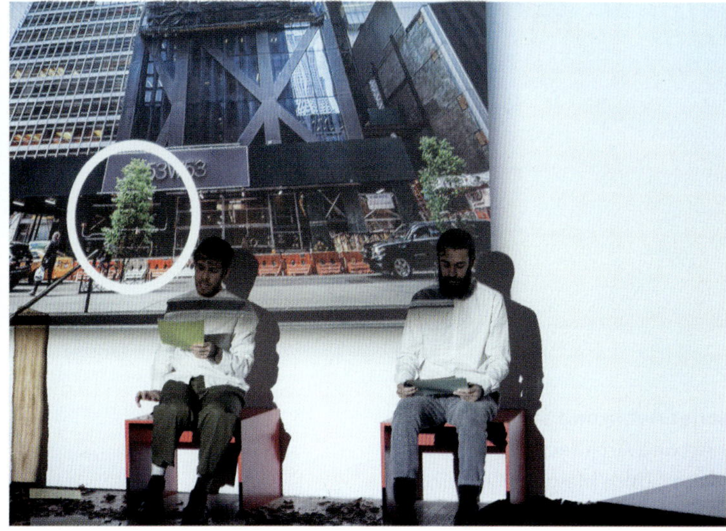

Lluís Alexandre Casanovas Blanco, Taller de Arquitectura's *City in the Space, Experience 1*, 2017. Performance view.

Cooking Sections, *Offsetted*, 2017. Performance view.

MAKING ROOM FOR ACTION

Since its inaugural edition, the Performa biennial has been driven by the desire to activate the city with commissions and live art that would engage directly with the built environment, from its day-to-day experience to its everlasting memories. As early as 2005, the biennial brought adventurous spectators to Governors Island, a military base south of Manhattan, which had not yet been redeveloped for public use (Melik Ohanian, Performa 05). It has also been returning to certain sites, re-envisioning them entirely each time. For instance, Times Square has hosted discreet interventions and encounters with passersby led by Polish experimental theater group Akademia Ruchu (Performa 13); became an urban stage for Arnold Schönberg's atonal opera *Erwartung*, reimagined by Robin Rhode (Performa 15); and served as the terminus of Mohau Modisakeng's procession across Manhattan (Performa 17).

In 2009, the first Hub was created by nOffice (Markus Miessen, Magnus Nilsson, and Ralf Pflugfelder). Serving as a lab for experimental building, the Hub has since become the ephemeral biennial's headquarters, offering a versatile space for art and socializing. Performa has also regularly hosted and participated in groundbreaking presentations exploring the use of performance to challenge architecture: Berlin group An Architektur presented *10 days for oppositional architecture towards post-capitalist spaces* during Performa 09, in the wake of the 2008 financial crisis; the 2010 panel discussion "Have You Kicked a Building Lately?" brought together architects Vito Acconci and Teddy Cruz, theorist Beatriz Colomina, and urban policy maker Elizabeth Berger; the 2012 symposium "Performing Architecture" featured RoseLee Goldberg, architect Elizabeth Diller, and architecture curator Pedro Gadanho at Princeton University.

In 2017, the biennial had an ambitious program of performances taking place in iconic and unexpected venues throughout the city and region (including Philip Johnson's legendary Glass House, a short train ride away from Manhattan in New Canaan, Connecticut). Titled *Circulations*, this platform spearheaded by Performa Curator Charles Aubin examined the rich tradition of liveness within architectural practices (see page 82).

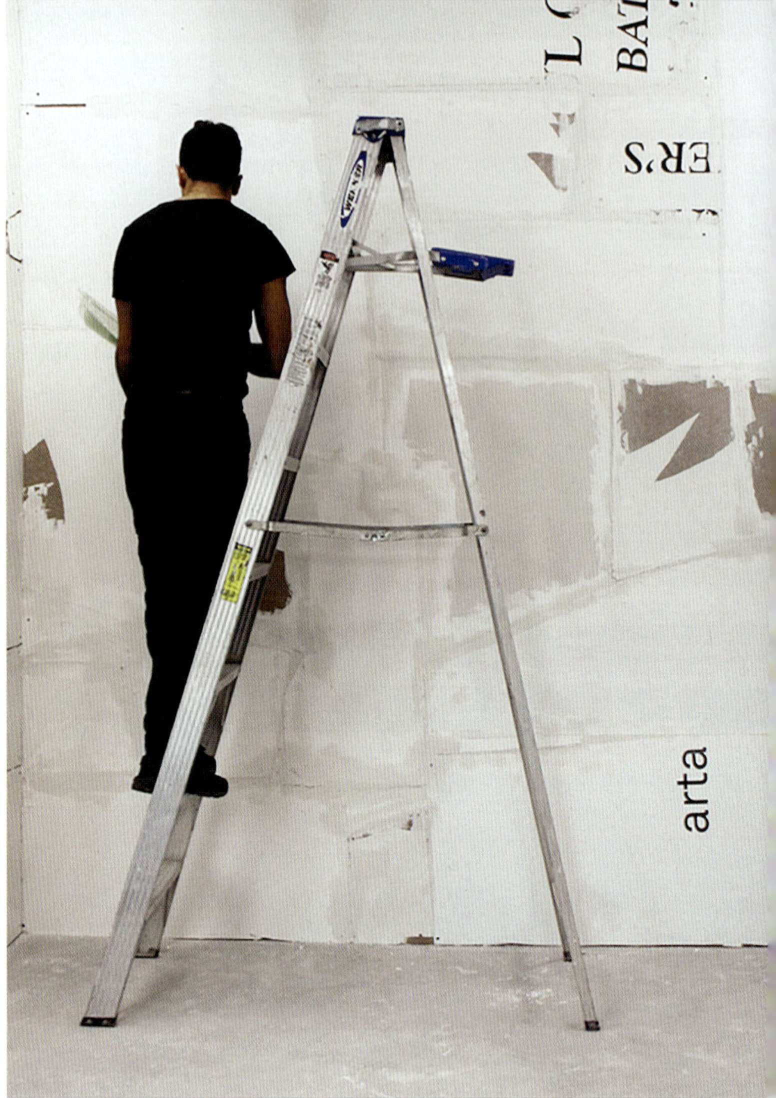

Circulations included a daylong symposium titled "Making Room for Action," held at the Hub. Architect and scholar Lluís Alexandre Casanovas Blanco opened with a lecture-performance on a short-lived experiment by Spanish practitioner Ricardo Bofill's multidisciplinary studio Taller de Arquitectura, operating in Madrid in 1969 and inspired by the writing of Antonin Artaud and its embodiment by American group The Living Theater.

Documentarist duo Ila Bêka & Louise Lemoine then screened *Selling Dreams* (2016), followed by a response by architect and theorist Ife Vanable. A panel discussion between architecture curator Giovanna Borasi, visual artist Yve Laris Cohen, and architect Thom Moran (T+E+A+M) moderated by Charles Aubin and Storefront for Art and Architecture Associate Curator Carlos Mínguez Carrasco completed the day. "Making Room for Action" ended with *Offsetted*, a lecture-performance by London artists Cooking Sections (Daniel Fernández Pascual & Alon Schwabe) on the financialization of urban trees-turned-"carbon reserves" planted in an effort to offset pollution.

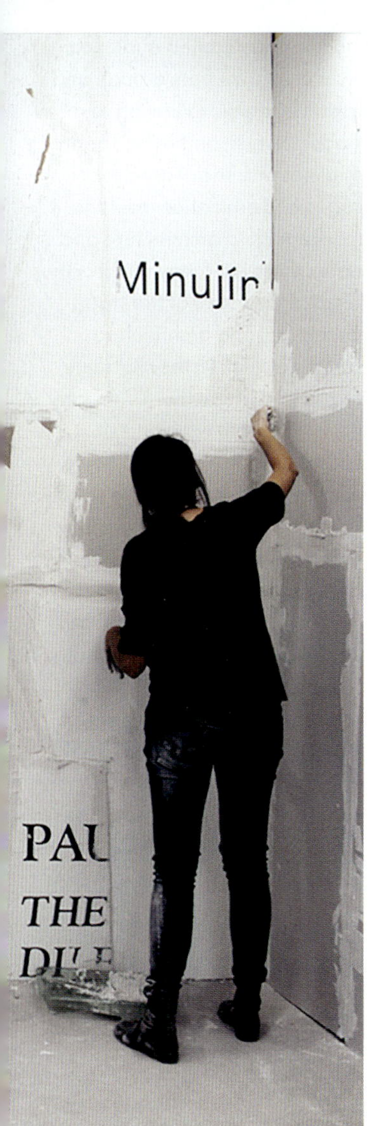

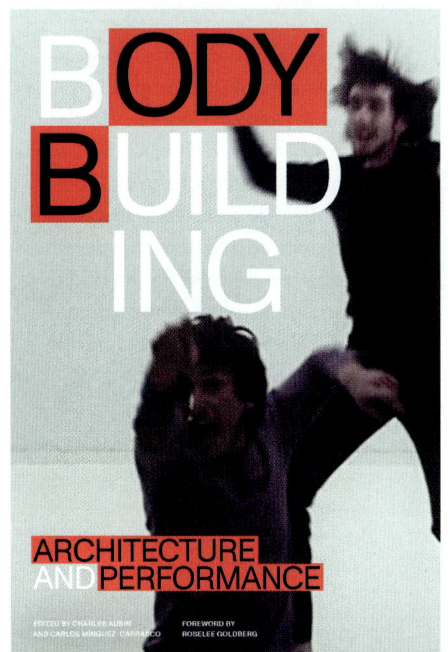

New Affiliates, *Drywall is Forever*, 2019. Video still.

Bodybuilding book cover. Performa, 2019.

BODYBUILDING

"Making Room for Action" served as a stepping stone for *Bodybuilding*, Performa's 2019 publication that examines architects' use of performance in their own practices. Through a selection of historical and contemporary examples, *Bodybuilding* traces an alternative lineage—one about those who opted to stage actions and ephemeral situations rather than erect buildings. For them, performance can be a method of collecting information crucial to the design process, a tool to transform users' experiences, or an instrument of critique.It expands and helps to rethink their discipline. *Bodybuilding* launched at the Performa 19 Hub on November 17, 2019, with *Drywall is Forever*, a lecture-performance by New York firm New Affiliates (Ivi Diamantopoulou and Jaffer Kolb), which explored the use and misuse of drywall by museums and commercial galleries. Made principally of gypsum, these affordable and lightweight temporary walls are easy to erect and discard. But gypsum is a finite resource and is impossible to recycle; after their temporary use for exhibitions, drywall accumulates in dumpsters and landfills. For several weeks in the fall of 2019, Diamantopoulou and Kolb collected leftover pieces of drywall from closed local exhibitions, brought the fragments back to their studio, and methodically fitted them as the walls of a new white cube, one no longer pristine but that bears the traces of its past applications. In this processual work, conducted in collaboration with the city's Department of Sanitation, the firm looked at the economies and flows of art-world byproducts.

ELIZABETH DILLER IN CONVERSATION WITH ROSELEE GOLDBERG

In a dialogue held at the Performa 17 Hub for "Making Room for Action," RoseLee Goldberg and Elizabeth Diller discussed how live work has informed the firm Diller Scofidio + Renfro throughout its four-decade-long practice, tracing how this critical approach to space in motion has shaped their building commissions.

ELIZABETH DILLER

Architecture and performance are the same to me. Our studio works in both disciplines on parallel tracks, and always has. Ric [Scofidio] and I started our studio in 1981 with an alternative practice in which we taught, wrote, and made installations. Our agendas followed our curiosity, independent of the architectural profession, which we felt at the time was intellectually bankrupt. We had little interest in making buildings, and so worked nearly exclusively across the arts, theater, and dance. But we maintained an interest in the discipline of architecture—in space-making. Architecture was bereft of a figure we could look to as a model. Much of our early performance work, our experiments with pictorial and textual forms of expression, narrative and non-narrative structures, and playful attacks on the discipline were inspired by Marcel Duchamp.

We contributed an installation to the "Apropos of Marcel Duchamp *1887/1987*" exhibition, mounted by the Philadelphia Museum of Art in celebration of the 100-year anniversary of Duchamp's birth. Our piece, A *Delay in* Glass, or *The Rotary Notary and His Hot Plate,* divided the stage in half with a rotating wall. A forty-five-degree mirror suspended above the upstage half produced unique perspectives for the audience, such as a plan view of the obscured part of the stage. In one scene, the Bachelor character is in bed, his headboard on the dividing centerline. The headboard allows only his head to be visible downstage, like a pillory. The audience can see the Bachelor's body as it takes direction from his disembodied head. Even from our first days in theater, we wanted to challenge the conventions of the stage and explore the interplay between the physical and the virtual, the real and the simulated, and mediated and unmediated experiences.

Our studio never thinks of architecture as a static form. We approach all projects four-dimensionally, considering the element of time as one would for any theatrical performance. But we also consider a mobile, uncontrolled audience, which has grown from a small and narrow academic following to a broader, diverse audience, spanning disciplines and social divides of all ages and education levels. In our approach to architecture and theater, there is a funny reciprocity. We make the space of the stage architectural and architectural space theatrical. At the High Line, for example, where there's already nothing to do but walk and sit, a sunken overlook allows visitors to indulge in "nothingness"—to simply stare at the taillights of cars below that are driving up 10th Avenue. At the Institute of Contemporary Art in Boston, the best moment in the entire building is in the mediatheque, where the space frames the view of the harbor—but only the water, with no surrounding context. The spectacle is the texture of water. It's mesmerizing. Many have mistaken it for a giant screensaver.

ROSELEE GOLDBERG

The art world of the seventies and into the eighties, with its focus on

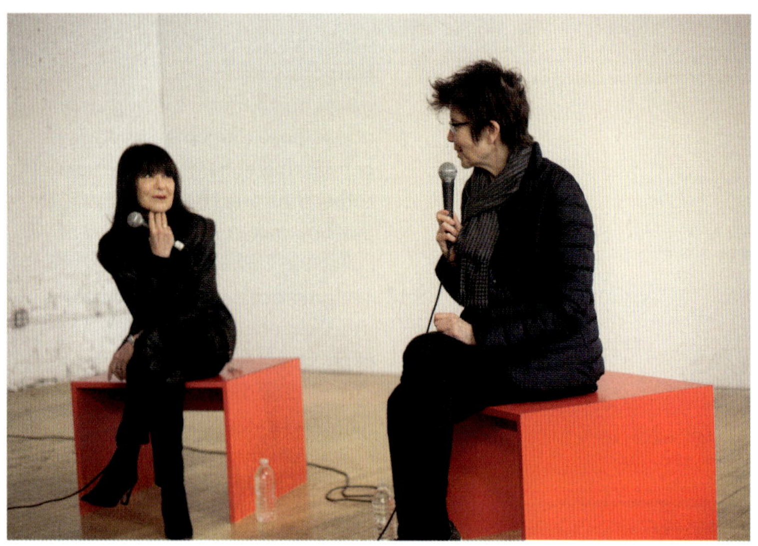

conceptual art, was an incredibly permissive place, and that permission was to work in unexpected ways. Can you describe further the separation between thinking like an architect and thinking like an artist, moving from one realm to the other?

ED

We never made the distinction between architecture, art, or performance. The only question we asked ourselves was: What's the right tool for any particular research? Sometimes the answer was to make a small artifact; sometimes, to work with dancers and film; sometimes we felt compelled to make a temporary installation in the public realm. And sometimes, the opportunity to permanently attach something to the ground was pretty interesting, too. We see these multiple disciplines as a kit of tools to help us navigate changing agendas and step from one medium into another.

One of my biggest early influences was Vito Acconci. When I first noticed Vito's performance work, it subverted gallery space—or was even located in the street. His work was promiscuous, agitating, weird, and very architectural. When he got interested in architecture and started to make buildings, my interest waned. It can be jarring when artists weave in and out of art forms that are ill-fitting. In our case, I don't think any of our interests ever displaced another. They were always parallel or intertwined, but they grew in scale and audacity. This often meant jumping off a cliff without a parachute and expecting a soft landing. We achieved some successes because of our sheer naïveté.

RLG

Looking back on this early work shows the origins of so many of your ideas that are apparent in your current material, how each concept has been developed. There's an accumulation of experience and expertise over time. All your tools have been so sharpened and so perfected that the results are better and better. I think it was Frederick Kiesler who said you have one good idea and you spend the rest of your life perfecting it. The Blur Building, the ICA in Boston, the Shed—each are places that seem always to pivot back and forth between the experience of space and the framing devices of the space, which also includes vantage points to view a building, to hear a building, to feel a building.

ED

A project that marked a critical turning point for us was the Blur Building for Expo.02 in 2002 on Lake Neuchatel, Switzerland. This was a national expo whose typical agenda was the exhibition of progress and technological advancement. Our site was on the side of a lake, but we wanted to build in the water rather than just use the lake as a backdrop, and, beyond that, to use the water as the main building material. The building was a kind of ether that you could inhabit—a big cloud that prevented you from seeing which way to go. The Swiss Expo

RoseLee Goldberg and Liz Diller in conversation. November 11, 2017.

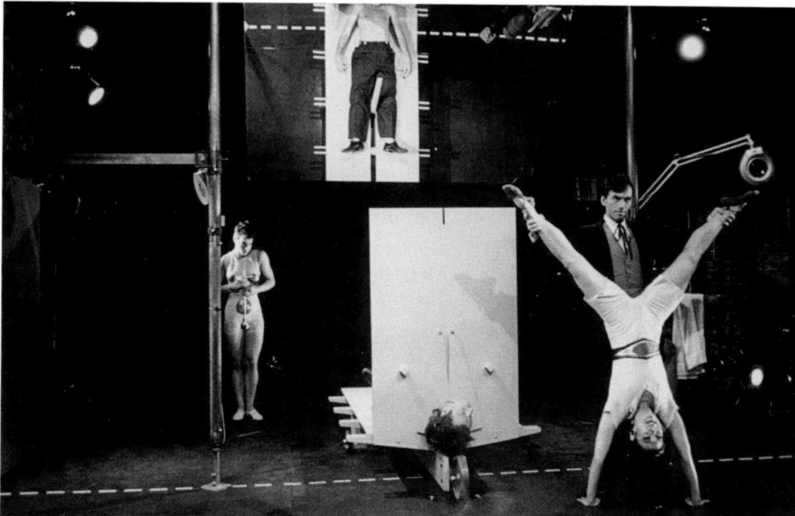

Susan Mosakowski, *The Rotary Notary and His Hot Plate*, set design by Diller + Scofidio, 1987. Performance view.

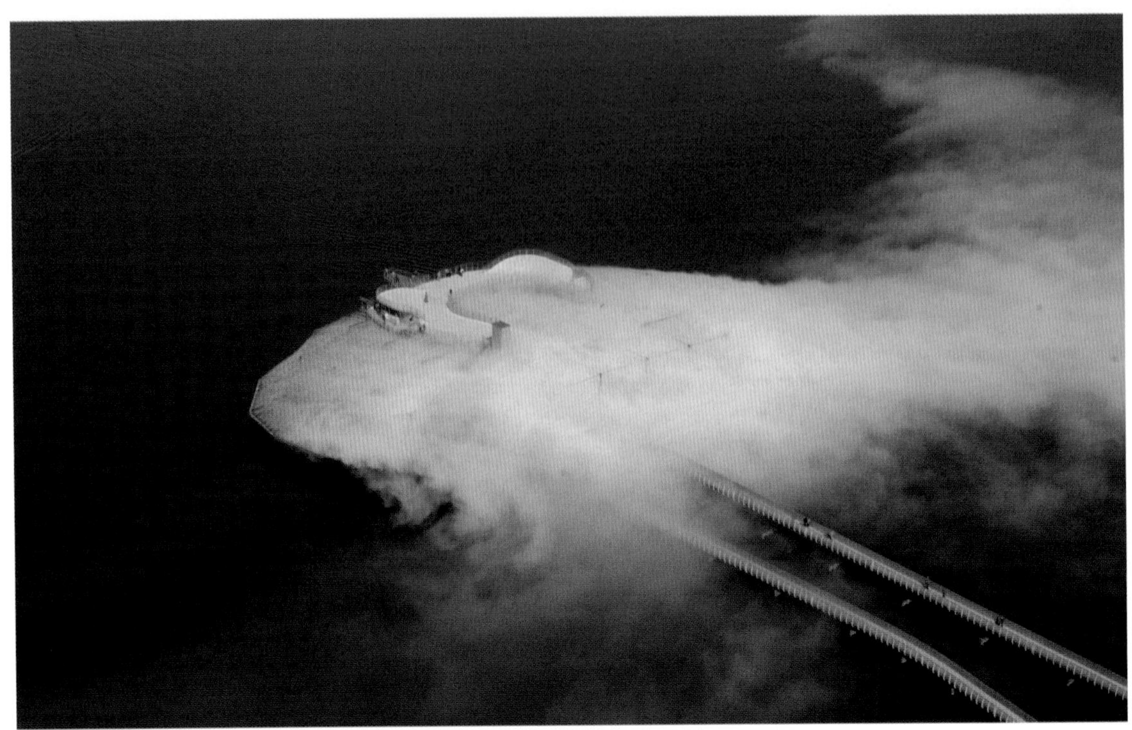

followed the Hanover Expo, which was a demonstration of the latest high-definition screens, generating more and more pixels per inch to create a spectacle. By contrast, the Blur Building was a decidedly low-definition experience. We were using technology to make an anti-spectacle, a theatrical space where there was nothing to see and nothing to do, except contemplate our dependence on vision as the master sense. It was an early form of artificial intelligence. There was a weather station on the structure that read the weather conditions—wind, temperature, humidity, dew point, wind speed, and direction—and responded in real time accordingly. It learned behaviors and got smarter as time went on. I was inspired by Hubert Damisch's writing on the theory of the cloud and the way fog is used in Victorian novels to build tension. The Swiss press at the time asked, "Why do you want to make fog for the Expo? We already have too much of it." Later, everyone came to embrace the project. Visiting Blur became mandatory for every school kid in Switzerland. It was seen by Expo visitors of all ages, cultural backgrounds, income levels, and levels of education. It became a symbol of Swiss pride; it was on stamps, posters, and liquor bottles.

Through Blur, we realized that our desire to make this environmental scale "architecture of atmosphere," with its sensory and scholarly agenda, appealed to just a fraction of the audience. There were endless alternate interpretations that were just as rich. Many visitors thought it was surreal; some thought it represented religious ascension; some thought it was a political statement representing Swiss "doubt." After that, we began to see our work through the lens of a broader audience. It wasn't satisfying enough to just have our art and architecture following. It was more fulfilling to think through many lenses at once. That's how we gauge success now—as work that can be peeled back in layers like an onion that many diverse audiences can engage.

RLG

Recently, you've gone back to your High Line and you created a mile-long performance there. It seems to have had more to do with the shape of this long meandering line than with any building. That seemed to be another kind of liberation for you:

Diller + Scofidio, The Blur Building. Expo.02, Lake Neuchâtel, Switzerland. 2002.

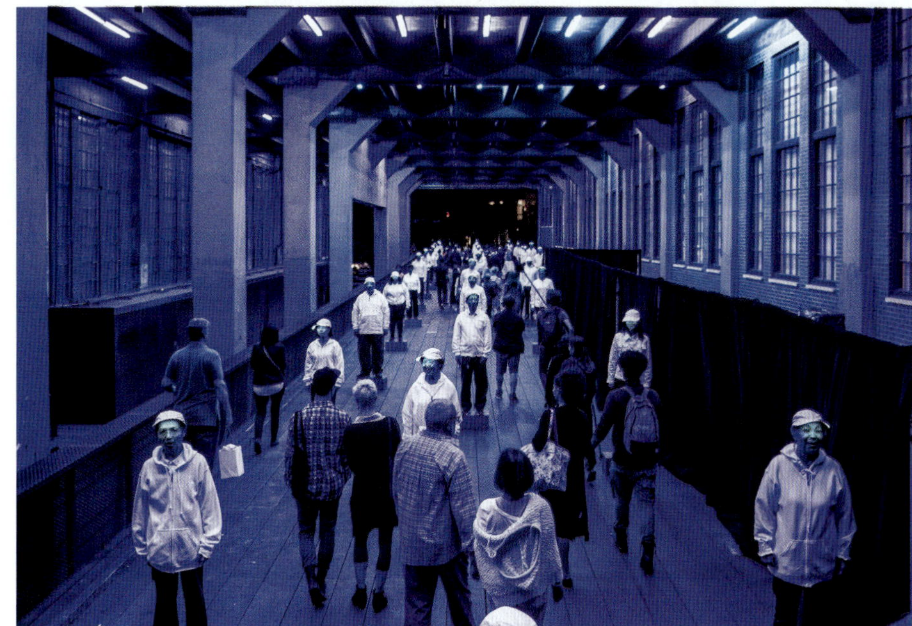

Diller Scofidio + Renfro, The Mile-Long Opera. The High Line, New York. 2018. Performance view.

"Okay, I did the Shed, but now we're going to ignore it, instead taking voices and music for a long walk outside." It seems like you found another outlet.

ED

The High Line is a never-ending project; it's perpetually unfinished. That space—that mile and a half—seemed to us to be a great urban stage to do something unusual. It was always gnawing at us to use it in an alternative way. But the true itch came from an uncomfortable feeling about the rapid transformation of the surrounding area. I thought a lot about the life cycle of the city—its decay and rebirth—full of opportunities and contradictions.

I wanted to do an opera. I actually don't like the form, but I wanted to confront it by liberating opera from the stage. In the end, it wasn't exactly an opera; it was a huge choral work. I co-created and co-directed it. DS+R co-produced it. We worked with David Lang, Anne Carson, Claudia Rankine, and a thousand professional and avocational singers from all five boroughs. We turned the park into a thirty-block-long urban stage for an immersive performance. Performers were above, below, next to, and under the mobile audience that strolled down the length of the park. There was a musical infrastructure that extended across the High Line with different acoustic atmospheres that you walked in and out of. The piece had a very intricate structure with a thousand stories that were sung and spoken to passersby.

The work was a contemplation of the speed of change of the contemporary city. The city was the backdrop and the protagonist. The work touched on two parallel themes: our nostalgia for an irretrievable past and our apprehension about an unknowable, alienating future. It was a critical, political piece presented poetically. The Shed was not big enough for it—it needed to be at the scale of the city.

As I mentioned, we think of buildings as performative, as stages also. They're not discrete, inert objects. Whether we're designing a theater, a museum, or a housing project, the same agenda tends to resurface despite the different circumstances. One thematic we always come back to is spectatorship. Whether we're working at the scale of the city, the institution, or a display, we are always rethinking the conventions of spectatorship.

THE BAUHAUS REVISITED AT PERFORMA 19

In 2019, Performa 19 celebrated the Bauhaus school, founded by the architect Walter Gropius a century earlier in Weimar, Germany. Gropius's manifesto called for the unification of all arts during a time of cultural recovery in impoverished postwar Germany, and so the experimental institution brought together architecture, metalwork, painting, sculpture, theater, and weaving, among other disciplines. The school attracted and influenced Europe's avant-garde, including Paul Klee, Ida Kerkovius, Johannes Itten, Gunta Stölzl, Wassily Kandinsky, Lyonel Feininger, Alma Buscher, and László Moholy-Nagy. Led by Oskar Schlemmer from 1923 to 1929, the stage workshop was the first performance course to be taught in an art institute. The 2019 biennial asked artists, curators, and writers how the fabled center continues to reverberate in the cultural landscape of the twenty-first century, and investigated which tools, precepts, ethics, and aesthetics should drive art colleges in the future.

In collaboration with Goethe-Institut New York, the Performa Institute engaged with the intense social and political environment in and around the Bauhaus. It examined the opportunities provided to both students and faculty to explore the intersections of art, industrial production, and technology and highlighted the revolutionary academy's legacy of interdisciplinary experimentation. The program took place at both Performa 19 Hubs—18 and 47 Wooster Street in SoHo.

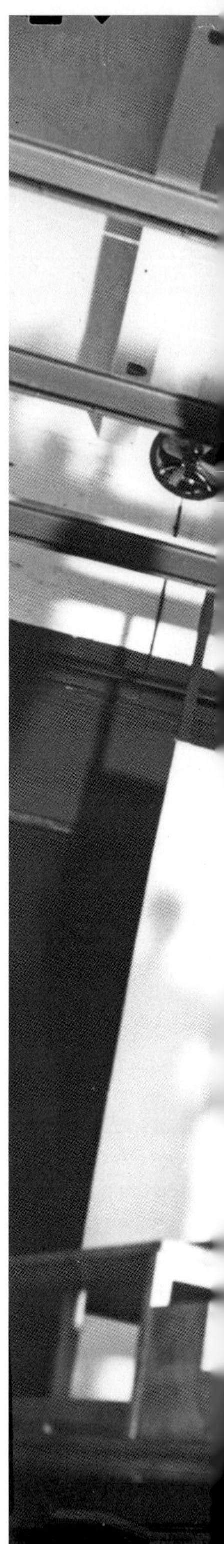

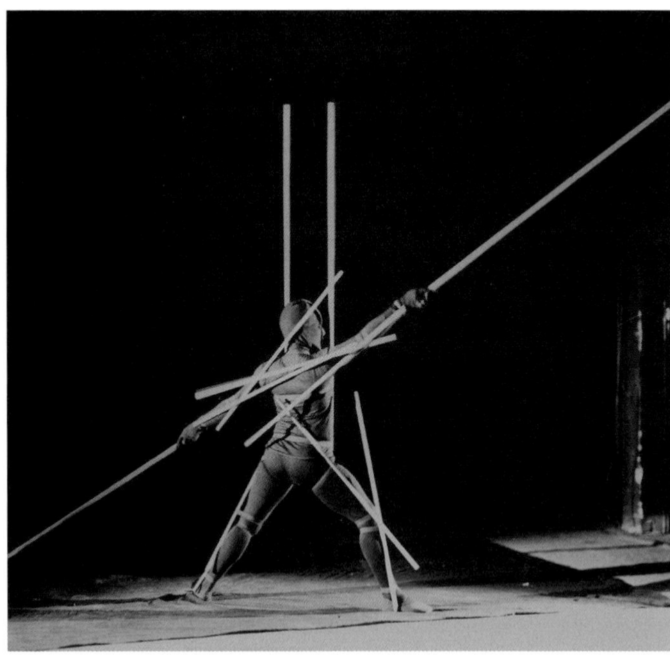

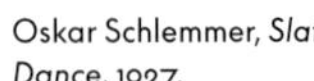

Oskar Schlemmer, *Slat Dance*, 1927.

Andor Weininger, Oskar Schlemmer, Hermann Röseler, and Werner Siedhoff, *Treppenwitz*, 1927.

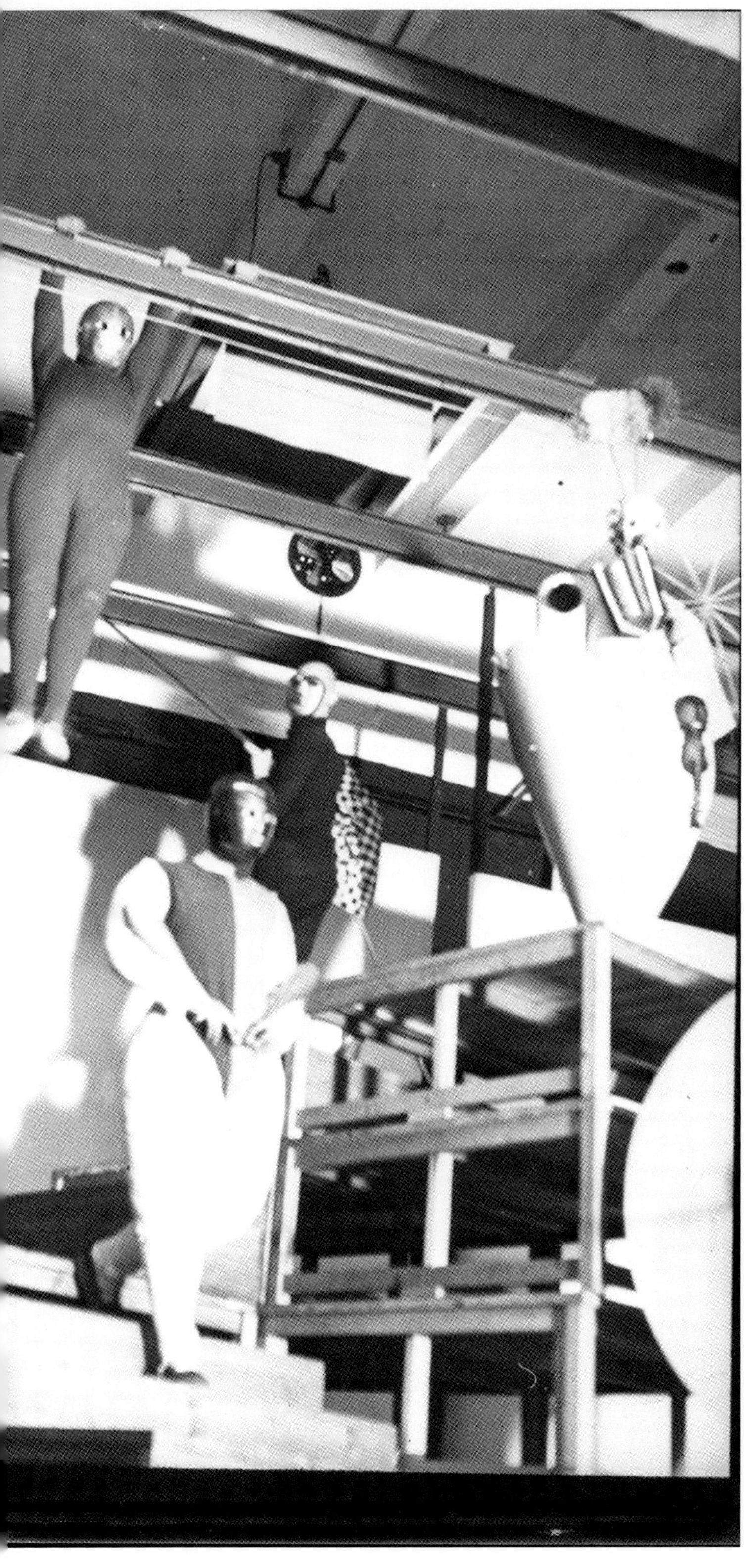

SUBVERSIVE THREADS

On a brisk Sunday, New York interior design collective RUN HOME (founded in the late 1990s by artist-fashion designer Susan Cianciolo and textile artist Kiva Motnyk) led an afternoon of quilting and natural dyeing. Accompanied by tea and cake, the workshop—itself a function of the Bauhaus's re-imagining of the medieval guild system—was a social affair in making and learning, drawing on the German avant-garde institution's concepts of craft, thrift, and the unification of arts. The intimate community created by this twenty-person workshop, if only existing for a few hours, brought together ideas of kinship, curiosity, and play to the otherwise stark white cube of the gallery.

Each participant sat down to a box of one-of-a-kind findings and fabrics, like tiny scissors and scraps of vintage floral brocades, to make their own quilt square, giving new life to found materials. This distinctly "off-the-grid" DIY approach recalled the wildly ingenious props and costumes created for the scene's raucous parties: a guest wore a functioning mini train set to one event; another dressed as a "nonsense" soldier from the legendary 1929 Metal Party, sporting a stockpot and ladle as a headpiece with spoons attached to the uniform's front to mimic epaulettes. In the same spirit, each participant walked away that afternoon with a wholly original creation, informed by new, bold, and boundless ways of making.

CHARLENE K. LAU

BAUHAUS AT THE MARGINS: GENDER, QUEER, AND SEXUAL POLITICS

Architectural historian and theorist Beatriz Colomina and art and cultural historian Elizabeth Otto were in conversation about the complex gender and sexual politics within the Bauhaus community. While Walter Gropius's hall of austere modernist aesthetics and inherent masculinity may come to mind in any discussion of the iconoclastic place, recent scholarship has shed light on lesser-known narratives within this circle that were at the nexus of concepts of gender, sexuality, and what might now be termed *queer identity*. Colomina spoke to undercurrents of perversity in the circle, and more broadly within architectural modernism, with the example of Italian playboy-architect Carlo Mollino, whose erotic Polaroids featured in Nairy Baghramian's installation *Entre deux actes II (Loge*

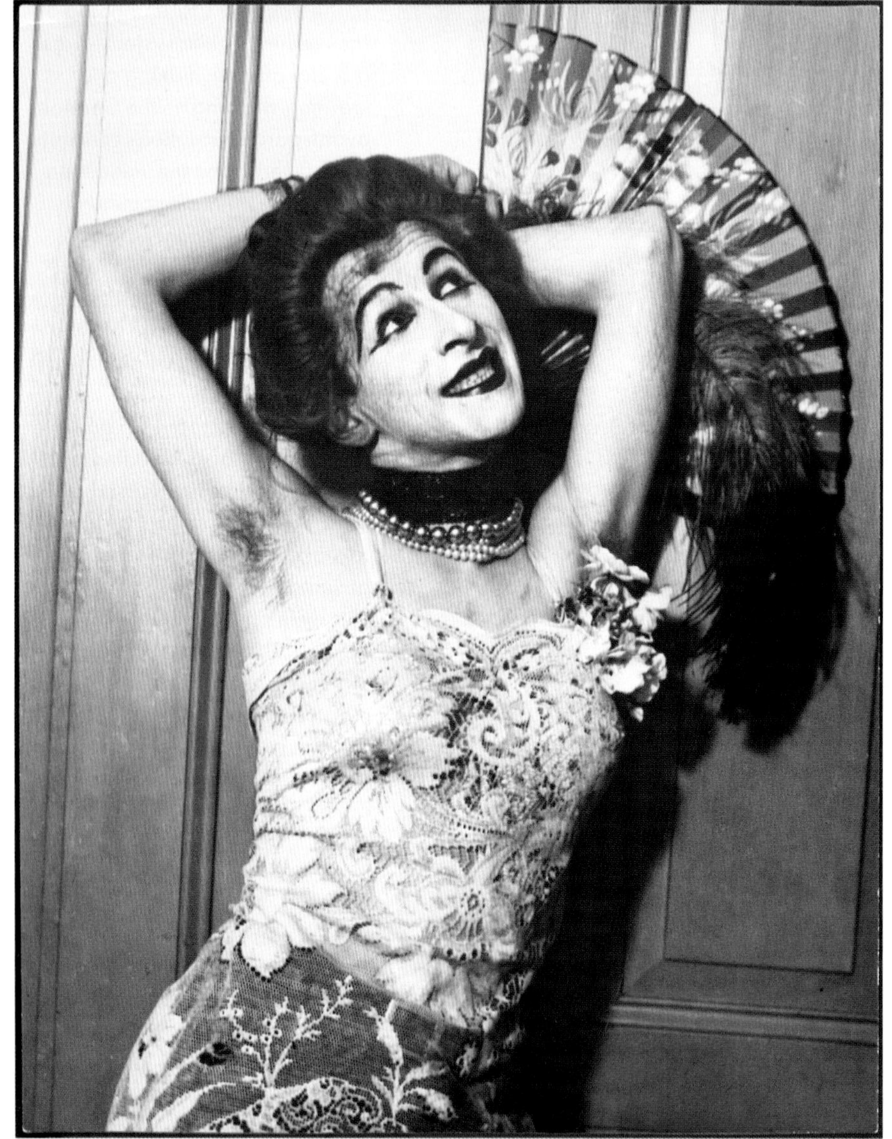

Max Peiffer Watenphul (1896–1976), *Frau mit Fächer (Groteske)* [Woman with Fan (Grotesque)], photograph, ca. 1928. Collection Galerie Berinson, Berlin.

Florence Henri, *Self-Portrait (in the Mirror)*, 1928.

des comédiennes) (2009–19) for Performa 19. Using extracts from her publication *Haunted Bauhaus: Occult Spirituality, Gender Fluidity, Queer Identities, and Radical Politics* (2019), Otto highlighted how the movement proposed a new sort of woman, one who would upend ideas of conventional femininity with her liberated style and dress. Photographs of female associates Marianne Brandt, Florence Henri, and Max Peiffer Watenphul documented female masculinity and practices such as drag, illustrating the fluidity and flexibility with which gender and sexuality were treated in the community. In this sense, the institution not only advanced revolutionary freedom and experimentation in art, craft, and design, but also in the very expression of the essence of the self. CHARLENE K. LAU

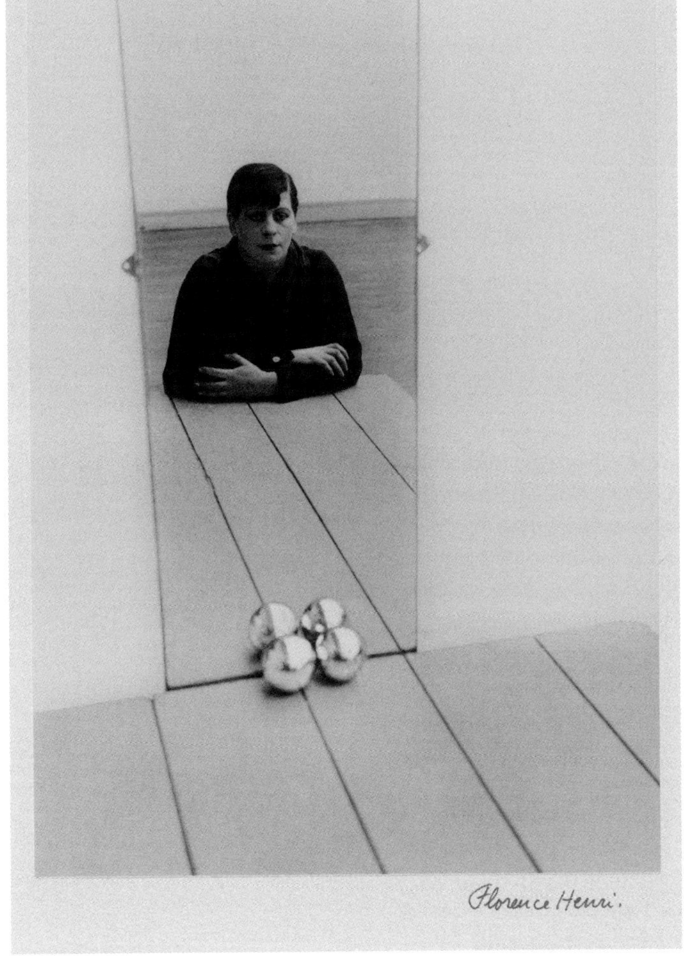

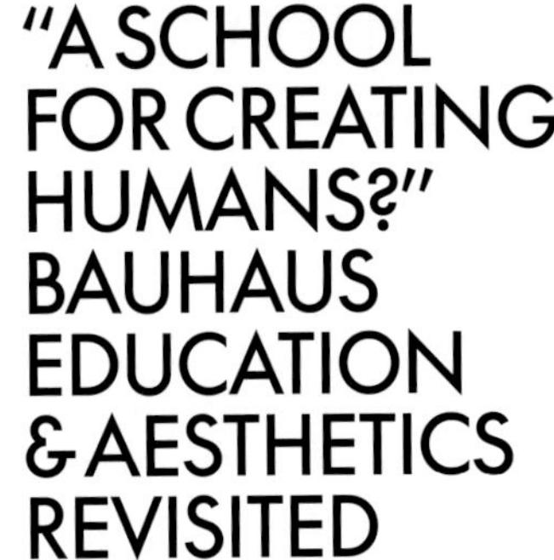

"A SCHOOL FOR CREATING HUMANS?" BAUHAUS EDUCATION & AESTHETICS REVISITED

What is the academic background for Gropius's understanding of the "human?" Who did he envision to be "liberated through creative forces?" In a talk led by scholar Nana Adusei-Poku, artist Coco Fusco, researcher Carmen Mörsch, and theorist Mabel O. Wilson discussed the pedagogical strategies and blind spots of the institution. The roundtable examined how we might learn from the institution while also push against the Bauhaus's limitations and establish ethical conditions for the art institution of the twenty-first century.

BAUHAUS SPIRIT: 100 YEARS OF BAUHAUS

The Goethe-Institut New York screened this 2018 documentary at their headquarters on Irving Place in Manhattan. Directed by German filmmakers Niels Bolbrinker and Thomas Tielsch, the footage explored the college's ideas of renewal as well as its failure in attempting to create a social utopia.

UNLIMITED BODIES

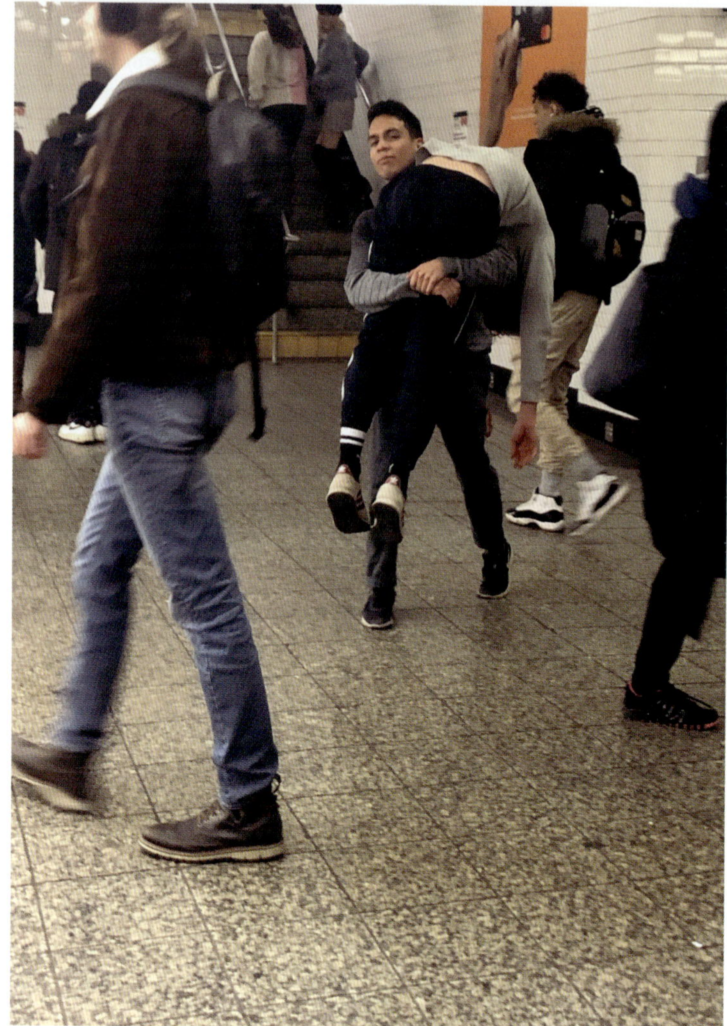

At the Bauhaus, a morning spent in the stage workshop was as important as an afternoon spent in the sculpture studio: Movement was just another method to explore space, volume, or weight. For Performa 19, art historian Sigrid Pawelke and choreographer and CalArts' Dean of the Sharon Disney Lund School of Dance Dimitri Chamblas proposed *UNLIMITED BODIES*, a week-long interdisciplinary experiment inspired by the sweeping pedagogies of the Bauhaus (1919–33) and Black Mountain College (1933–57), the progressive arts institution in North Carolina heavily influenced by the German school's holistic principles. Considering movement research as its backbone, this pedagogical exercise brought together participants from various backgrounds and disciplines to multiply perspectives and viewpoints. For the occasion, Performa hosted thirteen graduate students: four from CalArts's departments in Dance and Critical Studies; three from NYU's Visual Arts Administration course; two enrolled at the Institute for Applied Theatre Studies in Giessen, Germany; two graduates from Paris's Beaux-Arts school; one enrolled at the Columbia University's Astrophysics Laboratory; and one at Barnard College's Movement Lab.

The participants met up every morning at the Hub, where they conducted private workshops with daily noon sessions called "homeroom" open to the public. Each participant was asked to contribute an action, a visit, a person to meet, or a text to read. Among many other impromptu interventions, they went to Mount Sinai Hospital's Abilities Research Center and met with its staff, choreographed among the jostle of rush-hour subway crowds at the very busy Atlantic Avenue–Barclays Center subway station in Brooklyn, and imitated animal behaviors in Central Park, outside the American Museum of Natural History. The week concluded with a day of choreographic improvisations at the Hub. This intensive asked its members to fluidly change roles throughout the week, from participant to session leader or from artist to critic.

UNLIMITED BODIES's participants Cianci Kalid Melo Carrillo and Félix Touzalin at Atlantic Avenue–Barclays Center subway station, 2019. Performance view.

THE BLACK ACT MOVEMENT WORKSHOP

Collaborators Kia LaBeija and Taína Larot led a dynamic workshop of freestyle movement at the Hub. Inspired by the grid plan of Manhattan streets, participants were invited to move through the "Grid of Possibility" and the "Dueling Duet" in specific exercises utilized in the creation of LaBeija's Performa 19 Commission, *(Untitled) The Black Act*, shown at Performance Space New York (see page 266).

LISTENING SESSION BY NKISI

In the Bantu-Kongo cosmology, sound precedes sight: The act of seeing is considered the visual interpretation of an acoustic vibration, echoing within the listener like an underwater sonar. At the Performa 19 Hub, sound artist Melika Ngombe Kolongo, AKA Nkisi, used a listening session to break down the metaphysical power of vibrations at the core of her production.

The Berlin-based Belgian artist of Congolese descent paired her interest in central African cosmologies with the theories of late composer Gérard Grisey. Drawing on the French composer's notion of the "skin of time," Nkisi examined the perception of sonic rhythm and cosmic temporalities. Through a spectral approach to music, Grisey established scientific tools and computer-based processes to distill these notes down to the pure idea of sound perception.[1] For instance, in *Le Noir de l'Étoile*, he placed six percussionists around an audience to produce an atmospheric physical experience influenced by astrophysicists' discovery of pulsars, celestial objects that emit residual signals from supernova explosions.[2] Like in the Bantu-Kongo tradition, information drawn directly from space contemplation relies on nothing else but the reverberation of sound.

In her lecture-performance composed of excerpts and cosmograms, Nkisi drew a web of connections between eras and cultures, alternating in scales from her own intimate experience of sound to her highly physical live DJ sets. She demonstrated her experiments in modulating frequencies to create liminal zones between audibility and inaudibility. As she considers sound a living entity, she reveals how music may constrain and constrict space as easily as it can manipulate and extend time, as if it were, to use Grisey's words, a skin. For Nkisi, whether it comes to cosmic noise, a heartbeat, or even the texture of the human voice, a combination of extreme and multi-dimensional scales deepens the listener's experience of time and allows for renewed emotional connections. SIMON GÉRARD

1 Gérard Grisey and Joshua Fineberg, "Did you say spectral?," *Contemporary Music Review*, Volume 19, Issue 3: Music: Techniques, Aesthetics and Music (2000): 1–3.

2 Gérard Grisey, *Le Noir de l'Étoile* (1989–90), *Ricordi* nº R. 2758.

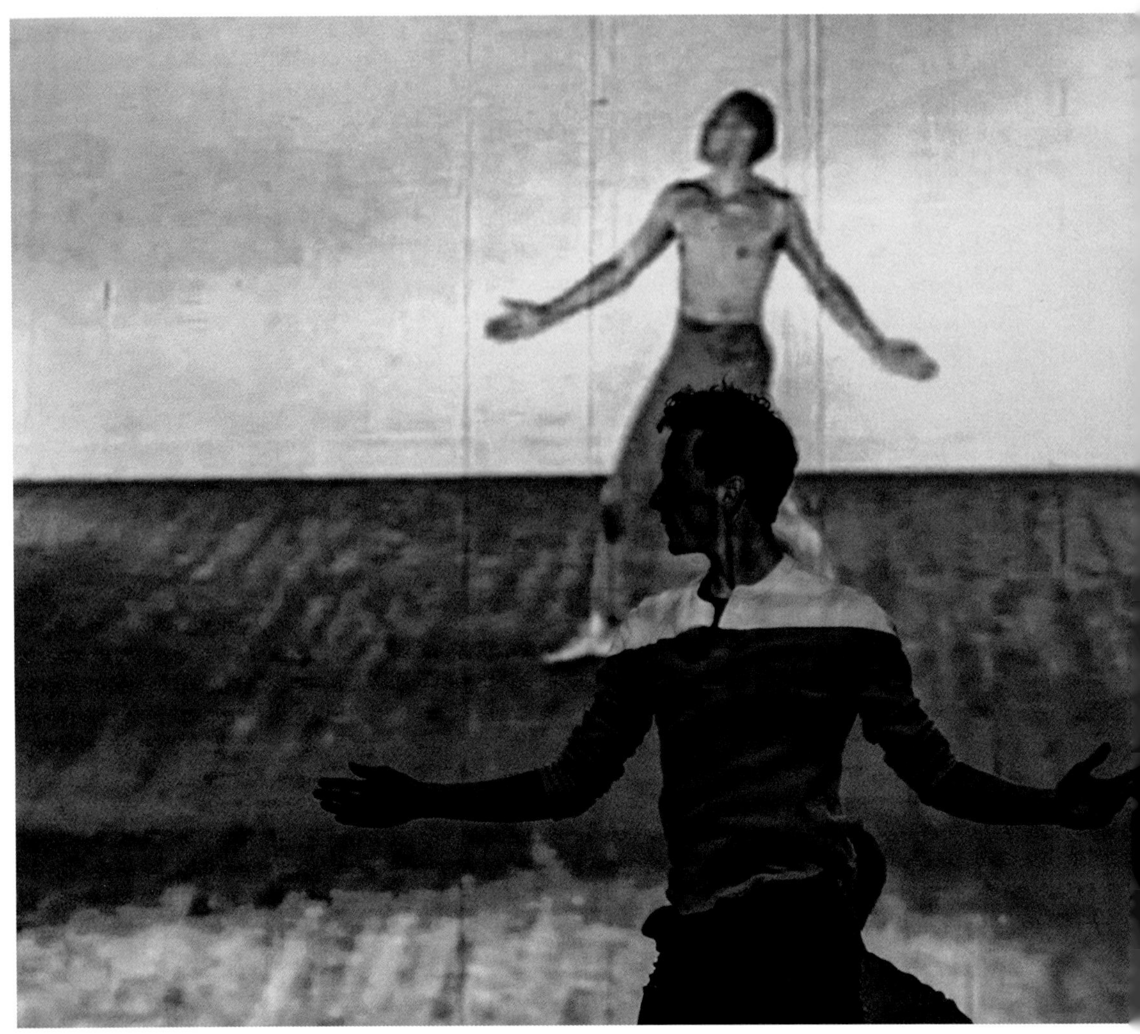

MONUMENTS: ECHOES IN THE DANCE ARCHIVE

American choreographer and researcher Adam Weinert presented an evening of archival film footage, performance, and discussion around his recent reconstruction of several historical works by American modern dance pioneer Ted Shawn (1891–1972). Onstage at the Bruno Walter Auditorium at the New York Public Library of Performing Arts, Weinert, along with performers John Alex McBride and J.M. Tate, presented movement studies that extrapolated from Shawn's choreographic notes, photographs, and reviews to bring *Death of Adonis* (1924), *Four Solos Based on American Folk Music* (1930), and *Dance of the Ages* (1938) back to life.

Adam Weinert, *Four Solos Based on American Folk Music* (Ted Shawn), 2019. Performance view.

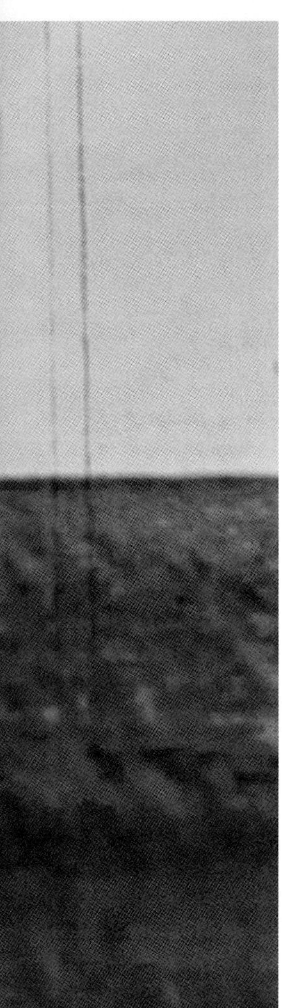

SHU LEA CHEANG ONSCREEN

"I consider sex as a political statement; sexuality is a construct, fluid gender is the norm," cyberfeminist filmmaker Shu Lea Cheang once said, placing her continual entanglements with the politics of queer identity at the core of her production.[1] The screening took this proclamation as a catalyst to connect the artist's early films made while living in New York in the 1980s and reconsider her pioneering work within art and technology. Originally shown inside laundromat washing machines at the Whitney Museum of American Art in 1990, the three-channel standalone work *COLOR SCHEMES* (1989) likened the different wash cycles to processes of cultural assimilation in American culture. The cast—including artists Jimmie Durham and Gloria Miguel—rehearsed and spoke out on instances of racist stereotyping and exclusion felt in both casting calls and everyday life. In one skit, Durham speaks of the challenges of being typecast in indigenous roles but also playing the "enemy": "I have also been a cowboy. But I did it for economic reasons. [...] This cowboy said to me: 'So you're an Indian and a cowboy? Be careful you don't kill yourself.'"

Then, the videos *Sex Fish* (1993) and *Sex Bowl* (1994) from Cheang's *Lesbian Shorts* series focused on interracial sexuality. The former paired sex with biology and fluidity: Ethereal music ushered in strobing black-and-white footage of two nude female bodies explicitly intertwined, one Black and one white (Cheryl Dunye and Alexandra Juhasz) interspersed with images of fish swimming in an aquarium, body parts submerged in water, cunnilingus, and public-bathroom-stall sex. Becoming percussive, the sounds in *Sex Fish* matched the chaotic cycling of scenes of sex and underwater action, messy like the unfettered desire ramped up onscreen.
On the other hand, *Sex Bowl*, as if the "turf" to *Sex Fish*'s "surf," compared sex to scoring and sport amongst segments of zoomed-in bowling alley action. A confident voice ran down a list of romantic exploits with various partners and their fetishes over a funk bassline and atonal operatic vocals, while snapshot portraits and fast cuts of humping and rubbing naked bodies displayed a liberated sensuality. The evening was rounded out with a lively conversation on Cheang's radical oeuvre between the artist and former Guggenheim and Smithsonian Museum curator John G. Hanhardt—who commissioned Cheang's ground-breaking net artwork *Brandon* (1998–99)—moderated by transgender studies scholar and filmmaker Susan Stryker. CHARLENE K. LAU

1 Ashley Wong, "Shu Lea Cheang: FLUIDØ Cypherpunk Film," *Sedition*, June 5, 2015. Accessed March 7, 2021. https://www.seditionart.com/magazine/shu-lea-cheang-fluido-film?lang=en.

GRAND FINALE MALCOLM MCLAREN AWARD

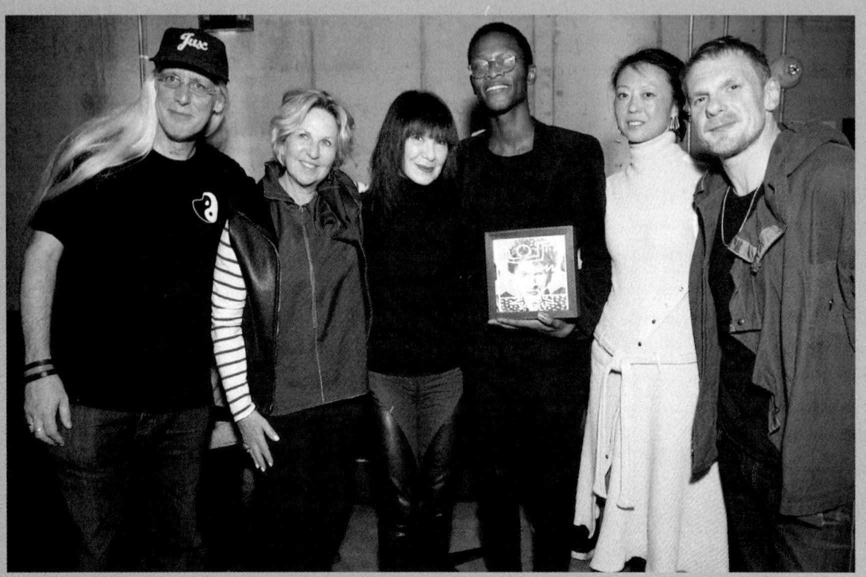

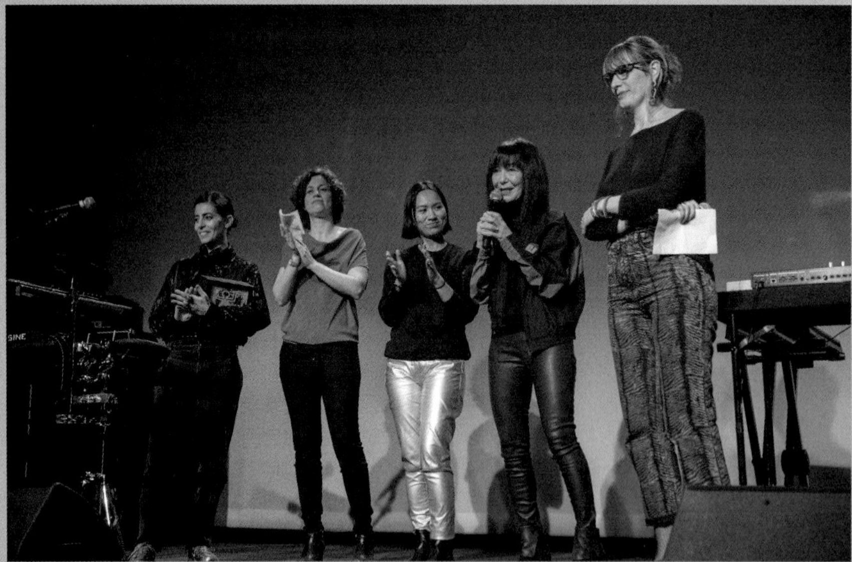

Carlo McCormick, Wendy Fisher, RoseLee Goldberg, Vuyo Sotashe, Young Kim, and Mark Beasley at the Grand Finale of Performa 17.

Maria Hassabi, Nikki Columbus, Lumi Tan, RoseLee Goldberg, and Ana Janevski at the Grand Finale of Performa 19.

In 2011, Performa created the Malcolm McLaren Award in memory of the spirited and irreverent punk icon. Working with curator Mark Beasley, McLaren had planned to deliver a Dada-inspired lecture-performance for Performa 11, but sadly passed away on April 8, 2010, before the work could be realized. In his honor, the Marc Newson-designed prize—presented during a ceremony on each biennial's closing-night Grand Finale—is granted to an artist who innovates and pushes the bounds of imagination with bold, thought-provoking live art. The inaugural winner was Iceland's Ragnar Kjartansson, for his epic opera *Bliss* (2011), followed by Ryan McNamara for the choreographic exploration *MEƎM: A STORY BALLET ABOUT THE INTERNET* (2013), and Edgar Arceneaux for his part re-enactment, part video installation *Until, Until, Until...* (2015).

For Performa 17, Cape Town-based Kemang Wa Lehulere received the award for *I cut my skin to liberate the splinter*, where he and five performers played sculpted musical instruments and danced movements borrowed from children's games at the East Village's Connelly Theater. In collaboration with South African theater director and choreographer Chuma Sopotela, *I cut my skin* examined the nation's colonial violence by using meaningful symbols from indigenous astrology, tribal wisdom, and religious rites. Cultural critic and curator Carlo McCormick handed the award to South African singer Vuyo Sotashe, who accepted on Wa Lehulere's behalf, and guests continued to celebrate all night with a DJ set spun by producer Venus X.

At the Performa 19 Grand Finale, Raymond Pettibon gave the McLaren Award to three participants across two Commissions: Iranian-born German sculptor Nairy Baghramian and Cyprian-born, New York-based choreographer Maria Hassabi, as well as multidisciplinary Swedish-Romanian artist Éva Mag. Co-commissioned by Performa and 1014, Baghramian and Hassabi's hybrid installation and live performance *Entre Deux Actes (Ménage à Quatre)* was set over two floors of a Fifth Avenue townhouse formerly inhabited by the Goethe-Institut. The two transformed the domestic interiors into a stage where bodies and architecture enmeshed, exchanging intimacy, desire, and fantasy between them. Mag's durational *Dead Matter Moves* had her and ten performers sculpting, shifting, and supporting clay-textile effigies, turning the historic space of the Judson Memorial Church gym into a messy factory floor for leaden figures.

Later, David J, founding member of the post-punk band Bauhaus, played a tribute to the centennial of the Bauhaus school. Butoh artist Vangeline and J performed an hour-long composition that featured voice samples from René Halkett, part of the original Staatliches Bauhaus at Weimar from 1923 to 1925. The set ushered revelers late into the brisk November darkness, saying goodnight to another biennial.

ABOUT PERFORMA

Founded in 2004 by art historian and curator RoseLee Goldberg, Performa is the leading organization dedicated to exploring the critical role of live performance in the history of twentieth-century art and to encouraging new directions in performance for the twenty-first century. Since launching New York's first performance biennial, Performa 05, in 2005, the organization has solidified its identity as a commissioning and producing entity. As a "museum without walls," Performa contributes important art-historical heft to the field by showing the development of live art in all its forms from many different cultural perspectives. In the past fifteen years, Performa has presented six hundred works, engaged more than seven hundred artists, and toured commissioned performances in twenty countries. Performa also produces exhibitions, an online magazine, conferences, lectures, and standalone programming that foster learning, critical discourse, and deeper engagement with performance.

CREDITS

PERFORMA BOARD OF DIRECTORS
RoseLee Goldberg, Founding Director
Toby Devan Lewis, Emeritus Board Chair
Rashid Johnson, Board Chair
Richard Chang, President
Barbara Hoffman, Secretary
Todd Bishop, Treasurer
Wendy Fisher
Ronald Guttman
Jeanne Greenberg Rohatyn
David Hallberg
Joyce Liu
Shirin Neshat
Roya Sachs
Neil Wenman

PERFORMA CURATORIAL ADVISORY COUNCIL
Marina Abramović
Massimiliano Gioni
Yuko Hasegawa
Chrissie Iles
Joan Jonas
Lois Keidan
William Kentridge
Joseph V. Melillo
Paul D. Miller
Meredith Monk
Hans Ulrich Obrist
Yoko Ono
Lisa Phillips
Catherine Wood
Octavio Zaya

PERFORMA STAFF
Founding Director & Chief Curator: RoseLee Goldberg
Managing Director & Executive Producer: Esa Vincenty Nickle
Senior Curator & Head of Curatorial Affairs: Kathy Noble
Senior Curator & Head of Publications: Charles Aubin
Senior Producer & Manager of Media Initiatives: Sasha Okshteyn
Associate Curator at Large: Job Piston
Curator at Large: Defne Ayas

PERFORMA ADVISORY COUNCIL
Laurie Beckelman
Anne Bergeron
Concetta Duncan

Stephanie French
Michael Kantrow
Nadine Peyser

PERFORMA OPERATING FUND AND PERFORMA INSTITUTE PROGRAMS CONTRIBUTORS

The Performa Board of Directors, the National Endowment for the Humanities, the Andrew W. Mellon Foundation, the David and Elaine Potter Foundation, the Crown Family Philanthropies, the Aspen Community Foundation, New York City Department of Cultural Affairs, the New York State Council on the Arts, the Aaron Copland Foundation, Performa Members Circles, the Performa Visionaries and all of the generous donors who support our annual gala celebrations.

PERFORMA 17 STAFF

Founding Director & Chief Curator: RoseLee Goldberg
Producing Director & International Affairs: Esa Vincenty Nickle
Curator: Adrienne Edwards
Curator: Charles Aubin
Special Projects Manager: Job Piston
General Manager: Eliza Coviello
Assistant to the Director: Maggie Chan
Manager of Individual Giving: Sarah Haimes
Marketing Manager: Gabrielle Saint-Amour
Andrew W. Mellon Curatorial Fellow: Lydia Brawner
Research & Archives: Marc Arthur
Biennial Producer: Maaike Gouwenberg
Producer: Raul Zbengheci
Associate Producer: Sasha Okshteyn
Associate Producer: Robert Wuss
Associate Producer: Bob Kalas
Curatorial Fellow Estonian Pavilion: Evelyn Raudsepp
Performa 17 Biennial Hub Manager: Stephanie Bokenfohr
Box Office Manager: Debbie Huang
Technical Producer: Todd Garrison
Production Assistant: Xica Aires
Production Fellow: Manuela Nebuloni
Development Assistant: Eva Sibinga
Grant Writer: Beth Allen
Marketing Assistant: Meytar Moran
Press Associate: Rosemary Reyes
Ticket Services & Front of House Assistant: Flore Herman
Administrative Intern: Bjorn Lee Varella
Design: Barbara Kruger with Project Projects
Website: Perry Garvin Studio
PR Agency: Sutton PR
Archival Photography: Paula Court
Video Documentation: Polemic

PERFORMA 17 COMMISSIONING FUND

Edgar Arcenaux, Maggie Barr, Anne Bergeron, Lauren Leilani Ching, Darren G. Fields, Davidoff Art InitiativeSandra C. Gil, Jason Jacques, Jonathan Jawno, Eileen O'Kane Kornreich, Miyoung Lee, Kevin Lu, Iris Marden, Richard J. Massey Foundation, Jessica Mitrani, Jorge Baron Muniz, Shoujou Piston, Andrew Renton, Tracey and Phillip Riese, Andy Romer, Karen Robinovitz, Robert M. Rubin, Rivka Saker, Arlene Shechet and Mark Epstein, South African Foundation for Contemporary Art, Stephen Friedman Gallery, Keith Yazmir, and Marcella Zimmermann.

SOUTH AFRICAN PAVILION COMMITTEE

Wendy Fisher (Committee Chair), Bob and Renee Drake - Robben Stichting, Liza Essers - Goodman Gallery, Patrick Gaspard, Jonathan Jawno, Pulane Kingston, Tracey and Phillip Riese, and Emile Stipp.

PERFORMA 17 PARTNERS

Aesop, Artnews Africa, BKLYN Studios, BOS Tea, Bronx Brewery, Brooklyn Brewery, CalArts, Create Blueprint, David Bowler Wines, Dig Inn, Frieze, the Glass House, Lagunitas Brewing Company, Louis/Dressner Selections, Material Vodka, NeueHouse, NYC Parks, Project Projects, PUBLIC Hotel, Sutton PR, and Turtle Conservancy.

PERFORMA 19 STAFF

Founding Director & Chief Curator: RoseLee Goldberg
Producing Director & International Affairs: Esa Vincenty Nickle

Senior Curator & Manager of Curatorial Affairs: Kathy Noble
Curator: Charles Aubin
Andrew W. Mellon Curatorial Fellow: Charlene K. Lau
Assistant to the Director & Curatorial Assistant: Brittany Richmond
Producer: Maaike Gouwenberg
Producer: Sasha Okshteyn
Associate Producer: Bob Kalas
Associate Producer: Debbie Huang
Associate Producer: JP Faienza
Technical Producer: Sascha von Oertzen
Advancement & Special Events: Julia Clark
Press & Marketing Manager: Evan Lenox
Hub Producer: Xica Aires
Curatorial Assistant: Uchenna Itam
Curatorial Fellow (Taiwanese Pavilion): Wang Han-Fang
Biennial Fellow: Thuthuka Sibisi
Production Fellow: Simon Gérard
Production Fellow: Anne Stolten
Social Media & Marketing Coordinator: Jametria Wright
Gala Coordinator: Sabrina Potterpin
Box Office Manager: Liz Hepp
Advancement Assistant: Sofia Ramirez
Finance & Administration: Matthew Corey
Grant Writer: Beth Allen
Administrative Coordinator: Bjorn Lee Varella
Design: Special - Offer
PR Agency: Pelham Communications
Archival Photographer: Paula Court
Video Documentation: Romke Hoogwaerts

PERFORMA 19 MAJOR FUNDERS
The Ford Foundation, the Andy Warhol Foundation for the Visual Arts, Toby Devan Lewis, and the Robert Rauschenberg Foundation

PERFORMA 19 PROGRAM SUPPORTERS
Barbro Osher Pro Suecia Foundation, New York City Department of Cultural Affairs, Crozier Fine Arts, David and Elaine Potter Foundation, Étant donnés Contemporary Art, a program of the French American Cultural Exchange (FACE) Foundation, Flemish Cultural Services, Fundación Almine y Bernard Ruiz-Picasso, FUSED (French U.S. Exchange in Dance), the Graham Foundation, German Academy, Goethe Institute, Agnes Gund, Hong Kong Arts Development Council, Iaspis/the Swedish Arts Grants Committee, Institut français, Elise Jaffe + Jeffrey Brown, Maria Bonnier Dahlin Foundation, Marian Goodman Gallery, Nowness, Red Bull Arts, Société Berlin, Swedish Arts Grants Committee and the Visual Arts Fund, Taipei Cultural Center in New York, Taiwan Ministry of Culture, and Taiwan Contemporary Culture Lab (C-Lab).

Sarah Arison, the Daniel Sachs Foundation, Charlie Ferrer, Liz and Jonathan Goldman, the Josie Club (Mickalene Thomas, Racquel Chevremont, Jet Toomer, and Nina Chanel Abney), Bruce Karatz, King's Fountain, Abigail Pucker, the Rosenkranz Foundation, Shelley and Donald Rubin, Spring Workshop, and the Young Arts Foundation.

PERFORMA 19 COMMISSIONING FUND

Noreen Ahmad, Carla Chammas and Judi Roaman, Füsun Eczacıbaşı, Dominique Lévy, Arthur and Jay Richardson, Tracey and Phillip Riese, Mikelle Rindflish and Matthew Borrowick, Victoria Rogers, Rivka Saker, Roger Silverstein, Hope Stringer, Ellen and William Taubman, Anne Tenenbaum and Thomas Lee, Joseph Rosenwald Varet and Esther Kim Varet, Madeline Weinrib, and Royal Norwegian Consulate General in New York.

PERFORMA 19 PARTNERS

2014, Abrons Art Center, Bonnier Konsthall, CalArts, C L E A R I N G New York / Brussels, Consulate General of Sweden in New York, Jeffrey Deitch, Embassy of Sweden, Galerie Nordenhake Stockholm, Hallands Konstmuseum, Institute for Contemporary Ideas and Art, the Kitchen, Lafayette Anticipations - Fondation d'entreprise Galeries Lafayette, NeueHouse, Performance Space New York, Royal Institute of Art (Stockholm), Taipei Fine Arts Museum, and Wallplay.

IMAGE CREDITS

All photographs are by Paula Court unless otherwise noted below.

PERFORMA 17
Pages 16 and 17: photo by Cameron Cuchulainn. Page 21: photo by Max Lakner. Courtesy BFA. Page 25: Courtesy William Kentridge and Marian Goodman Gallery. Page 39: photo by Cameron Cuchulainn. Page 41: Courtesy Zanele Muholi. Pages 44 and 45: photo by Cameron Cuchulainn. Page 63 and 65: photos by Cynthia Edorh. Courtesy the Metropolitan Museum of Art. Pages 68 and 69: Courtesy Yto Barrada. Page 78: © Van Vechten Trust. Page 89: photo by Michael Biondo. Page 91: © François Dallegret. Page 99, 100, and 101: photos by Jenica Heintzelman. Page 103, 104, 105, and 107: photos by Paula Lobo. Pages 120 and 121: photo by Cameron Cuchulainn. Page 137: photos by Ian Douglas. Courtesy Danspace Project. Page 145: photo by Cameron Cuchulainn. Page 147: photo by Colleen Tuite. Courtesy 1.5 Rooms. Page 149: photo by Cameron Cuchulainn

PERFORMA 19
Page 161: photo by Walter Wlodarczyk. Page 171: photo by Caroline Budge. Pages 172 and 173: photo by Eian Kantor. Page 184: Courtesy Nairy Baghramian. Page 185 and 187: photos by Sarah Blesener. Page 191: photo by Peter Moore, 1965. © 2021 Barbara Moore. Licensed by VAGA at Artists Rights Society (ARS), New York. Courtesy Paula Cooper Gallery, New York. Pages 196 and 197: photos by Al Giese, 1965. Robert Rauschenberg Foundation Archives, New York. © 2021 Hottelet/Giese. Licensed by Artists Rights Society (ARS), New York. Pages 200, 201, and 203: photos by Eian Kantor. Pages 209 and 211: photos by George Etheredge. Pages 214 and 215: Still image from Phantom Banquet VR 360. Courtesy Lap-See Lam. Pages 223, 224, and 225: photos by Carter Seddon. Courtesy 80WSE. Page 233: photo by Charles Aubin. Pages 234, 235, 239, 240, 241, 242, and 243: photos by Eian Kantor. Page 245: photo by Mark Waldhauser. Page 252 and 256: photos by Hyla Skopit. Courtesy Pace Gallery. © Torkwase Dyson. Page 258: photo by Maria Baranova. Courtesy Pace Gallery. © Torkwase Dyson. Pages 263, 264, and 265: photos by Eian Kantor. Page 269: photo by Julieta Cervantes. Courtesy Performance Space New York. Page 271, above: Courtesy Theatermuseum der Universität zu Köln. Page 271, below, left and right: photos by Atelier Grill. Courtesy Bauhaus-Archiv Berlin. Page 277: photo by T. Lux Feininger. Courtesy Bauhaus-Archiv Berlin. © Estate of T. Lux Feininger. Page 291: photo by Carter Seddon. Courtesy Paul Maheke and Galerie Sultana, Paris. © Goethe-Institut, New York.

PERFORMA AT LARGE
Page 296: photo by Anders Sune Berg. Courtesy Copenhagen Contemporary. Page 298 and 301: photos by Julieta Cervantes © 2015 The Museum of Modern Art, New York. Page 302: Courtesy ORF, Vienna. Page 306 and 308: Courtesy Electronic Arts Intermix (EAI). Page 311: photo by Dona Ann McAdams. Page 312: photo by Job Piston. Page 314: Courtesy Judy Chicago, Salon 94, and Jessica Silverman Gallery. Page 316: photo by Antonio Martinelli. Courtesy Fondazione Aldo Rossi. © Eredi Aldo Rossi. Pages 318, 320, 321, and 323: Courtesy Fortes D'Aloia & Gabriel, São Paulo/Rio de Janeiro. Page 326: Courtesy Rene Matić. Page 328: photo by Elise Galant. Page 334: photo by Walter Wlodarczyk. Page 341: Courtesy E.S.P. TV.

NOT FOR SALE
Page 349, above: © Naho Kubota. Page 349, below: photo by J. Dewait. Page 352 and 356: Courtesy Adam Pendleton. Page 358: photo by Stephanie Bokenfohr. Page 359: Courtesy Jaan Toomik and Temnikova & Kasela Gallery. Page 360: Courtesy Janus Films. Page 361: Courtesy The Nest Collective. Page 364: Courtesy Omar Berrada. Page 367: Courtesy Nemo Hill. Page 368: photo by Stephen Sewell. Courtesy Lluís Alexandre Casanovas Blanco. Page 369: photo by Ian Giles. Page 370: Courtesy New Affiliates. Page 371: Film still courtesy Taller de Arquitectura/Ricardo Bofill. Graphic design by Riley Hooker. Page 372: photo by Ian Giles. Page 373: photo by J. Vezuzzo. Courtesy Diller Scofidio + Renfro. Page 374: photo by Beat Widmer. Courtesy Diller Scofidio + Renfro. Page 375: photo by Timothy Schenck. Courtesy Diller Scofidio + Renfro. Page 376: photo by T. Lux Feininger. Page 377: photo by T. Lux Feininger. Harvard Art Museums/Busch-Reisinger Museum, Gift of Herbert Bayer. © T. Lux Feininger. © President and Fellows of Harvard College, BR48.123. Page 378: Courtesy Galerie Berinson, Berlin. Page 379: Archives Florence Henri. Courtesy Bauhaus-Archiv Berlin, © Galleria Martini & Ronchetti. Page 380: © François-Thibaut Pencenat. Page 382: photo by Zach Gross. Courtesy Adam Weinert. Page 384, above: photo by Max Lakner. Courtesy BFA. Page 384, below: photo by Walter Wlodarczyk.

PRODUCTION & FUNDING CREDITS

PERFORMA 17

Barbara Kruger's Performa 17 works *Untitled (Know, Believe, Forget)*, *Untitled (School)*, *Untitled (Skate)*, and *Untitled (The Drop)* were curated by RoseLee Goldberg with Job Piston and produced by Esa Nickle with Sasha Okshteyn. *Untitled (Know, Believe, Forget)* was presented on a billboard situated at 10th Avenue and 17th Street from November 1 to 19, 2017. *Untitled (Skate)* was presented at Coleman Playground Skate Park from November 1 to 19, 2017. *Untitled (The Drop)* took place at the Performa 17 Hub on November 2, 9, and 16, 2017. Support was provided by Volcom, Sprüth Magers, Larry Warsh, the Broad Art Foundation, Mary Boone, Susi Kenna, and the Performa Commissioning Fund. Special thanks to Eric Goode, the Park restaurant, the Turtle Conservancy, Steve Rodriguez, and EP+Co.

The South African Pavilion Without Walls for Performa 17 was curated by RoseLee Goldberg and supported by the Ford Foundation and the South African Pavilion Committee: Wendy Fisher, Fundação Sindika Dokolo, Liza Essers - Goodman Gallery, Patrick Gaspard, Emile Stipp, Tracey and Phillip Riese, Robben Stichting, Stephen Friedman Gallery, Jonathan Jawno, SAFFCA - Southern African Foundation for Contemporary Art, and Pulane Kingston.

Presented on November 5 and 6, 2017 at the Harlem Parish, *Ursonate* by William Kentridge was curated by RoseLee Goldberg and produced by Esa Nickle and Raul Zbengheci. Musical accompaniment by the Knights. French horn: Michael Atkinson. Percussion: Shane Shanahan. Soprano: Ariadne Greif. Set design: Sabine Theunissen. Set fabrication: Hatchet Design and Build. Video design: Janus Fouché. Video engineer: Brendan Bercik. Lighting design: Wild Dogs International and Andre Ferreira. Audio engineer: Anthony Fraser. It was supported by the Ford Foundation, the Broad Art Foundation, Marian Goodman Gallery, Liza Essers - Goodman Gallery, Wendy Fisher and the Performa 17 South African Pavilion Committee, and the Performa Commissioning Fund.

Presented on November 3–5, 2017 at the Connelly Theater, *I cut my skin to liberate the splinter* by Kemang Wa Lehulere was curated by RoseLee Goldberg. Production coordinator and performer: Ziphozenkosi Dayile. Choreographer and performer: Chuma Sopotela. Technician and performer: Lulama Qupe. Sound design: Daniel Bruce Gray. Performer: Asemahle Ntlonti. Trumpet: Lesedi Ntsane. Produced by Esa Nickle with Robert Wuss. Production Manager: Bob Kalas. Production Manager/ Lighting Design: Megan Lang. Sound Design: Mikey Deane. Supported by the Ford Foundation, Marian Goodman Gallery, Wendy Fisher and the Performa 17 South African Pavilion Committee, and the Performa Commissioning Fund. Special thanks to Josh Luxenburg and the Connelly Theater, Andrew Leslie Heyward, Josh Ginsburg, Kyle Crose, Five OHM Sound, Bryan William, and A4 Arts Foundation.

Curated by RoseLee Goldberg with Maaike Gouwenberg, Lydia Brawner, and Job Piston, *Masihambisane - On Visual Activism* by Zanele Muholi was supported by the Ford Foundation, Michael Hoeh, Abby Pucker, Yancey Richardson, the Performa Commissioning Fund, and the Performa 17 South African Pavilion Committee. The artist's photographic series *Somnyama Ngonyama* was on view on billboards and digital screens at City Point, Times Square, and six subway stations across New York City from November 2 to 14, 2017. Muholi's "Information Station" was presented on November 5 at the Leslie-Lohman Museum of Art. The artist was in conversation with Staceyann Chin at BAAD! Bronx Academy of Arts and Dance on November 7, and with Renee Cox at the Schomburg Center for Research in Black Culture on November 8. *Masihambisane - On Visual Activism* also included programs at PUBLIC Arts on November 4, the Stonewall Inn on November 8, and the Bronx Museum on November 10, 2017.

Presented on November 11, 2017, *Zion* by Mohau Modisakeng was curated by RoseLee Goldberg. Direction, text, and set design: Mohau Modisakeng. Score for Times Square: Neo Muyanga. Performers (Harambee Dance Group): Annalise Berthelot, Omari Contaste, Ibn Days, Aatifa Drayton, Shawn Hawkins, Rhea Henry Ford, Raven Holmes Dodge, Briana Kimble, Aphiwe Livi, Aphiwe Mphaleni, Joyce Smith, and Imani Wilburg-Folds. Musicians: Frank W Malloy III, Frank W Malloy IV, Lesedi Ntsane, and Linda Sikhakhane. Produced by Maaike Gouwenberg, Sasha Okshteyn, and Xica Aires. Associate producer: Ashleigh McLean (WHATIFTHEWORLD). Co-presented by Times Square Arts. Supported by the Ford Foundation, Times Square Arts, WHATIFTHEWORLD, Ron Mandos and the Performa 17

South African Pavilion Committee, and the Performa Commissioning Fund. Collaborators: AME Mother Zion Church, Harambee Dance Group, Harlem Arts Alliance, New York State of Opportunity – Council on the Arts, and NYC Cultural Affairs. Special thanks to Eclectic Props, Frank and Sandella Malloy, and Andrew Dinwiddie.

Presented on November 8, 2017 at WhiteBox, *RitualResist* by Kendell Geers was curated by Juan Puntes and Amanda Ryan. It was co-presented with WhiteBox and supported by Liza Essers - Goodman Gallery, Stephen Friedman Gallery, Jonathan Jawno, SAFFCA – Southern African Foundation for Contemporary Art, and Wendy Fisher and the Performa 17 South African Pavilion Committee.

Presented on November 18 and 19, 2017 at the Harlem Parish, *umBhovuzo: The Parable of the Sower* by Nicholas Hlobo was curated by RoseLee Goldberg. Produced by Maaike Gouwenberg with Esa Nickle. Production coordinator: Bob Kalas. Set fabrication: Standard and Supply. Supported by the Rolex Institute, Ford Foundation, Wendy Fisher and the Performa 17 South African Pavilion Committee, and the Performa Commissioning Fund. Special thanks to Stevenson Gallery, Lehmann Maupin Gallery, Raul Zbengheci, Bret Tonelli, Sasha Okshteyn, and Manuela Nebuloni.

Presented on November 2–4, 2017 at BKLYN Studios at City Point, *Black Paper* by Teju Cole was curated by Adrienne Edwards. Production and technical design/set: Robert Wuss. Video editing: Josh Begley. Sound and lighting provided by Prospect Lighting. Video and projectors provided by New City Video. Venue management: Company Agenda. Co-presented by BKLYN STUDIOS with support from the Ford Foundation and the Performa Commissioning Fund. Co-produced by the de Young Museum.

Presented on November 9–11, 2017 at the Black Lady Theatre, *THE TRACEY ROSE SHOW IN COLLABORATION WITH PERFORMA17 AND AFROGLOSSIA PRESENTS: THE GOOD SHIP JESUS VS THE BLACK STAR LINE HITCHING A RIDE WITH DIE ALIBAMA [WORKING TITLE]* by Tracey Rose was curated by Adrienne Edwards. Conceived and executed by Tracey Rose, Tito Valery, Alan Smithee, Christopher Wessels, Keitu Gwangwa, Chris Martin, Adrienne Edwards, the Black Lady Theatre, Maaike Gouwenberg, Audrey Rose, Sheila Lawler - Sheila's Creations, James Wilson, Lwandle Nzimande-Rose, Intikana Kekoeia, Lirael O'Neil, M. Lamar, Jahmal B. Golden, and Dan Gunn (Dan Gunn, Berlin). Invisible labor: Desmond Rose. Producer: Maaike Gouwenberg. Technical producer: Bob Wuss. Stage manager: Marija Misevičiūtė. Supported by the Ford Foundation, Fundação Sindika Dokolo, Liza Essers - Goodman Gallery, Wendy Fisher and the Performa 17 South African Pavilion Committee, and the Performa Commissioning Fund. With thanks to RoseLee Goldberg, Bonaventure Soh Bejeng Ndikung, and Koyo Kouoh.

Presented on November 13 and 14, 2017 at the Grace Rainey Rogers Auditorium at the Metropolitan Museum of Art, *Banana Stroke* by Wangechi Mutu was curated by Adrienne Edwards. Producer/cinematographer/editor: Andrew Dru Mungai. Music: Willy Rama Mbaji, Boaz Otieno Akech, Stephen Okoti Ngala, and Erick Baya Thoya. Sound record: Ronnie Mugambi and Maureen Adhiambo. Costume design: Ashaka Givens and Oana Botez. Production: Raul Zbengheci, Astrid Meek, and Hiroko Ishikawa. Set fabrication and consultation: Standard and Supply. Co-presented with Live Arts at The Metropolitan Museum of Art. Supported by the Ford Foundation, Gladstone Gallery, Victoria Miro Gallery, Susanne Vielmetter Los Angeles Projects, and the Performa Commissioning Fund. Special thanks to Barbara Gladstone, Victoria Miro, Susanne Vielmetter, Adrienne Edwards, RoseLee Goldberg, Sandra Jackson-Dumont, Limor Tomer, and Marsha Reid.

Presented on November 17–19, 2017 at the Connelly Theater, *Tree Identification for Beginners* by Yto Barrada was curated by Adrienne Edwards. Film by Yto Barrada. Director of photography: Steve Cossman. Animators: Yto Barrada and Steve Cossman. Editor: Kate Abernathy. Additional editor: Maxwell Paparella. Sound mixer: Matthew Curry. Producers: Maaike Gouwenberg and Sean Gullette. Technical producer: Bob Wuss. Curtain design: Yto Barrada. Curtain production: Victoria Mangianello with Jared Ellner and Johanna Castillo. Voices: Yto Barrada, Sanford Biggers, Allen Frame, Ashley Fure, Sean Gullette, Arana Hankin, Ishion Hutchinson, T. Geronimo Johnson, and Peter Benson Miller. Foley artists: Yto Barrada, Steve Cossman, and Rachel Abernathy-Guma.

Supported by the Ford Foundation, the Performa Commissioning Fund, and Pace Gallery. Special Thanks to Amistad Research Center, Mounira Bouzid El Alami, the American Academy in Rome, Noemie Bablet, Mono No Aware, Marc Glimcher, Tamara Corm, Elodie Pong, Operation Crossroads Africa, Adrienne Edwards, and Maaike Gouwenberg.

Presented on November 16, 2017 at the Harlem Parish, *MASS (HOWL, eon)* by Julie Mehretu and Jason Moran was curated by RoseLee Goldberg and Adrienne Edwards. Producer: Esa Nickle. Associate producer: Raul Zbengheci. Cornet and effects: Graham Haynes. Drums: Jamire Williams. Sound engineer: Sascha Von Oertzen. Editor: Charles Cohen. Video engineer: Brendan Bercik. Light design: Andre Ferreira (Wild Dogs International). Set fabrication: Standard and Supply. Supported by the Performa Commissioning Fund and Marian Goodman Gallery. Special thanks to Marian Goodman, Neal Benezra, Gary Garrells, Rachel Jans, Emily-Jane Kirwan, Jessica Rankin, Cade and Haile Mehretu Rankin, Tom Powel, Yasmine El Rashidi, Sarah Rentz, Damien Young, Clara Ranenfir, Deb Chaney, Janel Schultz, Marco Lawrence, Jennifer Lee, Mark Chariker, Martha Moszczynski, Elisabeth Melnyczuk, Charles Cohen, RoseLee Goldberg, and Adrienne Edwards.

Presented on November 3–5, 2017 at the Glass House, *Imitation of Lives* by Jimmy Robert was curated by Charles Aubin and Cole Akers. Co-commissioned by Performa and the Glass House for Performa 17. Performers: NIC Kay, Jimmy Robert, and Quenton Stuckey. Painting: *Loos / De Bruycker marble* (2017) by Lucy McKenzie. Costume design: Carmen Secareanu (robes) and Regina M. Rizzo (t-shirts). Voice coach: Emily Kron. Graphic design: David Knowles. Special thanks to Felix Burrichter, Ion Dumitrescu, Jason Farago, Davalois Fearon, Mario Gooden, Matthias Mau, Tom McDonough, Ben Pryor, and Mabel O. Wilson. Supported by the Performa Commissioning Fund and FUSED (French U.S. Exchange in Dance), a program of the New England Foundation for the Arts-National Dance Project and the Cultural Services of the French Embassy in New York in collaboration with FACE (French American Cultural Exchange), with lead funding from the Doris Duke Charitable Foundation, the Florence Gould Foundation, the French Ministry of Culture and Communication, and private donors. Additional support provided by Andy Romer. This project was selected and supported by the patronage committee for the arts of the FNAGP.

The Environment-Bubble by François Dallegret with Dimitri Chamblas and François Perrin was curated by Charles Aubin and François Perrin. It was presented on November 8, 2017 on the Empire Fulton Ferry Lawn at the Brooklyn Bridge Park, and on November 9, 2017 at Mineral Springs in Central Park. Produced by Maaike Gouwenberg with Sasha Okshteyn and Xica Aires. Inflatable architecture consultant: Jesse Seegers. Production assistant manager: Melisa Dougherty. Production assistants: Brendan Kirk, Victor Ziolkowski, and Wyatt Ininns. Production fellow (workshops): Manuela Nebuloni. Supported by the Canada Council for the Arts, Robert M. Rubin, the Performa Commissioning Fund, and the Cultural Services of the French Embassy in the United States. Co-produced by Guy Reziciner, SOLID LLC and presented in partnership with CalArts Dance. Special thanks to Bob Henderson, Polyfabrics.

The Newcomers by Alex Schweder and Ward Shelley, joined by Lena Kouvela and Sarah Burns, was staged at 28 Liberty on November 10–19, 2017. Supported by B&O Play and the Performa Commissioning Fund, it was co-presented with Fosun/28 Liberty. Special thanks to Blackwell.

Presented on November 11 and 12, 2017 at Marcus Garvey Park, *Marching On* was a project by Bryony Roberts and Mabel O. Wilson in collaboration with the Marching Cobras of New York. Commissioned by Storefront for Art and Architecture, it was presented with the Marcus Garvey Park Alliance and Performa. Artistic direction: Bryony Roberts and Mabel O. Wilson. Choreography: Terrel Stowers and Kevin Young of the Marching Cobras of New York. Performers: Nochamy Bamba, Nhazheir Bradley, Isaiah Coleman, Damian Creer Jr., Dion Creer, Afrika Garry, Asante Garry, Chuquira Gray, Steven Greene, Malcolm Hines, Enlee JeanLouis, Starasia McCormick, C'Niyah McCrary, Mya McCrary, Nyja Matthews, Beyoncé Miller, Khalil Moore, Helen Rahman, Jeremy Rosario, Destiny Rodriguez, Shaanan Tilman, and Anai Williams of the Marching Cobras of New York. Costume sourcing: Joseph Blaha and Morgen Warner. Cape construction: Colin Davis Jones Studios. Fabric printing: Design2Print. Graphic design:

ssistance: Mariam Abd El Azim (Storefront for Art and Architecture) nd Mayra Mahmood (Columbia GSAPP). Production assistance: asha Okshetyn and Maaike Gouwenberg (Performa). Marching On vas supported by the National Endowment for the Arts, the Graham oundation for Advanced Studies in the Fine Arts, and the Lower Manhattan Cultural Council.

Curated by Limor Tomer, *A Body in Places—The Met Edition* by Eiko Otake vas presented at the Met Cloisters on November 5; the Met Breuer on November 12; and the Metropolitan Museum of Art on November 19, 2017. Concept, video, and performance by Eiko Otake. Photography by William ohnston. Dramaturgy by Iris McCloughan. Presented in collaboration with Performa 17. *A Body in Places* was made possible with the support of the National Endowment for the Arts, the New York State Council on the Arts, he New York City Department of Cultural Affairs, the John S. and James . Knight Foundation, the New England Foundation for the Arts' National Dance Project, the Japan Foundation's Performing Arts Japan program, the MAP Fund, and Art Matters. Assistance at critical junctures was provided by the Pennsylvania Academy for the Fine Arts, Wesleyan University, and he Lower Manhattan Cultural Council. Further support was provided by he Doris Duke Charitable Foundation, which named Eiko an inaugural Doris Duke Artist. Development of community engagement strategies was ostered by the Danspace Platform 2016, which focused on Eiko and her olo project, and by the Cathedral of Saint John the Divine in New York, vhich designated Eiko Artist-in-Residence for its Dignity Initiative.

The Estonian Pavilion Without Walls was organized by Esa Nickle and Maaike Gouwenberg with Evelyn Raudsepp. Supported by the Estonian Ministry of Culture, Outset Estonia, and the Estonian Contemporary Art Development Center (ECADC), it was co-presented with the Estonian Contemporary Art Development Center (ECADC). Partners included the Kumu Art Museum, Center for Contemporary Arts, Estonia, Art in General, nd the New York Estonian House.

Presented on November 3 and 10, 2017 at the Estonian House New York, *Ainult liikmetele* (Members Only) by Flo Kasearu was organized by Esa Nickle and Maaike Gouwenberg with Evelyn Raudsepp. Co-presented by the Flo Kasearu House Museum, the Estonian House New York, and he Estonian Contemporary Art Development Center. Supported by he Performa Commissioning Fund, the Estonian Ministry of Culture, the Estonian Contemporary Art Development Center, and the Estonian House New York. Tour guides: Flo Kasearu and Kadri Sepp. Technical director: Tõnu Narro. Participants: Krista Altok, Tassa Uno, Habakukk Urve, Ruut Kaminski, Maret Kesküla, Paul Kuldkepp, Andres Männik, Mario Notton, ormi Notton, Naima Rauam, Kristi Roosmaa Tootell, Diina Tamm, Mare Valgemäe, Hele-Mai Varik, Oskar Varik Kuldkepp, Reet Värnik. Kitchen and bartender: Aarne Laanemaa and Maria Nigul, Tõnis Luik. Thank you to Eleanor O'Connell, Liisi Vanaselja, Liina M. Sarapik, Mardi Valgemäe, and he members of the Estonian House New York.

Presented on November 15–17, 2017 in a walking tour across the neighborhood of SoHo, *Open House Closing. A Walk* by Anu Vahtra was organized by Esa Nickle and Maaike Gouwenberg with Evelyn Raudsepp. Supported by the Performa Commissioning Fund, the Estonian Ministry of Culture, and the Estonian Contemporary Art Development Center, it was co-presented with the Estonian Contemporary Art Development Center.

Presented on November 11–12, 2017 at the Harlem Parish, *Going, Going* by Kris Lemsalu with Kyp Malone was organized by Maaike Gouwenberg with Evelyn Raudsepp. Lights: Andre Ferreira. Sound: Miles Robinson. Video: Brendan Berick. Technician: Tarvo Porroson. Supported by the Performa Commissioning Fund, the Estonian Ministry of Culture, and the Estonian Contemporary Art Development Center, it was co-presented with the Estonian Contemporary Art Development Center. Special thanks to Philly Abe, Astrid Bai, Doll Chao, Tõnu Narro, and Esa Nickle.

Presented on November 10–11, 2017 at Abrons Arts Center, *People Pie Pool* by Brian Belott was curated by Jens Hoffmann. Supported by the Performa Commissioning Fund and Gavin Brown's Enterprise, it was co-presented with Abrons Arts Center.

Lab at the Massachusetts Institute of Technology (Bjorn Sparrman, Jared Laucks and Skylar Tibbits). Co-commissioned and co-produced with the Brown Arts Initiative at Brown University, it was organized by Esa Nickle. Lead dancer and rehearsal director: Marissa Ruazol. Laban/Bartenieff movement instructor: Teresa Heiland. Dancers: Jonathan Gonzalez, Brooklynn Reeves, and Marissa Ruazol. Researcher: Bjorn Sparrman. Composition, electronics: Phillip Curtis. Costume designer: Karen Boyer. Associate producer: Raul Zbengheci. Fabrication: Standard and Supply. Assistants: Sophie Schwartz, Sophia Washburn, Marley Kirton, and Manuela Nebuloni. Special thanks to Peter Begler, Sean Flaherty, Valerie Green, Manuela Nebuloni, Marissa Ruazol, Aïda Ruilova, Bjorn Sparrman, Shannon Timms, Bret Tonelli, and Anne Bergeron.

Presented on November 16–18, 2017 at Danspace Project, *Moon Fate Sin* by Gillian Walsh was curated by Judy Hussie-Taylor. It was created with Emily Hoffman and performed by Maggie Cloud, Emily Hoffman, Justin Hyacinth, Mickey Mahar, and Gillian Walsh. Sound design by Wally Blanchard, Gillian Walsh, and Neal Medlyn. Lighting design by Carol Mullins. Costumes by earth_trauma. The accompanying *Moon Fate Sin* book was developed with Ben Van Buren and YIP; the Dance Torture Mixtape with producer Neal Medlyn. *Moon Fate Sin* was developed in research periods at the Watermill Center, MoMA PS1, and Museum Insel Hombroich. It was supported, in part, by the Mertz Gilmore Foundation's Late-Stage Stipend and a Foundation for Contemporary Arts Emergency Grant. The creation of *Moon Fate Sin* was made possible, in part, by the Danspace Project 2017–18 Commissioning Initiative, with support from the Jerome Foundation. *Moon Fate Sin* was co-presented by Danspace Project and Performa.

Presented on November 1–4, 2017 at the BAM Fisher at the Brooklyn Academy of Music, *Buffer* by Xavier Cha was curated by Holly Shen. Conception and direction by Xavier Cha. Music and sound design by Aaron David Ross. Libretto by Juliana Huxtable. Stage design by Paul Kopkau, Felix Burrichter, and Michael Bullock. Screenplay by Xavier Cha and Robert Moulthorp. Lighting design by Joe Levasseur. Costume design by Avena Gallagher. Produced in association with 47 Canal and Metro Pictures with support from the AHL Foundation. *Buffer* was co-presented by the Brooklyn Academy of Music and Performa.

Presented on November 3–5, 2017 at PARTICIPANT INC, *The Body is a House* by Narcissister was curated by Lia Gangitano.

House of Cards by Mei Lun Xue, Ryan Luke Johns, and Stephen Fan was presented at 1.5 Rooms on November 12, 2017.

Organized by Job Piston and Lydia Brawner with Discwoman, *Afterhours* took place at PUBLIC Arts at the PUBLIC Hotel on November 4 and 16, 2017. On November 4, the program opened with Zanele Muholi and the Sisonke collective followed by BEARCAT; on November 16, it was comprised of Tabita Rezaire, SHYBOI, and Richard Kennedy. Richard Kennedy's performance featured Quetzal Arias, Zeelie Brown, Isiah Cook, Xander Gaines, Rashonda Reeves, Erik Thurmond, and Tyler Wilcox. *Afterhours* was supported by PUBLIC Arts. Additional support provided by Hotel Americano, Chloe Wise, Dig Inn, Victoria Rogers, and Tiffany Zabludowicz.

PERFORMA 19

The Swedish Pavilion was made possible by Iaspis/the Swedish Arts Grants Committee, the Swedish Arts Council, the Consulate General of Sweden in New York, and the Embassy of Sweden in Washington, D.C. It was curated in collaboration with Bonniers Konsthall, Hallands Konstmuseum, ICIA - Institute for Contemporary Ideas and Art, Public Art Agency Sweden, and the Royal Institute of Art, with the generous support of Iaspis/the Swedish Arts Grants Committee, the Barbro Osher Pro Suecia Foundation, Maria Bonnier Dahlin Foundation, and the Swedish Arts Council.

The Taiwanese Pavilion was made possible by the Taiwanese Ministry of Culture and the Taipei Cultural Center in New York. It was curated in collaboration with Taipei Fine Arts Museum and Taiwan Contemporary Culture Lab (C-Lab).

Presented on November 11, 2019 at the Apollo Theater, *University Of Georgia Redcoat Band Live* by Paul Pfeiffer was curated by Kathy Noble

Sanford Stadium Redcoats. *University Of Georgia Redcoat Band Live* was co-commissioned with VIA Art Fund and supported by Agnes Gund, Shelley and Donald Rubin, and the Performa Commissioning Fund. Many thanks to Paula Cooper Gallery. Musical direction and composition by Brett Bawcum, Associate Director, Athletics Bands, the University of Georgia. Athens, Georgia producer and director of photography: Mo Costello. Performa producers: Esa Nickle and Sasha Okshteyn. Performa technical producer: Sascha von Oertzen. Technical consultant: Kevin Reuning. University of Georgia Acting Director of Athletic Bands: Brett Bawcum. Former Director of Athletic Bands, Professor of Music Education: Michael C. Robinson. Associate Director of Athletic Bands: Rob Akridge. Associate Director of Bands: Jaclyn Hartenberger. Director of Bands: Cynthia Johnston Turner. Director, Hugh Hodgson School of Music: Peter Jutras. Associate Dean of the Franklin College of Arts and Sciences: Jean Martin-Williams. Dean of the Franklin College of Arts and Sciences: Alan Dorsey. Director of the Lamar Dodd School of Art: Chris Garvin. Director of the School of Art Galleries: Katie Geha. Associate Professor of Contemporary Art, Lamar Dodd School of Art: Isabelle Loring Wallace. Assistant Athletic Director: John Bateman. J. Reid Parker Director of Athletics: Greg McGarity. University of Georgia President: Jere W. Morehead. Livestream production assistant Athletic Director - digital production: Mike Bilbow. Athens, Georgia production stage manager: lark Hackshaw. Senior broadcast engineer: Rick Freeman. Service manager: Paul Wlazlov, CTS. Streaming coordinator and director of live broadcast: Stephen Bridges. Lead audio engineer: Joshua "JP" Pruett. Assistant lead audio engineer: Robert Martinez. Video documentation production - Athens, Georgia director of photography: Mo Costello. Additional camera operators: David Glenn, Kia Pooler, Bryan Redding, and Justin Zweifach. Production assistants: Paron Payne and Khadif Sanders. Video documentation production workshop participants: Teryone Campbell, Nkela "Yoshi" DreKompena, Joshua Henderson, Malcolm Payne, Jaishan Richards, and Tyler Warren. Video documentation production workshop education team: Michael Bosby, Mo Costello, kara lynch, and Che Williams. Special thanks to Lemuel "Life" LaRoche, Tie Velasco, Scott Nesbit, Nicolas Allen, and Vicki Michaelis. Special thanks to the Apollo Theater team: Alisa Payne, Joe Levy, Diane Dispo-Klein, and Monet Fleming. Apollo Redcoats: Ryan Apa, Jennifer Aplin, Garison Baker, Josh Barron, Tatumn Behrens, Davis Bradley, Matthew Brown, Rylee Carfer, Davis Clark, Elizabeth Curry, Katie Beth Fowler, Eric Gluckman, Scotty Hall, Kayla Hanner, Maggi Hines, Kim Hoang, Luke Iddings, Noah Jackson, Josh Jimenez, Miaka Kemp, Hannah Kepner, Lucas Labado, Savannah Landry, Daniel Lopez, Sam Lopez, Stephanie Lopez, Sydney Loverde, Jamie Mancuso, Riley Maness, Josh Mishkin, Cesar Moncada, Tyler Moore, Evan Page, Isaac Parham, Cameron Pittman, Tyler Richmond, Jennifer Rogers, Callan Russell, Lino-Raye Sa'enz, Noah Shaw, Hannah Shuman, Justin Smith, Conner Sweat, Warren Walker, Mark Wang, Karena Washington, Brandon Waugh, Austin White, Kellie White, and James Wilson. Special thanks to Jackie Hartenberger and Jaime Diamond. Sanford Stadium Redcoats: Carson Adams, Jon Thomas Adcock, Kiyah Adkins, Daniel Agramonte, Adia Aidoo, Lydia Akin, Nicky Akin, Kelsey Albertini, Brynna Allen, Emily Alvarado, Jackson Alvarez, Rachel Anders, Lauren Anderson, Rachel Anderson, Thomas Anderson, Ivania Aparicio, Nic Aquila, Reagan Arntzen, Jonathan Ashley, Richie Augenstein, Alex Aull, Olin Aultman, Andrew Aziz, Conner Bacon, Colin Baillie, Kaitlyn Ballard, Andrew Barber, Anna Beth Barber, Laura Anne Beacham, Alyssa Beasley, Camille Becker, Nick Beech, Jacob Bell, Marshall Bellando, Megan Benton, Michael Berejikian, Julien Berger, Katelyn Berger, Sam Berman, Kerry Bethea, Gigi Biggs, Greer Blackmon, Cherith Blair, Drew Bodney, Ian Bonam, Nick Borkovich, Jacob Borland, Jared Bouland, Talie Bowles, Ethan Bowmar, Chloe Bragg, Sarah Kate Brewer, Sarah Bridges, Becca Brigdon, Will Broadwater, Izzy Brown, Logan Brown, Mikala Brown, Henry Browne, Grace Buhmeyer, Jaclyn Bulluck, Rush Burnes, Matthew Butler, Jonathan Buwalda, Scott Cameron, Oscar Campos, Stephanie Cannon, Grace Cantele, Daniel Carter, Eddie Carter, Julia Rae Castleberry, Bennett Caughran, Will Cawthon, Andrew Cerny, Emily Chancellor, Thomas Charyton, Peyton Ciesco, Scott Cohen, Jace Combs, Gracie Conner, Caroline Cook, Iain Cooke, Katie Cope, Seth Cope, Lillie Coppage, Ian Cornelius, Mackenzi Costley, Heather Countryman, Malia Craft, Shelby Crane, Brooklyn Craymer, Miruna Cristian, Cami Crosby, Emma Grace Crumbley, Emily Culpepper, Matt Curlee, Anna Dahlstrand, Spencer Daughtry, Janie Davis, Kellsie Davis, Tylan Davis, Jonovan Dawson, Justin Defalco, Bella Defelippi, Alyssa DeLoach, Laura Denton, Nathan Dial, Paul Dicicco, Emma Bay Dickinson, Caleb Dillehay, Jaser Doja, Wyatt Dover, Catherine Dukes, Madeline Dukes, Henry Dykes, Spencer Emous, Ethan Etheridge, Annie Evans, Clay Evans, Reagan Fields, Erich Fietkau, Reagan Finnerty, Justine Fitz, Chase Fiveash, Anna Floyd, Zack Flynn, Ansley Folds, Kelly Fry, Meredith Fuchs, Jonathan Fuller, Markisha Fuller, Amanda Galloway, Brenda Galvez, Trevor Garrett, Anna Gerald, Meggie Gilkey, Shae Gillespie, Jared Gilstrap, Alison Goddard, Nicholas Goldfarb, Carter Golovach, Shannon Graham, Kayla Graves, Lindsey Green, Leila Grist, Jennifer Grubbs, Amy Guzman-Reyes, Griffin Haarbauer, Brad Hagin, Will Halloran, Hannah Hankins, Tyler Hanson, Markell Hardee, Tucker Hardison, Derren Harwell, Elizabeth Harwood, Madison Haschak, Annabeth Hatfield, John Mark Hatfield, Camille Hay, Allison Hayman, Tobias Haymes, Carrie Hazard, Stephen Hedden, Tamaris Henderson, Julia Hernandez, Heidi Hicks, Natalie Hicks, Andrew Hixon, Jake Hobbs, Nick Hobbs, Lizy Hoepfinger, Grace Hohnadel, Hannah Hohnadel, Shawn Holman, Caitlyn Holmes, Jacob Hopkins, Olivia Horn, Ben Hornung, James Hughes, Kayla Hutcherson, Malaya Ilustrisimo, Tarik Itum, Nick Jackson, Nathan Jacobi, Parker Jamieson, Katie Jenkins, Cedric Johnson, Jamison Johnson, Jack Johnston, Grayson Jones, Kaitlyn Jones, Kathleen Jones, Myles Jones, Natalie Jones, Taylor Jordan, Eva Jourolmon, Zack Kalet, Ethan Keairnes, Brent Kelley, Addie Kelly, Logan Kendricks, Anya Kerkemeyer, Andrew Kilpatrick, Michael Kim, David Knight, Lizzie Knox, Rishi Kotian, Millie Kraft, Erin Kurtzer, Drew Lance, Ben Lane, Duncan Lane, Tyler Lane, Jackson Lankford, Emily Lanoue, Kipling Len, Allison Little, Emma Llewallyn, Robert Lloyd, Sean Loubser, Sam Lovell, Olivia Low, Sydney Lowe, Mallory Luense, Stephania Luna, Juan Luviano, Sophy Macartney, Gabby Mansour, Andrew Mappes, Sophie Marsh, Hannah Marston, Brenna Martin, Marcus Mascara, Mason Mascara, Ember Mayo, Mary Dru McCoy, Tryggvi McDonald, Matt McFadden, Bailey McGovern, Becca McGuire, Abigail McLain, Ansley McNeese, Alex Merritt, Julianne Merritt, JP Miller, Katie Miller, Nick Miller, Hunter Mills, Janie Millwood, Danielle Moeller, Carlie Moore, Miranda Moore, Bella Morgano, Natalie Morris, Ashley Mueller, Kristina Nash, Braelynn Neely, Jordan Newberry, Jackson Newton, Andy Nguyen, Anna Nguyen, Elizabeth Nicholson, Jesse Norton, Sarah Norton, Shannon O'Donnell, Matthew Olson, Roberto Ortiz, Gracie Page, Zane Page, Carissa Pangilinan, Anna Parker, Kat Parler, Richa Patel, Grace Pavan, Olivia Payne, Claire Pearson, Karson Pennington, Anthony Perrotto, Todd Perry, Quintin Peters, Victor Philippe, Benny Phillips, Zach Picard, Karyna Pillay, Kristin Pirkle, AJ Plante, Amberly Plummer, Grace Pulliam, Briana Purves, Sarah Quayle, Brandy Quick, Wesley Rains, Mike Ramirez, Ruben Ramirez, Smaran Ranjit, Jonathan Ray, Jordan Reidy, Kayla Reilly, Lee Thomas Richardson, Sam Riddle, Melody Rivers, Craig Rodgers, Josh Rohme, Anthony Roper, Isaiah Ross, Sydney Rowell, Caitlin Santos, Elaina Satterfield, Zach Schamis, Lauren Schermerhorn, Katie Schoeffner, Keith Schroeder, Ari Schulman, Nate Scott, Maggie Sears, Austin Seawright, Sarah Secrist, Hannah Selvaggi, Banta Sesay, Sarah Sewell, Elizabeth Shaffer, Sarah Sharp, DeAndra Shields, Taylor Shirk, Evan Shope, Emma Shuman, Tanner Shurek, Olivia Silva, Alex Skelton, Carmen Smith, Courtney Smith, Victoria Smith, Gwen Snell, Madeline Snipes, Grace Snuggs, Camron Sohn, Bailie Sorah, Addie Sparks, Andrew Speicher, Carter Stacy, Lizzy Stanford, Zack Starker, Lance Stechschulte, Raegan Strasser, Emily Suggs, Makenzie Sullivan, Tori Swyers, Kate Tabeling, Matthew Talbot, Delaney Talty, Rachel Tellano, Emily Teston, Colin Thomas, Loren Thomas, Brett Toutkoushian, Logan Trapnell, Mary Truett, Ansley Tucker, McKenzie Turner, Bella Tyre, Douglas Vines, Abby Wagner, Anna Wakeman, Grace Ward, Sydney Waters, Jonathan Webb, Alex Weekley, Anna Weissel, Chloe-Marie Westhafer, Taylor Wetterhan, Hannah Wetzel, Ana White, William Whitten, Keane Whittenburg, Emily Whittier, Morgan Wiggins, Brendan Williams, Sarah Willoughby, Stephen Willoughby, Abby Wolfe, Brant Yang, Taylor Yarbro, Emmalyne Zant, and George Zeliff.

Presented on November 15 and 16, 2019 at Abrons Arts Center, *The White Waters* by Su Hui-Yu was organized and produced by Maaike Gouwenberg, Han-Fang Wang, Debbie Huang, and JP Faienza. Artist/director: Su Hui-Yu. Choreographer/dancer: I-Ling Liu. Video production/producer: Liu Yueh-Ming, Huang Ching-Han. First assistant director: Liu Yueh-Ming. Director of cinematography: Chen Kuan-Yu. Production design: Su Hui-Yu, Liao Yin-Chiao. Costume design: Huang Ching-Han. Performer: Popcorn, Ling (Jong Yi-Ling). Acting instructor: Kuo Meng-Shin. Technical production/lighting design: Reza Behjat. Master electrician: Taylor Jensen. Fabrication: Nicholas Buckalew and Ada McNulty. Video system design: Ted Charles Brown and Brendan Bercik. Video programming: JP Faienza. Stage manager: Hannah Mitchell. Production manager: JP Faienza. Video crew: Starr Sanford, Jeremiah Brunnhoelzl. Abrons Art Center technical director: Rebecca Key. Abrons Art Center production

Ministry of Culture, Taipei Culture Center in New York, and the Performa Commissioning Fund, and co-commissioned by Taiwan Contemporary Culture Lab (C-Lab).

Presented on November 2, 2019 at Castle Williams, *The Immortals* by Samson Young (featuring DITHER, Eliza Li, and Michael Schiefel) was curated by RoseLee Goldberg and Kathy Noble and produced by Esa Nickle and Maaike Gouwenberg. Supported by the Hong Kong Arts Development Council, Spring Workshop, and the Performa Commissioning Fund and co-produced by Trust for Governors Island and the Center for Heritage Arts & Textile. Music, lyrics, animation, and costume design: Samson Young. Vocal performance and musical arrangement: Michael Schiefel. Vocal performance and Cantonese lyrics: Eliza Li. Guitars: DITHER Quartet (James Moore, Taylor Levine, Brendon Randall-Myers, and Liz Faure). Costume fabrication: Kwok Hang Lin, Cheung Chi Mau, Wong Kam Tai, Paola Sinisterra, Gabrielle Wong, Essa Lin, Kristy Chan, and Kimmie Pang. Sound design: Sascha von Oertzen. Cantonese opera costumer: Wu Lan Fong. Research assistant: Christie Wong. Production assistant: Vvzela Qu. Special thanks to Meredith Johnson and Shane Brennan.

Presented on November 19–24, 2019 at the Gym at Judson Memorial Church, *DEAD MATTER MOVES* by Éva Mag was curated by Kathy Noble with assistance from Uchenna Itam in collaboration with Bonniers Konsthall, Stockholm, and was produced by Sasha Okshteyn and Anne Stolten. Performers: Éva Mag, Elinor Tollerz Brattby, Rosemary Carroll, Matty Davis, Eryka Dellenbach, Sarah Donnelly, Kristen De Lillo, Alex Romania, Rakia Seaborn, Ogemdi Ude, Anh Vo. Costume fabrication: Lena Otterheim. Music composer: Peter Holm. Lighting designer: Sara Gosses. Rigger: Joe Diamond. *DEAD MATTER MOVES* was supported by Iaspis/the Swedish Arts Grants Committee, the Barbro Osher Pro Suecia Foundation, the Swedish Arts Council, Crozier Fine Arts, the Performa Commissioning Fund, and co-commissioned with Bonniers Konsthall, Stockholm. Special thanks to Movement Research, Martina Domonkos Klemmer, the Romanian Cultural Institute, Zac Mosley, Zach Laks, and Jeanne Davis at Judson Memorial Church.

Presented on November 6–10, 2019 at 1014, *Entre Deux Actes (Ménage À Quatre)* by Nairy Baghramian and Maria Hassabi with Janette Laverrière and Carlo Mollino was curated by Charles Aubin and produced by Maaike Gouwenberg with Anne Stolten. Performers: Leslie Cuyjet, Hristoula Harakas, Maria Hassabi, Alice Heyward, Mickey Mahar, Oisín Monaghan. Outfits: Victoria Bartlett. Lighting: Zack Tinkelman. Project manager: Natasha Katerinopoulos. Marian Goodman Gallery: Drew Moody, Timothy Bergstrom, and Nicolas Munich. JL Editions: Michel Ziegler. Perimeter 360: Jonathan Ellis and team. *Entre Deux Actes (Ménage À Quatre)* was co-commissioned with 1014 and co-produced with the Kitchen. It was supported by Marian Goodman Gallery and the Performa Commissioning Fund. Many thanks to Georg Blochmann, Benjamin Bergner, Katja Benz, Katja Wiesbrock Donovan, and Marian Goodman.

Presented on November 15–17, 2019 at the Gelsey Kirkland Arts Center, *Parts of Some Sextets, 1965/2019* by Yvonne Rainer was curated by Kathy Noble assisted by Brittany Richmond. It was supported by the Robert Rauschenberg Foundation and the Performa Commissioning Fund. Choreography: Yvonne Rainer. Reconstruction: Yvonne Rainer and Emily Coates. Performers: Rachel Berman, Emily Coates, Brittany Engel-Adams, Patrick Gallagher, Shayla-Vie Jenkins, Jon Kinzel, Liz Magic Laser, Nick Mauss, Mary Kate Sheehan, David Thomson, and Timothy Ward. Lighting designer: Les Dickert. Audio and sound engineer: Quentin Chiappetta. Producer and prop wrangler: Sasha Okshteyn. Production fellows: Simon Gérard and Anne Stolten. Stage manager: Anne Stolten. Audio technician: Daniel Shepard. Master electrician: David Levitt. Prop fabricator: CainCain. Mattress fabricator: Charles H. Beckley, Hand-made Custom Bedding. Many thanks to the Robert Rauschenberg Foundation; Baryshnikov Dance Foundation; Michael Chernov and Marissa Freeman at the Gelsey Kirkland Arts Center; Barbara Moore, who supplied photos by Peter Moore, an invaluable resource for the reconstruction of this dance; Glenn Phillips and Andrew Perchuk of the Getty Research Institute, which houses Rainer's archive; and Will Orzo, who transcribed innumerable Bentley Diary excerpts from one of Rainer's

Yu Cheng-Ta was curated by Charlene K. Lau, organized by Esa Nickle and Jo Hsiao, and produced by Bob Kalas. Museum designer: Emma Exley. Museum manager: Zoe McNichols. Photographer: Silver Chen. Director of photography: Daniel Rampulla. Audio: Chang Wang. Stylist: Max Ruelas. Makeup artist: Ayumi Takahashi. Visual designer: Peng Guan-Jie. Website designer: Wu I-Yeh. Video editor: Mel Hsieh. Music producer: Missy Mute. Project assistant: Chang Kang-Hua. *FAMEME* was supported by the Taiwanese Ministry of Culture, Taipei Culture Center in New York, and the Performa Commissioning Fund. The work was co-commissioned by the Taipei Fine Arts Museum and co-presented with Wallplay. Many thanks to Deng Yun-Chin, Samantha Shao, James Blaxland, Ming Wong, and Freya Chou.

Presented on November 2–24, 2019 on the fifth floor of 147 Spring Street in SoHo, *Nostalgia-Acts of Vanitas* by Ylva Snöfrid was curated by Kathy Noble, Anna van der Vliet, and Uchenna Itam and produced by Esa Nickle and Sasha Okshteyn. Performer/artist: Ylva Snöfrid. Building of furniture onsite: Rodrigo Mallea Lira (construction of furniture a collaboration between Ylva Snöfrid and Rodrigo Mallea Lira). Onsite producer: Vera Petukhova. *Nostalgia-Acts of Vanitas* was supported by Iaspis/the Swedish Arts Grants Committee, the Barbro Osher Pro Suecia Foundation, the Swedish Arts Council, and the Performa Commissioning Fund, and co-commissioned by the Institute for Contemporary Ideas and Art and co-produced by the Daniel Sachs Foundation.

Presented on November 16, 2019 at Essex Street Academy, *Sanctuary* by Bunny Rogers was curated by Kathy Noble and produced by Bob Kalas. Performers: Bunny Rogers, Dasha Nekrasova, Joseph Beers, Filip Olszewski, Allese Thomson, Juan F Moreira, Christobal Bernal, Kenny Mattucci, Kurt Beers. Stage manager: Emely Zepeda. Assistant stage manager: Bonnie McHeffey. Costume designer: Katja Andreiev. Makeup: Jaime Gruber. Lighting designer: Megan Lang. Audio technician: Julie Roinos. Florist: Gust at the Avenue J Florist. *Sanctuary* was supported by Société Berlin and the Performa Commissioning Fund. Special thanks to Essex Street Academy and Nick Tapiano.

Presented on November 12–16, 2019 at the Performa 19 Hub (18 Wooster), *Phantom Bouquet* by Lap-See Lam was curated by Sara Arrhenius and Charlene K. Lau and produced by Esa Nickle, Debbie Huang, and Sofia Curman. Performer: Tin Tay. Musicians: Li Qiong Lin, Shao Ji Tan, Qi Bin Chen, Jian Bo Xie. Voiceover script: Lap-See Lam and Wingyee Wu. Voiceover: Wingyee Wu. Sound designer and composer: Marlena Lampinen. Sound mixing and mastering: Linus Hillborg. VR producer: Sofia Curman. Real-time engine consultant: Martin Christensen. Motion capture studio: DevinSense. VR vocals: Ping-Kwan Lam. Textile fabrication: Emmy Rengfors. Frost sculpture fabrication: Neoset Designs. Neon fabrication: Vida Graphics and Signs. Food: Mission Chinese Food. Construction consultation: Joe Diamond. *Phantom Bouquet* was supported by Christel Engelbert, Chairwoman of the Maria Bonnier Dahlin Foundation, and the Performa Commissioning Fund. Additional support came from the Consulate General of Sweden in New York, the Embassy of Sweden in Washington, D.C., the Barbro Osher Pro Suecia Foundation, Galerie Nordenhake Stockholm, and Bonniers Konsthall. This project was co-produced by the Royal Institute of Art. Many thanks to Esther Eriksson, Dennis Härmä, and Hampus Larsson, the restaurant staff at New Peking City, Hang Chow, Mandarin City, Ming Garden, Ming Pal-ace, Bamboo Garden, Ho Wah, Hong Kong, Wing Shing, and Winner House.

Presented on November 2, 2019, from 5:50 pm to 6:25 am at the Performa 19 Hub (47 Wooster), *Sleep 1237* by Shu Lea Cheang was curated by Taiwan Contemporary Culture Lab (C-Lab) and Charlene K. Lau. It was produced by Charlene K. Lau, Han-Fang Wang, and Xica Aires. Performers: Martha Rosler, Lawrence Chua, Surya Mattu, Phumzile Sitole, McKenzie Wark, Jason Lucas, Morehshin Allahyari, Larissa Pham, Shu Lea Cheang, Prince Harvey, and Dennis Yi Tenen. Technical production: Osaro Ogedengbe. Sound technician: Asa Wember. Construction: Joe Diamond, Matthew Uhlmann, and Nazar Bezanyuk. Intermission music: Kaffe Matthews. Beer label design: Diana Duque. *Sleep 1237* was supported by the Taiwanese Ministry of Culture, the Taipei Cultural Center in New York, and the Performa Commissioning Fund and was co-commissioned with C-Lab. Many thanks to Galen Joseph-Hunter at Wave Farm, Debbie

"Atlas Unlimited: Acts VII–X" by Andros Zins-Browne and Karthik Pandian with Zakaria Almoutlak was curated by Nicola Lees and was on view at 80WSE from October 10 to November 3, 2019. It was made possible by the generous support of the Graham Foundation for Advanced Studies in the Fine Arts and the Cheswatyr Foundation. "Acts VII–X" were supported by residencies at Certain Bird, Vermont, and the ArtLab at Harvard University. Special thanks to designer Casey Lurie and conservator Daniela Murphy Corella.

Presented on November 20 and 21, 2019 at the Performa 19 Hub (18 Wooster), *Chemical Gliding, Keep Calm, Galvanize, Pray, Ashes, Manifestation, Unequal, Dissatisfaction, Capitalize, Incense Burner, Survival, Agitation, Hit* by Chou Yu-Cheng was curated by Wu Dar Kuen and Charlene K. Lau, and produced by Esa Nickle, Sasha Okshteyn, and Debbie Huang. Musical score: Ian Vanek. Musicians: Ian Vanek (drums) and Schuyler Maehl (bass). Supervisors: Brendan Kirk and Seth-Michael McMillian. Laborers: Gardner Allen and Alexis Ruiseco-Lombera. Forklift drivers: Kacey Card and Chris Haag. Construction: Joe Diamond. Prop wrangler: Han-Fang Wang. *Chemical Gliding, Keep Calm, Galvanize, Pray, Ashes, Manifestation, Unequal, Dissatisfaction, Capitalize, Incense Burner, Survival, Agitation, Hit* was supported by the Taiwan Ministry of Culture, and the Taipei Cultural Center in New York, as well as the Performa Commissioning Fund, and was co-commissioned by Taiwan Contemporary Culture Lab (C-Lab). Many thanks to Yang Chi-Chuan.

"WORKINGALLERY" by Gaetano Pesce was on view from October 25 to November 2, 2019 at Salon 94 Design. Its closing performance on November 2 was co-presented by Performa and Salon 94 Design.

Presented on November 8 and 9, 2019 at Abrons Arts Center, *A Catch Upon the Mirror* by Ed Atkins was curated by Kathy Noble and supported by the Performa Commissioning Fund.

Presented on November 21, 23, and 24, 2019 at the Alexander Hamilton U.S. Custom House, *AS DEEP AS I COULD REMEMBER, AS FAR AS I COULD SEE* by Tarik Kiswanson was curated by Charles Aubin and produced by Maaike Gouwenberg and Simon Gérard. Performers: Elle Chevremont, Omolara Dawodu, Marcel Kottmann, Lucy-Lou Marino, Todd Roosevelt Martin, Gold Ray Martin, Jada Rose-Pringle, Daria Ryzhova, Gaspar Souchard, Sara Tecle, and Akiro Thomas. Vocalists: "Every Voice Concert Choir" led by Nicole Becker, Jack Boge, Sophie D'Halleweyn, Kayla Fan, Jade Hayes, Xavier Daichi Kiyomi, Eliza Malterre, Madeline Ment, Leo Porter, Lorelei Rey, Ria Shivam, MaryGrace Uy, Eva Woodruff, and Kiesse Yengo-Passy. Music and sound design: Luciano Chessa, assisted by Eric Vanderzee. Stage manager: Tyler Considine. Sound advisor: Sascha von Oertzen. Wardrobe assistant: Hannah Kramm. *AS DEEP AS I COULD REMEMBER, AS FAR AS I COULD SEE* was supported by the Barbro Osher Pro Suecia Foundation, Swedish Arts Council, Fundación Almine y Bernard Ruiz-Picasso, Étant donnés Contemporary Art, Institut Français, Noreen Ahmad, and the Performa Commissioning Fund, co-produced by Hallands Konstmuseum, and co-commissioned by Lafayette Anticipations - Fondation d'entreprise Galeries Lafayette, Paris. Many thanks to Thuthuka Sibisi, Toby Wine at the Church Street School for Music, Amy Graves at the Brooklyn Children's Theater, Jevon S. Goldson, "Jerzey" at Lotus Creations Academy of Performing Arts, Michael Inge, and to all the parents for their incredible support of these young performers.

On view at PARTICIPANT INC from November 3 to December 22, 2019, "The Shank" by Glendalys Medina was curated by Lia Gangitano. The performance *Dear Me* took place on November 12 and 19. It was supported by the Performa Commissioning Fund.

Presented on November 14, 15, 16, 21, 22, and 23, 2019 at the Performa 19 Hub (47 Wooster), *Heaven on Fourth* by Huang Po-Chih was curated by Jo Hsiao and Charlene K. Lau and produced by Esa Nickle and Debbie Huang. Performers: Ann Dang, Andrea Granera, Mila Levine, Shamôr Peeler-Dean, Sarah Wang, James Yeh, and Jenny Xie. Writers: Huang Po-Chih, Karen Gu, Yen-Chiao Huang, Sarah Wang, and Jenny Xie. Translator: Brent Heinrich. Editor: James Yeh. Dramaturge: Chien-Han Hung. Bartender: Kimberly Anderson. Moonshine: Kings County Distillery. Construction: Joe Diamond. Photography and video: Hoho Lin. *Heaven on Fourth* was supported by the Taiwanese Ministry of Culture, the Taipei Cultural Center in New York, and the Performa Commissioning Fund, and was co-commissioned with the Taipei Fine Arts Museum. Many thanks to Colin Spoelman of Kings County Distillery, Han-Fang Wang, Michael Chu, Banyi Huang, and Jia, Kai, and Khokhoi of Red Canary Song.

Untitled by Yahon Chang was presented on November 7, 2019 at the Performa 19 Hub (18 Wooster).

Presented by Pace Live on November 19 and 22, 2019 at Pace Gallery, *I Can Drink the Distance: Plantationocene in 2 Acts* by Torkwase Dyson was curated by Mark Beasley. Collaborators: Dionne Brand, Dark Adaptive, Gaika, Arthur Jafa, Autumn Knight, Christina Sharpe, and Deja Smith.

Presented on November 23, 2019 at the Performa 19 Hub (18 Wooster), *before we die* by Cecilia Bengolea and Michèle Lamy was curated by Kathy Noble and produced by Maaike Gouwenberg with assistance by Bob Kalas. Performers: Ani Taj, Brandon Washington, Brandon Wen, BRAT, Cori Kresge, Dayanis Mondeja, Eloise DeLuca, Honey, Jendaya Dash, and Quenton Stuckey. Music by LAVASCAR (Michèle Lamy, Nico Vascellari, and Scarlett Rouge). Stage manager: Thuthuka Sibisi. Lighting: JP Faienza. Sound: Cara Stewart. Costume assistant: Brandon Wen. *Before we die* was supported by the Performa Commissioning Fund and was co-produced by Michèle Lamy.

Presented on November 7–9, 2019 at Performance Space New York, *(Untitled) The Black Act* by Kia LaBeija was curated by Kathy Noble and Job Piston, organized by Pati Hertling, and produced by Maaike Gouwenberg. Performers: Kia LaBeija, Daniella Agosto, Selena Ettienne, Khristina Cayetano, Taína Larot, and Terry Lovette. Artist/director: Kia LaBeija. Assistance movement director and creative producer: Taína Larot. Music director and composition: Kenn Michael. Percussion: Warren Benbow. Costume design: Kyle Luu. Costume design assistant: Tonya Huynh. Costume fabrication: Jessi Highet. Lighting design: Christina F. Tang. *(Untitled) The Black Act* was supported by Abigail Pucker, Victoria Rogers, Carole Server, and Jane Wesman, the Performa Commissioning Fund, and in part by a grant from the Jerome Foundation. This project was co-commissioned with Performance Space New York and co-produced with the Josie Club (Mickalene Thomas, Racquel Chevremont, Jet Toomer, and Nina Chanel Abney). Many thanks to Swarovski.

Presented on November 12 and 13, 2019 at the Harlem Parish, *Together* by Korakrit Arunanondchai, in collaboration with boychild, Alex Gvojic, and Aaron David Ross, was curated by RoseLee Goldberg and Job Piston and produced by Maaike Gouwenberg with assistance from Jessica Kursh and Sheridan Telford. Performers: Dylan Balka, Luna Beller-Tadiar, Trinity Dawn Bobo, Jendaya Dash, Cynthia Leung, Honey LaBeija, Jade Manns, Ashton Muniz, Shelby Nelson, Isaac Spector, Quenton Stuckey, Yasmin Venable, and Nicki Wong. Music and sound design: Aaron David Ross & Bonaventure. Lighting design: Nitemind. *Together* was supported by Liz and Jonathan Goldman, Bruce Karatz, and the Performa Commissioning Fund, with additional support by NOWNESS, the Rosenkranz Foundation, the Young Arts Foundation, and Joseph Varet and Esther Kim Varet. Many thanks to CLEARING, the Standard Hotel, Nitemind and Selina Hotels, Susan Brown, Nikki Mirsaeid, Djordje Gvojic, Rory Mulhere, Matt Taber, Nick Repasy, Vanessa Carlos, Hannah Jewett, Trailerdaddy, Op Sudasna, Supamas Phahulo, Varachit Nitibhon, and Tippawanna Nitibhon.

Presented on November 7–9, 2019 at Abrons Arts Center, *Sènsa* by Paul Maheke, Nkisi, and Ariel Efraim Ashbel was curated by Charles Aubin and Ali Rosa-Salas and produced by Maaike Gouwenberg and Simon Gérard. Performer: Paul Maheke. Sound: Nkisi. Lights: Ariel Efraim Ashbel. Costume: Firpal Jawanda. Stylist: Curtly Thomas. *Sènsa* was supported by Arts Council England, FUSED (French U.S. Exchange in Dance), and the Performa Commissioning Fund. The project was co-commissioned and co-presented by Abrons Arts Center, Red Bull Arts, and Performa. Many thanks to Charles Aubin, Stéphanie Busson, Laetitia Deering, Simon Gérard, Firpal Jawanda, Ali Rosa-Salas, Guillaume Sultana, and Curtly Thomas, as well as the ICA London and Abrons Arts Center and their technical teams.

Levant (2018) by Paul Maheke, with the participation of Ligia Lewis and Nkisi, was curated by Franziska Wildförster and was on view at Ludlow 38 - MINI/Goethe Curatorial Residencies from November 13 to December 15, 2019. It was produced by Lafayette Anticipations – Fondation d'entreprise Galeries Lafayette.

"Performa Archive" was presented at the Whitechapel Gallery in London from September 6, 2017 to March 4, 2018, and at Copenhagen Contemporary from June 20 to October 11, 2019. Curated by Dr. Nayia Yiakoumaki, it included video documentation of Performa commissions by Edgar Arceneaux, Yto Barrada, Jérôme Bel, Brian Belott, Sanford Biggers, Candice Breitz, Elmgreen & Dragset, Omer Fast, David Hallberg, Christian Jankowski, Isaac Julien, Jesper Just, Wyatt Kahn, Mike Kelley, William Kentridge, Jon Kessler, Ragnar Kjartansson, Kris Lemsalu, Arto Lindsay, Liz Magic Laser, Russell Maliphant, Kyp Malone, Mohau Modisakeng, Oscar Murillo, Kelly Nipper, Adam Pendleton, Yvonne Rainer, Raqs Media Collective, Robin Rhode, Jimmy Robert, Mika Rottenberg, Rozeal (formerly iona rozeal brown), Francesco Vezzoli, Kemang Wa Lehulere, and Tori Wrånes.

Presented on Radical Broadcast from March 7 to May 7, 2019, "Musical Chairs" was curated by Kathy Noble. It included video documentation of live performances from the Performa archives by Destroy All Monsters, Joan La Barbara, Julie Mehretu and Jason Moran, Meredith Monk, Shirin Neshat, Adam Pendleton, Genesis P-Orridge, and the X-Patsys.

Presented on Radical Broadcast from September 19 to October 31, 2019, "Fashion Television" was curated by Charlene K. Lau. It included moving-image works by General Idea, Cynthia Maughan, Bernadette Corporation, and Ryan Trecartin. Special thanks to Electronic Arts Intermix (EAI), New York.

Presented on Radical Broadcast from April 2 to May 14, 2020, "Time Share" was curated by Job Piston. It included moving-image works by Korakrit Arunanondchai and Alex Gvojic, Honey Balenciaga, Sam Banks, Vanessa Beecroft, Xavier Cha, Judy Chicago, Sara Cwynar, FlucT (Monica Mirabile and Sigrid Lauren), Christian Jankowski, Jane Jin Kaisen, Farrah Karapetian, Richard Kennedy, Shigeko Kubota, Zanele Muholi, Oscar Nñ, Robert Rauschenberg, Robin Rhode, Viva Ruiz, Jamilah Sabur, Jacolby Satterwhite, Nick Sethi, Ryan Trecartin, and Tori Wrånes. "Time Share" was supported by the NYC COVID-19 Response and Impact Fund of the New York Community Trust and by public funds from the New York City Department of Cultural Affairs, in partnership with the City Council.

Presented on Radical Broadcast from May 15 to September 7, 2020, "Bodybuilding" was curated by Charles Aubin and Carlos Mínguez Carrasco and was dedicated to the life and work of curator and art historian Germano Celant (1940–2020). It included works by Ant Farm, Basurama + Area Ciega, Ricardo Bofill, Cooking Sections, Coop Himmelblau, Decolonizing Architecture Art Residency, Diller Scofidio + Renfro and David Lang, Estudio Teddy Cruz + Fonna Forman, Fake Industries Architectural Agonism, Didier Fiúza Faustino, Anna and Lawrence Halprin, Haus-Rucker-Co, Hans Hollein, Arata Isozaki & Associates, Andrés Jaque / Office for Political Innovation, Francis Kéré and Christoph Schlingensief, Ugo La Pietra, Moore Grover Harper, New Affiliates, NLÉ, Office for Metropolitan Architecture, Gaetano Pesce, Julieanna Preston, raumlabor, visual artist Jimmy Robert, Bryony Roberts and Mabel O. Wilson with the Marching Cobras of New York, Aldo Rossi, Alex Schweder and Ward Shelley, SO – IL with Ana Prvački, Bernard Tschumi, Nomeda and Gediminas Urbonas, and Wolff Architects. "Bodybuilding" was supported by the NYC COVID-19 Response and Impact Fund of the New York Community Trust and by public funds from the New York City Department of Cultural Affairs, in partnership with the City Council.

Presented on Radical Broadcast from September 11 to November 30, 2020, "Threshold: Art in Times of Crisis" was curated by RoseLee Goldberg, Kathy Noble, Charles Aubin, Job Piston, and Brittany Richmond. It included moving-image works by ACT UP, Yael Bartana, Mykki Blanco/Zoe Leonard, Lee Bul, Kota Ezawa, William Greaves, Gran Fury, Lynn Hershman Leeson, William Kentridge, Glenn Ligon, Nicole Miller, Rabih Mroué, Shirin Neshat, Yoko Ono, Walid Raad and Souheil Bachar, Martha Rosler, Studios Kabako (Faustin Linyekula), Kara Walker, Carrie Mae Weems, David Wojnarowicz, and Artur Żmijewski. "Threshold: Art in Times of Crisis" was supported by the NYC COVID-19 Response & Impact Fund of the New York Community Trust and by public funds from the New York City Department of Cultural Affairs, in partnership with the City Council.

Presented on Radical Broadcast from December 1, 2020 to February 28, 2021, "*LEAN*" was curated by Legacy Russell. It included moving-image works by Justin Allen, Jen Everett, Devin Kenny, Kalup Linzy, Rene Matić, Sadé Mica, and Leilah Weinraub. "*LEAN*" was supported by the NYC COVID-19 Response and Impact Fund of the New York Community Trust and by public funds from the New York City Department of Cultural Affairs, in partnership with the City Council.

Upward Facing Control Table Top by FlucT (Sigrid Lauren and Monica Mirabile) was commissioned by Performa with Salon 94 and Maccarone Gallery for the exhibition "MIDTOWN" at the Lever House. Presented on May 3, 2017, it was performed by FlucT+ featuring Jerome AB, Destiny Be, Emil Bognar-Nasdor, Ciara Clements, Jendaya Dash, Kellian Delice, Joshua Dunn, Kathleen Dycaico, Jillian Goodwin, Erin Grant, Violetta Komyshan, Charlie Kolarich, Sigrid Lauren & Monica Mirabile of FlucT, Jes Nelson, Aaron Ricks, Cheryl Rosario, and Quenton Stuckey.

Beloved Country, Performa's 2016 gala on November 1, 2016, was produced by Esa Nickle. Technical direction: Raul Zbengheci. Event production: Jemma Moss. Food design: BITE. Company manager: Sasha Okshteyn. Installation: Joe Diamond. Set fabrication: Liz Fairleigh. It featured *Over the Rainbow*, a newly commissioned performance by Athi-Patra Ruga, and a musical performance by Dope Saint Jude. Performance producer: Ashleigh McLean (WHATIFTHEWORLD). Music: Angel-Ho. Musical director: Vuyo Sotashe. Costume for Athi-Patra Ruga: Unathi Mkonto. Costumes for Dope Saint Jude and Angel-Ho: threeASFOUR. Makeup: MAC Cosmetics. Hair: Bumble and bumble. Event planning: MF Productions. Program design: Sean Yendrys.

The Yoko Ono program for the Performa 17 Opening Night on November 1, 2017 was organized by Roya Sachs and Esa Nickle in consultation with Jon Hendricks. "Now or Never" by Yoko Ono was performed by Lizzi Bougatsos with Brian DeGraw and Josh Diamond. *Lighting Piece* (1955) was performed by Will Rawls. *Voice Piece for Soprano* (1961) was performed by Laurie Anderson. "Imagine" by John Lennon was performed by Vuyo (Vuyolwethu) Sotashe and the Ono Orchestra and arranged by Luciano Chessa. "Malaika" by Adam Salim was performed by Vuyo Sotashe with Joel Wenhart. Production: Esa Nickle with Raul Zbengheci Catering: BITE. Video design: Todd Garrison. Audio engineer: Anthony Fraser. Lighting designer: Andre Ferreira, Wild Dogs International. Video engineer: Brendan Bercik. Yoko Ono works production: Evelyn Raudsepp with Xica Arias and Manuela Nebuloni. Production support: Maaike Gouwenberg, Sasha Okshteyn, and Bob Kalas. Ono Orchestra: conductor: Luciano Chessa; violins: Pauline Kim Harris and Rachel Golub; viola: Isabel Hagen; cello: Meaghan Burke; bassoon: Sara Schoenbeck; flute: Alice Teyssier; bass: Patrick Duff; trombone: Peter Zummo; trumpet: Sam Nester; harp: Shelley Burgon; piano: Luciano Chessa. Special thanks to Yoko Ono for lending her works for the program.

Performa's 2018 gala on November 1, 2018 was organized by Roya Sachs and Esa Nickle and co-produced by Esa Nickle and Raul Zbengheci. Production assistants: Zoe McNichols, Ehm West, and Yitian Yan. Gala coordinator: Soigné Events. Sound engineer: Sascha von Oertzen. Lighting design: Tuce Yasak. Video engineer: Brendan Bercik. Video production: Andre Ferreira. Program design: Rachelle Viciere. Volunteers: Alison Kuo, Ridhima Mukim, and Dana Robinson. Food: Scott Skey and BITE. Logistics: Austen Boone, BITE. Christo and Jeanne-Claude archival footage/video editing: Anastas Petkov. Scenic direction: Ximena Garnica and Shige Moriya (LEIMAY). Performances by Kaoru Watanabe, LEIMAY, Miralda, and Sudan Archives. Special thanks to Valdimir Yavachev and Jonathan Henery of team XTO, Peter Oberlink and Baker Lee of SIR, and the team at SoundOff. A limited-edition plate and dessert performance was created by Antoni Miralda.

The Performa 2019 Opening Night on November 1, 2019 was organized by Roya Sachs and Esa Nickle and produced by Esa Nickle, Sasha Okshteyn, and Bob Kalas. Technical producer: JP Faienza. Gala coordinator: Soigné Events. Performances by Morgan Bassichis and Emily Coates. Dancers: Miguel Anaya, Reid Bartelme, Brittany Engel-Adams, and Megan Wright. Musical direction: Thuthuka Siblisi. Music by Benjamin Jephta, Lesedi, Dave Nelson and Marlon Patton, Immanuel Wilkins, and Ariel Zetina. Costumes by Reid & Harriet. Props: Anne Stolten. Loom: Textile Arts Center. Lighting designer: Christian LeMay. Print design: Sean Suchara. Food: BITE.

The Performa Telethon on November 18, 2020 was organized by the Performa team. Conceived and produced by Esa Nickle with E.S.P. TV and Roya Sachs. Producers: Sasha Okshteyn and Bob Kalas with Victoria Keddie and Scott Kiernan for E.S.P. TV. QVC Editions led by Kathy Noble. Additional support by Charles Aubin, Job Piston, and Brittany Richmond. Administration: Soigné Events. Design: Special—Offer. Public relations: Cultural Counsel. Video editing: Romke Hoogwaerts. Technical team: Andrew Devlin, Andre Ferreira, David Reichman, Daniel Neumann, Michael Hernandez-Stern, Lauryn Siegel, Nolan Roy, Nadine Regne. Special thanks to Pace Gallery, Mark Beasley, Andria Hickey, Gracia Ross, Gabriela Vidal-Irizarry, and Ugo Di Donato. Newly commissioned performances by Jennifer Rubell, Ragnar Kjartansson, Laurie Anderson, Madeline Hollander and David Hallberg, Keren Cytter, Kalup Linzy, Jason Moran, Ian Vanek, Marcel Dzama, Marco Brambilla, Hank Willis Thomas and Ebony Brown, Chloe Wise, Tamy Ben-Tor, and Rufus Wainwright. Live performances by Yvonne Rainer, Jacolby Satterwhite, Laura Ortman, Jérôme Bel, Emily Sundblad, Marc Razo, and Oyinda. Editions by Korakrit Arunanondchai, Barbara Kruger, Kia LaBeija, Michèle Lamy, Cindy Sherman, and Laurie Simmons. Hosted by Nick Hallet and Angela di Carlo.

NOT FOR SALE
The Performa Institute is supported by the David and Elaine Potter Foundation and the New York City Department of Cultural Affairs.

Commissioned by Performa and curated by Adrienne Edwards, *Just Back from Los Angeles: A Portrait of Yvonne Rainer* by Adam Pendleton premiered at Anthology Film Archives on January 9, 2017.

Presented on November 4, 2017 at the Performa 17 Hub, *Forever and a Day: Archiving Performa* was organized by Marc Arthur. It was supported by a grant from the National Endowment for the Humanities.

Presented on November 8, 2017 at the Performa 17 Hub, *Call for Action: Key Moments in Estonian Performance Art* was organized by Maaike Gouwenberg with Evelyn Raudsepp. The lecture and screening were presented by Anu Allas and Maria Arusoo and included moving-image works by Flo Kasearu, Raoul Kurvitz, Kris Lemsalu, Maria Metsalu, Kristina Norman, Jüri Okas, Ene-Liis Semper, Hanno Soans, Jaan Toomik, and Valie Export Society. Supported by the Performa Commissioning Fund, the Estonian Ministry of Culture, the Estonian Contemporary Art Development Center, the Art Museum of Estonia, and the Center for Contemporary Arts, Estonia (CCA), it was co-presented with the Estonian Contemporary Art Development Center.

Presented on November 6, 7, 12, and 13, 2017 at Anthology Film Archives, the *Afroglossia* film program was organized by Adrienne Edwards and Jed Rapfogel with Lydia Brawner. It was co-presented with Anthology Film Archives.

The *Tree Identification Walk* with Yto Barrada and Lisa Nett took place on November 11, 2017 at Prospect Park.

Curated by Adrienne Edwards, Kwani Trust's residency, *Everyone is Radicalizing*, took place at the Performa 17 Hub from November 13 to 17, 2017, and was supported by the Ford Foundation. Participants included Helon Habila, Lyle Ashton Harris, Billy Kahora, Kai Kresse, Funa Maduka, Neo Musangi, Wangechi Mutu, and Tavia Nyong'o. The film selection was co-organized with the African Film Festival New York. *Timbuktu 52 days* by Omar Berrada and *Black Listening* by Teju Cole were presented on November 17.

A Truncated History of the Universe for Dummies: A Dance Rant by Yvonne Rainer was presented on November 19, 2017 at the Performa 17 Hub.

Presented on November 3, 2018 at the Alvin Johnson/J.M. Kaplan Hall at the New School, *Julius Eastman's Symphony No. II Restored* was curated by Luciano Chessa. It was supported by G. Schirmer; Steel House in Rockland, Maine; and the Mannes School of Music at the New School. Special thanks to Mary Jane Leach, R. Nemo Hill, Dean Richard Kessler, and Music Director David Hayes.

Presented on November 11, 2017 at the Performa 17 Hub, *Making Room for Action* was organized by Charles Aubin and Carlos Mínguez Carrasco. Research assistants: Vera Petukhova, Gabrielle Printz, and Juliana Stadelmann. Speakers and participants included Ila Bêka & Louise Lemoine, Giovanna Borasi, Lluís Alexandre Casanovas Blanco, Yve Laris Cohen, Cooking Sections, Elizabeth Diller, RoseLee Goldberg, Thom Moran (T+E+A+M), and Ife Vanable. Special thanks to Marielle Pelissero, John A. Delgado (Prospect Park), and Chris Fox (Bigreuse). *Making Room for Action* was supported by the Graham Foundation for Advanced Studies in the Fine Arts and the Consulate General of Spain New York.

Edited by Charles Aubin and Carlos Mínguez Carrasco and published by Performa in 2019, *Bodybuilding: Architecture and Performance* was supported by the Graham Foundation, Elise Jaffe + Jeffrey Brown, and the Performa Institute with funds provided by the New York City Department of Cultural Affairs and the David and Elaine Potter Foundation. Additional support provided by the Royal Norwegian Consulate General in New York.

Drywall is Forever by New Affiliates was presented at the Performa 19 Hub (47 Wooster) on November 17, 2019. It was supported by the Performa Commissioning Fund and Goethe-Institut New York.

The Performa 19 Hub at 18 Wooster Street was generously hosted by Deitch Projects. Special thanks to Jeffrey Deitch.

Presented on November 10, 2019 at the Performa 19 Hub (18 Wooster), *Subversive Threads: A Quilting and Dyeing Workshop* by RUN HOME was organized by Charlene K. Lau. It was supported by the Performa Commissioning Fund and Goethe-Institut New York.

Presented on November 15, 2019 at the Performa 19 Hub (47 Wooster), *Bauhaus at the Margins: Gender, Queer, and Sexual Politics* with Beatriz Colomina and Elizabeth Otto was organized by Charlene K. Lau. It was supported by the Performa Commissioning Fund and Goethe-Institut New York.

Presented on November 16, 2019 at the Performa 19 Hub (47 Wooster), *"A School for Creating Humans?" Bauhaus Education and Aesthetics Revisited* with Coco Fusco, Carmen Mörsch, and Mabel O. Wilson was organized by Nana Adusei-Poku. It was supported by the Performa Commissioning Fund and Goethe-Institut New York. Special thanks to the Center for Curatorial Studies at Bard College.

Bauhaus Spirit: 100 Years of Bauhaus by Niels Bolbrinker and Thomas Tielsch was screened on November 9, 2019 at the Goethe-Institut New York.

Conceived by Dimitri Chamblas and Sigrid Pawelke, *UNLIMITED BODIES* took place across New York City on November 11–17, 2019. It was supported by the Performa Commissioning Fund, Goethe-Institut New York, and King's Fountain. Participants included Alexis Alleyne-Caputo, Anaïs Barras, June Chee, Allie Costa, Madison Hicks, Tatum Howey, Cianci Kalid Melo-Carrillo, Mun Wai Lee, Jiaoyang Li, Alice Nogueira, Allison Smith, Félix Touzalin, Siye Zhang, and François-Thibaut Pencenat. *UNLIMITED BODIES* was presented in partnership with the CalArts School of Dance, New York University, the University of Giessen, and Paris École des Beaux-Arts.

The Black Act Movement Workshop, led by Kia LaBeija and Taína Larot, took place at the Performa 19 Hub (47 Wooster) on November 20, 2019.

Presented on November 11, 2019 at the Performa 19 Hub (47 Wooster), Nkisi's *Listening Session* was organized by Charles Aubin. It was supported by the Performa Commissioning Fund and Goethe-Institut New York and was co-hosted by Performa and Red Bull Arts.

Monuments: Echoes in the Dance Archive by Adam Weinert was presented on November 12, 2019 at the Bruno Walter Auditorium at the New York Public Library for the Performing Arts.

Presented on November 2, 2019 at Anthology Film Archives, *Shu Lea Cheang Onscreen* was organized by Charlene K. Lau. It was supported by the Taiwanese Ministry of Culture and the Taipei Cultural Center in New York.

INDEX

ACKNOWLEDGMENTS

As with our previous biennial publications, *On the Town* is an essential companion piece: essential because images of new commissions can only be seen after the fact; because the extensive research and knowledge built into each Performa Biennial must be made available; because the remarkable relationships forged with each artist over an eighteen-month to two-year period are unmissable lessons; because stories as to how commissions evolved must be told; because images reignite memories and trigger fresh ideas; because thirty years from now art historians will look to these books as source material for understanding a moment in time.

Each page of this book is a tribute to the more than one hundred artists who have participated in our programs over the past five years and the curators who have worked with them.

My deepest appreciation goes to the remarkable team at Performa: Kathy Noble, Charles Aubin, Job Piston, Sasha Okshteyn, Bob Kalas, and Brittany Richmond, with special thanks to our multitalented Managing Director & Executive Producer, Esa Nickle, who has steered the ship through these unreal times. Thank you all for your incredible strength, imagination, kindness, creativity, and joyous goodwill. We held each other up in every way we could, making meetings over Zoom (or any platform, for that matter) a real pleasure. My heartfelt thanks also go to the people who have been part of the team: Adrienne Edwards, Mark Beasley, Lydia Brawner, Charlene K. Lau, Maaike Gouwenberg, Eliza Coviello, Raul Zbengheci, Debbie Huang, and many more. I thank you for your vision, camaraderie, and grace.

Performa's Board of Directors, infinitely encouraging and supportive, cannot be thanked enough. Toby Devan Lewis, Emeritus Board Chair, provides ongoing inspiration and leadership, as do many others without whom our organization simply could not produce the biennial, publications, and community that we do: Rashid Johnson, Richard Chang, Todd Bishop, Barbara Hoffman, Wendy Fisher, Ronald Guttman, David Hallberg, Joyce Liu, Shirin Neshat, Jeanne Greenberg Rohatyn, Roya Sachs, and Neil Wenman. I thank them, as well as our phenomenal supporters and fans, for their commitment and belief.

Thank you to photographer extraordinaire Paula Court, who has kept a record of Performa from the start, and my sincere thanks also go to Special Offer for their design of our website and constant reimagining of our online presence.

For this book itself, I would like to thank Charles Aubin, Senior Curator & Head of Publications, for his ambition to merge two biennials with all our programs since 2016 into one catalog. *On the Town* reflects both his deep intellectual engagement with the medium of performance and his ability to manage an intricate production with many moving parts. Taking over from Lydia Brawner, who laid the foundation for the Performa 17 entries, Charles has coaxed texts, photographs, and information essential to the recording of the critical years of our presentations from artists, curators, and writers. It was an immense task, brought to the page with the most sophisticated eye by our graphic designer, David Knowles. Their deep involvement shows on every page of this beautiful book. I also thank Jennifer Piejko for her diligence and dedication to this publication and many before.

Thank you to our co-publisher Gregory R. Miller & Co., who followed, advised on, and supported every single step of this complex enterprise, and to our distributor, Elisa Nadel at Artbook | D.A.P. They are enduring Performa friends and true believers in the importance of publishing on ephemeral art.

As always, my first and last thanks go to Dakota Jackson, and to Zoe Jackson and Pierce Jackson and their families. ROSELEE GOLDBERG

Published in 2021 by Performa
and Gregory R. Miller & Co.

PERFORMA

Performa
100 West 23rd Street, 5th floor
New York, NY 10011
www.performa-arts.org

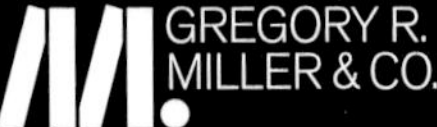

Gregory R. Miller & Co.
62 Cooper Square
New York, NY 10003
www.grmandco.com

Distributed worldwide by:
ARTBOOK | D.A.P.
75 Broad Street, Suite 630
New York, NY 10004
www.artbook.com

PERFORMA FOUNDING DIRECTOR AND CHIEF CURATOR
RoseLee Goldberg

EDITOR
Charles Aubin

EDITORIAL DEVELOPMENT FOR PERFORMA 17
Lydia Brawner

EDITORIAL RESEARCH
Charlene K. Lau and Quinn Schoen

EDITORIAL ASSISTANCE
Kelsey Brod and Camila Nichols

COPY EDITOR
Jennifer Piejko

INDEXER
Onni Nickle

PHOTOGRAPHER
Paula Court

IMAGE SOURCING AND RIGHTS MANAGEMENT
Dulce Lamarca and Victor Lozano

DESIGN
David Knowles

PRINT PRODUCTION
Willis Kingery

PRINTING
Szaransky Print Company
Poznań, Poland

TYPEFACE
Supreme LL

On the Town, A Performa Compendium: 2016-2021 is supported by the David and Elaine Potter Foundation, the Performa Board of Directors, and the New York City Department of Cultural Affairs.

ISBN 978-1-941366-35-6

Library of Congress Control Number: 2021944549

COVER
Kia LaBeija, *(Untitled) The Black Act*, 2019.
Performance view. Photo by Paula Court.